Lecture Notes in Computer Science 15560

Founding Editors

Gerhard Goos
Juris Hartmanis

AF173159

The series Lecture Notes in Computer Science (LNCS), including its subseries Lecture Notes in Artificial Intelligence (LNAI) and Lecture Notes in Bioinformatics (LNBI), has established itself as a medium for the publication of new developments in computer science and information technology research, teaching, and education.

LNCS enjoys close cooperation with the computer science R & D community, the series counts many renowned academics among its volume editors and paper authors, and collaborates with prestigious societies. Its mission is to serve this international community by providing an invaluable service, mainly focused on the publication of conference and workshop proceedings and postproceedings. LNCS commenced publication in 1973.

Edward A. Lee · Mohammad Reza Mousavi ·
Carolyn Talcott
Editors

Rebeca for Actor Analysis in Action

Essays Dedicated to Marjan Sirjani
on the Occasion of Her 60th Birthday

 Springer

Editors
Edward A. Lee (iD)
University of California
Berkeley, CA, USA

Mohammad Reza Mousavi (iD)
King's College London
London, UK

Carolyn Talcott
SRI International
Menlo Park, CA, USA

ISSN 0302-9743   ISSN 1611-3349 (electronic)
Lecture Notes in Computer Science
ISBN 978-3-031-85133-9   ISBN 978-3-031-85134-6 (eBook)
https://doi.org/10.1007/978-3-031-85134-6

The cover image shows the logo of Afra, an integrated environment for modeling and verifying Rebeca family designs. For more information, see: https://rebeca-lang.org/tools.

This Springer imprint is published by the registered company Springer Nature Switzerland AG
The registered company address is: Gewerbestrasse 11, 6330 Cham, Switzerland

If disposing of this product, please recycle the paper.

Preface

This volume is in honour of Marjan Sirjani's 60th birthday celebrating her various contributions to the specification and verification of concurrent and distributed actor-based systems. Marjan not only has had lasting contributions in research but also has trained generations of computer scientists and engineers and cared for every one of them. Wherever she has been, she has tried her best to create an environment for young minds to thrive. In this preface, we present our biased and personal account of some of the highlights of her lasting impact in these areas.

Marjan is the inventor of the Rebeca modelling languages, which is one of the best-known examples of actor-based languages with a formal semantics and a wealth of analysis and verification tools. Rebeca has been used in modelling and analysis of a wide range of systems, including in domains such as biomedical engineering, automotive, and aviation, to name a few.

Marjan loves connecting people and their research fields and creating crossdisciplinary teams and projects. Marjan co-created, together with Farhad Arbab and many colleagues and organisers, the International Conference on Fundamentals of Software Engineering (FSEN) conference series, which helped many young talents connect to the international research community. She created a unique environment for scholarly exchange. It is a fitting occasion to celebrate her achievements and her 60th birth anniversary in conjunction with the 20th anniversary of the FSEN conference series.

Throughout her career, Marjan trained a large group of students, collaborated within and across disciplinary boundaries with a vast network of collaborators (DBLP counts 150 people among her co-authors). The wide range of contributions in this festschrift reflects Marjan's broad expertise, interests, and network of friends, collaborators, and (former) students.

Marjan, thank you very much for your contributions and friendship; we look forward to your continued contributions to challenging problems.

January 2025

Mohammad Reza Mousavi
Edward A. Lee
Carolyn Talcott

Contents

Modelling Cyber-Physical Systems for Verification and Synthesis

Rong Gu[✉]

Mälardalen University, Västerås, Sweden
`rong.gu@mdu.se`

Abstract. Cyber-physical systems (CPS), such as cars and robots, are pervasive in our modern society. As CPS consist of heterogeneous components, analysis of such systems requires knowledge from different domains, such as mechanics, software engineering, control theory, and most recently artificial intelligence. However, practitioners and researchers of CPS lack a versatile framework that supports modelling all kinds of components in CPS and provides suitable verification and synthesis methods. The author proposes such a modelling framework and its implementation in this paper. This framework employs various formalisms to model the physical processes, controlling software, and external environment of CPS. The implementation of the framework is realised in UPPAAL, which supports symbolic and statistical model checking, as well as controller synthesis. This framework provides experts from different domains with analytical methods on both individual components and the entire system such that they can comprehensively consider the mutual influence of their design decisions. A case study of motion planning for autonomous vehicles demonstrates the applicability and versatility of the framework.

1 Introduction

Cyber-physical systems (CPS) are not pure software or hardware but orchestration of computers and physical processes [24]. A CPS has embedded computers that monitor and control physical processes. With feedback loops, physical processes can affect computations too. Such systems are often safety-critical, e.g., aircraft and vehicles, because an error may cause casualties and heavy financial loss. One feature of CPS that makes them hard to test and verify is the fusion of continuous dynamics and discrete logic in the digital controllers. Specifically, CPS need to keep perceiving the environment via sensors, transferring the data to the digital controller, and controlling their physical processes via actuators in a real-time manner. Therefore, CPS safety depends on the accuracy of sensors and actuators, the functional correctness of the controller, and the timing of performing actions. For example, airbags, as one of the most important safety innovations for the car industry, must be deployed within 15–30 ms and fully inflated within 60–80 ms. Failing to fulfil such kind of timing requirements may lead to catastrophic consequences. Security is another issue for CPS. In general,

E. A. Lee et al. (Eds.): Marjan Sirjani Festschrift, LNCS 15560, pp. 1–25, 2025.
https://doi.org/10.1007/978-3-031-85134-6_1

safety requires the system not to cause damage to itself and the environment, whereas security is concerned with external intrusion into the system. As CPS are often interconnected or connected to the Internet, the risk of cybersecurity and attacks surface. In 2015, a Jeep was attacked and remotely controlled by a hacker on a highway near St. Louis in the USA [34]. Therefore, methods for ensuring CPS safety and security have been one of the focuses of the research community and industries such as automotive companies.

Formal methods are well-known for providing rigorous analysis of safety-critical systems. Techniques such as model checking [2] have been proven to be useful for solving real-world problems [5]. Successful applications of formal methods on CPS can be generally divided into two aspects: verification and synthesis. *Formal verification* is about exploring the state space of the model and checking if the model satisfies the properties. *Synthesis* aims to find an implementation that satisfies the properties automatically, that is, the so-called *correctness by construction* introduced by Church in 1963 [9]. Since then, a great amount of effort has been made to address this problem [7,22,28]. The collaboration of Marjan Sirjani and the author is about CPS synthesis [14], which requires not only the system model but also the environment model. Objects in the environment can behave deterministically, non-deterministically, or stochastically. Formal models are therefore often employed because their rigorous semantics are indispensable for proving sound and complete synthesis methods.

As a formal model is an abstraction of the target system, one major concern is whether the formal model is faithful enough to the CPS. If the abstraction is too coarse or even false, crucial bugs can be neglected or false positive. If the abstraction is too fine, verification would need an unrealistic long period of computation time due to the unnecessary detail in the model. Therefore, building a model that reflects and only reflects the relevant aspects of the CPS is very important. However, the current studies either stay at the abstract level of models or contain nonlinear dynamics, which indeed model the system's behaviour precisely but are extremely hard, if not impossible, to be formally verified.

Another challenge in verifying and synthesising CPS controllers is the hybrid composition of CPS. A study in this domain may emphasise one kind of component, i.e., either the discrete controlling software or the continuous physical processes. However, the correctness of CPS depends on both their software and physical processes. When modelling the CPS behaviour as ordinary differential equations (ODEs), one can obtain the nonlinear dynamics of the system. It reflects how the CPS behaves in the physical world but is not what the computer system of CPS perceives. Sensors are the eyes and ears of CPS, from which the controlling software receives data periodically. Therefore, the world CPS perceives is discrete and can be erroneous.

Eduard Lee discusses the fidelity between models and their targets in the physical world [25]. Essentially, a model cannot 100% reflect its target. Figure 1 symbolically illustrates the different state spaces of the CPS dynamics in the physical world, and the CPS specification and implementation in the computer system. Control engineers use their tools like ordinary differential equations (ODEs) to model the system's behaviour. However, humans can only give an

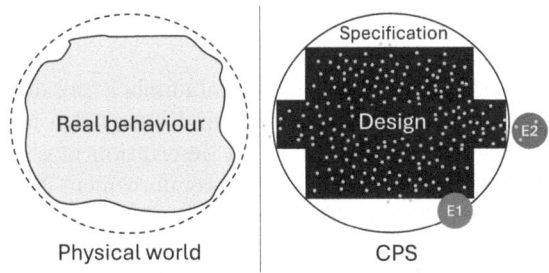

Fig. 1. An illustration of the differences among state spaces of the physical world and the CPS specification and implementation. E1 and E2 are the unsafe state spaces.

approximation of the physical world, like the dashed-line circle in Fig. 1. In the CPS, the solid-line circle represents the system specification, emulating the dashed-line circle in the physical world as faithfully as possible. Inside the solid-line circle, the black area shows the design space of the computer system in CPS. It may not 100% match the specification because computer systems are discrete but specifications can have nonlinear ODEs. Moreover, it might still not be what the CPS sees because sensors can have errors. In the end, the yellow dots represent the discrete states that CPS implementation has. It is not perfect because it is based on periodic and possibly erroneous sensory data but it is what the CPS really perceives. Due to measuring errors, the implementation might contain erroneous states that the specification does not consider (e.g., E2) or fails to detect the specified erroneous states (e.g., E1). Our goal of formal modelling is to integrate models of computer systems and physical processes, distinguish their differences, provide a separation of concerns, and find the right granularity of abstraction.

In a nutshell, the contributions of this paper are:

– A new modelling framework for CPS and the external environment. The framework provides various formalisms for modelling CPS's discrete controlling software and continuous physical processes separately or holistically.
– Methods for verification and synthesis on the symbolic state space or concrete state space of the model. Based on these methods, the author discusses the necessity and means of model pre-analysis before reinforcement learning.
– An implementation of the modelling framework in UPPAAL. The implementation provides model templates in the form of (stochastic) timed and hybrid automata games, and reusable functions.
– A case study of the modelling framework in autonomous driving. The case study demonstrates the applicability and versatility of the framework.

The remainder of the paper is organised as follows. Section 2 introduces the background knowledge for understanding this paper. Section 3 describes the problems that the new CPS modelling framework aims to solve. Section 4 introduces the modelling framework and how it is implemented in UPPAAL. Section 5 describes the case study, i.e., motion planning for autonomous vehicles. Section 6 presents the related work before Sect. 7 concludes the paper.

2   Preliminaries

In this paper, integers are denoted as $\mathbb{N}$ and real numbers are denoted as $\mathbb{R}$. This section is a brief introduction to the background knowledge for understanding this paper. First, the author gives a general description of the formalisms for modelling CPS. Next, the author introduces reinforcement learning (RL) and safety shields for RL, which are widely studied for ensuring the safety of RL.

2.1   Formalisms for Modelling CPS

Timed automata [1] is a formalism often used in modelling real-time systems, as it includes a continuous variable *time* that increases at a fixed rate of one. Formally, timed automata are defined as follows.

Definition 1. *A* timed automaton *is a tuple:*

$$TA = <L, l_0, C, \Sigma, E, Inv>, \tag{1}$$

where L is a finite set of locations, l_0 is the initial location, C is a finite set of non-negative real-valued variables (aka, clocks), Σ is a finite set of synchronisation channels, $E \subseteq L \times \mathcal{B}(C) \times \Sigma \times 2^C \times L$ is a finite set of edges, where $\mathcal{B}(C)$ is the set of guards over C, that is, conjunctive formulas of clock constraints of the form $x \bowtie n$ or $x - y \bowtie n$, where $x, y \in C$, $n \in \mathbb{N}$, $\bowtie \in \{<, \leq, =, \geq, >\}$, 2^C is a set of clocks in C that are reset, and $Inv : L \to \mathcal{B}(C)$ is a partial function assigning invariants to locations.

The semantics of a TA is defined as a *timed transition system*, where states consist of (l, v), l is a location and $v \in \mathbb{R}^C$ represents the variables' values on that location. An initial state is defined $s_0 = (l_0, v_0)$, where v_0 assigns zero to all variables in C. A timed transition system has two types of transitions:

- *delay transitions*: $(l, v) \xrightarrow{d} (l, v \oplus d)$, where $v \oplus d$ is an evaluation of clocks by incrementing them with $d \in \mathbb{R}^+$ such that $v \oplus d \models Inv(l)$, and
- *instantaneous transitions*: $(l, v) \xrightarrow{g,a,r} (l', v')$, where $g \in \mathcal{B}(C)$ evaluates to *true* at (l, v), $a \in \Sigma$, r resets a set of clocks in C such that $v' \models Inv(l')$.

When the continuous variables in C have various derivatives rather than one, hybrid automata are often employed. This formalism is often used in modelling hybrid systems consisting of discrete and continuous components, such as CPS. Formally, hybrid automata are defined as follows.

Definition 2. *A hybrid automaton is defined as the following tuple:*

$$HA = <L, l_0, V, \Sigma, E, Inv, F>, \tag{2}$$

where L is a finite set of locations, $l_0 \in L$ is the initial location, $V = C \cup X$ is a finite set of continuous variables, Σ is a finite set of channels, $E \subseteq L \times \mathcal{B}(C) \times \Sigma \times 2^X \times L$ is a finite set of edges, where $\mathcal{B}(C)$ is the set of guards

*over C, that is, conjunctive formulas of clock constraints of the form $c_1 \bowtie n$
or $c_1 - c_2 \bowtie n$, where $c_1, c_2 \in C$, $n \in \mathbb{N}$, $\bowtie \in \{<, \leq, =, \geq, >\}$, 2^X is a set of
variables in X whose values are changed, $Inv : L \to \mathcal{B}(C)$ is a partial function
assigning invariants to locations, and $F(l)$ is a set of ordinary different equations
(ODEs), e.g., $\dot{y} = f(x, t)$, $y, x \in X$, $t \in C$, assigned to location $l \in L$.*

Note that the non-clock continuous variables, that is, the ones in X, are only
used in ODEs[1]. Guards and invariants only have clocks. This is for enabling both
symbolic and statistical model checking in one model. Let's finish the introduction of formalisms before coming to model-checking techniques. Similar to TA,
the semantics of HA is also a transition system. However, the delay transitions
are different now because the continuous variables evolve based on ODEs. States
of a transition system of a HA are (l, c, x), where l is a location, $c \in \mathbb{R}^C$ are the
clocks' values, $x \in \mathbb{R}^X$ are other variables' values. Transitions are categorised:

- *delay transitions*: $(l, c, x) \xrightarrow{d} (l, c \oplus d, \int_0^d f(x, t)dt)$, where $c \oplus d$ increases clocks
  by $d \in \mathbb{R}^+$ such that $v \oplus d \models Inv(l)$, $\int_0^d f(x, t)dt$ integrates variables in X
  with respect to time according to $f(x, t) \in F(l)$, and
- *instantaneous transitions*: $(l, c, x) \xrightarrow{g, a, u} (l', c', x')$, where $g \in \mathcal{B}(C)$ evaluates
  to *true* at (l, c, x), u updates a set of variables in V such that $c' \models Inv(l')$.

Given a model composed of TA and HA, formal verification must be done in
different ways. The suitable model-checking techniques for TA and HA are introduced in the next section.

The semantics of TA and HA can have stochastic or nondeterministic interpretations of games. A game has two players who perform independently. One
can model CPS and the environment as a game, where CPS's goal is to reach the
destination safely and the environment keeps running regardless of how the CPS
moves. In other words, the mission of driving safely is the CPS's responsibility. A stochastic (resp, nondeterministic) environment may change the weather
throughout the day with a probability distribution (resp, arbitrarily). One can
use TA and HA to model the CPS and the environment with slight changes
in the model definitions. Transitions in TA and HA can be now categorised
into controllable ones (i.e., E_c) and uncontrollable ones (i.e., E_u). Controllable
transitions are taken by the CPS and uncontrollable ones are taken by the environment. Given such a model, CPS controller synthesis means to schedule the
controllable transitions such that the CPS reach the goal safely regardless of
how the environment acts. In the following sections, let's go through the techniques of verifying TA and HA before introducing two representative methods
of controller synthesis.

2.2   Symbolic and Statistical Model Checking

Model checking is a process of exploring the state space of a model (i.e., semantics) and checking if logic expressions (i.e., properties) are true in some or all

---

[1] Such non-clock continuous variables are the so-called *hybrid clocks* in UPPAAL [33],
which are used in the Sect. 4.2.

of the states. For example, given a model of a robot, one may want to check if collisions are avoided at all the states and if the destination is reached at some states. The former is called *safety* property and the latter is called *reachability* or *liveness* property [2]. According to the semantics of TA and HA, the states of such models are infinite and uncountable, which means it is impossible to exhaustively explore them all. However, modern model checkers transform the infinite state space of TA to a finite and countable one by using symbols. For example, UPPAAL [23] uses *zones* to represent the values of clocks of TA. Zones are the intervals of clocks, in which all the values of clocks are equivalent. In this paper, the infinite state space is referred to as concrete state space, corresponding to symbolic state space. Therefore, symbolic model checking means model checking the symbolic state space of a model.

Nevertheless, HA do not have such an abstraction over the concrete state space, and thus exhaustive verification of HA is still an undecidable problem [18]. However, one can use statistical model checking (SMC) [26] to estimate the probability of HA satisfying a property. Instead of exhaustive exploration, SMC randomly explores the concrete state space of a model, samples traces (i.e., sequences of states and transitions), and checks whether properties are true at these traces. Choices of transitions in the random exploration must follow the probability distributions of the model, which is often the uniform distribution if no particular one is defined. Statistically, given a confidence level and a sufficient amount of samples being collected, one can conclude the probability of the model satisfying a property, and this is how SMC works essentially. In this paper, the external environment of CPS has uncertainties. One can model them as nondeterministic or stochastic events, and use symbolic or statistical model checking for verification, respectively.

2.3   Controller Synthesis Methods

There are two classes of controller synthesis methods, i) exhaustive-search-based synthesis (ESS), and ii) reinforcement-learning-based synthesis (RLS).

Exhaustive-Search-Based Synthesis (ESS). As synthesis is about finding the optimal combination of actions, a natural method is to exhaustively explore all the possibilities and select the ones that are optimal, e.g., reaching the destination safely. Controller synthesis using ESS means an exhaustive exploration of the symbolic state space of the model of CPS and the environment, and collecting the state-action pairs that are safe and goal reaching. Since the state-space exploration is exhaustive, ESS is *sound* and *complete*, that is, the synthesised strategy must be correct, i.e., collision-free (soundness), and if a correct strategy exists, the method must be able to find it (completeness). However, a safe strategy can be *permissive* as it contains all the safe state-action pairs, including the inefficient ones. For example, when a CPS needs to finish a job at position A, a permissive strategy would allow the CPS to wait unnecessarily long, e.g., close to the maximum execution time, and then execute the job. Therefore, permissive strategies can be optimised.

Reinforcement-Learning-Based Synthesis (RLS). Reinforcement learning (RL) [32] lets the machine randomly run in the environment and learns by collecting and accumulating rewards from the environment. Based on this idea, RLS explores the concrete state space randomly via simulations instead of exhaustive exploration. Correspondingly, the purpose of state-space exploration now is not to collect optimal state-action pairs but to compute their rewards. In the end, an RL strategy means always choosing the action with the highest/lowest reward at each of the states. RLS does not have state-space explosion because the exploration is not exhaustive but the method is neither sound nor complete.

In this paper, the author employs these two classes of methods and combines them to show the ability and improved performance of the new CPS models.

3 Problem Description

CPS consist of cyber components (e.g., controlling software) and physical processes (e.g., throttles). A study of CPS may emphasize one aspect or the other, but the system's correctness depends on the integration of all components. Therefore, hybrid systems are often employed here to model CPS. Hybrid automata is a formal model of hybrid systems, which model the discrete controlling logic as transition systems and the continuous behaviour as ordinary differential equations (ODEs). However, model-checking hybrid automata with nonlinear ODEs remains an unsolvable problem so far [18]. One solution is to use over-approximation to abstract the hybrid system and verify the abstraction instead [11,15]. Methods of this solution effectively represent the nonlinear dynamics with (piece-wise) linear models and perform the verification. These methods have been proven useful in several applications where the difference between the linear and nonlinear models is tolerable. However, these methods often neglect the fact that no matter how accurately the ODEs reflect the system's behaviour, CPS are controlled by discrete software controllers, which obtain data from sensors and send commands to actuators periodically. Therefore, to verify CPS, one must take into account the discrete nature of controlling software. Nevertheless, even if the controlling software passes the verification, the CPS is not guaranteed to be safe, because sensors and actuators can have errors. For example, a pathfinding algorithm can generate a collision-free path that takes into account a vehicle's nonlinear dynamics. However, the vehicle's actual moving trajectory may inevitably deviate from the planned path due to the inaccurate accelerometers and gyroscopes. In summary, arguments for CPS's correctness are incomplete if they only concern one aspect of the system.

The environment where CPS works often contains uncertainties. For example, at an intersection of roads, the behaviour of other vehicles is not entirely predictable from an autonomous driving car's perspective. To prove the system safe, one may need to consider the worst-case scenarios and ensure the system would not enter unsafe states under those scenarios. However, to gain such kind of safety guarantee, one may need to sacrifice the system's performance, which is sometimes intolerable. In practice, customers of CPS only need to know if the system can be safe for most of the cases, e.g., 99.999%, especially when the environment is stochastic. Statistical model checking (SMC) [26] provides a way to formally verify hybrid automata and returns the probabilities of property satisfaction or violation. One can model CPS and the environment as a network of hybrid automata associated with probabilities or probability distributions, and then verify the model against temporal logic properties by using a SMC model checker, such as UPPAAL. Although SMC fulfils the need for knowing the probability of satisfaction, one cannot get to know the error causes, just like what symbolic model checking gives in counter-examples. If the problem comes from the environment, one may want to make the CPS more adaptable or change the operational design domain (ODD). If the problem comes from the CPS, one may want to know if it is a bug in the controlling software or the erroneous sensors. To achieve this, we need a modelling method that provides a separation of concerns but also a way of composing discrete and continuous features.

Before defining the research problem of this paper, let's define CPS as follows.

Definition 3 (CPS). *A CPS is a tuple (S, S_0, U, Act, f, T), where $S = (I, D)$ is the state space, where $I \subseteq \mathbb{N}^n$ is a set of discrete variables, and $D \subseteq \mathbb{R}^m$ is a set of continuous variables, $S_0 \subseteq S$ is the initial state set, $U \subseteq \mathbb{R}^k$ is the input space, $Act \subseteq \mathbb{N} \subset U$ is a set of discrete actions, $f : D \times U \to D$ is the dynamic function, and $T \subseteq I \times Act \times I$ is a transition relation.*

Intuitively, I *(Act)* is a set of discrete variables (actions) in the controlling software of the CPS. D *(U)* is a set of continuous variables (inputs) of the physical process. Although the variables in the controlling software can be integer or floating-point, they are all discrete. Variables and inputs of the physical process are real numbers because the motions of the CPS are continuous. The dynamic function f is often defined as ordinary differential equations (ODEs)[2]. *Act* is a set of CPS's actions that are invoked by the controlling software periodically or sporadically, such as retrieving data from memory shared with sensors. On the occurrence of an action in *Act*, the discrete variables in the controlling software may be changed, which is modelled by a transition in T.

Hybrid models have infinite state spaces and possibly nonlinear dynamics, which make exhaustive verification impossible. However, the controlling software should still be verifiable because it only has discrete variables and actions. Therefore, the modelling of CPS should integrate the discrete and continuous features of the system but also allow the separation of concerns such that the controlling software is verifiable, the accuracy validation of the sensors and actuators can be performed, and root cause analysis is possible.

As verification starts with an existing system, synthesis starts with specification and aims to generate a system that satisfies the specification. As aforementioned, synthesis algorithms can be categorised into searching and learning. As searching is exhaustive, searching-based synthesis is sound and complete but does not scale well. Learning uses random simulation so it is free from state-space explosion, but it loses soundness and completeness. Hence, modelling for

---

[2] In the literature, dynamic functions can also be defined as partial differential equations. The author uses ODEs in this paper.

controller synthesis needs a separation of concerns and supports different granularities of abstraction so that searching and learning can complement each other.

Definition 4. *Given a CPS, how to construct a formal model such that:*

(i) *The discrete controlling software and the continuous physical process can be integrated and analysed by suitable methods such that one can both estimate the success rate of the entire CPS and detect bugs in the components.*

(ii) *The accuracy of sensors and actuators can be evaluated, that is, the discrete variables in the controlling software are compared to the ground truth, which is represented by the continuous variables in the physical process.*

(iii) *A suitable granularity of discretisation can be decided such that verification and synthesis do not miss critical situations and can be finished within a reasonable time.*

4   CPS Modelling Framework and Implementation

This section describes the modelling of CPS and explains how the goals in Definition 4 are achieved.

4.1   Modelling Framework

Figure 2 depicts our CPS modelling framework, which has three components. The *controlling software* and *physical processes* are in the CPS, which work in an *environment*. The author uses different formalisms to model these components.

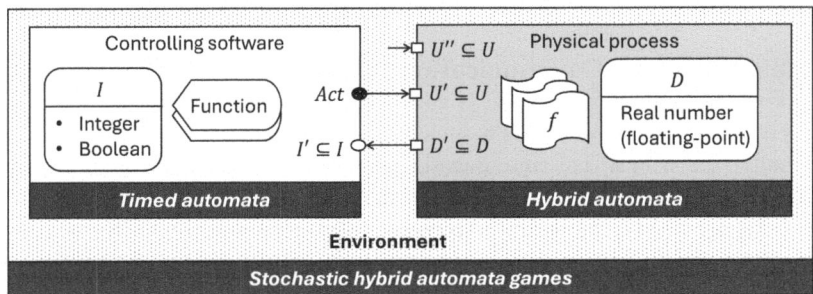

Fig. 2. CPS modelling framework. Variables, such as I and D, are defined in Definition 3.

Modelling of the Controlling Software. In line with Definition 3, the controlling software only has discrete variables in the dataset I. Periodically or sporadically, the controlling software performs actions and reads sensory data by calling functions. Therefore, the correctness of the controlling software depends on the functions and when to call them. Timed automata is the suitable formalism for modelling the controlling software as it can model functions as transitions among states and let time elapse before transitions are taken, which is perfect for modelling the periodic and sporadic calling of functions.

Modelling of the Physical Processes. Variables in the physical processes are real numbers as they are parts of the physical world. The dynamics of the physical processes are captured by the function f, which is an ODE in this paper. Actions from the controlling software may change the state of the physical processes. Therefore, hybrid automata is a suitable formalism for modelling physical processes because it supports discrete transitions among states and ODEs for describing the evolution of the continuous variables.

Modelling of the Environment. The environment includes all the entities outside CPS, such as roads, static obstacles, and moving obstacles. In general, these entities are not entirely predictable from the CPS's perspective, even if they are stationary. For example, a hole may suddenly appear on the road where the CPS is travelling. Such events are not predictable but one can have their probabilities based on historical data. The dynamics of moving obstacles also need to be modelled as ODEs. All these features make stochastic hybrid automata a suitable formalism for modelling the environment. Additionally, CPS and the environment are modelled as a *game* for controller synthesis. In the setting of games, two players act independently to reach their goals. If their goals are consistent, both players are cooperative; otherwise, they compete. Environments in this paper are neutral in the sense that their actions are not changed because of the CPS. The goal of controller synthesis is to calculate a set of actions at each of the states in the controlling software such that the CPS satisfies the requirements. If the environment is deterministic, one can obtain a safe, secure, and optimal controller. If the environment is non-deterministic or stochastic, our goal is to ensure the controller's safety and security before optimisation.

Modelling of Data Communication. Communication among the components of the modelling framework is various. Information from the environment is perceived by sensors of the CPS such as cameras. Pictures of the environment are usually stored in a real-time dataset that is able to respond to the controlling software within a time frame. Other kinds of sensors, like accelerometers and gyroscopes, are used to capture the physical information of the CPS, such as orientation and speed. The controlling software can obtain these data by accessing the memory of the sensors. The time for accessing the sensory memory can be neglected. However, when the CPS is distributed, which is often the case, the controlling system consists of components distributed in the CPS or even the environment and connected by a bus, e.g., CAN, or wirelessly. In either case, reading/writing the data costs time, aka, delays in communication, which can be a cause of faults.

Moreover, the mismatch of data types between the controlling software and physical processes is another challenge in modelling. Since physical processes are entities in the real world, the continuous variables in D are all real numbers, which are impossible to be exactly represented in the controlling software, a discrete world. Computer scientists decide to use floating-point numbers to represent real numbers, which means a truncation takes place when the real number is not a rational number or its digit lengths exceed the limit of the system, e.g., 32 bits or 64 bits. In the model-checking world, floating-point numbers are not welcome as they would overly bloat a model's state space and floating-point computations are not stable due to the *cancellation* effects [19].

The author is aware of the difficulty of using floating-point arithmetic in model checking [17] and does not aim to solve this problem in this paper. Instead, this paper proposes a way of representing floating-point numbers as integers at the model level. In the model of physical components, floating-point numbers are used to represent real numbers whereas the model of the controlling software uses integers to represent all the numbers. Specifically, in the model of controlling software, the *base* and *exponent* of floating-point numbers are defined as constant integers, and the *significand* of each floating-point number is stored as an integer.

$$3.1415 = \underbrace{314150}_{significand} \times \underbrace{10^{\overbrace{-5}^{exponent}}}_{base} \quad \overbrace{\phantom{10^{-5}}}^{scale} \tag{3}$$

For example, when the base is 10 and the exponent is -5, 3.1415 is stored as 314150. The representative integer of a floating-point number must multiply a number *scale* before it is involved in a computation. After the computation, the floating-point number is changed back to an integer by dividing it by *scale*. In the remainder of the paper, the author uses i2d to name the function converting integers to floating-point numbers, and d2i the other way around. These operations limit the length of floating-point numbers. However, they make the model of the controlling software verifiable by state-of-the-art model checkers like UPPAAL [23] and Modere [20].

4.2 Implementation of the Modelling Framework

This section introduces how the modelling framework is implemented. The author uses UPPAAL as the tool for implementation because it supports modelling timed automata, hybrid automata and timed games. It also integrates exhaustive model checking, statistical model checking, and synthesis. To illustrate the models, the author uses an autonomous vehicle (AV) as an example of CPS and a network of roads and the vehicles on it as the environment in this section.

Hybrid Automata of Physical Processes. Figure 3 depicts the hybrid automaton of the physical process of the AV and the variables in the model. Continuous variables are defined as hybrid clock in UPPAAL. Hybrid clocks can be used in ODEs but are abstracted away from the symbolic state space. Hence, this way of defining continuous variables allows the model to be analysed by symbolic and statistical model checking and used in search-based and learning-based synthesis, which are introduced in the following sections. The dynamics of the AV are modelled by the ODEs on the only location of the hybrid automaton,

Variable	Type	Unit	Description
d_x	hybrid clock	m	coordinate on X
d_y	hybrid clock	m	coordinate on Y
d_v	hybrid clock	m/s	velocity
d_acc	hybrid clock	m/s²	acceleration
d_h	hybrid clock	rad	yaw angle
i_jerk	int	m/s³	acceleration rate
i_turn	int	rad/s	angular velocity

$$d\_x' = \cos(d\_h) * d\_v \,\&\&$$
$$d\_y' = \sin(d\_h) * d\_v \,\&\&$$
$$d\_v' = d\_acc \,\&\&$$
$$d\_acc' = i2d(i\_jerk) \,\&\&$$
$$d\_h' = i2d(i\_turn)$$

(a) Hybrid automaton (b) Variables in the hybrid automaton

Fig. 3. An example of the physical-process model and its variables

which means the continuous variables keep evolving according to their derivatives during the verification and synthesis processes, respectively. Note that there are two integers in the model, namely `i_jerk` and `i_turn`. They are defined as integers because these variables are accessible by the controlling software. For

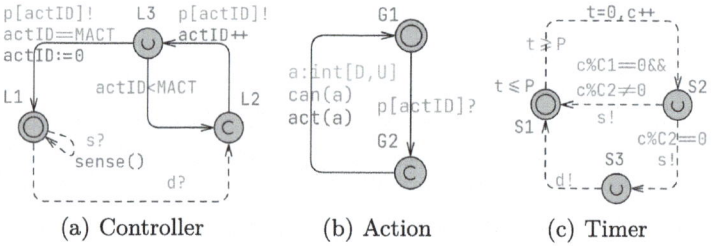

(a) Controller   (b) Action   (c) Timer

Fig. 4. An example of the controlling software model and its variables, where s, d, and p are broadcast synchronisation channels, sense(), can(), and act() are C-like code functions, t, c, a, and actID are variables, and D, U, C1, C2, and P are constants.

Table 1. Meanings of the variables, channels, and functions in Fig. 4

Declaration	Description	Declaration	Description
broadcast chan s	sensing syn	const uint8_t C2	time for decision making
broadcast chan p	action selection syn	const uint16_t P	maximum execution time
broadcast chan d	decision making syn	const uint16_t MACT	maximum action number
void sense()	update discrete variables	const double G	granularity of integration
bool can(int a)	can perform action a?	int32_t i_x	coordinate on X
bool act(int a)	change variables of a	int32_t i_y	coordinate on Y
clock t	count time	int32_t i_v	velocity
uint8_t c	count periods	int32_t i_acc	acceleration
const uint8_t D	lower boundry of action	int32_t i_h	heading
const uint8_t U	upper boundry of action	int32_t i_jerk	acceleration rate
const uint8_t C1	time for sensing	int32_t i_turn	turning rate

example, when the AV meets an obstacle, the controlling software calculates the right angle for avoiding that obstacle and steers the vehicle by changing i_turn. As mentioned in Sect. 4.1, floating-point numbers are stored as integers in the model. The latter must be changed back to floating-point numbers before being involved in any computation. Therefore, function i2d is used in the ODEs.

Timed Automata Games of Controlling Software. As shown in Fig. 4, the controlling software model consists of three templates of timed automata games, or simply timed games. For brevity, we use alphabets or simple words in those templates. The meaning of those alphabets and words are given in Table 1.

Variables in the models include clock t, which is zero in the beginning, and hybrid clocks, e.g., d_x and d_y, and their integer representatives, e.g., i_x and i_y. In principle, the hybrid clocks are only accessible by the physical process and thus should be declared in it. However, the author declares them as global variables that are accessible by all components for the sake of simplicity. One can declare the hybrid clocks inside the template of the physical processes, which makes them local variables, and it would not change the model's behaviour.

First, Timer starts to count time periodically. Every P time unit, Timer calls Controller, which executes two possible sequences of functions: i) sensing, and ii) sensing and decision making. Specifically, when it is time for sensing alone, Timer goes back to location S1 synchronising with Controller via channel s. When it is time for sensing and decision making, Timer synchronises with Controller on channels s and d sequentially, meaning that sensing must be done before decision making. The transition synchronised via channel s is along a self-loop edge of location L1, meaning that the controller does not need to make a decision now. Constants C1 and C2 distinguish the periods for case i) and case ii).

Algorithm 1: Numerical integration: update discrete variables

---

```
1  Function sense()
2      int steps := 1/G
3      double x := i2d(i_x)              // convert integer i_x to double x
4      double y, v, acc, heading ...     // convert the rest integers to double
5      double unit = C1 · G
6      while steps ≠ 0 do
7          acc := acc + i_jerk · unit
8          heading := heading + i_turn · unit
9          v := v + acc · unit
10         x := x + v · cos(heading) · unit
11         y := y + v · sin(heading) · unit
12         steps := steps - 1
13     i_x := d2i(x)                     // convert double x to integer i_x
14     i_y, i_v, i_acc, i_heading ... // convert the rest double to integers
15     return
```

Function sense() is for updating the discrete variables in the controlling software. In principle, continuous variables in the physical process are sampled by the controlling software via sensors. However, sampling a value from a hybrid clock makes the model impossible for symbolic verification in UPPAAL. Therefore, the author implements the sampling operation in function `sense()` (see Algorithm 1). Similar to the hybrid automata of physical processes (Fig. 3(a)), line 3 and line 4 convert variables like `i_x` to floating-point numbers. From line 7 to line 12, the results of the ODEs in the hybrid automata of the physical process are approximated by the numerical integration. Specifically, the floating-point numbers are gradually updated step by step with a changing unit $C1 \cdot G$, where $C1$ is the length of the sensing period and G is a predefined sampling granularity of the integration points (see Table 1). Although the numerical integration only approximates the integral, it reflects what the controlling software perceives, that is, periodically updated discrete variables. Between two consecutive sampling periods, the variables' values remain unchanged in the controlling software. After the numerical integration, line 13 and line 14 convert the floating-point numbers back to the globally declared integers. One can evaluate the difference between a numerically integrated integer and the corresponding continuous variable via statistical model checking, which is demonstrated in Sect. 5.

Now, we go back to the controlling software model in Fig. 4. Recall that `Timer` calls `Controller` every P time unit, and the latter executes sensing alone or sensing and decision-making sequentially. The decision-making process starts with synchronised transitions via channel `d`, after which `Timer` and `Controller` come to locations S3 and L2, respectively. The latter is a committed location meaning that the next transition must come from this location and happen immediately. Therefore, `Controller` leaves location L2 immediately and consecutively calls the action models via an array of channels named `p`. Simultaneously, `Action` transits to G2, another committed location. There, `Action` has multiple transitions to choose from, i.e., `a:int[D,U]`. Let's use acceleration as an example. When an AV controller decides to accelerate, it needs to choose a concrete value for the changing rate of acceleration, aka, *jerk*. As this value is chosen by the digital controller, it is defined as an integer in the model, i.e., `i_jerk` in Table 1. Correspondingly, the `Action` model has an integer `a` to represent the discrete variable attached to this action. Assuming the exemplary AV has five gears of acceleration, meaning that variable `i_jerk` has five possible values, then D is zero and U is four. In each round of decision-making, `Action` needs to check if any of the five gears are prohibited due to the physical limitation of the vehicle (i.e., function `can(a)`), choose from the feasible gears, and updates `i_jerk` accordingly in function `act(a)`. Note that only the transitions synchronised between `Controller` and `Action` are denoted by solid arrows as they are controllable from the CPS's point of view. Other edges are dashed arrows because those actions are from the environment, e.g., `Timer`. Obviously, `Action` presents all the feasible actions that are allowed by the physical laws but not all of them are optimal or safe. Controller synthesis is about finding the best actions in each round of decision-making such that the CPS can be safe, secure, and goal-reaching. The author is going to introduce controller synthesis in the following section.

Stochastic Hybrid Automata Games of the Environment. An environment contains two kinds of objects, static ones and dynamic ones. Examples of static objects are stationary vehicles, traffic signs, trees, and roadsides. These objects can be modelled as constants in the model, representing the objects' coordinates, such that they are not taken into the model state space. However, functions like collision checking can use those constants for calculation.

Dynamic objects are moving in the environment, like pedestrians and other vehicles. In the exemplary model, they are modelled as (stochastic) hybrid automata games depicted in Fig. 5. Dynamic objects can behave nondeterministically or stochastically. In either case, the CPS periodically senses the objects' status, like their positions, via the synchronisation channel s. Therefore, the hybrid automata in Fig. 5 stay at the initial location L0, where the continuous variables evolve according to the ODEs, until a synchronised transition is triggered by Timer via channel s!. Along this synchronised transition, the hybrid automata go to location L1, where the model diverges into two types, namely a nondeterministic model and a stochastic model. As shown in Fig. 5(a), the nondeterministic model arbitrarily chooses a transition between changing the variables of the model or doing nothing. Similarly, the stochastic model in Fig. 5(b) also has two feasible transitions from location L1. The difference is that the choice over these transitions is random now. Specifically, in this example, there is 80% of probability that the model changes the variables and 20% doing nothing. The verification and synthesis methods are different for these two kinds of models. The author is going to introduce these methods in the following sections.

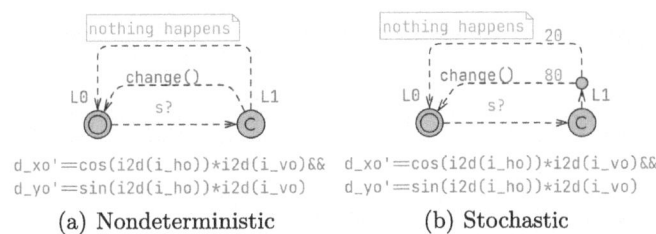

(a) Nondeterministic   (b) Stochastic

Fig. 5. An example of a dynamic object behaving in different ways

In summary, the physical process and controlling software of CPS as well as the objects in the environment are modelled as hybrid automata, timed automata games, and (stochastic) hybrid automata games, respectively. All of the models can be constructed in UPPAAL, which provides the corresponding methods for verification and synthesis. Next, the author introduces how the modelling framework is adopted in a platform that we developed for AV motion planning. The platform is called *CommonUppRoad* [16] because we combine UPPAAL with CommonRoad, a toolset that provides scenarios of AV driving, physical models of vehicles, and motion-planning algorithms[3]. In the next section, the author introduces how the modelling framework is adopted in CommonUppRoad.

5   Case Study: Motion Planning for Autonomous Vehicles

Previously, we developed CommonUppRoad to support engineers in designing motion-planning components of AV. The platform describes driving scenarios as XML files and visualises them. Figure 6(a) shows the visualisation of a scenario whose XML file structure is shown in Fig. 6(b). Briefly, roads have lanes that are separated by solid or dashed lines. Vehicles are free to change lanes when their boundaries are dashed lines. Moving vehicles are obstacles that move on predefined trajectories. The trajectories not only describe the vehicles' positions at each of the time points but also their velocities, headings, etc. The scenario can have static obstacles too, such as broken vehicles. The AD vehicle needs to travel safely, that is, never collide, never go off the road, and never break the traffic rules. Eventually, the AD vehicle must reach the goal area, which can be a target lane, an area, or even a goal state with a desired final position, speed, and heading. Motion planning is to find a set of actions for the AD vehicle at each of its states such that it can reach the goal safely.

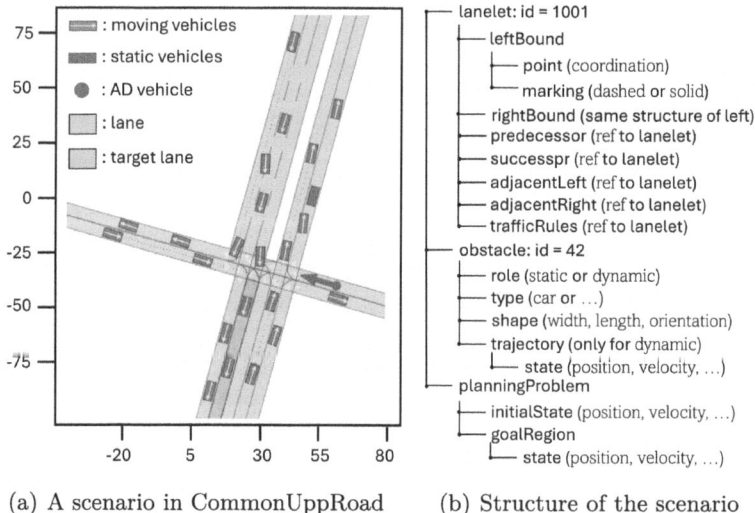

(a) A scenario in CommonUppRoad   (b) Structure of the scenario

Fig. 6. An example of driving scenarios in CommonUppRoad [16].

When addressing such a planning problem, one may first think of learning or a good searching algorithm to find the optimal combinations of state and

---

[3] https://sites.google.com/view/commonupproad.

actions, aka, state-action pairs. However, such solutions neglect two imperative factors that heavily influence the success of motion planning, that is, whether the model is correct and whether a motion plan exists.

First, as a cyber-physical system, the AD vehicle is controlled by a piece of digital controlling software, but its movement is continuous. As mentioned in the previous sections, the correctness of the model for such systems depends on both the digital and continuous components. Still, most learning algorithms focus on the continuous behaviour, e.g., the moving trajectory. However, a correct moving trajectory does not mean a safe AD vehicle. If the sensing periods of the controlling software are too long, the AD vehicle may deviate too much from the moving trajectory. If the decision-making periods are too short, learning spends too much time on trivial details. Additionally, real numbers cannot be 100% accurately presented in the controlling software. Sensors can have different levels of accuracy too. The mismatch of accuracy can lead to unexpected consequences. Second, the effort of learning can be futile if a valid motion plan does not exist at all. However, it is nontrivial to check the existence of a valid motion plan because the planning has multiple objectives, such as safety, progress, comfort, and traffic rule conformance. Nevertheless, since safety is the first and foremost objective, if we can find a counterexample that violates the safety requirement, we can quickly conclude the non-existence of valid motion plans. Model checking is a powerful tool to do it. In this section, the author uses the modelling method to formalise an AD vehicle and its driving scenario in CommonUppRoad, verify the model, and check the existence of motion plans before RL.

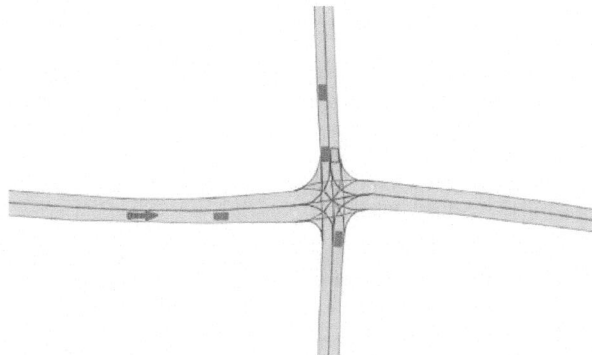

Fig. 7. Scenario for the experiments. ID in CommonRoad: DEU_Ffb-1_3_T-1.

5.1   Experiment Design

Figure 7 depicts the scenario for experiments, where the AD vehicle needs to enter the intersection, turn left, and drive to the goal area safely. To judge collisions and risky situations, the authors introduce two thresholds of distance in the model, namely TD and 3·TD. Once the distance between the AD vehicle and an obstacle is less than TD, a collision happens. Once the distance is less than 3·TD, a risky situation appears. To demonstrate the necessity of pre-analysis [12] prior to reinforcement learning, the author separates the models into four groups (Table 2).

Table 2. Experiment groups

Groups	Exponent	Periods		Description
		Sensing	Decision making	
I	1	1	4	Low sensory accuracy
II	4	2	4	Long sensing periods
III	4	1	1	Short decision-making periods
IV	4	1	4	Long decision-making periods

To show the difference that sensory accuracy makes, the exponent of floating-point numbers (see Eq. 3) is set to be one or four, and a threshold of sensory errors is a constant THD = 2. To show how model checking can benefit RL in choosing a suitable learning stepsize, the sensing periods are chosen from one and two time units, whereas the decision-making periods can be one or four time units. The modelling method in this paper integrates various formalisms and the corresponding verification and synthesis methods. This experiment is to show how the new modelling method enables pre-analysis before RL, strengthens the safety of RL, and improves the performance of RL. Therefore, the author creates the model templates, uses CommonUppRoad to convert the driving scenario in Fig. 7 to formal models, and performs the following operations in UPPAAL:

- *Pre-analysis*: as preparation for RL, the formal models are verified against the following queries, where MT is the maximum execution time, fabs returns the absolute value of the parameter, cv represents a continuous variable, aka, hybrid clock in UPPAAL, such as d_x in Fig. 3, iv is the corresponding integer representation of the continuous variable, and functions collide(), offroad(), and goal() returns *true* when the AD vehicle hits an obstacle, goes off the road, and reaches the goal, respectively.

$$Pr[\leq MT]([] \; fabs(cv-i2d(iv)) \leq THD\}) \qquad (4)$$

$$E<>!collide()\&\&!offroad()\&\&goal() \qquad (5)$$

Query (4) uses statistical model checking and returns the probability of satisfying the property in the brackets, that is, the difference between a continuous variable and its integer representation is always less or equal to the threshold of sensory accuracy tolerance. If the probability is lower than a certain value, e.g., 99%, one does not need to run RL because even if a motion plan is synthesised, the actual execution of the motion plan would still be wrong as the sensory error may cause a big deviation and makes the vehicle collide. Query (5) uses symbolic model checking and returns *true* if the model contains a trace having at least one state where the conjunction of the three functions is *true*. The trace is not necessarily optimal and the environment may influence the AD vehicle to deviate from the trace anyway. However, dissatisfaction of Query (5) indicates the non-existence of valid motion plans, and thus RL is not needed either.

- *Safety shield synthesis*: A safety shield for RL filters the unsafe actions such that the RL process and result are guaranteed to be safe [21]. UPPAAL provides the following query to synthesise a safety shield automatically.

$$\texttt{strategy safe=control:A[] !collide()\&\&!offroad()} \qquad (6)$$

Query (6) is similar to symbolic model checking. When executing this query, UPPAAL explores the symbolic state space of the model and collects the state-action pairs holding the safety property, i.e., never collide and never off the road. The environment's actions may influence the behaviour of the AD vehicle. Safety shields only select the system's actions and guarantee the system is safe regardless of how the environment's actions take place. One can use the keyword `under` in UPPAAL to restrict the model to only take the actions contained in a safety shield. For example, Query (7) verifies whether the AD vehicle can always eventually reach the goal when it is under the control of a safety shield.

$$\texttt{A<> goal() under safe} \qquad (7)$$

Unfortunately, Query (7) is not always true because the safety shield only guarantees safety but not reachability. RL can complement this shortcoming.
- *RL*: UPPAAL provides several RL algorithms, such as Q learning [32], or calls a user-defined RL algorithm from an external library [13]. This experiment employs the internal Q learning algorithm in UPPAAL. Specifically, Query (8) is executed, where `maxE(rf)` means the learning objective is to maximise the reward function `rf`, defined in Eq. (9), and `ls` and `vs` denote two sets of state variables used in RL. For example, the locations of all timed games are in the set `ls` and integer variables, such as the AD vehicle's coordinates `i_x` and `i_y`, are included in the set `vs`.

$$\texttt{strategy policy = maxE(rf)[} \leq \texttt{MT]\{ls\}->\{vs\}: <> gt} \geq \texttt{MT} \qquad (8)$$

$$\texttt{rf} = 100 \cdot \texttt{goal()} - 90 \cdot (\texttt{collide()||offroad()}) - 10 \cdot \texttt{risky()} \qquad (9)$$

When executing Query (8), UPPAAL runs Monte-Carlo simulation for state-space exploration and samples traces that satisfy the following property "`<> gt` $\geq$ MT", where `gt` is a global clock that is never reset. Therefore, the query gathers all the traces that finish the maximum execution time no matter whether they are safe or reach the goal, which means the RL results have no guarantees of safety or reachability.

– *Evaluation of RL results*: The experiment uses Queries (10) and (11) to check whether the AD vehicle can be always safe and eventually reach the goal, respectively, when it is controlled by strategy `policy`.

$$\text{A[] !collide() \&\& !offroad() under policy} \tag{10}$$

$$\text{A<> goal() under policy} \tag{11}$$

The experiment also runs Query (12) to use the safety shield `safe` for guarding RL. Specifically, UPPAAL also uses Monte-Carlo simulation for Query (12), however, only the state-action pairs that are contained in `safe` can be explored. Hence, the learning process as well as the result are guaranteed to be safe. Nevertheless, reachability is still not ensured, but symbolic analysis now is not possible because UPPAAL does not support symbolic verification of multi-level strategies. Instead, one can use statistical model checking, that is, Query (13), to see the probability of goal-reaching.

$$\text{strategy rSafe = maxE(rf)[} \leq \text{MT]: <> gt} \geq \text{MT under safe} \tag{12}$$

$$\text{Pr[} \leq \text{MT](<> goal()) under rSafe} \tag{13}$$

5.2　Results and Discussion

Table 3 shows the experiment results. As the experiment starts with a pre-analysis of the model, Queries (4) and (5) are executed first.

Table 3. Experiment result. Q stands for Query. NR means non-relevant. Green (resp. red) cells mean successful (resp. failed) synthesis or satisfactory (resp. dis-satisfactory) verification results.

Groups	Synthesis			Statistical		Symbolic			
	Q6	Q8	Q12	Q4	Q13	Q5	Q7	Q10	Q11
I	NR	NR	NR	75.5%	NR	1.7s	NR	NR	NR
II	NR	NR	NR	0.0%	NR	<1s	NR	NR	NR
III	>3h	81.4s	NR	96.4%	NR	62.1s	NR	<1s	<1s
IV	35.2s	103.1s	9.3s	99.9%	99.9%	3.3s	<1s	<1s	<1s

All groups satisfy Query (5), meaning that a valid motion plan potentially exists in the symbolic state space of the model. However, groups I and II do not reach the desired level of sensory accuracy, that is, the probabilities of satisfying Query (4) are too low. Running the rest of the queries for synthesis and verification is futile because low sensory accuracy implies the wrong execution of the motion plan in reality. Therefore, the results of other queries in groups I and II are NR, meaning non-relevant. However, the author did run Query (6), i.e., safety-shield synthesis, Query (12), i.e., RL with a safety shield, or Query (8), i.e.,

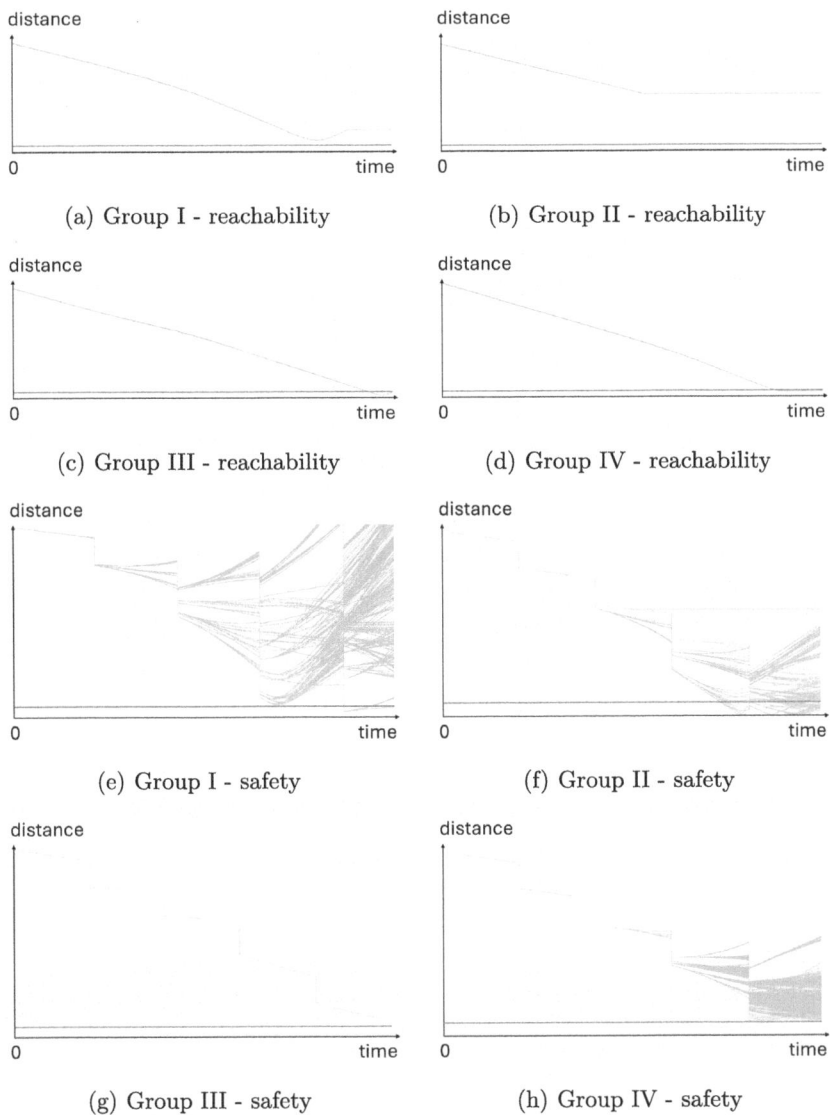

Fig. 8. Statistical model checking on safety shields and RL strategies. The red line is the distance threshold for judging collision and reaching the goal. (Color figure online)

pure RL, in all four groups and performed statistical model checking on the synthesis results to show the necessity of analysing sensory accuracy before motion planning. Safety-shield synthesis in group III cost more than three hours but did not generate any results. The author terminated the synthesis and marked it as a failure. The execution of Query (8) took several rounds before the result satisfied Queries (10) and (11). The computation times of Query (8) reported in Table 3 are the final rounds of execution in groups III and IV. However, the trial-and-error process cost even longer, which makes RL with safety shields a better choice. In group IV, RL with safety shields, that is, Query (6) and Query (12), cost 44.5 s in total, whereas pure RL cost more than 100 s.

Additionally, the author executed a random simulation to observe the AD vehicle's distances to the goal and a moving obstacle. Figure 8 show the results. Note that the reachability simulation of groups I, II, and IV are conducted on the strategy of Query (12), whereas in group III it is on the strategy of Query (8). Similarly, the safety simulation of groups I, II, and IV uses the strategy of Query (6) and group III uses the strategy of Query (8) again. Figure 8(a) and Fig. 8(b) show that the AD vehicle never really reaches the goal, that is, the distance to the goal is always above the threshold, even though it is trained by RL with safety shields. Nevertheless, Fig. 8(c) and Fig. 8(d) show the AD vehicle can reach the goal in groups III and IV. Similarly, the AD vehicle's distance to a moving obstacle can be less than the threshold of collision in Fig. 8(f) and Fig. 8(e), whereas in Fig. 8(g) and Fig. 8(h) it is always above the threshold. The problem of groups I and II is mentioned, i.e., the low sensory accuracy. Hence, although safety shields and controllers can be synthesised in the symbolic state space, the real behaviour captured by the continuous variables can still go wrong.

The experiment shows the importance of the model pre-analysis before RL. Through the pre-analysis, one can deepen his understanding of the model, reveal potential problems before training, and determine suitable lengths of periods for learning and sensing. In addition, in some cases, RL with safety shields can improve not only the safety aspect of training but also the performance, because the safety shields eliminate unsafe state-action pairs and restrict the state space.

6   Related Work

Surveys and systematic mapping studies have been conducted on CPS modelling, which collectively reveals the gaps in this research field [4,6]. The common formalisms of modelling CPS are Petri Nets, Hybrid Automata, and Discrete Events. However, studies using more than one formalism are not many because of the intricacy of CPS development [4,29]. The composition of heterogeneous components is thus one of the main themes in the research of CPS. Consequently, methods for module composition and identifying behaviour emerging from the composite systems/sub-systems are needed. Bliudze et al. [6] discuss the three steps of linking the physical process and computer system of a CPS, that is, CPS modelling, discretisation for execution, and implementation. Bakirtzis et al. [3] proposes categorical formalisms to find inconsistency errors in CPS models. Compared with these studies, this paper proposes a conceptual framework for modelling CPS that includes various formalisms for different components, and a concrete implementation of the framework in UPPAAL. The composition of the heterogeneous components is not an issue in this framework because all features are integrated into one model, but different verification and synthesis methods are selected in the backend depending on the users' choice of queries. In this holistic model, one can analyse the cyber parts and physical parts of CPS separately, or evaluate the behaviour of the entire system, like the success rate and sensory accuracy.

Verification is an important issue for CPS. The challenges stem from the heterogeneous nature of CPS. Studies either assume correct physical processes and focus on the cyber components [14,27,31], or neglect the computer system but work on the nonlinear dynamics of CPS directly [10,30]. Although these studies have conquered many problems in each of the sub-fields, the gap between the physical world and computer system (Fig. 1) still exists [4,8]. This insufficiency exists because researchers from different fields, such as control theory and software engineering, naturally focus on their interested facets of CPS. This paper attempts to draw the attention of researchers in different fields to the existing gap of research and provide a common ground and tool to work together.

7 Conclusion and Future Work

This paper proposes a CPS modelling framework for verification and synthesis. The framework employs timed automata for modelling the cyber components (aka, controlling software) of CPS, hybrid automata for modelling the physical processes, and stochastic hybrid automata for modelling the environment. All kinds of automata can be easily configured as games in this framework, which is the formalism for controller synthesis. Besides the multiple formalisms, this paper points out the discrepancy between discrete variables in cyber components and real numbers of physical processes. To deal with this mismatch, the framework uses integers as the discrete variables in cyber components and proposes a way of representing floating-point numbers as integers. This design reflects the discrete representation of the physical world, which is what the cyber components sense, and enables symbolic and statistical model checking in one model. The author proposes an implementation of the framework in UPPAAL, which supports modelling continuous variables as hybrid clocks. This feature is the foundation of the holistic model integrating cyber and physical components of CPS. A case study is done on an autonomous driving platform, CommonUppRoad, where vehicles are CPS. The case study shows how the modelling framework can be used in a concrete problem and the performance of verification and synthesis is proven to be improved via experiments.

One of the future works is investigating other applications of the modelling framework in other domains of CPS, such as health care and smart manufacturing. So far, the research of CPS modelling mainly focuses on the system, however, the modelling of the environment is worth studying as well. Modelling methods and the corresponding analytical techniques for dealing with nondeterministic and stochastic environments are important for the success of CPS.

Acknowledgments. The author acknowledges the support of the Swedish Knowledge Foundation via the project SATISFIES - Holistic Synthesis and Verification for Safe and Secure Autonomous Vehicles, grant nr. 20230047.

References

1. Alur, R., Dill, D.L.: A theory of timed automata. Theor. Comput. Sci. **126** (1994)
2. Baier, C., Katoen, J.P.: Principles of Model Checking. MIT Press, Cambridge (2008)
3. Bakirtzis, G., Vasilakopoulou, C., Fleming, C.H.: Compositional cyber-physical systems modeling. arXiv preprint arXiv:2101.10484 (2021)
4. Barišić, A., et al.: Multi-paradigm modeling for cyber-physical systems: a systematic mapping review. J. Syst. Softw. **183**, 111081 (2022)
5. ter Beek, M.H., et al.: Formal methods in industry. Form. Asp. Comput. (2024). https://doi.org/10.1145/3689374
6. Bliudze, S., Furic, S., Sifakis, J., Viel, A.: Rigorous design of cyber-physical systems: linking physicality and computation. Softw. Syst. Model. **18**, 1613–1636 (2019)
7. Bloem, R., Jobstmann, B., Piterman, N., Pnueli, A., Saár, Y.: Synthesis of reactive (1) designs. J. Comput. Syst. Sci. **78**(3), 911–938 (2012)
8. Broman, D., Lee, E.A., Tripakis, S., Törngren, M.: Viewpoints, formalisms, languages, and tools for cyber-physical systems. In: Proceedings of the 6th International Workshop on Multi-Paradigm Modeling, pp. 49–54 (2012)
9. Church, A.: Application of recursive arithmetic to the problem of circuit synthesis. J. Symb. Logic **28**(4) (1963)
10. Cleaveland, M., Lindemann, L., Ivanov, R., Pappas, G.J.: Risk verification of stochastic systems with neural network controllers. Artif. Intell. **313**, 103782 (2022)
11. Fan, C., Miller, K., Mitra, S.: Fast and guaranteed safe controller synthesis for nonlinear vehicle models. In: International Conference on Computer Aided Verification, pp. 629–652. Springer, Cham (2020)
12. Gu, R.: Model checking for reinforcement learning in autonomous driving: one can do more than you think! In: Luckcuck, M., Xu, M. (eds.) Proceedings Sixth International Workshop on Formal Methods for Autonomous Systems, Manchester, UK, 11th and 12th of November 2024. Electronic Proceedings in Theoretical Computer Science, vol. 411, pp. 160–177. Open Publishing Association (2024). https://doi.org/10.4204/EPTCS.411.11
13. Gu, R., Jensen, P.G., Seceleanu, C., Enoiu, E., Lundqvist, K.: Correctness-guaranteed strategy synthesis and compression for multi-agent autonomous systems. Sci. Comput. Program. **224**, 102894 (2022)
14. Gu, R., Moezkarimi, Z., Sirjani, M.: Guess and then check: controller synthesis for safe and secure cyber-physical systems. In: International Conference on Formal Techniques for Distributed Objects, Components, and Systems, pp. 230–238. Springer, Cham (2024)
15. Gu, R., Seceleanu, C., Enoiu, E., Lundqvist, K.: Model checking collision avoidance of nonlinear autonomous vehicles. In: Formal Methods: 24th International Symposium, FM 2021, pp. 676–694. Springer, Cham (2021)
16. Gu, R., Tan, K., Høeg-Petersen, A.H., Feng, L., Larsen, K.G.: Commonupproad: a framework of formal modelling, verifying, learning, and visualisation of autonomous vehicles (2024). https://arxiv.org/abs/2408.01093
17. Hartmanns, A.: Correct probabilistic model checking with floating-point arithmetic. In: International Conference on Tools and Algorithms for the Construction and Analysis of Systems, pp. 41–59. Springer, Cham (2022)

18. Henzinger, T.A., Kopke, P.W., Puri, A., Varaiya, P.: What's decidable about hybrid automata? J. Comput. Syst. Sci. **57**(1), 94–124 (1998)
19. Ivančić, F., Ganai, M.K., Sankaranarayanan, S., Gupta, A.: Numerical stability analysis of floating-point computations using software model checking. In: Eighth ACM/IEEE International Conference on Formal Methods and Models for Codesign (MEMOCODE 2010), pp. 49–58. IEEE (2010)
20. Jaghoori, M.M., Movaghar, A., Sirjani, M.: Modere: the model-checking engine of Rebeca. In: Proceedings of the 2006 ACM Symposium on Applied Computing, pp. 1810–1815 (2006)
21. Könighofer, B., Lorber, F., Jansen, N., Bloem, R.: Shield synthesis for reinforcement learning. In: Leveraging Applications of Formal Methods, Verification and Validation: Verification Principles: 9th International Symposium on Leveraging Applications of Formal Methods, ISoLA 2020, Rhodes, Greece, 20–30 October 2020, Proceedings, Part I 9, pp. 290–306. Springer, Cham (2020)
22. Křetínský, J., Meggendorfer, T., Prokop, M., Rieder, S.: Guessing winning policies in LTL synthesis by semantic learning. In: International Conference on Computer Aided Verification, pp. 390–414. Springer, Cham (2023)
23. Larsen, K.G., Pettersson, P., Yi, W.: UPPAAL in a nutshell. Int. J. Softw. Tools Technol. Transfer **1**, 134–152 (1997)
24. Lee, E.A.: The past, present and future of cyber-physical systems: a focus on models. Sensors **15**(3), 4837–4869 (2015)
25. Lee, E.A.: Fundamental limits of cyber-physical systems modeling. ACM Trans. Cyber-Phys. Syst. **1**(1), 1–26 (2016)
26. Legay, A., Lukina, A., Traonouez, L.M., Yang, J., Smolka, S.A., Grosu, R.: Statistical model checking. In: Computing and Software Science: State of the Art and Perspectives, pp. 478–504. Springer, Cham (2019)
27. Lin, S., et al.: Towards building verifiable CPS using lingua franca. ACM Trans. Embed. Comput. Syst. **22**(5s), 1–24 (2023)
28. Pnueli, A., Rosner, R.: On the synthesis of an asynchronous reactive module. In: International Colloquium on Automata, Languages, and Programming, pp. 652–671. Springer, Cham (1989)
29. Putnik, G.D., Ferreira, L., Lopes, N., Putnik, Z.: What is a cyber-physical system: definitions and models spectrum. FME Trans. **47**(4) (2019)
30. Qin, X., Xia, Y., Zutshi, A., Fan, C., Deshmukh, J.V.: Statistical verification of cyber-physical systems using surrogate models and conformal inference. In: 2022 ACM/IEEE 13th International Conference on Cyber-Physical Systems (ICCPS), pp. 116–126. IEEE (2022)
31. Sirjani, M., Lee, E.A., Khamespanah, E.: Verification of cyberphysical systems. Mathematics **8**(7), 1068 (2020)
32. Sutton, R.S.: Reinforcement Learning: An Introduction. A Bradford Book (2018)
33. UPPAAL: UPPAAL documentation. https://docs.uppaal.org/
34. Wired: Hackers remotely kill a jeep on the highwaywith me in it (2015). https://www.wired.com/2015/07/hackers-remotely-kill-jeep-highway/

20 Years of Actor Model Checking with Rebeca From Dining Philosophers to Micro-services

Ehsan Khamespanah[1]([✉]) and Mohammad Mahdi Jaghoori[2]

[1] School of ECE, University of Tehran, Tehran, Iran
e.khamespanah@ut.ac.ir
[2] Dockmeh B.V., Amsterdam, The Netherlands

Abstract. Micro-service architecture, combined with message-passing tools such as Kafka, is nowadays widely used in software systems. However, this leads to highly concurrent behavior, making it susceptible to subtle design flaws. In this paper, we survey the two decades of research and development in the actor-based modeling language Rebeca and its model checking toolset, and explore how it can be leveraged to ensure the correctness of software with these modern designs.

1 Introduction

Software verification has not yet found its way to the software development process in the industry. Despite the widespread use of unit and integration testing in practice, the testing and verification of end-to-end communication between various software components is quite difficult and is often left out. This issue is particularly critical in modern architectures like micro-services [3], where asynchronous message passing is a key feature.

In this paper, we leverage two decades of research in Rebeca [25,28], a class-based imperative interpretation of the actor model [1], to address this challenge. We demonstrate how Rebeca can be used to abstractly model software systems with micro-services architecture. To illustrate this, we use a practical example of an online retail system, and use the Rebeca model checking toolset and identify a subtle bug that manifests only under specific circumstances, namely when Kubernetes auto-scaling and Kafka load balancing are triggered.

Kafka [19] is a widely used messaging platform in the industry, if not the most common. Kafka implements the so-called pub-sub mechanism and offers at-least-once delivery by default, but it also supports at-most-once and exactly-once delivery configurations. Each message is published under a topic, and consumers can choose to subscribe to certain topics and thus receive only those messages. With its first-in-first-out message ordering, Kafka essentially implements the asynchronous message passing characteristic of the actor model and Rebeca. Kafka, however, provides additional features, for instance, allowing multiple service instances to form a consumer group for distributed message processing, thereby balancing the processing load. We present an abstract model of

E. A. Lee et al. (Eds.): Marjan Sirjani Festschrift, LNCS 15560, pp. 26–43, 2025.
https://doi.org/10.1007/978-3-031-85134-6_2

this Kafka behavior in Rebeca and use it to verify the correctness of our example system under load balancing conditions.

Our example also assumes a platform like Kubernetes [8], which provide various practical features for running and orchestrating the micro-service instances comprising a software system. One of the fundamental advantages of Kubernetes is its fault-tolerance mechanisms. For example, if a service crashes, Kubernetes spins up a new instance immediately, enabling automatic recovery, especially in the case of transient errors. Kubernetes can additionally be configured to horizontally scale up the number of instances of a given service when under high load. Our running example will demonstrate that while an implementation might function correctly with a single service instance, auto-scaling together with Kafka's load balancing can potentially lead to a violation of safety properties, causing the application to malfunction. For the purpose of this discussion, we do not model Kubernetes in Rebeca. To capture the effect of auto-scaling, we run the model checking on two settings of before and after auto-scaling.

In the following sections, we first provide a detailed introduction to Rebeca and how it can be used in modeling distributed systems. We provide a survey of how model checking techniques were applied to Rebeca and present the evolution of the Rebeca model checking suite. We then present our case study of an online retail system, demonstrating how Rebeca can be used to identify potential issues in a practical context. We also discuss how we model Kafka in Rebeca, and present the results of our model checking.

Related Work. Formal verification approaches and standards in the cloud computing were studied in 2018 [30]. A more recent review of application of formal verification focuses on microservices autoscaling [16]. Correctness of microservice architecture has been previously subject of research where a formal model of Kubernetes was given in [32]. Recent research have focused on formal modeling and verification of Kafka [23,31,34] but these are not considering Kafka in the context of micro-services or auto-scaling. Camilli [4] suggests an approach to integrate formal verification of message communication via Kafka into the software development process. All the trends mentioned above and the research presented in this paper consider different aspects of the modern software architectures and software development process. Integrating these novelties, especially that of Camilli [4] with ours provides a promising horizon on bringing verification to the industrial practice of software engineering.

2 Rebeca Introduction

Rebeca [25,28] is a class-based imperative interpretation of the actor model [1]. In Rebeca, the behavior of a system is modeled as a collection of reactive objects with isolated states, communicating via asynchronous message passing. Rebeca has a Java-like syntax which makes it easy to learn and use by practitioners. In addition to assertion-based verification, it is equipped with an LTL model checker, integrated into the Afra [18] toolset (cf. Sect. 3).

To make our explanation of Rebeca easier to follow, we explain the Rebeca features over a running example, i.e. an online retail system. This system is a platform that facilitates the buying and selling of products over the Internet. This system typically consists of various components, including a user-friendly interface for customers, a shopping cart, payment gateways, and back-end processes for managing orders, inventory, and shipping. Customers can browse products, add items to their cart, and complete transactions securely from the comfort of their homes. For retailers, it provides tools to manage product listings, track inventory, handle customer inquiries, and analyze sales data.

We implement the core behavior of a retail system as illustrated in the event diagram of Fig. 1. It demonstrates that the primary activity of a customer is browsing, which may sometimes lead to placing an order. A placed order is checked for item availability. If the items are available, they are shipped to the customer. As depicted in Fig. 1, the events of this model can be associated with four different actors.

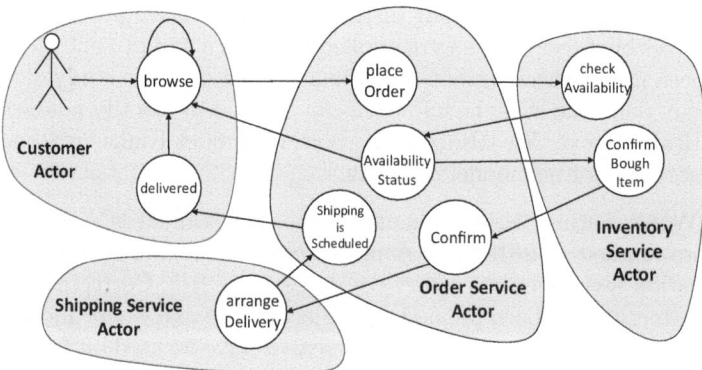

Fig. 1. The event diagram of the online retail system including the main actors involved

To implement the online retail system of Fig. 1 in Rebeca, Four different actor types have to be defined. A Rebeca model consists of a set of reactive class definitions –as the actor types– and the main block –which contains actor instances of the defined reactive classes. The body of a reactive class includes the declaration of its known actors, state variables, and message servers. Message servers consist of the declaration of their corresponding parameters and statements of the message servers. The statements can be assignment to state variables, conditionals, enumerated loops, non-deterministic assignments, and method calls. Method calls are sending asynchronous messages to other actors (or to themselves). In this section, the four actors of our example communicate directly, whereas we extend this in Sect. 4 to introduce an abstract model of Kafka.

To illustrate Rebeca syntax for reactive class definition, the implementation of **Customer** reactive class is presented in Listing 2.1. A reactive class has an argument of type integer denoting the maximum size of its message queue.

Although message queues are unbounded in the semantics of Rebeca, to ensure that the state space is finite, we need a user-specified upper bound for the queue size. The queue size of Customer is set to 3, as depicted in line 1.

A customer is allowed to send requests to the order service; so, its known rebec is defined as a variable of type OrderService in line 2. It also has buying state variable which is used to figure out the buying status of the customer. Upon construction of an instance of Customer reactive class, it starts browsing as depicted in line 4. Two message servers browse and delivered in Customer model the behavior of browsing an online shop and receiving the result of previously placed orders. Using the nondeterministic assignment of line 6, a customer nondeterministically decides between buying an item and continuing browsing. Buying an item takes place by sending placeOrder message to orderService actor, shown in line 8. As depicted in the message server delivered, delivery of an item results in setting buying to false and continue browsing from the customer site. This way, a customer is allowed to continue browsing only after finishing processing of its previous request.

Listing 2.1. The Rebeca model of the Customer reactive class

```
 1  reactiveclass Customer(3) {
 2    knownrebecs { OrderService orderService; }
 3    statevars { boolean buying; }
 4    Customer() { self.browse(); }
 5    msgsrv browse() {
 6      buying = ?(true, false);
 7      if(buying)
 8        orderService.placeOrder(self, ?(0, 1), ?(1, 2));
 9      else
10        self.browse();
11    }
12    msgsrv delivered(boolean success) {
13      buying = false;
14      self.browse();
15    }
16  }
```

The main duty of OrderService reactive class is dispatching requests to the inventory service and shipping the confirmed items to the customers, modeled using four message servers of OrderService, depicted in Listing 2.2. The message server placeOrder checks availability of the requested item. The result of checking availability is reported to OrderService by sending availabilityStatus. In the case of not having enough items, customer is informed by sending delivered message with parameter false to it. If the requested items exists, buying is confirmed and shipping process is started as depicted in line 17.

Listing 2.2. The Rebeca model of the OrderService reactive class

```
 1  reactiveclass OrderService (4) {
 2    knownrebecs {
```

```
3      InventoryService inventory;
4      ShippingService shipping;
5    }
6    msgsrv placeOrder(Customer cu, byte product, byte qty) {
7      inventory.checkAvailability(cu, product, qty);
8    }
9    msgsrv availabilityStatus(Customer cu, boolean available, byte
         product, byte qty) {
10     if(available) {
11       inventory.confirmBoughtItem(cu, product, qty);
12     } else {
13       cu.delivered(false);
14     }
15   }
16   msgsrv confirm(Customer cu, byte product, byte qty) {
17     shipping.arrangeDelivery(cu, product, qty);
18   }
19   msgsrv shippingIsScheduled(Customer cu) {
20     cu.delivered(true);
21   }
22 }
```

As shown in Listing 2.3, an instance of InventoryService has two products, and the number of available items of products are stored in stockLevel state variable. As shown in line 5, the initial number of items is set to 5 for both of them. The message server checkAvailability informs order service the existence of enough items by sending availabilityStatus message to the order service using the sender keyword. As depicted in line 9, the sender of this message is cast to OrderService to be able to send messages to it. Completing the process of buying items and updating the number of available items takes place in the message server confirmBoughtItem.

Listing 2.3. The Rebeca model the InventoryService reactive class

```
1  reactiveclass InventoryService (4) {
2    statevars { int[2] stockLevel; }
3    InventoryService() {
4      for (int i = 0; i < 2; i++) {
5        stockLevel[i] = 5;
6      }
7    }
8    msgsrv checkAvailability(Customer cu, byte product, byte qty) {
9      ((OrderService)sender).availabilityStatus(cu,
           stockLevel[product] >= qty, product, qty);
10   }
11   msgsrv confirmBoughtItem(Customer cu, byte product, byte qty) {
12     stockLevel[product] -= qty;
13     ((OrderService)sender).confirm(cu, product, qty);
14   }
15 }
```

The model of `ShippingService` of Listing 2.4 shows how shipping confirmed items is modeled in the `arrangeDelivery` message server.

Listing 2.4. The Rebeca model of the `ShippingService` reactive class

```
1  reactiveclass ShippingService (3){
2    msgsrv arrangeDelivery(Customer customer, byte product, byte
       quantity) {
3      ((OrderService)sender).shippingIsScheduled(customer);
4    }
5  }
```

Finally, the main block of Listing 2.5 models an environment that two customers browse the online retail system, and one instance of the other three services is responsible for serving them. Section 4 presents the results of model checking this example and its further extensions.

Listing 2.5. The main block of the online retail system

```
1  main {
2    Customer customer1(orderService):();
3    Customer customer2(orderService):();
4    OrderService orderService(inventoryService, shippingService):();
5    InventoryService inventoryService():();
6    ShippingService shippingService():();
7  }
```

3   The Story of Rebeca Model Checker

3.1   Early Developments

The initial attempts to enable verification of Rebeca models started two decades ago by translating these models into other well-known modeling languages and using their respective model checkers. The first approach involved using NuSMV, the model checker for SMV language, to verify Rebeca against CTL properties [26]. Although this translation supported limited features, e.g., only boolean variables, it did enable the compositional verification that was proposed for Rebeca [27]. This means that a big Rebeca model can be broken down into smaller components to avoid state-space explosion. Having proven the correctness of each component using this tool, then one can theoretically prove the correctness of their composition.

A visual editor, Roudabeh, was also developed to simplify the modeling and model checking process. Roudabeh not only integrates the Rebeca-to-SMV tool into a visual environment but also enables compositional verification. The system topology can be visualized as a graph, where nodes represent rebecs and edges depict the bindings between them. Having selected a component to include some rebecs, the tool automatically generates a Rebeca model for the chosen system part. The environment is then extracted based on the selected rebecs, and the translation to SMV is performed automatically. The tool runs NuSMV in the background, managing the program's input/output and uses it for model checking Rebeca models.

Subsequently, a new translator from Rebeca to Promela was developed, allowing the use of the SPIN model checker to verify LTL properties [29]. Since the process-based nature of Promela is closer to the actor model, this provided a more natural translation and therefore supported more of Rebeca features. Later, Sarir [10] was implemented as a translator of Rebeca to mCRL2, a process algebra enhanced with data types. The main motivation was to exploit the verification tools and theories developed for mCRL2 in Rebeca. The minimization tools of mCRL2 proved to be more effective in certain cases than the Promela translation with SPIN model checker.

3.2   Mature Dedicated Toolset

In 2005, Rebeca got its own dedicated model checking engine, Modere [12]. Modere uses Nested Depth First Search (NDFS) algorithm for exploring the state-space and checking LTL formulas on-the-fly. To avoid stack overflow, Modere uses the non-recursive implementation of the NDFS and handles the search stack manually. Modere only considers the fair sequences of execution. An infinite sequence is considered (weakly) fair when all the actors of the model are infinitely often executed or disabled [2]. Practically, it means in every loop representing an infinite execution, all actors with a non-empty message queue must contribute at least one transition. By dividing the state of the system into inter-process and intra-process hash tables, similar to the method used in SPIN, Modere benefits from up to 60% reduction in the memory usage for storing transition systems. As mentioned in [12], Modere has been used for the model checking of models from networking, distributed systems, an some other models from different domains and handles state spaces of up to 10 million states.

Modere supports two state-space reduction techniques, namely Partial-Order and Symmetry Reduction [13]. In Rebeca, each state's potential future states are determined by the interleaving of enabled actions (i.e., processing a message) from various rebecs. However, it's not always necessary to consider all possible interleaved sequences of these actions. The partial order reduction method [6] proposes that the execution of certain enabled actions can be deferred to a future state without impacting the correctness property's satisfiability. Consequently, by avoiding the complete interleaving of the enabled actions, some states can be omitted from the exhaustive state exploration in model checking.

Symmetry, on the other hand, exists in the graph representation of a state space if a permutation on the states exists such that the resulting graph is isomorphic to the original one. Such a permutation partitions the state space into equivalence classes. Thus, one needs to store only one representative for each class of states. The difficulty in applying this technique is finding the equivalence classes without constructing the whole state space. The actor-based nature of Rebeca helps us define state permutations based on rebec indices [14]. We have proven that symmetry in communication graph of a Rebeca model translates into symmetry in the state space (inter-rebec symmetry). Additionally, we introduced some syntactic restrictions that can be applied by the modeler to expose the internal symmetry of some rebecs. We gave polynomial time algorithms for statically detecting inter- and intra-rebec symmetry in Rebeca models [24].

Partial order techniques exploit the independence of actions, while symmetry based reduction techniques are based on structural symmetries in the system. Based on this fact, Modere implements the abstract framework for combining these two techniques proposed in [5].

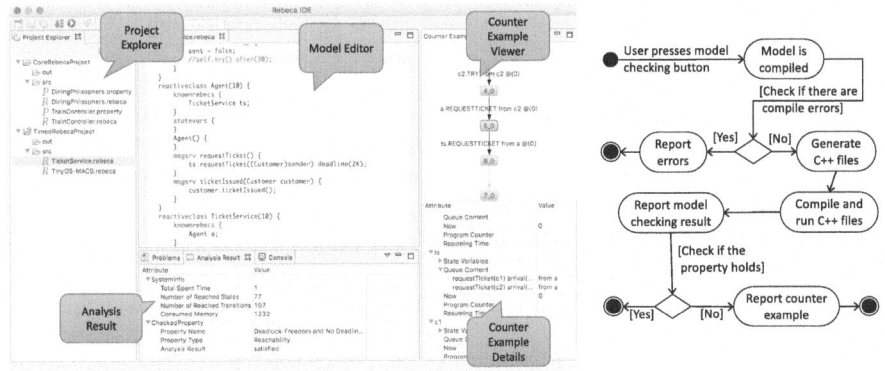

Fig. 2. Afra. Graphical user interface (left); Model checking process (right) [18]

Khamespanah et al. [18] introduced Afra some years later as an integrated environment designed for modeling and verifying Rebeca models, primarily using Modere at the core. Afra is an Eclipse-based tool and supports the modeling and model checking of Rebeca models. It includes a standard enriched editor, an easy-to-trace counterexample viewer, modular temporal property definitions, and the ability to export models and their transition systems to other formats. Given a Rebeca model file, the properties that must be satisfied by the model are specified in another file, known as the property file. Afra generates C++ code representing the model and the properties and places them next to the C++ engine of Modere. This combination is then compiled and executed (see Fig. 2). The result of the model checking is then parsed and presented in the IDE. Having an integrated development environment is a key step in enabling the adoption of Rebeca in practical software engineering practice.

3.3   Further Extensions: Timed and Probabilistic Model Checking

After successful application of Rebeca in various domains [9,15,20], Rebeca and consequently Rebeca Model Checker have been extended with the concepts of real time and probabilistic verification.

To address discrete time, Timed Rebeca (TRebeca) allows one to specify computation time, message delivery time, message expiration, and period of occurrence of events [21]. In the initial implementation, the transformation of TRebeca models to Realtime Maude is used for the model checking of TRebeca models [22]. Then, the Floating Time Transition System (FTTS) is introduced to significantly reduce the state space generated when model checking Timed Rebeca (TRebeca) models in [17]. In this work, we also proposed a new notion for equivalence relation between two states to make the transition systems finite, called shift equivalence relation. Intuitively, in shift equivalence relation two states are equivalent if and only if they are the same except for the parts related to the time and shifting the times of those parts in one state makes it the same as the other one.

In an independent work, PRebeca is proposed as an extension of Rebeca to model probabilistic and nondeterministic behavior [33]. In PRebeca, one can specify the probability of losing a message in the communication. Additionally, alternate operations can be specified in the definition of message servers where each alternative is selected based on the specified probabilities. In combination with real-time in PTRebeca [11], computations and message delays are also probabilistic. PTRebeca is the first actor-based language that supports time, probability, and nondeterminism in modeling distributed systems with asynchronous message passing.

For model checking timed models, Modere has been extended with FTTS semantics and timed CTL properties. The semantics of PTRebeca is however defined as Timed Markov Decision Processes. Afra automatically generates a Markov Automaton from a PTRebeca model in the form of the input language of the Interactive Markov Chain Analyzer (IMCA) [7]. Then IMCA can be used as a back-end model checker for performance analysis of PTRebeca models. PTRebeca models can thus be analyzed against PCTL, expected reachability, and probabilistic reachability properties.

4 Verifying Modern Software Architectures in Rebeca

Micro-service architecture is a software architectural style that structures an application as a collection of loosely coupled services. In this architecture, services are fine-grained, and the communication protocols are lightweight. The aim of using micro-service architecture is to enhance the modularity, scalability, and maintainability of software systems. Each service in a micro-service architecture is autonomous, responsible for a specific business capability, and can be developed, deployed, and scaled independently.

A common pattern in micro-services architecture is that services communicate by message passing. For example, Kafka is a very common tool for this purpose. This is, among others, due to Kafka's guarantee on the ordering of messages, automatic load balancing between the recipients of a message (consumer groups), and more. The model presented in Sect. 2 is essentially equivalent to such an architecture. As long as there is only one instance of each service, this will be already an abstraction of Kafka. Model checking with Afra proves that there is no deadlock in this model and additionally we verify that the number of available items never falls below zero (see Sect. 4.3).

In the rest of this section, we introduce an abstract model of Kafka and show the effect of horizontal upscaling of the services as Kubernetes would do. We present an implementation containing a fixed number of service instances and a Kafka broker as a new reactive class. The proposed model of Kafka can partition messages and distributes them between the various service instances.

4.1 Implementing Kafka in Rebeca

One abstract model of Kafka in Rebeca is shown in Listing 4.1. In this implementation, two reactive classes are defined: `KafkaConsumer` and `KafKa`. Any reactive class that wants to subscribe to Kafka must declare `KafkaConsumer` as its superclass. This way, it inherits a reference to `Kafka` as its knownrebecs and must implement the `receive` message server to handle incoming messages from Kafka. The `Kafka` reactive class simulates the behavior of the Kafka message broker, featuring a message buffer –i.e. `data`– which supports three topics and a fixed size of 10. In this implementation, each message is represented as a tuple of three bytes, and the number of currently received data in each topic is stored in the `dataSize` state variables. To model the concept of "consumers subscribing to topics", we define `waitingConsumers` where we store per topic, at most 2 consumers that are ready to receive a message on that topic.

Sending messages to Kafka is handled in the `receive` message server. Upon receipt, new data is added to the messages list of its corresponding topic. If a consumer is ready to receive a message, it sends `getMessage` to Kafka. If there is already a message in the buffer, it is delivered. But, if no data is available, the consumer is added to the list of waiting consumers. Upon receiving a new message, it will be delivered to the first waiting consumer.

It is worth noting that at this level of abstraction, we have modeled the exactly-once delivery scheme. To enable model checking, we have fixed the size of the message queue in Kafka and allow at most two waiting consumers, that is, only two partitions within the consumer group. In a typical application, a value like the order ID would be used as the partitioning key. In our model, every order is sent only once and therefore we can abstract away the concept of the partitioning key. So Kafka is free to deliver the messages to any of the subscribers in the consumer group. This model can safely handle both cases of one or two consumers, as we prove deadlock freedom and correctness in the sequel.

4.2 Adding Kafka to the System

Introducing a message broker between the customer and the order service requires changes in both the `Customer` and `OrderService` reactive classes. As demonstrated in Listing 4.3, when a customer wants to purchase an item, it publishes a message to Kafka (line 14) and then await a response on a relevant topic (line 15). Then `Customer` reactive class now has a state variable, `buying`,

Listing 4.1. The Rebeca model of Kafka

```
 1 abstract reactiveclass KafkaConsumer(5) {
 2   knownrebecs { Kafka kafka; }
 3   abstract msgsrv receive(byte data1, byte data2, byte data3);
 4 }
 5 reactiveclass Kafka(10) {
 6   statevars {
 7     byte[3][10][3] data;
 8     byte[3] dataSize;
 9     KafkaConsumer[3][2] waitingConsumers;
10   }
11   msgsrv sendMessage(byte topicId, byte data1, byte data2, byte
        data3) {
12     int size = dataSize[topicId];
13     data[topicId][size][0] = data1;
14     data[topicId][size][1] = data2;
15     data[topicId][size][2] = data3;
16     dataSize[topicId]++;
17     if(waitingConsumers[topicId][0] != null) {
18       KafkaConsumer consumer = waitingConsumers[topicId][0];
19       waitingConsumers[topicId][0] = waitingConsumers[topicId][1];
20       waitingConsumers[topicId][1] = null;
21       sendDataToConsumer(consumer, topicId);
22     }
23   }
24   msgsrv getMessage(KafkaConsumer consumer, byte topicId) {
25     if(dataSize[topicId] == 0) {
26       for(int cnt = 0; cnt < 2; cnt++)
27         if(waitingConsumers[topicId][cnt] == null) {
28           waitingConsumers[topicId][cnt] = consumer;
29           return;
30         }
31     }
32     sendDataToConsumer(consumer, topicId);
33   }
34   void sendDataToConsumer(KafkaConsumer consumer, byte topicId) {
35     byte data1 = data[topicId][0][0];
36     byte data2 = data[topicId][0][1];
37     byte data3 = data[topicId][0][2];
38     dataSize[topicId]--;
39     int size = dataSize[topicId];
40     for(int cnt = 0; cnt < 9; cnt++) {
41       data[topicId][size][0] = data[topicId][size + 1][0];
42       data[topicId][size][1] = data[topicId][size + 1][1];
43       data[topicId][size][2] = data[topicId][size + 1][2];
44     }
45     consumer.receive(data1, data2, data3);
46   }
47 }
```

which indicates whether the customer is currently in the buying phase. Once the response from Kafka is received, the consumer resumes browsing and the `buying` flag is reset to `false`.

Listing 4.2. The Rebeca model the `Customer` reactive class that publishes messages in Kafka

```
1  env byte ORDERSERVICE_TOPIC_ID = 2;
2  reactiveclass Customer extends KafkaConsumer(3) {
3    statevars {
4      byte topicId;
5      boolean buying;
6    }
7    Customer(byte myTopicID) {
8      topicId = myTopicID;
9      self.browse();
10   }
11   msgsrv browse() {
12     buying = ?(true, false);
13     if(buying) {
14       kafka.sendMessage(ORDERSERVICE_TOPIC_ID, topicId, ?(0, 1),
                ?(1, 2));
15       kafka.getMessage(self, topicId);
16     } else
17       self.browse();
18   }
19   msgsrv receive(byte data1, byte data2, byte data3) {
20     buying = false;
21     self.browse();
22   }
23 }
```

The same set of modifications is needed to make `OrderService` compatible with Kafka. It starts by waiting for an incoming message from a customer (line 7). Upon receiving a request from a customer, it asks the inventory service about the availability of items. Once there are enough items, the order service confirms buy request and ships the items. When shipment is scheduled, the customer informs regarding the status of its placed order (line 32). In the case of not having enough items, the customer is informed about rejecting its order (line 21).

Listing 4.3. The Rebeca model the `OrderService` reactive class that publishes messages in Kafka

```
1  reactiveclass OrderService extends KafkaConsumer(4) {
2    knownrebecs {
3      InventoryService inventory;
4      ShippingService shipping;
5    }
6    statevars { byte product, qty, consumerTopicId; }
7    OrderService() { self.startReceiving(); }
8    msgsrv startReceiving() {
```

```
 9      kafka.getMessage(self, ORDERSERVICE_TOPIC_ID);
10    }
11    msgsrv receive(byte data1, byte data2, byte data3) {
12      consumerTopicId = data1;
13      product = data2;
14      qty = data3;
15      inventory.checkAvailability(product, qty);
16    }
17    msgsrv availabilityStatus(boolean available) {
18      if(available) {
19        inventory.confirmBoughtItem(product, qty);
20      } else {
21        kafka.sendMessage(consumerTopicId, -1, 0, 0);
22        consumerTopicId = 0;
23        product = 0;
24        qty = 0;
25        kafka.getMessage(self, ORDERSERVICE_TOPIC_ID);
26      }
27    }
28    msgsrv confirm() {
29      shipping.arrangeDelivery(product, qty);
30    }
31    msgsrv shippingIsScheduled() {
32      kafka.sendMessage(consumerTopicId, 1, 0, 0);
33      consumerTopicId = 0;
34      product = 0;
35      qty = 0;
36      kafka.getMessage(self, ORDERSERVICE_TOPIC_ID);
37    }
38  }
```

4.3   Model Checking Multiple Scenarios

We defined a correctness assertion formula for this model to ensure that the number of items in the inventory service never drops below zero. Model checking against this property in a setting where we have one instance of each service resulted in the generation of 75,800 states, with no counterexample found, confirming the correctness of the model.

Auto-Scaling. In modern systems, micro-services are often deployed on Kubernetes or comparable systems. As previously mentioned, Kubernetes offers numerous advantages, particularly for systems managing large volumes of data or requiring high throughput. Such systems can be configured to spin up new instances of a service once it is under high load. In such a situation, Kafka will notice the change in the size of the consumer group and automatically distributes the load accordingly. By dividing the topics into partitions based on the message keys, Kafka allows the consumers to receive independent messages and process them in parallel without affecting the producers.

The proposed Rebeca model of Kafka supports the distribution of data across multiple consumers. To create the effect of auto-scaling, we change the main section to introduce two instances of OrderService. This allows for serving customers concurrently across both service instances. While the model with a single instance of OrderService operates correctly, model checking of the updated model reveals a counterexample. Specifically, in a trace with 671 steps, the number of items in the inventory drops below zero. Upon reviewing the counterexample, it becomes clear that the issue arises because checking and updating the number of items in the inventory service is not an atomic operation. This leads to a race condition between the two instances of OrderService, causing incorrect values to be set for the remaining number of items.

There are multiple solutions to this issue. A typical approach is to include more data inside the messages such that the services are stateless as far as possible. In our example, there is a simpler solution, that is, to make the check-and-update operations atomic. This solution can be implemented by updating OrderService and InventoryService as shown in Listing 4.4. Model checking of the updated model illustrates that it works correctly after the generation of 517,400 states.

Listing 4.4. The Rebeca model the OrderService reactive class that publishes messages in Kafka

```
 1  reactiveclass OrderService extends KafkaConsumer(4) {
 2    ...
 3    msgsrv availabilityStatus(boolean available) {
 4      if(available) {
 5        shipping.arrangeDelivery(product, qty);
 6      } else {
 7        kafka.sendMessage(consumerTopicId, -1, 0, 0);
 8        kafka.getMessage(self, ORDERSERVICE_TOPIC_ID);
 9        consumerTopicId = 0;
10        product = 0;
11        qty = 0;
12      }
13    }
14  }

16  reactiveclass InventoryService(4) {
17    ...
18    msgsrv checkAvailability(byte product, byte qty) {
19      boolean available = stockLevel[product] >= qty;
20      if(available)
21        stockLevel[product] -= qty;
22      ((OrderService)sender).availabilityStatus(available);
23    }
24  }
```

Table 1 presents the model checking result for various implementations of the model discussed above, each with different numbers of customer and order

Table 1. The model checking results of the various configurations.

	Conf.	#States	#Transitions	Memory	Time	Result
Without Kafka	1O 2C	49,234	86,843	3.6 MB	1 s	✓
	1O 3C	3,179.106	6,595,513	254 MB	32 s	✓
Kafka + Non-Atomic	1O 2C	75,800	160,850	6 MB	2 s	✓
	1O 3C	2,939,637	7,159,382	258 MB	01:21	✓
	2O 2C	2,088	3,792	180 KB	<1 s	✗
Kafka + Atomic	1O 2C	60,840	128,194	4.8 MB	1 s	✓
	1O 3C	24,014,164	68,210,899	2.3 GB	14:41	✓
	2O 2C	517,400	1,282,359	45 MB	15 s	✓

service instances. In the following, *Conf.* shows the configuration of the model, represented by the number of order services (O) and customers (C). For instance 1O 2C indicates one instance of `OrderServices` and two instances of `Customers`. The host of Afra for these experiments is a Macbook Pro with the Apple M1 chip and 16GB of RAM storage. Out of the eight experiments, only one case resulted in the violation of the correctness property.

4.4   Discussion

Even though we provided an abstract model of Kafka tailored to the running example, it is possible to create a more generic implementation of Kafka. By covering more of Kafka features, we can apply model checking to the designs of numerous modern software systems. To address the challenge of state-space explosion, the compositional verification approach of Rebeca can be very useful. To this end, natural candidate components include "Kafka and producer service" or "Kafka and consumer service".

Even though we did not model Kubernetes in this paper, its fault tolerance and auto-scaling features have been previously studied in the context of formal methods. We considered various scaling configurations by manually changing the Rebeca model definition. This can be automated to run the Rebeca model multiple times based on predefined auto-scaling scenarios.

The abstract Rebeca model as provided in this paper can be used as a starting point in designing new software systems. Decisions on how the communication between various actors (aka micro-services) should be implemented are typically stored as the so-called ADRs (architectural decision records). The Rebeca model generated at the architectural level can be included in the ADR descriptions. These can be used to generate end-to-end test cases for the future system. These tests can be integrated into the continuous integration pipeline of the system and applied on an end-to-end level where messages are produced on Kafka based on the Rebeca model, and the expectation is that correct Kafka messages must be produced by the system under test.

5   Conclusions

We looked back at the evolution of Rebeca model checking over the past two decades. From its initial stages of translating models into other known modeling languages for verification, until Rebeca got its own dedicated model checking tool. Manual compositional verification combined with automatic state-space reduction techniques, such as Partial-Order and Symmetry Reduction, have proven very useful for managing the complexity of model checking in large systems.

The use of Rebeca in the software development process can help to develop bug-free systems. We made an abstract model of a modern architecture involving micro-services on Kubernetes and using Kafka for communication. We believe that this can be a starting point to improve the applicability of formal methods and verification, and in particular the Rebeca model checker, by integrating it into architectural designs and continuous integration pipelines of software systems. This will be one step towards the adoption of software verification by the software industry.

References

1. Agha, G.: Actors: A Model of Concurrent Computation in Distributed Systems. MIT Press, Cambridge (1986)
2. Baier, C., Katoen, J.: Principles of Model Checking. MIT Press, Cambridge (2008)
3. Balalaie, A., Heydarnoori, A., Jamshidi, P.: Microservices architecture enables devops: migration to a cloud-native architecture. IEEE Softw. **33**(3), 42–52 (2016)
4. Camilli, M.: Continuous formal verification of microservice-based process flows. In: Muccini, H., et al. (eds.) ECSA 2020. CCIS, vol. 1269, pp. 420–435. Springer, Cham (2020). https://doi.org/10.1007/978-3-030-59155-7_31
5. Emerson, E.A., Jha, S., Peled, D.: Combining partial order and symmetry reductions. In: Proceedings of the Tools and Algorithms for Construction and Analysis of Systems, Third International Workshop, TACAS 1997. LNCS, vol. 1217, pp. 19–34. Springer, Cham (1997)
6. Godefroid, P.: Partial-order methods for the verification of concurrent systems: an approach to the state-explosion problem. Ph.D. thesis, Universite De Liege (1995)
7. Guck, D., Han, T., Katoen, J.-P., Neuhäußer, M.R.: Quantitative timed analysis of interactive Markov chains. In: Goodloe, A.E., Person, S. (eds.) NFM 2012. LNCS, vol. 7226, pp. 8–23. Springer, Heidelberg (2012). https://doi.org/10.1007/978-3-642-28891-3_4
8. Hightower, K., Burns, B., Beda, J.: Kubernetes: Up and Running Dive into the Future of Infrastructure. O'Reilly Media, Inc., Sebastopol (2017)
9. Hojjat, H., Nakhost, H., Sirjani, M.: Formal verification of the IEEE 802.1d spanning tree protocol using extended Rebeca. In: Arbab, F., Sirjani, M. (eds.) Proceedings of the First IPM International Workshop on Foundations of Software Engineering, FSEN 2005, Tehran, Iran, 1–3 October 2005. Electronic Notes in Theoretical Computer Science, vol. 159, pp. 139–154. Elsevier (2005)
10. Hojjat, H., Sirjani, M., Mousavi, M.R., Groote, J.F.: Sarir: a Rebeca to mCRL2 translator. In: Seventh International Conference on Application of Concurrency to System Design (ACSD 2007), Bratislava, Slovak Republic, 10–13 July 2007, pp. 216–222. IEEE Computer Society (2007)

11. Jafari, A., Khamespanah, E., Sirjani, M., Hermanns, H., Cimini, M.: PTRebeca: modeling and analysis of distributed and asynchronous systems. Sci. Comput. Program. **128**, 22–50 (2016)
12. Jaghoori, M.M., Movaghar, A., Sirjani, M.: Modere: the model-checking engine of Rebeca. In: Haddad, H. (ed.) Proceedings of the ACM Symposium on Applied Computing (SAC 2006), Dijon, France, 23–27 April, pp. 1810–1815. ACM (2006)
13. Jaghoori, M.M., Sirjani, M., Mousavi, M.R., Khamespanah, E., Movaghar, A.: Symmetry and partial order reduction techniques in model checking Rebeca. Acta Informatica **47**(1), 33–66 (2010)
14. Jaghoori, M.M., Sirjani, M., Mousavi, M.R., Movaghar, A.: Efficient symmetry reduction for an actor-based model. In: Chakraborty, G. (ed.) ICDCIT 2005. LNCS, vol. 3816, pp. 494–507. Springer, Heidelberg (2005). https://doi.org/10.1007/11604655_56
15. Jahandideh, I., Ghassemi, F., Sirjani, M.: Hybrid Rebeca: modeling and analyzing of cyber-physical systems. In: Cyber Physical Systems. Model-Based Design: 8th International Workshop, CyPhy 2018, and 14th International Workshop, WESE 2018, Turin, Italy, 4–5 October 2018, Revised Selected Papers 8, pp. 3–27. Springer, Cham (2019)
16. Jawaddi, S.N.A., Johari, M.H., Ismail, A.: A review of microservices autoscaling with formal verification perspective. Softw. Pract. Exp. **52**(11), 2476–2495 (2022)
17. Khamespanah, E., Sirjani, M., Kaviani, Z.S., Khosravi, R., Izadi, M.J.: Timed Rebeca schedulability and deadlock freedom analysis using bounded floating time transition system. Sci. Comput. Program. **98**, 184–204 (2015)
18. Khamespanah, E., Sirjani, M., Khosravi, R.: Afra: an eclipse-based tool with extensible architecture for modeling and model checking of Rebeca family models. In: Fundamentals of Software Engineering - 10th International Conference, FSEN 2023, Tehran, Iran, 4–5 May 2023, Revised Selected Papers. Lecture Notes in Computer Science, vol. 14155, pp. 72–87. Springer, Cham (2023)
19. Kreps, J., Narkhede, N., Rao, J., et al.: Kafka: a distributed messaging system for log processing. In: Proceedings of the NetDB, Athens, Greece, vol. 11, pp. 1–7 (2011)
20. Razavi, N., Sirjani, M.: Compositional semantics of system-level designs written in SystemC. In: Arbab, F., Sirjani, M. (eds.) FSEN 2007. LNCS, vol. 4767, pp. 113–128. Springer, Heidelberg (2007). https://doi.org/10.1007/978-3-540-75698-9_8
21. Reynisson, A.H., et al.: Modelling and simulation of asynchronous real-time systems using timed Rebeca. Sci. Comput. Program. **89**, 41–68 (2014). https://doi.org/10.1016/J.SCICO.2014.01.008
22. Sabahi-Kaviani, Z., Khosravi, R., Ölveczky, P.C., Khamespanah, E., Sirjani, M.: Formal semantics and efficient analysis of timed Rebeca in real-time maude. Sci. Comput. Program. **113**, 85–118 (2015). https://doi.org/10.1016/J.SCICO.2015.07.003
23. Sinha, S., Kang, E.: Formal modeling and analysis of apache kafka in alloy 6. In: International Conference on Rigorous State-Based Methods, pp. 25–42. Springer, Cham (2024)
24. Sirjani, M., SeyedRazi, H., Movaghar, A., Jaghoori, M.M., Forghanizadeh, S., Mojdeh, M.: Model checking CSMA/CD protocol using an actor-based language. WSEAS Trans. Circuit Syst. **3**(4), 1052–1057 (2004)
25. Sirjani, M., Jaghoori, M.M.: Ten years of analyzing actors: Rebeca experience. In: Formal Modeling: Actors, Open Systems, Biological Systems: Essays Dedicated to Carolyn Talcott on the Occasion of Her 70th Birthday, pp. 20–56 (2011)

26. Sirjani, M., Movaghar, A., Iravanchi, H., Jaghoori, M.M., Shali, A.: Model checking in Rebeca. In: Proceedings of the International Conference on Parallel and Distributed Processing Techniques and Applications, PDPTA 2003, Las Vegas, Nevada, USA, 23–26 June, vol. 4, pp. 1819–1822. CSREA Press (2003)

27. Sirjani, M., Movaghar, A., Shali, A., de Boer, F.S.: Model checking, automated abstraction and compositional verification of Rebeca models. J. Univ. Comput. Sci. (JUCS) **11**(6), 1054–1082 (2005)

28. Sirjani, M., Movaghar, A., Shali, A., De Boer, F.S.: Modeling and verification of reactive systems using Rebeca. Fund. Inform. **63**(4), 385–410 (2004)

29. Sirjani, M., Shali, A., Jaghoori, M.M., Iravanchi, H., Movaghar, A.: A front-end tool for automated abstraction and modular verification of actor-based models. In: Proceedings of the International Conference on Application of Concurrency to System Design (ACSD 2004), Hamilton, Canada, 16–18 June, pp. 145–150. IEEE Computer Society (2004)

30. Souri, A., Navimipour, N.J., Rahmani, A.M.: Formal verification approaches and standards in the cloud computing: a comprehensive and systematic review. Comput. Stand. Interfaces **58**, 1–22 (2018)

31. Sun, M., Chen, Z.: Formal modeling and verification of kafka producer-consumer communication in mediator. In: Science and Information Conference, pp. 603–619. Springer, Cham (2024)

32. Turin, G., Borgarelli, A., Donetti, S., Damiani, F., Johnsen, E.B., Tarifa, S.L.T.: Predicting resource consumption of kubernetes container systems using resource models. J. Syst. Softw. **203**, 111750 (2023)

33. Varshosaz, M., Khosravi, R.: Modeling and verification of probabilistic actor systems using prebeca. In: ICFEM, pp. 135–150. Springer, Cham (2012)

34. Xu, J., Yin, J., Zhu, H., Xiao, L.: Formalization and verification of Kafka messaging mechanism using CSP. Comput. Sci. Inf. Syst. **20**(1), 277–306 (2023)

Responsibility in Actor-Based Systems

Christel Baier[1,2] , Sascha Klüppelholz[1] , and Johannes Lehmann[1,2(✉)]

[1] Technische Universität Dresden, Dresden, Germany
{christel.baier,sascha.klueppelholz,johannes_alexander.lehmann}@tu-dresden.de
[2] Centre for Tactile Internet with Human-in-the-Loop (CeTI), Dresden, Germany

Abstract. The enormous growth of the complexity of modern computer systems leads to an increasing demand for techniques that support the comprehensibility of systems. This has motivated the very active research field of formal methods that enhance the understanding of *why* systems behave the way they do. One important line of research within the verification community relies on formal notions that measure the degree of responsibility of different actors. In this paper, we first provide a uniform presentation of recent work on responsibility notions based on Shapley values for reactive systems modeled by transition systems and considering safety properties. The paper then discusses how to use these formal responsibility notions and corresponding algorithms for three different types of actor sets: the *module-based notion* serves to reason about the impact of system components on the satisfaction or violation of a safety property. Responsibility values for *value-based actor sets* and *action-based actors* allow for the identification of program instructions and control points that have the most influence on a specification violation. Beyond the theoretical considerations, this paper reports on experimental results that provide initial insights into applicability and scalability.

1 Introduction

Ensuring the correctness of software is of ever-increasing importance. This has given rise to a variety of formal techniques that aim to prove that software adheres to its specification. The classical verification task is to determine whether a model satisfies a logical formula. Algorithmic techniques such as model checking [6,15,16] can solve this task for systems represented by a finite-state model and temporal logical specifications. Moreover, if a model checker finds a specification violation, it can return a *counterexample*, which is an execution sequence

---

J. Lehmann—Authors are listed in alphabetical order.

The authors are supported by the DFG through the DFG grant 389792660 as part of TRR 248 (see https://perspicuous-computing.science) and the Cluster of Excellence EXC 2050/1 (CeTI, project ID 390696704, as part of Germany's Excellence Strategy) and by BMBF (Federal Ministry of Education and Research) in DAAD project 57616814 (SECAI, School of Embedded and Composite AI) as part of the program Konrad Zuse Schools of Excellence in Artificial Intelligence.

E. A. Lee et al. (Eds.): Marjan Sirjani Festschrift, LNCS 15560, pp. 44–69, 2025.
https://doi.org/10.1007/978-3-031-85134-6_3

for which the specification does not hold. Some verification techniques also support the generation of a mathematical *certificate* in case that the specification holds. Such certificates offer the possibility to check the verification result independently from the verification process. Examples are inductive variants, derivations in deductive systems or mathematical proofs [10,25,26,32,34,35].

Although such certificates and counterexamples can provide useful insights, they are often complex and can enhance the comprehensibility of the system behaviors only to a very limited extent. This motivated research on additional techniques that provide comprehensible and more coherent explanations for *why* a system behaves the way it does. Most notable is the work on methods that extract additional debugging information from counterexamples [2,7,8,20,21,29,31]. The majority of this work is based on formal notions of *counterfactual causality* and inspired by Halpern and Pearl's pioneering work on actual causality for structural equation models [22–24]. The main idea of the counterfactual principle for cause-effect relations is that the effect would not have happened if the cause had not occurred. Related to these works on causality-based explanations of counterexamples is research on formal notions to quantify the *(degree of) responsibility*. Such quantitative notions aim to measure the individual influence of actors of a system on (potential or actually observed) effects on the systems behavior.

Research on responsibility notions in the verification context is motivated by natural questions. For instance, if a system fails to meet its specification, which system component is most responsible? Or, which lines of program code are erroneous and lead to the specification violation? Such questions naturally arise from a *backward-looking* perspective where an execution sequence with undesired behavior has been observed or has been reported in the form of a counterexample by a model checker. Opposed to this is the *forward-looking* perspective where all potential executions of the system are taken into account and one asks for responsibilities for all potential specification violations (or, conversely, the satisfaction of the specification if the system meets its specification). The forward-looking perspective is not only useful for classical functional specifications from the safety-liveness spectrum, but also for reasoning about non-functional properties, e.g. by asking for the system components that have most impact on the expected energy consumption. The distinction between the forward- and backward-looking perspective goes to van de Poel [36] who studied responsibility under philosophical aspects. Among others, it has been taken up for multi-agent systems and game structures under partial observability assumptions [4,39].

Orthogonal to the distinction between forward- and backward-looking approaches are the different possibilities to measure the individual impact of actors on effects. The most popular concepts that have been used in the verification context are *intervention-based approaches* (e.g. those used in [11,12,14]) and more recent approaches that rely on *Shapley values* (e.g. those used in [2,4,5,33]). Responsibility notions of the intervention-based approaches rely on the general concept of responsibility introduced by Chockler and Halpern [13] and derive the degree of responsibility from the smallest number of changes to the system model ("interventions") that make an event a cause of another one with respect to Halpern and Pearl's notion of causality. On the other hand, Shapley values [37] are a game-theoretic concept that has been introduced for one-shot cooperative games which assign a numerical game value to any coalition (i.e. subset) of players. These values represent the outcome the players of a coalition can achieve when cooperating with each other. Roughly speaking, the Shapley value of a player a measures the individual impact of a by its average contribution to the outcomes of coalitions that include player a. The idea of using Shapley values in the verification context is to assign to each coalition of actors of a system (e.g. the system components) the game value 1 if these actors can enforce the specification by resolving their nondeterministic choices in an appropriate way, and 0 otherwise. For other types of responsibility in AI systems and causality-based explanations in the verification context, see, e.g. the survey articles [3,11,17].

This article focuses on responsibility notions defined by Shapley values. More concretely, we present the notions of forward [33] and backward responsibility [2] of *actors* in transition systems on the satisfaction or violation of safety properties in a uniform way. In this setting, the actors are logical units of a system, formalised here by sets of states that constitute a partition of the state space or a fragment thereof. The idea is that each actor controls the nondeterministic choices in the states assigned to her. Beyond the works [2,33] that concentrate on the theoretical foundations, we discuss the generation of natural actor sets, which are either *module-based*, *value-based*, or *action-based*. The proposed techniques for generating actor sets operate on the syntactic description of the system by a program code written in a *reactive module language*. Value-based actors are determined by partial assignments for the program's variables and can, for instance, serve to identify the control points or instructions of a program that have the most influence on a specification violation. Our techniques for module-based actors and action-based actors rely on model transformations. The reason is that each state of a transition system can have transitions of multiple modules. Thus, modules cannot be treated as actors directly. Here we propose a model transformation that generates a new program with an auxiliary scheduler module that serves to split such states where two or more modules can make a move. Likewise, reasoning about the responsibility of actions requires a tailored model transformation.

The remainder of this paper is structured as follows. Section 2 presents our notations for transition systems, safety games and Shapley values. Section 3 provides a summary of the results presented in [33] and [2] for safety properties (rephrased in a uniform manner). In Sect. 4, we show how actors can be derived from a reactive module specification. Section 5 reports on experimental studies that have been carried out a prototypical implementation and provide insights on how the proposed responsibility notions can be used to locate errors in system models. Section 6 concludes with a brief summary and a discussion on future research directions.

2   Preliminaries

We briefly present the notations for transition systems, safety games and Shapley values. More details about transition systems and (safety) games can be found for example in the text books [6,15,18,19].

Transition Systems. A *transition system* is a tuple $T = (S, \rightarrow, s_{init}, \xi)$ where S is a finite set of *states*, $\rightarrow \subseteq S \times S$ the *transition relation* on S, $s_{init} \in S$ the *initial state*, and $\xi \subseteq S$ a set of *bad states*. We assume that the states in ξ are absorbing. A *run* on T is an infinite sequence of states $\rho = \rho_0 \rho_1 \ldots \in S^\omega$, where $\rho_0 = s_{init}$ and for all $i \in \mathbb{N}$, we have $\rho_i \rightarrow \rho_{i+1}$. The states in ξ induce a safety property "never reach ξ", which is satisfied for a run $\rho = \rho_0 \rho_1 \ldots \in S^\omega$ if $\rho_i \cap \xi = \varnothing$ for all $i \in \mathbb{N}$ and satisfied for T if all runs satisfy the safety property.

We call $\hat\rho = \hat\rho_0 \ldots \hat\rho_k \in S^*$ a counterexample to the safety property "never reach ξ" if $\hat\rho$ is the prefix of a run with $\hat\rho_k \in \xi$. Additionally, we may assume that $\hat\rho$ is loop-free, i.e. $\hat\rho_i \neq \hat\rho_j$ for all $i \neq j$.

Safety Games. A *safety game* is a tuple $G = (S_{Safe}, S_{Reach}, \rightarrow, s_{init}, \xi)$, where S_{Safe} and S_{Reach} are disjoint sets of states such that the states in S_{Safe} are controlled by player *Safe*, while the states in S_{Reach} are controlled by player *Reach*, $\rightarrow$ is the *transition relation* on $S = S_{Safe} \cup S_{Reach}$, $s_{init} \in S$ is the *initial state* and $\xi \subseteq S$ is the set of *bad states*. A *play* $\rho \in S^\omega$ is an infinite sequence $\rho_0 \rho_1 \ldots$ such that $\rho_0 = s_{init}$ and $(\rho_i, \rho_{i+1}) \in \rightarrow$ for all $i \in \mathbb{N}$. A play ρ is *winning* for *Reach* if $\rho_i \in \xi$ for some $i \in \mathbb{N}$, otherwise it is winning for *Safe*. A strategy for *Safe* is a function $\sigma \colon S_{Safe} \rightarrow S$ with $(s, \sigma(s)) \in \rightarrow$ for all $s \in S_{Safe}$ (and strategies for *Reach* are defined similarly). A pair of strategies $(\sigma_{Safe}, \sigma_{Reach})$ for *Safe* and *Reach* induces a play $\rho = \rho_0 \rho_1 \ldots$ with $\rho_{i+1} = \sigma_{Safe}(\rho_i)$ if $\rho_i \in S_{Safe}$ and $\rho_{i+1} = \sigma_{S_{Reach}}(\rho_i)$ otherwise. A strategy for *Safe* is winning if, for all strategies of *Reach*, the induced play is winning for *Safe* (and winning strategies for *Reach* are defined similarly). For any game G, we write $val(G) = 1$ if there exists a winning strategy for *Safe* and $val(G) = 0$ otherwise. The winning region $Win(G)$ contains all states from which *Safe* has a winning strategy. Computing the winning region takes linear time in the number of states and transitions of the model. [18, Theorem 12].

Shapley Values. Shapley values [37] are a prominent concept to measure the individual impact of agents on the outcome of plays in a game. They have been introduced for cooperative games with real-valued outcomes. For the purposes of this paper, simple cooperative games with monotonic Boolean functions for the possible outcomes are sufficient.

Let $\mathcal{A} = \{a_1, \ldots, a_n\}$ be a set of players. A *simple cooperative game* is a monotonic function $\gamma \colon 2^{\mathcal{A}} \mapsto \{0, 1\}$. For a simple cooperative game γ, the Shapley values are defined by the function $Shap_\gamma \colon \mathcal{A} \rightarrow [0, 1]$ given by

$$Shap_\gamma(a) = \sum_{C \subseteq \mathcal{A} \setminus \{a\}} \frac{(|\mathcal{A}| - |C| - 1)! \cdot |C|!}{|\mathcal{A}|!} \Big(\gamma(C \cup \{a\}) - \gamma(C) \Big).$$

For $a \in \mathcal{A}$ and $C \subseteq \mathcal{A} \setminus \{a\}$, we call (C, a) a *switching pair* if $\gamma(C \cup \{a\}) - \gamma(C) = 1$, i.e. if $\gamma(C \cup \{a\}) = 1$ and $\gamma(C) = 0$. Critical pairs correspond to the non-zero summands in the above sum.

Remark 2.1. The Shapley value is characterised by the axioms of *efficiency*, *symmetry*, *additivity* and the *dummy* axiom [38]. These axioms make it particularly suitable for responsibility allocation. The efficiency axiom requires that the sum of responsibilities allocated to the players is equal to the value of the grand coalition, i.e. $\sum_{a \in \mathcal{A}} Shap_\gamma(a) = \gamma(\mathcal{A})$. For simple cooperative games, if γ is winnable, then $\gamma(\mathcal{A}) = 1$. The symmetry axiom requires that if $a, b \in \mathcal{A}$ are players such that $\gamma(C \cup \{a\}) = \gamma(C \cup \{b\})$ for all player sets $C \subseteq \mathcal{A}$, then $Shap_\gamma(a) = Shap_\gamma(b)$. The dummy axiom requires that if $a \in \mathcal{A}$ is a player such that $\gamma(C) = \gamma(C \cup \{a\})$ for all player sets set $C \subseteq \mathcal{A}$, then $Shap_\gamma(a) = 0$. The additivity axiom concerns the sum of (possibly non-simple) cooperative games and is irrelevant for the case of simple cooperative games.

3   Forward and Backward Responsibility

Following previous works on notions for (the degree of) responsibility in operational models [2,4,33], we present definitions for the forward and backward responsibility of *actors* on the satisfaction (and the violation, respectively) of a safety property. The idea is that every actor controls a set of states and resolves the non-deterministic choices within these states. Moreover, there can be other states that are not assigned to any actor. These can be auxiliary states that have been introduced for modelling purposes or states whose behavior is given by an adversarial environment (see Sect. 4.4). The responsibility notions will then assign numerical values to the actors.

Definition 3.1 (Actor). Let $\mathcal{T} = (S, \rightarrow, s_{init}, \notdivides)$ be a transition system. A *responsibility signature* is a triple $(\mathcal{A}, S_{Aux}, S_{Adv})$ where S_{Aux} and S_{Adv} are disjoint subsets of the state space S and $\mathcal{A}$ a partition of $S \setminus (S_{Aux} \cup S_{Adv})$. The elements of $\mathcal{A}$ are called *actors*. The states in S_{Aux} are called *auxiliary states* and the states in S_{Adv} the *adversarial states*.

In Sect. 4, we propose three schemes for extracting actor sets from a reactive module specification. First, actors can be extracted from modules, such that each module is represented by an actor (Sect. 4.2). In Sect. 4.3, value-based actors are constructed, where each actor corresponds to a partial variable assignment. For both module- and value-based actors. S_{Aux} and S_{Adv} will be empty. An instance where S_{Aux} and S_{Adv} are nonempty are action-based actors (Sect. 4.4). For these, every actor represents one action of the program.

For the remainder of this section, we suppose a fixed responsibility signature $(\mathcal{A}, S_{Aux}, S_{Adv})$ and define the (degree of) responsibility for the actors $a \in \mathcal{A}$.

As in [2,4,33], these notions rely on Shapley values for one-shot cooperative games given by a function $\gamma \colon 2^{\mathcal{A}} \rightarrow \{0, 1\}$ that assign to every coalition of agents an outcome. Intuitively, the outcome $\gamma(C) = 1$ for a coalition $C \subseteq \mathcal{A}$ indicates that the actors in C can cooperate to prevent the violation of the safety property, while $\gamma(C) = 0$ means that the actors in A do not have such a strategy.

Definition 3.2 (Safety games for coalitions of agents – forward). Let $\mathcal{T} = (S, \rightarrow, s_{init}, \frac{i}{2})$ be a transition system, $(\mathcal{A}, S_{Aux}, S_{Adv})$ a responsibility signature and $C \subseteq \mathcal{A}$. We define the game

$$\mathsf{GameFw}(\mathcal{T}, S_{Aux}, C) = (C \cup S_{Aux}, S \setminus (C \cup S_{Aux}), \rightarrow, s_{init}, \frac{i}{2}).$$

This construction preserves the structure of the transition system. State ownership is assigned based on whether they are in the coalition. Additionally, Player *Safe* controls all auxiliary states. If Player *Safe* wins, this indicates that the states in C and the auxiliary states are sufficient to enforce the safety property.

As the function name indicates, this construction is tailored for forward responsibility. For backward responsibility we incorporate the a given counterexample $\hat{\rho}$ into the construction.

Definition 3.3 (Safety games for coalitions of agents – backward). Let $\mathcal{T}$, $(\mathcal{A}, S_{Aux}, S_{Adv})$ and C be as in Definition 3.2 and let $\hat{\rho} = \hat{\rho}_0 \dots, \hat{\rho}_k$ be a counterexample. We define the game

$$\mathsf{GameBw}(\mathcal{T}, S_{Aux}, \hat{\rho}, C) = (C \cup S_{Aux}, S \setminus (C \cup S_{Aux}), \rightarrow_{Bw}, s_{init}, \frac{i}{2})$$

with $\hat{\rho}_i \rightarrow_{Bw} \hat{\rho}_{i+1}$ for $i \in \{0, \dots, k-1\}$ if $\hat{\rho}_i \notin (C \cup S_{Aux})$ and

$s \rightarrow_{Bw} s'$ if $s \rightarrow s'$ and either $s \notin \hat{\rho}$ or $s \in C \cup S_{Aux}$.

The transition relation $\rightarrow_{Bw}$ in Definition 3.3 is modified to "engrave" the counterexample. For every state $\hat{\rho}_i$ on the counterexample that is not part of C or S_{Aux}, we remove all transitions except for the one to $\hat{\rho}_{i+1}$. As the counterexample represents a specific execution, this ensures that we adhere to the behaviour observed during this execution. By only engraving the counterexample for states not in C or S_{Aux}, we selectively analyse which counterexample states could have changed the outcome by behaving differently.

The safety games defined in Definitions 3.2 and 3.3 are now used to introduce simple cooperative games where the players are the actors of the transition system. In this cooperative game, the value of a coalition C is then given by the (non-)existence of a winning strategy in the safety game assigned to C.

Definition 3.4 (Foward and backward cooperative games). Let $\mathcal{T}$ be a transition system and let $(\mathcal{A}, S_{Aux}, S_{Adv})$ be an actor set. The *forward cooperative game* is the function $\mathsf{CoopFw}_{\mathcal{T}} : 2^{\mathcal{A}} \rightarrow \{0, 1\}$ given by

$$\mathsf{CoopFw}_{\mathcal{T}}(C) = \mathit{val}(\mathsf{GameFw}(\mathcal{T}, S_{Aux}, C)).$$

If $\hat{\rho}$ is a counterexample then the *backward cooperative game* is the function $\mathsf{CoopBw}_{\mathcal{T}}^{\hat{\rho}} : 2^{\mathcal{A}} \rightarrow \{0, 1\}$ given by

$$\mathsf{CoopBw}_{\mathcal{T}}^{\hat{\rho}}(C) = \mathit{val}(\mathsf{GameBw}(\mathcal{T}, S_{Aux}, \hat{\rho}, C)).$$

The individual contribution of an actor a to the satisfaction (and the violation, respectively) of the given safety property can now be defined as the Shapley value of a (see Sect. 2 for the definition) in the forward and the backward cooperative game, respectively.

Definition 3.5 (Responsibility). Let $\mathcal{T} = (S, \rightarrow, s_{init}, \lightning)$ be a transition system and $(\mathcal{A}, S_{Aux}, S_{Adv})$ a responsibility signature. The *forward responsibility of* $a \in \mathcal{A}$ is $Shap_{\mathsf{CoopFw}_{\mathcal{T}}}(a)$. If $\hat{\rho}$ is a counterexample then the *backward responsibility of* $a \in \mathcal{A}$ with respect to $\hat{\rho}$ is $Shap_{\mathsf{CoopBw}_{\mathcal{T}}^{\hat{\rho}}}(a)$.

Remark 3.6. The dual of the safety property *"never $\lightning$"* is the reachability property *"eventually $\lightning$"*. For forward responsibility, the degree of responsibility is the same for both the safety and reachability property due to the zero-sum nature of cooperative games [33]. For backward responsibility, this is not the case, as the counterexample to the safety property does not form a counterexample to the reachability property.

Remark 3.7. The definition of backward responsibility as introduced in Definition 3.5 corresponds to *pessimistic* responsibility in [2] for the case where the actors are singeltons and constitute a partition of the state space S. Besides pessimistic responsibility, [2] also introduces the concept of *optimistic* responsibility. Optimistic and pessimistic responsibility differ in how they deal with the states that are neither on the counterexample nor in C. For pessimistic responsibility, these states are controlled by *Reach*, whereas for optimistic responsibility, they are controlled by *Safe*. For optimistic responsibility, [2] shows that for every transition system $\mathcal{T}$ and counterexample $\hat{\rho}$, there is a constant c such that every actor either has responsibility 0 or c. Thus, optimistic responsibility can be seen as a Boolean concept where each state is either responsible or not. We focus here on the more interesting (and computationally harder) concept of pessimistic responsibility.

Example 3.8. Consider the transition system from Fig. 1. It models the tracks leading into a train station. There are two platforms: p_1 and $\lightning$ – the latter must not be reached, as it is undergoing maintenance. The switches are controlled by three actors, called here Alice, Bob and Charlie. Alice controls the switches s_0 and s_1, Bob controls s_2 and s_3 and Charlie controls s_4, s_5 and s_6. This induces the responsibility signature $(\{A, B, C\}, \varnothing, \varnothing)$ for $A = \{s_0, s_1\}$, $B = \{s_2, s_3\}$ and $C = \{s_4, s_5, s_6\}$. We omit s_7 and $\lightning$, as they do not have any outgoing transitions. With respect to forward responsibility, the pair $(A, \varnothing)$ is switching: Obviously, $\varnothing$ is not a winning coalition, whereas $\{A\}$ is by going from s_0 to s_1 and then to p_1, from where $\lightning$ is unreachable. On the other hand, $(B, \varnothing)$ and $(C, \varnothing)$ are not switching pairs. Instead, $(B, \{C\})$ and $(C, \{B\})$ are switching: If s_2 is reached, B moves s_3, if s_3 is reached, B goes to s_4 and if s_4 is reached, C goes to p_1.

As B and C are not individually winning and A is, we have two additional switching pairs: $(A, \{B\})$ and $(A, \{C\})$. Given these switching pairs, computing the Shapley value yields a responsibility value of $\frac{2}{3}$ for Alice and $\frac{1}{6}$ each for Bob and Charlie. This makes sense, as Alice is able to route the train to p_1 on her

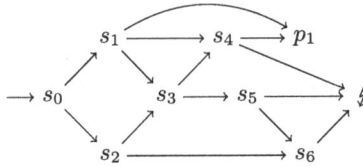

Fig. 1. Model of the tracks leading into a train station. The switches are controlled by the three controllers Alice, Bob and Charlie. The train must not reach ⚡, as this track is already occupied.

own, whereas Bob and Charlie needs to cooperate to achieve the same thing, giving them individually less power.

3.1   Algorithms and Complexity

The most relevant algorithmic task is the computation of the responsibility value of a given actor. Besides this task, called the *computation problem*, [2,33] also study the complexity of the positivity and the threshold problem.

In the *positivity problem*, the question is whether the responsibility of a given actor is positive. The *threshold problem* asks whether the responsibility of a given actor is greater than or equal to a given threshold.

The complexity of these three algorithmic problems has been studied in [33] for the case of forward responsibility and different types of properties. The results of [33] have then be adapted for the case of backward responsibility and single-ton actors [2]. The hardness results presented in [2] carry over to the more general case considered here. The upper complexity bounds are achieved by similar algorithms as presented in [33] for forward responsibility and their adaptions presented in [2] for backward responsibility and singleton actors.

As a consequence of [2,33], we obtain the following results for the setting considered in this article. For the positivity problem, an NP upper bound is obtained by the observation that agent a has positive responsibility if and only if there is at least one switching pair (C, a). Thus, the positivity problem is solvable by a simple nondeterministic polynomial time-bounded guess-and-check algorithm that first guesses a coalition $C \subseteq \mathcal{A} \setminus \{a\}$ and then checks whether (C, a) is switching by solving the safety games for the coalitions C and $C \cup \{a\}$. NP-hardness has been achieved via a reduction from 3SAT. This yields:

Proposition 3.9 (Complexity of the positivity problem). The forward positivity problem as well as the backward positivity problem are NP-complete.

Given known polynomially time-bounded algorithms for solving safety games, the threshold and the computation problem are solvable in exponential time by a naïve algorithm that considers all coalitions $C \subseteq 2^{\mathcal{A}}$, computes the winning regions in the induced safety games and then computes the Shapley values of the agents according to the definition as a sum that ranges over all coalitions.

This naïve approach can be rephrased to obtain polynomially space-bounded algorithms for the threshold and the computation problem.

NP-hardness of the threshold problem is a direct consequence of the NP-hardness of the positivity problem (Proposition 3.9). #P-hardness of the computation problem has been shown by reduction from the counting problem of how many valuations satisfy exactly one clause of a 3SAT formula.

Proposition 3.10 (Complexity of the threshold and the computation problem). For both forward and the backward responsibility, the threshold problem is NP-hard, while the computation problem is #P-hard. Furthermore, the threshold and the computation problem are solvable by polynomially space-bounded algorithms.

The NP- and #P-hardness results are caused by the inherent difficulty in dealing with the exponential growth of the number of coalitions. The above sketched algorithm runs exponentially in the number of actors, but polynomial in the number of states of the transition system. Thus, the major bottleneck is the size of the actor set rather than the size of the transition system. If the number of actors is small, then the computation of responsibility values is feasible even for large state spaces as our experimental studies (see Sect. 5) indicate. In the following section, we present three methods for deriving small actor sets from a system specification.

4   Extracting Actors from a Reactive System Specification

This section presents three methods for deriving actor sets from a program's specification. Transition systems are usually specified in a higher-level modelling language, from which an explicit transition system is then built. The methods presented in this section build actor sets from different elements of such a modelling language. These elements correspond to semantic units of the final system, so it is natural to group them into actors. Additionally, responsibility values for elements in this higher-level language are easy to interpret, as they abstract the complexity of the underlying transition system.

A popular formalism for program specification are reactive modules [1]. Here, the program consists of a set of modules, which each have variables and guarded commands. Commands can either be local or synchronised with commands in other modules. Reactive modules make it easy to describe non-determinism, which is why they lend themselves well to modelling transition systems.

In the following, we first introduce the syntax and (informal) semantics of a simple reactive modules language. We then provide three schemes that construct actors that correspond to program components of a reactive modules program. These schemes produce actors that correspond to the modules, variable values or actions of a given program. We provide an example for each scheme to demonstrate its usefulness.

4.1 The Reactive Modules Language

The syntax of the reactive modules language is given by the following rules:

$$\langle\text{program}\rangle ::= \frac{1}{2} = \langle\text{bexp}\rangle; \ \langle\text{module}\rangle^*$$
$$\langle\text{module}\rangle ::= \texttt{module} \ \langle\text{decl}\rangle^* \langle\text{command}\rangle^* \ \texttt{endmodule}$$
$$\langle\text{decl}\rangle ::= \langle\text{id}\rangle : [\langle\text{int}\rangle . . \langle\text{int}\rangle] \ \texttt{init} \ \langle\text{int}\rangle;$$
$$\langle\text{command}\rangle ::= [\langle\text{act}\rangle] \ \langle\text{bexp}\rangle \texttt{->} \langle\text{updates}\rangle;$$
$$\langle\text{act}\rangle ::= \varepsilon \ | \ \langle\text{id}\rangle$$
$$\langle\text{updates}\rangle ::= \varnothing \ | \ (\langle\text{assignment}\rangle \ \texttt{\&})^* \langle\text{assignment}\rangle$$
$$\langle\text{assignment}\rangle ::= \langle\text{id}\rangle := \langle\text{exp}\rangle$$

Here, $\langle\text{id}\rangle$ is an alpha-numeric identifier, $\langle\text{int}\rangle$ is an integer, $\langle\text{exp}\rangle$ is an expression composed of integer and the operators $+$, $-$, $\cdot$, $/$ and mod and $\langle\text{bexp}\rangle$ is a Boolean expression composed of *true*, *false*, the operators $\wedge$, $\vee$ and $\iff$ applied to Boolean expressions and the operators $=$, $\neq$, $<$, $\leq$, $\geq$ and $>$ applied to expressions. The left-hand side of an assignment must refer to a variable declared in the same module.

An example is given in Fig. 2. The program has two modules – A and B. They have variables x and y, respectively. As long as a variable's value is less than 5, it can be incremented. The command for this does not contain an action, which means it is executed without synchronisation. If there are multiple available commands, one is selected non-deterministically. For example, in state $\{x \mapsto 3, y \mapsto 2\}$, there are transitions to $\{x \mapsto 4, y \mapsto 2\}$ and $\{x \mapsto 3, y \mapsto 3\}$. Additionally, there are commands with synchronising action reset. This can only be executed if both commands are enabled, i.e. if $x = 5$ and $y = 5$. If one module has multiple commands with the same action, one such command with active guard is chosen non-deterministially. A synchronising action may also be used in more than two modules, in which case the action can only be taken if there is an enabled command in each such module. If an action occurs in multiple modules, we call it a synchronising action.

```
module A                    module B
  x: [0..5] init 0;           y: [0..5] init 0;
  [] x<5 -> x:=x+1;           [] y<5 -> y:=y+1;
  [reset] x=5 -> x:=0;        [reset] y=5 -> y:=0;
endmodule                   endmodule
```

Fig. 2. Example program in the reactive modules language

Semantics. Let P be a program and φ_ξ a Boolean expression over the program variables that specifies the invariant of the safety condition "φ_ξ is never reached" (in the following, this is abbreviated to *safety invariant* φ_ξ). Then the operational semantics of P and φ_ξ is a transition system $\mathcal{T}(P, \varphi_\xi) = (S, \rightarrow, s_{init}, \xi)$. We assume that every command in P has an action – commands with the empty action ε can be assigned a new, unique action to ensure this holds. The state space S is the set of variable assignments, i.e. functions that assign to each variable an element of its domain. For $s \in S$ and variable v, we denote by $s(v)$ the value that v takes in s. For states $s, s' \in S$, we have $s \rightarrow s'$ if there exists an action α and a set of commands C such that

- every command in C has action α,
- for every module that contains a command with action α, exactly one such command is contained in C,
- s satisfies the guard of every command in C and
- s' is the result of applying the updates of all commands in C to s simultaneously.

Finally, ξ contains those states that satisfy φ_ξ.

4.2   Module-Based Actors

A natural instance of an actor set of a parallel system is given by its components, i.e. the modules of a reactive module language. However, modules specify transitions, not states, so one cannot assign each state to an individual module: In some states, actions from multiple modules may be active. Thus, the formalisation of responsibility notions for the modules in our state-based approach where actors are sets of states requires some transformations. To this end, we propose adding a scheduler module. Its purpose is to resolve the inter-module nondeterminism, while otherwise preserving the program's structure. As commands with synchronising actions cannot be assigned to a single module, they are handled separately – the scheduler non-deterministically enables either a module or synchronising action.

We need to ensure that the scheduler never chooses a module or synchronising action that is not currently enabled. This would lead to a deadlock that is not present in the original program. To avoid this, we construct a guard condition for each module and each synchronising action that is only true if the program element can be executed.

Definition 4.1 (Module and action guards). Let P be a program with modules $M_1, \ldots, M_n$ and synchronising actions $\alpha_1, \ldots, \alpha_m$. Then $\mathsf{Guard}(M_i)$ denotes the disjunction of the guards of all commands with non-synchronising action in M_i. Furthermore, $\mathsf{Guard}(M_i, \alpha_j)$ denotes the disjunction of the guards of all commands with action α_j in M_i and we define $\mathsf{Guard}(\alpha_j) = \bigwedge_{i \in \{1, \ldots, n\}} \mathsf{Guard}(M_i, \alpha_j)$.

We now introduce the function $\mathsf{WithSched}$, which takes a program and returns an equivalent program with a scheduler module.

Definition 4.2 (Scheduler construction). Let P be a program with modules $M_1, \ldots, M_n$ and synchronising actions $\alpha_1, \ldots, \alpha_m$. The scheduler module has a single variable declaration

    active: [0..n+m] init 0;

For every module M_i, the scheduler contains the two commands

    [choose_M_i] active=0 & Guard(M_i) -> active := i;
    [act_M_i] active=i -> active := 0;

For every synchronising action α_i, the scheduler contains the two commands

    [choose_α_i] active=0 & Guard(α_i) -> active := n+i;
    [α_i] active=n+i -> active := 0;

The program WithSched(P) contains all modules from P and the scheduler module. In every module M_i, we replace all non-synchronising actions (including the empty action) with act_M_i.

The scheduler alternates between two states. When `active` is 0, it non-deterministically chooses which module or synchronising action to activate. Note that the guards ensure only modules and synchronising actions are chosen that can then actually be executed. If $1 \leq$ `active` $\leq n$, the corresponding module M_i is then activated, because all non-synchronising commands in the module have action act_M_i. Similarly, if $n <$ `active` $\leq n + m$, the corresponding synchronising action is executed. This construction preserves safety invariants, as shown in the following lemma.

Lemma 4.3 (Soundness of the scheduler transformation). Let P be a program and $\varphi_\natural$ a safety invariant. Then the semantics of P is given by the transition system $\mathcal{T}(P, \varphi_\natural) = (S, \rightarrow, s_{init}, \natural)$ and $\natural$ is reachable in $\mathcal{T}(P)$ if and only if $\natural'$ is reachable in $\mathcal{T}(\mathsf{WithSched}(P), \varphi_\natural) = (S', \rightarrow', s'_{init}, \natural')$.

Proof. Assume that $\natural$ is reachable in $\mathcal{T}(P, \varphi_\natural)$. Then there exists some run $\rho = \rho_1 \rho_2 \ldots \rho_n$ with $\rho_n \in \natural$. For $i \in \{1, \ldots, n-1\}$, we define $\mathcal{I}(i) = k$ if the transition from ρ_i to ρ_{i+1} was produced by an internal command of module M_k and $\mathcal{I}(i) = n + \ell$ if it was produced by synchronising action α_ℓ. We abbreviate variable `active` with a. Then

$$\rho' = \rho_1[a \mapsto 0] \; \rho_1[a \mapsto \mathcal{I}(1)] \; \ldots \; \rho_{n-1}[a \mapsto 0] \; \rho_{n-1}[a \mapsto \mathcal{I}(n-1)] \; \rho_n[a \mapsto 0]$$

is a run in $\mathcal{T}(\mathsf{WithSched}(P), \varphi_\natural)$ and $\rho_n[a \mapsto 0] \in \natural'$, as $\rho_n \in \natural$ and thus satisfies $\varphi_\natural$. Therefore, $\natural'$ is reachable in $\mathcal{T}(\mathsf{WithSched}(P), \varphi_\natural)$.

Now assume that $\natural'$ is reachable in $\mathcal{T}(\mathsf{WithSched}(P), \varphi_\natural)$. The scheduler module alternates between `active` $= 0$ and `active` > 0. Moreover, as every other module only has synchronising actions with the scheduler module, the scheduler module is active in every step. Therefore, any run in $\mathcal{T}(\mathsf{WithSched}(P), \varphi_\natural)$ has the form ρ' shown above. Then ρ is a run in $\mathcal{T}(P, \varphi_\natural)$ that reaches $\natural$.

The value of `active` indicates which module or action is active in a given state. This gives a natural partition of the state-space into module-based actors.

Definition 4.4 (Module-based actors). Let P be a program with modules $M_1, \ldots, M_n$ and synchronising actions $\alpha_1, \ldots, \alpha_m$. Let φ_i be a safety invariant and let S be the state space of $T(P, \varphi_i)$. The *module-based responsibility signature* has form $(\mathcal{A}, \varnothing, \varnothing)$ for $\mathcal{A} = \{a_i \mid i \in \{0, \ldots, n+m\}\}$, where $a_i = \{s \in S \mid s(\texttt{active}) = i\}$. We call a_0 the *scheduler actor*, a_i for $1 \le i \le n$ the *actor of module* M_i and a_{n+j} for $1 \le j \le m$ the *actor of synchronising* α_j.

```
module Window                          module Ada
    // 1: rock-proof glass                 // 1: throw!
    // 2: normal glass                      // 2: don't throw!
    // 3: broken                            a: [0..2] init 0;
    w: [0..3] init 0;
                                            [] a=0 -> a:=1;
    [install] w=0 -> w'=r;                  [] a=0 -> a:=2;
    [a_throws] w=1 -> ∅;                    [a_throws] a=1 -> a:=2;
    [a_throws] w=2 -> w:=3;             endmodule
    // similar for j_throws
endmodule                              module Julia
                                            // 1: throw!
                                            // 2: don't throw!
module Rebeca                               j: [0..2] init 0;
    // 1: rock-proof glass
    // 2: normal glass                      [] j=0 -> j:=1;
    r: [0..2] init 0;                       [] j=0 -> j:=2;
                                            [j_throws] j=1 -> j:=2;
    [] r=0 -> r:=1;                     endmodule
    [] r=0 -> r:=2;
    [install] r>0 -> ∅;
endmodule
```

Fig. 3. Model of Ada and Julia throwing rocks at a potentially rock-proof window

Example 4.5. To understand module-based actors, consider the code in Fig. 3. Here, Ada and Julia may throw a rock at a window. However, Rebeca, the window fitter, may decide to install rock-proof glass. The situation is modelled in such a way that these choices are first made locally in the module and then transferred to the window after that using synchronising actions.

In our scenario, Rebeca first installs normal (non-rock-proof) glass, after which Ada decides that she wants to throw a rock, breaking the window. Analysing responsibility yields the following for the module actors: $Ada \mapsto \frac{1}{6}$, $Julia \mapsto \frac{1}{6}$ and $Rebeca \mapsto \frac{2}{3}$. This is because Rebeca could have prevented the window from being broken on her own. Meanwhile, even if Ada decided not to throw her rock, Julia might still throw her rock, so they need to collaborate to prevent the window from breaking. In this example, neither the scheduler nor the synchronising actions have any responsibility.

4.3   Value-Based Actors

We now show how actors can be constructed based on the values of some of the program variables. For this, we select some variables and then place those states in the actor where the chosen variables have the same value.

Definition 4.6 (Value-based actors). Let P be a program, φ_{ξ} a safety invariant, $V = \{v_1, \ldots, v_k\}$ some of the variables of P with domains $D_1, \ldots, D_k$ and S the state space of $\mathcal{T}(P, \varphi_{\xi})$. The *value-based responsibility signature* has form $(\mathcal{A}, \varnothing, \varnothing)$ for

$$\mathcal{A} = \left\{ a_{(d_1, \ldots, d_k)} \mid (d_1, \ldots, d_k) \in D_1 \times \ldots \times D_k \right\},$$

where $a_{(d_1, \ldots, d_k)} = \left\{ s \in S \mid s(v_i) = d_i, i = 1, \ldots, k \right\}$.

Remark 4.7. Module-based actor groups are a special case of value-based actors, where $V = \{\texttt{active}\}$ for the variable $\texttt{active}$ of the scheduler.

One obvious instance of value-based actor sets is obtained taking V to be the set of all control variables (program counters) or a subset thereof. The induced responsibility notions can help to identify the control locations that are most critical for the satisfaction of the safety property.

```
module Clock
  t: [8..20] init 8;

  [tick] t<20 -> t:=t+1;
endmodule

module Car
  loc: [0..13] init 0;

  // Malmö
  [tick] loc=0 -> loc=1;
  [tick] loc=0 -> loc=2;

  // Helsingborg
  [tick] loc=1 -> loc=3;
  [tick] loc=1 -> loc=4;

  // ... (see right)
endmodule
```

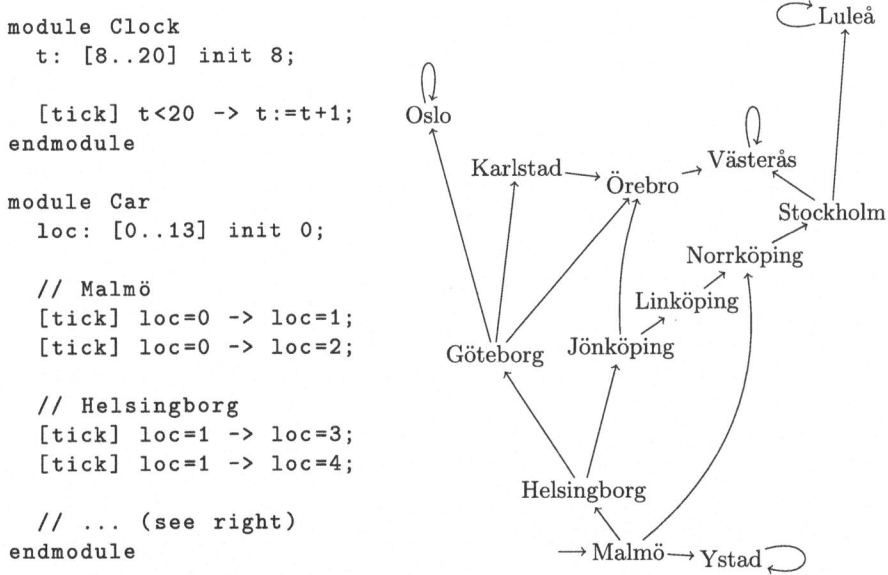

Fig. 4. Model of Ada and Rebeca's drive from Malmö to Västerås.

Example 4.8. Ada and Rebeca are driving from Malmö to Västerås. Ada is behind the wheel, but does not know Swedish geography, while Rebeca knows the way, but is very tired. Rebeca therefore wants to know when she needs to be awake. For this, she models the major roads in southern Sweden. The code for this is given in Fig. 4, as is a graph that shows the area modelled by Rebeca.

They start at 8:00 and want to arrive by 20:00. Rebeca therefore uses the property "never $t = 20 \wedge loc \neq$ Västerås", where variable t tracks the current time and loc tracks the current location. She groups states based on the value of $time$ and computes the forward responsibility.

This reveals that the actors $time = 8$, $time = 9$, $time = 10$ and $time = 13$ have positive responsibility. Therefore, Rebeca can safely sleep in the hours between that, as it is impossible for any important decisions to occur in these times. The actor $time = 13$ has positive responsibility because the route Malmö → Helsingborg → Jönköping → Linköping → Norrköping → Stockholm reaches Stockholm at 13:00. Rebeca needs to ensure that Ada takes the correct turn in Stockholm to avoid travelling to Luleå in Sweden's arctic north.

4.4   Action-Based Actors

Module-based responsibility is often not sufficiently granular and value-based responsibility only makes sense in models where a few distinguished variables represent different components of a program. In this section, we propose a method for generating actors that correspond to the actions in a program. However, there is no one-to-one correspondence between actions in a program and the states in its semantics. Furthermore, unlike for modules, we cannot apply the scheduler construction like we did for modules: This would transfer all non-deterministic choices of the program to the scheduler, thus providing no insight into which actions are responsible for an outcome.

We propose a transformation on transition systems that makes the responsibility of each action explicit. We then define a responsibility signature where each actor corresponds to an action.

The Action-Separation Construction. Most states in a transition system have multiple outgoing transitions corresponding to different actions. Our goal is to determine which of these actions are responsible for whether the property is fulfilled. For this, we separate the actions of each state into separate auxiliary states. This allows us to individually measure whether each action has an impact on the satisfaction of the property.

We first give an intuition of the technique and then provide a formal definition. The construction is illustrated in Fig. 5 for a single state s in a transition system. Figure 5a shows the state in the original transition system. It has three outgoing transitions α, β and γ to three new states t_1, t_2 and t_3. The transformation is depicted in Fig. 5b. State s has been expanded into several states. The states $s_{\alpha?}$ provides two options: Either we enable action α and transition to s_α or we directly proceed to $s_{\beta?}$, which provides the same two options for β. If we choose to enable action α, we can choose action α in state s_α, which leads to state t_1 as in the original transition system. However, we can also choose to not take α and proceed in $s_{\beta?}$. These states are depicted as squares because they

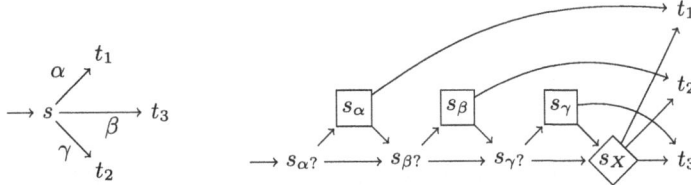

(a) Before apply-
ing the transfor-
mation.

(b) After applying the transformation. Square
states always behave cooperatively, the diamond state always behaves adversarial.

Fig. 5. Action-separation transformation applied to a state with three actions.

always behave cooperatively, i.e. they always try to fulfil the safety property,
regardless of whether they are in the coalition.

If we have not taken any action, we finally reach to s_X. This state is depicted
as a diamond to symbolise that it always behaves adversarially, i.e. it always tries
to violate the safety invariant.

Because states s_α, s_β, s_γ and s_X have fixed behaviour, they never have positive responsibility. State $s_{\alpha?}$ has positive responsibility if enabling α is critical
for satisfying the property in some context C. For this, it is necessary that the
context C and α together are sufficient for enforcing the property and that the
context alone is insufficient.

Note that the second condition does not hold if both β and γ are also sufficient
for enforcing the property in context C: The demonic state s_X must choose one
of the actions and if every choice leads to satisfying the property, then none of
the actions are responsible. This also means that an action in a state with a
single action never has any responsibility.

Having introduced the intuition for a single state, we now provide a formalisation for an entire transition system.

Definition 4.9 (Action-separation construction). Let P be a program and
$\varphi_{!}$ a safety invariant. Then the semantics of P is $\mathcal{T}(P, \varphi_{!}) = (S, \rightarrow, s_{init}, !)$.
Assume that P has no unnamed actions. Let ℓ be a function that maps each
transition to the action that produced it. If there are multiple actions that produce the same transition, we arbitrarily choose one of them. The set of actions
available in s is denoted by $Act(s) = \{\alpha \in Act \mid \exists t \in S: s \rightarrow t, \ell((s,t)) = \alpha\}$.

The function $\mathsf{ActionSeparated}(\mathcal{T}) = (S', \rightarrow', s'_{init}, !')$ produces a transition
system where the actions are separated. Here, $S' = S_? \cup S_! \cup S_X$, where $S_? =
\{s_{\alpha?} \mid s \in S, \alpha \in Act(s)\}$, $S_! = \{s_\alpha \mid s \in S, \alpha \in Act(s)\}$ and $S_X = \{s_X \mid s \in S\}$.
Given an arbitrary ordering of the actions $\alpha_1, \ldots, \alpha_k$ of $s \in S$, we denote by
$\mathsf{First}(s) = s_{\alpha_1?}$ the first ?-state and by Next with $\mathsf{Next}(s, \alpha_i) = s_{\alpha_{i+1}?}$ for $i < k$
and $\mathsf{Next}(s, \alpha_k) = s_X$ the ?-state of the next action (or s_X if the last action is
reached).

The transition relation $\to'$ is composed of the following elements for each $s \in S$:

- $s_{\alpha?} \to s_\alpha$ for $\alpha \in Act(s)$,
- $s_{\alpha?} \to \mathsf{Next}(s, \alpha)$ for $\alpha \in Act(s)$,
- $s_\alpha \to t$ for $(s, t) \in\to, \ell((s, t)) = \alpha$,
- $s_\alpha \to \mathsf{Next}(s, \alpha)$ for $\alpha \in Act(s)$ and
- $s_X \to t$ for $(s, t) \in\to$.

Furthermore, $s'_{init} = \mathsf{First}(s_{init})$ and $\natural' = \{\mathsf{First}(s) \mid s \in \natural\}$

Similar to the scheduler transformation for module-based actors, one can show that this transformation preserves safety invariants.

Lemma 4.10 (Soundness of the action-separation transformation). Let P and $\varphi_\natural$ be as above with semantics $\mathcal{T}(P, \varphi_\natural) = (S, \to, s_{init}, \natural)$. The action-separation transformation yields transition system $\mathsf{ActionSeparated}(\mathcal{T}(P, \varphi_\natural)) = (S', \to', s'_{init}, \natural')$. Then $\natural$ is reachable in $\mathcal{T}(P, \varphi_\natural)$ if and only if $\natural'$ is reachable in $\mathsf{ActionSeparated}(\mathcal{T}(P, \varphi_\natural))$.

Proof. Assume that $\natural$ is reachable in $\mathcal{T}(P, \varphi_\natural)$. Then there exists a loop-free run $\rho = \rho_1 \ldots \rho_n$ with $\rho_n \in \natural$. For $i \in \{1, \ldots, n-1\}$, we define $\alpha(i) = \alpha$ when $\ell((\rho_i, \rho_{i+1})) = \alpha$. The run ρ' that reaches $\natural'$ in $\mathsf{ActionSeparated}(\mathcal{T}(P, \varphi_\natural))$ is constructed as follows. Here, ρ'_{last} refers to the last state of ρ'.

For every $i \in \{1, \ldots, n-1\}$, we first append $\mathsf{First}(\rho_i)$. This is a state of form $\rho_{i,\alpha?}$ for some action α. While $\rho'_{last} = \rho_{i,\alpha?}$ for $\alpha \neq \alpha(i)$, we append $\mathsf{Next}(\rho'_{last}, \alpha)$. Eventually, we have $\alpha = \alpha(i)$, as α is an action in state ρ_i. We then append $\rho_{i,\alpha}$. By construction, there exists a transition to $\mathsf{First}(\rho_{i+1})$. Finally, we append $\mathsf{First}(\rho_n)$ and have $\rho'_{last} \in \natural'$ in $\mathsf{ActionSeparated}(\mathcal{T}(P, \varphi_\natural))$ because $\rho_n \in \natural$ in $\mathcal{T}(P, \varphi_\natural)$.

Now assume that $\natural'$ is reachable in $\mathsf{ActionSeparated}(\mathcal{T}(P, \varphi_\natural))$. Then there exists a loop-free run $\rho = \rho_1 \ldots \rho_n$ with $\rho_n \in \natural'$. We construct a run ρ' that reaches $\natural$ in $\mathcal{T}(P, \varphi_\natural)$ as follows. We sequentially consider every state $\rho_i \in \rho$. If there is an $s \in S$ such that $\rho_i = \mathsf{First}(s)$, we append s to ρ'. Otherwise, we proceed without appending any state to ρ'.

As the last state ρ_{last} of ρ reaches $\natural'$, it has form $\rho_{last} = \mathsf{First}(s)$ for some $s \in S$ with $s \in \natural$. Therefore, s is the last state of ρ' and ρ' therefore reaches $\natural$ in $\mathcal{T}(P, \varphi_\natural)$.

It remains to show that ρ' is a run $\mathcal{T}(P, \varphi_\natural)$. The initial state of the transition system $\mathsf{ActionSeparated}(\mathcal{T}(P, \varphi_\natural))$ is $\mathsf{First}(s_{init})$, so s_{init} is the first state in ρ'. We now show that ρ' adheres to the transition relation $\to$.

Consider consecutive states $s, t \in \rho'$. We show that $(s, t) \in\to$. Let $\rho_i, \rho_j \in \rho$ be the states with $\mathsf{First}(s) = \rho_i$ and $\mathsf{First}(t) = \rho_j$. Note that ρ is loop-free and therefore, ρ_i and ρ_j are well-defined.

From ρ_i, one can only reach states of the forms $s_{\alpha?}$, s_α and s_X (for action α) and states of form $\mathsf{First}(t')$ for $t' \in S$. Therefore, all states between ρ_i and ρ_j have the form $s_{\alpha?}$, s_α or s_X. Now consider the state ρ_{j-1}. We have $\rho_{j-1} \neq s_{\alpha?}$ for any action α, as ?-states do not have transitions to states of form $\mathsf{First}(t')$

for any $t' \in S$. If we have $\rho_{j-1} = s_X$, then there is a transition between s_X and ρ_j in ActionSeparated($\mathcal{T}(P, \varphi_{\sharp})$). This implies that there is a transition between s and t in $\mathcal{T}(P, \varphi_{\sharp})$. Alternatively, $\rho_{j-1} = s_\alpha$. In this case, there is a transition between s_α and ρ_j in ActionSeparated($\mathcal{T}(P, \varphi_{\sharp})$). This once again implies that there is a transition between s and t in $\mathcal{T}(P, \varphi_{\sharp})$. Therefore, ρ is a run and we have proved the lemma.

Definition 4.11 (Action-based actors). Let P be a program with actions Act and let $\varphi_{\sharp}$ be a safety invariant. Let $\mathcal{T}(P, \varphi_{\sharp}) = (S, \rightarrow, s_{init}, \sharp)$ be the semantics of P. The *action-based responsibility signature* has form $(\mathcal{A}, S_{Aux}, S_{Adv})$ for

$$\mathcal{A} = \{a_\alpha \mid \alpha \in Act\} \text{ with } a_\alpha = \{s_{\alpha?} \mid s \in S\},$$
$$S_{Aux} = \{s_\alpha \mid \alpha \in Act, s \in S\},$$
$$S_{Adv} = \{s_X \mid s \in S\}.$$

Example 4.12. For her birthday, Rebeca was gifted a puzzle box. The box displays a number – initially 0 – and has three buttons: The first button increments the number by 2, the second one multiplies the number by 6 and then increments it by 1 and the third button squares the current number. The box will open and reveal Rebeca's gift if, after exactly twenty button presses, the display shows 60. Rebeca is wondering whether all the buttons are useful for reaching this goal.

```
module PuzzleBox
  counter: [0..61] init 0;
  steps: [0..20] init 0;

  [btn1] true -> counter:=counter+2 & steps:=steps+1;
  [btn2] true -> counter:=counter*7+1 & steps:=steps+1;
  [btn3] true -> counter:=counter*counter & steps:=steps+1;
endmodule
```

Fig. 6. Model of Rebeca's puzzle box. For the sake of simplicity, overflow checks are omitted here.

To find out, she models the entire box as a reactive module. The code is shown in Fig. 6. We assume that values larger than 61 are clamped to 60 in the model (this is omitted for simplicity in the code shown). This does not affect the model's semantics, as none of the actions decrease the value of `counter`. Therefore, 60 is unreachable as soon as a value larger than 60 is reached.

Rebeca chooses the safety property *"never* `counter` $\neq 60 \wedge$ `steps` $= 20$*"* and computes forward action-based responsibility for the three actions `btn1`, `btn2`, `btn3`. This reveals that `btn2` has no responsibility, whereas the other two actions both have responsibility $\frac{1}{2}$.

This result is to be expected, since the goal is to reach an even number. Pressing the third button always produces an odd number and none of the buttons give a way to turn an odd number into an even number. Therefore, pressing the fourth button is never necessary when trying to reach 60. Armed with this knowledge, Rebeca is quickly able to solve the box and get to her gift.

5   Experimental Evaluation

In this section, we report on initial experiments for actor-based responsibility. We use the prototypical implementation from [2] enriched with functionality to support actors. Our tool relies on the probabilistic model checker PRISM [27] for building the transition system and for counterexample generation. The input language of PRISM is similar to the guarded command language introduced in Sect. 4. It is possible to specify stochastic behaviour in PRISM's language, but we do not make use of this. Actors can be specified manually or extracted from the PRISM source code automatically using the techniques described in Sect. 4. The implementation supports the naïve approach of iterating over all coalitions to compute the responsibility values. In addition to this, the tool contains a randomised procedure, which samples coalitions and approximate the responsibility values rather than computing the precise values.

The naïve algorithm has to consider every coalition and therefore has exponential runtime. There are several optimisations that improve runtime, in particular by reducing the number of games that need to be solved in total. Algorithm 1 outlines how responsibility is computed in the implementation and illustrates the following optimisations:

- The set of minimal winning coalitions is pre-computed. This ensures no game is solved twice. The precomputation results are reused when computing the responsibility of other states.
- A game for coalition C is only solved if no subset of C is already known to be winning. If a winning subset exists, this directly implies that C is also winning. To this end, the coalitions are analysed in ascending size, therefore ensuring that all subsets of C have been analysed before C itself is analysed.
- Only *minimal* winning coalitions are stored. Usually, this set is fairly small, which ensures that checks for whether a coalition is winning take little time.

Furthermore, actors are excluded if they do not contain any non-determinism, e.g. because they have just a single outgoing transitions. Additionally, in the implementation, the major steps are parallelised to take advantage of modern multi-core processors.

The experimental studies as reported in this section investigate how responsibility is distributed among different actors when considering the three different types of actor classes. We study the general applicability of the approach and show how responsibility values can be used to guide debugging and diagnostic processes. Furthermore, we investigate the scalability of our approach for an increasing number reachable states in the transition system and increasing numbers of actors. All experiments were performed on a MacBook Pro running macOS 13.3 with an 8-core M2 chip and 24 GB of memory. The code, example files (small examples from the previous sections), as well as all relevant data files are made available for download via [30].

Algorithm 1 Algorithm for computing responsibility that uses pre-computation to reduce the number of games that need to be solved. Here, SHAPLEY(k) computes the Shapley weight for a coalition of size k and SOLVE_GAME() determines the winner of the induced game for coalition C. We assume that the underlying transition system with actor set Act and a safety property is available in all functions.

```
 1: function RESPONSIBILITIES()
 2:     W ← MINIMAL_WINNING()
 3:     for a ∈ Act:
 4:         r ← RESPONSIBILITY(W, a)
 5:         PRINT(r)

 6: function RESPONSIBILITY(W, a)
 7:     r ← 0.0
 8:     for C ⊆ Act \ {a}:
 9:         if ¬WINNING(W, C):
10:             if WINNING(W, C ∪ {a}):
11:                 r ← r + SHAPLEY(|C|)
12:     return r

13: function MINIMAL_WINNING()
14:     W ← ∅
15:     for i ∈ {0, . . . , |S|}:
16:         for C ⊆ Act with |C| = i:
17:             if ¬IS_WINNING(W, C):
18:                 if SOLVE_GAME(C):
19:                     W ← W ∪ {C}
20:     return W

21: function IS_WINNING(W, C)
22:     for w ∈ W:
23:         if w ⊆ C:
24:             return true
25:     return false
```

5.1   Case Study: Bounded Retransmission Protocol

The first case study is on a non-probabilistic (i.e. purely a non-deterministic) variant of the bounded retransmission protocol [28] from the PRISM benchmark suite. The goal is to send a message, split into a number of frames, via an unreliable communication channel. The PRISM code contains modules for a sender, a receiver, two communication channels and a checker module, which determines whether the message was transmitted correctly. If transmission fails, the frame is to be re-transmitted, but only a bounded number of times. When the number of retransmissions reaches its maximum, the protocol aborts. Both sender and receiver can be different locations, for example idle, next_frame or retransmit. Those locations are encoded as values of respective variables. Those values are used to define our variable-value-based actors. Messages can be lost non-deterministically at different locations during the execution of the protocol.

We consider here a counterexample in which sending fails repeatedly during the transmission of the first frame, causing the message transmission to ultimately fail when the maximum number of retries is reached. Our analysis reveals that the location wait_ack has responsibility $\frac{2}{3}$, while next_frame and retransmit both have responsibility $\frac{1}{6}$. This is unexpected, as the sender module does not behave non-deterministically in the wait_ack location. In a second investigation, we therefore construct actors based on the location of the sender and the transmission channel. This reveals that the responsible actors all represent the beginning of transmission in the channel. This hints at some problem in the channel – and indeed, the channel may non-deterministically lose the frame, as it is the case in our counterexample.

5.2   Analysis of the Scheduler Construction

Module-based actors divide responsibility between a scheduler module, synchronising actions and the modules of the program. In Example 4.5 only the modules have positive responsibility, whereas scheduler and shared actions have none. In this section, we evaluate how the scheduler construction allocates responsibility for examples taken from [2] and in parts originating in the QComp benchmark suite [9], again adapted to the non-probabilistic setting.

Name	Scheduler module	Synchronous actions	Modules
alternating_bit	0.50	0.00	0.50
brp	0.00	1.00	0.00
dining_philosophers_a	1.00	0.00	0.00
dining_philosophers_b	0.50	0.00	0.50
3_generals_a	1.00	0.00	0.00
3_generals_b	0.08	0.00	0.92

Fig. 7. Distribution of module-based responsibility among the scheduler module, the synchronising actions and the modules of the respective model.

The results are shown in Fig. 7. The model `brp` is the only one where synchronising actions have positive responsibility. This is because `brp` is the only model among our examples where multiple commands with the same synchronising action may be enabled simultaneously. In the other modules, this is not the case. Therefore, once the scheduler has chosen a synchronising action, the next step is deterministic – only one command (in every module) is enabled.

For `dining_philosophers` and `3_generals`, we provide two variants. The original versions with suffix _a allocate all responsibility to the scheduler. To understand why, consider one philosopher in `dining_philosopher_a`. Assuming she does not hold any forks, she has two available commands:

```
[Phil1TakesFork1] !has_fork_1 -> has_fork_1 := true;
[Phil1TakesFork2] !has_fork_2 -> has_fork_2 := true;
```

The forks are modelled by additional modules that provide commands with actions `Phil1TakesFork1` and `Phil1TakesFork2`, making them synchronising actions. Therefore, by choosing one of these actions, the scheduler has already resolved all non-determinism and the behavior of the philosopher and the fork are fully deterministic. In `dining_philosophers_b`, on the other hand, the fork selection process is split into two stages. In the first stage, the philosopher chooses which fork she wants and stores the result in an internal variable. In a second step, the philosopher then uses a synchronising action to transmit that she took the fork. Now, the scheduler only chooses which philosopher acts. The choice between left and right fork is made in the philosopher module. Therefore, it makes sense that responsibility is split between the scheduler and the modules here.

For 3_generals, the explanation is similar. In the original model, choices are made and transmission happens simultaneously, whereas in the modified protocol, choices are made locally first and then transmission happens.

These examples demonstrate that module-based responsibility is very sensitive to the specific modelling details. If only the scheduler is responsible, it is often possible to refine the model to better represent where choices are actually made.

5.3   Performance

As outlined in Sect. 3.1, computing responsibility is exponential in the number of actors and linear in the size of the transition system. In the following, we investigate tool performance. For this, we investigate the time taken to actually *compute* responsibility only[1].

We use the following three synthetic model families in this investigation. For all three, the states emerge from the evaluation of a variable ranging from 0 to n.

- **linear**: each state has several transitions which increment the variable value by different step sizes. The goal is to avoid the state where the variable value is n. The state space is partitioned into m actors such that states with the same index modulo m belong to he same actor.
- **random**: every state has transitions to six random other states. Several states are marked as ⚡ and we add a few additional transitions to ensure a counterexample exists. The states are randomly partitioned into evenly-size actors.
- **tree**: states are arranged as a binary tree. The root is the initial state, every tenth leaf is in ⚡ and states are partitioned into evenly-sized actors.

Safety games are solved by iteratively enlarging the winning region. Therefore, **linear** and **tree** are extreme cases for the algorithm – **linear** requires many iterations, whereas in **tree**, the winning region grows rapidly in each iteration.

Figure 8a shows the computation time for constant model size $n = 100\,000$ and varying numbers of actors. Performance differs between the models, but for all three models it becomes evident that the runtime grows exponentially in the number of actors.

Figure 8b shows the computation time for varying model sizes from $n = 50\,000$ to $n = 500\,000$. The number of actors is 7 in every case. Due to the

---

[1] Note that we do not report here on the overhead runtimes for exporting and re-importing the model. The responsibility computation is not (yet) fully integrated into PRISM or any other model checker, which makes the current prototypical implementation rather inefficient at this point. An integration would avoid the expensive and unnecessary data exchange via the file system.

overhead costs for exporting and re-importing, we did not scale our experiments beyond this point. For $n = 500\,000$, this step took four minutes already. One can observe a strong linear correlation between the size of the transition system and the runtime.

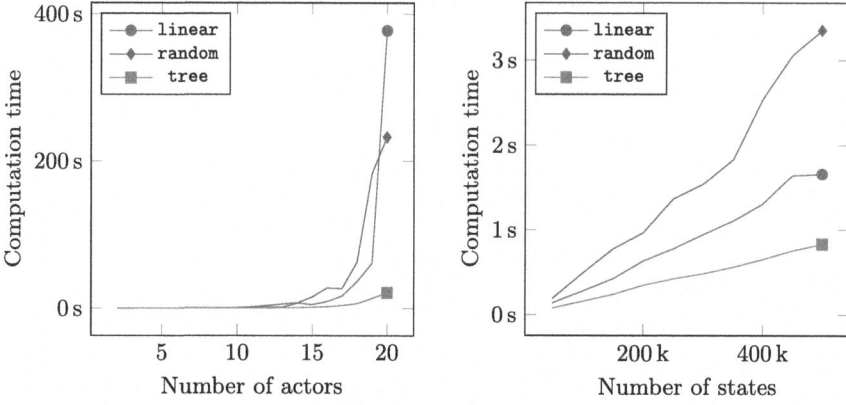

(a) Runtime for different number of actors and constant state space size 100 k.

(b) Runtime for different state space size and fixed number of 7 actors.

Fig. 8. Runtimes for the computing responsibility values for the three model families `linear`, `random` and `tree` for increasing numbers of actors and states.

Our results show that by choosing a coarse actor signature, it is possible to analyse large models with hundreds of thousands of states. Currently, transferring the data between model checker and the implementation creates a bottleneck, but this can be avoided by integrating responsibility directly into a model checker.

6   Conclusion

This article builds on previous work on responsibility notions for (sets of) states on the satisfaction or violation of safety properties from the forward [33] and backward [2] perspective. The focus here was on the view of actors and natural definitions of actor sets that exploit structural system features (like modules or actions) and can be derived from the syntax of reactive programs. Module-based actors are constructed by adding a scheduler module, value-based actors group states together in which one – or multiple – distinguished variables have the same value and action-based actor groups rely on an action-separation technique. The experimental results carried out with a prototypical implementation served to provide insights in the scalability and how the presented responsibility notions can be used for debugging purposes.

Future Work. The action-separation technique presented for action-based actors can be explored further. For example, it could be useful to build finer-grained actors that represent actions in individual states, instead of just considering actions globally. This would enable ascribing responsibility to individual transitions in the transition system.

While the focus of this article is on safety properties, analogous definitions for the responsibility of actors on the satisfaction or violation of other properties, e.g. reachability, Büchi or LTL-formulas, can be provided [33]. Some of concepts presented in Sect. 4 would need to be adapted as e.g. the soundness of the scheduler and action separation transformation (Lemma 4.3 and Lemma 4.10) does not hold when switching from safety to LTL properties.

The complexity results show that an efficient algorithm is unlikely to exist. However, there might be branch-and-bound techniques and other heuristics for finding switching pairs that provide a speed-up over the current implementation, which naïvely enumerates all coalitions.

References

1. Alur, R., Henzinger, T.A.: Reactive modules. Formal Methods Syst. Des. **15**, 7–48 (1999). https://doi.org/10.1023/A:1008739929481

2. Baier, C., van den Bossche, R., Klüppelholz, S., Lehmann, J., Piribauer, J.: Backward responsibility in transition systems using general power indices. In: Proceedings of the AAAI Conference on Artificial Intelligence, vol. 38, pp. 20320–20327 (2024). https://doi.org/10.1609/aaai.v38i18.30013

3. Baier, C., et al.: From verification to causality-based explications (invited talk). In: 48th International Colloquium on Automata, Languages, and Programming (ICALP), LIPIcs. Schloss Dagstuhl - Leibniz-Zentrum für Informatik, vol. 198, pp. 1:1–1:20 (2021). https://doi.org/10.4230/LIPICS.ICALP.2021.1

4. Baier, C., Funke, F., Majumdar, R.: A game-theoretic account of responsibility allocation. In: Zhi-Hua Zhou (ed.) Proceedings of the Thirtieth International Joint Conference on Artificial Intelligence, IJCAI 2021. Main Track. International Joint Conferences on Artificial Intelligence Organization, pp. 1773–1779 (2021). https://doi.org/10.24963/ijcai.2021/244

5. Baier, C., Funke, F., Majumdar, R.: Responsibility attribution in parameterized Markovian models. In: Thirty-Fifth AAAI Conference on Artificial Intelligence (AAAI), pp. 11734–11743. AAAI Press (2021). https://doi.org/10.1609/AAAI. V35I13.17395

6. Baier, C., Katoen, J.-P.: Principles of Model Checking. MIT Press (2008). ISBN 978-0-262-02649-9

7. Ball, T., Naik, M., Rajamani, S.K.: From symptom to cause: localizing errors in counterexample traces. In: Proceedings of the 30th ACM SIGPLAN-SIGACT Symposium on Principles of Programming Languages, POPL 2003, New Orleans, Louisiana, USA, pp. 97–105. Association for Computing Machinery (2003). https://doi.org/10.1145/604131.604140. ISBN 1581136285

8. Beer, I., Ben-David, S., Chockler, H., Orni, A., Trefler, R.J.: Explaining counterexamples using causality. Formal Methods Syst. Des. **40**(1), 20–40 (2012). https://doi.org/10.1007/S10703-011-0132-2

9. Budde, C.E., et al.: On correctness, precision, and performance in quantitative verification. In: Margaria, T., Steffen, B. (eds.) ISoLA 2020. LNCS, vol. 12479, pp. 216–241. Springer, Cham (2021). https://doi.org/10.1007/978-3-030-83723-5_15

10. Chang, B.-Y.E., Chlipala, A., Necula, G.C.: A framework for certified program analysis and its applications to mobile-code safety. In: Emerson, E.A., Namjoshi, K.S. (eds.) VMCAI 2006. LNCS, vol. 3855, pp. 174–189. Springer, Heidelberg (2005). https://doi.org/10.1007/11609773_12

11. Chockler, H.: Causality and responsibility for formal verification and beyond. In: Gössler, G., Sokolsky, O. (eds.) First Workshop on Causal Reasoning for Embedded and safety-critical Systems Technologies (CREST). EPTCS, vol. 224, pp. 1–8 (2016). https://doi.org/10.4204/EPTCS.224.1

12. Chockler, H., Grumberg, O., Yadgar, A.: Efficient automatic STE refinement using responsibility. In: Ramakrishnan, C.R., Rehof, J. (eds.) TACAS 2008. LNCS, vol. 4963, pp. 233–248. Springer, Heidelberg (2008). https://doi.org/10.1007/978-3-540-78800-3_17

13. Chockler, H., Halpern, J.Y.: Responsibility and blame: a structural-model approach. J. Artif. Intell. Res. **22**, 93–115 (2004). https://doi.org/10.1613/JAIR.1391

14. Chockler, H., Halpern, J.Y., Kupferman, O.: What causes a system to satisfy a specification? ACM Trans. Comput. Log. **9**(3), 20:1–20:26 (2008). https://doi.org/10.1145/1352582.1352588

15. Clarke, E.M., Grumberg, O., Peled, D.A.: Model Checking, 1st edn. MIT Press (2001). http://books.google.de/books?id=Nmc4wEaLXFEC. ISBN 978-0-262-03270-4

16. Clarke, E.M., Henzinger, T.A., Veith, H., Bloem, R. (eds.): Handbook of Model Checking. Springer (2018). https://doi.org/10.1007/978-3-319-10575-8. ISBN 978-3-319-10574-1

17. Dastani, M., Yazdanpanah, V.: Responsibility of AI systems. AI Soc. **38**(2), 843–852 (2023). https://doi.org/10.1007/S00146-022-01481-4

18. Fijalkow, N., et al.: Games on graphs. CoRR abs/2305.10546 (2023). https://doi.org/10.48550/ARXIV.2305.10546

19. Grädel, E., Thomas, W., Wilke, T. (eds.): Automata Logics, and Infinite Games. LNCS, vol. 2500. Springer, Heidelberg (2002). https://doi.org/10.1007/3-540-36387-4

20. Groce, A., Chaki, S., Kroening, D., Strichman, O.: Error explanation with distance metrics. Int. J. Softw. Tools Technol. Transfer **8**, 229–247 (2006). https://doi.org/10.1007/s10009-005-0202-0

21. Groce, A., Visser, W.: What went wrong: explaining counterexamples. In: Ball, T., Rajamani, S.K. (eds.) SPIN 2003. LNCS, vol. 2648, pp. 121–136. Springer, Heidelberg (2003). https://doi.org/10.1007/3-540-44829-2_8

22. Halpern, J.Y., Pearl, J.: Causes and explanations: a structural-model approach. Part I: Causes. Br. J. Philos. Sci. (2005)

23. Halpern, J.Y., Pearl, J.: Causes and explanations: a structural-model approach. Part II: Explanations. Br. J. Philos. Sci. (2005)

24. Halpern, J.Y.: A modification of the Halpern-Pearl definition of causality. In: IJCAI, pp. 3022–3033. AAAI Press (2015)

25. Henzinger, T.A., Necula, G.C., Jhala, R., Sutre, G., Majumdar, R., Weimer, W.: Temporal-safety proofs for systems code. In: Brinksma, E., Larsen, K.G. (eds.) CAV 2002. LNCS, vol. 2404, pp. 526–538. Springer, Heidelberg (2002). https://doi.org/10.1007/3-540-45657-0_45

26. Hofmann, M., Neukirchen, C., Rueß, H.: Certification for μ-calculus with winning strategies. In: Bošnački, D., Wijs, A. (eds.) SPIN 2016. LNCS, vol. 9641, pp. 111–128. Springer, Cham (2016). https://doi.org/10.1007/978-3-319-32582-8_8

27. Kwiatkowska, M., Norman, G., Parker, D.: PRISM 4.0: verification of probabilistic real-time systems. In: Gopalakrishnan, G., Qadeer, S. (eds.) CAV 2011. LNCS, vol. 6806, pp. 585–591. Springer, Heidelberg (2011). https://doi.org/10.1007/978-3-642-22110-1_47

28. Kwiatkowska, M., Norman, G., Parker, D.: The PRISM benchmark suite. In: 9th International Conference on Quantitative Evaluation of SysTems, pp. 203–204. IEEE CS Press (2012). https://doi.org/10.1109/QEST.2012.14

29. Landsberg, D., Chockler, H., Kroening, D., Lewis, M.: Evaluation of measures for statistical fault localisation and an optimising scheme. In: Egyed, A., Schaefer, I. (eds.) FASE 2015. LNCS, vol. 9033, pp. 115–129. Springer, Heidelberg (2015). https://doi.org/10.1007/978-3-662-46675-9_8

30. Lehmann, J.: Tool to compute actor-based responsibility (2024). https://doi.org/10.5281/zenodo.13738447

31. Leitner-Fischer, F., Leue, S.: SpinCause: a tool for causality checking. In: International Symposium on Model Checking of Software (SPIN), pp. 117–120. ACM (2014). https://doi.org/10.1145/2632362.2632371

32. Leroy, X.: A formally verified compiler back-end. J. Autom. Reason. **43**(4), 363–446 (2009). https://doi.org/10.1007/s10817-009-9155-4. http://xavierleroy.org/publi/compcert-backend.pdf

33. Mascle, C., Baier, C., Funke, F., Jantsch, S., Kiefer, S.: Responsibility and verification: importance value in temporal logics. In: 36th Annual ACM/IEEE Symposium on Logic in Computer Science (LICS), pp. 1–14. IEEE (2021). https://doi.org/10.1109/LICS52264.2021.9470597

34. Namjoshi, K.S.: Certifying model checkers. In: Berry, G., Comon, H., Finkel, A. (eds.) CAV 2001. LNCS, vol. 2102, pp. 2–13. Springer, Heidelberg (2001). https://doi.org/10.1007/3-540-44585-4_2

35. Necula, G.C.: Proof-carrying code. In: van Tilborg, H.C.A., Jajodia, S. (eds.) Encyclopedia of Cryptography and Security, 2nd edn., pp. 984–986. Springer, Cham (2011). https://doi.org/10.1007/978-1-4419-5906-5_864

36. van de Poel, I.: The relation between forward-looking and backward-looking responsibility. In: Vincent, N.A., van de Poel, I., van den Hoven, J. (eds.) Moral Responsibility: Beyond Free Will and Determinism, pp. 37–52. Springer, Dordrecht (2011). https://doi.org/10.1007/978-94-007-1878-4_3. ISBN 978- 94-007-1878-4

37. Shapley, L.S.: A value for n-person games. Contrib. Theory Games **2** (1953)

38. Winter, E.: The shapley value. Handb. Game Theory Econ. Appl. **3**, 2025–2054 (2002)

39. Yazdanpanah, V., Dastani, M., Jamroga, W., Alechina, N., Logan, B.: Strategic responsibility under imperfect information. In: Elkind, E., Veloso, M., Agmon, N., Taylor, M.E. (eds.) Proceedings of the 18th International Conference on Autonomous Agents and MultiAgent Systems, AAMAS 2019, Montreal, QC, Canada, 13–17 May 2019. International Foundation for Autonomous Agents and Multiagent Systems, pp. 592–600 (2019). http://dl.acm.org/citation.cfm?id=3331745

Semantics and Formal Analysis of Lingua Franca CPS Specifications in Rewriting Logic

Mircea Marin[1], Peter Csaba Ölveczky[2(✉)], Mario Reja[1], Mikheil Rukhaia[3], and Kyungmin Bae[4]

[1] West University of Timişoara, Timişoara, Romania
[2] University of Oslo, Oslo, Norway
peterol@ifi.uio.no
[3] Institute of Applied Mathematics, Tbilisi State University, Tbilisi, Georgia
[4] POSTECH, Pohang, South Korea

Abstract. In this paper we formalize in rewriting logic the intended discrete-event semantics of the Lingua Franca coordination language for cyber-physical systems in the simplified setting where each reaction has exactly one trigger. We then show how such Lingua Franca models can be simulated and model checked using Maude, and provide functionality that should make the formal analysis easy to perform also for the Maude non-expert. We illustrate such Maude verification on a number of existing Lingua Franca models, including of a car driver assistance system and of train door controllers. To the best of our knowledge, this is the first verification framework for Lingua Franca that captures the intended semantics of the language, and which therefore provides correct (and state-space efficient) model checking analysis for Lingua Franca.

1 Introduction

It is an honor to be invited to celebrate Marjan Sirjani's scientific achievements and contributions to the formal methods community. Although Marjan's scientific contributions are too numerous to be discussed here, the overall goal of much of her work is shared by the "Maude community" to which some of us belong: The quest for *intuitive* and *expressive* "modeler-friendly" *formal* modeling languages and *practical* formal analysis methods for modern distributed systems. To achieve this goal, Marjan developed the actor-based Rebeca modeling language for distributed systems [48], extended it to timed [1], hybrid [23], and probabilistic systems [22], and subjected these languages to an impressive range of applications. One of those applications inspired the work presented in this paper.

A remarkable community-building contribution of Marjan's is that of establishing a respected biennial international formal methods conference, Fundamentals of Software Engineering (FSEN), in Iran, thereby exposing researchers in

Iran to cutting-edge formal methods research. Those of us who have attended FSEN loved the conference and its excursions in friendly and beautiful Iran.

The second author of this paper (Ölveczky) first met Marjan in Tehran in 2011. They decided to collaborate on two papers providing formal semantics and analysis to Timed Rebeca using Real-Time Maude [46,47]. Ölveczky has also been a program committee member of FSEN since 2013, and even got the FSEN Best Paper Award in 2019 [21]. He also fondly remembers his pre-FSEN'19 excursion, when Marjan and her daughter Ladan encouraged their lovely friend Hanieh Rahmati to show him the subtle charms of the Bandar Abbas region.

Marjan and two of us, Bae and Ölveczky, also have in common that all three of us have collaborated with Edward A. Lee. Our paths also crossed when Edward gave an invited talk, based on a paper by him and Marjan [24], at the FACS'18 conference that Bae and Ölveczky chaired.

Edward and others recently developed the *Lingua Franca* [30,33,36] coordination language for CPSs, based on the *reactor* model of computation [31,32]. Reactors are deterministic actors (with local variables) whose *reactions* are triggered by, and may produce, *discrete events*. The semantics of Lingua Franca resembles that of *discrete-event* systems [15,20,25], which is a timed version of the *synchronous-reactive* model of computation [13]. Essentially, an event may trigger a reaction that generates new events which trigger other reactions *at the same logical time* and/or in the future, and so on. A key property of Lingua Franca is that, despite the fact that multiple reactions at the same logical time may be executed in different orders, the end result is deterministic.

Example 1. Figures 1 and 2 present a simple Lingua Franca specification, taken from [33]. (See Sect. 2.1 for a brief introduction to Lingua Franca). The *reaction* to startup (shown as a circle) in the *reactor* y outputs the value 1 to both of its output ports (dbl and inc) upon startup. The reaction in the reactor relay just writes the value read in its input port r upon receiving an input to its output port out. The reactor x has a state variable s whose value is doubled when the top-most reaction of x is executed, triggered by the presence of an event in x's input port dbl. When the second reaction is triggered, the value of s is increased by the value of the input port inc. All of these reaction executions take place at the *same logical time*. To achieve determinism, reactions that happen at the same logical time *in the same reactor* must be executed in the order of declaration; i.e., in our example the final value of s will be 3.

Even this simple example poses some questions: Upon receiving input at inc, when can the second reaction (inc) in x be executed? If, as in our case, an input always is present at dbl at the same logical time, then the last reaction must wait until the first reaction in x finishes executing. However, if instead relay only produces outputs when some condition holds (e.g., its input is an even number), then the second reaction in x cannot "wait" for the first reaction. The paper [36] defines constraints of reaction executions in the form of an *acyclic precedence graph* (APG), that must be dynamically maintained, so that all executions at the same logical time are consistent with the APG. □

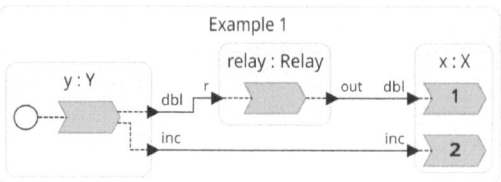

Fig. 1. Graphical representation of the Lingua Franca specification in Fig. 2.

```
1    target C;                              22   }
2                                           23
3    reactor X {                            24   reactor Y {
4        input dbl: int;                    25       output dbl:int;
5        input inc: int;                    26       output inc:int;
6        state s:int = 1;                   27       reaction(startup) -> dbl, inc {=
7        reaction(dbl) {=                    28           lf_set(dbl, 1);
8            self -> s *= 2;                 29           lf_set(inc, 1);
9        =}                                 30       =}
10       reaction(inc) {=                   31   }
11           self -> s += inc;              32
12           printf("%d\n", self -> s);     33   main reactor {
13       =}                                 34       x = new X();
14   }                                      35       r = new Relay();
15                                          36       y = new Y();
16   reactor Relay {                        37
17       input r:int;                       38       y.dbl -> r.r;
18       output out:int;                    39       r.out -> x.dbl;
19       reaction(r) -> out {=              40       y.inc -> x.inc;
20           lf_set(out, r -> value);       41   }
21       =}
```

Fig. 2. Lingua Franca specification of the "relay" system in [33].

There are two timelines in play: "logical" time and "physical" time. *Logical actions* are triggered by reactors, whose timing the system "controls," and *physical actions* may happen nondeterministically at any (physical) time.

Even though Lingua Franca is *deterministic*, it needs model checking analysis to analyze systems with physical actions, which could happen *nondeterministically* in time (and in values). This need has been addressed by Edward A. Lee, Sanjit Seshia, and their collaborators in [30], and by Marjan, Edward, and Ehsan Khamespanah in [49]. In the latter, the authors first extend Timed Rebeca with priorities on both actors and on the message servers of an actor. They then present Timed Rebeca models corresponding to the Lingua Franca specifications of three different versions of a simple train door controller system. The Berkeley group encodes Lingua Franca computations as SMT constraints, and uses bounded model checking to analyze Lingua Franca specifications.

In this paper we pay homage to Marjan's work and to her collaboration with Edward A. Lee by presenting a rewriting logic [37] semantics for a subset of Lingua Franca that roughly corresponds to those tackled in [30,49], except that we assume that each reaction can be triggered by exactly *one* (unique) trigger. This assumption makes it much easier to formalize the Lingua Franca semantics. Our object-based semantics is executable in the Maude system [17], and therefore makes possible a wide range of analysis methods for Lingua Franca, including simulation, reachability analysis, and LTL model checking.

The work reported in this paper differs from the work in [49] as follows:

- Edward A. Lee places great emphasis on Lingua Franca being deterministic. However, since Sirjani et al. [49] just let the Timed Rebeca computational model also be the computational model for Lingua Franca, the semantics in [49] is a nondeterministic "event-based" semantics which also takes "intermediate" steps into account. Since rewriting logic has both *equations* (which do not generate transitions or new states) and *rewrite rules* (which do), we can define the desired deterministic "logical-time" semantics for Lingua Franca. This also leads to much fewer states encountered during model checking.
- Sirjani et al. extend Timed Rebeca with priorities on actors and on each actor's message servers to capture constraints on the executions. Since they only give their translation for three examples, we do not know how they would use the priorities on other specifications, such as the one given in Fig. 3, where a lexicographic comparison on ⟨actor-priority, message-server-priority⟩ pairs is not sufficient to capture the constraints (see [35]). We instead dynamically build and maintain the *acyclic precedence graph* (APG) in each step, and make sure that the executions satisfy the constraints of the APG.
- Although, like [30,49], we leave the treatment of the interplay between physical and logical time for future work, we present a fairly general method for specifying the time and value nondeterminism of physical actions.

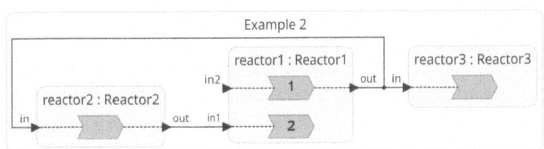

Fig. 3. Graphical representation of another Lingua Franca specification.

We cover a subset of Lingua Franca similar to that in [30], but do not consider hierarchical Lingua Franca models or models where reactions may have multiple triggers. We provide an operational semantics for Lingua Franca, whereas [30] provides an "axiomatic semantics" SMT encoding of Lingua Franca computations. This semantics corresponds to the undesired "event-based" semantics, whereas we give the "logical-time" semantics, where all the reactions that happen at the same logical time are performed in a single transition. The authors of [30] use their semantics for time-bounded model checking (which sometimes captures all possible behaviors), whereas we perform both time-bounded and unbounded reachability analysis and LTL model checking.

We give some background to rewriting logic, Maude, and Lingua Franca in Sect. 2. Section 3 first defines the subset of Lingua Franca that we consider, and then shows how Lingua Franca models can be represented as Maude terms. Section 4 presents our "big-step" (logical-time) semantics of Lingua Franca computations in Maude, and Sect. 5 explains how Lingua Franca specifications can be formally analyzed in Maude. Section 6 shows how we have applied our framework to (a small variation of) the automated driving assistance system example in [30] and all three variations of the train door system in [49]. Finally, Sect. 7 discusses related work and Sect. 8 gives some concluding remarks.

Due to space limitations, we have to leave out much detail, and refer to our longer report [35] for more details and explanations. Our executable semantics and all case studies, with their analysis commands, are available at https:// github.com/symbolicsafety/lf-maude.

2   Preliminaries

2.1   Lingua Franca

Lingua Franca (LF) [33,36] is a coordination language designed to enrich mainstream programming languages with deterministic reactive concurrency and timed behavior. LF is based on *reactor-oriented* programming [32,34], where *reactors*, modeling system components, can be seen as deterministic actors with a discrete-event execution semantics and explicitly declared ports and connections. LF is concerned only with coordination: the logic of each component is specified in a target programming language such as C, C++, Python, TypeScript, or Rust.

A *reactor* consists of local state variables, reactions, actions, timers, and/or ports. A *reaction* reaction (*triggers*) *uses* -> *effects* {= *body* =} executes when any of its *triggers* is present. A trigger can be (the presence of an *event* at) an input port, a *timer*, or an *action*. A timer is used to generate periodic events, and an action is used to schedule future events. startup is an action that happens at startup. *effects* is a set of ports and actions that the reaction *may* write to (resp., schedule), and *body* specifies the reaction's behavior in the target language.

All events are time-stamped with *tags*, which are pairs $\langle t, m \rangle$, where t is a *time value* and $m \in \mathbb{N}$ is a *micro-step* index, and are ordered lexicographically along a single logical time line. An event may also carry an additional value. The events produced by a reaction by writing to ports have the same timestamp as its triggering event. This means that a reaction itself is logically instantaneous.

A *connection* from an output port to an input port is declared using ->, with an optional delay specified using after. Without a specified delay, an event travels from an output port to an input port logically instantaneously. An output port may be connected to multiple input ports, but an input port can only be connected to a single output port.

A *timer* timer *t*(*offset*, *period*) is used to trigger reactions by scheduling events at regular intervals (given by *period*) relative to a start time (*offset*).

Actions are used to schedule future events. *Logical actions* schedule events for the future with a specified delay (controlled by the program). If the delay is zero, the event will be scheduled at the next micro-step. *Physical actions* represent *external* events from the "physical" environment, the timing (and values) of which is not controlled by the program. LF therefore considers two timelines: *logical time* and *physical time*. The relation between the two timelines is subtle [33,51].

Reactions are executed in the order of the tags ("timestamps") of their triggering events. When a reaction executes, it may read inputs, change the reactor's local state variables, generate new outputs, and/or schedule future events. A certain output may or may not be generated in a reaction execution (depending, e.g., on the values of the inputs and/or the reactor's local state variables).

A reaction execution may create new events *with the same tag* ("time"), which will trigger other reaction executions at the same (logical) time, and so on. LF has a discrete-event-style semantics, where all reaction executions at the same logical time are considered to be executed simultaneously. Such execution is impossible if there are circular dependencies among the reaction executions at the same logical time. Therefore, LF requires that the following constraint ($\mathbf{c_1}$) is satisfied:

($\mathbf{c_1}$) if a reaction r_1 of one reactor declares that it *may* produce an event that triggers a reaction r_2 of another reactor, then at any logical time t at which r_1 is triggered, r_1 must execute (and finish) before r_2 starts executing.

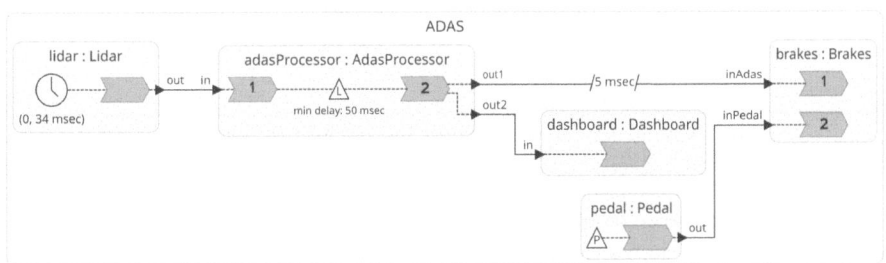

Fig. 4. Graphical representation of the ADAS system specification.

Example 2. Figures 4 and 5 show a version of the LF specification of an advanced driver assistance system (ADAS) in [30] from which we have omitted the camera component (since our semantics currently does not support multiple reaction triggers). In this system, a LiDAR periodically sends "data from the environment" to an ADAS processor. If an object is close to the vehicle, a warning message is displayed on the dashboard. If it is too close, the ADAS processor signals to the brakes reactor to apply the brakes. The user can also press the brake pedal.

In Fig. 4, reactors are represented as rectangles with round corners, ports as black triangles, and reactions as chevrons labeled with numbers indicating the order of their declaration in a reactor. Timers are rendered as clocks and actions as white triangles with a label: L for logical actions, and P for physical actions.

```
1   target C;                                39    =}
2                                            40  }
3   reactor Lidar {                          41
4     output out: int                        42  reactor Pedal {
5     state frame: int = 0                   43    output out: int
6     timer t(0, 34 msec)                    44    physical action a
7                                            45
8     reaction(t) -> out {=                  46    reaction(a) -> out {=
9       lf_set(out, frame);                  47      lf_set(out, 1);
10      self -> frame++;                     48    =}
11    =}                                     49  }
12  }                                        50
13                                           51  reactor Brakes {
14  reactor AdasProcessor {                  52    input inAdas: int
15    input in: int                          53    input inPedal: int
16    output out1: int                       54    state brakesApplied: int = 0
17    output out2: int                       55
18    state requestStop: bool = false        56    reaction(inAdas) {=
19    logical action a(50 msec): int         57      self -> brakesApplied = inAdas -> value;
20                                           58    =}
21    reaction(in) -> a {=                   59    reaction(inPedal) {=
22      self -> requestStop = true;          60      self -> brakesApplied = inPedal -> value;
23      lf_schedule(a, 0);                   61    =}
24    =}                                     62  }
25                                           63
26    reaction(a) -> out1, out2 {=           64  main reactor {
27      if (self -> requestStop)             65    lidar = new Lidar()
28        lf_set(out1, 1);                   66    adasProcessor = new AdasProcessor()
29      else                                 67    brakes = new Brakes()
30        lf_set(out2, 4);                   68    dashboard = new Dashboard()
31    =}                                     69    pedal = new Pedal()
32  }                                        70
33                                           71    lidar.out -> adasProcessor.in
34  reactor Dashboard {                      72    adasProcessor.out1 -> brakes.inAdas after 5
35    input in: int                                  msec
36    state received: bool = false           73    adasProcessor.out2 -> dashboard.in
37    reaction(in) {=                        74    pedal.out -> brakes.inPedal
38      self -> received = true;             75  }
```

Fig. 5. LF specification of the ADAS example.

Immediate connections from a port to another are drawn as continuous lines between them, and connections with a delay t are shown as ▶————/t/———▶.

The LF specification in Fig. 5 models the ADAS system with reactors lidar, brakes, adasProcessor, dashboard, and pedal of types Lidar, Brakes, AdasProcessor, Dashboard, and Pedal, respectively. Line 6 sets a timer t to trigger at time 0 and then every 34 milliseconds. When triggered, the reaction outputs the value of the LiDAR frame through the output port out. The adasProcessor reactor uses a Boolean state variable requestStop and declares a *logical* action a. When an event arrives in its input port, the reaction sets this state variable to true and schedules the logical action immediately (line 23). The logical action a has an additional delay of 50 ms before it triggers (line 19). When triggered, the second reaction sends an event to *one* of its output ports, depending on the value of requestStop. The pedal reactor has a *physical* action a that models input from the environment. Line 72 shows a delay of 5 ms in the connection from adasProcessor's output port out1 and brakes' input port. □

LF aims to ensure a *deterministic* result of the executions (at any logical time). Since multiple reactions *in the same reactor* may be triggered at the same time, and since these reactions share the reactor's local variables, LF prioritizes the executions of reactions in the same reactor by imposing the following constraint:

(c_2) a reaction r_1 that is declared before another reaction r_2 *in the same reactor* is fully executed before r_2 executes, if both are triggered at the same time.

The above constraints (c_1) and (c_2) can be captured as an *acyclic precedence graph* (APG) [36] in which the nodes are reactions and the edges are dependencies between them. Any execution of all the reactions triggered at the same logical time must be consistent with the APG.

Example 3. The following graph shows the APG of the system in Fig. 3 w.r.t. to an event at input port in2 of reactor reactor1, where solid arrows represent (c_1)-dependencies and dotted arrows represent (c_2)-dependencies:

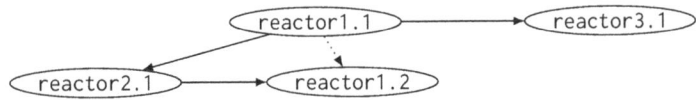

2.2 Maude

Maude [17] is a declarative language and high-performance tool for formally specifying and analyzing concurrent systems in rewriting logic [37]. A Maude module specifies a *rewrite theory* $\mathcal{R} = (\Sigma, E, L, R)$, where:

- Σ is a *signature*, declaring sorts, subsorts, and function symbols;
- E is a set of equations of the form $t = t'$ **if** *cond*, where t and t' are Σ-terms and *cond* is a conjunction of equations;
- L is a set of rule *labels*; and
- R is a set of *rewrite rules* of the form $l : t \longrightarrow t'$ **if** *cond*, where $l \in L$, t and t' are Σ-terms, and *cond* is a conjunction of equations and rewrites.

States are specified as elements of algebraic data types defined by the equational theory (Σ, E), and system transitions are specified by the rewrite rules R.

We summarize Maude's syntax and refer to [17] for details. Operators are declared **op** $f : s_1 \ldots s_n$ -> s and can have user-definable syntax, using '_' for argument positions. An operator with the **ctor** attribute is a data constructor. A binary function symbol can be declared to be *associative* (**assoc**), *commutative* (**comm**), and/or to have an *identity element* t (**id:** t), so that computations are performed *modulo* these properties. Unconditional and conditional equations and rewrite rules are introduced with, respectively, the keywords **eq** and **ceq**, and **rl** and **crl**. An equation $f(t_1, \ldots, t_n) = t$ with the **owise** ("otherwise") attribute can be applied to a term $f(\ldots)$ only if no other equation with a left-hand side $f(u_1, \ldots, u_n)$ can be applied. Mathematical variables are declared with the keywords **var** and **vars**, or on-the-fly as *var:sort*.

class C | att_1 : s_1, ... , att_n : s_n declares a *class* C with attributes att_1 to att_n of sorts s_1 to s_n. A term <o : C | att_1 : val_1, ..., att_n : val_n> denotes an *object* of class C, where o (of sort Oid) is the object's *identifier*, and val_1 to val_n are the attribute values. A *configuration* is a *multiset* of objects and messages and has sort Configuration. For example, a rewrite rule

```
rl [1] :  < O : C | a1 : x, a2 : w, a3 : z >  =>  < O : C | a1 : x + w, a2 : w, a3 : z > .
```

defines a set of transitions where object O of class C updates its attribute a1 to x + w. Attributes whose values do not change and do not affect the next state, such as a3, may be omitted in a rule. A *subclass* B of C (**subclass** B < C) inherits the attributes and rules of its superclass C.

Maude provides a variety of analysis methods. The rew command simulates one behavior of the system. The command search [n] t_0 =>* *pattern* such that *cond* searches for up to n states reachable from state t_0 that match *pattern* and satisfy the condition *cond*. The linear temporal logic (LTL) model checking command red modelCheck(t_0, ϕ) checks whether all paths from state t_0 satisfy the LTL formula ϕ. Formulas are built using (possibly parametric) state propositions of sort Prop and standard LTL operators, such as ~ (negation), \/, /\, ->, [] ("always"), <> ("eventually"), U ("until"), W ("weak until"), and O ("next").

Real-time systems can be specified in rewriting logic as real-time rewrite theories [44]. Ordinary rewrite rules then model *instantaneous* change, and time advance is modeled by "tick" rules crl [*tick*] : {t} => {u} in time τ if *cond*, where τ is a term of sort Time, t and u are terms of sort System, the *entire* state has the form {s}, so that time advances uniformly in the whole system.

The Real-Time Maude tool [41,43] offers a range of time-specific analysis methods for real-time rewrite theories, including time-bounded and unbounded reachability analysis and LTL model checking, as well as *timed* CTL model checking [29]. However, since Real-Time Maude currently is being upgraded, we use the Maude tool in this paper. This requires "hard-coding" some of the model transformations performed by Real-Time Maude, e.g., for time-bounded analysis.

3   Representing Lingua Franca Models in Maude

This section first discusses the subset of Lingua Franca (LF) that we target, and then explains how an LF specification is represented as a Maude term.

3.1   Targeted Subset of Lingua Franca

The other formalizations [30,49] of LF do not consider physical actions as such, and therefore do not take into account both physical and logical time. We therefore also do not support physical actions to their fullest generality and also only consider one timeline. However, to analyze systems with (time-and-value-nondeterministic) physical actions, we propose a fairly general framework where we treat physical actions in logical time as follows:

– Each physical action has a user-defined period and finite range of possible "values" that the physical action may take as parameter.
– At the end of each period, a nondeterministic choice is made whether or not the physical action happens at this time.
– If the action happens, its "value" is selected nondeterministically.

We also support that a physical action always triggers at the end of its "period," to periodically trigger events with parameter values selected nondeterministically.

The goal of this paper is not to formalize C or Python in Maude. Sirjani et al. [49] translate the C code in LF reactions by hand to Timed Rebeca code, and Lin et al. [30] treat a very limited subset of C. Therefore, we provide a simple iterative programming language to specify the control logic of the reactions.

We do not treat hierarchical models, and, to significantly simplify the formalization of the LF semantics, we assume that each reaction has exactly one trigger and that a trigger can trigger at most one reaction.

3.2 Representing Lingua Franca Models in Maude

Representing LF Models. We represent an LF model in an object-oriented style, where each reactor is modeled as an object of the following class:

```
class Reactor | inports : Configuration,    outports : Configuration,
                  state : ReactorState,    reactions : ReactionList,
                  timers : Configuration,    actions : Configuration .
```

The attributes `inports` and `outports` contain the reactor's input ports and output ports, respectively. `state` denotes the reactor's local state as a set of pairs *var* |-> *value*, `reactions` is a *list* of the reactor's reactions, and `timers` and `actions` contain objects for the timers and the actions declared in the reactor.

A port object has a single attribute `value`:

```
class Port | value : Value .
```

A reaction is represented as **reaction when** *triggers* --> *possibleOutputs* {*code*}:

```
sorts ReactionList Reaction .           subsort Reaction < ReactionList .

op nil : -> ReactionList [ctor] .
op __ : ReactionList ReactionList -> ReactionList [ctor assoc id: nil] .

op reaction when_-->_do'{_'} : OidSet OidSet ReactionBody -> Reaction [ctor] .
op reaction when_do'{_'} : OidSet ReactionBody -> Reaction .
var RB : ReactionBody .           var OS : OidSet .
eq reaction when OS do {RB} = reaction when OS --> none do {RB} .
```

An immediate *connection* (resp., with delay *d*) from port *p* of reactor *r* to port *p'* of reactor *r'* is denoted $r : p$ --> $r' : p'$ (resp., $r : p$ -- d --> $r' : p'$):

```
sort Connection .           subsort Connection < Configuration .

op _:_-->_:_ : ReactorId PortId ReactorId PortId -> Connection [ctor] .
op _:_--_-->_:_ : ReactorId PortId Time ReactorId PortId -> Connection [ctor] .
```

```
sorts PortId IPortId BPortId VarId IVarId BVarId ReactorId TimerId
      ActionId IActionId BActionId ReactionId .
subsorts  ReactorId ReactionId < Oid .  subsorts IPortId BPortId < PortId .
subsorts IVarId BVarId < VarId .       subsorts IActionId BActionId < ActionId .
```

Since `Connection` is a subsort of `Configuration`, a configuration can contain connections in addition to objects.

A timer is modeled in Maude as an object of the following class:

```
class Timer | offset : Time, period : TimeInf .
```

Physical and logical actions are represented by objects of the respective classes `PhysicalAction` and `LogicalAction`:

```
class Action | minDelay : Time,  minSpacing : Time,  policy : ActionPolicy,  payload : Value .
class PhysicalAction .              class LogicalAction .
subclasses PhysicalAction LogicalAction < Action .
```

Language for Reaction Code. We define a simple programming language for the reaction code. The basic types are Boolean values, time values, and natural numbers. Constants are denoted `[4]` and `[true]`, etc., and we build expressions using the usual arithmetic and comparison operators. Port names (sort `IPortId` for integer-typed ports and `BPortId` for Boolean-typed ports), variable names, and action names also are considered to be expressions:

```
sorts NatValue TimeValue BoolValue Value IntExpr BoolExpr Expr .
subsort NatValue < TimeValue .        subsort TimeValue BoolValue < Value .

op [_] : Nat -> NatValue [ctor] .    op [_] : Time -> TimeValue [ctor] .
op [_] : Bool -> BoolValue [ctor] .

subsort IntExpr BoolExpr < Expr .      subsort NatValue IPortId IVarId IActionId < IntExpr .
subsort BoolValue BPortId BVarId BActionId < BoolExpr .

ops _+_ _*_ : IntExpr IntExpr -> IntExpr [ctor] .
ops _<_ _>_ _<=_ _>=_ : IntExpr IntExpr ->  BoolExpr [ctor] .
op _===_ : Expr Expr -> BoolExpr [ctor] .
```

Our language (whose programs are terms of sort `ReactionBody`) consists of assignment of expressions to variables (*var* := *expr*), sending the value of an expression to an output port (*port* <- *expr*), scheduling an event, sequencing (;), conditionals, and while loops:

```
sort ReactionBody .
op skip : -> ReactionBody [ctor] .
op _;_ : ReactionBody ReactionBody -> ReactionBody [ctor assoc id: skip] .
op _:=_ : VarId Expr -> ReactionBody [ctor] .
op if_then_fi : BoolExpr ReactionBody -> ReactionBody [ctor] .
op if_then_else_fi : BoolExpr ReactionBody ReactionBody -> ReactionBody [ctor] .
op while_do_done : BoolExpr ReactionBody -> ReactionBody [ctor] .
op _<-_ : PortId Expr ->  ReactionBody [ctor] .
op schedule : ActionId IntExpr Expr -> ReactionBody [ctor] .
```

Example 4. The following Maude module defines `init` as the Maude representation of (the initial state of) the LF model of the ADAS system in Fig. 5:

```
omod ADAS-WITHOUT-CAMERA is including LF-REPR .
 ops frame received brakesApplied requestStop : -> IVarId [ctor] .
 ops lidar adasProcessor dashboard pedal brakes : -> ReactorId [ctor] .
 ops in in1 in2 out out1 out2 inAdas inPedal : -> IPortId [ctor] .
 op a : -> IActionId .              op t : -> TimerId [ctor] .
 op init : -> Configuration .
 eq init
  = < lidar : Reactor | inports : none,  outports : < out : Port | value : [0] >,
                        state : (frame |-> [0]),  actions : none,
                        timers : < t : Timer | offset : 0, period : 34 >,
                        reactions : reaction when t --> out do
                                   {(out <- frame) ; (frame := frame + [1])} >
    < adasProcessor : Reactor | inports : < in : Port | value : [0] >,
                        outports : < out1 : Port | value : [0] >
                                   < out2 : Port | value : [0] >,
                        state : requestStop |-> [0],  timers : none,
                        actions : < a : LogicalAction | minDelay : 50, minSpacing : 0,
                                                        policy : defer, payload : [0] >,
                        reactions :
                         (reaction when in --> a do
                            {(requestStop := [1]) ; schedule(a, [0], [0])})
                          reaction when a --> out1 ; out2 do
                        {if requestStop === [1] then (out1 <- [1]) else (out2 <- [4]) fi} >
    < dashboard : Reactor | inports : < in : Port | value : [0] >, outports : none,
                        state : received |-> [0],  timers : none,  actions : none,
                        reactions : reaction when in do {received := in} >
    < pedal : Reactor | inports : none, outports : < out : Port | value : [0] >,
                        timers : none,  state : empty,
                        actions : < a : PhysicalAction | minDelay : 0, minSpacing : 0,
                                                        policy : defer, payload : [0] >,
                        reactions : reaction when a --> out do {out <- [1]} >
    < brakes : Reactor | inports : < inAdas : Port | value : [0] > < inPedal : Port | value : [0] >,
                        outports : none,  timers : none,  actions : none,
                        state : (brakesApplied |-> [0]),
                        reactions : (reaction when inAdas do {brakesApplied := inAdas})
                                    (reaction when inPedal do {brakesApplied := inPedal}) >
    (lidar : out --> adasProcessor : in)
    (adasProcessor : out1 -- 5 --> brakes : inAdas)
    (adasProcessor : out2 --> dashboard : in)
    (pedal : out --> brakes : inPedal) .
endom
```

4   Maude Semantics of Lingua Franca Behaviors

This section explains how we have formalized the discrete-event ("synchronous big-step") semantics of LF behaviors in Maude.

To execute the system, we add an *event queue* to the state. The elements of this queue are pairs $\langle events, tag \rangle$, where *events* is a *set* of events, and *tag* is a tag $\langle t, m \rangle$. We prefer to "count down" the tags in the queue when time advances: a tag $\langle t, m \rangle$ in the event queue denotes that the corresponding events will be served ("executed") *in time t from "now"*. The queue is ordered by tags, and when the *first* events in the queue have a tag $\langle 0, n \rangle$, for some $n \geq 0$, they are served.

We use two rewrite rules to formalize the dynamics of LF:

– The `tick` rewrite rule advances time (in one step) until the next event(s) should be served. That is, if the smallest ("remaining-time") tag in the event queue is $\langle t, m \rangle$, with $t > 0$, then time advances by time t.

– The step rewrite rule performs one "big step" of the system (in one step) when the events at the head of the event queue have tag $\langle 0, n \rangle$, for some n. This rule executes all the reactions triggered by those events, and all those reactions triggered by events generated (and arriving without delay) by the execution of these reactions, and so on. The execution builds and dynamically maintains the APG for all these events, and makes sure that the reaction executions are consistent with the APG. As indicated elsewhere, this is tricky, since even if a triggered reaction r is a successor of another reaction r' in the APG, the reaction r' may or may not be triggered in this step.

We use a *function* to perform the reaction executions, so that the actual execution schedule of the reactions in the step is nondeterministic (more precisely: determined by the Maude interpreter). Because of the determinism of LF, the result should be the same independent of which schedule is "chosen" by Maude, as long as it is consistent with the APG. The future events resulting from actions triggered in this step, and from generated outputs traveling through delayed connections, are inserted into the event queue.

We also include a model of the nondeterministic environment, represented by the physical actions, which adds three more rewrite rules. In our model, each action has a (user-given) period, and at the end of each period, a nondeterministic choice is made as to whether or not the action "happens".

Due to space limitations, we do not show the variable declarations (see [35]), but follow the convention that variables are written with all capital letters.

4.1   States of the Execution

The states in our executions are terms of sort GlobalState of the form

```
{< env : Environment | physicalActions : physicalActions >
 reactors    connections
 < queue : EventQueue | queue : queue >}
```

where *physicalActions* consists of a PhysAct object for each physical action in the system (see below); *reactors* are the objects of class Reactor modeling the reactors; *connections* are the immediate and delayed connections between ports; and *queue* is the queue of events scheduled to trigger reactions.

An *event* is represented by a term event(r, a, v) of sort Event, where r is the reactor which should handle the event, a is the trigger (which could be a timer, an action, or an event/input port that went through a delayed connection), and v is the "value" of the event. A *set* of such events is a term of sort Events, and a set *events* of events with ("remaining") tag is represented by the term *events* at tag(t,n). A queue is a ::-separated list of such tagged event sets:

```
sort Event Events Tag TaggedEvents EQueue .  subsort Event < Events .  subsort TaggedEvents < EQueue .

op noEvent : -> Events [ctor] .
op event : ReactorId ActionTrigger Value -> Event [ctor] .
op __ : Events Events -> Events [assoc comm id: noEvent ctor] .

op tag : Time Nat -> Tag [ctor] .        op _at_ : Events Tag -> TaggedEvents [ctor] .
op empty : -> EQueue [ctor] .            op _::_ : EQueue EQueue -> EQueue [ctor assoc id: empty] .
```

```
class EventQueue | queue : EQueue .      op schedule : Events Time EQueue -> EQueue .
```

`schedule` inserts a set of events, with a given delay, into the event queue.

Initial States. Initially, the event queue should include the first event generated by each timer and other actions that take place initially (typically `startup` actions). We have therefore defined functions `addInitialTimers` and `addStartup` that insert the events generated by timers and initial actions (see [35] for details).

Example 5. The initial execution state for the system in Example 1, which has a `startup` action but no timers, is therefore defined as follows:

```
op initSystem : -> GlobalSystem .
eq initSystem =
    {< env : Environment | physicalActions : none >
     init
     < queue : EventQueue | queue : addStartup(startup, init, empty) >} .
```

where `init` is the Maude representation of the LF specification (see [35]).   □

4.2   Simulating Physical Actions

We use objects of class `PhysAct` to simulate physical actions using logical time:

```
class PhysAct | leftOfPeriod : TimeInf,      period : TimeInf,
                possibleValues : ValueSet, timeNonDet : Bool .
```

The identifiers $(r . a)$ of these objects denote the corresponding actions (r denotes the reactor and a the action). `leftOfPeriod` denotes the time remaining of its period (when the action may or may not "happen"), `period` denotes its period, and `possibleValues` its finite range of possible values. A physical action always triggers (at the end of its period) if its attribute `timeNonDet` is `false`.

The following rewrite rules model the behaviors of a physical action when its period ends (`leftOfPeriod` is 0). Then the action either does *not* happen (rule `noAction`) or it happens (rule `actionHappens`). In the latter case, the value V of the action is selected nondeterministically from the set V , VS of possible values (since the set union operator ',' is declared associative and commutative). The equation inserts the corresponding event with delay 0 into the event queue:

```
rl [noAction] :
   < O : PhysAct | leftOfPeriod : 0, period : P, timeNonDet : true >  =>
   < O : PhysAct | leftOfPeriod : P > .

rl [actionHappens] :
   < (RI . AI) : PhysAct | leftOfPeriod : 0, period : P, possibleValues : (V : VS) >  =>
   < (RI . AI) : PhysAct | leftOfPeriod : P > scheduleAction(event(RI, AI, V)) .

msg scheduleAction : Event -> Msg .

eq < O : Environment | physicalActions : CONF scheduleAction(EVENT) >
   < O2 : EventQueue | queue : QUEUE >
 = < O : Environment | physicalActions : CONF >
   < O2 : EventQueue | queue : schedule(EVENT, 0, QUEUE) > .
```

Example 6. The ADAS system has a timer, but no `startup` actions; its initial
state can therefore be defined

```
eq initSystem
= {< env : Environment | physicalActions : < (pedal . a) : PhysAct | leftOfPeriod : 5, period : 5,
                                                                      possibleValues : [69] : [71],
                                                                      timeNonDet : true > >
    init
    < queue : EventQueue | queue : addInitialTimers(init, empty) >} .
```

`init` denotes the reactor objects and connections in Example 4. The physical
action `a` in the `pedal` reactor chooses every 5 time units whether or not to happen;
if it happens, it chooses its "value" to be either `[69]` or `[71]`.   □

4.3   Advancing (Logical) Time

The following rewrite rule `tick` advances (logical) time by `T`, which is the
shortest time until either some physical action timer (`leftOfPeriod`) expires
or the events at the head of the queue should be served/executed (`T := min(T1,
smallestTimer(CONF1))`). The condition `T > 0` makes sure that this rule cannot
fire when some events are ready to be served. As a result, the tags of all events
in the event queue and all physical action timers are decreased by `T`:

```
crl [tick] :
    {< E : Environment | physicalActions : CONF1 >
     REACTORS-AND-CONNECTIONS
     < Q : EventQueue | queue : (EVENTS at tag(T1, N)) :: QUEUE >}
    =>
    {< E : Environment | physicalActions : decreaseTimers(CONF1, T) >
     REACTORS-AND-CONNECTIONS
     < Q : EventQueue | queue : (EVENTS at tag(T1 monus T, N))
                                :: decreaseTags(QUEUE, T) >}      in time T
   if T := min(T1, smallestTimer(CONF1)) /\ T > 0 .
```

A similar rewrite rule, described in [35], advances time when the event queue
is empty and there are physical actions.

4.4   The `Step` Rule

When the tag of the events `EVENTS` *at the head of the event queue* is `tag(0,N)`, the
rewrite rule `step` performs (in one step) all the reactions that happen at this logical time because of the events `EVENTS`. The condition `smallestTimer(CONF1) > 0`
ensures that the rules `noAction` or `actionHappens` are performed *before* the rule
`step` if a physical action period ends at the same time:

```
crl [step] :
    {< E : Environment | physicalActions : CONF1 >
     REACTORS-AND-CONNECTIONS
     < Q : EventQueue | queue : (EVENTS at tag(0, N)) :: QUEUE >}
    =>
    {< E : Environment | physicalActions : CONF1 >
     NEW-NETWORK
     < Q : EventQueue | queue : NEW-QUEUE >}
   if  smallestTimer(CONF1) > 0
   /\ networkQueue(NEW-NETWORK, NEW-QUEUE) :=
          executeStep(EVENTS, REACTORS-AND-CONNECTIONS, QUEUE) .

sort Network+Queue .              op networkQueue : Configuration EQueue -> Network+Queue [ctor] .
```

This rewrite rule leaves the work of executing the reactions to the *function* executeStep, which returns a pair consisting of the resulting reactor objects (and connections) (NEW-NETWORK) and the updated event queue (NEW-QUEUE), to which the future events generated in the step have been added.

executeStep calls generateAPG(EVENTS, NETWORK) to generate the APG induced by the events EVENTS, and adds the EVENTS (i.e., their "values") to the corresponding input ports and actions (addEventsToPorts(EVENTS, NETWORK)). The function executeStep then calls another function executeStep (with different signature) with the APG and updated network:

```
op executeStep : Events Configuration EQueue -> Network+Queue .
eq executeStep(EVENTS, NETWORK, QUEUE)
 = executeStep(generateAPG(EVENTS, NETWORK), addEventsToPorts(EVENTS, NETWORK), QUEUE) .
```

This new executeStep, which executes all the reactions, is described in Sect. 4.6.

4.5   Generating and Updating the APG

We represent the nodes of the APG as objects of the class

```
class APGNode |  pre : ReactionIdSet,  succ : ReactionIdSet,  status : ExecutionStatus .
```

Each such node contains data about a *reaction*, and its identifier has the form $(r.a)$, with r the reactor name and a its trigger. The attributes pre and succ denote the (identifiers of the) reactions that precede (resp., succeed) it in the APG. The execution status status is either executed, absent, unknown, or present.

For a set events EVENTS and a network state (i.e., reactors and connections) NETWORK, the operation generateAPG(EVENTS, NETWORK) computes the APG with all direct dependencies between its nodes established:

```
op generateAPG : Events Configuration -> Configuration .
eq generateAPG(EVENTS, NETWORK)
 = addVerticalDeps(addDeps(initializeAPG(EVENTS, NETWORK), NETWORK), NETWORK)
```

The function initializeAPG generates an object < $(r.t)$: APGNode | pre : none, succ : none, status : present > for each event in its first argument.

The function addDeps function defines the set of direct (c_1)-successors for every node of the dynamic APG.

```
op addDeps : Configuration Configuration -> Configuration .
eq addDeps(< (REACTOR . TRIGGER) : APGNode | succ : SUCC >
           GRAPH,
           NETWORK < REACTOR : Reactor |
                     reactions : RECS  (reaction when TRIGGER --> 0 ; OS do {BODY}) RECS2 >
           (REACTOR : 0 --> REACTOR2 : 02))
 = addDeps(< (REACTOR . TRIGGER) : APGNode | succ : SUCC ; (REACTOR2 . 02) >
           addSucc(GRAPH, (REACTOR2 . 02), (REACTOR . TRIGGER)),
           NETWORK < REACTOR : Reactor | >) .

eq addDeps(GRAPH, NETWORK) = GRAPH [owise] .
```

addDeps adds a new dependency as long as there is a node (REACTOR . TRIGGER) in the APG, where the reaction (to) TRIGGER in REACTOR *may* cause an output to

REACTOR's output port O, *and* there is an *immediate* connection (REACTOR : O -->
REACTOR2 : O2). A new dependency from (REACTOR . TRIGGER) to (REACTOR2 . O2)
is added, and we remove the connection (REACTOR : O --> REACTOR2 : O2) from
the recursive call. When a "fixed-point" has been reached (i.e., we cannot add
new dependencies), the second (owise) equation ends the function call.

The addSucc function adds the reverse dependency: (REACTOR . TRIGGER) is
added to the set of predecessors of (REACTOR2 . O2). If no APGNode exists for
(REACTOR2 . O2), a new node is created with status set to unknown.

The function addVerticalDeps adds the (c_2)-dependencies between reactions
in the same reactor.

The function updateGraph is applied after a reaction execution. If, after executing the reaction, we can decide whether a node with status unknown can be
changed to either present or absent (also "transitively"), then updateGraph does
so.

4.6 Executing Reactions

The workhorse executeStep function executes all the reactions in a big step.
executeStep simultaneously updates the APG and executes reactions: it checks
the APG and finds a reaction that can be executed, executes that reaction, and
updates the APG based on the results of executing that reaction. executeStep
does this until it reaches a point where no reaction can be executed.

The arguments to this function are: (i) the APG, (ii) the reactor objects and
the connections ("the network"), and (iii) the event queue.

In the following equation, a reaction is executed. This is possible because:

- The APG says that this reaction has input present (and not absent, unknown,
  or already executed).
- All its predecessor reactions PRE in the APG that can be executed already have
  been executed (presetOK(PRE, GRAPH), see [35], checks whether each reaction
  in the preset PRE has status executed or absent in the APG GRAPH).

The function executeReaction executes the reaction (REACTOR . TRIGGER).
This function returns a triple result(OBJECT, OUTPUTS, RESULT-QUEUE) consisting of the new state of the REACTOR object (OBJECT), the outputs generated by
executing the reaction (OUTPUTS), and the resulting event queue RESULT-QUEUE.

As a result of executing this reaction:

- The status of the reaction's APG node is set to executed.
- The APG is updated with the outputs OUTPUTS produced by executing this
  reaction. The above function updateGraph is used to modify the APG according to the result (i.e., outputs) generated by the reaction execution.
- The new network (propagateImmediateOutputs(...)) remains more or less
  the same, except that (i) the state of the reactor whose reaction was executed
  has changed (values of local variables updated) to OBJECT, and (ii) outputs
  are propagated to the corresponding input ports.

- The event queue is updated by scheduling all future events; i.e., outputs generated (OUTPUTS) that are connected to inputs with *delayed* connections (scheduleDelayedInputs(...)).

```
op executeStep : Configuration Configuration EQueue -> Network+Queue .

ceq executeStep(< (REACTOR . TRIGGER) : APGNode | status : present, pre : PRE >   GRAPH,
                NETWORK
                < REACTOR : Reactor | reactions : REACTIONS1
                                      reaction when TRIGGER --> OS do {BODY}
                                      REACTIONS2 >,
                QUEUE)
  =
    executeStep(< (REACTOR . TRIGGER) : APGNode | status : executed >
                updateGraph(GRAPH, REACTOR, OS, NETWORK < REACTOR : Reactor | >, OUTPUTS),
                propagateImmediateOutputs(OUTPUTS, NETWORK OBJECT),
                scheduleDelayedInputs(OUTPUTS, NETWORK, RESULT-QUEUE))
  if presetOK(PRE, GRAPH)   /\
        result(OBJECT, OUTPUTS, RESULT-QUEUE) :=
          executeReaction(< REACTOR : Reactor | reactions : REACTIONS1
                                      reaction when TRIGGER --> OS do {BODY}
                                      REACTIONS2 >,
                          TRIGGER, QUEUE) .
```

When no more reaction can be executed, executeStep returns the new reactor objects (and unchanged connections) NETWORK and the updated event queue QUEUE:

```
eq executeStep(GRAPH, NETWORK, QUEUE) = networkQueue(NETWORK, QUEUE) [owise] .
```

The function executeReaction calls another function executeReactionBody that executes the program BODY of the reaction:

```
op executeReaction : Object ActionTrigger EQueue -> ReactorOutputsFutureevents .

sort ReactorOutputsFutureevents .
op result : Object Events EQueue -> ReactorOutputsFutureevents [ctor] .

ceq executeReaction(< REACTOR : Reactor | reactions : REACTIONS1
                                      (reaction when TRIGGER --> OS do {BODY})
                                      REACTIONS2 >,
                    TRIGGER, QUEUE)
  = executeReactionBody(< REACTOR : Reactor | >, BODY, noEvent, QUEUE) if not (TRIGGER :: TimerId) .
```

The function executeReactionBody executes each program statement as expected. We show the cases for while loops, and for producing output to a port ((IPORT <- IEXPR)), and refer to [35] for the other cases.

The evaluation of while loops is as expected. Notice that we also need to provide the input ports (INPORTS) and the actions (ACTIONS) to the function eval, that finds the value of an integer expression is a given context, since port names and action names also can be seen as integer expressions:

```
op executeReactionBody : Object ReactionBody Events EQueue -> ReactorOutputsFutureevents .

eq executeReactionBody(< REACTOR : Reactor | state :  VALUATION,
                                      inports : INPORTS, actions : ACTIONS >,
                    (while BEXP do BODY1 done) ; BODY, OUTPUTS, QUEUE)
  =
    executeReactionBody(< REACTOR : Reactor | >,
                    if evalB(BEXP, VALUATION, INPORTS ACTIONS) then
                      (BODY1 ; (while BEXP do BODY1 done) ; BODY) else BODY fi,  OUTPUTS, QUEUE) .
```

The program statement IPORT *texttt*<− IEXPR generates an output to output port IPORT with value (the evaluation of) IEXPR. In this case we add the event/output event(REACTOR, IPORT, eval(IEXPR, ...)) to the generated outputs:

```
eq executeReactionBody(< REACTOR : Reactor | state : VALUATION,
                                    outports : CONF < IPORT : Port | >,
                                    inports : INPORTS, actions : ACTIONS >,
                        (IPORT <- IEXPR) ; BODY, OUTPUTS, QUEUE)
 =
   executeReactionBody(< REACTOR : Reactor | outports : CONF
                           < IPORT : Port | value : [eval(IEXPR, VALUATION, INPORTS ACTIONS)] > >,
                       BODY,
                       event(REACTOR, IPORT, [eval(IEXPR, VALUATION, INPORTS ACTIONS)]) OUTPUTS,
                       QUEUE) .
```

5   Maude Analysis of Lingua Franca Specifications

This section explains how LF models can be formally analyzed in Maude, even by non-experts in Maude.

Our semantics of LF is defined as a real-time rewrite theory [44]. Such theories can be analyzed by the Real-Time Maude tool [41,43]. However, since Real-Time Maude currently does not support version 3 of Maude, we analyze our models directly in Maude. We therefore have to "manually" do the theory transformations performed by Real-Time Maude for the different analysis methods.

Our tick rules do not limit the time that can elapse in the system, and therefore do not support *time-bounded* analysis. Furthermore, with our tick rules, the states in Maude executions are state/clock pairs of the form {*state*} in time t, where t denotes the total time elapsed in the behavior. Since time typically can advance beyond any bound, the reachable "clocked" state space in *unbounded* analyses is usually infinite, even when the reachable "state-only" space is finite. Section 5.1 explains how we modify the tick rules to support: (i) *time-bounded* analysis, and (ii) *unbounded* analysis without adding the "clock" to the states.

Section 5.3 presents some generic functions that make it easy for the LF modeler to define her reachability and LTL model checking queries, without requiring her to understand the Maude representation of her model.

5.1   Time-Bounded Analysis

To perform *time-bounded* analysis up to a time bound timeBound, we modify the tick rules to *not* advance time in the system beyond the time bound, by (i) changing each tick rule

```
crl [tick] : {t} => {u} in time τ if cond .
```

to

```
crl [tick] : {t} in time T => {u} in time T + τ if T + τ <= timeBound and cond .
```

where T is a variable not appearing elsewhere in the rule, and (ii) starting the analysis with initial states of the form `initSystem in time 0`.

The user of our framework does not need to modify the tick rules: she just includes the module `TIME-BOUNDED-DYNAMICS` and gives the desired time bound to the constant `timeBound`. She can then use the `rew` command to simulate *one* behavior of her system up to the given time bound, and to perform time-bounded reachability analysis and LTL model checking. Time-bounded reachability analysis, searching for a state pattern *pattern* satisfying some condition *cond*, can then be given as follows (where T is a variable of sort `Time` not appearing in *pattern*):

```
search [1] initSystem in time 0 =>* pattern in time T such that cond .
```

Example 7. Assuming that the initial state `initSystem` in Example 6 for the ADAS system is defined in a module `TEST-ADAS`, we define the following module to perform time-bounded analysis of the ADAS system up to time 55:

```
omod TIME-BOUNDED-ADAS is  including TEST-ADAS .  including TIME-BOUNDED-DYNAMICS .
  eq timeBound = 55 .
endom
```

We can then simulate one behavior of the system up to time 55:

```
Maude> rew initSystem in time 0 .

result ClockedSystem:
{< brakes : Reactor | state : (brakesApplied |-> [1]),    ... >
  ...
 < env : Environment | ... >
 < queue : EventQueue |
     queue : ((event(lidar, t, [0]) at tag(13, 0)) ::
              event(adasProcessor, a, [0]) at tag(29, 0)) >}   in time 55
```

We can search for states reachable in a time interval [*lowerBound*, `timeBound`] using search commands of the form

```
search [1] initSystem in time 0 =>* pattern in time T such that T >= lowerBound and cond .
```

5.2   Unbounded Analysis

To perform *unbounded* (in terms of time bounds; reachability analysis can still be restricted to only consider behaviors up to d rewrite steps) analysis, without carrying the "system clock" in the Maude state, we just remove the "in time" part of the tick rules, which will then have the form

```
crl [tick] : {t}  => {u} if cond .
```

and use `initSystem` as the initial state, so that a search command has the form

```
search [1] initSystem =>* pattern such that cond .
```

The   user   of our framework can use the module `UNBOUNDED-ANALYSIS-DYNAMICS` to perform unbounded analysis.

Example 8. The following module can be used to perform *unbounded* analysis of the relay system in Example 1, assuming that the initial state initSystem in Example 5 is defined in a module TEST-RELAY:

```
omod UNCLOCKED-RELAY is  including TEST-RELAY .  including UNBOUNDED-ANALYSIS-DYNAMICS .
endom
```

We can then check whether it is possible to reach a state in which the variable s of the reactor x has the value 2; i.e., a state in which the reaction dbl has been executed, but where the reaction inc has not yet been executed:

```
search [1] initSystem =>* {REST:Configuration
                           < x : Reactor | state : (s |-> [2]), ATTS:AttributeSet >} .

No solution.
```

In the desired "big-step" semantics, such a state should *not* be reachable; however, an "event-based" semantics like in [30,49] would find this bad state.   □

In LTL model checking, it is sufficient to define the labeling function for the atomic propositions on "unclocked" states, and then add an equation

```
eq STATE in time TIME |= PROP  =  STATE |= PROP .
```

to extend the labeling function to "clocked" states.

5.3 Specifying Properties

We define functions that make it easy for the user to define her analysis commands.

The following function allows us obtain the value of the local variable *var* in reactor *r* in the global execution state *state* as the term valueOf *r* . *var* in *state*:

```
op valueOf_._in_ : ReactorId VarId GlobalSystem -> Value [frozen (3)] .
op valueOf_._in_ : ReactorId VarId ClockedSystem -> Value [frozen (3)] .

eq valueOf REACTOR . VAR in
    {CONF < REACTOR : Reactor | state : ((VAR |-> VALUE) ; RS), ATTS:AttributeSet >} = VALUE .

eq valueOf REACTOR . VAR in SYSTEM in time T = valueOf REACTOR . VAR in SYSTEM .
```

Example 9. The search in Example 8 for a reachable state in which the value of the state variable s is [2] can be written

```
Maude> search [1] initSystem =>* SYSTEM:GlobalSystem such that
                    valueOf x . s in SYSTEM:GlobalSystem == [2] .
```

For LTL model checking, we have defined the following generic parametric atomic propositions:

- *var* in *reactor* is *value*, which holds in each state where the local state variable *var* in the reactor *reactor* has the value *value*, and
- *event* isInQueue, which holds in a state if *event* currently is present in the execution's event queue.

```
omod MODEL-CHECK-LF is including MODEL-CHECKER .  including UNBOUNDED-ANALYSIS-DYNAMICS .
  subsort ClockedSystem < State .

  op _in_is_ : VarId ReactorId Value -> Prop [ctor] .
  op _isInQueue : Event -> Prop [ctor] .

  eq {REST < REACTORID : Reactor | state : (VAR |-> VAL) ; RS >}
     |= VAR in REACTORID is VAL = true .

  eq {REST < 0 : EventQueue | queue : (EQ1 :: (EVENT EVENTS at TAG) :: EQ2) >}
     |= EVENT isInQueue = true .
endom
```

Example 10. We can model check the desired property in our relay example that in *all* behaviors from `initSystem` (there should be only *one* behavior), we will reach a state in which the variable `s` is `[3]` *and* remains so forever:

```
Maude> red modelCheck(initSystem, <> [] (s in x is [3])) .

result Bool: true
```

Example 11. We use time-bounded LTL model checking to verify that the brakes have been applied in *all possible* behaviors within time 55 in the ADAS system:

```
Maude> red modelCheck(initSystem in time 0,  <> (brakesApplied in brakes is [1])) .

result Bool: true
```

If we instead set `timeBound` to `54`, this command returns a counterexample.   □

6   Case Studies

This section shows how we use the techniques in Sect. 5 to analyze the case studies described in [30, 49].

The ADAS system is the running example in the verification paper [30] by the UC Berkeley group, who also show five variations in which the properties do not hold. We analyze all six versions of this example, although without the camera component, with the expected outcome.

In [49], Sirjani et al. translate three versions of a train door controller system in LF to Timed Rebeca with priorities. Important properties that such a system should satisfy are that the train doors must be locked when the train is moving (safety) and that the train eventually will be able to move (liveness). We analyze all three versions, with the desired results. This is in contrast to the analysis in [49] where the authors find inconsistent states in their event-based semantics that are not reachable in the deterministic discrete-event semantics of LF. Furthermore, in [49] they hardcode that the "open" button is pushed every 2 time units. We analyze the system with a more general user model, and show under what circumstances the train door will eventually be locked.

6.1   ADAS System

The LF specification of the ADAS driver assistance system in [30] (without the camera) is introduced in Example 2, its Maude representation is given in Example 4, and Example 6 shows the initial execution state, where the physical action corresponding to pressing the brake pedal nondeterministically chooses every 5 time units whether or not the driver presses the brake pedal at that time.

The key property is that the brakes are always applied within time 55. The model checking analysis in Example 11 verifies that this indeed holds.

The authors of [30] also introduce the following five bugs in their model:

1. Output to the wrong port: line 28 in the ADAS model in Fig. 5 is changed from lf_set(out1, 1) to lf_set(out2, 1).
2. The connection from the lidar to the adasProcessor is missing.
3. Timing: the offset of the timer t is 11 instead of 0; the delay of the action a is 51 instead of 50; and the delay of the connection adasProcessor.out1 -> brakes.inAdas is 6 instead of 5.

We introduced each error into our Maude representation of the LF model, and performed the model checking command in Example 11, with timeBound 55, on each of these variations. This analysis returned a counterexample in each case.

6.2   Train Door Controllers

First Version. The following LF specification, also shown in Fig. 6, of a simple train door controller is given in [49]:

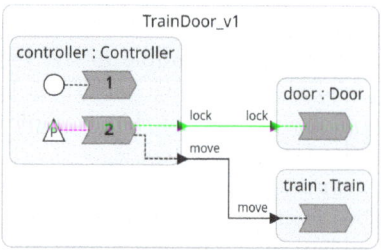

Fig. 6. First version of the train door controller in [49].

```
 1   reactor Controller {                    20       =}
 2      output lock: bool                    21   }
 3      output move: bool                    22
 4      physical action external: bool       23   reactor Door {
 5      reaction(startup) {=                 24      input lock: bool
 6         //initialize system               25      state locked: bool = false
 7      =}                                   26      reaction(lock) {=
 8                                           27         self -> locked = lock -> value;
 9      reaction(external) -> lock, move {=  28      =}
10         lf_set(lock, external -> value);  29   }
11         lf_set(move, external -> value);  30
12      =}                                   31   main reactor {
13   }                                       32      controller = new Controller()
14                                           33      train = new Train()
15   reactor Train {                         34      door = new Door()
16      input move: bool                     35      controller.lock -> door.lock
17      state moving: bool = false           36      controller.move -> train.move
18      reaction(move) {=                    37   }
19         self -> moving = move -> value;
```

The only action that does something is a physical action where the environment (the driver?) may nondeterministically generate a Boolean-valued event (true to lock the doors and move the train; false in the opposite case). The train and door reactors have a Boolean flag denoting their current "state."

The term init gives the Maude representation of this LF specification:

```
eq init
= < controller : Reactor | inports : none,  state : empty,  timers : none,
                    outports : < lock : Port | value : [false] >
                               < move : Port | value : [false] >,
                    actions : < startup : LogicalAction | minDelay : 0, minSpacing : 0,
                                                    policy : defer,  payload : [0] >
                              < external : PhysicalAction | minDelay : 0,  minSpacing : 0,
                                                    policy : defer,
                                                    payload : [false] >,
                    reactions : (reaction when startup do {skip})
                                reaction when external --> lock ; move do
                                         {(lock <- external ) ; (move <- external)} >
  < train : Reactor | inports : < move : Port | value : [false] >, outports : none,
                    state : (moving |-> [false]),  timers : none,  actions : none,
                    reactions : reaction when move do {moving := move} >
  < door : Reactor | inports : < lock : Port | value : [false] >, outports : none,
                    state : (locked |-> [false]),  timers : none,  actions : none,
                    reactions : reaction when lock do {locked := lock} >
  (controller : lock --> door : lock)
  controller : move --> train : move .
```

The execution environment adds the following model of the physical action: every 5 time units it is chosen nondeterministically whether or not the action takes place, and if so, it nondeterministically selects the value [true] or [false]:

```
eq initSystem
= {< env : Environment | physicalActions :
        < (controller . external) : PhysAct | leftOfPeriod : 0,  period : 5,  timeNonDet : true,
                                  possibleValues : ([true] : [false]) > >
     init   < queue : EventQueue | queue : addStartup(startup,init, empty) >} .
```

We check the safety of the system by performing *unbounded* reachability analysis to check whether a dangerous state, in which the train is moving (moving is [true]) while the door is open (locked is [false]), can be reached:

```
Maude> search initSystem =>*
```

```
{REST:Configuration
  < train : Reactor | state : (moving |-> [true]), ATTS1:AttributeSet >
  < door : Reactor | state : (locked |-> [false]), ATTS2:AttributeSet >}  .

No solution.
```

Our analysis shows that no such dangerous state is reachable. In contrast, Sirjani et al. [49] encounter a dangerous state (since the door-opening may happen "before" the train-stopping, even though both reactions happen at the same logical time) in their event-based "small-step" semantics.

Second Version. The second version in [49] tries to make the system even safer by introducing a safety margin: They delay the opening of doors (after the train has stopped) and the start of the train (after the doors are locked) by 100ms.

Like [49], our analysis shows that we can reach bad "non-instantaneous" states in which the doors are open while the train is moving. We refer to [35] for details.

Third Version. The third version in [49] only deals with the doors: they close before being locked and are unlocked before being opened. This version adds a passenger who can push the green button next to the door as a physical action (Fig. 7):

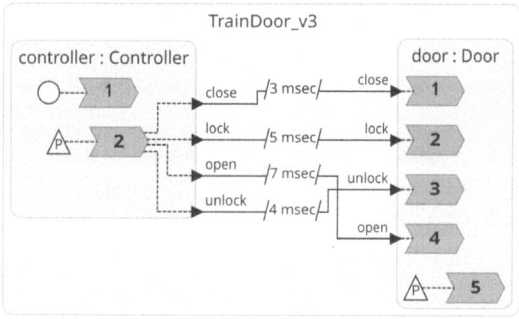

Fig. 7. Third version of the train door controller in [49].

2
342nonenone

```
1   reactor Controller {                10
2       output lock: bool               11      reaction(external) -> close, lock, open,
3       output open: bool                       unlock {=
4       output unlock: bool             12          if (external -> value == true) {
5       output close: bool              13              lf_set(close, true);
6       physical action external: bool  14              lf_set(lock, true);
7       reaction(startup) {=            15          } else {
8           //initialize system         16              lf_set(open, true);
9       =}                              17              lf_set(unlock, true);
```

```
18         }                                39      =}
19      =}                                  40      reaction(open) {=
20  }                                       41          if (self -> locked == false)
21                                          42              self -> isOpen = true;
22  reactor Door {                          43      =}
23      input lock: bool                    44      reaction(extOpen) {=
24      input unlock: bool                  45          if (self -> locked == false)
25      input open: bool                    46              self -> isOpen = true;
26      input close: bool                   47      =}
27      state locked: bool = false          48  }
28      state isOpen: bool = false          49
29      physical action extOpen: bool       50  main reactor {
30      reaction(close) {=                  51      controller = new Controller()
31          self -> isOpen = false;         52      door = new Door()
32      =}                                  53      controller.lock -> door.lock after 5 msec
33      reaction(lock) {=                   54      controller.unlock -> door.unlock after 4
34          if (self -> isOpen == false)        msec
35              self -> locked = true;      55      controller.open -> door.open after 7 msec
36      =}                                  56      controller.close -> door.close after 3 msec
37      reaction(unlock) {=                 57  }
38          self -> locked = false;
```

We refer to [35] for the initial state init of this system. For the physical actions, the driver *must* give a signal every 10 time units (timeNonDet : false), and the passenger *may* push the "open door" button every 11 time units:

```
eq initSystem =
= {< env : Environment |
       physicalActions : < (controller . external) : PhysAct | leftOfPeriod : 0,  period : 10,
                                                               possibleValues : ([true] : [false]),
                                                               timeNonDet : false >
                          < (door . extOpen) : PhysAct | leftOfPeriod : 0,  period : 11,
                                                          possibleValues : ([true]),
                                                          timeNonDet : true > >
      init    < queue : EventQueue | queue : empty >} .
```

The doors are initially open. The main question is whether a push-happy passenger can make the train doors be unlocked forever. We use unbounded LTL model checking, with the atomic propositions defined in Sect. 5.3, to check whether a locked door can be reached in all possible behaviors:

```
Maude> red modelCheck(initSystem, <> (locked in door is [true])) .

result ModelCheckResult: counterexample(...)
```

As expected, this returned a counterexample, since the property does not always hold, especially since the driver can choose not to want to close the door.

What we need is a more sophisticated temporal logic property: If the controller wants to close the door, and therefore (i) does not send "open door" signals and (ii) sends infinitely many "lock door" signals, then eventually the door must be locked, no matter what the potentially push-happy passenger does:

```
Maude> red modelCheck(initSystem,
          (((~ event(controller,external, [false]) isInQueue) W (locked in door is [true]))
          /\ ([] <> (event(controller, external, [true]) isInQueue)))
          -> <> (locked in door is [true])) .
```

This command returns a counterexample (and hence a passenger can prevent the door from eventually locking) if the passenger can push the button every 2 time units, and returns true for longer periods.

7 Related Work

Formal Semantics and Verification for Lingua Franca. We refer to the introduction for a comparison with the work by Sirjani et al. [49].

Lin et al. [30] provide an "axiomatic" semantics for a similar subset of LF as SMT constraints, and encode *bounded* (timed) temporal logic model checking for LF models as SMT constraints that can be solved by SMT solvers. As [49], they formalize the "event-based" semantics of LF, where each reaction invocation defines a transition [30, p. 8]. They also provide a non-operational semantics, which does not support simulating the system. In contrast, we provide the intended discrete-event semantics, and an executable operational model. They can apply their method directly to LF models, whereas we must generate the corresponding Maude representation of an LF model by hand. Unlike us, Lin et al. [30] also support hierarchical models and reactions with multiple triggers. They support only time-bounded model checking, while we support both unbounded and time-bounded analysis. Nevertheless, they show that you often can compute the bound that ensures that all possible behaviors are covered by bounded model checking. Lin et al. support analyzing LTL properties involving both actions and states, whereas we only support state-based LTL properties. Lin et al. also provide *timed* (or *metric*) temporal logic model checking, whereas we only provide (possibly time-bounded) ("non-metric") temporal logic model checking. However, the Real-Time Maude tool has a timed CTL model checker [29], and our models should be directly analyzable in Real-Time Maude. Finally, Lin et al. have verified many more LF specifications than we have.

Deantoni et al. [19] propose an operational semantics for LF on GEMOC MoCCML [14,18]. They define a set of rewrite rules to manipulate program states and a set of domain-specific events (DSEs) that specify observable atomic actions in execution traces. In this approach, a sequence of DSEs defines a big-step semantics, while a sequence of rewrites defines a small-step semantics. Their big-step transitions reflect observable behaviors but do not represent the intended "synchronous" transitions. The paper [19] focuses on debugging of LF specifications using execution traces from the semantics, but does not present any formal analysis of such specifications, except to mention that this can be done by connecting to the CADP model checker. In contrast: in our approach, each synchronous transition captures all events occurring at the same logical time, and we perform various formal analyses for LF models.

Rewriting Logic Semantics and Analysis for Timed Modeling Languages. Rewriting logic has proved useful as a semantic framework in which many programming and modeling languages can be given a formal semantics [16,39]. Likewise, real-time rewrite theories and Maude and Real-Time Maude have provided a formal semantics and analysis capabilities to a wide range of timed modeling languages (see, e.g., [42] for a dated overview, and [7,26,27] for some recent work).

Many of these language are "asynchronous" and have been given a "standard" event-driven asynchronous semantics (e.g., [3,40]). Work on providing a rewriting semantics to synchronous real-time modeling language includes our work on Ptolemy II discrete-event models [9] and the family of Synchronous AADL languages used to specify synchronous CPS designs in AADL [11,28].[1]

The work most closely related to the one presented in this paper is the Real-Time Maude formalization of the semantics of Ptolemy II discrete-event models [9]. However, defining the semantics of such discrete-event models was much easier, as any order of executing the actors worked, since different actors/(re)actions did not share state. Therefore, generating and dynamically maintaining an APG while executing a step, and making sure that the execution order of reactions is consistent with the APG, was not needed.

Synchronous AADL [8,11,12,28] employs a relatively simple synchronous semantics: all components operate in lockstep, based on inputs from the *previous* round, and in each iteration, *every* component is triggered *exactly once* and does not trigger other actions that must be executed "at the same time". Furthermore, different components do *not* share variables in Synchronous AADL.

8 Concluding Remarks

We have exploited the fact that rewriting logic supports both transitions (through rewrite rules) and functions (through equations) to formalize the semantics of the Lingua Franca coordination language for CPSs. We have shown how this allows us to use Maude to perform both unbounded and time-bounded reachability analysis and LTL model checking of Lingua Franca specifications, and defined functions to make it easy for the Maude non-expert to do so. We have also shown how a number of Lingua Franca specifications of CPSs, such as train door controllers and a driver assistance system for cars, can be verified in Maude.

In contrast to other verification frameworks for Lingua Franca, our semantics captures the desired "big-step" logical-time semantics of Lingua Franca, rendering our analyses of Lingua Franca models sound. However, defining such a discrete-event-style semantics for Lingua Franca is nontrivial, and requires simultaneously updating the precedence graph and executing the reactions.

Like the other verification frameworks for Lingua Franca, we only consider a single timeline, albeit supporting a reasonably general model of nondeterministic physical actions. We should therefore in future work formalize and integrate the semantics of PTIDES-like two-timeline models for CPSs.

It turns out that assuming that each reaction has exactly one unique trigger is a quite significant restriction, since many of the subtle issues of LF arise because of multiple reaction triggers. We must therefore formalize the LF semantics for that more general setting; the present work provides a good starting point for such an effort. We should also support model checking *timed/metric* temporal logic formulas as well as temporal logic formulas over both actions and states, since many of the properties verified by Lin et al. [30] are such "mixed" properties. We should also perform benchmarking, which could validate our conjecture that

---

[1] Synchronous AADL languages identify a synchronous subset of AADL for specifying and analyzing synchronous designs, and apply synchronizers for CPSs [2,5,6,10,38] to obtain correct-by-construction distributed models.

analysis based on our "big-step" semantics should be much more efficient than analysis based on the event-based semantics in [30, 49].

In our framework, we *periodically* choose nondeterministically whether or not a physical action takes place, which allows us to use explicit-state analysis. We should in future work allow physical actions to happen at *any* time (in a dense time domain). This will require developing *symbolic* analysis methods, e.g., based on rewriting combined with SMT solving [4, 45, 50], for Lingua Franca.

We should also automate the transformation from Lingua Franca to Maude, and formalize distributed implementation approaches for Lingua Franca.

Finally, Maude's support for metaprogramming and distributed Maude sessions should make it possible to *implement* a Lingua Franca specification, possibly with Maude as target language, in a distributed setting. Lingua Franca could then be a language for coordinating multiple distributed Maude sessions.

Acknowledgments. We thank Edward A. Lee for very useful discussions about Lingua Franca and the anonymous reviewers for their very helpful comments on a previous version of this paper. This work was supported by NATO SPS program project G6133 ("SymSafe"). Rukhaia and Marin were also supported by the Shota Rustaveli National Science Foundation of Georgia under the project FR-21-16725. Bae has been partially supported by the National Research Foundation of Korea (NRF) grant (No. RS-2021-NR060080), and Institute of Information & Communications Technology Planning & Evaluation (IITP) grant (No. RS-2024-00439856), both funded by the Korea government (MSIT).

References

1. Aceto, L., Cimini, M., Ingólfsdóttir, A., Reynisson, A.H., Sigurdarson, S.H., Sirjani, M.: Modelling and simulation of asynchronous real-time systems using Timed Rebeca. In: 10th International Workshop on the Foundations of Coordination Languages and Software Architectures (FOCLASA 2011). EPTCS, vol. 58, pp. 1–19 (2011)
2. Al-Nayeem, A., Sun, M., Qiu, X., Sha, L., Miller, S.P., Cofer, D.D.: A formal architecture pattern for real-time distributed systems. In: Proceedings of the RTSS, pp. 161–170. IEEE, USA (2009)
3. AlTurki, M., Dhurjati, D., Yu, D., Chander, A., Inamura, H.: Formal specification and analysis of timing properties in software systems. In: International Conference on Fundamental Approaches to Software Engineering, pp. 262–277. Springer (2009)
4. Arias, J., Bae, K., Olarte, C., Ölveczky, P.C., Petrucci, L., Rømming, F.: Symbolic analysis and parameter synthesis for networks of parametric timed automata with global variables using Maude and SMT solving. Sci. Comput. Program. **233** (2024)
5. Bae, K., Meseguer, J., Ölveczky, P.C.: Formal patterns for multirate distributed real-time systems. Sci. Comput. Program. **91**, 3–44 (2014)
6. Bae, K., Ölveczky, P.C.: MSYNC: a generalized formal design pattern for virtually synchronous multirate cyber-physical systems. ACM Trans. Embed. Comput. Syst. (TECS) **20**(5s), 1–26 (2021)
7. Bae, K., Ölveczky, P.C.: Formal model engineering of distributed CPSs using AADL: From behavioral AADL models to Multirate Hybrid Synchronous AADL. In: Proceedings of the International Conference on Formal Aspects of Component Software (FACS 2023). Lecture Notes in Computer Science. Springer (2023)

8. Bae, K., Ölveczky, P.C., Al-Nayeem, A., Meseguer, J.: Synchronous AADL and its formal analysis in Real-Time Maude. In: Proceedings of the ICFEM 2011. LNCS, vol. 6991. Springer, Heidelberg (2011)

9. Bae, K., Ölveczky, P.C., Feng, T.H., Lee, E.A., Tripakis, S.: Verifying hierarchical Ptolemy II discrete-event models using Real-Time Maude. Sci. Comput. Program. **77**(12), 1235–1271 (2012)

10. Bae, K., Ölveczky, P.C., Kong, S., Gao, S., Clarke, E.M.: SMT-based analysis of virtually synchronous distributed hybrid systems. In: Proceedings of the HSCC, pp. 145–154. ACM, New York (2016)

11. Bae, K., Ölveczky, P.C., Meseguer, J.: Definition, semantics, and analysis of Multirate Synchronous AADL. In: Proceedings of the FM 2014. LNCS, vol. 8442. Springer (2014)

12. Bae, K., Ölveczky, P.C., Meseguer, J., Al-Nayeem, A.: The SynchAADL2Maude tool. In: Proceedings of the FASE 2012. LNCS, vol. 7212. Springer, Heidelberg (2012)

13. Benveniste, A., Berry, G.: The synchronous approach to reactive and real-time systems. Proc. IEEE **79**(9), 1270–1282 (1991)

14. Bousse, E., Degueule, T., Vojtisek, D., Mayerhofer, T., Deantoni, J., Combemale, B.: Execution Framework of the GEMOC Studio (Tool Demo). In: Proceedings of the 2016 ACM SIGPLAN International Conference on Software Language Engineering, pp. 84–89 (2016)

15. Cassandras, C.G.: Discrete Event Systems, Modeling and Performance Analysis. Irwin (1993)

16. Chen, X., Roşu, G.: 𝕂—a semantic framework for programming languages and formal analysis. In: 5th International School on Engineering Trustworthy Software Systems (SETSS 2019), pp. 122–158. Springer, Cham (2020)

17. Clavel, M., Durán, F., Eker, S., Meseguer, J., Lincoln, P., Martí-Oliet, N., Talcott, C.: All About Maude – A High-Performance Logical Framework. Lecture Notes in Computer Science, vol. 4350. Springer, Heidelberg (2007)

18. Combemale, B., De Antoni, J., Larsen, M.V., Mallet, F., Barais, O., Baudry, B., France, R.B.: Reifying concurrency for executable metamodeling. In: Software Language Engineering: 6th International Conference, SLE 2013, Indianapolis, IN, USA, 26–28 October 2013, Proceedings 6, pp. 365–384. Springer (2013)

19. Deantoni, J., Cambeiro, J., Bateni, S., Lin, S., Lohstroh, M.: Debugging and verification tools for Lingua Franca in GEMOC studio. In: 2021 Forum on Specification & Design Languages (FDL), pp. 01–08. IEEE (2021)

20. Edwards, S., Hui, J.: The sparse synchronous model. In: Forum for Specification and Design Languages (FDL 2020). IEEE (2020)

21. González-Burgueño, A., Ölveczky, P.C.: Formalizing and analyzing security ceremonies with heterogeneous devices in ANP and PDL. In: Proceedings of the Fundamentals of Software Engineering (FSEN 2019). Lecture Notes in Computer Science, vol. 11761, pp. 129–144. Springer (2019)

22. Jafari, A., Khamespanah, E., Sirjani, M., Hermanns, H., Cimini, M.: PTRebeca: Modeling and analysis of distributed and asynchronous systems. Sci. Comput. Program. **128**, 22–50 (2016)

23. Jahandideh, I., Ghassemi, F., Sirjani, M.: Hybrid Rebeca: Modeling and analyzing of cyber-physical systems. In: International Workshop on Cyber Physical Systems: Model-Based Design (CyPhy 2018 and WESE 2018). Lecture Notes in Computer Science, vol. 11615, pp. 3–27. Springer (2018)

24. Lee, E.A., Sirjani, M.: What Good are Models? In: Bae, K., Ölveczky, P.C. (eds.) Formal Aspects of Component Software (FACS 2018). Lecture Notes in Computer Science, vol. 11222, pp. 3–31. Springer (2018)
25. Lee, E.A., Zheng, H.: Leveraging synchronous language principles for heterogeneous modeling and design of embedded systems. In: Proceedings of the EMSOF 2007 (2007)
26. Lee, J., Bae, K., Ölveczky, P.C.: An extension of HybridSynchAADL and its application to collaborating autonomous UAVs. In: International Symposium on Leveraging Applications of Formal Methods. LNCS, vol. 13703, pp. 47–64. Springer (2022)
27. Lee, J., Bae, K., Ölveczky, P.C., Kim, S., Kang, M.: Modeling and formal analysis of virtually synchronous cyber-physical systems in AADL. Int. J. Softw. Tools Technol. Transf. **24**(6), 911–948 (2022)
28. Lee, J., Kim, S., Bae, K., Ölveczky, P.C.: HybridSynchAADL: Modeling and formal analysis of virtually synchronous CPSs in AADL. In: Proceedings of the CAV 2021. LNCS, vol. 12759, pp. 491–504. Springer, Heidelberg (2021)
29. Lepri, D., Ábrahám, E., Ölveczky, P.C.: Sound and complete timed CTL model checking of timed Kripke structures and real-time rewrite theories. Sci. Comput. Program. **99**, 128–192 (2015)
30. Lin, S., et al.: Towards Building Verifiable CPS using Lingua Franca. ACM Trans. Embed. Comput. Syst. **22**(5s), 1–24 (2023)
31. Lohstroh, M., et al.: Reactors: A deterministic model for composable reactive systems. In: 8th International Workshop on Model-based Design of Cyber Physical Systems (CyPhy 2019). LNCS, vol. 11971. Springer (2019)
32. Lohstroh, M.: Reactors: A Deterministic Model of Concurrent Computation for Reactive Systems. Ph.D. thesis, EECS Department, University of California, Berkeley (2020)
33. Lohstroh, M., Menard, C., Bateni, S., Lee, E.A.: Toward a Lingua Franca for Deterministic Concurrent Systems. ACM Trans. Embed. Comput. Syst. (TECS) **20**(4), 1–27 (2021)
34. Lohstroh, M., et al.: Actors revisited for time-critical systems. In: Proceedings of the 56th Design Automation Conference 2019 (DAC 2019), pp. 152:1-152:4. ACM (2019)
35. Marin, M., Ölveczky, P.C., Reja, M., Rukhaia, M., Bae, K., Dundua, B.: Semantics and formal analysis of Lingua Franca CPS specifications in rewriting logic (2024). http://olveczky.se/lf2maude-techrep.pdf
36. Menard, C., Lohstroh, M., Bateni, S., Chorlian, M., Deng, A., Donovan, P., Fournier, C., Lin, S., Suchert, F., Tanneberger, T., et al.: High-performance deterministic concurrency using Lingua Franca. ACM Trans. Archit. Code Optim. **20**(4), 1–29 (2023)
37. Meseguer, J.: Conditional rewriting logic as a unified model of concurrency. Theoret. Comput. Sci. **96**(1), 73–155 (1992)
38. Meseguer, J., Ölveczky, P.C.: Formalization and correctness of the PALS architectural pattern for distributed real-time systems. Theoret. Comput. Sci. **451**, 1–37 (2012)
39. Meseguer, J., Rosu, G.: The rewriting logic semantics project. Theoret. Comput. Sci. **373**(3), 213–237 (2007)
40. Ölveczky, P.C., Boronat, A., Meseguer, J.: Formal semantics and analysis of behavioral AADL models in Real-Time Maude. In: Proceedings of the FMOODS/-FORTE 2010. LNCS, vol. 6117, pp. 47–62. Springer (2010)

41. Ölveczky, P.C., Meseguer, J.: Semantics and pragmatics of Real-Time Maude. High.-Order Symb. Comput. **20**(1–2), 161–196 (2007)
42. Ölveczky, P.C.: Semantics, simulation, and formal analysis of modeling languages for embedded systems in Real-Time Maude. In: Formal Modeling: Actors, Open Systems, Biological Systems. Lecture Notes in Computer Science, vol. 7000, pp. 368–402. Springer (2011)
43. Ölveczky, P.C.: Real-Time Maude and its applications. In: Proc. WRLA 2014. LNCS, vol. 8663. Springer (2014)
44. Ölveczky, P.C., Meseguer, J.: Specification of real-time and hybrid systems in rewriting logic. Theoret. Comput. Sci. **285**(2), 359–405 (2002)
45. Rocha, C., Meseguer, J., Muñoz, C.: Rewriting modulo SMT and open system analysis. J. Log. Algebraic Methods Program. **86**(1), 269–297 (2017)
46. Sabahi-Kaviani, Z., Khosravi, R., Ölveczky, P.C., Khamespanah, E., Sirjani, M.: Formal semantics and efficient analysis of Timed Rebeca in Real-Time Maude. Sci. Comput. Program. **113**, 85–118 (2015)
47. Sabahi-Kaviani, Z., Khosravi, R., Sirjani, M., Ölveczky, P.C., Khamespanah, E.: Formal semantics and analysis of Timed Rebeca in Real-Time Maude. In: Formal Techniques for Safety-Critical Systems (FTSCS 2013). Communications in Computer and Information Science, vol. 419, pp. 178–194. Springer (2013)
48. Sirjani, M.: Rebeca: Theory, applications, and tools. In: Formal Methods for Components and Objects (FMCO 2006). LNCS, vol. 4709. Springer (2006)
49. Sirjani, M., Lee, E.A., Khamespanah, E.: Verification of cyberphysical systems. Mathematics **8**(7), 1068 (2020)
50. Yu, G., Bae, K.: A flexible framework for integrating Maude and SMT solvers using Python. In: Proceedings of the International Workshop on Rewriting Logic and its Applications (WRLA 2024). Lecture Notes in Computer Science, vol. 14953. Springer (2024)
51. Zhao, Y., Lee, E.A., Liu, J.: A programming model for time-synchronized distributed real-time systems. In: Proceedings of the RTAS 2007. IEEE (2007)

Parallel Composition of Constraint Automata

Benjamin Lion[1]([envelope]) and Farhad Arbab[2,3]

[1] INRIA, Rennes, France
benjamin.lion@inria.fr
[2] Computer Security, CWI, Amsterdam, The Netherlands
[3] LIACS, Leiden University, Leiden, The Netherlands

Abstract. In this paper, we introduce the parallel composition of Constraint Automata (CA), a variant of the original composition of Constraint Automata better suited to compactly represent highly concurrent compositional models, such as Reo. By relegating the crux of composition to run-time, our parallel composition maintains the integrity of the constituent parts of a composite model, allowing dynamic modification of CA models. We discuss the run-time structure of the parallel composition with its implementation in Maude, and the notion of maximality for a composite transition with respect to various criteria. We show the utility of parallel composition in formal analysis through Maude search queries.

1 Introduction

Reo [2] is an exogeneous coordination language in which interaction protocols are built compositionally out of a set of (user defined) primitive channels. In Reo, a channel denotes a constraint on the flow of data through the two ports at its boundary, and as such it represents a binary interaction protocol. Composing such channels (i.e., binary protocols) yields more complex interaction protocols which accord an intuitive graphical representation as connectror circuits. A small set of very simple primitive channels suffices to compose arbitrarily complex protocols. Over the years, several semantics have been defined to express the dataflow nature of primitive channels, and how primitives compose to create complex circuits.

Constraint Automata (CA) [7] were introduced as an operational semantics for Reo, primarily intended to express the semantics of Reo circuits for the purpose of formal verification through model checking [6, 20]. Subsequently, variants of CA and other automata-based models inspired by CA were also used as operational models based on which Reo compilers translate Reo circuits into executable code [15–17], to model quality of service [3, 27, 31], as well as in the

---

Dedication. This paper is dedicated to Marjan Sirjani in celebration of her technical and leadership contributions to advancing computer science.

E. A. Lee et al. (Eds.): Marjan Sirjani Festschrift, LNCS 15560, pp. 102–126, 2025.
https://doi.org/10.1007/978-3-031-85134-6_5

synthesis of Reo circuits from CA [28] and from specification of concurrency protocols expressed in other models, such as UML sequence diagrams [5] and BPMN business process models [4]. However, like most (but not all) formal semantics of Reo [14], the original composition operator in CA is inherently sequential as it captures the highly concurrent nature of Reo only indirectly through explicit enumeration of all valid combinations of states and transitions of the constituents that comprise a composite model. Such enumeration results in a combinatorial explosion that becomes an obstacle, especially when CA are to be used as an operational model for simulation or execution.

Moreover, the composition operation on CAs loses the structure of the composite CAs by merging states and transitions. The lack of means to isolate individual CAs after composition limits the kinds of structural runtime analysis that can be performed. Indeed, the ability to isolate a specific CA out of a composition can lead to insightful understanding of how a process behaves within its changing environment (i.e., the other CAs in that or another composition).

The original constraint automata model was meant to capture the semantics of Reo circuits for static verification. In this paper, we present a parallel composition operator on CA, a variant of the original composition of CA meant for execution, dynamic reconfiguration, and dynamic verification. As an executable, verifiable, and reconfigurable model, the parallel composition must satisfy the following list of properties:

1. soundness: every trace produced at runtime is sound with respect to the specification;
2. completeness: every trace possible in the specification is reachable at runtime;
3. realistic: a step from runtime composition succeeds only if it consists of a set of operations that enact permissible dataflow. While soundness states which steps are allowed, the realistic property states the operations that achieve such permissible steps;
4. structure preserving: the runtime structure reflects the (modular) structure of the specification;
5. expressive: the runtime is sufficiently expressive to contextualize the execution (e.g., optimize for throughput, for fairness, for maximal progress);
6. verifiable: the executable model is formal and can support verification.

We evaluate the related work from the perspective of the above list of objectives, and show how our new model adequately addresses all of them.

Existing compilers for Reo either use a static composition (as in the Treo compiler [8,13]), or some form of hybrid composition (as in the Lykos compiler [16]) that partitions the set of constraint automata into synchronous subsets. The first approach is not structure preserving, as the composition is done statically. Similarly, although less restrictive, the second approach assumes static composition of synchronous subsets, which is also not structure preserving. Moreover, the runtime composition of synchronous subsets is not associative, i.e., CAs at runtime must execute in a specific order for the runtime to avoid deadlock. In our case, the runtime allows arbitrary multisets of CAs to run in parallel (in

Sect. 2.2), which preserves the full structure of the original specification expression. Our underlying composition operator forms a multiset of connector and is therefore commutative and associative, which is closer to the original composition operator in Reo. Our model supports equational reasoning, e.g., in Maude, to equationally rewrite a synchronous subset to a simpler component (as we show in Sect. 3.2).

The Dreams framework [32] is an approach that composes CAs at runtime. In the Dreams framework, coordination is achieved by a consensus among a distributed set of CAs. In the Dreams framework, ports are not explicit: they are attributes of actors. We chose to make ports explicit structural constructs in our framework, instead of attributes of CAs. Consequently, there is no need in our model to run a centralized consensus algorithm among CAs, as one failure detected at a port triggers an error whose propagation prunes wrong choices (see Sect. 2.2). To achieve the goal of providing a realistic runtime, our execution engine makes sure that transitions in CAs run in the order of the dataflow through ports.

The constraint satisfaction approach [9,10] takes a different perspective on the problem of coordination: every constraint is a logical formula, and a centralized solver provides a sequence of consistent solutions to those constraints over time. The benefit of such approach is that its logic is expressive enough to encode higher order constraints such as context dependent constraints. However, not every solution found declaratively by a solver necessarily reflects a realistic dataflow through a Reo connector, as it may violate causality. We show an algorithm that solves the assignment of data to ports while still preserving causality (i.e., a port gets a value before being used) that reflects the realistic nature of dataflow through Reo connectors.

In addition to the points already mentioned above, our runtime provides two new features. First, our use of rewriting logic opens new avenues for verification of the correctness of connectors. Our Maude runtime provides a syntax to perform reachability queries on a composition of connectors. This way, one can search (see Sect. 3.2) to verify if a CA state is reachable from an initial state, within a context (i.e., a composition of CAs).

Second, the structure and modularity of our runtime opens possibilities to express new kinds of components. For instance, we can model components that reconfigure a component with a rewriting rule that triggers its reconfiguration in a specific state. Moreover, in our rewriting logic framework we can combine CAs with non-CA models in heterogeneous specifications.

The structure preserving feature of our executable environment forces our product to be lazy, at runtime. Therefore, the Maude implementation provides a "just in time" composition of the constraint automata that is sound with respect to the static composition in existing work. A similar strategy is used in tools such as Uppaal [22]. Uppaal checks a temporal formula in CTL using a network of timed automata. The underlying calculus of networks of timed automata uses a quotient formula and constraint solving methods. In our Maude implementation, verification is done via reachability queries on the composition. The language for reachability queries is quite liberal, and can be any pattern of the system's description. Instead of asking, as in Uppaal "is this formula true within the context of the composition $A_1 \mid \cdots \mid A_n$?", we ask "is the pattern X reachable after execution of the composition $A_1 \mid \cdots \mid A_n$?". We leave as future work the development of a dedicated syntax for useful search queries (and a calculus similar to that in Uppaal to further simplify the search). See [1] for a work to relate the verification of CTL formulas and reachibility queries on a network of automata.

2   Parallel Composition of Constraint Automata

In this section, we give a brief introduction to constraint automata as first presented in [7], and then extended with memory in [18]. Constraint automata have been applied in the fields of design and verification of networks of interacting components [7,19,20].

We start with few prerequisites, introduce our notation, and then present in Sect. 2.1 the syntax and semantics for constraint automata. We give two properties that are generally assumed: the fact that the constraint labeling a transition restricts the data flowing at all ports of a constraint automaton (i.e., there is no data flow through a port that does not appear in the transition); and that a silent transition is implicit in every state. We say that a constraint automaton is *guard covered* if it satisfies the first property and *independent* if it satisfies the second.

Next, in Sect. 2.2, we present an algorithm to compose constraint automata in parallel. The algorithm ensures that the assignment of values to ports is sound with respect to the static product of constraint automata.

Prerequisites. We use $\mathbb{D}$ to denote the set of all data elements, and $\mathcal{N}$ the set of all variable names. In our context, a variable name can be either a port name (regardless of its input/output directionality), or a memory name.

We write an assignment as a function of signature $\mathcal{N} \mapsto \mathbb{D}$. Conceptually, an assignment is a collection of simultaneous events that occur at the ports and memories in $\mathcal{N}$.

A stream of assignments is an element of $(\mathcal{N} \to \mathbb{D})^{\omega}$, which denotes an infinite sequence of assignments. For $\sigma : X \to Y$, we use $dom(\sigma)$ to refer to the domain of σ, i.e., the set X.

2.1   Constraint Automata

Reo connectors synchronize through shared ports. The standard operational specification of a Reo connector is defined as a constraint automaton. In this section, we give a brief introduction to constraint automata with memory; for more precise description, see [18].

A constraint automaton has labeled transitions among its states. The label of a transition is a formula that we call a *guard*. A guard consists of a set of free memory and port variables, and a constraint that restricts the data assignments to those variables. The state based description of a constraint automaton, therefore, encodes sequences of solutions to interaction constraints, formally modeled as solutions to the guards labeling its transitions.

Guards (Syntax). For $* \notin \mathbb{D}$, we use $\mathsf{Some}\ d$ to denote an element of $\mathbb{D}_{\star}$ that has a value $d \in \mathbb{D}$, and use $\star$ to denote the absence of such a value.[1] We use $\mathcal{N} = \mathcal{N}_P \cup \mathcal{N}_L \cup \mathcal{N}_M \cup \mathcal{N}_{M\bullet}$ as a set of variables, where $\mathcal{N}_P, \mathcal{N}_L$, and $\mathcal{N}_M$ are mutually disjoint. A term, typically denoted as $t_1, t_2, ...$, is an an element of $\mathcal{N} \cup \mathbb{D}_{\star}$. We syntactically differentiate between *port* names, typically denoted as $p_1, p_2, ... \in \mathcal{N}_P$, *data variables* names, typically denoted as $x_1, x_2, ... \in \mathcal{N}_L$, *current memory* names, denoted as $m_1, m_2, ... \in \mathcal{N}_M$, and *next memory* names, which we denote as $m_1^\bullet, m_2^\bullet, ... \in \mathcal{N}_{M\bullet}$. We assume that the two sets $\mathcal{N}_M$ and $\mathcal{N}_{M\bullet}$ are in a bijection, i.e., every memory name $m \in \mathcal{N}_M$ has a next memory name $m^\bullet \in \mathcal{N}_{M\bullet}$ and vice versa. Note that, for simplicity, we do not consider function symbols in the set of terms.

The set of *guards* G is the set of all equality of terms $t_1 = t_2$ closed under the conjunction operator, i.e., given $g_1 \in G$ and $g_2 \in G$, then $g_1 \wedge g_2 \in G$. Note that, for simplicity, we do not consider predicate symbols. We assume $\mathbb{D}$ to contain at least one data element d, and we write as a shorthand notation $\top := \star = \star$ and $\bot := \star = \mathsf{Some}\ d$. We use $\mathcal{N}(g)$ to denote the set of free variable names in $g \in G$. Given a guard g such that $v \in \mathcal{N}(g)$, we write $g[v \mapsto d]$ for the new formula where the free variable v is substituted by a constant $d \in \mathbb{D}_{\star}$.

Similarly, an empty memory cell is encoded with the constraint $m = \star$. Finally, we denote the firing of a port as $p = \mathsf{Some}\ x$, where x is a data variable in $\mathcal{N}_L$.

Guards (Semantics.) We use the standard satisfaction relation between guards and assignments. Port and memory variables are interpreted in the domain $\mathbb{D}_{\star}$, i.e., can be assigned the $\star$ value, and data variables are interpreted in the domain $\mathbb{D}$, i.e., are always assigned to $\mathsf{Some}\ d$ for $d \in \mathbb{D}$.

Given a guard $g \in G$, we say that $\Gamma \in \mathcal{N} \to \mathbb{D}_{\star}$ satisfies g, and write $\Gamma \models g$, defined inductively on g as:

- $\Gamma \models t_1 = t_2$ if and only if $\Gamma(t_1) = \Gamma(t_2)$ (where $\Gamma(t) = t$ if t is a constant symbol in $\mathbb{D}_{\star}$); and
- $\Gamma \models g_1 \wedge g_2$ if and only if $\Gamma \models g_1$ and $\Gamma \models g_2$.

Constraint Automata (Syntax). A *constraint automaton* is a tuple $A = (Q, \mathcal{V}, \to, Q_0)$, where Q is a set of *state* names, $\mathcal{V} \subseteq \mathcal{N}$ is a set of variable names, $\to\ \in Q \times G \times Q$ is a set of *transitions* labeled with a guard $g \in G$ such that

---

[1] The datatype $\mathbb{D}_{\star}$ is traditionally called an option datatype, where elements in $\mathbb{D}$ are injected with the constructor Some and the $\star$ element is not in $\mathbb{D}$. The use of the syntactic Some constructor makes pattern matching easier to extract the value from $\mathbb{D}_{\star} \setminus \mathbb{D}$.

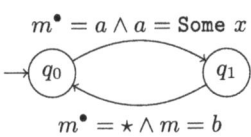

Fig. 1. CA for Fifo(a,b)

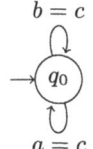

Fig. 2. CA for Merger(a,b,c)

$\mathcal{N}(g) \subseteq \mathcal{V}$, and $Q_0 \in 2^Q$ is a set of *initial* states. We use the shorthand notation $q \xrightarrow{g} q'$ for transitions $(q, g, q') \in \rightarrow$.

Note that in the standard definition of constraint automata, a transition is also labeled with the set $\mathcal{N}(g) \cap \mathcal{N}_P$ of free port variables in the guard, called the port synchronization set. As this set can be recovered, we drop it from transition labels in our notation.

In Fig. 1 and Fig. 2, we show two constraint automata for the Fifo and the Merger, respectively. Starting in initial state q_0, the Fifo constraint automaton accepts any assignment of a non-empty value to the port variable a, which is also stored in the memory $m^\bullet$. Next, the Fifo automaton assigns to the port variable b the value in m and sets the memory value back to $\star$. Note that the syntax Some x enforces the value assigned to a to be an element different from $\star$.

The Merger constraint automaton accepts, non-deterministically, any assignment of equal values to port variables c and b or to port variables a and c. As explained in the semantics paragraph below, any port variable that does not occur in a guard but is in the signature of the constraint automaton gets the silent $\star$ assignment. We show in Table 1 and Table 2 a prefix for an execution of, respectively, the Fifo and the Merger constraint automata.

Constraint Automata (Semantics). The semantics of a constraint automaton captures the series of data flowing at ports and memory locations of that constraint automaton. In the case where there is no data flow, we use the constraint $p = \star$ to denote that p is assigned the silent element $\star$.

Let $A = (Q, \mathcal{V}, \rightarrow, Q_0)$ be a constraint automaton. A *run* $\sigma \in \rightarrow^\omega$ of the automaton A, is an infinite sequence of consecutive transitions. We refer to the ith element of σ as $\sigma_i = q_i \xrightarrow{g_i} q_{i+1}$ and we impose that $\sigma_0 = q_0 \xrightarrow{g_0} q_1$ with $q_0 \in Q_0$. An *execution* of a run σ is a stream of observations $\gamma \in (\mathcal{V} \rightarrow \mathbb{D})^\omega$ such that for all $i \in \mathbb{N}$, $\gamma(i) \models g_i$, and for all $m \in \mathcal{V} \cap \mathcal{N}_M$, $\gamma(i+1)(m) = \gamma(i)(m^\bullet)$. The second condition semantically relates the two memory variables $m \in \mathcal{V} \cap \mathcal{N}_M$ and $m^\bullet \in \mathcal{V} \cap \mathcal{N}_{M^\bullet}$ as, respectively, the current and the next values of the same memory variable m. If a guard g_i does not constrain a port variable $p \in \mathcal{V} \cap \mathcal{N}_P$, we semantically assume that the variable is restricted to $\star$, i.e., that the port p does not fire. If a guard g_i does not constrain a next memory variable $m^\bullet \in \mathcal{V} \cap \mathcal{N}_{M^\bullet}$, we semantically assume $m = m^\bullet$, i.e., that the data value of the memory is propagated to the next step of the execution. If the run contains a guard that is unsatisfiable, then no execution exists for this run.

Table 1. An execution for `Fifo(a,b)`.   **Table 2.** Execution for `Merger(a,b,c)`.

a	m	b
d_1	d_1	$\star$
$\star$	d_1	$\star$
$\star$	d_1	d_1
$\dots$	$\dots$	$\dots$

a	b	c
d_1	$\star$	d_1
$\star$	d_2	d_2
$\star$	$\star$	$\star$
$\dots$	$\dots$	$\dots$

The *behavior* $L(A)$ of a constraint automaton A is the set consisting of all executions of all runs on A, i.e., a subset of $(\mathcal{V} \to \mathbb{D})^\omega$. Note that the standard semantics of constraint automata restricts the set $\mathcal{V}$ to the set of port names only, whereas our semantics also deals with memory variables. As this difference is not the main motivation in this paper, we ignore such detail.

Composition. Given two constraint automata $A_i = (Q_i, \mathcal{V}_i, \to_i, Q_{0,i}), i \in \{1,2\}$ such that $(\mathcal{V}_1 \setminus \mathcal{N}_P) \cap (\mathcal{V}_2 \setminus \mathcal{N}_P) = \emptyset$ (i.e., only port variables may be shared), we call $A = (Q_1 \times Q_2, \mathcal{V}_1 \cup \mathcal{V}_2, \to, Q_{0,1} \times Q_{0,2})$ the composition of A_1 and A_2, and write $A = A_1 \times A_2$ where:

$$\frac{q_1 \xrightarrow{g_1} q_1' \qquad q_2 \xrightarrow{g_2} q_2'}{(q_1, q_2) \xrightarrow{g_1 \wedge g_2} (q_1', q_2')} \tag{1}$$

The behavior of a composite constraint automaton $A_1 \times A_2$ is equal to the merging of the behaviors of its operands A_1 and A_2 (see a similar proof in [7]), i.e., $L(A_1 \times A_2) = L(A_1) \bowtie L(A_2)$, where $\sigma \in L(A_1) \bowtie L(A_2)$ if and only if there exists $(\sigma_1, \sigma_2) \in L(A_1) \times L(A_2)$, such that for all $i \in \mathbb{N}$, $k \in \{1,2\}$, and $v \in \mathcal{V}_k$, $\sigma_k(i)(v) = \sigma(i)(v)$. When $\mathcal{V}_1 = \mathcal{V}_2$, the product leads to the intersection of executions, i.e. $L(A_1) \bowtie L(A_2) = L(A_1) \cap L(A_2)$.

Properties. Recall that we semantically enforce that every port variable of a constraint automaton that does not appear in a guard is assigned $\star$. We can also syntactically enforce this property by considering guards that cover all variables. A guard g covers a set of variables V if every variable in the set V appears free in g.

Theorem 1 (Guard-covered). *A constraint automaton $A = (Q, \mathcal{V}, \to, Q_0)$ is semantically equivalent to another constraint automaton, called guard-covered, for which all guards cover $\mathcal{V}$. The guard-covered property is preserved through composition.*

Proof. If a variable in $\mathcal{V}$ does not appear free in g, the satisfaction relation that is accepted by the semantics of the constraint automaton either imposes that $p \mapsto \star$ if the variable is a port variable, or $m = m^\bullet$ for a memory variable. Adding those clauses as conjuncts to g does not change the semantics, and makes g cover $\mathcal{V}$.

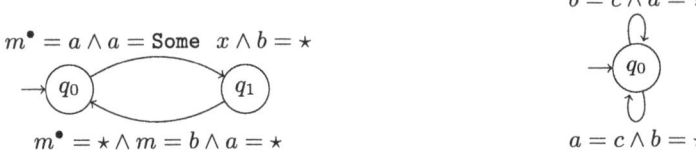

Fig. 3. Guard-covered CA for `Fifo(a,b)`

Fig. 4. Guard-covered CA for `Merger` (a,b,c)

Figures 3 and 4 show the two guard-covered constraint automata for the Fifo and the Merger, respectively.

The standard definition of constraint automata in [7] has three rules for composition: the two other rules encode the *independent* transitions of one constraint automaton while the other one stays in the same state. Instead, we eliminate the two independence rules and impose a syntactic constraint on constraint automata to recover independent transitions. A constraint automaton is *independent* if every one of its states has a self-loop transition with the guard $\top$. Consequently, the behavior of an independent automaton is closed under insertion of arbitrary silent steps for ports, while it preserves its memory values across a run.

Theorem 2 (Independence). *A constraint automata $A = (Q, \mathcal{V}, \rightarrow, Q_0)$ for which the transition relation contains, for all $q \in Q$, the transition $q \xrightarrow{\top} q$ is closed under insertion of arbitrarily many (possibly infinite) assignments of silent value to ports, while preserving memory values. The independence property is preserved through composition.*

Proof. The guard $\top$ is semantically equivalent to the conjunction of a clause $p = \star$ for every $p \in \mathcal{V} \cap \mathcal{N}_P$ and a clause $m^\bullet = m$ for every $m \in \mathcal{V} \cap \mathcal{N}_M$. Thus, an execution can be extended with arbitrarily many assignments that satisfy the new $\top$ constraints, from any state. Because the conjunction of two $\top$ constraints is still $\top$, the independence is preserved through composition.

Figures 5 and 6 show the two independent constraint automata for the Fifo and the Merger, respectively.

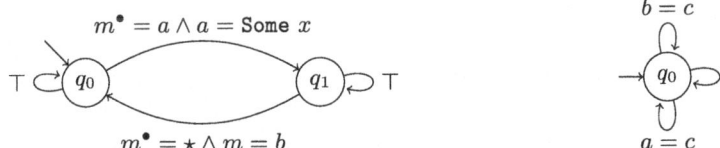

Fig. 5. Independent CA for `Fifo(a,b)`

Fig. 6. Independent CA for `Mergerr` (a,b,c)

We consider, for the next section, guard-covered and independent constraint automata. A naive way to run constraint automata in parallel is to find a solution to the composite guard $g_1 \wedge g_2$ as the union of a solution to g_1 and a solution to g_2. As variables occur free in g_1 and g_2, such approach may need to enumerate a large susbet of $\mathbb{D}$ before finding a satisfying assignment. Instead, we translate a declarative constraint (now expressed as a guard) into a set of operations on port structures. Thus, each constraint automaton may run those operations, in an order that preserves the dataflow, so that a resulting solution is found if it exists. We explain these operations in the next section.

2.2   Parallel Product

We first review a few undesirable properties of a static implementation of the composition operation defined by Rule 1. First, observe that this static product is not *structure preserving*. Indeed, the conjunction of guards loses the original structure of the composition operands: the guard $g_1 \wedge g_2$ may decompose into several conjuncts, different from the original g_1 and g_2.

Second, the solution to the guard labeling a transition is obtained from an oracle that somehow solves the composite constraint. Such a solution may not be *realistic* in the sense that it does not emerge out of (and may not respect) the data flow through ports.

We present an algorithm that composes constraint automata in parallel while preserving the structure of the composition as a multiset of constraint automata, and that uses the dataflow at ports to find a global solution to the composite constraint.

We assume, for this section, that variables are partitionned into input and output variables. Let $A = (Q, \mathcal{V}, \rightarrow, Q_0)$ be a constraint automaton, and $\mathcal{V} = \mathcal{V}_I \cup \mathcal{V}_O$ be a partition of port variables in $\mathcal{V}$ such that $\mathcal{V}_I \cap \mathcal{V}_O = \emptyset$. A variable in $\mathcal{V}_I$ is an input variable, and a variable in $\mathcal{V}_O$ is an output variable. Every port is therefore either an input or an output (this distinction does not matter for memory variables). Note that port variables may not partition on a composite constraint automaton: an internal port may simultaneously serve as both an input and an output. One can hide and eliminate internal ports to recover the partition of ports [16].

Finally, we assume a well-formedness condition for constraint automata, namely that guards labeling the transitions of the constraint automata are *directed*. Given an input/output partition $\mathcal{V} = \mathcal{V}_I \cup \mathcal{V}_O$ of ports, a guard is directed if all equalities in the guard are of the following form: $l = k$ with $l \in \mathcal{V}_O \cup \mathcal{N}_{M\bullet} \cup \mathcal{N}_L$ and $k \in \mathcal{V}_I \cup \mathcal{N}_M \cup D_\star$. This assumption allows us to interpret an equality as a dataflow assignment: from input or current a memory value or constants (right-hand side), to output or next memory value or a local variable (left-hand side). Every primitive cosntraint automaton in Reo can be written in this form.

Operations on Ports and Constraint Automata. Constraint automata place constraints on the data that flow through its ports. Operationally, the dataflow results from actions of constraints automata on its ports. We are therefore after a mechanism to find a global solution to a composite constraint by

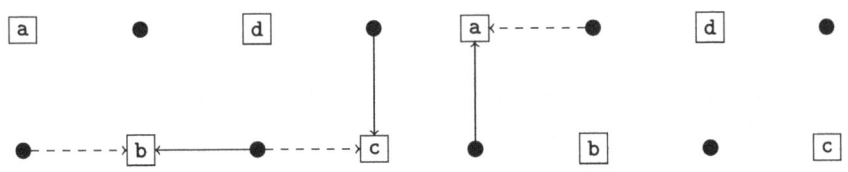

Fig. 7. Two composite actions for the parallel product of the constraint automata Prod(a), Fifo(a, b), Merger(b, c, d), and Cons(c, d).

locally performing a consistent set of get/put operations on port structures. To give an idea of how solutions are constructed, we draw operations graphically as in Fig. 7.

Ports are represented graphically with square boxes with letters. Constraint automata are black circles, and may do operations on ports. Operations are graphically represented with directed arrows, from constraint automata (black dots) to ports (squares with letters): dashed arrows represent *put* operations and full arrows represent *take* operations. Note that the arrows in Fig. 7 do not represent data flow, but rather the "flow" of operations, i.e., the sequences of operations that a constraint automaton performs on its ports.

On the left part of Fig. 7, the bottom left black circle represents the Fifo(a, b) constraint automaton, as it puts (dashed arrow) some value in port b, while the merger takes (filled arrow) a data item from b, puts that data item in c, and the consumer gets the data item from c.

On the right part of Fig. 7, the Prod(a) constraint automaton puts some data item on port a, and the Fifo(a, b) constraint automaton gets that data item from port a.

We identify two challenges in the dynamic assignment of values to ports as presented here. First, the order in which put and take operations are performed matters: a take operation on a port must always follow after a put places a value in that port; moreover, ports should be updated in the order of the dataflow (i.e., first b, then c for the example in Fig. 7). As we show in the next subsection, we enforce such ordering at runtime.

Second, local operations on ports (such as puts and gets) may lead to a global state that blocks the composition: some synchronous transitions can no longer proceed because of a value assigned to a port. If such a state arises, the runtime reaches a failure state which means that the current sequence of local transitions does not contribute to a global transition. In case of a failure, the runtime needs to backtrack to explore alternatives.

With those two concerns in mind, we present an algorithm that performs the parallel product of constraint automata at runtime, i.e., it finds a solution for a composite transition if such solution exists.

Algorithm. Every port is a data structure with two buffers: a sync and a data buffer. For a port P, we use $P(sync) \in \{\bot, \top\}$ to refer to the sync buffer, and $P(data) \in D_\star$ to the data buffer of P. We write $p < q$ when p is smaller than q. The ordering is inherent in synchronous regions that are consistent with dataflow causality (i.e., an output cannot occur before an input, and the input cannot be synchronously linked with an output). We assume that, in every constraint automaton, an input port is smaller than an output port to which it is synchronously related (i.e., the data from the input is directly put in the output). For instance, in the case of Merger(a,b,c), a and b are input ports synchronously related to the output port c, so it must be that $a < c$ and $b < c$. On the other hand, a Fifo(a,b) imposes no such ordering constraints as a and b are not synchronously related. In such cases, ordering can be arbitrary. As such, is not incorrect to assume a total ordering on ports. A total order is sufficient for soundness (i.e., realizable dataflow), although it is not necessary. This property helps to solve the first challenge identified above, namely that the operations on ports are done in an order that respects the direction of data flow through ports.

We explain the main operations in Algorithm 1. For $i \in [1,n]$, let A_i be a guard covered and independent constraint automaton. We fix an initial state q_i for automaton A_i, with the initial assignments μ_i. The data and sync states of every port are also initialized to $\perp$ and $\star$, respectively. We require that every port as input for a constraint automaton is also used as an output for another constraint automaton, i.e., $\bigcup_{i \in [1,n]} V_{i,I} = \bigcup_{i \in [1,n]} V_{i,O}$. Dataflow must abide by some basic principles: causality and preservation of data. Causality means that no data item can spontaneously appear out of nowhere in a flow: every data item must have a cause, i.e., it must come from some source (either a memory or an input port). Preservation of data means that no data item can disappear while it flows, i.e., every data item must get disposed into a sink (either a memory or an output port).

The algorithm consists of an infinite loop, each iteration of which consists of an atomic update from a composite transition. The first step is to form a composite transition: given the state q_i of automaton A_i, one outgoing transition from q_i is selected for the iteration. Note that it is not required that each automaton performs a transition (as automata are assumed to be independent, see Theorem 2).

For each transition t_i from the newly formed composite transition, let g_i be its guard. The algorithm derives a series of operations O_i: if $p \in V(g_i) \cap V_I$, then $take(p) \in O_i$, if $p \in V(g_i) \cap V_O$, then $put(p) \in O_i$. These operations are later used to trigger changes in the buffers of their respective ports. The guard that labels the transition is updated such that its memory variable m is replaced with the memory value $\mu_i(m)$. This list of operations is added to a global list opList.

The ordering of the optList ensures that operations on ports will correspond to data flow. As such, operations are sorted from operation of the smallest port to the highest port given the ordering relation on ports. This ensures that operations on input ports of channels are performed before operations on their respective output ports (by the assumption of ordering of ports of constraint automata). Next, the algorithm orders a $put(p)$ operation before a $take(p)$ operation for every p. This ensures that the automaton that takes the data from a port will be able to read the value that has already been put in that port.

The *check* operation on opList returns *Fail* if there is not a $put(p)$ for every $take(p)$, and vice versa. The algorithm, thus, ensures the dataflow property that ports cannot retain data beyond a single atomic step.

Then, in sequence, for each operation o in the list, if the operation is a *take* operation, the *sync* buffer of the port is updated, the memory content of the port updates internal memory of the automaton, and port variables in g are updated with the new value. New memory assignments found in g then lead to updates of μ. If the operation is a *put* operation, the *data* buffer gets the value from the port variable.

Two possibilities exist for a round to be inconsistent: either the guard evaluates to false, or data fails to flow, i.e., a port produces without consuming, or consumes without producing, a value. In both cases, the algorithm resets the internal memory to the initial μ_i, and resets all port buffers. It then skips to the end of the loop and repeats the round with a new composite transition.

If no inconsitency is found in the guard or in the state of a port, each participating automaton moves to its next state, all memory variables for ports are reset, memories are updated, and all ports are reset.

Then the round ends and a new round starts, with updated memories and reset ports. We show in the next section how the runtime composition is implemented in Maude. We directly start with a set of operations for constraint automata, and therefore omit the translation from guards to list of operations.

Theorem 3 (soundness). *The sequence of assignments of ports given by Algorithm 1 forms prefixes of an execution of the corresponding composite constraint automaton.*

Proof (Proof sketch). As shown in [25], the independence property of Reo primitives (i.e., the possibility to do a self loop with a $\top$ label) makes every two composition kappa-compatible (i.e., there is always an outgoing transition for any state), and are sufficient conditions for the existence of an algorithm to perform a step-by-step runtime composition. Remains to show that Algorithm 1 qualifies as such, which is the motivation of this sketch proof.

The proof amounts to showing that, within an iteration, all assignments of values to ports conform with a solution of a composite transition in the statically composed CA. As every CA is independent, any finite sequence of transitions in the composition can be completed into an infinite sequence whose tail consists of an infinite sequence of silent self-loop transitions $q \xrightarrow{\top} q$.

Suppose that we start in a state $(q_1, ..., q_n)$. Due to the independence property, it is sufficient to consider a step to be a tuple of n transitions $(t_1, ..., t_n)$, each starting in its respective state q_1, ..., q_n. Some t_i may be silent (i.e., self loop with $\top$ label). In the algorithm, we consider the subset of k non-silent transitions as $T = [t_1, ..., t_k]$. The algorithm checks that the conjunction of all guards labeling t_i for $i \in [1, n]$ is satisfiable.

We start, with the loop from line 4 to line 8 to substitute in all guards g_i all current memory variables by their respective values μ_i. Then, we build a list of operations on ports occurring free in guards g_i, i.e., for every input port p we have an operation $take(p)$ and for every output port, an operation $put(p)$.

The condition on line 11 ensures that every $take(p)$ occurs in opList if and only if a $put(p)$ occurs in opList. If not, the loop is aborted and a new composite transition is considered. Since no dataflow occurs at any port, the semantics is sound for such a case. Moreover, the ordering on line 10 ensures that, for $p < q$ every $take(p)$ occurs in the list before a $put(q)$; and for every port p, every $put(p)$ occurs before a $take(p)$. This is important to operationally solve the guard in the next loop.

The loop from line 14 to line 23 takes a list of operations correctly ordered and substitutes the free variables in g_i with their values. Given the order of operations in the opList, a put operation on every port p_i happens before a $take$ operation on the same port; and for two ports whose values are synchronously related (i.e., as required by the data constraint of a constraint automaton), a $take$ happen before a put. Thus, the order of substitution of variables with values in *directed equalities* of guards g_i makes, in each iteration, it possibile to find new assignments for output ports (i.e., stored in $p_i(data)$). At the end of the loop, all variables in guards g_i labeling a transitions t_i have been removed and the guard is grounded.

The next iteration checks if one of the guards is false or if a port is in an inconsistent state (i.e., has sent but not received, or received but not sent). If this is the case, then all operations are reverted and no dataflow occurs.

Otherwise, every automaton takes a step, updating all local memories and states. Every port is reinitialized for the next round. The dataflow that occurs is a solution to the conjunction of all the guards labeling local transitions, and therfore sound.

3   Implementation in Maude

In this section, we present the details and evaluate an implementation in Maude of the runtime product of parallel constraint automata. Rewriting logic is a powerful framework for modeling concurrent systems [29,30]. Moreover, implementations of rewriting logic, such as Maude [11], make system specifications both executable and analyzable. In our Maude implementation, the internal logic of a constraint automaton is expressed equationally, and the dynamics of its transitions is given as rewriting rules.

Our implementation in Maude enables two levels to make a preference-aware system more specific: by selecting a subset of best actions either at the constraint automaton level (i.e., which transition to offer first in the algorithm), or at the system level (i.e., which composite transition to select when several are possible).

Our rewriting specification of constraint automata has the following benefits. First, performing lazy composition keeps the representation of an interacting system small. Second, step-wise runtime composition renders our runtime framework modular, where run-time replacement of individual component automata becomes possible (as long as the update complies with some rules). Finally, our

---

Algorithm 1. Pseudo code for parallel composition

Require: Constraint automata A_1, ..., A_n, in states q_1, ..., q_n, with initial memory
$\mu_1, ..., \mu_n$; ports $p_1, ..., p_m$ with $p_i(sync) = \bot$ and $p_i(data) = \star$; and $\bigcup_{i \in [1,n]} V_{i,I} = \bigcup_{i \in [1,n]} V_{i,O}$.

```
 1: repeat
 2:     pick a new composite transition T = [t_1, ..., t_k] for t_i in A_i in state q_i
 3:     opList = []
 4:     for t_i ∈ [t_1, ..., t_k] do
 5:         convert the guard g_i on transition t_i into a list O_i of operations on ports
 6:         g_i[m ↦ μ_i(m)]
 7:         update μ with new values found from g
 8:         add O_i to opList
 9:     end for
10:     order opList into a single list of operations
11:     if check(opList) = Fail then
12:         continue
13:     end if
14:     for o in opList do
15:         let t_i be the transition that lead to action o, labeled with guard g_i
16:         if o = take(p_i) then
17:             p_i(sync) ↦ ⊤
18:             g_i[p_i ↦ p_i(data)]
19:         else if o = puts(p_i) then
20:             update μ_i with new values found from g_i
21:             p_i(data) ↦ μ_i(p_i)
22:         end if
23:     end for
24:     if one of the g_i is ⊥ or one of the port is in inconsistent state then
25:         μ_i is reinitialized to the initial μ_i
26:         for  p in all A_i do
27:             p(sync) ↦ ⊥ and p(data) ↦ ⋆
28:         end for
29:         continue
30:     end if
31:     for t_i ∈ [t_1, ..., t_k] do
32:         forall p in A_i, μ_i(p) ↦ ⋆
33:         forall m in A_i, μ_i(m) ↦ μ_i(m•)
34:         q_i ↦ q'_i with q'_i the post state of t_i
35:     end for
36:     for  p in all A_i do
37:         p(sync) ↦ ⊥ and p(data) ↦ ⋆
38:     end for
39: until True
```

Ensure: Consecutive data flow at ports $p_1, ..., p_m$ that satisfy a composite transition
in $A_1, ..., A_n$.

runtime framework more closely matches the architecture of a distributed framework, where entities are physically separate and no party may have access to the whole description of the entire system.

The running time of an execution may, in constrast, be slower than for the case of a static product. We discuss the challenges of our approach below.

Prerequisite. The framework that we use has been developped for simulation and analysis of interacting *agents* with cyber-physical aspects [26]. In this current work, we use this framework to implement our parallel constraint automata. We implement both ports and constraint automata as instances of an *agent*, which is similar to an object:

```
[id : class | state ; flag ; actions]
```

where id is a unique identifier for the agent of type Class. Every agent has a state, that contains key/value pairs. A Boolean flag indicates whether or not an agent is available for composition (i.e., flag is true). The set of actions that an agent can perform in a round is given by actions, where an action in our case consists of *put* and *take* operations on ports.

A system of agents is simply a multiset of agents. The run of a system is given by the main rewrite rule:

```
crl[transition] : [sys]    => [sys']
    if agentsReady?(sys)   /\
       saAtom := getSysActions(sys) /\
       saComp := buildComposite(saAtom) /\
       p(actseq, sys') ; actseqs := kbestActions(saComp, k,
          sys)
```

where

- sys and sys' are multisets of agents before and after taking a composite transition, respectively;
- agentsReady? returns true if all agents have their flag set to true, i.e., ready to proceeed;
- getSysActions collects the list of actions for each agent in sys;
- buildComposite builds the list of composite actions (i.e., composite transitions); and
- kbestActions returns the k best acceptable composite actions, i.e., that do not bring the composition sys into an error state. The notion of *best* action is liberal in our framework (as it makes use of preferences), but not detailed in this paper. See [26] for more details.

We give, in Sect. 3.1, the definition of a port as an agent, and a channel as an agent.

3.1   Port and Constraint Automaton as Agents

In order to achieve the goals set in the introduction, the runtime should accommodate for the concurrency inherent in the dataflow of a Reo circuit. Previous work [12] shows that constraint automata is not adequate to simulate the concurrent aspect of Reo models, and proposes multilabeled petri nets as an alternative. Instead, we implement the parallel extension of constraint automata described in the previous section in the rewriting framework we have developed in Maude.

Existing executable environments for Reo [8] focuse on compilation of input circuits into an executable code. A challenge not addressed in such work is the construction of a compositional runtime where each part of a Reo circuit can be compiled independently and run concurrently. This capability is important, for instance, to reconfigure a circuit during its execution. Also, in such a framework, one can keep the structure of a Reo circuit at runtime, mix different semantics for Reo channels (e.g., guarded commands, constraint automata, etc.), while allowing for simulation and verification through reachability queries.

We present, in the next paragraphs, the structure of our runtime environment to simulate, verify, and dynamically reconfigure Reo circuits. More precisely, we introduce two primitive sorts both encoded as agents in our framework: PORT and CONNECTOR. As shown in the previous subsection, a system specification is a multiset of agents, which is instantiated as a multiset of connectors and ports, through which data flow. Every channel primitive in Reo translates into a constraint automaton. Now we assign an agent to simulate every such constraint automaton. In addition, we have agents that simulate ports.

The code and examples discussed in this section are accessible at [24].

Port as Resource. A port is a point of synchronization in Reo, and its typical behavior is to atomically forward data from its input connector to its output connector. We fix a port identifier to be of the form P(i) where i:Float is a floating point number. We later use the identifier of a port to define the operation of linearization and use the natural ordering of Float to order actions.

A port contains a structure with two buffers that implement the atomic passing of data from its input to its output connector. One buffer collects the data item that the input connector may *put*, and the other contains the request from the output connector to *take* a data item. Only when the two buffers are full should the port allow both put(d) and take actions.

Interface of a port:

```
[P(i) : Port | state ; flag ; action]
```

where:

- i is a float number that identifies a port. We use float in order to easily introduce new ports, and yet preserve a meaningful ordering over ports;
- state contains key/value pairs that collectively identify a state. For instance, the key k("sync") is mapped to a Boolean value that is k("true") when a take operation has been performed; the key k("data") contains the data value given by some put(d) operation; and the key k("blocked") maps to true if the port has been blocked by another component;
- the flag will be set to true (as a port is always ready to proceed) and the action fields will be set to empty, as a port *reacts* to actions of other agents.

Connectors as Agents. We give three instances of primitive Reo connectors: a SYNC, a FIFO, and a MERGER. Other primitive connectors, such as a replicator, syncdrain, etc., are defined similarly. We show in the next section some more complex connectors, such as the alternator, defined as a composition of primitive connectors.

A SYNC agent has two ports on which it acts synchronously. The action of a SYNC agent consists of an atomic sequence of two actions: a take on its input port, and a put on its output port. The composite action succeeds if and only if the two parts involved in the action allow it to succeed, and the value *put* in the output port corresponds to the value *taken* from the input port.

A FIFO agent has two ports on which it acts in sequence. A FIFO agent has two actions, a take action that stores a data item from its input port into a memory, and a put action that outputs that data item through its output port. The take action succeeds only if the current memory cell is empty, and the put action succeeds only if the current memory cell is full. As a result, the FIFO agent alternates between taking a value from its input port, and putting that value into its output port.

A MERGER is a ternary connector that acts, for each of its input ports, as a synchronous channel with its output port. Moreover, the MERGER relates its two input ports with a relation of exclusion, i.e., the two input ports cannot fire at the same time. A MERGER with the list of ports P(1), P(2), P(3) has two actions: an action that forwards a data item from port P(1) to port P(3), and an action that forwards a data item from port P(2) to port P(3). These two actions are exclusive, as they cannot occur at the same time. Moreover, the merger always enables both actions, which raises some non-determinism at the system level (i.e., to chose which of the two actions to perform). Similarly to the SYNC channel, a MERGER agent instantiates the value for the put action at runtime, once the result of the take action is known. We use the ? symbol to denote a value that will be put at a port but that is not already known (because it is not already taken from an input port).

A PROD and a CONS agent implement a producer and consumer, respectively. Each of these agents has a single port, on which it always performs, respectively, a put and a take action. The PROD agent puts natural numbers as values on its port, and increments the value when the put action succeeds. We use such canonical sequences of increasing natural numbers to verify certain firing properties of a Reo circuit. When a put action succeeds for a PROD agent, its state is updated to contain the message that has been sent in the k("sent") field. Similarly, when a take action succeeds for a CONS agent, its state is updated to contain the message that has been received in the k("recv") field.

Runtime Composition. As expected, runtime composition has several drawbacks: if there are n automata to compose, each with one transition, there are 2^n possible combination of composite transitions. This is easily understood as a tuples of size n, where the ith location tells whether the transition has been selected or not (i.e., 1 means that the transition of the ith automata is in the product). The enumeration of all possibilities, therefore, leads to 2^n cases.

Note that we can prune some compositions that are not *well-formed*. By construction, we know that every put(d) action on a port P(i) must be in the atomic set of a take action on that same port. Thus, any combination that has one but not the other can already be removed.

The next operation that speeds up runtime composition is called *lineariza-tion*. This operation takes a list of transitions (aSeq), and reorders it so that the runtime checks and applies each transition in sequence. To do so, we use the name of the port, as a float number, to order the transitions: action on ports with a smaller port numbers will be run first at runtime. As we require that a channel has increasing port numbers, we ensure that, if possible, data will flow from its input to its output.

In Maude, the implementation of linearization is done as follows:

```
ceq linearization(aSeq) = orderActionPort(seq) linearization(
    aSeq')
    if  seq := getActionsFromPort(aSeq, getSmallestPort(aSeq))
        /\
        aSeq' := filterOut(aSeq, makeSet(seq)) /\ aSeq =/= nil

eq orderActionPort(aSeq) = putValue(aSeq) takeValue(aSeq) .it
```

where

- orderActionPort orders, from right to left, actions on the same port. The ordering for a given port places first *put* actions, then *take* actions so that the *take* action will eventually have the data from a preceding *put* action;
- linearization is recursively applied on the remaining actions.

3.2 Execution and Analysis

We show the utility of our framework by example applications within three different categories: verification with reachability queries, normalisation of connectors, and dynamic reconfiguration. The fact that all three use cases can be investigated within the same framework is also a benefit compared with existing works.

The first category is the most intuitive one, as it provides a way to simulate Reo circuits. Our example in this category is the alternator connector.

The second category uses the algebraic nature of Maude: we equationally define the equivalence of circuits, and therefore simplify a system to a smaller one. For instance, the composition of two sync channels can be rewritten as a single sync channel as the two circuits are behaviorally equivalent.

The third category of examples explores the use of rewrite rules to do dynamic reconfiguration: a new component is added to the system at runtime each time a reconfigurable rule is triggered. As an example in this category, we show how to model an unbounded fifo.

Dataflow Properties. We first use our framework to verify dataflow properties of a binary alternator connector. A binary alternator has two input ports and an output port. In our example, we connect each input port to a producer and the output port to a consumer process. The behavior of a binary alternator is as follows: it synchronizes its two input ports to ensure that both producers connected to these ports have data items to offer. It then places the data items from its input ports in its output port in a fixed, predefined order; thus, what the alternator produces through its output port is an alternating sequence of the data items that it obtains from its two input ports. A property of the alternator is therefore that no two data items of one producer is observed in its output next to each other.

We give the specification of the alternatorScenario, and then check some of its properties. The alternatorScenario consists of two `Prod` agents that communicate with a `ConsList` agent through an alternator protocol:

```
alternator =
[PortList(1.0, 1.5, 1.8, 2.0, 2.5, 2.8, 3.0, 3.5, 4.0)
 Prod(P(1.0)) Prod(P(2.0)) ConsList(P(4.0))
 Replicator(P(1.0), P(1.5), P(1.8))
 SyncDrain(P(1.5), P(2.5))
 Sync(P(1.8), P(3.0))
 Merger(P(3.0), P(3.5), P(4.0))
 Replicator(P(2.0), P(2.5), P(2.8))
 Fifo(P(2.8), P(3.5), empty)]
```

All the channels, with the exception of `Prod` and `ConsList` in the above are primitives that constitute the internals of an alternator. The `ConsList` agent records the sequence of data received. We assume that $\text{Prod}(P(i))$ sends data $nd(i)$ to its port (where **nd** stands for *natural data* to denote natural numbers).

We show two search commands on an alternator: one that looks for consecutive data in the consumer that are different (i.e., alternating), and one that looks for consecutive data that come from the same agent.

The execution of the following search result returns no solution in a reasonable amount of time, leading to the conclusion that no consecutive data of the same producer can be output from the alternator:

```
search [1] in SCENARIO : alternator =>* [sys::Sys
  [ConsList(P(4.0)) : Consumer |
    M2::MapKD, k("data") |-> nd(i::Nat) nd(j::Nat) ; false ;
      null]]
    such that i::Nat == j::Nat = true .
```

One solution is found, however, when searching two consecutive data items coming from different producers. The following search query asks to find a rewriting sequence that leads the consumer observe two consecutive data with different values.

```
search [1] in SCENARIO : alternator =>* [sys::Sys
  [ConsList(P(4.0)) : Consumer |
```

```
  M2::MapKD, k("data") |-> nd(i::Nat) nd(j::Nat) ; false ;
      null]]
  such that i::Nat =/= j::Nat = true .
```

Simplification of Circuits. If one proves that the behavior of two circuits are the same, one would like to simplify the system term to the smaller and simpler of the two specifications. For instance consider the composition of two consecutive sync channels:

```
eq init = [
  [Prod(P(1.0)) : Producer | k("data") |-> 1.0 ; false ;
      null]
  [Cons(P(3.0)) : Consumer | k("data") |-> nodata; false ;
      null]
  [P(1.0) : Port | state ; false ; null]
  [P(2.0) : Port | state ; false ; null]
  [P(3.0) : Port | state ; false ; null]
  [Sync(P(1.0), P(2.0)) : Channel | state ; false ; null]
  [Sync(P(2.0), P(3.0)) : Channel | state ; false ; null]
] .
```

The above expression can provably be simplified by replacing the two Sync channels with a single Sync channel, and removing the intermediate port. We can give the following equation in Maude:

```
var i j k : Float .

ceq [sys] = [
    [P(i) : Port | state ; false ; null]
    [P(k) : Port | state ; false ; null]
    [Sync(P(i), P(k)) : Channel | state ; false ; null] sys
      ']
  if
[P(i) : Port | state ; false ; null]
[P(j) : Port | state ; false ; null]
[P(k) : Port | state ; false ; null]
[Sync(P(i), P(j)) : Channel | state ; false ; null]
[Sync(P(j), P(k)) : Channel | state ; false ; null] sys' :=
    sys .
```

Then, the reduction of the term init is the new term:

```
init = [
[Prod(P(1.0)) : Producer | k("data") |-> 1 ; false ; null]
[P(1.0) : Port | state ; true ; null]
[P(3.0) : Port | state ; true ; null]
[Cons(P(3.0)) : Consumer | k("data") |-> nodata ; false ;
    null]
[Sync(P(1.0), P(3.0)) : Channel | state ; false ; null]]
```

Dynamic Updates. As we showed earlier, a Reo circuit can be simulated, and the state space can be explored within our framework implemented in Maude. We now present an additional feature, namely the possibility to dynamically reconfigure a circuit. Dynamic reconfiguration has already been explored in some previous tools supporting simulation of Reo circuit [21]. However, that implementation required an ad hoc plugin to interface the main environment. In our case, the simulation, verification, and reconfiguration are all done in the same environment, expressed with rewriting logic.

We show, as a use case, how we can use our bounded Fifo channel (with capacity of 1) to implement an unbounded fifo that triggers a reconfiguration at the system level each time it receives a data. We add two rewrite rules together with the specification of the unbounded fifo: add-buffer and rem-buffer.

The first rewrite rule adds a buffer whenever the UnboundedFifo is full:

```
crl [add-buffer] :
 [UnboundedFifo(P(n1), P(n2)) : Channel | M, k("state") |->
    nd(1) ; false ; null] sys] =>
 [[P((n1 + n2) / 2.0) : Port | defaultState ; false ; null]
 [UnboundedFifo(P(n1), P((n1 + n2) / 2.0)) : Channel | k("
    data") |-> nodata, k("state") |-> nd(0) ; false ; null]
 [Fifo(P((n1 + n2) / 2.0), P(n2)) : Channel | M, k("state")
    |-> nd(1) ; false ; null] sys] .
    if [Fifo(P(n2), P(n3)) : Channel | M, k("state") |-> nd(1)
    ; false ; null] sys' := sys .
```

Then, the initial term init given by a Prod, a Cons, and an UnboundedFifo leads to the following system after 9 rewrites:

```
Maude> cont 9 .
    rewrites: 8105 in 3ms cpu (3ms real) (2041047 rewrites/
        second)
    result Global: [
    [Prod(P(1.0)) : Producer | k("data") |-> nd(1), k("msg")
        |-> nd(1) ; false ; null]
    [P(1.0) : Port | k("data") |-> nodata, k("sync") |-> bd(
        false) ; true ; null]
    [P(1.5) : Port | k("data") |-> nodata, k("sync") |-> bd(
        false) ; true ; null]
    [P(2.0) : Port | k("data") |-> nodata, k("sync") |-> bd(
        false) ; true ; null]
    [Cons(P(2.0)) : Consumer | k("data") |-> nd(1) ; false ;
        null]
    [Fifo(P(1.5), P(2.0)) : Channel | k("data") |-> nodata, k
        ("state") |-> nd(0) ; false ; null]
    [UnboundedFifo(P(1.0), P(1.5)) : Channel | k("data") |->
        nd(1), k("state") |-> nd(1) ; false ; null]]
```

As we can see, an intermediate empty fifo has been added to the system, which will then take the value from the UnboundedFifo, and forward it to the Cons. If

Prod produces values faster than Cons consumes them, the UnboundedFifo will interleave new Fifo, in order, to implement the unbounded behavior.

The second rule to *remove* empty buffers is:

```
rl [rem-buffer] :
  [[UnboundedFifo(P(n1), P((n1 + n2) / 2.0)) : Channel | M
    ; false ; null]
    [P((n1 + n2) / 2.0) : Port | k("data")|-> nodata, k("
      sync") |-> bd(false) ; true ; null]
    [Fifo(P((n1 + n2) / 2.0), P(n2))          : Channel | k
      ("data") |-> nodata, k("state") |-> nd(0) ; false ;
      null] sys] =>
  [[UnboundedFifo(P(n1), P(n2))              : Channel | M ;
    false ; null] sys] .
```

As shown after running the search command

```
search [1] init =>*
  [[Prod(P(1.0)) : Producer | k("data") |-> nd(1), k("msg")
      |-> nd(1) ; false ; null]
    [P(1.0) : Port | k("data") |-> nodata, k("sync") |-> bd(
      false) ; true ; null]
    [P(2.0) : Port | k("data") |-> nodata, k("sync") |-> bd(
      false) ; true ; null]
    [Cons(P(2.0)) : Consumer | k("data") |-> nd(1) ; false ;
      null]
    [UnboundedFifo(P(1.0), P(2.0)) : Channel | k("data") |->
      nd(1), k("state") |-> nd(1) ; false ; null]] .
```

the added buffer has been removed by the *rem-buffer* rewrite rule when it was emptied by the consumer. Thus, we successfully implemented an unbounded fifo by using two additional rewrite rules.

4   Conclusion

Reo is a powerful channel-based language that models coordination among processes. Constraint automata is an operational semantics for Reo channels, that supports model checking techniques. Unfortunately, constraint automata are not suitable for simulation and dynamic reconfiguration, and their (static) product violates architectural fidelity: the requirement to perform the product statically not only creates a state space explosion, it also loses the internal structure of composition of the components in a system. We presented in this paper the PCA model: a modified version of constraint automata that preserves architectural fidelity and enables simulation, verification, and dynamic reconfiguration of Reo circuit. We demonstrated the utility of the PCA with an implementation in Maude and a series of examples.

Given the capabilities of the execution environment presented in the paper, the algebraic nature of the specification of Reo channels in Maude opens new avenues for new connector. For instance, *physical* aspects of components can be algebraically encoded, and would supplement Reo's existing exogeneous coordination primitives. Thus, time sensitive circuits could be simulated, verified, and could profit from the possibility of dynamic reconfiguration. A first step has been taken in this direction in the PhD thesis [23]. We leave as future work the improvements to our current Maude implementation to support more examples (e.g., cyber-physical Reo circuits), to optimize further the search queries for verification, and to take full advantage of the rewriting features provided by Maude for, e.g., dynamically reconfigurable circuits.

Acknowledgement. The authors are extremely grateful to Carolyn Talcott for her immensely valuable guidance and input during the development of the Maude framework that underlies the PCA implementation presented in this paper. Any remaining errors of fact, in implementation, or presentation are, of course, the authors'.

References

1. Aceto, L., Burgueño, A., Larsen, K.G.: Model checking via reachability testing for timed automata. In: Steffen, B. (ed.) TACAS 1998. LNCS, vol. 1384, pp. 263–280. Springer, Heidelberg (1998). https://doi.org/10.1007/BFB0054177
2. Arbab, F.: Reo: a channel-based coordination model for component composition. Math. Struct. Comput. Sci. **14**(3), 329–366 (2004). https://doi.org/10.1017/S0960129504004153
3. Arbab, F., Chothia, T., van der Mei, R., Meng, S., Moon, Y.J., Verhoef, C.: From coordination to stochastic models of QoS. In: Field, J., Vasconcelos, V.T. (eds.) COORDINATION 2009. LNCS, vol. 5521, pp. 268–287. Springer, Heidelberg (2009). https://doi.org/10.1007/978-3-642-02053-7_14
4. Arbab, F., Kokash, N., Meng, S.: Towards using Reo for compliance-aware business process modeling. In: Margaria, T., Steffen, B. (eds.) ISoLA 2008. CCIS, vol. 17, pp. 108–123. Springer, Heidelberg (2008). https://doi.org/10.1007/978-3-540-88479-8_9
5. Arbab, F., Meng, S.: Synthesis of connectors from scenario-based interaction specifications. In: Chaudron, M.R.V., Szyperski, C., Reussner, R. (eds.) CBSE 2008. LNCS, vol. 5282, pp. 114–129. Springer, Heidelberg (2008). https://doi.org/10.1007/978-3-540-87891-9_8. ISBN 978-3-540-87891-9
6. Baier, C., Blechmann, T., Klein, J., Klüppelholz, S., Leister, W.: Design and verification of systems with exogenous coordination using vereofy. In: Margaria, T., Steffen, B. (eds.) ISoLA 2010. LNCS, vol. 6416, pp. 97–111. Springer, Heidelberg (2010). https://doi.org/10.1007/978-3-642-16561-0_15
7. Baier, C., Sirjani, M., Arbab, F., Rutten, J.J.M.M.: Modeling component connectors in Reo by constraint automata. Sci. Comput. Program. **61**(2), 75–113 (2006). https://doi.org/10.1016/J.SCICO.2005.10.008
8. Dokter, K., Lion, B.: The Reo Language repository (2017). https://github.com/ReoLanguage/Reo
9. Clarke, D., Proença, J.: Coordination via interaction constraints I: local logic. In: Bonchi, F., Grohmann, D., Spoletini, P., Tuosto, E. (eds.) Proceedings 2nd Interaction and Concurrency Experience: Structured Interactions, ICE 2009, Bologna, Italy, 31st August 2009. EPTCS, vol. 12, pp. 17–39 (2009). https://doi.org/10.4204/EPTCS.12.2

10. Clarke, D., Proença, J., Lazovik, A., Arbab, F.: Channelbased coordination via constraint satisfaction. Sci. Comput. Program. **76**(8), 681–710 (2011). https://doi.org/10.1016/J.SCICO.2010.05.004

11. Clavel, M., et al. (eds.) All About Maude - A High-Performance Logical Framework, How to Specify, Program and Verify Systems in Rewriting Logic. Lecture Notes in Computer Science, vol. 4350. Springer (2007). https://doi.org/10.1007/978-3-540-71999-1. ISBN 978-3-540-71940-3

12. Dokter, K.: Multilabeled petri nets. In: Arbab, F., Jongmans, S.-S. (eds.) FACS 2019. LNCS, vol. 12018, pp. 106–126. Springer, Cham (2020). https://doi.org/10.1007/978-3-030-40914-2_6

13. Dokter, K., Arbab, F.: Rule-based form for stream constraints. In: Di Marzo Serugendo, G., Loreti, M. (eds.) COORDINATION 2018. LNCS, vol. 10852, pp. 142–161. Springer, Cham (2018). https://doi.org/10.1007/978-3-319-92408-3_6

14. Jongmans, S.-S.T.Q., Arbab, F.: Overview of thirty semantic formalisms for Reo. Sci. Ann. Comput. Sci. **22**(1), 201–251 (2013). https://doi.org/10.7561/SACS.2012.1.201

15. Jongmans, S.-S.T.Q., Arbab, F.: Centralized coordination vs. partially distributed coordination with Reo and constraint automata. Sci. Comput. Program. **160**, 48–77 (2018). Fundamentals of Software Engineering (selected papers of FSEN 2015). https://doi.org/10.1016/j.scico.2017.06.004. ISSN 0167-6423

16. Jongmans, S.-S.: Automata-theoretic protocol programming: parallel computation, threads and their interaction, optimized compilation [at a] high level of abstraction. PhD thesis. Leiden University, Netherlands (2016)

17. Jongmans, S.-S.T.Q., Arbab, F.: PrDK: protocol programming with automata. In: Chechik, M., Raskin, J.-F. (eds.) TACAS 2016. LNCS, vol. 9636, pp. 547–552. Springer, Heidelberg (2016). https://doi.org/10.1007/978-3-662-49674-9_33

18. Jongmans, S.-S.T.Q., Kappé, T., Arbab, F.: Constraint automata with memory cells and their composition. Sci. Comput. Program. **146**, 50–86 (2017). https://doi.org/10.1016/J.SCICO.2017.03.006

19. Klüppelholz, S., Baier, C.: Symbolic model checking for channel-based component connectors. Sci. Comput. Program. **74**(9) (2009). https://doi.org/10.1016/J.SCICO.2008.09.020

20. Kokash, N., Krause, C., de Vink, E.P.: Reo + mCRL2: a framework for model-checking dataflow in service compositions. Formal Aspects Comput. **24**(2), 187–216 (2012). https://doi.org/10.1007/S00165-011-0191-6

21. Krause, C., Maraikar, Z., Lazovik, A., Arbab, F.: Modeling dynamic reconfigurations in Reo using high-level replacement systems. Sci. Comput. Program. **76**(1), 23–36 (2011). https://doi.org/10.1016/J.SCICO.2009.10.006

22. Laroussinie, F., Larsen, K.G.: Compositional model checking of real time systems. In: Lee, I., Smolka, S.A. (eds.) CONCUR 1995. LNCS, vol. 962, pp. 27–41. Springer, Heidelberg (1995). https://doi.org/10.1007/3-540-60218-6_3

23. Lion, B.: An algebra for interaction of cyber-physical components. Ph.D. thesis (2023)

24. Lion, B.: The maude implementation of Reo (2024). https://benjaminlion.fr/reo.zip

25. Lion, B., Arbab, F., Talcott, C.: Runtime composition of systems of interacting cyber-physical components. In: Madeira, A., Martins, M.A. (eds.) WADT 2022. LNCS, vol. 13710, pp. 141–162. Springer, Cham (2023). https://doi.org/10.1007/978-3-031-43345-0_7. ISBN: 978-3-031-43345-0

26. Lion, B., Arbab, F., Talcott, C.: A rewriting framework for interacting cyber-physical agents. In: Margaria, T., Steffen, B. (eds.) ISoLA 2022, Part III. LNCS, vol. 13703, pp. 356-372. Springer, Cham (2022). https://doi.org/10.1007/978-3-031-19759-8_22

27. Meng, S., Arbab, F.: QoS-driven service selection and composition using quantitative constraint automata. Fundam. Inform. **95**(1), 103–128 (2009). https://doi.org/10.3233/FI-2009-144

28. Meng, S., Arbab, F., Baier, C.: Synthesis of Reo circuits from scenario-based interaction specifications. Sci. Comput. Program. **76**(8), 651–680 (2011). https://doi.org/10.1016/J.SCICO.2010.03.002

29. Meseguer, J.: Conditioned rewriting logic as a united model of concurrency. Theor. Comput. Sci. **96**(1), 73–155 (1992). https://doi.org/10.1016/0304-3975(92)90182-F

30. Meseguer, J.: Twenty years of rewriting logic. J. Log. Algebraic Methods Program. **81**(7–8), 721–781 (2012). https://doi.org/10.1016/j.jlap.2012.06.003

31. Moon, Y.-J., Silva, A., Krause, C., Arbab, F.: A compositional model to reason about end-to-end QoS in Stochastic Reo connectors. Sci. Comput. Program. **80**, 3–24 (2014). https://doi.org/10.1016/J.SCICO.2011.11.007

32. Proença, J., Clarke, D., de Vink, E.P., Arbab, F.: Dreams: a framework for distributed synchronous coordination. In: Ossowski, S., Lecca, P. (eds.) Proceedings of the ACM Symposium on Applied Computing, SAC 2012, Riva, Trento, Italy, 26–30 March 2012, pp. 1510–1515. ACM (2012). https://doi.org/10.1145/2245276.2232017

Privacy-Aware Modeling and Analysis of Social Networks Using Rebeca

Zahra Moezkarimi[1]([⊠]) [iD] and Fatemeh Ghassemi[2,3] [iD]

[1] Mälardalen University, Västerås, Sweden
zahra.moezkarimi@mdu.se
[2] University of Tehran, Tehran, Iran
[3] Tehran Institute for Advanced Studies (TeIAS), Tehran, Iran

Abstract. Social network users control the flow of information through their privacy settings. Such privacy settings specify the possibility of interaction or the visibility of each user's activity to other users. We extend the Rebeca language with 1) annotations for specifying the user's privacy policies on send and receive message actions, and 2) conditional statement on the knowledge of actors. The annotation of a send message statement identifies possible observers while the annotation of a message server defines the possible senders of that message. Rebecs perceive knowledge by observing messages and they can react accordingly. By integrating epistemic logic into conditional statements, we can model the behaviors influenced by the knowledge of an actor. We define the semantics in terms of labeled transition systems enriched by indistinguishability relations, called Social Network Semantic Model (SNSM). This semantic model addresses both operational and epistemic aspects of social networks which enables us to find scenarios leading to private data disclosure using model checking. We illustrate the applicability of our approach through a simple case study on Instagram.

Keywords: Privacy Policies · Social Networks · Rebeca Modeling Language · Operational Semantics · Model Checking

1 Introduction

People use social networks to communicate and share common interests. This could be from typical private communications to business and scientific collaboration. Among the most popular social networks are Facebook (ca. 3 billion active users), YouTube (ca. 2.5 billion active users), WhatsApp (ca. 2.5 billion active users), and Instagram (ca. 2.5 billion active users) [1]. This huge amount of interaction provide people with novel ways of virtual communication. Hence, a huge amount of information is online and accessible.

To: Marjan, whose endless support and encouragement have been my constant inspiration. – Fatemeh
To: Marjan, with gratitude for all her unwavering kindness. – Zahra.

© The Author(s), under exclusive license to Springer Nature Switzerland AG 2025
E. A. Lee et al. (Eds.): Marjan Sirjani Festschrift, LNCS 15560, pp. 127–148, 2025.
https://doi.org/10.1007/978-3-031-85134-6_6

Due to the high volume of interactions on social media, many areas has been transformed such as marketing and education, by allowing people to interact in fast and innovative ways. While this has brought about many positive changes, it has also led to challenges such as the spread of fake news and online harassment through fake profiles. Among these concerns, protecting user privacy and preventing the leakage of personal information have become especially important. To address these issues, social media platforms are working on creating better privacy settings that give users more control over their data. Additionally, they are ensuring that their data processing and storage practices comply with regulations such as GDPR [25] to protect user privacy. However, there is still a lack of understandable formal approaches to ensure that social networks behave as expected when these privacy policies are adopted by users. For instance, even when privacy settings are configured correctly, there could still be information leaks that don't match what users expect. We introduce a unified formal framework to model and analyze these networks while considering the user's privacy settings that affect user interactions on social networks. We do not cover the analysis of data protection during storage and processing in this paper, but there is potential to explore these areas in future research.

Rebeca (Reactive Object Language) [21,24] is an actor-based modeling language designed for modeling and formal verification of reactive, concurrent, and distributed systems. In Rebeca, reactive objects, or rebecs, function similarly to actors [2,7], communicate through asynchronous message passing. In social networks, multiple agents interact through asynchronous message passing, responding to one another based on the messages they receive. This behavior aligns with the principles of the actor model. We extend the Rebeca modeling language to allow users to define their privacy settings, called PRIVATEREBECA. This extension allows users to define who can observe their send message actions and specify from whom they can receive messages using two distinct annotations. Rebecs perceive knowledge by observing send messages which can affect their behaviors. We integrate epistemic logic into conditional statements to infer about the knowledge of rebecs and consequently, model the behaviors influenced by the knowledge of an actor following the approach of [15]. We borrow the logical framework introduced in [13] with a minor modification. The framework combines model μ-calculus with past and epistemic logic. We substitute the belief operator with the knowledge operator to focus on reasoning about data disclosure [14].

We define the semantics of PRIVATEREBECA in terms of labeled transition systems enriched by indistinguishability relations on states, called Social Network Semantic Model (SNSM) [14]. The indistinguishability relation shows the states that cannot be distinguished by a rebec based on its knowledge and enables epistemic reasoning. Privacy policies on send actions can be viewed as renaming functions which rename such actions to τ, i.e., hide information, from an unintended observer, similar to how social networks manage privacy. However, instead of merely concealing data, this approach can also be used for misrepresentation or lying (similar to [15] and [13]), meaning displaying false information or actions rather than the real ones. Transitions of SNSMs carry actions decorated with renaming functions capturing the privacy policy of the user for each action within a social network. The indistinguishably relation is constructed based on the renaming functions. We verify the disclosure of private data as properties specified by an epistemic formula on SMSNs to find scenarios leading to privacy violation. We show the effect of adding the privacy feature to a language by formulating the operational semantic rules that induce the transition relation of SNSMs, using the semantic template rules of the Transparent Actor [6] model. This model offers a structured approach to define actor-based language semantics through a set of operational semantic template rules in which design decision points are explicitly identified. We demonstrate that the template rules are sufficiently general to support the extension with privacy policies. However, for the extension involving epistemic reasoning at the conditional statement, we identify a deviation.

Our framework is not only useful to understand what users know locally in a social network but also what they can infer about others' behaviors and privacy practices based on their observations. Using our framework, we can specify and enforce privacy policies, similar to those used by social networks, and also can investigate potential information leakage that might implicitly compromise user privacy. We can summarize our contributions as follows:

– Extending the Rebeca modeling language to incorporate privacy policies and epistemic reasoning;
– Providing a set of operational rules to induce the semantic model suitable for analyzing information leakage in social networks;
– Utilizing a modular approach to defining our operational semantic rules using the Transparent Actor template rules to investigate the effect of the new feature of the language;
– Illustrating the applicability of our approach through a case study on Instagram.

To illustrate the concepts, we present Example 1 as a running example, which we build upon throughout the paper.

Example 1. Consider a simplified version of the social network *Instagram* in which users communicate through sending/receiving messages. Each user has a profile consisting of their name, age, sets of followers, following, blocked users, and a set of posts. Each user also has a unique publicly accessible username, i.e., everyone can see (know). For every available send and receive action within the network, users can determine who is allowed to observe their sent actions and from whom they prefer to receive actions.

Note that in this paper we statically append policies to actions in each reactive class in the Rebeca model. However, the framework is general enough to support dynamic policy definitions, enabling different policies to be assigned during the instantiation of rebecs. It means that the policies could be different for different instances of a reactive class.

2   Preliminaries

We first review the core Rebeca language, and then explain the semantic model introduced in [14] for social networks addressing their operational and epistemic aspects. As we extend Rebeca for modeling the privacy rules in social networks, we use the approach of [6] to give the semantic rules of the extended language. This approach explicitly highlights the parts of the language that are influenced by the new feature.

2.1   Rebeca

Actors, as defined in the literature [2,7], serve as the fundamental units of concurrency. Rebeca (Reactive Object Language) [21,24] is an actor-based modeling language for modeling and formal verification of concurrent reactive systems. In Rebeca models, reactive objects, called rebecs, are the units of computations that interact with each other through asynchronous message passing. They can also send messages to themselves to trigger periodic behaviors. Each rebec operates as a single-threaded entity, consisting of variables, methods (known as message servers), and a dedicated message queue to handle incoming messages. A rebec's response to a message is defined within its message servers, and messages are processed by dequeuing them from the head of the queue and executing the corresponding message server in a non-preemptive manner. During the execution of a message server, the state of a rebec can be modified through assignment statements.

A Rebeca model is composed of several reactive classes along with a main section. Each reactive class defines the type of a group of rebecs, which are instantiated in the main block. Although the message queues in Rebeca's semantics are conceptually unbounded, users must specify an upper bound on the queue size to ensure a finite state space during model checking. Reactive classes include constructors, named identically to the class, which are responsible for initializing the actor's state variables and placing the initial messages into the actor's message buffer. They also incorporate various message servers to define the behavior of the rebecs associated with that reactive class.

Rebeca offers an operational interpretation of the actor model using a Java-like syntax. Its design principles make it adaptable, allowing the core language to be extended for specific domains [22]. For instance, various extensions of Rebeca have been developed to address specific aspects, including probabilistic systems [8], real-time systems [11,23], cyber-physical systems [9], and wireless networks [27]. For simplicity, this paper uses Rebeca, but our extension is equally applicable to other extensions without any modifications as privacy is an orthogonal feature.

2.2   Transparent Actor

Transparent Actor is a semantic framework for actor-based languages introduced in [6] to explicitly identifies the decision points governing communication, coordination, and task scheduling in distributed systems based on the actor model.

This framework makes network explicit and provides a set of semantic operational template rules in which the decision points are identified. These template rules are organized within three levels: *actors*, *abstract network*, and *composition*. There are two decision points at the actor level: one for receiving and one for taking a message. For example, when the mailbox is full, the message can be either dropped or overwrite the old messages. The design decision for taking a message from the mailbox realises the scheduling of tasks within an actor. There is one decision point at the abstract network level expressing how messages are delivered to their recipients. For example, in Timed Rebeca, messages are delivered respecting the order of their time-tags while in Rebeca the order of sending (in one actor) determines the order of transfer. The decision point at the composition level shows in which order actors are executed.

By building our semantic rules on the foundation of Transparent Actor template rules, we can explicitly clarify the relation between the privacy feature of a language and the identified decision points.

2.3   Social Network Semantic Model

Our semantic model is based on the policy-aware epistemic framework for social network (Social Network Semantic Model - SNSM) proposed in [14]. The framework is based on the annotated labelled transition system (ALTS) [4] which is an extension of labelled transition systems. ALTS is a combination of a transitions system and a Kripke structure [5] capturing the operational and epistemic aspects of systems respectively. Agents construct a set of conceptual relations during their interactions in social networks, conceived as a *social graph*. These relations affects on their following interactions based on their privacy policies captured within the labels of SNSM.

Definition 1 (Social Graph). *A social graph is a pair $(ID, r_1, ..., r_n)$, where ID represents the set of agent identifiers, and each relation $r_i \subseteq ID \times ID$ represents a set of pairs of identifiers, i.e., edges. The set of all social graphs is denoted by SG.*

To show the propagation of information using a particular type of relation, we define a projection operator on social graphs.

Definition 2 (Projection Function). *Given $sg = (ID, r_1, \ldots, r_n)$, its projection onto the relation r_x, denoted by $sg \downarrow r_x : ID \to P(ID)$, is a function where for all $, j \in ID, j \in sg \downarrow r_x(i)$ if and only if $(i, j) \in r_x$.*

To provide an intuition, consider two types of relationships Follow and Block among users on *Instagram*. The social graph on this network can be modeled as *Instagram* $= (ID, followers, followings, block)$, where the *followers* relation defines which agents follow an agent, *followings* defines which agents an agent follow and the *block* relation denotes which agents are blocked by the agents. The followers of the agent $Bob \in ID$ are thus denoted by *Instagram* $\downarrow followers(Bob)$.

We use actions to model interactions between users and evaluation of social networks, i.e., the operational behavior of systems. These actions can be decorated with renaming functions indicating what each user can see and know, i.e. the information released to each user.

Definition 3 (Decorated Action). *Consider two sets, A and C, which represent actions and contexts, respectively. A decorated action [14] $d \in DAct$ is defined as a pair(a, f) where $a \in A$ is an atomic action and $f : A \times C \to A$ is a renaming function that maps each combination of an action and a context to a potentially different action. The context identifies various factors influencing the visibility of actions and data. We consider the context as $C = ID \times SG$ for social networks.*

We consider a specific action $\tau \in A$ in our semantics as an unobservable action. It is used to model information hiding, meaning that nothing can be observed or perceived by other agents. The privacy policies of an agents describe how the activities of an agent can be observed by others. We use the renaming functions to specify the privacy policies.

Definition 4 (Privacy Policies). *In our semantic model, the renaming function is defined as $DAct \times (ID \times SG) \to DAct$.*

For our *Instagram* social network in Example 1, an agent Alice would like to specify that only her followers can see her messages. We can model it as a function f such that for all $i \in Instagram \downarrow Follow(Alice)$, $f(msg, i, Instagram) = msg$ while $f(msg, i, Instagram) = \tau$ when $i \notin Instagram \downarrow Follow(Alice)$. The latter means that those who are not Alice's followers cannot see her messages or even notice that anything has occurred at all.

Definition 5 (Social Network Semantic Model (SNSM). [14]) *A SNSM is defined as a quadruple $\langle Conf, \to, Ind, conf_0 \rangle$, where:*

- *$Conf \subseteq SG \times S \times DAct^*$ is the set of configurations (sg, s, π), each consisting of:*
  - *$sg \in SG$, the social graph,*
  - *$s \in S = \coprod_{n \leq N} S_n$ represents the local states of all agents, where S is the set of local states for each agent, and N is the maximum number of agents in the specification (which may vary across different configurations).*
  - *$\pi \subseteq DAct^*$ represents the history of decorated actions.*
- *$\to \subseteq Conf \times DAct \times Conf$ is the transition relation.*
- *$Ind \subseteq Conf \times ID \times Conf$ is the indistinguishability relation.*
- *$Conf_0$ is the initial configuration.*

Indistinguishability relations capture agents' uncertainty and enable epistemic reasoning about past actions. These relations are established between states that the agent cannot distinguish based on its knowledge. These relations can be formally constructed automatically using the rules provided in [14] and will be described next.

Definition 6 (Indistinguishability Relations [14]). *The indistinguishability relation* $\cdots \subseteq DAct^* \times ID \times DAct^*$ *is the smallest relation defined by the following deduction rules. We let* $h \overset{i}{\cdots} h'$ *to denote* $(h, i, h') \in \cdots$, *where* $i \in ID$.

$$(\epsilon)\frac{}{\epsilon \overset{i}{\cdots} \epsilon} \qquad (\textbf{match})\frac{h \overset{i}{\cdots} h' \quad f(a, i, sg) = f'(b, i, sg)}{h \frown (a, f) \overset{i}{\cdots} h' \frown (b, f')}$$

$$(\textbf{hid0})\frac{h \overset{i}{\cdots} h' \quad f(a, i, sg) = \tau}{h \frown (a, f) \overset{i}{\cdots} h'} \qquad (\textbf{hid1})\frac{h \overset{i}{\cdots} h' \quad f(a, i, sg) = \tau}{h \overset{i}{\cdots} h' \frown (\tau, f)}$$

The rule (ϵ) is self-explanatory. For deduction rule (match), assume that an agent i is on a run of the protocol (i.e., h) that is indistinguishable from an alternative run (i.e., h') from the original up to the current state. Consider that the agent i observes $f(a, i, sg)$, and the indistinguishable run also ends with the same observable action (i.e., $f'(b, i, sg)$), then she remains uncertain about her state in the social network. This implicitly assumes that the observing agent has the set of all plausible local privacy policies for each action in her local knowledge [14].

Additionally, the rule (match) preserves ignorance meaning that if an agent u is uncertain whether she is in state s_1 or s_2, and an action a is possible from both s_1 and s_2, leading to states s_1' and s_2', respectively, the uncertainty will persist between the new states s_1' and s_2' for the agent u. The deduction rules (hid0) and (hid1) state that if an action a is hidden from an agent (i.e., it appears as τ), the agent should not notice anything when a occurs. In most social networks, applying privacy policies means hiding a message or data from unintended audiences. However, there are cases (e.g. an extension of Diaspora for photo sharing [17]) where agents may need to modify certain information. In such cases, the deduction rule (match) is used.

Note that it is proved that the indistinguishability relations created using Definition 6 satisfy S5 knowledge properties, meaning that they are reflexive, symmetric and transitive [14].

3   PrivateRebeca: Privacy-Aware Actor Language Based on Rebeca

We introduce PRIVATEREBECA as an extension of Rebeca, inheriting the core features of actor-based languages. The communication takes place through asynchronous message passing, and the computation is message-driven (messages trigger message handler activation). We consider non-preemptive execution of message servers (like most actor-based languages); meaning that an actor cannot handle another message unless it completes the handling of its previous message.

3.1 PrivateRebeca The Syntax

Our syntax is an extension of the Rebeca syntax, specifically tailored for privacy policies. It enhances Rebeca by utilizing keywords that modify the visibility and flow of messages, allowing for more granular control over access and information flow. This visibility/flow control is crucial for conducting epistemic analysis, such as evaluating information leakage within networks. This extension enables the specification of privacy requirements within the syntax of Rebeca to ensure that sensitive information is handled according to the defined policies. By this approach, we enforce privacy policies. The syntax of PRIVATEREBECA is given in Fig. 1. We have highlighted the extended syntax to core Rebeca in blue.

$$\text{Model} ::= \langle\text{Class}\rangle^+ \text{ Main}$$

$$\text{Main} ::= \text{main } \{\langle\text{C r}(\langle\text{const}\rangle^*);\rangle^+\}$$

$$\text{Class} ::= \text{reactiveclass C } \{\text{Vars Method}^+\}$$

$$\text{Vars} ::= \{\text{statevars } \langle\text{T v;}\rangle^*\}$$

$$\text{Method} ::= \text{@senders(Rebecset) @observations(pred) msgsrv name } \{\text{Stmt}^*\text{end}\}$$

$$\text{Rebecset} ::= \text{public(Rebecset, Rebecset) | private(Rebecset, Rebecset) | } r \text{ | null}$$

$$\text{Stmt} ::= \text{v} = expr; \text{ | } v =?(expr_1, expr_2); \text{ | r.name @observers(Rebecset); |}$$

$$\text{if}(expr|\phi) \text{ }\{\text{Stmt}^+\} \text{ else } \{\text{Stmt}^+\} \text{ | for(T v in v)}\{\text{Stmt}^+\} \text{ | skip;}$$

$$\phi ::= \top \text{ | } Y \text{ | } \phi \wedge \phi \text{ | } \neg\phi \text{ | } \langle\!\langle\overline{pred}\rangle\!\rangle\phi \text{ | } K_r\phi \text{ | } \nu Y.\phi(Y)$$

Identifiers C, T, *name*, v, *const*, *expr*, r, ϕ, and *pred* resp. denote class, type, message server name, variable, constant, expressions, rebec id, epistemic formula, and predicate. $\langle\ \rangle$ denotes meta parenthesis, $+$ and $*$ denote resp. one or more and zero or more repetitions.

Fig. 1. PRIVATEREBECA Syntax. (Color figure online)

A model is defined by a set of Rebeca classes and a main block. Each Rebeca class is declared by keyword reactiveclass. We define the state variables of a class by using statevars. We treat the names of rebecs as their identifiers in PRIVATEREBECA, and in contrast to Rebeca, we do not define the rebecs to whom it can send a message by using knownrebecs. Rebecs maintain this set locally as their state variables which can be updated dynamically based on their relations like *Follow*. The message servers are defined by msgsrv annotated by the policy of the actor on the receive action. The policy @senders(rs) denotes the set of rebec identifiers rs that can be the sender of the message (from whom the rebec instances of the class would like to receive the message). The body of message servers is specified by a list of statements: assignment, non-deterministic assignment, conditional, send, for and skip. Execution of a send statement r.name@observers(rs) expresses that a message corresponding to name is sent to the rebec r with the policy @observers(rs) (on the send action).

The policy denotes the actors that can observe the send action. For each message server, we also use the annotation @observation(p) to express the knowledge constructed in a rebec (as a predicate p) upon observation of a message for which its server is declared. If nothing is specified, it means the default value is the name of the message without parameters.

We use privacy functions public and private with two parameters of $\mathcal{P}(ID)$, to identify a set of rebec identifiers. The function public(rs_1, rs_2) returns $rs_1 \setminus rs_2$ while private(rs_1, rs_2) returns $rs_1 \cup rs_2$. By composing these two functions, the admissible observers for each action can be defined. Based on this set, the privacy policies as renaming functions can be derived.

```
1   reactiveclass InstagramInfo
2   {
3     statevars {List<ID> users;}
4     InstagramInfo(List<ID> u){
5       users = u;
6     }

8     @senders(public(ID,null))
9     msgsrv search(){
10      sender.getUsers(users)
11      @observers(sender);
12    }

14    @senders(public(ID,null))
15    msgsrv postStory(string s){}
16  }
17  reactiveclass InstagramUser
18  {
19    statevars {
20      string name;
21      InstagramInfo center;
22      List<InstagramUser>
23        followers, followings, block;}

25    InstagramUser(ID c,string na){
26      name = na;center=c;
27      center.search()
28      @observers(center);
29      //@observers(null);
30      //@observers(private(center,self))
31    }

33    @senders(center)
34    msgsrv getUsers(List<ID> ids){
35      for(ID i in ids){
36        i.FollowRequest()
37        @observers(null);}
```

```
38    }

40    @senders(public(ID,block))
41    msgsrv FollowRequest(){
42      int flag = ?(0,1);
43      if (flag){
44        sender.accept()
45        @observers(public(followers,block))
46        followers.add(sender);
47        self.postStory(self)
48        @observers(null); }
49      else{
50        block.add(sender);}
51    }

53    @senders(public(ID,block))
54    @observations(story(id))
55    msgsrv postStory(ID id){
56      for (ID i in followings){
57        if (K_self(《story(i)》T))
58        {center.postStory(i)
59        @observers(public(followers,block));}}
60    }

62    @senders(public(ID,block))
63    msgsrv accept(){
64      followings.add(sender);
65    }
66  }

68  main(){
69    InstagramInfo c () :([Ali,Emy,Bob]);
70    InstagramUser Ali (c,"Gamer");
71    InstagramUser Emy (c,"");
72    InstagramUser Bob (c,"Fox");
73  }
```

Fig. 2. Specification of users on Instagram

Rebecs construct knowledge upon observing send actions within the system. The knowledge may affect the behavior of the rebec. We extend the conditional statement in Rebeca with conditions on the knowledge of the rebec using the epistemic logic on past observations. In the main block, the instances of the reactive classes are created by initializing the actual values of the constructor parameters.

Example 2 Consider the social network *Instagram* from Example 1 in which users communicate through sending messages such as follow requests, posting stories and accepting requests. We specify the user behaviors of Instagram in Fig. 2.

We have two reactive classes InstagramInfo which has a list of users and handles search requests and InstagramUser that represents individual users. The profile of each user is modeled by the state variables like a name (user's unique username), and the lists of followers, followings, and block. Each user (rebec) of InstagramUser can interact with other users through e.g. follow requests, posting stories and accepting requests (Followrequest, postStory and accept message servers, respectively). In the constructor (lines 25–31), each user will send a message to the rebec center of InstagramInfo to search other users (line 27); the observers of the search message is only center (line 28). We can equivalently either indicate that the observer is null or private(center,self) (lines 29, 30) as the sender and receiver are added by default to the observers (see the rule SEND in Table 2). In response, the center will provide the list of users by sending back a message getUser by setting the observers to sender (meaning that it is a private message and only the sender of the search request can see it (lines 10–11)). In the getUsers message server, the user will send to all users a follow request (FollowRequest) privately (line 36). In reply to a follow request, a user will accept it (line 44) non-deterministically using the non-deterministic assignment (line 42) and will add it to the list of her followers (in FollowRequest message server) (line 46) and sends a story privately to itself (line 47–48). The user may non-deterministically block the sender of the follow request (line 50).

The user also publishes another story upon handling a postStory message to the rebec center. A user posts any observed story that it knows from its followings (lines $56 - 60$). The conditional statement in line 57 reasons on the knowledge of the user by the epistemic formula $K_{self}(\langle\!\langle\overline{story(i)}\rangle\!\rangle\top^{\urcorner})$ meaning that whether the rebec itself knows that in past a story with an identifier i of its followings has been published. The annotation at line 54 indicates that upon observing a message with the name $postStory(id)$ by a sender, it perceives the predicate $story(id)$.

Each message server has a @senders annotation. For instance, this annotation before FollowRequest indicates that a user can receive a follow request from any user in the network except those that it has blocked (line 40).

3.2 PrivateRebeca Semantics

We define the semantics of PRIVATEREBECA in terms of a SNSM $\langle Conf, \rightarrow$, $Ind, conf_0\rangle$ by providing the operational semantic rules following the approach of Transparent Actor at three levels: actor, network, and composition, and the rules for the indistinguishability relations revised for our framework based on the ones provided in Sect. 2. The set of configurations $Conf = ID \rightarrow LocalSt \times NetLocal \times DAct^*$ are defined as the composition of the local states of rebecs, the local state of the abstract network, and the history of decorated actions. Let Msg denote the set of communicated messages defined as a triple of the sender identifier, the message name, and the receiver identifier. For simplicity, we assume that messages have no parameter. We use the dot notation to access elements of a message tuple. We assume that $m.sndr$ specifies the sender identifier while $m.name$ denotes the message name. The set of decorated actions is defined as $DAct = \{(m, f), (\tau, f_\tau) \mid m \in Msg\}$ where the renaming function $f : A \times ID \rightarrow A$ and $A = \{m, \tau \mid m \in Msg\}$. The action τ denotes an internal action, and m shows sending the message m. The specific renaming function f_τ is an identify function meaning that $\forall_{i \in ID, a \in A} f_\tau(a, i) = a$. The social graph counterpart of each configuration (c.f. Definition 5) is derivable from the local states of rebecs as we will discuss later. The transition relation $\rightarrow \subseteq Conf \times DAct \times Conf$ over the configurations is defined by the transition relation rules given at the composition level. These transitions are defined based on transitions over the local states of rebecs and the abstract network. The transition relation rules over local states of rebecs, abstract network, and composition, are depicted in Table 1.

Transition Relation Rules of the Actor Level. Assume Var is the set of variable identifiers and $Value$ is the set of possible values for variable identifiers. We define a valuation function (environment) as $Env : Var \rightarrow Value$. Let $domain(e)$ denote the domain variables of the environment e and $e[x \mapsto y]$ denote updating e with the mapping x to y. We use the type $Buffer$ to address the rebec message queue and network buffer with FIFO policy in the semantics. We assume the buffers are unbounded, but in practice they are bounded in the model checker tools like Afra [10]. We consider a set of operations on the type $Buffer$: $insert$, $remove$, $include$, and $size$.

We define the transition relation of rebecs as $\longrightarrow\!\!\!\!\!\rhd \subseteq LocalSt \times \Phi \times DAct \times LocalSt$ where $LocalSt \subseteq Env \times Buffer \times Stmt^*$ is the set of local states of rebecs, $DAct = \{(\tau, f_\tau)\} \cup \{(m!, f), (m?, f_\tau) \mid m \in Msg\}$ that $m!$ and $m?$ denote the sending and receipt of the message m, and Φ is the set of epistemic logic formulae. The transitions at this level are restricted to an epistemic conditions on the knowledge of a rebec. The local state of a rebec is defined by the triple (e, b, π) where $e \in Env$ is a valuation function with the domain of state variables, and the special variable $self$ that shows the identifier of the rebec, $b \in Buffer$ is the rebec queue, and $\pi \in Stmt^*$ is the remaining statements from a message server that should be executed. Empty sequence, denoted by ϵ, shows that a rebec is not executing any message server.

The rule RECEIVE I specifies that a rebec can always receive the message $m \in Msg$ if it is allowed to receive messages with the name $m.name$ from the sender $m.sndr$ as defined by the policy on the receive action using the annotation @senders. We assume that these policies for the message names of a reactive class are integrated into the function $sndrPolicy$ such that $sndrPolicy(m.name) = fn$, where the message server $m.name$ is annotated by @senders(fn). The expression

Table 1. Operational Semantics of PRIVATEREBECA; $\alpha = \{(m!, f) \mid m \in Msg\} \cup \{(\tau, f_\tau)\}$ for some f and $\beta = \alpha \cup \{(m?, f_\tau) \mid m \in Msg\}$.

Actor	(STMTEXEC)	$\dfrac{e, \pi \xrightarrow{\phi:\alpha} e', \pi'}{(e, b, \pi) \xrightarrow{\phi:\alpha} (e', b, \pi')}$
	(TAKE)	$\dfrac{m = head(b)}{(e, b, \epsilon) \xrightarrow{\top:(\tau, f_\tau)} (e, remove(b, m), MsgSrv(m.name))}$
	(RECEIVE I)	$\dfrac{m.sndr \in eval(sndrPolicy(m.name), e)}{(e, b, \pi) \xrightarrow{\top:(m?, f_\tau)} (e, insert(b, m), \pi)}$
	(RECEIVE II)	$\dfrac{m.sndr \notin eval(sndrPolicy(m.name), e)}{(e, b, \pi) \xrightarrow{\top:(m?, f_\tau)} (e, b, \pi)}$
Network	(RECEIVE)	$b \xrightarrow{m?} insert(b, m)$
	(TRANSFER)	$\dfrac{include(b, m) \quad \exists x \in ID \cdot m = head(getBuff(b, x))}{b \xrightarrow{m!} remove(b, m)}$
Composition	(ACTORPROG)	$\dfrac{(s, n, h) \models \phi \quad s(x) \xrightarrow{\phi:\beta} (e', b', \pi')}{(s, n, h) \xrightarrow{\beta} (s[x \mapsto (e', b', \pi')], n, h \frown \beta)}$
	(COMM I)	$\dfrac{s(x) \xrightarrow{\top:(m!, f)} (e', b', \pi') \quad n \xrightarrow{m?} n'}{(s, n, h) \xrightarrow{(m, f)} (s[x \mapsto (e', b', \pi')], n', h \frown (m, f))}$
	(COMM II)	$\dfrac{n \xrightarrow{m!} n' \quad y \in m.rcv \quad s(y) \xrightarrow{\top:(m?, f_\tau)} (e', b', \pi')}{(s, n, h) \xrightarrow{(\tau, f_\tau)} (s[y \mapsto (e', b', \pi')], n', h \frown (\tau, f_\tau))}$

$eval(fn, e)$ computes fn using the evaluation e:

$$eval(\mathsf{null}, e) = \emptyset$$
$$eval(r, e) = \{e(r)\}$$
$$eval(\mathsf{public}(fn_1, fn_2), e) = eval(fn_1, e) \setminus eval(fn_2, e)$$
$$eval(\mathsf{private}(fn_1, fn_2), e) = eval(fn_1, e) \cup eval(fn_2, e)$$

The rule RECEIVE II expresses that a rebec cannot receive a message m from a sender that it is not allowed to receive from (as the message is not inserted into the rebec queue).

According to the rule TAKE, a rebec can take a message from the head of its queue when it is not busy handling any other messages, i.e., when it has no remaining statement to execute (ϵ). The rebec handles the taken message by executing the statements of its corresponding message server $MsgSrv(m.name)$. As a result of the *take*, the content of b is updated by calling $remove(b, m)$.

The rule STMTEXEC shows how the local state of a rebec changes upon execution of a statement. This change is defined by the semantics of the statement with no effect on the rebec queue. The semantics of the statements are given by the relation $\hookrightarrow$, as shown in Table 2. The function $eval(expr, e)$ used in the rule ASSIGN, evaluates the given $expr$ based on the rebec environment e. We denote the successful termination of a single statement by $\top$. Rebecs construct knowledge upon observing send actions. The observing rebecs are defined through the @observers(fn) annotation placed after the send statements. Rule SEND uses the function $eval(fn, e)$ to compute the observing set fn specified by the composition of public and private functions, based on the rebec environment e. The rule defines the appropriate renaming function f such that the send message action is only observable to those rebecs specified by fn, the sender, and the receiver. The rules CONDE I and CONDE II transfers the conditions on the knowledge of the rebec from the statement on the transitions as these conditions can only be evaluated with respect to the current configuration of the system. The semantic rules of non-deterministic assignment and for statement are straightforward and not given for brevity.

Transition Relation Rules of the Abstract Network Level. We define the transition relation of the abstract network by $\longrightarrow \subseteq NetLocal \times Act \times NetLocal$ where $NetLocal = Buffer$ is the set of network local states and $Act = \{m!, m? \mid m \in Msg\}$. For brevity, we use "network" instead of "abstract network". We assume that the network buffer has the function $getBuff(b, x)$ which returns a buffer of the pending messages in the network buffer b with the rebec x as their sender. The order of sending is preserved in this buffer. So, the function $head(getBuff(b, x))$ returns the first pending message sent by x.

The network-level transition relation rules are shown in Table 1. The rule RECEIVE specifies that the network can always receive a message. The rule TRANSFER defines that the network dispatches the buffered messages to their recipients. This rule transfer messages with the transfer policy of FIFO order for each sender who has at least one pending message in the network buffer. The selection among those senders is nondeterministic.

Transition Relation Rules of the Composition. We define the transition relation for the composition level by $\rightarrow \subseteq Conf \times DAct \times Conf$ where $Conf = ID \rightarrow LocalSt \times NetLocal \times DAct^*$ is the set of configurations. A configuration is (s, n, h) where $s : ID \rightarrow LocalSt$ is a mapping from actor identifiers to their local states, $n \in NetLocal$ is the network local state, and $h \in DAct^*$ is the history of decorated actions. The rules at this level define the semantics of (1) communication between rebecs and network, (2) progress of rebecs, given in Table 1. A rebec locally evolves when either it takes a message from its buffer or it executes the statements of a message server as indicated by the rule ACTOR-PROG. Executing a send statement results in communication from the sending rebec to the network (rule COMM I), and then from the network to the receiving actor (rule COMM II).

Table 2. Operational Semantics of PRIVATEREBECA statements: $\alpha = \{(m!, f) \mid m \in Msg\} \cup \{(\tau, f_\tau)\}$ for some f.

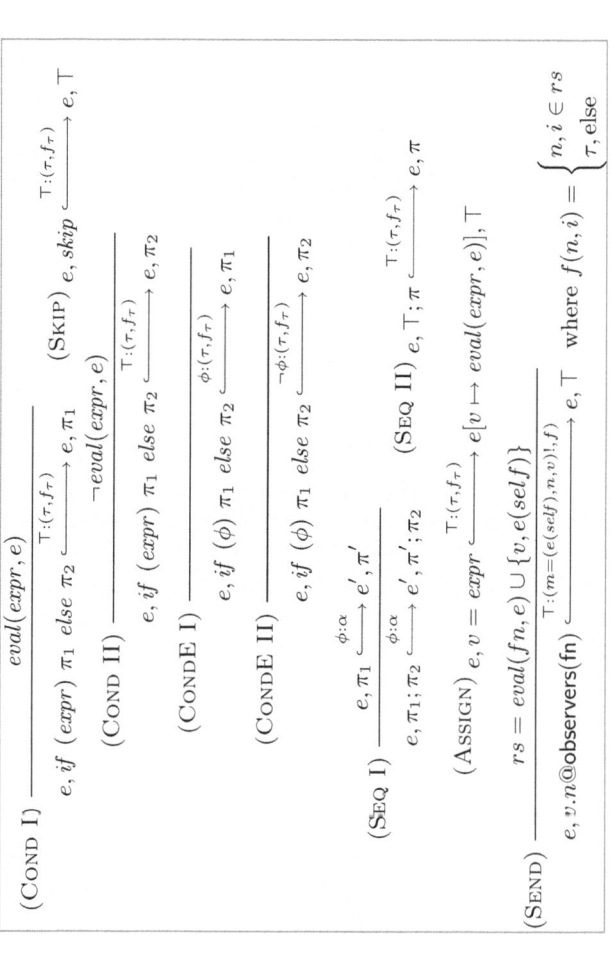

Initial Configuration. The initial configuration is achieved by initializing the state variables of rebecs to their default values, e.g., variables of type List are set to empty, and then executing the statements of constructors of rebecs in the order instantiated in the main block.

Discussion. We show the mapping between the configurations of PRIVATEREBECA's semantics and the configuration defined by Definition 5 and discuss the context of decorated actions in our semantics in comparison with Definition 3. The social graph counterpart of each configuration in PRIVATEREBECA's semantics is derivable from the local states of rebecs. In other words, (s, n, h) can be conceived as the triples (sg, s', h) which is consistent to the definition of configuration in Definition 5. Assume the social graph is defined as $sg = (ID, r_x, r_y, \ldots)$, where the variables x and y as a list of IDs are defined in the local states of the rebecs. These variables specify the social graph relations like r_x and r_y (e.g., followers) that are partially known to a rebec and are used to define the privacy policies. Formally, $sg \downarrow r_x(i) = e(x)$ where $s(i) = (e, b, \pi)$.

The context in the renaming function of decorated actions in Definition 3 is a pair of an identifier and the social graph. As the privacy policies are specified with respect to the local variables of rebecs (which induce the relations of social graph), the context at the level of semantics of PRIVATEREBECA is simpler.

By using the semantic template rules of Transparent Actor, we can explicitly show the connection between the new feature of the extended language to the identified decision points at the framework; the policies on send actions affect the semantics of send statement. Policies on receive actions relates to the decision point for receiving at the actor level. The only decision point identified for the rule ACTORPROG is how actors are scheduled. In Rebeca, rebecs are executed non-deterministically, so no constraint to enforce any order among the rebecs is needed. Transparent Actor assumes that actors can execute their statements locally. But for executing conditional statements on knowledge, such statements cannot be executed without considering the history of rebec on observed messages. This rule deviates from the ones given in Transparent Actor.

Indistinguishability Relation. We revise the indistinguishability relation $\cdots \subseteq DAct^* \times ID \times DAct^*$ in our framework as our renaming function is simpler due to the simpler context. We let $h \overset{i}{\cdots} h'$ to denote $(h, i, h') \in \cdots$, where $i \in ID$.

$$(\epsilon)\frac{}{\epsilon \overset{i}{\cdots} \epsilon} \qquad (\textbf{match})\frac{h \overset{i}{\cdots} h' \quad f(m, i) = f'(m', i)}{h \frown (m, f) \overset{i}{\cdots} h' \frown (m', f')}$$

$$(\textbf{hid0})\frac{h \overset{i}{\cdots} h' \quad f(m, i) = \tau}{h \frown (m, f) \overset{i}{\cdots} h'} \qquad (\textbf{hid1})\frac{h \overset{i}{\cdots} h'}{h \overset{i}{\cdots} h' \frown (\tau, f_\tau)}$$

Example 3. A part of the semantics model of Fig. 2 from Example 2 is depicted in Fig. 3. We use the abbreviations a, b, c, e, n in the figure to denote Ali, Bob, c (center), Emy, and network, respectively. The initial configuration c_0 denotes that there are three messages in the queue of rebec c, and others are empty (not shown in the figure). Rebec c takes the first message, i.e., search from its queue resulted by application of rules ACTORPROG and TAKE. There is a self-loop indistinguishability relation in c_0 induced by the rule (ϵ). As the take action is also not observable to any rebec, by the rule (**hid1**), still the configurations c_0 and c_1 are indistinguishable. In c_1, rebec c sends a message getUsers to Ali induced by rule COMM I. This send message action is observable to both Ali and c, but not Bob and Emy. So the configurations c_1 and c_2 are still indistinguishable by Emy and Bob, resulted by the rule (**hid1**). Due to the transitivity property of indistinguishability relation, c_0 and c_2 are also indistinguishable by Emy and Bob. In c_2, there is a non-deterministic choice between network and c to take a message from their queue. Note that as the indistinguishability relations are reflexive, we have a self-loop at each configuration which is omitted in Fig. 3.

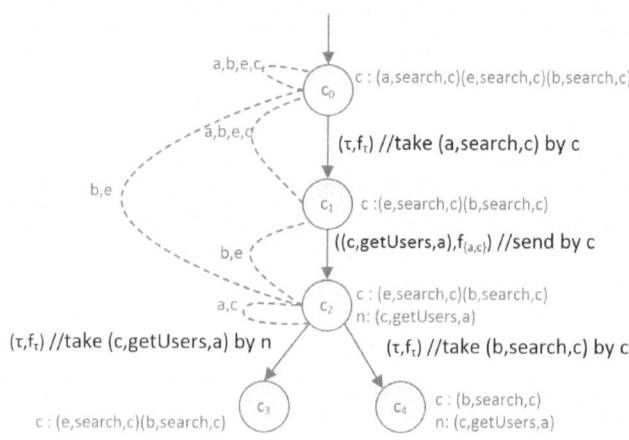

Fig. 3. Partial semantic model of Fig. 2. Indistinguishability relations are shown in blue. Abbreviations a, b, c, e, n denote Ali, Bob, c (center), Emy, and network, respectively. The state variables and empty buffers are not shown in the configurations.

4   Analysis of Social Network

We employ the logical framework, introduced in [13] with a minor modification. The framework combines model μ-calculus with past and epistemic logic (of knowledge). The grammar of logical formulae is given below. Assume the set of atomic proposition $\mathcal{A}$, ranged over by a, is defined based on the predicates on messages (specified by the annotation @observation(pred) before the message server m): $\mathcal{A} = \{pred(m) \mid m \in Msg\}$.

$$\phi \ ::= \ \top \ \mid \ Y \ \mid \ \phi \wedge \phi \ \mid \ \neg\phi \ \mid \ \langle\!\langle a \rangle\!\rangle \phi \ \mid \ \langle\!\langle \overline{a} \rangle\!\rangle \phi \ \mid \ K_i \phi \ \mid \ \nu Y.\phi(Y)$$

In the above-given grammar, logical connectives have their traditional intuitive meanings; Y stands for the class of recursive variables; $\langle\!\langle a \rangle\!\rangle \phi$, means that it is possible to perform an observable a-transition preceded/proceeded by some unobservable actions, after which the formula ϕ holds, we call such a sequence, an observable a-trace; $\langle\!\langle \overline{a} \rangle\!\rangle \phi$, means that in the immediate past an a-trace has taken place, before which the formula ϕ holds; $K_i \phi$ means that principal i knows that ϕ holds and $\nu Y.\phi(Y)$ denotes the maximal fixed point of the equation $Y = \phi(Y)$, where Y should occur positively in ϕ meaning that every free occurrence of Y in ϕ is under an even number of negations [26]. This restriction guarantees the existence of a fixed point. The well-known operators $[\![a]\!]$, $\vee$, and the minimal fixed point μY which are the dual operators of $\langle\!\langle a \rangle\!\rangle$, $\wedge$, and νY, respectively can be defined easily. The operator $\phi^{\dashv}$ meaning that ϕ held somewhere in the past can be defined as $\mu Y.\phi \vee (\bigvee_{a \in A} \langle\!\langle \overline{a} \rangle\!\rangle Y)$ [15].

The semantics of epistemic logic is interpreted with respect to the SNSM $\langle Conf, \rightarrow, Ind, conf_0 \rangle$ derived from a PRIVATEREBECA model. Let $\xrightarrow{\tau}^{*}$ be the reflexive transitive closure of $\xrightarrow{(\tau, f_\tau)}$ transitions, and $\overset{a}{\Rightarrow}$ denote an a-transition, preceded or proceeded by a set of τ-transitions, i.e., $\xrightarrow{\tau}^{*} \xrightarrow{a} \xrightarrow{\tau}^{*}$. We call $\overset{a}{\Rightarrow}$ an a-labeled weak transition. The semantic definitions for various constructs of our logic are given below.

We define the semantics of the logic by using the function $[\![\phi]\!]_\rho \subseteq Conf$, where the environment ρ maps the free variables of ϕ to a subset of $Conf$. Thus, $c \models \psi$ iff $c \in [\![\psi]\!]_\rho$ for all ρ.

$$[\![\top]\!]_\rho = Conf$$
$$[\![\phi_1 \wedge \phi_2]\!]_\rho = [\![\phi_1]\!]_\rho \cap [\![\phi_2]\!]_\rho$$
$$[\![\neg\phi]\!]_\rho = \mathcal{S} \setminus [\![\phi]\!]_\rho$$
$$[\![\langle\!\langle a \rangle\!\rangle \phi]\!]_\rho = \{c' \in Conf \mid \exists m \exists c' \cdot a = pred(m) \wedge c \xrightarrow{(m,f)} c' \wedge c' \in [\![\phi]\!]_\rho\}$$
$$[\![\langle\!\langle \overline{a} \rangle\!\rangle \phi]\!]_\rho = \{c' \in Conf \mid \exists m \exists c' \cdot a = pred(m) \wedge c' \xrightarrow{(m,f)} c \wedge c' \in [\![\phi]\!]_\rho\}$$
$$[\![K_i \phi]\!]_\rho = \{c \in Conf \mid \forall c' \in Conf \cdot c \overset{i}{\cdots} c' \in Ind \Rightarrow c' \in [\![\phi]\!]_\rho\}$$
$$[\![X]\!]_\rho = \rho(X)$$
$$[\![\nu X.\phi(X)]\!]_\rho = \bigcup\{C' \subseteq Conf \mid C' \subseteq [\![\phi(X)]\!]_{\rho[X \mapsto C']}\}$$

Example 4. Consider the configuration c_i reachable after that Ali, Emy, and Bob handled their getUsers messages and their consequence FollowRequest messages such that Emy has rejected all follow requests ($block = \{Ali, Bob\}$), Ali has accepted Bob but rejected Emy ($block = \{Emy\}, followers = \{Bob\}$)), and Bob has only rejected Ali ($block = \{Ali\}, followers = \{Emy\}$)). Assume that c_i and c_j are indistinguishable by Emy where the local states of rebes and network for the configuration c_i and c_j are the same. Upon accepting a follow request, rebecs send a postStory to themselves which is not observable to any one (see line 47–48 in Fig. 2). As Bob and Ali have accepted a follow request, they both have a postStory message in their queues in configuration c_i (abbreviated by PS).

A possible execution from c_i is shown in Fig. 4. As we aim to reason on the knowledge of Emy, only the distinguishability relation of Emy is shown. First Ali takes its postStory message from its queue (leading to c_1), and executes the for-loop and conditional statements at lines 56–57 (reaching to c_2"). As the only observable story to Ali was his own previous story as the consequence of accepting a follow request, it will send a story with content of its identifier to center (leading to c_3). We assume that the identifier of Ali is 1. This story is observable to both Ali and Bob. Then, Bob handles its postStory assuming that the identifier of Bob is 2 (reaching to c_4) and executes the for-loop and conditional statements (reaching to c_5). As Bob has previously observed the story of Ali, the condition $K_2(\langle\!\langle \overline{story(1)} \rangle\!\rangle \top^{\neg})$ is satisfied in c_5. So, Bob can send a story with the content of Ali's identifier to center which is observable to Emy (reaching to c_6). All actions except the last one are not observable to Emy. By application of (**hid0**) and (**hid1**), the relation of between c_i and c_j is preserved in the following configurations $c_1 - c_5$. Similarly, the configurations c_i, c_j and $c_1 - c_5$ are all indistinguishable by Emy (transitivity property). For brevity, we depict only some of them. As the story of Bob is visible to Emy, c_6 is not related to c_j. Based on the semantics of knowledge operator, $K_3(\langle\!\langle \overline{story(1)} \rangle\!\rangle \top^{\neg})$ holds in c_6 , where the identifier of Emy is 3, as c_6 satisfies $\langle\!\langle \overline{story(1)} \rangle\!\rangle \top$. In other words, there is a data disclosure on the story of Ali. We remark that in c_5, Bob can also story his own identifier.

5   Related Work

The use of epistemic logic to reason about knowledge and beliefs in multi-agent systems has a rich history, with seminal contributions by Fagin et al. [5]. Epistemic approaches argue about knowledge or belief of agents about the environment, themselves and other agents. So, they can take into account this knowledge in their decisions and interactions (having epistemic aspects in the operational part). Epistemic logic has been extensively explored in the context of privacy, with a vast body of work addressing various aspects of privacy reasoning. Among these, we can mention a recent contribution by Rajaona et al. [18] discussing key foundational concepts and introducing Phoebe, a proof-of-concept model checker designed to verify privacy properties in security protocols.

Privacy concerns in social networks have also been extensively studied, particularly in the context of data protection regulations such as GDPR [25]. However, a formal foundation for model checking of privacy compliance from a user perspective have received less attention. We can think of privacy policies as hiding information in social interactions. There are models that address information propagation in social networks using epistemic logic. In [19], authors propose

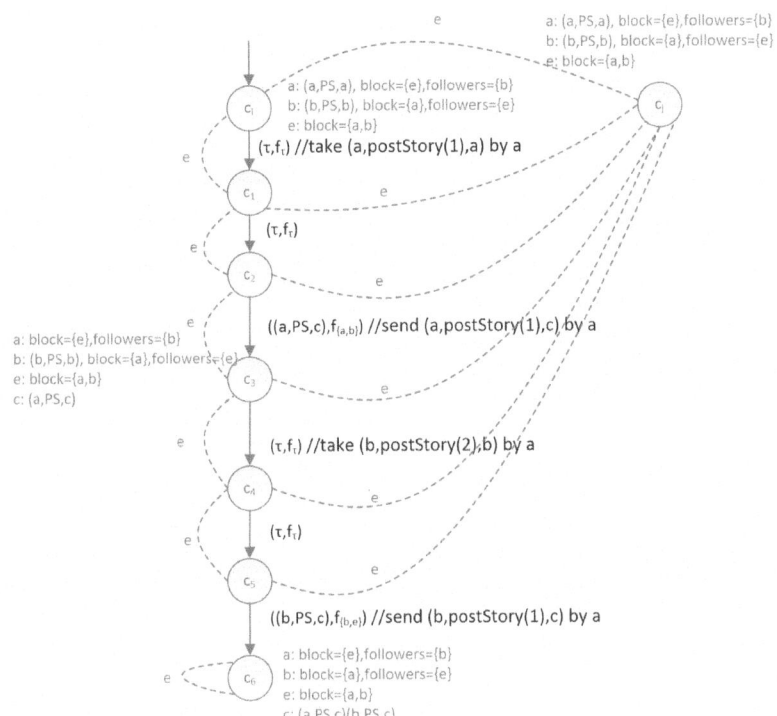

Fig. 4. Partial semantic model of Fig. 2 reachable after handling getUsers and FollowRequest messages. All indistinguishability relations are not shown. Abbreviations a, b, c, e, n denote Ali, Bob, c, Emy, and network, respectively.

Social Epistemic Model (SEM), which focuses on knowledge flow in social networks. It consists of a bipartite structure, with one part representing social relationships and the other part containing agents within an epistemic model. SEM utilizes dynamic epistemic semantics to depict social actions, communication channels, and knowledge propagation but does not address privacy policies and assumes the network structure is common knowledge. Dynamic Epistemic Friendship Logic (DEFL) [20] is another one which models the dynamics of knowledge and friendship on Facebook. DEFL enables reasoning about communication effects within symmetric social networks. Another work is Epistemic Threshold Model (ETM) [3] that capture the dynamics of threshold models (a model for information propagation) and the influence of agents' knowledge within the system. ETM allows for the modeling of both the network structure and agent behaviors, facilitating the exploration of various social relationships. However, the model does not account for the changing nature of network structures or incorporate privacy policies.

In [16], an epistemic framework is proposed for specifying and reasoning about privacy policies in social networks that is the only one that considered privacy as well. This framework uses a social network model (SNM) with a network structure and knowledge base for each agent, defining both local and global privacy policies. While it describes the social network's behavior from structural, epistemic, and privacy perspectives, policy changes require manual updates to the semantic rules.

We have provided privacy-aware extensions of actor-based models that build on: i) the policy-aware epistemic framework for social networks proposed in [14] that automatically generates and updates agents' knowledge, reasons about action sequences, and enforces local privacy policies via decorated actions, ii) the modular definition of semantic rules based on transparent actors [6], which clarifies communication and coordination policies in actor models, and iii) specify protocols based on users' knowledge in Rebeca inspired from [13,15] (considering epistemic aspects in the operational part and specification of the protocols).

6   Conclusion and Future Work

We extended the modeling language of Rebeca with three annotations to capture user's privacy policies in social networks. The first annotation observers, attached to the send statements, indicates the observers of a messages. This annotation is converted into a renaming functions which control the observability of messages, i.e., the flow of information. Rebec obtain new information upon observing the send actions within a social network. The second annotation senders, attached to message server declarations, is converted into a receive policy at the actor level which controls the receipt of a message. The third annotations is observation to express the knowledge constructed in a rebec as a predicate upon observation of a message. We also extended the conditional statement with epistemic formulae on the knowledge of the rebec to behave based on the perceived knowledge. We provided a set of semantic rules by using the Transparent Actor semantic template rules which induce the operational part of a SNSM from a given PRIVATERE-BECA model. This semantic model enables to verify the privacy properties as epistemic formulae. Using the template rules of Transparent Actor reveals the applicability of this semantic framework to address the new language feature of privacy specification. Furthermore, we can explicitly show that the connection between the new feature to the identified decision points at the framework; the policies on send action affect the semantics of send statement. Policies on receive actions relates to the decision point for receiving at the actor level. However, for extension with epistemic reasoning at the conditional statement, we identify a deviation at the composition level.

For future work, we plan to extend the Rebeca's tool to enhance its capabilities for information leakage analysis by model checking epistemic logic. We will also take into account Timed Rebeca [11,23] to perform temporal analysis. Additionally, we will provide a broader range of examples and conduct detailed analyses of real-world case studies. We do not have shared memory; for example, when a follow request is sent and accepted by the receiver, the sender's list of followings is not immediately updated. The shared information in social networks can also be modeled by extending the actor model with shared memory following the approach of [12]. Such an extension with the feature of shared memory is orthogonal with the feature of privacy which is the focus of this work. Considering the feature of shared memory is also among our future work. Finally, we plan to investigate similar properties for other distributed systems, such as opacity in multi-robot systems.

References

1. Most popular social networks worldwide as of April 2024, by number of monthly active users (2024). https://www.statista.com/statistics/272014/global-social-networks-ranked-by-number-of-users/. Accessed 26 Aug 2024
2. Agha, G.: Actors: A Model of Concurrent Computation in Distributed Systems. MIT Press, Cambridge (1986). https://doi.org/10.7551/mitpress/1086.001.0001
3. Baltag, A., Christoff, Z., Rendsvig, R.K., Smets, S.: Dynamic epistemic logics of diffusion and prediction in social networks. Stud. Log. **107**(3), 489–531 (2019). https://doi.org/10.1007/s11225-018-9804-x
4. Dechesne, F., Mousavi, M.R., Orzan, S.: Operational and epistemic approaches to protocol analysis: bridging the gap. In: Dershowitz, N., Voronkov, A. (eds.) LPAR 2007. LNCS (LNAI), vol. 4790, pp. 226–241. Springer, Heidelberg (2007). https://doi.org/10.1007/978-3-540-75560-9_18
5. Fagin, R., Halpern, J.Y., Moses, Y., Vardi, M.Y.: Reasoning About Knowledge. MIT Press, Cambridge (2003). https://dl.acm.org/doi/10.5555/995831
6. Ghassemi, F., Sirjani, M., Khamespanah, E., Mirani, M., Hojjat, H.: Transparent actor model. In: 11th IEEE/ACM International Conference on Formal Methods in Software Engineering, FormaliSE 2023, Melbourne, Australia, 14–15 May 2023, pp. 97–107. IEEE (2023). https://doi.org/10.1109/FORMALISE58978.2023.00018
7. Hewitt, C., Bishop, P., Steiger, R.: A universal modular actor formalism for artificial intelligence. In: Proceedings of the 3rd International Joint Conference on Artificial Intelligence, pp. 235–245. Morgan Kaufmann Publishers, Inc. (1973). http://ijcai.org/Proceedings/73/Papers/027B.pdf
8. Jafari, A., Khamespanah, E., Sirjani, M., Hermanns, H.: Performance analysis of distributed and asynchronous systems using probabilistic timed actors. Electron. Commun. Eur. Assoc. Softw. Sci. Technol. **70** (2014). https://doi.org/10.14279/TUJ.ECEASST.70.984
9. Jahandideh, I., Ghassemi, F., Sirjani, M.: Hybrid Rebeca: modeling and analyzing of cyber-physical systems. In: Chamberlain, R., Taha, W., Törngren, M. (eds.) CyPhy/WESE -2018. LNCS, vol. 11615, pp. 3–27. Springer, Cham (2019). https://doi.org/10.1007/978-3-030-23703-5_1
10. Khamespanah, E., Sirjani, M., Khosravi, R.: Afra: an eclipse-based tool with extensible architecture for modeling and model checking of Rebeca family models. In: Hojjat, H., Ábrahám, E. (eds.) FSEN 2023. LNCS, vol. 14155, pp. 72–87. Springer, Cham (2023). https://doi.org/10.1007/978-3-031-42441-0_6
11. Khamespanah, E., Sirjani, M., Sabahi-Kaviani, Z., Khosravi, R., Izadi, M.: Timed Rebeca schedulability and deadlock freedom analysis using bounded floating time transition system. Sci. Comput. Program. **98**, 184–204 (2015). https://doi.org/10.1016/j.scico.2014.07.005

12. Martin, B., Shapiro, M.: Shared memory for the actor model. In: COMPAS 2022 - Conférence francophone d'informatique en Parallélisme, Architecture et Système. Laboratoire Modélisation, Informatique et Système - de l'Université de Picardie Jules Verne, Amiens, France (2022). https://inria.hal.science/hal-04004775
13. Moezkarimi, Z., Ghassemi, F.: Efficient analysis of belief properties in process algebra. J. Log. Algebraic Methods Program. **141**, 101001 (2024). https://doi.org/10.1016/j.jlamp.2024.101001, https://www.sciencedirect.com/science/article/pii/S2352220824000555
14. Moezkarimi, Z., Ghassemi, F., Mousavi, M.R.: A policy-aware epistemic framework for social networks. J. Log. Comput. **32**(6), 1234–1271 (2022). https://doi.org/10.1093/logcom/exac025
15. Mousavi, M.R., Varshosaz, M.: Telling lies in process algebra. In: 2018 International Symposium on Theoretical Aspects of Software Engineering (TASE), pp. 116–123 (2018)
16. Pardo, R., Balliu, M., Schneider, G.: Formalising privacy policies in social networks. J. Log. Algebraic Methods Program. **90**, 125–157 (2017). https://doi.org/10.1016/j.jlamp.2017.02.008, https://www.sciencedirect.com/science/article/pii/S235222081730038X
17. Picazo-Sanchez, P., Pardo, R., Schneider, G.: Secure photo sharing in social networks. In: De Capitani di Vimercati, S., Martinelli, F. (eds.) ICT Systems Security and Privacy Protection, pp. 79–92. Springer, Cham (2017)
18. Rajaona, F., Boureanu, I., Ramanujam, R., Wesemeyer, S.: Epistemic model checking for privacy. In: 2024 IEEE 37th Computer Security Foundations Symposium (CSF), pp. 1–16 (2024). https://doi.org/10.1109/CSF61375.2024.00020
19. Ruan, J., Thielscher, M.: A logic for knowledge flow in social networks. In: Wang, D., Reynolds, M. (eds.) AI 2011. LNCS (LNAI), vol. 7106, pp. 511–520. Springer, Heidelberg (2011). https://doi.org/10.1007/978-3-642-25832-9_52
20. Seligman, J., Liu, F., Girard, P.: Facebook and the epistemic logic of friendship (2013). https://arxiv.org/abs/1310.6440
21. Sirjani, M.: Rebeca: theory, applications, and tools. In: de Boer, F.S., Bonsangue, M.M., Graf, S., de Roever, W.-P. (eds.) FMCO 2006. LNCS, vol. 4709, pp. 102–126. Springer, Heidelberg (2007). https://doi.org/10.1007/978-3-540-74792-5_5
22. Sirjani, M., Jaghoori, M.M.: Ten years of analyzing actors: Rebeca experience. In: Agha, G., Danvy, O., Meseguer, J. (eds.) Formal Modeling: Actors, Open Systems, Biological Systems. LNCS, vol. 7000, pp. 20–56. Springer, Heidelberg (2011). https://doi.org/10.1007/978-3-642-24933-4_3
23. Sirjani, M., Khamespanah, E.: On time actors. In: Ábrahám, E., Bonsangue, M., Johnsen, E.B. (eds.) Theory and Practice of Formal Methods. LNCS, vol. 9660, pp. 373–392. Springer, Cham (2016). https://doi.org/10.1007/978-3-319-30734-3_25
24. Sirjani, M., Movaghar, A., Mousavi, M.: Compositional verification of an object-based model for reactive systems. In: AVoCS 2001 (2001). https://rebeca-lang.org/assets/papers/2001/CompositionalVerificationOfAnObject-BasedModelForReactiveSystems.pdf
25. Voigt, P., Von dem Bussche, A.: The EU General Data Protection Regulation (GDPR): A Practical Guide. Springer, Heidelberg (2017). https://doi.org/10.1007/978-3-319-57959-7
26. Winskel, G.: A note on model checking the modal nu-calculus. Theor. Comput. Sci. **83**(1), 157–167 (1991)
27. Yousefi, B., Ghassemi, F., Khosravi, R.: Modeling and efficient verification of wireless ad hoc networks. Formal Aspects Comput. **29**(6), 1051–1086 (2017). https://doi.org/10.1007/s00165-017-0429-z

Ranch: Rebeca On Chip

Meyssam Rostamzadeh[1](✉), Mahboubeh Samadi[1], Fatemeh Ghassemi[1,2],
and Hossein Hojjat[1]

[1] Tehran Institute For Advanced Studies, Khatam University, Tehran, Iran
meyssam.rostamzadeh@gmail.com
[2] University of Tehran, Tehran, Iran

Abstract. Actor-based languages have attracted much interest in industry and academia. In particular, Rebeca is an actor-based language which offers model checking back-end to ensure absence of any unwanted behavior in the model. After ensuring that a model is correct, an important challenge is the correct implementation of the actor model on the computer. In this work, we present Ranch, a prototype tool that correctly compiles a subset of Rebeca into assembly. In the conducted tests, the target of the translation is ARM Cortex-M3 microcontrollers. With formal verification of this compilation, Ranch guarantees that the Rebeca model and the implementation have the same operational semantics. Our experiments show how Ranch translates some Rebeca models into real hardware and demonstrate the applicability of our approach.

Keywords: Actor based languages · Correct Compilation · Model Checking

1 Introduction

Actor models [1,2] are a model for distributed systems in which distributed components do not share any variable and can merely communicate through message-passing. In actor models, each actor has a mailbox with a unique address to store the received messages. An actor's behavior is defined using a set of message handlers that specify how the actor reacts to the received message.

Rebeca [3] is an actor-based modelling language that has been used in industry and academia for modeling and verification of various distributed systems. Notable case studies include complex cyber-physical systems [4], connected vehicles [5], healthcare [6] and transportation systems [7]. Rebeca has formal semantics and the Afra [8] model checker is an integrated environment for modeling and verifying Rebeca models. After ensuring that there is no unwanted behavior in the Rebeca model of a system, the next step is to implement the system using an actor-based language like Akka [9]. After that, by using a compiler, the code will be translated to the final hardware target (such as computer or

---

To: Marjan. My academic mother, who always believes in me.
Even during my worst days, even after my painful rejections. – Hossein.

cyber-physical system) for execution. The path from a correct model to hardware is error prone: a correct model of the system may be translated incorrectly to the final implementation due to incorrect translation of the Rebeca model to programming language. Or, an incorrect compilation process may introduce unwanted incorrect behavior in the final assembly code on the hardware.

In this paper, we propose a provably correct mapping of Rebeca to an assembly language for execution on real hardware. We show the correctness of this translation both theoretically and empirically. We use a prototype tool, called *Ranch* (R̲ebeca o̲n c̲hip), to convert a subset of Rebeca [10] as a source modeling language into the ARM assembly language as a target language. We assume that the input Rebeca model is verified (e.g. using Afra IDE) and hence its syntax is correct and the required properties are satisfied by the specified model. We aim to integrate Ranch into Afra in the future.

For simplicity, we use a subset of Rebeca including sending a message, taking a message, conditional and assignment statements. We aim to extend the proposed compiler to translate all statements of Rebeca in the future. The main contributions of this paper are as follow:

- We give a mapping from Rebeca to ARM assembly language and explain how statements such as send a message, take a message, assignment and conditional statements are translated to assembly. We also give the semantics of assembly instructions (Sect. 3).
- We prove that Ranch preserves the operational semantics of Rebeca and hence the semantics of Rebeca and ARM assembly language are equivalent (Sect. 5).
- We show the applicability of our approach on some experiments using various examples (Sect. 6).

2   Preliminaries

In this section, we first give some preliminaries about Rebeca as an actor-based language, and then explain the ARM assembly language.

2.1   Rebeca

Rebeca [3,11] is an actor-based language used for modeling and verification of distributed systems. Rebeca's syntax is like Java and it is supported by the model-checking tool called Afra [8]. Actors, called *rebecs*, have no shared variables and communicate through asynchronous message passing. The in-order message delivery is guaranteed in such models meaning that two messages sent directly from one rebec to another will be delivered and processed in the same order that they were sent. Each rebec has a unique address and a message queue. A rebec sends messages to a target rebec using its address, and the message is inserted into the queue of the target rebec. Each rebec handles its received messages from its queue in a FIFO order.

$$
\begin{aligned}
\text{Model} &::= \langle \text{Class} \rangle^{+} \text{ Main} \\
\text{Main} &::= \textsf{main } \{\text{ActorInstance}^{+}\} \\
\text{ActorInstance} &::= \text{C actor} : (\langle \text{const} \rangle^{*}) \\
\text{Class} &::= \textsf{reactiveclass } \text{C } \{\text{KnownRebecs Vars Method}^{+}\} \\
\text{KnownRebecs} &::= \textsf{knownrebecs } \{\langle \text{Type v} \rangle^{*}\} \\
\text{Vars} &::= \textsf{statevars } \{\langle \text{Type v;} \rangle^{*}\} \\
\text{Method} &::= \textsf{msgsrv } \text{name } \{\text{Stmt}^{*}\} \\
\text{Stmt} &::= \text{v} := expr; \mid \text{x.name;} \mid \textsf{if}(expr) \{\text{Stmt}^{+}\} \textsf{ else } \{\text{Stmt}^{+}\};
\end{aligned}
$$

Fig. 1. Core Rebeca syntax: C, name, v, const, $expr$, and actor denote class, type, handler name, variable, constant, expressions, and actor name. $\langle \, \rangle$ denotes meta parenthesis, $+$ and $*$ denote one or more and zero or more repetitions.

In this paper, we focus on a subset of Rebeca [10] (core Rebeca) where message servers (methods) have no parameters, and each rebec can only send/take messages, and execute assignment and conditional statements. In the following, we explain the syntax and semantics of core Rebeca.

Syntax. The syntax of core Rebeca is shown in Fig. 1 where an actor-based model is defined by a set of actor classes and a main block. Each actor class is defined by reactiveclass. A reactive class has a numeric argument in parenthesis next to the reactiveclass name which denotes the maximum size of its queue. The body of the reactive class includes the declaration of its known rebecs (knownrebecs), state variables (statevars), message servers (msgsrv), and a constructor. The state variables can be initialized in the constructor. The known rebecs denote a set of rebecs to whom an actor can send a message. The body of the message server includes assignments, conditional statements, and *send* statements. We use $x.name$ to express that a message corresponding to the message server *name* is sent to actor x. Rebecs can also send messages to themselves by using the reserved word self.

Example 1. Figure 2 shows a system composed of a counter and an alarm where their queue's lengths are three. The known rebec of counter is an instance of Alarm class (line 3), and accum is a state variable (line 5). The variable accum is initialized to zero, and counter sends a message inc to itself in its constructor (lines 8–9). By receiving the inc message, the counter checks the value of accum (line 12, line 15), and then sends another inc message to itself (line 19). If accum equals one, it is reset to zero (line 13). Otherwise, it is set to one and then the counter sends a message notify to its known rebec of class Alarm (line 17). In the main block, the known rebecs and actual values of parameters are initialized (lines 34–35). So, the known rebec a of counter c is initialized by the first pair of parenthesis while the second pair of parenthesis indicates that no parameter is passed to the constructor (line 34).

```
1   reactiveclass Counter(3) {        19        self.inc();
2                                     20      }}
3     knownrebecs{Alarm a;}           21
4                                     22   reactiveclass Alarm(3) {
5     statevars{int accum;}           23
6                                     24     knownrebecs { }
7     Counter(){                      25
8       accum=0;                      26     statevars { }
9       self.inc();}                  27
10                                    28     msgsrv notify (){
11    msgsrv inc(){                   29       // Play the alarm
12      if(accum == 1) {              30       }}
13          accum = 0;                31
14      }                             32   main
15      else {                        33   {
16          accum = 1;                34      Counter c(a):();
17          a.notify();               35      Alarm a():();
18      }                             36   }
```

Fig. 2. A system model in Rebeca

Semantics. We rely on a set of notations to define the semantics of core Rebeca. For an arbitrary set A, we use A^* to show the set of all sequences from the elements of A, and ϵ to denote an empty sequence. We use $\phi[i]$ to show the ith element of $\phi \in A^*$, and $|\phi|$ to show the length of ϕ. We also use $\phi_1; \phi_2$, where $\phi_1, \phi_2 \in A^*$, to denote a sequence achieved by appending ϕ_2 to ϕ_1. We assume *ID* is the set of possible rebec identifiers and *Msg* is the set of messages communicated among rebecs, ranged over by m. We model the mailbox of rebecs as a sequence of messages, ranged over by q, where $q \in Msg^*$. Each message $m \in Msg$ has three parts: sender identifier, message name (method), and receiver identifier. We use $m.name$ to denote the message name of m and $body(m.name)$ to denote the statements within the method (message server) of $m.name$. Let *Var* denote the set of variables, ranged over by i, and *Val* the set of all possible values for the variables, ranged over by v. We define a valuation function as $e : Var \rightarrow Val$ and the set of function valuations by *Eval*. We use $e[i := v]$ to denote updating $e(i)$ by v while other variables are not changed. We employ $eval(expr, e)$ to show the value of an expression $expr$ computed based on the variable evaluation e.

The semantics of core Rebeca is defined in terms of a transition system $\langle S, \rightarrow, s_0 \rangle$, where S is the set of global states, $\rightarrow \subseteq S \times S$ is the set of transition relations, and s_0 is the initial state. We define each part in the following.

$$\text{(SEND)} \quad \frac{s(x) = (e, q, y.n; \pi) \qquad s(y) = (e', q', \pi')}{s \to s[x \mapsto (e, q, \pi), y \mapsto (e', q'; (x, n, y), \pi')]}$$

$$\text{(TAKE)} \quad \frac{s(x) = (e, m; q, \epsilon)}{s \to s[x \mapsto (e, q, body(m.name))]}$$

$$\text{(COND 1)} \quad \frac{s(x) = (e, q, \textit{if } (expr) \ \pi_1 \textit{ else } \pi_2; \pi) \qquad eval(expr, e)}{s \to s[x \mapsto (e, q, \pi_1; \pi)]}$$

$$\text{(COND 2)} \quad \frac{s(x) = (e, q, \textit{if } (expr) \ \pi_1 \textit{ else } \pi_2; \pi) \qquad \neg eval(expr, e)}{s \to s[x \mapsto (e, q, \pi_2; \pi)]}$$

$$\text{(ASSIGN)} \quad \frac{s(x) = (e, q, i := expr; \pi)}{s \to s[x \mapsto (e[i := eval(expr, e)], q, \pi)]}$$

Fig. 3. Semantics of core Rebeca where $x, y \in ID$, $q, q' \in Msg^*$, $\pi, \pi' \in Stmt^*$, and $e, e' \in Eval$

Global States. A global state $s \in S$ is defined as $s : ID \to LocalState$, a mapping from actor identifiers to their local states, where $LocalState \subseteq Eval \times Msg^* \times Stmt^*$. The local state of each rebec is defined by a triple (e, q, π) where e is a evaluation function whose domain is the state variables of the rebec, $q \in Msg^*$ specifies the rebec's mailbox, and $\pi \in Stmt^*$ is a sequence of statements remained from a message server that should be executed.

Transition Relation. Figure 3 shows the operational semantic rules that induce the transition relation.

- SEND rule explains that upon executing the send statement $y.n$ by x, the message (x, n, y) is inserted into the queue of rebec y.
- TAKE rule expresses that a rebec can take a message from the head of its queue when it has no statement to execute. Upon taking a message, it starts executing the statements of its corresponding message server.
- CONDITIONAL rules define the semantic of the conditional statement. Based on the evaluation of the condition *expr*, either the *then* or *else* statements are selected for execution.
- ASSIGN rule expresses that the value of v is set to the evaluation of *expr*.

Initial State. In the initial state s_0, each rebec has a constructor message in its queue, and the state variables of rebecs are initialized to their default values, e.g., integer variables are set to 0.

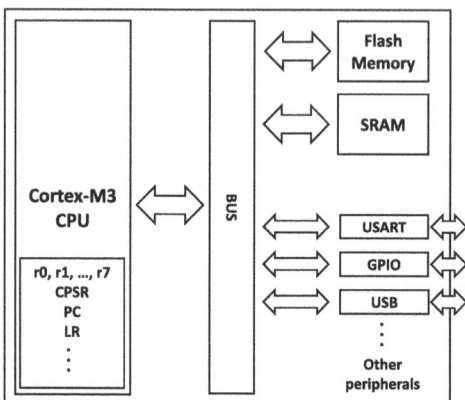

Fig. 4. Simplified ARM STM32F1xx Architecture

2.2   Hardware Description

We used the STM32F1xx microcontroller as our target Hardware, which incorporates the Cortex-M3 CPU based on the ARMv7-M architecture specification. Figure 4 shows a simplified version of STM32F103xx Architecture (for the full version see [12]). The STM32 ARM microcontroller consists of a CPU, flash memory, SRAM (Static Random Access Memory), and several peripherals. A peripheral refers to any module built into the ARM microcontroller that interacts with the CPU to perform specific functions. Examples of peripherals include GPIO (General Purpose Input/Output) and communication interfaces like USB (Universal Serial Bus) and USART (Universal Synchronous/Asynchronous Receiver-Transmitter). Each peripheral has its buffer and set of internal registers, which the CPU can access as needed. The CPU manages peripheral operations by reading from and writing to the peripheral dedicated registers. For instance, to check if a new byte has been received via the USART peripheral, the CPU can check a specific status bit in the USART status register. If this bit reads as 1, it indicates that a new byte has been received and is stored in the USART's internal buffer. Then, the CPU can retrieve and load the byte into SRAM for further processing.

The ARM Cortex-M3 CPU contains 16 general-purpose registers, with registers r_0 to r_7 being the primary ones used for general operations like storing data and performing arithmetic. The Program Counter (PC) is a special register that holds the address of the next instruction to be executed, controlling the program flow. The Link Register (LR) stores the return address when a subroutine is called. Also, the Current Program Status Register (CPSR) holds important status bits. One of these is the Zero bit (Z), which is set when the result of an arithmetic or logical operation is zero. This bit is specially used in evaluating conditions and controlling the flow of the program based on comparison results. Hereafter, CPSR is used as shorthand for its Zero bit (Z) for simplicity.

ARM instruction	Description
ldr r_i, [r_j]	load the value from the location of memory specified by r_j and write it into register r_i
str r_i, [r_j]	store the current value of r_i into the location of memory specified by r_j
mov r_i, #v	store the immediate value of v into register r_i
cmp r_i, r_j	compare the value in register r_i with the value in r_j
b label	an unconditional jump to the line of assembly code specified by *label*
bl label	jump to the line of assembly code specified by *label* and store the current value of PC in the Link register (lr)
bx lr	jump to the line of assembly code specified by the Link register

Fig. 5. ARM Assembly Instructions

It is important to note that the CPU is responsible for all data transfers between peripherals and SRAM, and peripherals cannot directly write to SRAM. Other hardware components, such as clock management, are not detailed here for brevity.

Instruction Set Architecture (ISA) is the interface between an architecture (e.g. ARM, x86, MIPS) and the software. The ISA basically defines the low-level operations a processor can perform. Assembly language directly corresponds to ISA of an specific architecture. The assembler translates assembly commands like **add** and **sub** into instructions the processor can execute. By selecting an architecture, we determine the corresponding assembly language for code generation. The assembly that our tool generates consists of the basic minimal components needed for the compilation as follows:

- *Instructions*: consist of mnemonics and operands as defined in the syntax of instruction;
- *Directives*: like .global for accessing global variables;
- *Identifiers*: like label for a jump to a place in code (i.e., calling functions);

Example 2. Given an assembly instruction ldr r_i, [r_j], the mnemonic is ldr and registers r_i, r_j are operands.

Figure 5 shows some ARM assembly instructions that are used in this paper. Fixed numbers are denoted with the # sign as it is a standard in the assembly language. The detailed syntax of other instructions is available in [13]. For instance, ldr r_i, [r_j] loads a value at memory address specified by r_j and writes it into register r_i. By str r_i, [r_j], the current value in register r_i is written in the memory address specified by r_j.

$$\{Stmt; \pi\}_{asm} = \{Stmt\}_{asm}; \{\pi\}_{asm} \qquad \{\textbf{msgsrv } name \{Stmt^*\}\}_{asm} = \textbf{\textit{msgsrv\_name}}$$
$$\{Stmt^*\}_{asm}$$
$$\texttt{bx lr}$$

$$\{a := v\}_{asm} = \begin{cases} \texttt{ldr} & \texttt{r}_i, \ \texttt{\#v} \\ \texttt{ldr} & \texttt{r}_j, \ \texttt{@a} \\ \texttt{str} & \texttt{r}_i, \ \texttt{[r}_j\texttt{]} \end{cases} \qquad \{y.n\}_{asm} = \begin{cases} \texttt{ldr} & \texttt{r}_i, \ \texttt{@f}_{xny} \\ \texttt{mov} & \texttt{r}_j, \ \texttt{\#1} \\ \texttt{str} & \texttt{r}_j, \ \texttt{[r}_i\texttt{]} \end{cases}$$

$$\{take \ m\}_{asm} = \begin{cases} \texttt{ldr} & \texttt{r}_i, \ \texttt{@f}_{m.name} \\ \texttt{ldr} & \texttt{r}_j, \ \texttt{[r}_i\texttt{]} \\ \texttt{cmp} & \texttt{r}_j, \ \texttt{\#1} \\ \texttt{beq} & \texttt{m.name} \end{cases} \qquad \{if \ expr \ \pi_1 \ else \ \pi_2\}_{asm} = \begin{cases} \{\texttt{expr}\}_{\texttt{asm}} \\ \texttt{cmp} \quad \texttt{r}_{res}, \ \texttt{\#0} \\ \texttt{beq else\_branch} \\ \{\pi_1\}_{\texttt{asm}} \\ \texttt{b end} \\ \texttt{else\_branch :} \\ \{\pi_2\}_{\texttt{asm}} \\ \texttt{end :} \end{cases}$$

Fig. 6. Translation of Rebeca Constructs into Assembly where $\texttt{r}_i$, $\texttt{r}_j$, $\texttt{r}_{res}$ denote arbitrary general purpose registers, and $\texttt{r}_{res}$ denotes the register where the evaluation result of $\texttt{expr}$ is stored.

3   Ranch: Rebeca to Assembly Translation

This section introduces *Ranch* as a compiler that translates core Rebeca to an ARM assembly language. We first explain how a Rebeca model is mapped into an ARM assembly program, then give the semantics of the translated assembly instructions. Details of implementation will be covered in the next section.

3.1   Mapping of Rebeca to Assembly

In this section, we explain how actors, message servers, messages, and statements in a core Rebeca model are mapped into an ARM assembly language.

Actor. Each actor in Rebeca is mapped to a separate chip (i.e., ARM microcontroller) with its own CPU, registers, memory, and clock. These chips are connected through different communication mediums, e.g., hardwire or Bluetooth, using different protocols such as TCP.

$$\{a == v\}_{asm} = \begin{cases} \text{ldr} \quad \text{r}_i, \text{ @a} \\ \text{ldr} \quad \text{r}_j, \text{ [r}_i\text{]} \\ \text{cmp} \quad \text{r}_j, \text{ #v} \\ \text{beq} \quad \text{eq\_branch} \\ \text{mov} \quad \text{r}_k, \text{ #0} \\ \text{b} \quad \text{end} \\ \text{eq\_branch :} \\ \text{mov} \quad \text{r}_k, \text{ #1} \\ \text{end :} \end{cases} \qquad \{\neg a\}_{asm} = \begin{cases} \{a == 0\}_{asm} \\ \text{cmp} \quad \text{r}_{res}, \text{ #0} \\ \text{beq} \quad \text{true\_branch} \\ \text{mov} \quad \text{r}_i, \text{ #0} \\ \text{b} \quad \text{end} \\ \text{true\_branch :} \\ \text{mov} \quad \text{r}_i, \text{ #1} \\ \text{end :} \end{cases}$$

Fig. 7. Translation of Simple Expressions into Assembly: equality and negation

Message. Message sending and receiving among actors are managed through a flag manipulation. A *flag* is a Boolean variable that has a set or reset status.

- For each message $(x, n, y) \in Msg$, we define a flag variable f_{xny} in the generated code of actor x. When actor x sends the message name n to actor y, flag f_{xny} is set which triggers sending (x, n, y) from the corresponding chip x to the corresponding chip y.
- For each message server n inside actor y, we also define a flag variable f_n inside the generated code of actor y. Upon receiving a message $(x, n, y) \in Msg$, flag f_n is set which triggers the execution of message server n.

Message Server. Each message server n in core Rebeca maps to a function in assembly which starts with the label `msgsrv_n` and ends with the `bx lr` instruction. The body of n including assignment, conditional statements, and sending a message are also translated to a set of assembly instructions.

Statements. Figure 6 shows how different statements in core Rebeca including sending a message, taking a message, assignment, and conditional statements are translated into a sequence of ARM assembly instructions. For each statement *str* in core Rebeca, we use $\{str\}_{asm}$ to denote its translation into the assembly language. We also use the notation @ before a variable (resp. flag) to denote the memory address where that variable (resp. flag) is stored.

- **Assignment:** For an assignment $a := v$, first, the address of a is loaded into a temporary register, and then, the value of v is written to that address.

- **Send:** When actor x executes a send statement $y.n$, flag f_{xny} is set which triggers the message sending from the corresponding chip x to the corresponding chip y. Details about changing the value of a flag variable is similar to the **Assignment** explanation.

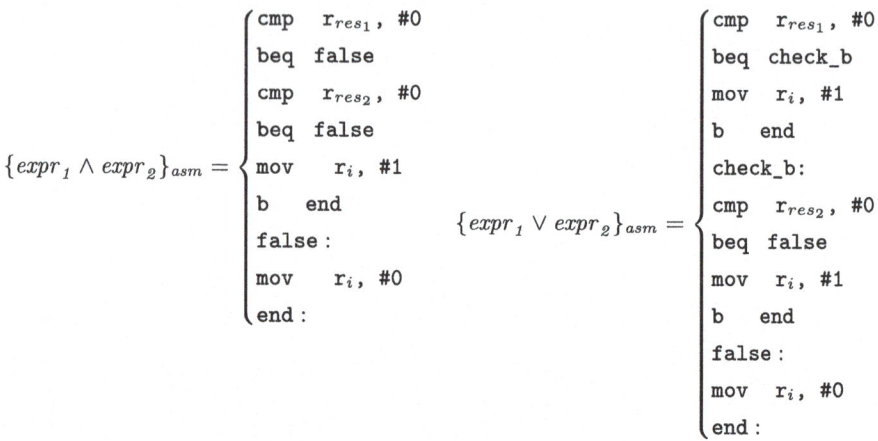

Fig. 8. Translation of Conjunction and Disjunction into Assembly

- **Take:** When actor y takes a message (x, n, y) from the head of its queue, flag f_n is set which results in the execution of the function `msgsrv_n`. The details about how the message is taken from the queue and how setting the flag leads to the execution of the function `msgsrv_n` are covered in the implementation section.

- **Conditional:** For a conditional statement "if expr then π_1 else π_2", we use $\{expr\}_{asm}$ to denote the assembly translation of $expr$, $\{\pi_1\}_{asm}$ to denote the assembly translation of π_1, and $\{\pi_2\}_{asm}$ to denote the assembly translation of π_2. We label the corresponding location of $\{\pi_2\}_{asm}$ by `else_branch` and the end of conditional statement by **end**. The evaluation of $expr$ is loaded into a temporary register r_{res} and compared with zero. If r_{res} equals zero, the program branches to the location labeled by `else_branch` and executes the instructions of $\{\pi_2\}_{asm}$. Otherwise, the instructions of $\{\pi_1\}_{asm}$ are executed and the program jumps to the location labeled by **end**. The expression $expr$ can be in the form of equality, logical negation, conjunction and disjunction of two expressions. Figure 7 shows the assembly translation of equality and logical negation expressions, and Fig. 8 shows the assembly translation of conjunction and disjunction of two expressions. We remark that Ranch can only compile nested expressions which consist of a few simple expressions. The reason is that currently, Ranch uses only 8 general purpose registers for storing intermediate results.

Remark. In core Rebeca, actors execute concurrently. Afra constructs the state-space of Rebeca and investigates all possible interleavings and execution paths. In the real-world parallel execution of corresponding assembly code of actors, each chip (corr. actor in Rebeca) has its own CPU and clock. In this way, assembly instructions (corr. Rebeca statements) are executed with different speeds on

Notation	Description
r_{index}	refer to a general-purpose register inside a chip ($0 \leq$ index < 8).
$[r_i]$	indicate that data in register r_i is a memory address
$\langle label \rangle$	refer to a line in the assembly code labeled by label
@v	refer to the memory address where the variable v (resp. flag) is stored

Fig. 9. Notations used in the Semantics of Assembly Programs

various chips. So, we observe an execution of instructions among actors which is the same as an arbitrary execution path in the state-space of Rebeca.

3.2 Assembly Program Semantics

Let *Chip* denote a set of ARM chips ranged over by c, d, and *Addr* denote a set of memory addresses ranged over by adr. We assume N denote a set of integers, and *Reg* denotes a set of registers including $r_0, \ldots, r_7, cpsr, pc, lr$. We define $\mu : Addr \rightarrow N$ as a valuation function of memory, and $\rho : Reg \rightarrow N$ as a valuation function of registers. Each register $r_i \in Reg$ stores a 32-bit value. Let $\rho[r_i := v]$ denote that the register evaluation is identical to ρ except that the value of register r_i is set to v. Similarly, $\mu[adr := v]$ denotes that the memory evaluation is identical to μ except that the memory value at the location adr is set to v. We define $code : N \rightarrow \sigma$ which indicates the assembly instruction σ of a given value (of pc). We also use $\langle label \rangle$ to denote the location of an instruction labeled by *label* in the assembly program. Figure 9 shows the description of these notations.

The semantics of an ARM assembly language is defined in terms of a transition system $\langle S, \rightarrow, s_0 \rangle$, where S is a set of global states, $\rightarrow \subseteq S \times S$ is a set of transition relations, and s_0 is the initial state. A global state $s \in S$ is defined as a mapping from chips to their local states. The local state of an ARM chip is defined by a tuple (μ, ρ) where μ specifies the memory values and ρ denotes the values of registers. In the initial state s_0, the memory is empty and registers are initialized to their default values. Figure 10 shows the transition relation over the global states of an assembly program which is defined based on the transition relations over the local states of chips.

4   Ranch Implementation

4.1   Transformation Approach

To translate a Rebeca model into the real world implementation, it's crucial to distinguish between design elements (e.g., message server logic) and real-world constraints (e.g., hardware specific details). We divide the code corresponding to a Rebeca actor, which will be compiled and run on hardware, into two parts: *Base code* and *Main code*. The *Base code* handles hardware-specific details, such

$$\text{LOAD} \ \frac{s(c) = (\mu, \rho) \quad code(\rho(pc)) = \texttt{ldr } r_2, [r_1]}{s \rightarrow s[c \mapsto (\mu, \rho[r_2 := [r_1], pc := pc + 4])]}$$

$$\text{STORE} \ \frac{s(c) = (\mu, \rho) \quad code(\rho(pc)) = \texttt{str } r_2, [r_1]}{s \rightarrow s[c \mapsto (\mu[[r_1] := r_2], \rho[pc := pc + 4])]}$$

$$\text{COMPARE-1} \ \frac{s(c) = (\mu, \rho) \quad code(\rho(pc)) = \texttt{cmp } r_1, \#\texttt{v} \quad \rho(r_1) = \texttt{v}}{s \rightarrow s[c \mapsto (\mu, \rho[pc := pc + 4, z := 1])]}$$

$$\text{COMPARE-2} \ \frac{s(c) = (\mu, \rho) \quad code(\rho(pc)) = \texttt{cmp } r_1, \#\texttt{v} \quad \rho(r_1) \neq \texttt{v}}{s \rightarrow s[c \mapsto (\mu, \rho[pc := pc + 4, z := 0])]}$$

$$\text{BRANCH} \ \frac{s(c) = (\mu, \rho) \quad code(\rho(pc)) = \texttt{b label}}{s \rightarrow s[c \mapsto (\mu, \rho[pc := \langle \texttt{label} \rangle])]}$$

$$\text{BRANCH AND LINK} \ \frac{s(c) = (\mu, \rho) \quad code(\rho(pc)) = \texttt{bl label}}{s \rightarrow s[c \mapsto (\mu, \rho[lr := pc + 4, pc := \langle \texttt{label} \rangle])]}$$

$$\text{BRANCH AND EXCHANGE} \ \frac{s(c) = (\mu, \rho) \quad code(\rho(pc)) = \texttt{bx lr}}{s \rightarrow s[c \mapsto (\mu, \rho[pc := lr])]}$$

$$\text{BRANCH EQUAL} \ \frac{s(c) = (\mu, \rho) \quad code(\rho(pc)) = \texttt{beq label} \quad \rho(z) = 1}{s \rightarrow s[c \mapsto (\mu, \rho[pc := \langle \texttt{label} \rangle])]}$$

Fig. 10. Semantics of Assembly Instructions

as communication ports used to connect to neighbor actors, keeping those hidden from the *Main code*. This separation allows the message servers to be compiled into assembly, as Rebeca abstracts away hardware specifics-e.g., calling "a.notify()" for sending a message to the actor *a* regardless of how underlying hardware operations are managed. Ranch translates the input Rebeca model for each actor into an inline assembly that we call *Main code*. The *Main code* is added to the *Base code*, and the resulting code is compiled using a standard ARM toolchain. In this section, we explain the details of the two parts along with the functional behavior of the final code that runs on hardware.

Base Code. *Base code* is a predefined template responsible for the initialization of hardware, along with the prerequisites for general actor functions. The *Base code* includes hardware initialization, such as setting up the clock and communication peripherals, as well as prerequisites for the operation of the actors, such as managing of the circular FIFO queue. The *Base code* for STM32F1xx microcontroller as a C++ project is available at [14].

For each actor, the *Base code* can have different configurations and even be developed for a different architecture.

Main Code. The logic and processing mechanisms that define an actor's reactions are mainly encapsulated in the definition of message servers. We compile message servers to assembly instructions, we call the *Main code*, which is added to the *Base code* as inline assembly. The entire code is then compiled by the standard ARM toolchain and transferred to the microcontroller.

4.2 Functional Description of Ranch

Ranch's functionality is built around the interaction between *Base code* and *Main code*, which results in the execution of the actor on hardware. In the following, we explain how these components work together to achieve an exact translation of actor behaviors into hardware execution.

The *Main code* is added into the *Base code* as inline assembly within the main "while" routine and interfaces with the *Base code* through a system of flags. Given that our hardware is single-thread, each cycle of the while routine first executes the routines of the *Base code*, such as checking communication ports, before proceeding to execute the *Main code*. Figure 11 shows the pseudo-code of the main routine of the *Base code*.

In each cycle of while routine, the *Base code* monitors the message sending flags, communication ports, and input FIFO queue. If a message arrives on a port, it will be stored in the input FIFO queue. If the *Main code* sets a send message flag in the previous cycle of its execution, the *Base code* sees the flag and initiates the transmission of the corresponding message on the corresponding port. Also, the *Base code* checks the FIFO queue, and if there is a message, it sets the flag related to that message server, resulting in the *Main code* running that message server in the next cycle of execution. Since in our source language, messages are only requests for the execution of message servers and don't carry any data, there is no data to be passed to the *Main code* and the only data sharing between the *Base code* and *Main code* are sender's ID, flags and state variables. However, this is not a limitation of the compilation, and data exchange could easily be implemented if needed.

The *Main code*, on the other hand, loads and checks the flags each time it executes. If a flag has been set, it erases the flag and runs the corresponding message server. During the execution of message servers, if there is a request to send a message to an actor, a flag corresponding to that message will be set, initiating the procedure of sending the message in the next cycle of execution of the *Base code*.

```
1   main{
2   SystemClock_Config();
3   MX_GPIO_Init();
4   MX_USART1_UART_Init();
5   MX_USART2_UART_Init();
6       .
7       .    \\other HW.inits
8       .
9
10  while(1)
11      {
12          check_USART_1_routine();
13          check_USART_2_routine();
14              .
15              .    \\other HW ports
16              .
17          check_send_flags();
18          check_FIFO_queue();
19          asm(
20              .
21              .    \\assembly of Main code
22              .
23              );
24      }
25  }
```

Fig. 11. Pseudo-code of the *Base code*

The sequential execution of message servers is guaranteed by our hardware's single-threaded architecture. In each run of the "check FIFO queue" routine, only one message is read, and only one flag is set. As a result, in the next cycle of the main code execution, only one message server will be executed.

Additionally, processing messages in FIFO order is managed by the *Base code*, allowing the implementer the flexibility to choose the type of input queue structure. In our experiments, we utilize a circular FIFO, as stated in the Rebeca language specification.

5   Operational Guarantees of Ranch

In this section, we prove that the semantics of Rebeca is preserved during compilation. In other words, a Rebeca model and its corresponding assembly code exhibit similar observable behaviors. We consider the execution of Rebeca statements and taking a message from the queue by rebecs as the observable behaviors. There are many notions of behavioral equivalence where the strong bisimilarity is the strongest relation indicating that the two models can mimic each other step after step. As each Rebeca observable behavior is translated into a sequence of assembly instructions, we treat the instructions except the last one

$$\text{(SEND)} \quad \frac{s_i(c) = (\mu, \rho) \quad code(\rho(pc)) = \{y.n\}_{asm}[0]}{s_i \xrightarrow{\tau} s_{i+1} \xrightarrow{\tau} s_{i+2} \xrightarrow{send} s_{i+3}}$$

$$\text{(TAKE)} \quad \frac{s_i(c) = (\mu, \rho) \quad code(\rho(pc)) = \{take \ m\}_{asm}[0]}{s_i \xrightarrow{\tau} s_{i+1} \xrightarrow{\tau} s_{i+2} \xrightarrow{\tau} s_{i+3} \xrightarrow{take} s_{i+4}}$$

$$\text{(COND 1)} \quad \frac{s_i(c) = (\mu, \rho) \quad code(\rho(pc)) = \{if \ expr \ \pi_1 \ else \ \pi_2\}_{asm}[0]}{s_i \xrightarrow{\tau} \ldots \xrightarrow{\tau} s_{i'} \xrightarrow{\tau} s_{i'+1} \xrightarrow{\tau} s_{i'+2} \xrightarrow{conditional} s_{i'+3}}$$

$$\text{(COND 2)} \quad \frac{s_i(c) = (\mu, \rho) \quad code(\rho(pc)) = \{if \ expr \ \pi_1 \ else \ \pi_2\}_{asm}[0]}{s_i \xrightarrow{\tau} \ldots \xrightarrow{\tau} s_{i'} \xrightarrow{\tau} s_{i'+1} \xrightarrow{\tau} s_{i'+2} \xrightarrow{conditional} s_{i'+3}}$$

$$\text{(ASSIGN)} \quad \frac{s_i(c) = (\mu, \rho) \quad code(\rho(pc)) = \{a := v\}_{asm}[0]}{s_i \xrightarrow{\tau} s_{i+1} \xrightarrow{\tau} s_{i+2} \xrightarrow{assign(a,v)} s_{i+3}}$$

Fig. 12. Sequence of transitions that are generated by executing $\{st\}_{asm}$ or $\{take \ m\}_{asm}$

in this sequence as internal actions (denoted by τ). We exploit branching bisimilarity [15], the strongest equivalence handling internal actions, indicating that the two models can mimic each other step after step preceded/proceeded by some internal actions. We establish that any Rebeca model $\mathcal{M}_r$ is branching bisimilar to $\{\mathcal{M}_r\}_{asm}$.

Let TS_r denote the transition system of the Rebeca model $\mathcal{M}_r$ and TS_a denote the transition system of $\{\mathcal{M}_r\}_{asm}$. The transitions of TS_r and TS_a are derived by the rules in Fig. 3 and Fig. 10, respectively, and they do not carry a label. We assume that the transitions generated for the statements sending, $a := v$, and if carry the labels $send$, $assign(a, v)$, and $conditional$, respectively. We also label transitions as the consequence of taking messages by $take$.

Each statement st or taking a message is translated into a sequence of instructions in assembly given by $\{st\}_{asm}$ (or $\{take \ m\}_{asm}$) (shown in Fig. 6). These instructions generate a sequence of transitions in TS_a. We assume that the last transition in this sequence carries the corresponding label we assigned in TS_r (called assumption †) and the other non-last transitions have the τ label. Figure 12 shows the sequence of such transitions that are generated and their assigned labels. For the conditional statement $\{if \ expr \ \pi_1 \ else \ \pi_2\}_{asm}$, if $\{expr\}_{asm}$ holds, then $\{\pi_1\}_{asm}$ will be executed. Some τ transitions are generated for $\{expr\}_{asm}$ (denoted by $s_i \xrightarrow{\tau} \ldots \xrightarrow{\tau} s_{i'}$). The number of τ transitions depend on the expression $\{expr\}_{asm}$ as shown in Fig. 7 and Fig. 8. The set of actions (labels) in TS_r are $Act = \{send, take, conditional, assign(a, v)\}$, and $Act \cup \{\tau\}$ in TS_a. Let $\xrightarrow{\tau}^*$ be reflexive and transitive closure of τ-transitions:

- $t \xrightarrow{\tau}^* t$;
- $t \xrightarrow{\tau}^* s$, and $s \xrightarrow{\tau} r$, then $t \xrightarrow{\tau}^* r$.

Definition 1 (Branching Bisimilarity). *Let $\langle S, \rightarrow, s_0 \rangle$ be a labeled transition system where $\rightarrow \subseteq S \times Act \times S$, and Act is the set of actions. A binary relation $\mathcal{R} \subseteq S \times S$ is called a branching bisimulation if and only if, for any states $s_1, s_1', s_2, s_2' \in S$ and $\alpha \in Act$, the following transfer conditions hold:*

- $s_1 \mathcal{R} s_2 \wedge s_1 \xrightarrow{\alpha} s_1' \Rightarrow (\alpha = \tau \wedge s_1' \mathcal{R} s_2) \vee (\exists s_2', s_2'' \in S : s_2 \xrightarrow{\tau}^* s_2'' \xrightarrow{\alpha} s_2' \wedge (s_1 \mathcal{R} s_2'') \wedge (s_1' \mathcal{R} s_2'))$,
- $s_1 \mathcal{R} s_2 \wedge s_2 \xrightarrow{\alpha} s_2' \Rightarrow (\alpha = \tau \wedge s_1 \mathcal{R} s_2') \vee (\exists s_1', s_1'' \in S : s_1 \xrightarrow{\tau}^* s_1'' \xrightarrow{\alpha} s_1' \wedge (s_1'' \mathcal{R} s_2) \wedge (s_1' \mathcal{R} s_2'))$.

Two states s and t are called branching bisimilar, denoted by $s \simeq_{br} t$, if and only if there exists a branching bisimulation relating s and t.

The labeled transition system $TS_2 = \langle S', \rightarrow, s_0' \rangle$ is branching bisimilar to $TS_1 = \langle S, \rightarrow s_0 \rangle$ denoted by $TS_1 \simeq_{br} TS_2$, iff $s_0 \simeq_{br} s_0'$.

Theorem 1. *TS_r is branching bisimilar to TS_a where TS_r is the transition system of the Rebeca model $\mathcal{M}_r$ and TS_a is the transition system of $\{\mathcal{M}_r\}_{asm}$.*

Proof. A global state of TS_r maps each actor identifier of $\mathcal{M}_r$ to its local state, denoted by s, with the triple (e, q, π). Similarly, a global state of TS_a maps each chip of $\{\mathcal{M}_r\}_{asm}$ to its local state, denoted by s', with the tuple (μ, ρ). We define an auxiliary function $deploy : ID \rightarrow Chip$ which maps each actor identifier in $\mathcal{M}_r$ to a chip in $\{\mathcal{M}_r\}_{asm}$.

We construct the relation $\mathcal{R}$ and prove that this relation satisfies the transfer conditions of branching bisimulation given in Definition 1.

$$\mathcal{R} = \{(s, s') \mid \forall x. \exists e, q, \pi, \mu, \rho \cdot s(x) = (e, q, \pi) \wedge s'(deploy(x)) = (\mu, \rho) \wedge$$
$$VarEQ(e, \mu) \wedge QueueEQ(x, q, \mu) \wedge StmtEQ(\pi, \rho)\}$$

where $VarEQ$ expresses that the evaluation of variables in a rebec is equivalent to the value of variables in the memory of the corresponding chip.

$$VarEQ(e, \mu) = \forall i \in domain(e) \cdot e(i) = \mu(@i)$$

The predicate $QueueEQ$ indicates that the queue of rebec x in $\mathcal{M}_r$ contains the messages of the queue of its corresponding chip in $\{\mathcal{M}_r\}_{asm}$, denoted by $Queue(\mu)$, and the messages that their corresponding flags are set in the sender's chip.

$$QueueEQ(x, q, \mu) = \exists \delta \in Msg^* \cdot q = Queue(\mu); \delta \wedge FlagsSet(x, \delta)$$

The messages that are sent within message servers of $\mathcal{M}_r$, result in setting some flags in $\{\mathcal{M}_r\}_{asm}$. During execution of assembly, setting a send flag in the sender's chip initiates the process of delivering the message to the recipient chip. The message is then enqueued into the recipient chip's queue. As a result, for rebec x in $\mathcal{M}_r$ with a queue q, the queue of its corresponding chip in $\{\mathcal{M}_r\}_{asm}$, denoted by $Queue(\mu)$, may not contain all the messages of q yet. There exists a sequence of messages like δ such that $q = Queue(\mu); \delta$ and the corresponding flags of message in δ are set, denoted by $FlagsSet(x, \delta)$. In this way, for each message $\delta[i] = (y, n, x)$, its corresponding flag $@f_{ynx}$ is set which means that the messages have not yet been added to the queue of the chip corresponding to rebec x while the corresponding send flag has already been set in the corresponding chip of rebec y. The order of messages in δ reflects the order that flags are checked by the base code.

$$FlagsSet(x, \delta) = \forall 0 \leq i < |\delta|.\exists y, n \cdot \delta[i] = (y, n, x) \wedge$$
$$\exists \mu', \rho', f_{ynx} \cdot s'(deploy(y)) = (\mu', \rho') \wedge \mu'(@f_{ynx}) = 1$$

StmtEQ declares that the statements that are executed in a rebec are equivalent to the assembly instructions in the corresponding chip, where $code(\rho(pc)) = Base\ code$ indicates that $\rho(pc)$ shows the start address of the Base code routines as denoted in Fig. 11.

$$StmtEQ(\pi, \rho) = ((\pi = \epsilon) \Leftrightarrow code(\rho(pc)) = Base\ code) \wedge$$
$$(\exists st, \pi'.(\pi = st; \pi') \Leftrightarrow \forall 0 \leq i < |\{st\}_{asm}| \cdot code(\rho(pc) + i) = \{st\}_{asm}[i])$$

For an arbitrary pair $(s_i, s_i') \in \mathcal{R}$, assume that $s_i \xrightarrow{\alpha} s_{i+1}$. The following cases can be distinguished based on the induced transition relations:

- **Send Message Transition:** By this rule, it holds that there exists $x \in ID$ such that $s_i(x) = (e, q, y.n; \pi)$, $s_i(y) = (e^*, q^*, \pi^*)$, and there exists s_{i+1} such that $s_i \xrightarrow{send} s_{i+1}$ and $s_{i+1} = s_i[x \mapsto (e, q, \pi)][y \mapsto (e^*, q^*; (x, n, y), \pi^*)]$. From $(s_i, s_i') \in \mathcal{R}$, we imply that there are chips $c = deploy(x)$ and $d = deploy(y)$ such that $s_i'(c) = (\mu, \rho)$ and $s_i'(d) = (\mu^*, \rho^*)$ where $code(\rho(pc))$, $code(\rho(pc) + 1)$, and $code(\rho(pc) + 2)$ contain three instructions for $\{y.n\}_{asm}$ given in Fig. 6, which set the value of flag f_{xny} to true. These instructions induce three transitions $s_i' \xrightarrow{\tau} s_{i+1}' \xrightarrow{\tau} s_{i+2}' \xrightarrow{send} s_{i+3}'$ using the SOS rules in Fig. 10 and assumption † in TS_a. In this way, it holds that $s_{i+3}' = s_{i+2}'[c \mapsto (\mu[@f_{xny} := 1], \rho)]$ hence, $(s_i, s_{i+1}') \in \mathcal{R}$, $(s_i, s_{i+2}') \in \mathcal{R}$, and $(s_{i+1}, s_{i+3}') \in \mathcal{R}$.

- **Take Message Transition:** By this rule, there exists $x \in ID$ such that $s_i(x) = (e, m; q, \epsilon)$, and there exists s_{i+1} such that $s_i \xrightarrow{take} s_{i+1}$ and $s_{i+1} = s_i[x \mapsto (e, q, body(m.name))]$. From $(s_i, s_i') \in \mathcal{R}$, we conclude that there is a chip $c = deploy(x)$ such that $s_i'(c) = (\mu, \rho)$ where $\mu(@f_{m.name}) = 1$, $\mu.q[0] = m$ denotes that the first message in $\mu.q$ is m, and $code(\rho(pc)) = Base\ code$. Thus, upon executing a set of instructions within the base code, it finally reaches the code for checking the FIFO. As $\mu.q[0] = m$, according to $\{take\ m\}_{asm}$ in Fig. 6, four assembly instructions are executed which load the value of flag $f_{m.name}$ into a register and check if the value of flag $f_{m.name}$ is true, the program jumps to the location labeled by $m.name$. These four instructions induce four transitions $s'_i \xrightarrow{\tau} s'_{i+1} \xrightarrow{\tau} s'_{i+2} \xrightarrow{\tau} s'_{i+3} \xrightarrow{take} s'_{i+4}$ using the SOS rules in Fig. 10 and assumption † in TS_a such that $s'_{i+4} = s'_{i+3}[c \mapsto (\mu, \rho[pc := \langle label_{m.name} \rangle])]$. Trivially, it holds that $code(\rho(pc))$ refers to the message server $m.name$, and hence $(s_i, s'_{i+1}) \in \mathcal{R}$, $(s_i, s'_{i+2}) \in \mathcal{R}$, $(s_i, s'_{i+3}) \in \mathcal{R}$, and $(s_{i+1}, s'_{i+4}) \in \mathcal{R}$.

Conditional Transition: By the conditional rules, it holds that $s_i \xrightarrow{conditional} s_{i+1}$, where $s_i(x) = (e, q, if\ (expr)\ \pi_1\ else\ \pi_2; \pi)$. If $eval(expr, e)$ then $s_{i+1} = s_i[x \mapsto (e, q, \pi_1; \pi)]$. From $(s_i, s'_i) \in \mathcal{R}$, we conclude that there is a chip $c = deploy(x)$ such that $s'_i(c) = (\mu, \rho)$ where $code(\rho(pc))$ indicates the first instruction of $\{if\ (expr)\ \pi_1\ else\ \pi_2\}_{asm}$. As $\{expr\}_{asm}$ is true, at least six assembly instructions are executed based on the expression $\{expr\}_{asm}$. These six instructions induce six transitions $s'_i \xrightarrow{\tau} s'_{i+1} \xrightarrow{\tau} s'_{i+2} \xrightarrow{\tau} s'_{i+3} \xrightarrow{\tau} s'_{i+4} \xrightarrow{\tau} s'_{i+5} \xrightarrow{conditional} s'_{i+6}$ using the SOS rules in Fig. 10 and assumption † in TS_a such that $s'_{i+6} = s'_{i+5}[c \mapsto (\mu, \rho[pc := \langle label_{\pi_1} \rangle])]$. In this way, $code(\rho(pc))$ indicates the first instruction of $\{\pi_1\}_{asm}$. Hence, we can conclude that $(s_i, s'_{i+1}) \in \mathcal{R}$, $(s_i, s'_{i+2}) \in \mathcal{R}$, $(s_i, s'_{i+3}) \in \mathcal{R}$, $(s_i, s'_{i+4}) \in \mathcal{R}$, $(s_i, s'_{i+5}) \in \mathcal{R}$, and $(s_{i+1}, s'_{i+6}) \in \mathcal{R}$. The case when $\neg eval(expr, e)$ holds is discussed with the similar fashion.

- **Assignment Transition:** By this rule, it holds that $s_i \xrightarrow{assign\ (a,v)} s_{i+1}$, where $s_i(x) = (e, q, a := v; \pi)$ and $s_{i+1} = s_i[x \mapsto (e[a := v], q, \pi)]$. From $(s_i, s'_i) \in \mathcal{R}$, we conclude that there is a chip $c = deploy(x)$ such that $s'_i(c) = (\mu, \rho)$ and $code(\rho(pc))$, $code(\rho(pc) + 1)$, and $code(\rho(pc) + 2)$ contain three instructions of $\{a := v\}_{asm}$ given in Fig. 6. These three instructions induce three transitions $s'_i \xrightarrow{\tau} s'_{i+1} \xrightarrow{\tau} s'_{i+2} \xrightarrow{assign(a,v)} s'_{i+3}$ using the SOS rules in Fig. 10 and assumption † in TS_a such that $s'_{i+3} = s'_{i+2}[c \mapsto (\mu[@a := v], \rho)]$. Hence, we can conclude that $(s_i, s'_{i+1}) \in \mathcal{R}$, $(s_i, s'_{i+2}) \in \mathcal{R}$, and $(s_{i+1}, s'_{i+3}) \in \mathcal{R}$.

We must also prove the transfer conditions of branching bisimulation relation when $s'_i \xrightarrow{\alpha} s'_{i+1}$. Based on assumption †, two cases can be considered:

- $\alpha = \tau$: this transition corresponds to an assembly instruction that does not complete the translation of a Rebeca statement. Since these instructions change the content of the registers, trivially, $(s_i, s'_{i+1}) \in \mathcal{R}$.

- $\alpha \neq \tau$: this transition corresponds to an instruction that completes the translation of a Rebeca statement. Four cases can be considered. We discuss the case when $\alpha = take$ and other cases can be discussed in a similar way. In this case, this transition corresponds to the last instruction of $\{take\ m\}_{asm}$, i.e., `beq m.name`, and there exists $c \in Chip$ such that $s'_i(c) = (\mu, \rho)$ and

$\mu(@f_{m.name}) = 1$ which indicates that $\mu.q[0] = m$. By execution of beq m.name, the assembly program jumps to the location labeled by $m.name$. So, $s'_{i+1} = s'_i[c \mapsto (\mu, \rho[pc := \langle label_{m.name} \rangle)]$. As $(s_i, s'_i) \in \mathcal{R}$, we imply that there exists $x \in ID$ such that $s_i(x) = (e, m; q, \epsilon)$. Concluding that $s_i \xrightarrow{take} s_{i+1}$, and $s_{i+1} = s_i[x \mapsto (e, q, body(m.name))]$. Trivially, it holds that $(s_{i+1}, s'_{i+1}) \in \mathcal{R}$.

□

6   Evaluation and Experimental Results

To demonstrate the practical applicability of our approach, we conducted experiments using various examples that represent typical concurrent systems. We used an off-the-shelf STM32F1xx evaluation board for our experiments. Since in our experiments, the hardware setup is identical for all actors, we reused the same *Base code* across all actors with only minor adjustments like configuring which port connected to which neighbor actor.

6.1   Practical Demonstrations

Case 1. Consider the system model in Rebeca (Fig. 2) which consists of two actors "Counter" and "Alarm". Ranch generates two assembly codes for two actors as shown in Fig. 13. The corresponding *Main code* for the Counter actor has three main parts:

- retrieving memory addresses for global variables and flags (lines 1 to 4);
- checking flags (lines 5 to 9);
- the body of the message server (lines 11 to 34);

At the beginning of the *Main code*, the memory location of global variables and flags already defined in the *Base code* are shared with the *Main code* in lines 1 through 4. After that, in lines 5 through 9, the process of checking the flag corresponding to the "inc" message server is executed. To perform this, the current value of the flag is first loaded into register r3 and then compared to one (line 7). The equality means that there is a request for executing this message server, and the instruction in line 8 will cause a jump to the line labeled by msgsrv_inc (line 10), initiating the execution of the message server's body (lines 11 to 34). At the end of the code block of the message server (line 34), the bx lr instruction causes the program to jump back to line 9 (one line after the previous jump), which directly branches to the end of the *Main code*. If the flag is not set, the instruction in line 8 will not cause a jump, and the execution proceeds to line 9 and again branches to the end of the *Main code*. If multiple message servers exist, the procedures for checking the corresponding flags would be added before the final jump to the end (line 9).

The assembly structure for the Alarm actor follows the same pattern as the Counter actor, including retrieving memory addresses (lines 1 and 2), checking the flag (lines 3 to 7), and the body of the only message server (lines 9 to 13).

In this case, once the flag is set, the program jumps to the start of the body of the message server (line 8). In the source Rebeca code, the body of the message server "notify" is empty (Fig. 2, line 12). In Fig. 13, line 12, a call to the function function_play_alarm, that is defined inside the *Base code*, manually added to activate the alarm. It is important to note that this function is hardware-dependent and external to the functionality of the *Main code*. To show playing the alarm in our hardware implementation, we set a GPIO pin in the corresponding hardware of the Alarm actor. After the message server finishes execution, the program flow returns to line 7 and then to line 14, where the current cycle of execution of the *Main code* ends.

Case 2. Here, we demonstrate the well-known "dining philosophers" problem. There are three philosophers and three forks. Each philosopher and fork is implemented as a separate actor. Each philosopher requests two forks. When both forks become available, the philosopher takes them and begins eating. Once the eating is completed, the philosopher releases the forks. The dining philosophers problem has various versions. In our implementation, based on the version provided on the Rebeca website [16], each philosopher requests to eat immediately after finishing their previous meal.

Figure 14 shows the Rebeca code for modeling dining philosophers, where we have omitted the message server bodies for brevity. We define two reactive classes, **philosopher** and **fork**. Each philosopher is connected to two forks, represented by the known rebecs forkL and forkR as left and right forks (line 2). During instantiating in the main block, each philosopher is instantiated with two fork actors as parameters. For example, the first philosopher phil0 is connected to fork0 as the left and fork2 as the right fork (line 35). Similarly, each fork actor is connected to two philosopher actors (line 18), specified during instantiation (lines 39 to 41).

Each philosopher first requests the left fork by sending a message to run the request message server inside the left fork. Due to the pre-defined order on requests (philosopher "phil0" requests the right fork first), deadlock is avoided. Inside the request message server, if the fork is not assigned already, it accepts the request and sends a message to trigger the philosopher's permit message server. Inside the permit, the philosopher checks which fork sent the message. If the left fork responds, the philosopher requests the right fork; if the right fork responds, the philosopher starts eating. After eating, the leave message server releases both forks by sending a message to trigger their release message server, where the fork checks for pending requests from the other philosopher.

```
1   .global accum
2   .global sender
3   .global flag_inc
4   .global flag_notify_a
5   ldr r2, =flag_inc
6   ldr r3, [r2]
7   cmp r3, #1
8   beq msgsrv_inc:
9   b label_end
10  msgsrv_inc:
11  mov r0, #0
12  ldr r1, =flag_inc
13  str r0, [r1]
14  ldr r2, =accum
15  ldr r3, [r2]
16  mov r4, #1
17  cmp r3, r4
18  beq else_label1
19  mov r0, #0
20  ldr r1, =accum
21  str r0, [r1]
22  b end_label1
23  else_label1:
24  mov r0, #1
25  ldr r1, =accum
26  str r0, [r1]
27  mov r0, #1
28  ldr r1, =flag_notify_a
29  str r0, [r1]
30  end_label1:
31  mov r0, #1
32  ldr r1, =flag_inc
33  str r0, [r1]
34  bx lr
35  label_end:
```

(a) Counter actor

```
1   .global sender
2   .global flag_notify
3   ldr r1, =flag_notify
4   ldr r2, [r1]
5   cmp r2, #1
6   beq msgsrv_notify
7   b label_end
8   msgsrv_notify:
9   mov r0, #0
10  ldr r1, =flag_notify
11  str r0, [r1]
12  bl function_play_alarm
13  bx lr
14  label_end:
```

(b) Alarm actor

Fig. 13. Generated *Main code* for counter and alarm example

Figure 15 shows a photo of six STM32 evaluation boards running dining philosophers. Here we set neighbors of each actor according to the Rebeca implementation as shown in Fig. 14 (lines 35–41); That is, counting counterclockwise, the arrangement is Philosopher 0 (P0), Fork 0 (F0), Philosopher 1 (P1), Fork 1 (F1), Philosopher 2 (P2), and Fork 2 (F2). We utilized an onboard LED to show the current status of each philosopher (eating or waiting) and each fork (assigned or not assigned to any neighbor philosopher). Communication between actors is handled via the USART peripheral, as it requires no additional hardware. Each

```
1   reactiveclass Philosopher(3)   23      boolean lAssign;
    {                              24      boolean rAssign;
2   knownrebecs{                   25      boolean leftReq;
3       Fork forkL;                26      boolean rightReq;
4       Fork forkR;                27  }
5   }                              28  Fork(){}
6   statevars{                     29  msgsrv request(){}
7       boolean eating;            30  msgsrv release(){}
8       boolean fL;                31
9       boolean fR;                32  }
10  }                              33
11  Philosopher(){}                34  main {
12  msgsrv arrive(){}              35  Philosopher phil0(fork0,
13  msgsrv permit(){}                      fork2):();
14  msgsrv eat(){}                 36  Philosopher phil1(fork0,
15  msgsrv leave(){}                       fork1):();
16  }                              37  Philosopher phil2(fork1,
17  reactiveclass Fork(3) {                fork2):();
18  knownrebecs{                   38
19      Philosopher philL;         39  Fork fork0(phil0, phil1):();
20      Philosopher philR;         40  Fork fork1(phil1, phil2):();
21  }                              41  Fork fork2(phil2, phil0):();
22  statevars{                     42  }
```

Fig. 14. Rebeca code for dining philosophers example (msgsrv's body removed). philosopher 0's forks were swapped (line 35) to prevent deadlock.

Fig. 15. Dining philosophers on chip

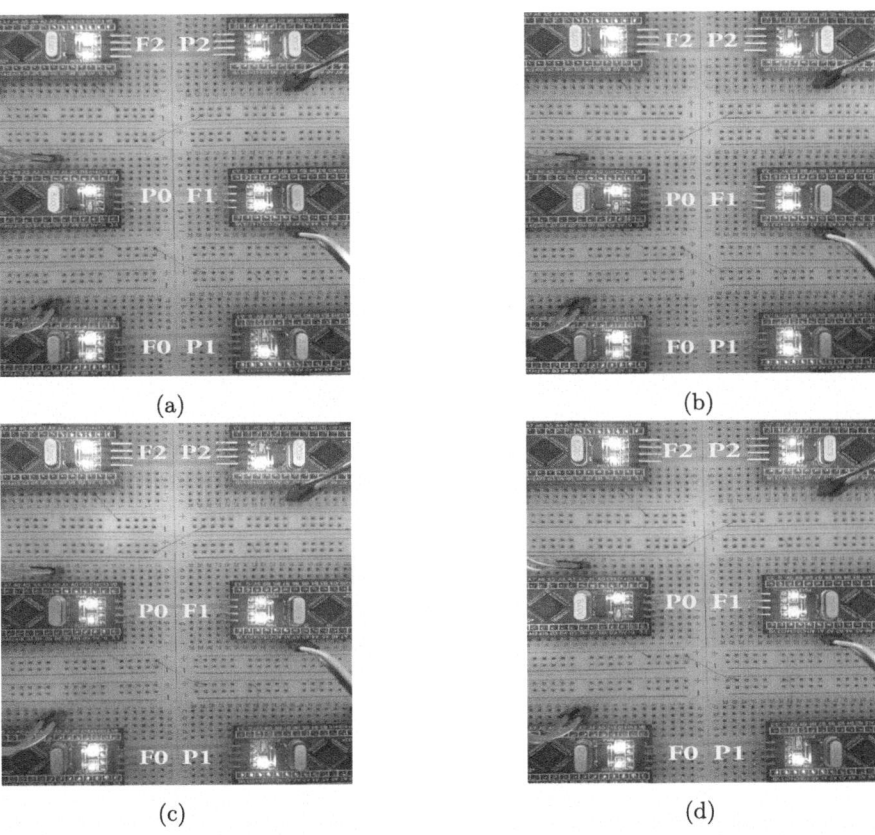

(a)

(b)

(c)

(d)

Fig. 16. Execution of dining philosophers

board is connected via two USART ports to its two neighbors. Since all six boards are identical, we used the same *Base code* for each, with the only difference being the *Main code* added before the generation of executable binary. The philosopher *Main code* was added to the *Base code* and programmed on three boards, while the fork *Main code* was used for the other three. Due to the quick transitions between "eating" and "waiting" states, a delay was added before each execution cycle of the *Main code* to capture the philosopher's status in the picture. Each time the system is powered on, a unique solution emerges, equivalent to an arbitrary trace within the state space resulting from model checking. Figure 16 illustrates a sample execution involving six actors in real-time, with philosophers and forks labeled as P1, P2, P3, and F1, F2, and F3, respectively. The red LED is a power indicator and the green LED is controlled by the chip. For philosopher actors, the green LED shows the status of the actor (LED is ON when the actor is in the eating state and otherwise is OFF) and for the fork actors, it indicates whether the fork is assigned to one of its neighbors or not. In the initial round of message passing between actors (Fig. 16a), the green LED of

P2 is ON, and for P0 and P1 it is OFF, indicating that P2 acquires both of its forks (F0 and F2) while the other philosophers remain waiting. The green LED for all three forks is ON because in all states of the system, every fork will assign itself to one of its neighbors as expected. In Fig. 16b, P2 releases its forks, and P1 enters the eating state, indicating that F1 had been assigned to P1 already. Now, P2 and P0 are waiting and P0 has acquired F2 and will be entering the eating state when P1 ends eating, as can be viewed In Fig. 16c. in Fig. 16d, P0 subsequently releases its forks, enabling P2, who already possesses F1, to obtain both forks and enter the eating state.

The generated *Main code* for each actor is shown in Fig. 17 and Fig. 18, excluding the message servers. For each message server, a dedicated figure is provided in Fig. 19 through Fig. 24, displaying both the source code and its corresponding assembly translation. Because of the size of generated assembly, we just show the Rebeca code For "permit", "request" and "release" message servers. the generated assembly for these three message servers comes in Appendix A.

As shown in Fig. 17, a dedicated flag is assigned for each message server of the philosopher actor (lines 5 to 8) and for each message server inside each neighbor actor (lines 9 to 12). At the start, all flags are checked (lines 13 to 28). If a flag is set, the code jumps to the corresponding message server, executes its body, and returns with **bx lr** to check other flags. Since the *Base code* sets at most one flag at a time, only one message server is executed in each cycle of execution of the *Main code*. The same procedure happens in the *main code* for the fork actor (Fig. 18), i.e., all flags are checked (lines 11 to 18), the code jumps to the relevant message server if a flag is set, and returns with **bx lr** after execution.

The "arrive" message server in Fig. 19, contains just one statement of sending a message to a neighbor actor in line 3, and the corresponding assembly comes in lines 5 to 7. Note that, due to the lack of optimization, the size of the generated assembly can get quite large. For example, in the "permit" message server in Fig. 20 the assembly generated for calculating the expression (**fL && !(fR)**) in line 10 results in 29 lines of code, because an if-else structure is used to evaluate each part of the expression: **!fR**, **fL**, and the **&&** operation, as mentioned in Fig. 7 and Fig. 8.

In Fig. 21, the "eat" message server is simple: it goes into eating mode by setting the "eating" variable to true (lines 5–7) and then requests the "leave" message server to run (lines 8–10) to end eating and free both forks.

The three remaining message servers in Fig. 22, 23 and Fig. 24 are structurally similar to the previous ones, and analysis of them is left to the reader.

6.2   Evaluation and Discussion

As seen in the first case of Counter and Alarm, while the Rebeca model correctly represents the Alarm actor behavior, an additional function must be added for playing the alarm on the hardware. This highlights a key challenge transitioning from an abstract model to a physical system. While the logical behavior of actors are correctly captured, hardware-specific details must be addressed. This neces-

```
 1  .global eating              26  ldr r1, [r0]
 2  .global fL                  27  cmp r1, #1
 3  .global fR                  28  beq msgsrv_leave
 4  .global sender              29  b label_end
 5  .global flag_arrive         30  msgsrv_arrive:
 6  .global flag_permit         31  .
 7  .global flag_eat            32  .
 8  .global flag_leave          33  .
 9  .global flag_request_forkL  34  bx lr
10  .global flag_release_forkL  35  msgsrv_permit:
11  .global flag_request_forkR  36  .
12  .global flag_release_forkR  37  .
13  ldr r0, =flag_arrive        38  .
14  ldr r1, [r0]                39  bx lr
15  cmp r1, #1                  40  msgsrv_eat:
16  beq msgsrv_arrive           41  .
17  ldr r0, =flag_permit        42  .
18  ldr r1, [r0]                43  .
19  cmp r1, #1                  44  bx lr
20  beq msgsrv_permit           45  msgsrv_leave:
21  ldr r0, =flag_eat           46  .
22  ldr r1, [r0]                47  .
23  cmp r1, #1                  48  .
24  beq msgsrv_eat              49  bx lr
25  ldr r0, =flag_leave         50  label_end:
```

Fig. 17. Generated *Main code* for philosopher actor (msgsrv's body removed)

```
 1  .global lAssign             17  cmp r1, #1
 2  .global rAssign             18  beq msgsrv_release
 3  .global leftReq             19  b label_end
 4  .global rightReq            20  msgsrv_request:
 5  .global sender              21  .
 6  .global flag_request        22  .
 7  .global flag_release        23  .
 8  .global flag_permit_philL   24
 9  .global flag_permit_philR   25  bx lr
10                              26  msgsrv_release:
11  ldr r0, =flag_request       27  .
12  ldr r1, [r0]                28  .
13  cmp r1, #1                  29  .
14  beq msgsrv_request          30
15  ldr r0, =flag_release       31  bx lr
16  ldr r1, [r0]                32  label_end:
```

Fig. 18. Generated *Main code* for fork actor (msgsrv's body removed)

sity was the main reason for separating the *Base code*, responsible for handling hardware-specific operations, from the *Main code*.

```
1   msgsrv arrive ()
2   {
3       forkL.request ();
4   }
```

(a) Rebeca code

```
1   msgsrv_arrive :
2   mov r0, #0
3   ldr r1, =flag_arrive
4   str r0, [r1]
5   mov r0, #1
6   ldr r1, =flag_request_forkL
7   str r0, [r1]
8   bx lr
```

(b) generated assembly

Fig. 19. The "arrive" message server.

```
1   msgsrv permit ()                        9       else {
2   {                                      10           if (fL && !(fR)) {
3       if (sender == forkL) {             11               fR = true;
4           if (!fL) {                     12               self.eat ();
5               fL = true;                 13           }
6               forkR.request ();          14       }
7           }                              15   }
8       }
```

Fig. 20. The Rebeca code for "permit" message server.

```
1   msgsrv eat ()
2   {
3       eating = true;
4       self.leave ();
5   }
```

(a) Rebeca code

```
1   msgsrv_eat :
2   mov r0, #0
3   ldr r1, =flag_eat
4   str r0, [r1]
5   mov r0, #1
6   ldr r1, =eating
7   str r0, [r1]
8   mov r0, #1
9   ldr r1, =flag_leave
10  str r0, [r1]
11  bx  lr
```

(b) generated assembly

Fig. 21. The "eat" message server.

During the execution of the second case of the dining philosopher's problem on the hardware, we observe that the philosophers simply alternate between eating and waiting. There is a case in the "leave" message server (Fig. 22, lines 6 and 7) where two consecutive requests are generated for sending messages to the two neighbor fork actors. In our implementation, this does not pose a problem because after the execution of the *Main code*, the *Base code* (in Fig. 11 line 17) checks all flags, appends any internally requested messages to the end of the queue and send requested messages through the appropriate peripherals. Before

```
1   msgsrv leave ()
2   {
3       fL = false;
4       fR = false;
5       eating = false;
6       forkL.release();
7       forkR.release();
8       self.arrive();
9   }
```

(a) Rebeca code

```
1   msgsrv_leave:
2   mov r0, #0
3   ldr r1, =flag_leave
4   str r0, [r1]
5   mov r0, #0
6   ldr r1, =fL
7   str r0, [r1]
8   mov r0, #0
9   ldr r1, =fR
10  str r0, [r1]
11  mov r0, #0
12  ldr r1, =eating
13  str r0, [r1]
14  mov r0, #1
15  ldr r1, =flag_release_forkL
16  str r0, [r1]
17  mov r0, #1
18  ldr r1, =flag_release_forkR
19  str r0, [r1]
20  mov r0, #1
21  ldr r1, =flag_arrive
22  str r0, [r1]
23  bx  lr
```

(b) generated assembly

Fig. 22. The "leave" message server.

```
1   msgsrv request ()
2   {
3       if (sender == philL) {
4           if (!leftReq) {
5               leftReq = true;
6               if (!rAssign) {
7                   lAssign = true;
8                   philL.permit();
9               }
10          }
11      }
12      else {
13          if (!rightReq) {
14              rightReq = true;
15              if (!lAssign) {
16                  rAssign = true;
17                  philR.permit();
18              }
19          }
20      }
21  }
```

Fig. 23. The Rebeca code for the "request" message server..

the next cycle of *Main code* execution, all flags are reset to zero. Currently, all flags are treated as Boolean variables. Consequently, compiling Rebeca codes with two consecutive sends to the same actor for executing the same message server during a single message server execution is not supported.

It is important to note that while we guarantee a correct mapping from the verified Rebeca code to assembly, this does not eliminate potential hardware-

```
1  msgsrv release()                      11      if (sender == philR &&
2  {                                                 rAssign){
3      if (sender == philL &&   12          rAssign = false;
           lAssign){               13          rightReq = false;
4          leftReq = false;        14          if (leftReq) {
5          lAssign = false;        15              lAssign=true;
6          if (rightReq) {         16              philL.permit();
7              rAssign=true;       17          }
8              philR.permit();     18      }
9          }                       19  }
10     }
```

Fig. 24. The Rebeca code for the "release" message server.

related issues that may not surface during model checking. The key point is that if unexpected behavior occurs, the implementer can rule out errors in the translation and focus on timing, delays, interrupts, CPU load, power fluctuations, or other hardware-related factors in the real-world environment.

7   Related Work

Correct compilation is a major area of research. There are provably correct compilers for programming languages such as C language (Compcert [17]) and Java [18]. Similar to our paper, the approach of those compilers is to prove a solid mapping between the semantics of the programming language and the target language. The correctness of the compilers in [17] and [18] is proved using an interactive theorem prover. We leave proving the correctness of our mapping using a theorem prover as our future work.

There were also efforts in code generation from modelling languages. The paper [19] proposes a code generation method for getting Delphi code from Z specification. In [20] the authors introduce a technique for translating TLA+ specifications to Elixir programs. Many of these works require manual refinement and user interaction. Although we do not cover the full Rebeca language, we believe that our automatic translation is a benefit of our approach.

8   Conclusion and Future Work

We introduced Ranch, a prototype compiler that translates a subset of Rebeca to an ARM processor. We proved our translation to be correct. We carried out some experiments for small actor programs such as dining philosophers. We plan to enhance our approach in several key areas as part of future work. First, we aim to extend support for a larger subset of the Rebeca language, allowing more complex models to be compiled and executed. Currently, message servers do not accept input parameters, and messages do not carry data. Additionally, local variables within message servers are not supported. We intend to address these limitations and use our tool for more realistic cases. Furthermore, we will explore the implementation of multiple actors on a single chip, which may introduce challenges such as managing shared resources and starvation among actors.

A Appendix

Figure. 25, 26 and 27 show the generated assembly code for the remaining message servers of Example 2 in the Sect. 6.

```
 1   msgsrv_permit:
 2   mov r0, #0
 3   ldr r1, =flag_permit
 4   str r0, [r1]
 5   ldr r0, =sender
 6   ldr r1, [r0]
 7   cmp r1, #1
 8   beq else_label1
 9   ldr r0, =fL
10   ldr r1, [r0]
11   cmp r1, #0
12   beq else_label2
13   mov r2, #0
14   b end_label2
15   else_label2:
16   mov r2, #1
17   end_label2:
18   cmp r2, #0
19   beq else_label3
20   mov r0, #1
21   ldr r1, =fL
22   str r0, [r1]
23   mov r0, #1
24   ldr r1, =flag_request_forkR
25   str r0, [r1]
26   b end_label3
27   else_label3:
28   end_label3:
29   b end_label1
30   else_label1:
31   ldr r0, =fL
32   ldr r1, [r0]
33   cmp r1, #0
34   beq else_label2
35   mov r2, #1
36   b end_label2
37   else_label2:
38   mov r2, #0
39   end_label2:
40   ldr r0, =fR
41   ldr r1, [r0]
42   cmp r1, #0
43   beq else_label3
44   mov r3, #1
45   b end_label3
46   else_label3:
47   mov r3, #0
48   end_label3:
49   cmp r3, #0
50   beq else_label4
51   mov r4, #0
52   b end_label4
53   else_label4:
54   mov r4, #1
55   end_label4:
56   cmp r3, #0
57   beq else_label5
58   cmp r4, #0
59   beq else_label5
60   mov r0, #1
61   ldr r1, =fR
62   str r0, [r1]
63   mov r0, #1
64   ldr r1, =flag_eat
65   str r0, [r1]
66   b end_label5
67   else_label5:
68   end_label5:
69   end_label1:
70   bx lr
```

Fig. 25. Generated assembly for the "permit" message server.

```
1   msgsrv_request:
2   mov r0, #0
3   ldr r1, =flag_request
4   str r0, [r1]
5   ldr r0, =sender
6   ldr r1, [r0]
7   cmp r1, #1
8   beq else_label1
9   ldr r0, =leftReq
10  ldr r1, [r0]
11  cmp r1, #0
12  beq else_label2
13  mov r2, #0
14  b end_label2
15  else_label2:
16  mov r2, #1
17  end_label2:
18  cmp r2, #0
19  beq else_label3
20  mov r0, #1
21  ldr r1, =leftReq
22  str r0, [r1]
23  ldr r0, =rAssign
24  ldr r1, [r0]
25  cmp r1, #0
26  beq else_label4
27  mov r3, #0
28  b end_label4
29  else_label4:
30  mov r3, #1
31  end_label4:
32  cmp r3, #0
33  beq else_label5
34  mov r0, #1
35  ldr r1, =lAssign
36  str r0, [r1]
37  mov r0, #1
38  ldr r1, =flag_permit_philL
39  str r0, [r1]
40  b end_label5
41  else_label5:
42  end_label5:
43  b end_label3
44  else_label3:
45  end_label3:
46  b end_label1
47  else_label1:
48  ldr r0, =rightReq
49  ldr r1, [r0]
50  cmp r1, #0
51  beq else_label6
52  mov r2, #0
53  b end_label6
54  else_label6:
55  mov r2, #1
56  end_label6:
57  cmp r2, #0
58  beq else_label7
59  mov r0, #1
60  ldr r1, =rightReq
61  str r0, [r1]
62  ldr r0, =lAssign
63  ldr r1, [r0]
64  cmp r1, #0
65  beq else_label8
66  mov r3, #0
67  b end_label8
68  else_label8:
69  mov r3, #1
70  end_label8:
71  cmp r3, #0
72  beq else_label9
73  mov r0, #1
74  ldr r1, =rAssign
75  str r0, [r1]
76  mov r0, #1
77  ldr r1, =flag_permit_philR
78  str r0, [r1]
79  b end_label9
80  else_label9:
81  end_label9:
82  b end_label7
83  else_label7:
84  end_label7:
85  end_label1:
86  bx lr
```

Fig. 26. The generated assembly for the "request" message server.

```
1   msgsrv_release:
2   mov r0, #0
3   ldr r1, =flag_release
4   str r0, [r1]
5   ldr r0, =sender
6   ldr r1, [r0]
7   cmp r1, #1
8   beq else_label1
9   mov r2, #1
10  b end_label1
11  else_label1:
12  mov r2, #0
13  end_label1:
14  ldr r0, =lAssign
15  ldr r1, [r0]
16  cmp r1, #0
17  beq else_label2
18  mov r3, #1
19  b end_label2
20  else_label2:
21  mov r3, #0
22  end_label2:
23  cmp r2,#0
24  beq else_label3
25  cmp r3,#0
26  beq else_label3
27  mov r4,#1
28  b end_label3
29  else_label3:
30  mov r4,#0
31  end_label3:
32  cmp r4,#0
33  beq else_label5
34  mov r0, #0
35  ldr r1, =leftReq
36  str r0, [r1]
37  mov r0, #0
38  ldr r1, =lAssign
39  str r0, [r1]
40  ldr r0, =rightReq
41  ldr r1, [r0]
42  cmp r1, #0
43  beq else_label6
44  mov r0, #1
45  ldr r1, =rAssign
46  str r0, [r1]
47  mov r0, #1
48  ldr r1, =flag_permit_philR
49  str r0, [r1]
50  b end_label6
51  else_label6:
52  end_label6:
53  b end_label5
54  else_label5:
55  end_label5:
56  ldr r0, =sender
57  ldr r1, [r0]
58  cmp r1, #2
59  beq else_label7
60  mov r2, #1
61  b end_label7
62  else_label7:
63  mov r2, #0
64  end_label7:
65  ldr r0, =rAssign
66  ldr r1, [r0]
67  cmp r1, #0
68  beq else_label8
69  mov r3, #1
70  b end_label8
71  else_label8:
72  mov r3, #0
73  end_label8:
74  cmp r2,#0
75  beq else_label9
76  cmp r3,#0
77  beq else_label9
78  mov r4,#1
79  b end_label9
80  else_label9:
81  mov r4,#0
82  end_label9:
83  cmp r4, #0
84  beq else_label10
85  mov r0, #0
86  ldr r1, =rAssign
87  str r0, [r1]
88  mov r0, #0
89  ldr r1, =rightReq
90  str r0, [r1]
91  ldr r0, =leftReq
92  ldr r1, [r0]
93  cmp r1, #0
94  beq else_label11
95  mov r0, #1
96  ldr r1, =lAssign
97  str r0, [r1]
98  mov r0, #1
99  ldr r1, =flag_permit_philL
100 str r0, [r1]
101 b end_label11
102 else_label11:
103 end_label11:
104 b end_label10
105 else_label10:
106 end_label10:
107 bx lr
```

Fig. 27. The generated assembly "release" message server.

References

1. Hewitt, C.: Viewing control structures as patterns of passing messages. Artif. Intell. **8**(3), 323–364 (1977)
2. Agha, G.: Actors - A Model of Concurrent Computation in Distributed Systems, MIT Press series in Artificial Intelligence (1990)
3. Sirjani, M., Movaghar, A., Shali, A., de Boer, F.: Modeling and verification of reactive systems using rebeca, Fundam. Informaticae 63 (4) (2004) 385–410. doi:rec/journals/fuin/SirjaniMSB04.bib
4. Jahandideh, I., Ghassemi, F., Sirjani, M.: Hybrid rebeca: modeling and analyzing of cyber-physical systems (2021)
5. Sharifi, Z., Khosravi, R., Sirjani, M., et.al.: Towards formal analysis of vehicle platoons using actor model. In: 25th IEEE International Conference on Emerging Technologies and Factory Automation (2020)
6. Zarneshan, M., Ghassemi, F., Khamespanah, E., Sirjani, M., Hatcliff, J.: Specification and verification of timing properties in interoperable medical systems (2022)
7. Bagheri, M., Akkaya, I., Khamespanah, E.: Coordinated actors for reliable self-adaptive systems. In: Formal Aspects of Component Software (2017)
8. Khamespanah, E., Sirjani, M., Khosravi, R.: Afra: an eclipse-based tool with extensible architecture for modeling and model checking of rebeca family models. In: Hojjat, H., Ábrahám, E. (eds.) FSEN 2023. LNCS, vol. 14155, pp. 72–87. Springer, Cham (2023). https://doi.org/10.1007/978-3-031-42441-0_6
9. https://akka.io . Accessed 05 Sept 2024
10. Ghassemi, F., Sirjani, M., Khamespanah, E., Mirani, M., Hojjat, H.: Transparent actor model. In: 11th International Conference on Formal Methods in Software Engineering (FormaliSE), ACM (2023). https://doi.org/10.1109/FormaliSE58978.2023.00018
11. Sirjani, M.: Rebeca: theory, applications, and tools. In: de Boer, F.S., Bonsangue, M.M., Graf, S., de Roever, W.P. (eds.) FMCO 2006. LNCS, vol. 4709, pp. 102–126. Springer, Cham (2006). https://doi.org/10.1007/978-3-540-74792-5_5
12. Stm32f103 datasheet. https://www.st.com/resource/en/datasheet/stm32f103c8.pdf. Accessed 05 Sept 2024
13. Armv7-m-refernce-manual. https://developer.arm.com/documentation/ddi0403/ee. Accessed 05 Sept 2024
14. Ranch repository. https://github.com/meyssamrostamzadeh/Ranch. Accessed 05 Sept 2024
15. van Glabbeek, R., Weijland, W.P.: Branching time and abstraction in bisimulation semantics. J. ACM **43**(3), 555–600 (1996)
16. https://rebeca-lang.org/allprojects/CoreRebecaExamples/DiningPhilosophers . Accessed 05 Sept 2024
17. Krebbers, R., Leroy, X., Wiedijk, F.: Formal C semantics: CompCert and the C standard. In: Klein, G., Gamboa, R. (eds.) ITP 2014. LNCS, vol. 8558, pp. 543–548. Springer, Cham (2014). https://doi.org/10.1007/978-3-319-08970-6_36
18. Lochbihler, A.: Verifying a compiler for java threads. In: Gordon, A.D. (ed.) ESOP 2010. LNCS, vol. 6012, pp. 427–447. Springer, Heidelberg (2010). https://doi.org/10.1007/978-3-642-11957-6_23

19. Khalafinejad, S., Mirian-Hosseinabadi, S.: Translation of Z specifications to executable code: Application to the database domain, Inf. Softw. Technol. 55 (6) (2013) 1017–1044. https://doi.org/10.1016/J.INFSOF.2012.12.007
20. Moreira, G., Vasconcellos, C.D., Kniess, J.: Fully-tested code generation from TLA+ specifications. In: de Almeida Maia, M., et al (eds.), SAST 2022: 7th Brazilian Symposium on Systematic and Automated Software Testing, Uberlandia, Brazil, October 3–7, 2022, pp. 19–28. ACM (2022). https://doi.org/10.1145/3559744.3559747

Animating Rebeca

Maurice H. ter Beek[1]([⊠]) [iD] and José Proença[2]([⊠]) [iD]

[1] CNR–ISTI, Pisa, Italy
maurice.terbeek@isti.cnr.it
[2] CISTER and University of Porto, University of Porto, Porto, Portugal
jose.proenca@fc.up.pt

Abstract. Rebeca is 20+ years old. Introduced by Marjan Sirjani and colleagues for modelling and analysing actor-based systems, it comes with a variety of tool support, including dedicated model checkers, simulators, and code generators. When encountering Rebeca for the first time, either as a student, as a researcher, or as a practitioner from industry, one needs to grasp the subtleties of Rebeca's semantics, which includes variants with probabilities and time.

This paper presents a user-friendly web-based front-end, based on the Caos library for Scala, to animate different operational semantics of (timed) Rebeca. This can facilitate the dissemination and awareness of Rebeca, provide insights into the differences among existing semantics, and support quick experimentation of new variants (e.g., when the order of received messages is preserved). The tool is illustrated by means of a ticket service use case from the literature.

Keywords: Rebeca · operational semantics · web front-end · animation · actors · time

1 Introduction

The _Reactive objects language_ (Rebeca) [21,24,25] is a high-level language designed for modelling and analysing concurrent and distributed systems based on the actor model of computation, which views systems as a collection of autonomous objects (actors) that communicate via asynchronous message passing.

Actors or _reactive objects_ (rebecs) constitute its primary modelling components, which are particularly useful for modelling and analysing reactive systems in which components react to incoming messages. Rebeca has a 25-year history [27,28], which traces back to the agent-based language Planner proposed by Hewitt [13], further developed into a concurrent object-based language by Agha [2], and formalised into a theory of actor computation by Agha et al. [3,4].

Rebecs communicate in a non-blocking fashion via asynchronous message passing between senders and receivers. Each rebec has a set of variables that store values, a set of methods (called message servers) and a message bag to

E. A. Lee et al. (Eds.): Marjan Sirjani Festschrift, LNCS 15560, pp. 182–194, 2025.
https://doi.org/10.1007/978-3-031-85134-6_8

store the received messages (along with their arrival times and their deadlines). Operationally, a rebec may take a message (with the least arrival time) from its message bag and execute the corresponding message server. Each rebec operates concurrently and can process one message at a time.

Throughout the years, several extensions of Rebeca have been introduced for the modelling and analysis of systems from specific domains, among which pRebeca [31] for probabilistic systems, Timed Rebeca [26] for real-time systems, PTRebeca [15] for probabilistic timed systems, and Hybrid Rebeca [17] for cyber-physical systems. In particular, Timed Rebeca extends core Rebeca with a global notion of time [1,20,23,26], which is achieved by synchronisation of (local) time of the actors (rebecs) involved. In Timed Rebeca, the primitives *delay* and *after* are used to model the progress of time while executing a message server.

Timed Rebeca is supported by the tool Afra [19], which offers a comprehensive IDE for specifying and verifying Rebeca models. It unifies the Java artifacts from various Rebeca-related projects and offers tools for model creation, property specification, model checking, and counterexample visualisation. Like other Eclipse-based plugins, the Afra interface is divided into a project browser, a model and property editor, and a view for model-checking results. Afra operates on the full space of global states (including local states and time) and transitions according to three types of possible actions (including taking a message, executing a message, and progressing time).

Besides Afra, there is a rich ecosystem of tools around Rebeca [24],[1] including generators for back-end model checkers such as SMV [29], mCRL2 [14], and McErlang [11], a dedicated model checker Modere [16], and a more recent Jacco model checker for Java actors [32] based on Rebeca's existing toolset.

As a result of this proliferation of extensions and tools for Rebeca, those who encounter Rebeca for the first time—either as a student, as a researcher, or as a practitioner from industry—need to grasp a number of subtleties of Rebeca's semantics, possibly including intricacies of probabilities and time.

We recently developed the Caos Scala framework (*Computer aided design of structural operational semantics*) [22], which can help ease these first contacts to Rebeca. Caos supports the creation of interactive JavaScript-based websites meant to animate operational semantics. These websites can provide both a quick feedback for developers and good insights to newcomers of a specific language.

Caos has been used, e.g., to animate and guide the development of the semantics of choreographic languages [8–10,18] and reactive systems [6,7,30], as well as to teach students about the semantics of C-like languages and of a concurrent process calculus.[2] A survey from 2020 with the participation of 130 formal methods experts—including three Turing Award winners, all five FME Fellowship Award winners, and 17 CAV Award winners—acknowledges the importance of supporting tools for teaching formal methods, since "an overwhelming majority of answers judged the use of tools essential when teaching formal methods" (75.4% of the respondents answered "major role") when asked "whether, and to

---

[1] https://rebeca-lang.org/tools.
[2] Many examples are listed here: https://github.com/arcalab/caos.

which extent, students should be exposed to software tools when being taught formal methods" [12, Section 6: Formal Methods in Education]. Moreover, tools "allow students to quickly link theory with practice" [5].

Contribution. We present a user-friendly web-based front-end for Rebeca based on Caos, which we call RebeCaos, to animate different operational semantics of (Timed) Rebeca and take away a little chaos from those who are new to the Rebeca theory and its supporting tools. More generally, this may facilitate further dissemination and awareness of Rebeca, provide insights into the differences among existing semantics, and support quick experimentation of new variants (e.g., when the order of received messages is preserved). RebeCaos is illustrated by means of a ticket service use case from the literature.

Outline. After this Introduction, Sect. 2 provides the syntax and semantics of core Rebeca, extended with time and dynamism, followed by the introduction of RebeCaos, a novel tool animating Rebeca, in Sect. 3. Before a dedication to Marjan Sirjani, we conclude the paper and present ideas for future work.

2 Rebeca: Syntax and Semantics

This section provides a quick introduction to Rebeca's syntax and semantics, starting with a simple toy example ⌷, presented in Fig. 1, borrowed from Hojjat et al. [14],[3] with a few adaptations. This program resembles a typical object-oriented one, where all objects are actors (called *rebecs*) and method invocation is asynchronous. In this concrete system there is a single **reactive class Example** that is instantiated twice in the **main** block on the right. The first instance is called ex1 and the second ex2. Two groups of arguments can be passed: the first to provide other rebecs that can be used to call methods to, and the second to provide values to initialise the rebec (via the initial method).

```
reactiveclass Example {          // available methods
  // rebecs to who it can send    msgsrv initial() {
  knownrebecs {                     counter=0;
    Example ex;                      ex.add(1);
  }                                }                      // Starting point to
  // internal state variables      msgsrv add(int a) {    // run the system
  statevars {                        if ( counter < 100 ) main {
    int counter;                       {counter = counter + a;}   Example ex1(ex2):();
  }                                }                        Example ex2(ex1):();
                                 }                        }
```

Fig. 1. Simple toy example ⌷ borrowed from Hojjat et al. [14].

---

[3] The electronic version of this paper includes hyperlinks to examples that open in our online tool, marked with the symbol ⌷.

In this system both **Example** instances initialise their counter to zero, and ask each other to increment their counter by one. The order in which they increment their counter is not fixed, and in the end both rebecs will have their counter set to one. The syntax and semantics will be precisely described below.

2.1 Syntax

We provide the abstract syntax of Rebeca from [20] below, writing $\langle \ldots \rangle$ for (meta) parenthesis, superscript $*$ for (zero or more) repetitions, $\langle \ldots \rangle^*$ for (zero or more) repetitions separated by commas, $\langle \ldots \rangle^+$ for (one or more) repetitions separated by commas, $[\ldots]$ for indicating that the text within the brackets is optional, identifiers *className*, *rebecName*, *methodName*, *v*, *literal*, *delay*, and *type* for denoting class name, rebec name, method name, variable, integer number, delay method, and type, respectively, *e* for denoting an (arithmetic, Boolean, or nondeterministic choice) expression, and parameter *t* for an expression with natural number result. The special variables *self* holds a reference to the current rebec, and *sender* holds a reference to the rebec that called the ongoing method.

$$
\begin{aligned}
Model ::&= Class^* \ Main \\
Main ::&= \textbf{main} \ \{ \ InstanceDcl^* \ \} \\
InstanceDcl ::&= className \ rebecName(\langle rebecName \rangle^*) : (\langle literal \rangle^*); \\
Class ::&= \textbf{reactiveclass} \ className \ \{ \ KnownRebecs \ Vars \ MsgSrv^* \ \} \\
KnownRebecs ::&= \textbf{knownrebecs} \ \{ \ VarDcl^* \ \} \\
Vars ::&= \textbf{statevars} \ \{ \ VarDcl^* \ \} \\
VarDcl ::&= type \ \langle v \rangle^+; \\
MsgSrv ::&= \textbf{msgsrv} \ methodName(\langle type \ v \rangle^*) \ \{ \ Stmt^* \ \} \\
Stmt ::&= v = e; \ | \ v=?(e, \langle e \rangle^+); \ | \ Call; \ | \ \textbf{if} \ (e) \ \{ \ Stmt^* \ \} \ [\textbf{else} \ \{ \ Stmt^* \ \}] \\
& | \ \ \textbf{delay}(t); \ | \ v = \textbf{new} \ className(\langle rebecName \rangle^*) : (\langle literal \rangle^*); \\
Call ::&= rebecName.methodName(\langle e \rangle^*) \ [\textbf{after}(t)] \ [\textbf{deadline}(t)]
\end{aligned}
$$

Timed Extension. The syntactic constructs that address time in the syntax above are marked with a light green background. These include a **delay**(*t*), which is a statement that causes its rebec to wait *t* time before proceeding; an **after**(*t*), whose value shows how long it takes for a message to be delivered to its receiver; and a **deadline**(*t*), which provides the timeout for a message, i.e., stating that it will remain valid for *t* time. Furthermore, a special variable *now* holds the local time value of each rebec, incremented in the semantic rules below. An example of a system with time will be presented later in Fig. 3, borrowed from Khamespanah et al. [20], describing a a Ticket service.

Dynamic Extension. At execution time, new rebecs can be created with the **new** keyword, similar to object-oriented languages such as Java. This part is marked in the syntax above with a darker blue background. When using this extension, each rebec can know both a static set of rebecs, declared in the **knownrebecs** block, and a dynamic set of rebecs, used and modified like other regular variables. For instance, "x = **new Example** (ex):(); x.add(3);" creates a new rebec of the **Example** class and calls its add method. We do not include a larger example in this paper, but some examples can be found in RebeCaos.

2.2 Semantics

We follow mainly the semantics of Timed Rebeca programs presented by Reynosson et al. [23], also used by others [1, 20]. This semantics uses both (1) an operational semantics to specify how the configuration of a system evolves when a pending message is processed, and (2) a natural semantics to evaluate a block of statements in a method. We start by describing the former, defining a configuration in a running system, followed by the evaluation of a given sequence of statements with both the timed and the dynamic extension.

Operational Semantics for the Scheduler. Assume a fixed set of rebec names R and let $r, s \in R$ range over these names. A configuration of a system is a pair $\langle Env, B \rangle$ where Env is a set of Rebeca states σ_r for each $r \in R$, and B is a multiset of pending messages. A *state* $\sigma_r \in Env$ of a rebec r is a mapping from variables to values, including the special variables *now* (representing the local time of a rebec) and *sender* (representing the rebec that called the ongoing method). A *message* in B is a tuple $\langle r, m(\overline{v}), s, TT, DL \rangle$ representing a pending call to a method m with arguments $\overline{v}$, called by a rebec s to a rebec r, sent at time TT and expiring at time DL. The SOS rule of Timed Rebeca is formalised below, specifying a scheduling of messages, i.e., the selection of the next pending message and consequently the next rebec to run:

$$[\text{SCHED}] \quad \frac{(\sigma_r(m), \sigma_r[now = max(TT, \sigma_r(now)), [\overline{arg} = \overline{v}], sender = s], Env, B)}{\left\langle \begin{array}{c} \{\sigma_r\} \uplus Env, \\ \{(r, m(\overline{v}), s, TT, DL)\} \uplus B \end{array} \right\rangle \xrightarrow{[s] \; r.m(\overline{v}) \, @ \, TT..DL} \left\langle \begin{array}{c} \sigma'_r \cup Env', \\ B' \end{array} \right\rangle} \quad Cnd$$

where condition $Cnd = TT \leq min(B) \wedge \sigma_r(now) \leq DL$ and $\uplus$ denotes the disjoint union. The function $\Downarrow$ evaluates a sequence of statements, described below. The label of the transition $[s] \; r.m(\overline{v}) \, @ \, TT..DL$ is used in our prototype implementation but not included in the reference publications [1, 20, 23]. It states that rebec s called method $m(\overline{v})$ of rebec r, and the message must be processed between time TT and DL.

The initial configuration $\langle Env, B \rangle$ is given by the **main** block: for each instance declaration $C \; r(\overline{k}) : (\overline{v})$, the environment Env includes a state $\sigma_r = \{now \mapsto 0, self \mapsto r\} \cup \{r_i \mapsto k_i \mid r_i \in C.\textbf{knownrebecs}, k_i \in \overline{k}\} \cup \{x_i \mapsto v_i \mid x_i \in C.\textbf{statevars},$

$v_i \in \overline{v}$ }, and the messages B include ($-$, $initial(v), r, 0, +\infty$). These *initial* methods are given higher priority within each rebec, which we leave out of the SCHED rule for simplicity, as is done in the above mentioned reference publications.

Natural Semantics for Statements. The effect of Timed Rebeca statements is given by the function $\Downarrow$, formalised below. This function receives a tuple (st, σ, Env, B) with a sequence of statements st, an initial state σ, the states of the neighbours Env, and the initial set of pending messages B. It returns a triple (σ', Env', B') with an updated state σ', environment Env', and messages B'. Here *eval* is a function that evaluates expressions in a given environment as expected, the value of special variable *self* is the name of the rebec, and σ is assumed not to be contained in Env.

$$[\text{SEND}]\ (x.m(\overline{v})\ \textbf{after}(d)\ \textbf{deadline}(DL), \sigma, Env, B)\ \Downarrow$$
$$(\sigma, Env, \{(\sigma(x), m(eval(\overline{v}, \sigma)), \sigma(self), \sigma(now) + d, \sigma(now) + DL)\} \cup B)$$

$$[\text{DELAY}]\ (\textbf{delay}(d), \sigma, Env, B)\ \Downarrow\ (\sigma[now = \sigma(now) + d], Env, B)$$

$$[\text{ASSIGN}]\ (v = e, \sigma, Env, B)\ \Downarrow\ (\sigma[v = eval(e, \sigma)], Env, B)$$

$$[\text{COND1}]\ \frac{eval(e, \sigma) = true \quad (S_1, \sigma, Env, B)\ \Downarrow\ (\sigma', Env', B')}{(\textbf{if}\ (e)\ \textbf{then}\ S_1\ \textbf{else}\ S_2, \sigma, Env, B)\ \Downarrow\ (\sigma', Env', B')}$$

$$[\text{COND2}]\ \frac{eval(e, \sigma) = false \quad (S_2, \sigma, Env, B)\ \Downarrow\ (\sigma', Env', B')}{(\textbf{if}\ (e)\ \textbf{then}\ S_1\ \textbf{else}\ S_2, \sigma, Env, B)\ \Downarrow\ (\sigma', Env', B')}$$

$$[\text{SEQ}]\ \frac{(S_1, \sigma, Env, B)\ \Downarrow\ (\sigma', Env', B'), \ (S_2, \sigma', Env', B')\ \Downarrow\ (\sigma'', Env'', B'')}{(S_1; S_2, \sigma, Env, B)\ \Downarrow\ (\sigma'', Env'', B'')}$$

$$[\text{CREATE}]\ \frac{r \text{ is a fresh rebec name}}{(v = \textbf{new}\ C(\overline{x}), \sigma, Env, B)\ \Downarrow}$$
$$(\sigma[v = r], \sigma_r[now = \sigma(now), self = r] \cup Env,$$
$$(r, initial(eval(\overline{x}, \sigma)), \sigma(self), \sigma(now), +\infty) \cup B)$$

3 RebeCaos by Example

This section describes RebeCaos, a pedagogical tool that animates the semantics of Rebeca as just presented in Sect. 2.2. RebeCaos is implemented in Scala, compiled into JavaScript, and it uses the Caos library [22] to generate the web-based front-end and to present the full state space exploration. The resulting tool consists of an interactive webpage that does not rely on a server, and that can easily be used in any browser with JavaScript support.

We describe how to use RebeCaos guided by two examples: a dynamic variation of the simple toy example⌃, listed in Fig. 1, and a timed example of a ticket service⌃, borrowed from Reynisson et al. [23].

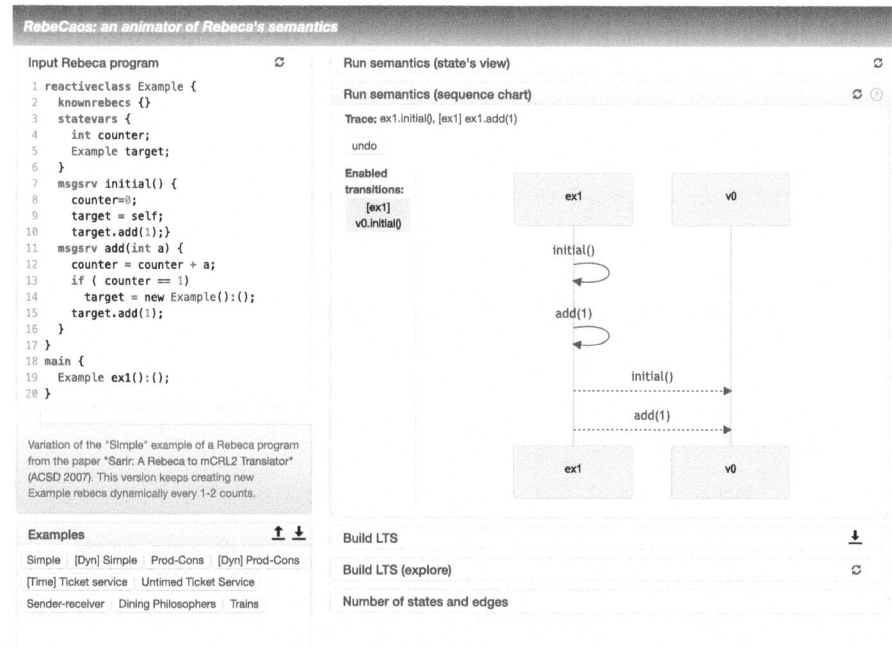

Fig. 2. Screenshot of the interface of RebeCaos.

3.1   Interface of RebeCaos

RebeCaos can be opened by navigating to https://fm-dcc.github.io/rebecaos, where the user can view an interface similar to the screenshot in Fig. 2. Here we use the second example, called "[Dyn] Simple"⌃, which is a variation of the simple toy example from Fig. 1 that dynamically creates new instances. This interface includes several *widgets*, each of which can be collapsed (such as Run semantics (state's view)) or expanded (such as Run semantics (sequence chart)). Clicking the title of a widget toggles between these modes and reloads its content. In the screenshot, we provide the above mentioned variation of the simple toy example in the widget Input Rebeca Program, as well as an interactive step-by-step execution of its semantics using sequence charts. Other examples, including the ones mentioned throughout the paper, can be loaded from the Examples widget.

3.2   Running Step-by-Step

The widget Run semantics (sequence chart) in Fig. 2 supports a guided step-by-step execution of an input Rebeca program, following closely the semantics presented in Sect. 2.2. The sequence diagram depicts the sequence of *called* and *processed* methods; in this case, the rebec ex1 already processed the methods initial() and add(1), marked with a solid line, and also created a new rebec v0 and called its method add(1). On the other hand, neither of the initial and the add methods have been processed yet, marked with a dashed arrow.

The column on the left of the sequence chart lists the *enabled transitions*; in this case there is only one enabled transition named "[ex1] v0.initial()", representing a pending method call initial to rebec v0 by triggered by rebec ex1. The method add(1) is not yet enabled because initial methods have precedence over all other methods of the same rebec.

By iteratively clicking on an enabled transition we can grow the sequence chart, producing a trace in which solid arrows are ordered based on when they are processed, while dashed arrows are randomly ordered at the bottom, representing the multiset of pending messages, i.e., called but not yet processed.

An alternative widget to build a trace of a Rebeca program is Run semantics (state's view), not depicted in the screenshot. This has the same buttons to select enabled transitions, but instead of the sequence chart it depicts the precise state of each rebec and the multiset of pending messages.

3.3   Running All Steps

It is often convenient to automatically traverse all possible states, instead of manually creating possible traces. This is performed by the widget Build LTS, illustrated in Fig. 4 to capture the state space of the Ticket Service ⍈ program in Fig. 3.[4] This concrete program was used, e.g., by Khamespanah et al. [20], and it produces the infinite state space partially represented in Fig. 4 on the left side.

Our implementation performs a breath-first traversal, stopping after a finite number of steps. By using an adaptation of this program without time references ⍈ , included in the examples of our tool, the state space becomes finite, depicted in Fig. 4 on the right side. The highlighted node on top corresponds to the highlighted node in the state space of the timed version, since the initial parts of these two graphs are identical. Interestingly, the finite state space on the right side for the untimed version has the same shape as the state space produced by Khamespanah et al. [20] for the timed version, where they use an optimisation that collapses states that are similar, i.e., with a behaviour that keeps on repeating itself after some time. This optimisation is not currently implemented in RebeCaos.

---

[4] The widget Build LTS (explore) (cf. Fig. 2) is similar to Built LTS but the state space is drawn iteratively, requiring the user to click the states that (s)he wants to expand.

```
reactiveclass TicketService {        reactiveclass Customer {           reactiveclass Agent {
  knownrebecs {                        knownrebecs {                      knownrebecs {
    Agent a;                             Agent a;                           TicketService ts;
  }                                    }                                    Customer c;
  statevars {                          msgsrv initial() {                 }
    int issueDelay;                      self.try();                      msgsrv requestTicket() {
  }                                    }                                    ts.requestTicket()
  msgsrv initial(int d) {              msgsrv try() {                         deadline (5);
    issueDelay = d;                      a.requestTicket();               }
  }                                    }                                  msgsrv ticketIssued(byte id) {
  msgsrv requestTicket() {             msgsrv ticketIssued(byte id) {       c.ticketIssued(id);
    delay(issueDelay);                   self.try() after(30);            }
    a.ticketIssued (1);               }                                  }
  }                                  }                                    main {
}                                                                           Agent a(ts,c):();
                                                                            TicketService ts(a):(3);
                                                                            Customer c(a):();
                                                                          }
```

Fig. 3. Ticket Service with time extensions⌁ borrowed from Khamespanah et al. [20].

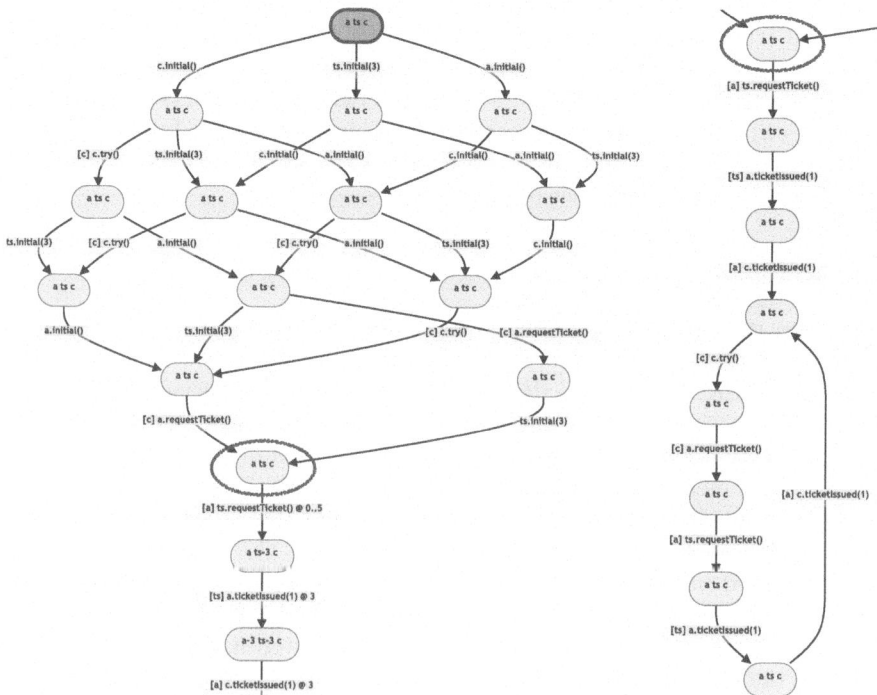

Fig. 4. Full state exploration of the ticket service (left) and an untimed version (right); the former continues infinitely below and the latter shows how this infinite sequence becomes a loop by showing the different behaviour from the highlighted state "a ts c".

3.4 Beyond RebeCaos

Existing tools for Rebeca, such as Afra [19], use an extended version of the syntax presented in Sect. 2.1. These extensions have not yet been implemented in RebeCaos, since most of them are not needed for many of the examples from the literature. These extensions include, e.g., arrays, syntactic macros (with the env keyword), and type casting.

Furthermore, as mentioned in the Introduction, Rebeca has been equipped with a probabilistic semantics (cf., e.g., [15, 31]) and this also has not been implemented in RebeCaos so far. RebeCaos moreover provides neither support for model checking nor for code generation, mainly because RebeCaos is not meant to substitute an IDE for Rebeca, but rather to provide an easy entry point.

We believe that RebeCaos can be useful, not only to help teaching and explaining the insights of Rebeca, but also as a relatively easy and intuitive tool for core Rebeca to experiment with new extensions or with variations. One could, for instance, implement a semantics that preserves the order of method calls, replacing the multiset of pending messages B by a queue; or attempt to define a type-checking algorithm that verifies conformity with a given behavioural type. Performing such experiments with RebeCaos may provide quicker feedback to developers, and help convince others that the new experiments make sense.

4 Conclusion

We presented RebeCaos, a user-friendly web-based front-end tool based on the Caos library for Scala and we illustrated by means of several examples how to animate Rebeca extended with time and dynamism. As future work, we might extend the syntax and semantics of Rebeca currently supported by RebeCaos, e.g., with a means to deal with probabilistic extensions of Rebeca, or with entirely novel extensions such as an experimental type-checking algorithm for verifying conformity with a given behavioural type.

Dedication

This paper is dedicated to Marjan Sirjani, the mother of Rebeca. While so far neither of us has written a paper together with Marjan, our paths have crossed several times.

Maurice recalls her expertise and kind professionalism during a European project review earlier in his career as well as their smooth and pleasant collaboration as PC co-chairs of COORDINATION 2022 and as co-editors of the associated special issue in Logical Methods in Computer Science. Since then many meetings have followed.

José recalls meeting Marjan for the first time at FOCLASA 2008, in Reykjavik, at the beginning of her Icelandic teaching position and his early work as a PhD student. Marjan visited many times his small group in CWI, in Amsterdam, as part of the warm Iranian cluster that brought him many wonderful moments.

As a tribute to Marjan, we decided to reanimate Rebeca. We hope that Marjan finds her child Rebeca as attractive as ever!

Acknowledgements. This work was funded by the MUR PRIN 2020TL3X8X project T-LADIES (Typeful Language Adaptation for Dynamic, Interacting and Evolving Systems) and by the CNR project "Formal Methods in Software Engineering 2.0", CUP B53C24000720005. This work is also supported by the CISTER, ISEP/IPP Research Unit (UIDP/UIDB/04234/2020), financed by National Funds through FCT/ MCTES (Portuguese Foundation for Science and Technology), and by the EU/Next Generation, within the Recovery and Resilience Plan, within project Route 25 (TRB/2022/00061 – C645463824-00000063).

References

1. Aceto, L., Cimini, M., Ingólfsdóttir, A., Reynisson, A.H., Sigurdarson, S.H., Sirjani, M.: Modelling and simulation of asynchronous real-time systems using timed Rebeca. In: Mousavi, M.R., Ravara, A. (eds.) Proceedings of the 10th International Workshop on the Foundations of Coordination Languages and Software Architectures (FOCLASA'11). EPTCS, vol. 58, pp. 1–19 (2011). https://doi.org/10.4204/EPTCS.58.1

2. Agha, G.A.: ACTORS: A Model of Concurrent Computation in Distributed Systems. MIT Press Series in Artificial Intelligence, MIT Press (1986). https://doi.org/10.7551/mitpress/1086.001.0001

3. Agha, G., Mason, I.A., Smith, S., Talcott, C.: Towards a theory of actor computation. In: Cleaveland, W.R. (ed.) CONCUR 1992. LNCS, vol. 630, pp. 565–579. Springer, Heidelberg (1992). https://doi.org/10.1007/BFb0084816

4. Agha, G.A., Mason, I.A., Smith, S.F., Talcott, C.L.: A foundation for actor computation. J. Funct. Program. **7**(1), 1–72 (1997). https://doi.org/10.1017/S095679689700261X

5. ter Beek, M., Broy, M., Dongol, B.: The role of formal methods in computer science education. ACM Inroads **15**(4), 58–66 (2024). https://doi.org/10.1145/3702231

6. ter Beek, M.H., Cledou, G., Hennicker, R., Proença, J.: Can we communicate? Using dynamic logic to verify team automata. In: Chechik, M., Katoen, J.P., Leucker, M. (eds.) FM 2023. LNCS, vol. 14000, pp. 122–141. Springer, Cham (2023). https://doi.org/10.1007/978-3-031-27481-7_9

7. ter Beek, M.H., Hennicker, R., Proença, J.: Team automata: overview and roadmap. In: Castellani, I., Tiezzi, F. (eds.) COORDINATION 2024. LNCS, vol. 14676, pp. 161–198. Springer, Cham (2024). https://doi.org/10.1007/978-3-031-62697-5_10

8. Cledou, G., Edixhoven, L., Jongmans, S.S., Proença, J.: API generation for multiparty session types, revisited and revised using Scala 3. In: Ali, K., Vitek, J. (eds.) Proceedings of the 36th European Conference on Object-Oriented Programming (ECOOP'22). LIPIcs, vol. 222, pp. 27:1–27:28. Schloss Dagstuhl - Leibniz-Zentrum für Informatik (2022). https://doi.org/10.4230/LIPIcs.ECOOP.2022.27

9. Edixhoven, L., Jongmans, S.S.: Realisability of branching pomsets. In: Tapia Tarifa, S.L., Proença, J. (eds.) FACS 2022. LNCS, vol. 13712, pp. 185–204. Springer, Cham (2022). https://doi.org/10.1007/978-3-031-20872-0_11

10. Edixhoven, L., Jongmans, S.S., Proença, J., Cledou, G.: Branching pomsets for choreographies. In: Aubert, C., Di Giusto, C., Safina, L., Scalas, A. (eds.) Proceedings of the 15th Interaction and Concurrency Experience (ICE 2022). EPTCS, vol. 365, pp. 37–52 (2022). https://doi.org/10.4204/EPTCS.365.3

11. Fredlund, L., Svensson, H.: McErlang: a model checker for a distributed functional programming language. In: Proceedings of the 12th International Conference on Functional Programming (ICFP 2007), pp. 125–136. ACM (2007). https://doi.org/10.1145/1291151.1291171

12. Garavel, H., ter Beek, M.H., van de Pol, J.: The 2020 expert survey on formal methods. In: ter Beek, M.H., Ničković, D. (eds.) FMICS 2020. LNCS, vol. 12327, pp. 3–69. Springer, Cham (2020). https://doi.org/10.1007/978-3-030-58298-2_1

13. Hewitt, C.: Description and Theoretical Analysis (Using Schemata) of Planner: A Language for Proving Theorems and Manipulating Models in a Robot. Technical report AITR-258, MIT (1972), http://hdl.handle.net/1721.1/6916

14. Hojjat, H., Sirjani, M., Mousavi, M.R., Groote, J.F.: Sarir: a Rebeca to mCRL2 translator. In: Proceedings of the 7th International Conference on Application of Concurrency to System Design (ACSD 2007), pp. 216–222. IEEE (2007). https://doi.org/10.1109/ACSD.2007.62

15. Jafari, A., Khamespanah, E., Sirjani, M., Hermanns, H., Cimini, M.: PTRebeca: modeling and analysis of distributed and asynchronous systems. Sci. Comput. Program. **128**, 22–50 (2016). https://doi.org/10.1016/J.SCICO.2016.03.004

16. Jaghoori, M.M., Movaghar, A., Sirjani, M.: Modere: the model-checking engine of Rebeca. In: Proceedings of the 21st Symposium on Applied Computing (SAC 2006), pp. 1810–1815. ACM (2006). https://doi.org/10.1145/1141277.1141704

17. Jahandideh, I., Ghassemi, F., Sirjani, M.: Hybrid Rebeca: modeling and analyzing of cyber-physical systems. In: Chamberlain, R., Taha, W., Törngren, M. (eds.) CyPhy/WESE -2018. LNCS, vol. 11615, pp. 3–27. Springer, Cham (2019). https://doi.org/10.1007/978-3-030-23703-5_1

18. Jongmans, S.S., Proença, J.: ST4MP: a blueprint of multiparty session typing for multilingual programming. In: Margaria, T., Steffen, B. (eds.) ISoLA 2022. LNCS, vol. 13701, pp. 460–478. Springer, Cham (2022). https://doi.org/10.1007/978-3-031-19849-6_26

19. Khamespanah, E., Sirjani, M., Khosravi, R.: Afra: an Eclipse-based tool with extensible architecture for modeling and model checking of Rebeca family models. In: Hojjat, H., Ábrahám, E. (eds.) FSEN 2023. LNCS, vol. 14155, pp. 72–87. Springer, Cham (2023). https://doi.org/10.1007/978-3-031-42441-0_6

20. Khamespanah, E., Sirjani, M., Sabahi-Kaviani, Z., Khosravi, R., Izadi, M.: Timed Rebeca schedulability and deadlock freedom analysis using bounded floating time transition system. Sci. Comput. Program. **98**, 184–204 (2015). https://doi.org/10.1016/J.SCICO.2014.07.005

21. Khosravi, R., Khamespanah, E., Ghassemi, F., Sirjani, M.: Actors upgraded for variability, adaptability, and determinism. In: de Boer, F.S., Damiani, F., Hähnle, R., Johnsen, E.B., Kamburjan, E. (eds.) Active Object Languages: Current Research Trends. LNCS, vol. 14360, pp. 226–260. Springer, Cham (2024). https://doi.org/10.1007/978-3-031-51060-1_9

22. Proença, J., Edixhoven, L.: Caos: a reusable scala web animator of operational semantics. In: Jongmans, S.S., Lopes, A. (eds.) COORDINATION 2023. LNCS, vol. 13908, pp. 163–171. Springer, Cham (2023). https://doi.org/10.1007/978-3-031-35361-1_9

23. Reynisson, A.H., et al.: Modelling and simulation of asynchronous real-time systems using Timed Rebeca. Sci. Comput. Program. **89**, 41–68 (2014). https://doi.org/10.1016/J.SCICO.2014.01.008
24. Sirjani, M.: Rebeca: theory, applications, and tools. In: de Boer, F.S., Bonsangue, M.M., Graf, S., de Roever, W.-P. (eds.) FMCO 2006. LNCS, vol. 4709, pp. 102–126. Springer, Heidelberg (2007). https://doi.org/10.1007/978-3-540-74792-5_5
25. Sirjani, M., Jaghoori, M.M.: Ten years of analyzing actors: Rebeca experience. In: Agha, G., Danvy, O., Meseguer, J. (eds.) Formal Modeling: Actors, Open Systems, Biological Systems. LNCS, vol. 7000, pp. 20–56. Springer, Heidelberg (2011). https://doi.org/10.1007/978-3-642-24933-4_3
26. Sirjani, M., Khamespanah, E.: On time actors. In: Ábrahám, E., Bonsangue, M., Johnsen, E.B. (eds.) Theory and Practice of Formal Methods. LNCS, vol. 9660, pp. 373–392. Springer, Cham (2016). https://doi.org/10.1007/978-3-319-30734-3_25
27. Sirjani, M., Movaghar, A.: An Actor-Based Model for Reactive Systems: Rebeca. Technical report CS-TR-80-01, Sharif University of Technology (2001)
28. Sirjani, M., Movaghar, A., Mousavi, M.R.: Compositional verification of an actor-based model for reactive systems. In: Proceedings of the 1st Workshop on Automated Verification of Critical Systems (AVoCS 2001), pp. 114–118. Oxford University (2001). https://rebeca-lang.org/assets/papers/2001/CompositionalVerificationOfAnObject-BasedModelForReactiveSystems.pdf
29. Sirjani, M., Shali, A., Jaghoori, M.M., Iravanchi, H., Movaghar, A.: A front-end tool for automated abstraction and modular verification of actor-based models. In: Proceedings of the 4th International Conference on Application of Concurrency to System Design (ACSD 2004), pp. 145–150. IEEE (2004). https://doi.org/10.1109/CSD.2004.1309125
30. Tinoco, D., Madeira, A., Martins, M.A., Proença, J.: Reactive graphs in action. In: Marmsoler, D., Sun, M. (eds.) FACS 2024. LNCS, vol. 15189, pp. 97–105. Springer, Cham (2024). https://doi.org/10.1007/978-3-031-71261-6_6
31. Varshosaz, M., Khosravi, R.: Modeling and verification of probabilistic actor systems using pRebeca. In: Aoki, T., Taguchi, K. (eds.) ICFEM 2012. LNCS, vol. 7635, pp. 135–150. Springer, Heidelberg (2012). https://doi.org/10.1007/978-3-642-34281-3_12
32. Zakeriyan, A., Khamespanah, E., Sirjani, M., Khosravi, R.: Jacco: more efficient model checking toolset for Java actor programs. In: Boix, E.G., Haller, P., Ricci, A., Varela, C.A. (eds.) Proceedings of the 5th International Workshop on Programming Based on Actors, Agents, and Decentralized Control (AGERE! 2015), pp. 37–44. ACM (2015). https://doi.org/10.1145/2824815.2824819

Verify Engineering Models, Not Scientific Models

Shaokai Lin$^{(\boxtimes)}$ and Edward A. Lee$^{(\boxtimes)}$

UC Berkeley, Berkeley, CA 94720, USA
{shaokai,eal}@berkeley.edu

Abstract. Driving progress in science and engineering for centuries, models are powerful tools for understanding systems and building abstractions. However, the goal of models in science is different from that in engineering, and we observe the misuse of models undermining research goals. Specifically in the field of formal methods, we advocate that verification should be performed on engineering models rather than scientific models, to the extent possible. We observe that models under verification are, very often, scientific models rather than engineering models, and we show why verifying scientific models is ineffective in engineering efforts. To guarantee safety in an engineered system, it is the engineering model one should verify. This model can be used to derive a correct-by-construction implementation. To demonstrate our proposed principle, we review lessons learned from verifying programs in a language called Lingua Franca using Timed Rebeca.

Keywords: Formal Verfication · Lingua Franca · Rebeca

Prologue

This paper is dedicated to our friend, colleague, and mentor, Marjan Sirjani, and offered as a contribution to her Festschrift. Marjan's work on formal methods for software engineering has been and continues to be an inspiration.

1 Scientific and Engineering Models

In science, the objective of a model is to match a real-world system. In contrast, in engineering, the objective of a real-world system (an implementation) is to match a model [15]. A digital logic diagram, for example, is an engineering model; a circuit gets constructed to match the model. Differential equations giving currents and voltages in a circuit over time are commonly used as a scientific model; the equations are crafted to match the physical circuit. But even these equations could be used as an engineering model, giving for example a specification of an analog circuit. The actual components used will not be perfectly linear and will not have the resistances, capacitance, and inductance

© The Author(s), under exclusive license to Springer Nature Switzerland AG 2025
E. A. Lee et al. (Eds.): Marjan Sirjani Festschrift, LNCS 15560, pp. 195–211, 2025.
https://doi.org/10.1007/978-3-031-85134-6_9

perfectly matching the model. When using models, it is important to understand whether they are being used as engineering models or scientific models. Are the resistances wrong in the model or in the physical circuit? One of the two must be true.

This paper argues that formal verification, by its very nature, should focus on verifying engineering models, not scientific ones. As George Box famously said, "all models are wrong, but some are useful" [6]. Here, Box was referring to scientific models. The corresponding statement for engineering models is, "all physical, real-world implementations are wrong, but some are useful" [14]. An engineering model is, or at least attempts to be, right, not wrong. It is a specification, an idealization, and an implementation can only approximate it.

Formal verification, by its nature of being formal, can only make assertions about *models*. For scientific models, therefore, since the model itself is always wrong, proving "correctness" of a wrong model has questionable value. On the other hand, proving that a design (a specification) is correct can be extremely useful. Indeed, most success stories for formal verification concern synchronous digital logic (an engineering model) and software (another engineering model). The physical realization in both cases is "electrons sloshing in silicon" [15], about which nothing is proved.

In this paper, we examine a major innovation of Sirjani and her colleagues, Timed Rebeca (TR), a language and formalism for describing and analyzing timed systems. We argue that the timing features of TR are more useful when viewed as an engineering model than when viewed as a scientific model. To support the case, we show the relationship between the timing constructs of TR and an implementation (vs. modeling) language with similar timing constructs, Lingua Franca (LF). We show that, with the addition of priorities for message handlers, TR can model the timing constructs of Lingua Franca and therefore can be used to effectively formally verify engineering models specified using LF.

For example, the TR after delay gives a time offset between the sending and the receiving of a message between actors. If this after delay is intended to model physical communication latencies, then it is being used as a scientific model. The model is correct only if the physical communication latencies actually match. If, on the other hand, it is used to specify a logical offset between the sender's view and the receiver's view of changing data, then it is being used as an engineering model. The implementation is correct only if it actually delivers the specified logical offset. Such delays are used in LF in the latter sense, not the former, whereas in TR, we have seen them used both ways.

A significant limitation remains, however. Formal verification can only be performed on closed models. For systems that interact with an uncontrolled environment that is not designed, we have no choice but to provide a scientific model of that environment. Any proof of the correctness of a design, therefore, is predicated on the assumptions about the environment. These assumptions are made evident by making a clear separation between models of the environment and models of the system under design. The weaker those assumptions, the stronger the confidence provided by the verification results.

2   Scientific and Engineering Models in Timed Rebeca

Timed Rebeca [21] is an extension of the Rebeca modeling language [22] (an implementation of the Hewitt-Agha actor model [1,2,8]) that adds a notion of time. In this extension, time is an integer, messages are sent and arrive at (possibly distinct) times and message handlers (optionally) take time to execute. Three operators are added to the Rebeca language to model time: `delay`, `deadline`, and `after`. A delay statement models the passing of time of an actor during the execution of a message server. The `after` operator indicates time that elapses before a message is delivered to its destination. The `deadline` operator models message loss if the destination is busy due to `delay` statements and does not handle an incoming message before the deadline expires.

In addition to these operators, Timed Rebeca strengthens the semantics that define the order in which message handlers are invoked. Because of these operators, each message delivered to an actor has a time associated with it, and the destination actor will handle messages in temporal order, unless it is busy due to a `delay` statement, in which case it will handle the message at the time the delay expires. If two messages are delivered with the same time, then the handler order is nondeterministic unless the programmer specifies priorities. The ability to specify priorities was added later specifically to support the kind of modeling we describe in this paper [9,24].

Reynisson et al. [21] give a ticket service example (Fig. 1), where an agent accepts requests for tickets from an environment and issues requests for a ticket to two ticket services. If the first ticket service does not respond with a ticket within a specified amount of time (defined by the `checkIssuedPeriod` environment variable, defined on line 1 and used on line 14), then it tries the second ticket service. The `TicketService` actor uses the `delay` operator to nondeterministically delay responding by either `serviceTime1` or `serviceTime2` (lines 38 and 39). Here, there is a mix of scientific and engineering modeling. The value of `checkIssuedPeriod` is an engineering *specification*. It defines how long the `Agent` actor should wait before giving up on the requested ticket service. On the other hand, the `serviceTime1` or `serviceTime2` variables model communication and computation time, which are *assumptions* derived from the environment through scientific means (measurement, for example). When performing verification on this model, the results of the verification can only be considered valid for these two particular assumed delays. If the actual observed delays deviate from these assumed delays, which could always happen due to the nature of scientific modeling, the verification model is no longer applicable.

Later, Sirjani and Khamespanah note the distinction between engineering models and scientific models and describe a Timed Rebeca example for components of a network on chip [23]. Specifically, the model consists of a Manager, which generates network traffic, and a Router, which routes traffic according to a specified policy. In this example, the precise times given in `after`, `delay`, and `deadline` statements can be interpreted as specifications for the time taken by a synchronous digital circuit implementation of the router. No time units are given in the paper, but in this engineering-model interpretation, they could be

```
 1  env int requestDeadline,
        checkIssuedPeriod,
        retryRequestPeriod,
        newRequestPeriod, serviceTime1,
        serviceTime2;
 2
 3  reactiveclass Agent {
 4    knownrebecs { TicketService ts1;
        TicketService ts2; }
 5    statevars { int attemptCount;
 6    boolean ticketIssued; int token; }
 7    msgsrv initial() {
 8      self.findTicket(ts1); }
 9    msgsrv findTicket(TicketService ts){
10      attemptCount += 1; token += 1;
11      ts.requestTicket(token) deadline(
          requestDeadline);
12      // Check if a reply to the
13      // request has been received.
14      self.checkTicket() after(
          checkIssuedPeriod);}
15    msgsrv checkTicket() {
16      if (!ticketIssued
17        && attemptCount == 1) {
18        self.findTicket(ts2);
19      } else if (!ticketIssued
20        && attemptCount == 2) {
21        self.retry() after(
            retryRequestPeriod);
22      } else if (ticketIssued) {
23        ticketIssued = false;
24        self.retry() after(
            newRequestPeriod);
25      }
26    }
```

```
22    msgsrv ticketIssued(int tok){
23      if (token == tok) {
24        ticketIssued = true; }}
25    msgsrv retry() {
26      attemptCount = 0;
27      self.findTicket(ts1);}
28  }
29  reactiveclass TicketService {
30    knownrebecs { Agent a; }
31    msgsrv initial() { }
32    msgsrv requestTicket(int token){
33      // The ticket service sends
34      // the reply after a non-
35      // deterministic delay of
36      // either serviceTime1 or
37      // serviceTime2.
38      int wait = ?(serviceTime1,
          serviceTime2);
39      delay(wait);
40      a.ticketIssued(token);
41    }
42  }
43  main {
44    Agent a(ts1, ts2):();
45    TicketService ts1(a):();
46    TicketService ts2(a):();
47  }
```

Fig. 1. Timed Rebeca model for a ticket service, from [21].

clock cycles or SI units (such as nanoseconds) as measured by the clock of a synchronous digital circuit.

We argue here that the Timed Rebeca constructs, `delay`, `deadline`, and `after`, are much more useful in an engineering model than in a scientific model, except when explicitly modeling an uncontrolled environment. Using `after` to model communication delays, for example, is questionable for systems using modern network communication. The delays can be nondeterministically chosen, but for verification to be tractable, a small number of possible delays must be used. Moreover, these delays refer to clock measurements of time at distinct points in the network. Reynisson et al. [21] assume perfect (or near perfect) clock synchronization, but perfect clock synchronization is not possible. On the other hand, when these numbers refer to a *logical* clock instead of physical clocks, and the time ordering of events is a *semantic* property of the system rather than an emergent property of the implementation, then verification results can be trusted subject only to the condition that the system implementation correctly realizes the semantics. We show how to do that in this paper.

Fig. 2. Two accidental deployments of emergency escape slides (image from *The Telegraph*, Sept. 9, 2015).

3 Running Example

In this section, we introduce an example (somewhat artificial and grossly oversimplified) which is a distributed system in which the order of events is of critical importance. There are many practical examples that have this character, but we pick this one because it is vivid, simple, and challenging to get right, all at the same time.

Consider automating the opening and closing of an aircraft door. Modern passenger planes are equipped with emergency escape slides that are automatically deployed if the door is opened while the door is "armed." When the doors are closed for departure, flight attendants arm them. At arrival, once they have verified that a ramp is right outside the door, the flight attendants disarm the door before an operator opens it. The process currently is manual, with a red or green flag displayed in a window on the door to indicate whether it is armed or not.

Suppose we wish to automate the process so that the door can be opened remotely. There might be multiple systems on the aircraft that issue a command to open the door. Some of these, such as a cockpit control, might want to ensure that a ramp is present and the door is disarmed before it is opened, while others, such as a fire alarm system, might want to open the door whether it is armed or not.

The door will be equipped with a networked microprocessor that provides just two services, disarm and open (we leave out arming and closing, which are not needed to make our points). Assume the door starts in the armed and closed state. What should the microprocessor do when it receives an open command over the network? It is critical to be sure that if the open command has an associated disarm command, or if there is a ramp present at the door, that the door should be disarmed before it is opened. We have to guard against errors

due to networking or computation delays, otherwise we might find ourselves in
the life-threatening situations depicted in Fig. 2.

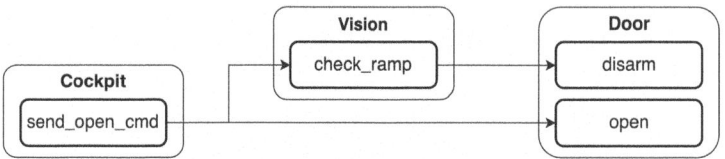

Fig. 3. Aircraft door system schematic using the Actor model.

Suppose that when a cockpit control issues an instruction to open the door,
the actual opening is delayed until a ramp is present. As shown in Fig. 3, a computer vision system might check for a ramp. Suppose further that the Cockpit,
Vision, and Door components are realized as Hewitt-Agha actors. We immediately have a problem because the order of message delivery and handling in the
Hewitt-Agha model is nondeterministic. It is highly sensitive to delays in the
network and in intermediate computations. With the design in Fig. 3, the open
message will very likely arrive before disarm message, resulting in catastrophe.

```
1  reactiveclass Cockpit(10) {
2    knownrebecs { Vision v; Door d; }
3    Cockpit() {
4      self.send_open_cmd();
5    }
6    msgsrv send_open_cmd() {
7      // Send open message.
8      d.open(true);
9      v.check_ramp(true);
10     // Repeat after 100 ms.
11     self.send_open_cmd() after(100);
12   }
13 }
14 reactiveclass Vision(10) {
15   knownrebecs { Door d; }
16   msgsrv check_ramp(boolean trigger) {
17     // Use vision to detect ramps.
18     // Assume a ramp is present.
19     d.disarm(true);
20   }
21 }
```

```
22 reactiveclass Door(10) {
23   statevars {
24     // 0: closed_armed,
25     // 1: closed_disarmed,
26     // 2: open,
27     // 3: open_deployed
28     int status;
29   }
30   Door() { status = 0; }
31   @priority(1)
32   msgsrv disarm(boolean disarm) {
33     // Disarm the door.
34     if (status == 0) status = 1;
35   }
36   @priority(2)
37   msgsrv open(boolean open) {
38     // Actuate door opener.
39     if (status == 0)
40       status = 3;
41     else if (status == 1)
42       status = 2;
43   }
44 }
45 main {
46   @priority(1) Cockpit c(v, d):();
47   @priority(2) Vision  v(d)    :();
48   @priority(3) Door    d()     :();
49 }
```

Fig. 4. Timed Rebeca model for the aircraft door system using priorities.

Figure 4 shows a Timed Rebeca model that uses a combination of temporal semantics and explicit priorities to ensure correct ordering of message handlers. The constructor for the Cockpit component starts things off by sending itself a send_open_cmd on line 4. It then repeatedly invokes this same message handler every 100 time units on line 11. This, effectively, models an environment, where the time units for the repeat may represent a worst case maximum frequency for events. We have, therefore, a scientific model of an environment that encodes an assumption about its worst case behavior. To trust any verification results with this model, we must convince ourself that any time intervals larger than this will not result in violations of the properties of interest.

In this (simplified) model, the Door actor has a state variable status (line 28) that takes on the value 3 if the door opens and the slides are deployed (Fig. 2). Since this model only includes the cockpit control, and it assumes that the Vision actor always sees a ramp (line 19), then we would like to verify that status never reaches value 3. Using Afra, the Timed Rebeca model-checking tool, we can verify that this requirement is satisfied. However, the requirements would not be satisfied without the @priority annotations on lines 31, 36, 46, 47, and 48. The priority annotations are a recent addition in Timed Rebeca [9,24]. They can be specified at the level of message servers (lines 31, 36) and at the level of actor instances (lines 46, 47, and 48). Semantically, a smaller priority value indicates higher execution priority. Components with the same priority get executed in a nondeterministic order when they are enabled. Priorities specified on message servers are treated separately from priorities specified on actors.

In this model, the only temporal operator is on line 11. Hence, all message transport and message handling is assumed to be instantaneous. Without the priorities, there is a risk that the open message handler of Door will be invoked before the check_ramp handler of Vision or, if not, before the disarm handler of Door. This, again, would result in catastrophe.

In a distributed system, enforcing these priorities is not trivial. The Lingua Franca language, described in the next section, infers priorities based on data dependencies and enforces them at runtime. Without LF, a distributed implementation of this design will be quite difficult to realize. Moreover, the enforcement aspect of the implementation will be error prone, weakening the verification results. We may have formally verified the design, but without a strong assurance that the implementation matches the design, the verification result is not very useful.

Given the temporal semantics of Timed Rebeca, it is tempting to instead model the timing of an implementation and verify that model. It may be, for example, that instead of assuming unrealistic instantaneous computation and message transport, the delays experienced in a physical implementation will lead to a safe design. The Timed Rebeca model in Fig. 5 attempts to check this. To open the aircraft door, the Cockpit actor calls the send_open_cmd handler, which sends two messages. It first sends a check_ramp message to the Vision actor (line 11) using an after delay to model the network delay. It then waits 5 time units (line 13) before sending an open message (line 16), again

```
1  reactiveclass Cockpit(10) {
2    knownrebecs {
3      Vision v; Door d;
4    }
5    Cockpit() {
6      self.send_open_cmd();
7    }
8    msgsrv send_open_cmd() {
9      // Send message to check ramp.
10     // Max network latency = 2ms.
11     v.check_ramp(true) after(2);
12     // Delay to avoid accidents.
13     delay(5);
14     // Send open message.
15     // Max network latency = 2ms.
16     d.open(true) after(2);
17     // Repeat after 100 ms.
18     self.send_open_cmd() after(100);
19   }
20 }
21 reactiveclass Vision(10) {
22   knownrebecs { Door d; }
23   msgsrv check_ramp(boolean trigger) {
24     // Computation time = 2 ms.
25     delay(2);
26     // Use vision to detect ramps.
27     // Assume a ramp is present.
28     // Max network latency = 2
29     d.disarm(true) after(2);
30   }
31 }
```

```
32 reactiveclass Door(10) {
33   statevars {
34     // 0: closed_armed,
35     // 1: closed_disarmed,
36     // 2: open,
37     // 3: open_deployed
38     int status;
39   }
40   Door() { status = 0; }
41   msgsrv disarm(boolean disarm) {
42     // Disarm the door.
43     if (status == 0) status = 1;
44   }
45   msgsrv open(boolean open) {
46     // Actuate door opener.
47     if (status == 0)
48       status = 3;
49     else if (status == 1)
50       status = 2;
51   }
52 }
53 main {
54   Cockpit c(v, d):();
55   Vision  v(d)    :();
56   Door    d()     :();
57 }
```

Fig. 5. Using `after` and `delay` to avoid accidentally deploying emergency slides, model network latencies, and model execution time.

using an `after` delay to model the network delay. The Vision actor models its computation time on line 25 and the network delay of its relay to Door on line 29. Again, we can use Afra to verify that the Door actor never reaches `status == 3`.

This model, however, exposes a critical flaw in this style of design. If we assume the `after` delays are worst-case scientific models of network delay, then we have a problem. If the `open` message from the Cockpit happens to experience less delay, say one time unit instead of two, then the model becomes nondeterministic, and the door may be opened before it is disarmed. To correct for this, we could increase the delay on line 13. In fact, this model mixes scientific models (lines 11, 16, 25, and 29) with engineering modeling (line 13). The scientific models must be interpreted as worst-case behaviors, and we have to do careful reasoning, separate from the formal verification, to assure ourselves that lower values will not hurt. On the other hand, the engineering model on line 13 has the opposite semantics. It must be interpreted as a lower bound, a *requirement* on the system design to ensure that accidental deployment of emergency slides never occurs. The formal verification performed by Afra does not help with this reasoning but only tells us whether the desired condition is satisfied for the particular delays chosen.

The ultimate root cause of the problem is mixing *engineering* models with *scientific* models in an undisciplined way. We illustrate how to correct this by clearly separating the model of the environment from the model of the system under design, and by exclusively using engineering models for the system under design.

4 Overview of Lingua Franca

Lingua Franca (LF) [19] is a polyglot coordination language designed to augment multiple mainstream programming languages (also called target languages), currently C, C++, Python, TypeScript, and Rust, with deterministic reactive concurrency and the capability to specify timed behavior. LF is supported by a runtime system that enables concurrent and distributed execution of reactive programs, which can be deployed on various platforms, including in the cloud, at the edge, in containers, and even on resource-constrained bare-metal embedded platforms.

A Lingua Franca program defines interactions between components known as reactors [17], with the logic for each reactor written in plain target code. Lingua Franca's code generator then produces one or more programs in the target language, which are compiled using standard toolchains. When the application has parallelism, it runs on multiple cores without losing determinism. For distributed applications, multiple programs and scripts are generated to deploy these programs on multiple machines and/or containers. The network communication fabric connecting these components is also synthesized as part of the code generation and compilation process.

4.1 Reactor-Oriented Programming

Lingua Franca programs consist of reactors, which are stateful entities with event-driven routines. Reactors adopt advantageous semantic features from established models of computation, namely actors [3], logical execution time [10], synchronous reactive languages [5], and discrete event systems [13] (such as DEVS [25] and SystemC [16]). The reaction routines belonging to reactors can process inputs, generate outputs, alter the reactor's state, and schedule future events. Reactors resemble actors [3], which are software components that communicate through message passing. However, unlike traditional actors, these messages have timestamps, and the concurrent interaction of reactors is deterministic by default. Any nondeterministic behavior must be explicitly programmed if needed.

Figure 6 shows a Lingua Franca program realizing the aircraft door service described in the previous section. The textual code shown at the bottom of the figure is Lingua Franca code, and the diagram above it is automatically generated by the tools and updated dynamically as the code is edited. In this example, the main program is *federated* (line 2), which means that each of the top-level reactors, Cockpit, Vision, and Door, will be code generated into its

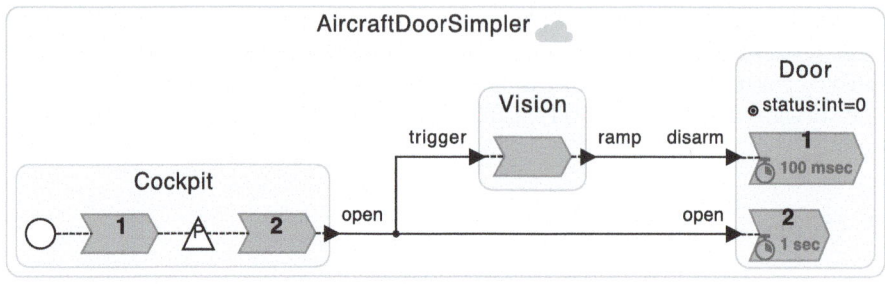

```
 1  target C // or Python, Rust, etc.
 2  federated reactor {
 3      c = new Cockpit()              30  reactor Door {
 4      v = new Vision()               31      input open: bool
 5      d = new Door()                 32      input disarm: bool
 6      c.open -> d.open               33      state status: int = 0
 7      c.open -> v.trigger            34      // This reaction should be first
 8      v.ramp -> d.disarm             35      reaction(disarm) {=
 9  }                                  36          // Disarm the door.
10  reactor Cockpit {                  37          if (self->status == 0) {
11      physical action command        38              self->status = 1;
12      output open: bool              39          }
13      reaction(startup) -> command {= 40     =} deadline(100 ms) {=
14          // Set up cockpit UI controls. 41        // Handle the deadline violation
15          // Target language code here... 42     =}
16      =}                             43      reaction(open) {=
17      reaction(command) -> open {=   44          // Actuate door opener.
18          // Target language code here. 45       if (self->status == 0) {
19          // E.g., send open message. 46              self->status = 3;
20          lf_set(open, true);        47          } else if (self->status == 1) {
21      =}                             48              self->status = 2;
22  }                                  49          }
23  reactor Vision {                   50      =} deadline(1 s) {=
24      input trigger: bool            51          // Handle the deadline violation
25      output ramp: bool              52      =}
26      reaction(trigger) -> ramp {=   53  }
27          // Target language code here...
28      =}
29  }
```

Fig. 6. Aircraft door system schematic and Lingua Franca specification.

own program in the target language (specified on line 1). These programs, called *federates*, can be containerized for better isolation and fault tolerance and/or distributed to distinct hardware, for example to exploit specialized hardware in the Vision reactor. This Vision reactor accesses a camera with a computer vision system that detects a ramp outside the door and disarms the door before opening it.

The grey chevrons in inside reactors in the diagram represent *reactions*, which are triggered by inputs, timers, or events on an event queue and are able to produce outputs. The business logic inside reactions is written in the target language that is chosen. A typical implementation of these reactors could use, for example, the Python target, which can leverage existing packages such as Tensorflow lite for the vision component, if it is to be realized on the edge, or it could use an API to realize the vision component in the cloud, or it could use the C target together with OpenCV, the open computer vision library (this code would go on line 27). Legacy code and libraries are easy to use in LF by simply invoking their APIs in the reaction bodies.

In principle, a federated LF program could use different target languages for each of the federates, such as Python for the Vision federate and C or Rust for the other components, but this capability only exists currently in concept demonstration form.

Cockpit uses a common pattern for LF programs that react to asynchronous events from the environment. It has a *physical action*, defined on line 11, which is used to inject asynchronous external events from the environment. The reaction to the *startup* event on line 13 can be used to set up any external interactions, for example enabling an interrupt service routine to handle sensor events or cockpit switches. When these events occur, the service routine schedules the physical action, which gets assigned a timestamp drawn from a local physical clock. The code on line 17 will then be invoked in reaction to such events.

A key property of Lingua Franca is that every reactor handles events in timestamp order, and when events bear the same timestamp, they will appear simultaneously at the reactor. Moreover, reactions are logically instantaneous. If they produce outputs in reaction to inputs, as the Vision does, those outputs have the same timestamp as the input. Consequently, LF semantics assures that the Door reactor will not react to an open command until the results of the Vision reactor are delivered to it. Moreover, when a reactor is presented with multiple simultaneous inputs, reactions will be invoked in the lexical order. Hence, given simultaneous disarm and open events, the Door reactor will react first to the disarm event (line 35) and then to the open event (line 43). As we have seen in the previous section, it is not trivial to ensure such behavior in an actor network, even one extended with time, as in Timed Rebeca. It is, nevertheless, possible, as we will show.

The Door reactor also includes two *deadline* declarations, which serve two purposes. First, they guide the LF scheduler to prioritize reaction invocations with nearer deadlines. Second, they provide fault handling code, on lines 40 and 50, which is invoked instead of the regular reaction code if and when the deadline is violated.

In this example, the federated reactors can be deployed on separate machines and reactions in different reactors can be executed by multiple threads in parallel. More importantly, for the same given input values and timing, the partial order constraints on the execution of reactions ensures determinism. This modular design of reactors, determinism, and flexibility in deployments make LF suitable for describing time-sensitive applications.

4.2 Specifying Timing Behavior

Lingua Franca makes a distinction between two timelines, **logical time** and **physical time** [18]. **Logical time** is represented by a tag (timestamp and microstep in superdense time [7,20]) that tracks the processing of events within the system. It is a marker for the sequence and timing of events as understood by the system's logic. **Physical time** tracks the actual movement of physical clocks, not to be confused with the conceptual clocks used in synchronous-reactive models. In LF's model of time, logical time, by default, lags behind physical time, meaning that the system's logical processing waits for the physical time to advance before proceeding.

Lingua Franca programs can explicitly specify a variety of timing behaviors in time-sensitive systems. These timing behaviors include time-triggered events, constraints on asynchronous events (such as minimum spacing), and deadlines. The timing behavior specification in Lingua Franca allows deterministic execution for timed events and user inputs. Reactions to events are executed in order based on the logical time (i.e., the tag).

The *physical action* in the Cockpit reactor (line 11), represented in the diagram by a triangle with a "P", captures external asynchronous inputs, assigning them a logical timestamp based on the physical time, as measured by a local clock. Lines 40 and 50 give deadlines, which specify a maximum acceptable gap between the logical time and physical time of a reaction invocation. These are also shown in the diagram as red markers in the reactions of the Door reactor.

Like Timed Rebeca, Lingua Franca supports **after delays** on connections between reactors (not used in this example). These increment the timestamp of an event conveyed along the connection. They are part of the program logic, not a scientific model of communication delays. This manipulation can be used to ameliorate that effects of the fundamental tradeoff between consistency and availability in a distributed system [12].

For federated programs, Lingua Franca offers two distinct coordination strategies [4]. The default coordinator is a centralized component called the RTI (for runtime infrastructure) that guarantees that events are processed in the proper semantic order regardless of communication delays, computation time, or clock synchronization. An alternative coordinator is decentralized and guarantees proper semantic order only under clearly stated assumed bounds on communication latency, computation times, and clock synchronization error. This coordinator also provides hooks to handle faults that occur when these assumptions are violated. Deadline statements in LF can also be viewed as clearly stated assumptions coupled with fault handlers to deal with violations of those assumptions.

In short, Lingua Franca offers deterministic behavior under clearly stated assumptions, mechanisms to detect when these assumptions are violated, and fault handlers so that applications can react appropriately to violation of the assumptions. This determinism applies even with parallel and distributed execution of LF programs, bringing the key advantages of determinism [11]: repeatability, consensus, predictability (sometimes), fault detection, simplicity, unsurprising behavior, and composability. For applications that require (or benefit from) nondeterminism, LF includes explicitly nondeterministic constructs that can be used. This is a notable contrast with most other concurrent and distributed computing frameworks, which give you nondeterminism by default and leave it to the designer to build deterministic behavior when needed.

5   Verifying an Engineering Model Using Timed Rebeca

```
1  reactiveclass Cockpit(10) {
2    knownrebecs {
3      Door door;
4      Vision Vision;
5    }
6    statevars { boolean open_value; }
7    Cockpit() {
8      // Schedule a physical action.
9      self.reaction_1();
10   }
11   @globalPriority(2)
12   msgsrv reaction_1() {
13     open_value = true;
14     door.read_port_open(open_value)
            after(0);
15     Vision.read_port_trigger(
            open_value) after(0);
16   }
17 }
18 reactiveclass Vision(10) {
19   knownrebecs { Door door; }
20   statevars {
21     boolean ramp_value;
22     boolean trigger_value;
23     boolean trigger_is_present;
24   }
25   Vision() {
26     trigger_is_present = false; }
27   @globalPriority(4)
28   msgsrv reaction_1() {
29     // Assume a ramp is detected
30     ramp_value = true;
31     door.read_port_disarm(ramp_value
            ) after(0);
32   }
33   @globalPriority(3)
34   msgsrv read_port_trigger(boolean
            _trigger_value) {
35     trigger_value = _trigger_value;
36     trigger_is_present = true;
37     self.reaction_1();
38   }
39 }
```

```
40 reactiveclass Door(10) {
41   statevars {
42     int status;
43     boolean open_value;
44     boolean open_is_present;
45     boolean disarm_value;
46     boolean disarm_is_present;
47   }
48   Door() {
49     status = 0;
50     open_is_present = false;
51     disarm_is_present = false;
52   }
53   @globalPriority(6)
54   msgsrv reaction_1() {
55     if (status == 0) status = 1;
56     disarm_is_present = false; }
57   @globalPriority(8)
58   msgsrv reaction_2() {
59     // Deploy emergency slides.
60     if (status == 0) status = 3;
61     else if (status == 1) {
62       status = 2; }
63     open_is_present = false; }
64   @globalPriority(7)
65   msgsrv read_port_open
            (boolean _open_value) {
66     
67     open_value = _open_value;
68     open_is_present = true;
69     self.reaction_2(); }
70   @globalPriority(5)
71   msgsrv read_port_disarm
            (boolean _disarm_value) {
72     
73     disarm_value = _disarm_value;
74     disarm_is_present = true;
75     self.reaction_1(); }
76 }
77 main {
78   Cockpit c(d, v):();
79   Vision  v(d):();
80   Door    d():();
81 }
```

Fig. 7. Timed Rebeca model encoding the semantics of the Lingua Franca model.

In this section, we show how to use Timed Rebeca to verify an engineering model of the aircraft door system, rather than a model mixing engineering requirements and scientific assumptions. Figure 7 shows a Timed Rebeca model encoding the semantics of the Lingua Franca program shown in Fig. 6. Strictly speaking, this Timed Rebeca model encodes the behavior of the LF program at the *instant* when the Cockpit component schedules the physical action command. We discuss the challenge of environmental modeling in Sect. 6.

Since the LF program is an engineering model, we interpret all reaction dependencies and temporal semantics as *requirements* on the system design.

Therefore, in the Timed Rebeca model, we ensure that the same requirements hold for all message servers that represent LF reactions. In the LF model, when a physical action command is scheduled, the disarm and open input ports of Door should receive messages logically simultaneously, despite the fact that the Vision component sits between the open port and the disarm port. This temporal requirement necessitates that Vision reaction must be invoked before both reactions in Door, regardless of actual network delays and execution times.

In addition, to preserve determinism, LF requires that all reactions within the same reactor execute in the order of their declarations. This means that when reactions in the Door components are triggered logically simultaneously, the reaction labelled 1 must execute before the reaction labelled 2, as explained in Sect. 4.1. Therefore, based on the requirements above, LF defines a unique correct sequence of reaction invocations upon the arrival of a physical action:

Cockpit reaction 2 → Vision reaction 1 → Door reaction 1 → Door reaction 2.

A correctly implemented LF runtime must deliver this sequence during program execution, and ensuring that an LF runtime is implemented correctly is nontrivial. When formally verifying the engineering model, however, the LF semantics can be *assumed*, which simplifies verification significantly.

To encode this well defined sequence in Timed Rebeca, we use the @globalPriority annotation, which gives a Timed Rebeca message server a priority value respected across reactive classes. These priorities provide partial ordering constraints that, according to Lingua Franca semantics, allow parallel execution while respecting dependencies. This is suitable in our use case, as LF's requirements on the order of reaction invocations spans across reactors. We give the four reactions in the sequence global priorities of 2, 4, 6, and 8 respectively (lines 11, 27, 53, 57 in Fig. 7). We set a reaction's priority to twice its invocation order so that auxiliary handlers (lines 34, 65, 71), which encode the semantics of LF ports, can execute before the reactions they trigger.

We verify this engineering model in Afra, which confirms that status can never be 3, even under all possible network latencies and execution times. As long as the implementation correctly follows the LF semantics, we can fully trust this verification result.

6   Challenges

One challenge that arises is that, in order to perform verification, Timed Rebeca programs must usually include a model of the environment in which they operate. A verifiable TR system is closed. All inputs to the designed part of the system have to be modeled. They can be modeled nondeterministically using Timed Rebeca, but in order for bounded model checking to be tractable, the number of nondeterministic choices must be limited. We avoided this problem in the previous section by using a degenerate environment model, where the environment makes exactly one request for service. But for many cases, this will not be sufficient. For example, it may be important to consider the rate at which requests for service can occur. These rates can be bounded in Lingua Franca, which may make the modeling easier, but this remains to be explored.

Since we cannot design the environment in which an engineered system runs, a model of the environment is necessarily a scientific model, not an engineering model. The model can make *assumptions*, enabling a kind of "assume-guarantee" reasoning, but the model cannot be a *specification* of the environment. There is an art, therefore, to constructing models of the environment. Ideally, each such model represents the weakest possible assumptions such that verification remains tractable and the assumptions can reasonably be assumed to hold. In practice, patterns of environment behaviors will need to be verified separately, because any single model with weak enough assumptions to admit all possible behaviors of the environment will lead to intractable verification problems.

7   Conclusion

We observe that models used for verification in practice sometimes conflate engineering models and scientific models, and that there is significant risk that this confusion compromises the trustworthiness of the verification results. We argue that systems under design should be modeled with engineering models, which are specifications of correct behavior, rather than scientific models, which approximate implementations. When this can be done, the results of formal verification can show definitively the correctness of a design. It is a separable problem to determine whether an implementation correctly realizes the specification. A key limitation, however, is that designs can only be verified under assumptions about the environment in which they operate, and that models of the environment are inevitably scientific models, not engineering models.

We have shown that Lingua Franca programs can serve as effective engineering models for a deterministic version of actor networks, and that Timed Rebeca can be used to verify these models. Using Timed Rebeca's ability to model nondeterminism, scientific models of the operating environment can be combined with the engineering models of the design, yielding verification results that are trustworthy under clearly stated assumptions about the operating environment of the designed system.

Acknowledgments. The work in this paper was supported in part by the National Science Foundation (NSF), award #CNS-2233769 (Consistency vs. Availability in Cyber-Physical Systems) and the iCyPhy Research Center (Industrial Cyber-Physical Systems), supported by Denso, Siemens, and Toyota.

Disclosure of Interests. The authors have no competing interests to declare that are relevant to the content of this article.

References

1. Agha, G.: ACTORS: A Model of Concurrent Computation in Distributed Systems. The MIT Press Series in Artificial Intelligence, MIT Press, Cambridge, MA (1986)
2. Agha, G.: Concurrent object-oriented programming. Commun. ACM **33**(9), 125–140 (1990)
3. Agha, G.A.: Abstracting interaction patterns: a programming paradigm for open distributed systems. In: Stefani, E.N., J.-B. (eds.) Formal Methods for Open Object-based Distributed Systems, IFIP Transactions, pp. 135–153. Chapman and Hall (1997). https://doi.org/10.1007/978-0-387-35082-0_10
4. Bateni, S., et alisk and mitigation of nondeterminism in distributed cyber-physical systems. In: ACM-IEEE International Conference on Formal Methods and Models for System Design (MEMOCODE) (2023). https://doi.org/10.1145/3610579.3613219
5. Benveniste, A., Caspi, P., Edwards, S.A., Halbwachs, N., Le Guernic, P., De Simone, R.: The synchronous languages 12 years later. Proc. IEEE **91**(1), 64–83 (2003)
6. Box, G.E.P., Draper, N.R.: Empirical Model-Building and Response Surfaces. Wiley Series in Probability and Statistics, Wiley, Hoboken (1987)
7. Cataldo, A., Lee, E.A., Liu, X., Matsikoudis, E., Zheng, H.: A constructive fixed-point theorem and the feedback semantics of timed systems. In: Workshop on Discrete Event Systems (WODES) (2006). http://ptolemy.eecs.berkeley.edu/publications/papers/06/constructive/
8. Hewitt, C.: Viewing control structures as patterns of passing messages. J. Artif. Intell. **8**(3), 323–363 (1977)
9. Khosravi, R., Khamespanah, E., Ghassemi, F., Sirjani, M.: Actors upgraded for variability, adaptability, and determinism. In: de Boer, F., Damiani, F., Hähnle, R., Broch Johnsen, E., Kamburjan, E. (eds.) Active Object Languages: Current Research Trends. LNCS, vol. 14360, pp. 226–260. Springer, Cham (2024). https://doi.org/10.1007/978-3-031-51060-1_9
10. Kirsch, C.M., Sokolova, A.: The logical execution time paradigm. In: Chakraborty, S., Eberspächer, J. (eds.) Advances in Real-Time Systems, pp. 103–120. Springer, Heidelberg (2012). https://doi.org/10.1007/978-3-642-24349-3_5
11. Lee, E.A.: Determinism. ACM Trans. Embed. Comput. Syst. (TECS) **20**(5), 1–34 (2021). https://doi.org/10.1145/3453652
12. Lee, E.A., Akella, R., Bateni, S., Lin, S., Lohstroh, M., Menard, C.: Consistency vs. availability in distributed cyber-physical systems. ACM Trans. Embed. Comput. Syst. (TECS) **22**(5s), 1–24 (2023). https://doi.org/10.1145/3609119. presented at EMSOFT, September 17-22, 2023, Hamburg, Germany
13. Lee, E.A., Liu, J., Muliadi, L., Zheng, H.: Discrete-event models. In: Ptolemaeus, C. (ed.) System Design, Modeling, and Simulation using Ptolemy II. Ptolemy.org, Berkeley, CA (2014). http://ptolemy.org/books/Systems
14. Lee, E.A., Sirjani, M.: What good are models? In: Formal Aspects of Component Software (FACS). vol. LNCS 11222. Springer (2018)
15. Lee, E.A.: Plato and the Nerd – The Creative Partnership of Humans and Technology. MIT Press, Cambridge (2017)
16. Liao, S., Tjiang, S., Gupta, R.: An efficient implementation of reactivity for modeling hardware in the scenic design environment. In: Proceedings of the 34th annual Design Automation Conference, pp. 70–75 (1997)

17. Lohstroh, M., Romeo, Í.Í., Goens, A., Derler, P., Castrillon, J., Lee, E.A., Sangiovanni-Vincentelli, A.: Reactors: a deterministic model for composable reactive systems. In: Chamberlain, R., Edin Grimheden, M., Taha, W. (eds.) CyPhy/WESE -2019. LNCS, vol. 11971, pp. 59–85. Springer, Cham (2020). https://doi.org/10.1007/978-3-030-41131-2_4

18. Lohstroh, M., Lee, E.A., Edwards, S., Broman, D.: Logical time for reactive software. In: Workshop on Timing-Centric Reactive Software (TCRS), in Cyber-Physical Systems and Internet of Things Week (CPSIoT). ACM (2023). https://doi.org/10.1145/3576914.3587494

19. Lohstroh, M., Menard, C., Bateni, S., Lee, E.A.: Toward a lingua franca for deterministic concurrent systems. ACM Trans. Embed. Comput. Syst. (TECS) 20(4), Article 36 (2021). https://doi.org/10.1145/3448128

20. Maler, O., Manna, Z., Pnueli, A.: Prom timed to hybrid systems. In: de Bakker, J.W., Huizing, C., de Roever, W.P., Rozenberg, G. (eds.) REX 1991. LNCS, vol. 600, pp. 447–484. Springer, Heidelberg (1992). https://doi.org/10.1007/BFb0032003

21. Reynisson, A.H., et al.: Modelling and simulation of asynchronous real-time systems using timed Rebeca. Sci. Comput. Program. 89, 41–68 (2014). https://doi.org/10.1016/j.scico.2014.01.008

22. Sirjani, M., Jaghoori, M.M.: Ten years of analyzing actors: Rebeca experience. In: Agha, G., Danvy, O., Meseguer, J. (eds.) Formal Modeling: Actors, Open Systems, Biological Systems. LNCS, vol. 7000, pp. 20–56. Springer, Heidelberg (2011). https://doi.org/10.1007/978-3-642-24933-4_3

23. Sirjani, M., Khamespanah, E.: On time actors. In: Ábrahám, E., Bonsangue, M., Johnsen, E.B. (eds.) Theory and Practice of Formal Methods. LNCS, vol. 9660, pp. 373–392. Springer, Cham (2016). https://doi.org/10.1007/978-3-319-30734-3_25

24. Sirjani, M., Lee, E.A., Khamespanah, E.: Verification of cyberphysical systems. Mathematics 8, 1–20 (2020). https://doi.org/10.3390/math8071068

25. Zeigler, B.P., Moon, Y., Kim, D., Ball, G.: The DEVS environment for high-performance modeling and simulation. IEEE Comput. Sci. Eng. 4(3), 61–71 (1997)

Black-Box Protocol Testing Using Rebeca and Automata Learning

Stefan Marksteiner[1,2]([⊠]) [iD] and Mikael Sjödin[2] [iD]

[1] AVL List Gmbh, Graz, Austria
stefan.marksteiner@avl.com
[2] Mälardalen University, Västerås, Sweden
{stefan.marksteiner,mikael.sjodin}@mdu.se

Abstract. Industrial and critical infrastructure devices should be scrutinized with rigorous methods for inconsistencies with a specification. At the same time, this specification should also be correct, otherwise the specification conformance is of little value. On the example of eMRTDs (electronic Machine-Readable Travel Documents) we demonstrate an approach that combines model-checking a specification for correctness in terms of security with learning an implementation model using automata learning. Once the specification is modeled, we automatically mine a model of the implementation and check the model for compliance with the verified specification using simulation and trace preorder. Underspecification of the standard is in this setting modeled as non-deterministic behavior, so one of the possibilities has to simulate the implementation in order for the latter to be compliant. We also present a working tool chain realizing this method. When adopting the tool chain accordingly, the method might be used in practice for checking the correctness of any reactive system.

Keywords: Automata Learning · Rebeca · Compliance Checking · Model Checking · Formal Methods · NFC · eMRTD · Afra

1 Introduction

1.1 Motivation

Electronic Machine Readable Documents (eMRTDs) are critical infrastructure and should therefore be correct and secure systems. This means that they should be scrutinized with rigorous methods for inconsistencies with a specification. At the same time, this specification should also be correct, otherwise the specification conformance is of little value. We therefore strive for a methodology to

The authors want to thank Marjan Sirjani, the receiver of this Festschrift and PhD advisor of the main author for teaching Rebeca and helping with the first steps of modeling the system described in this paper. Congratulations to the jubilee! We further acknowledge the support of the Swedish Knowledge Foundation via the industrial doctoral school RELIANT, grant nr: 20220130.

automatically checking both a specification for its correctness and an implementation to be compliant to the former. In practice we present a practical approach to connect model checking for a correct specification for eMRTD communication (via Near-Field Communications – NFC) with automata learning to mine a model of an implementation to check its conformance with the verified model. We thereby emphasize on security properties (i.e., protected information may only be read with proper authentication, etc.). With appropriate adapter classes, the method might be used for checking the correctness of many reactive systems. Having the interaction of two reactive systems (an eMRTD and a reader device) as target of examination, we use the Rebeca modeling language [28] (particularly *Core Rebeca*) to create a checkable specification model, since modeling these kind of systems is the very purpose of Rebeca. The latter, in conjunction with its Java-like syntax makes the modeling process fairly easy (compared to the decription syntax of other model checking systems) and, therefore, well-maintainable.

1.2 Contribution

This paper combines formal methods with systems engineering and testing to create a tool chain for checking implementations for their correctness and security. Our main contributions are:

– An approach for combining model-checking a specification for correctness with learning an implementation model
– An automated tool chain for the complete process, once a specification is modeled
– A verified specification model for eMRTDs

We use three formal methods: automata learning, equivalence checking (particularly simulation and trace preorder), and model checking. We use these methods in an automated tool chain and apply it to a practical use case, namely checking eMRTDs for their specification conformance and verifying the specification for security properties. Relying on Rebeca to model the standard, we produce a more secure (assured by model checking) and maintainable (through the traits of Rebeca) specification model to be used for checking the behavioral correctness of mined implementation models.

1.3 Approach

Starting from existing work on learning a behavioral model using automata learning and comparing it with a (partial) specification [19,20], we use Rebeca to create a partial model of the International Civil Aviation Organization's (ICAO) Doc 9303 part 9 standard [25], which was done by hand in the contributions mentioned before. This document defines the structure of an eMRTD (including mandatory and optional elements, like stored document and personal data, biometrics, etc.) and how to access this data via the NFC protocol (ISO/IEC 14443-4 [10]) and standardized integrated-circuit interfaces (ISO/IEC 7816-4

[11]). It is important to note that despite using the standard that defines the data structure for eMRTDs, we actually model the behavior of inter-reacting systems: one hosting and one accessing the data structures defined in the standard. We already outlined the specifics in another paper [20]. Rebeca's integration environment (Afra) comes with a specific model checker (Modere) [28]. This allows to verify the model for properties using Linear Temporal Logic (LTL) or Computational Tree Logic (CTL). The checker also creates a state space that represents the model (based on two communicating reactive systems). On the other hand we use active automata learning with the Learnlib library [13] to mine Mealy machine models of eMRTD implementations (i.e., the electronic representations of passports). We use a self-written converter to transform the Rebeca state space model into a Mealy-styled LTS (see Sect. 4.3). We can then check whether the learned implementation model is included (using simulation or trace preorder – see Sect. 4) in the verified specification. We use the MCRL2 toolset's [4] *ltscompare* tool to perform this analysis. If both the specification is successfully verified and the implementation is inside the specified behavior (i.e., preorder is successful), we can claim that the examined system is assured to fulfill the verified properties. We modeled security properties (e.g., authentication before access to sensitive data – see Sect. 4.2) and implemented this into a tool-supported process (see Fig. 1).

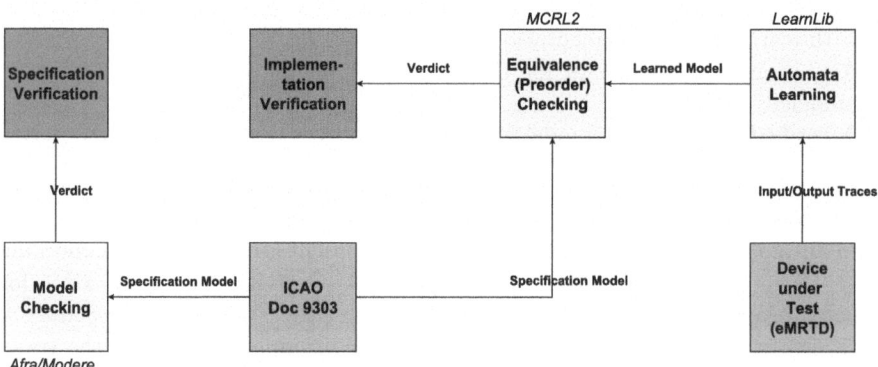

Fig. 1. Overview of the approach. Green are processes, blue are external inputs, and amber are outputs (i.e., results), the arrow labels are artifacts (input artifacts for arrows from blue to green boxes, output artifacts from green to amber boxes. The italic labels next to the green boxes denote the used tool sets/frameworks. (Color figure online)

1.4   Limitations

Due to a lack of an available implementation, the authentication method is limited to Basic Access Control (BAC), while the other standardized methods, namely Password Authenticated Connection Establishment (PACE) and Terminal Authentication (TA) are not included in the models.

2   Preliminaries

Here we give a brief overview of some fundamental concepts used in this paper, as well as some basic descriptions of used tools and methods. We also give some definitions to well-known concepts to show our interpretation and avoid ambiguities.

2.1   Labeled Transition Systems and Mealy Machines

There are some basic approaches to model reactive systems. We use two of them, particularly Labeled Transitions Systems (LTS) and Mealy Machines. Transition systems describe a system's behavior in a graph-based manner by defining a set of states the system is in and a set of transitions that realize changes of these states, normally denoted by actions (i.e., inputs) and a transition function, along with initial states and atomic propositions (i.e., properties of the system in a certain state). An LTS contains also a labelling function that assigns actions to transitions. Formally, an LTS is defined as $LTS = (Q, Act, \rightarrow, I, AP, L)$, with Q being the set of states, Act a set of actions, $\rightarrow$ a transition function, I the set of initial states, AP a set of atomic propositions and L a labelling function [2]. Finite State Machines (FSMs), also called automata, are similar to LTS, but their number of states and transitions is finite (a restriction not applicable to LTS), often used in a deterministic version, so called deterministic finite automata (or acceptor - DFA). This means that every input must have exactly one result in each state whereas, LTS do not have to be deterministic and can be seen as non-deterministic automata [8]. To model real-world, reactive systems, automata types that provide input and output are used. The two most common are Mealy [21] and Moore machines [23], where the difference lies in the output being produced by transitions (Mealy) or by states (Moore). For easier access to learning algorithms, we use Mealy machines. In a Mealy Machine, each input from a set (the alphabet) must be matched with a transition (i.e., change to a certain state, which can also be the original one) and an output. A Mealy Machine is defined as $M = (Q, \Sigma, \Omega, \delta, \lambda, q_0)$, with Q being the set of states, Σ the input alphabet, Ω the output alphabet (that may or may not be identical to the input alphabet), δ the transition function ($\delta : Q \times \Sigma \rightarrow Q$), λ the output function ($\lambda : Q \times \Sigma \rightarrow \Omega$) – or a merger of both functions ($Q \times \Sigma \rightarrow Q \times \Omega$) – and q_0 the initial state. The transitions can be viewed also as tuples $\langle p, q, \sigma, \omega \rangle$ with $p, q \in Q$, $\sigma \in \Sigma$, and $\omega \in \Omega$ as elements of the combined input/transition function. State machines can be viewed as LTS by interpreting input/output pairs as labels of an LTS [29].

2.2   Types of Equivalence

To check the conformity of a system with a standard, we look for standard conform behavior of the system. The idea is to compare the behavior of a system with a specification. Using formal methods, we use behavioral equivalence checks of a learned (see Sect. 2.3) model of the implemented system with a correct (see

Sect. 2.5) specification model. Since we treat our models as LTS, we concentrate on equivalences for LTS. There are different types of formally defined equivalences, of which we use simulation and trace preorder, as well as bisimulation and trace equivalence [2]. The difference between preorder and equivalence relations is that preorder is reflexive and transitive, whereas equivalence is reflexive, transitive and symmetric (i.e., an equivalence is a symmetric preorder) [5]. Formally defined:

Definition 1 (Simulation Preorder). *Simulation preorder of two LTS ($LTS_1 \preceq LTS_2$) is defined as exhibiting a binary relation $R \subseteq Q \times Q$, such that [2]:*

A) $\forall s_1 \in I_1 \cdot (\exists s_2 \in I_2 \cdot (s_1, s_2) \in R)$.
B) for all $(s_1, s_2) \in R$ must hold
    1) $L_1(s_1) = L_2(s_2)$
    2) if $s_1\prime \in Post(s_1)$ then there exists $s_2\prime \in Post(s_2)$ with $(s_1\prime, s_2\prime) \in R$

Where $Post$ is the set of successor states of another state $Post(s) = \bigcup_{\alpha \in ACT} Post(s, \alpha)$ and $Post(s, \alpha) = \{s\prime \in Q | s \rightarrow s\prime\}$ [2]. For preorder, the respective relation may be unidirectional, whereas for equivalence, it is bidirectional. That means that when comparing two LTS (LTS_1 and LTS_2) with simulation preorder ($LTS_1 \preceq LTS_2$), LTS_2 has to simulate every behavior of LTS_1, but not vice versa; with bisimulation equivalence ($LTS_1 \sim LTS_2$) LTS_1 has to simulate LTS_2's behavior and vice versa. For preorder, the behavior of a system LTS_1 has to be included in another system LTS_2, but the latter might display additional behavior not included in the former. Additionally there is trace preorder, which mandates that the set of traces of LTS_1 has to be included in the one of LTS_2, which might or might not contain additional traces:

Definition 2 (Trace preorder).
$Traces(LTS_1) \subseteq Traces(LTS_2)$

For bidirectional relations, there are equivalence relations with the same principles as preorder, namely bisimilarity and trace equivalence.

Definition 3 (Bisimilarity). *of two LTS ($LTS_1 \sim LTS_2$) has a binary relation $R \subseteq QxQ$, such that [2]:*

A) $\forall s_1 \in I_1 \exists s_2 \in I_2 \cdot (s_1, s_2) \in R$ and $\forall s_2 \in I_2 (\exists s_1 \in I_1 \cdot (s_1, s_2) \in R$.
B) for all $(s_1, s_2) \in R$ must hold
    1) $L_1(s_1) = L_2(s_2)$
    2) if $s_1\prime \in Post(s_1)$ then there exists $s_2\prime \in Post(s_2)$ with $(s_1\prime, s_2\prime) \in R$
    3) if $s_2\prime \in Post(s_2)$ then there exists $s_1\prime \in Post(s_1)$ with $(s_1\prime, s_2\prime) \in R$

Trace equivalence is the symmetric version of trace preorder, which means that two transitions systems produce the same traces for each same input.

Definition 4 (Trace equivalence). $Traces(LTS_1) = Traces(LTS_2)$

2.3 Automata Learning

(Active) Automata Learning is a method of deriving a system model by querying a system with input data. Originally, it was described by Angluin in her work on learning regular sets [1], where she introduces the Learner-Teacher-Framework. In this framework, a learning system might ask a teacher two kinds of questions about the scrutinized system (System-under-learning – SUL):

- *Membership queries* and
- *Equivalence queries.*

Thereby, it is assumed that the teacher possesses a correct automaton of the SUL. The naming stems from the original purpose of learning Deterministic Finite Acceptors (DFA), a state machine type that describe regular languages. The DFA does or does not accept (hence acceptor) arbitrary sequences of symbols from a specific alphabet by deciding if the sequence (i.e., word) is a well-formed part of the respective language. Therefore, membership queries denote such input words, where the teacher answers whether or not they are accepted. The learner uses the respective output in a systematic way to infer a state machine. This also works for real-world reactive systems, but instead of generating queries to learn a DFA, the target is usually to learn a Mealy or Moore type automaton. Given the nature of these, the answer to membership queries is not yes or no, but rather the output of the automaton according to the output function, i.e. a query consists of an input word W_σ that consists of symbols from the input alphabet ($\sigma \in \Sigma | W_\sigma = \langle \sigma_1, \sigma_2..\sigma_n \rangle$) and delivers an output word W_ω consisting of symbols from the output alphabet ($\omega \in \Omega | W_\omega = \langle \omega_1, \omega_2..\omega_n \rangle$) according to the output function λ (simultaneously traversing through the sates according to δ). If there is enough data to construct a state machine, the learner might ask the teacher whether the constructed state machine (hypothesis) corresponds to the actual system. This type of question is called equivalence query. The teacher answers with yes, if the hypothesis is correct (i.e., the hypothesis automaton is equivalent to the SUL automaton). Otherwise, the answer is a counterexample in form of an input word and the respective output word from the SUL automaton, that deviates from the hypothesis automaton's output word. Since the original L* algorithm, many improvements in learning methodologies have been developed, most notably the closure strategy of Rivest and Schapire [26]. More recent improvements include the replacement of the originally used observation tables by tree structures that represent distinctive features between states and allow for more efficient membership query generation. Notable algorithms using trees include Kearns-Vazirani (KV) [15], Direct Hypothesis Construction (DHC) [22], TTT[12], and L# [30]. When learning real-world systems, the assumption of possessing a correct SUL automaton is not feasible, especially for black-box learning settings (which is one of the main use cases for automata learning). Therefore, generally equivalence queries are replaced by conformance tests, i.e. a *sufficient*[1] amount of (potentially long) queries after a certain strategies, e.g., random walks [18].

---

[1] What is sufficient heavily depends on the specific use case and cannot be determined generally.

2.4   LearnLib

Learnlib [13] is arguably the most widely used library for automata learning (however, there are others, e.g., AALpy [24] or Libalf [3]). Written in Java, It features the most used automata learning algorithms (L*, Rivest-Schapire, AAAR, ADT, KV, DHC and TTT) and an addon L# implementation is available [17]. Also, it contains classes for conformance testing strategies (complete depth-bounded exploration, random words, random walk, W-method, Wp-method) and interfaces for providing connectors to SULs. It further contains AutomataLib, which contains tools for automata analysis and manipulation (e.g., minimizing automata).

2.5   Model Checking

Model checking is an automated methodology that (efficiently) explores all states (i.e., system scenarios) of (state-based) system model. Traversing through the states, it can check if certain system properties are satisfied in a certain state based on a sound fundament of graph theory, data structures, and logic [2]. The checkable properties can be stated in different kinds of logic like Linear Temporal Logic (LTL) or Computation Tree Logic (CTL), or the branching-time logic CTL* that encompasses both of the former. For its availability in the used model checker, we concentrate on LTL formulas. These are propositional logic [27] formulas with temporal modalities. Those modalities are

- *always* ($\Box$): the proposition must hold in any state
- *eventually* ($\Diamond$): the proposition must hold in some subsequent state (could hold before)
- *next* ($\bigcirc$): the proposition must hold in the immediately subsequent state and
- *until* ($\mathcal{U}$): the proposition A_1 must hold until another defined proposition A_2 occurs ($A_1 \mathcal{U} A_2$).

The respective proposition is embedded in a propositional formula. LTL formulas can also be nested. This allows for describing state conditions that must and must not occur in any state-based model. We use model checking in LTL for verifying the security properties (particularly authentication) of a specification model.

2.6   Rebeca

Rebeca is a modeling language that can be used to model reactive systems with a Java-like syntax [28]. It possesses its own modeling IDE (Afra [16]), which has also a built-in model checker (Modere [14]) that uses LTL statements for checking Rebeca models. A Rebeca model mainly consists of *reactive classes*, which model the behavior of a specific actor. These classes can have (internal) functions and (externally callable) message servers. Both allow local variables and basic statements like arithmetic and logic operations, assignments, conditionals, comparisons, casting, and instance operators that work like in the Java programming language. Additionally, it has non-deterministic assignment operator to model behavior that may take one of multiple paths. Additionally, a reactive class can have state variables that are maintained in any state of the model. These state variables can also be checked with Modere. Instances of a class are called reactive actors or Rebecs. Each class can have a list of known Rebecs with which its instances can interact by sending messages to its message servers. A class has also a message queue of defined size that holds (and sequences) messages for its specific server functions. This queue is also used for checking purposes like deadlock detection – if the system reaches a state where the message queue of the Rebec that is to take action at that point is empty, the system stalls in a deadlock. For model checking, a property file is defined that contains property definitions (i.e. atomic propositions that are statements formed from state variables of Rebecs), assertions (simple logic formulas that are always checked in any model checker execution) and LTL formulas (that can be executed one-by-one). The model checker also creates a state space of all visited states in an XML format, which is also convertible to the Graphviz format. The model checker thereby creates a state for every execution of a message server. This means that for a model of two interacting reactive systems, the resulting state machine shows mutual calling of the two Rebecs, with the possibility of a Rebec also calls its own message server (i.e., a self-loop). The state variables referenced in the property file are included as atomic propositions of the sate (they show up in the state if they are true and do not show up if they are false). Local functions and variables are not part of LTS generated from the state space.

2.7 Near Field Communication

Near Field Communication (NFC) is a wireless communication standard for passive (powerless), small embedded devices such as Radio-Frequency Identification (RFID) and chip cards (also known as smart cards). A proximity coupling device (PCD) creates an induction field that powers up a proximity integrated circuit card (PICC) and modulates the communication signals onto the induction field for transfer between PCD and PICC. ISO/IEC 14443-4 [10] defines the messages types for data transmission (information or I blocks), signaling (supervisory or S blocks), and acknowledgements (receive-ready or R blocks), along with protocol mechanisms like block numbering, chaining, error correction, etc.

2.8 Integrated Circuit Access

ISO/IEC 7816-4 [11] defines data structures for transmission (both wired and wireless) to and from integrated circuit cards, including PICCs in the NFC protocol. Potential defined operations are data access, reading and writing data, as well as administrative and security functions, including authentication. For data access, PICCs are usually segmented into different applications (comparable to directories in a file system) that can be accessed via *Dedicated Files (DFs)*. The actual data resides in *Elementary Files (EFs)*. Both are usually accessed through a *SELECT* command. Once (potentially a DF and) an EF is (successfully) selected it can be manipulated via *READ*, *WRITE* and similary commands. Since the access to certain data should be protected, also the *GETCHALLENGE* and *AUTHENTICATE* commands are defined. The former is to initiate an authentication process, while the second concludes it. How that authentication works in particular is subject to the respective application and out of scope of the standard, usually some cryptographic operation based on a (symmetric or asymmetric) secret is conducted on the value obtained with the GETCHALLENGE command and returned in the AUTHENTICATE command. It is also expected that, after the authentication process, the commands for file selection and manipulation are secured (i.e., usually encrypted). It is also common that a successful authentication is tied to the application (i.e., DF) and could also differ on different applications on the same PICC.

The answer to any request contains the (encrypted or unencrypted) return data and a (always unencrypted status code, consisting of two bytes. In our work with eMRTDs, we have learned (and modeled) the following status codes as answers to specific queries:

- *9000* - OK
- *6300* - No information given (seen at authentication attempts with wrong credentials)
- *6700* - Error with no information given (when trying to perform write operations without authentication)
- *6982* - Security status not satisfied (i.e., lack of authentication)
- *6985* - Conditions of use not satisfied (when trying to authenticate without an application selected)
- *6986* - Command not allowed (when trying to read without a file selected)
- *6988* - Insecure messaging DOs (when encrypting data with a wrong key)
- *6A82* - File not found
- *6D00* - Instruction code not supported or invalid (when sending malformed commands)

2.9   Electronically Machine-Readable Travel Documents

Electronically Machine-Readable Travel Documents (eMRTDs) refer to the data stored on passport integrated circuits, accessible via NFC. The data structure is standardized in ICAO Doc 9303 part 9 [25]. It defines four applications: eMRTD, travel records, visa records, and additional biometrics. They are grouped into *LDS1* (only the eMRTD application) and *LDS2* (all other applications). Only the first is mandatory. Since we found only LDS1 on examined passports, we concentrate on this group. In the common area of the device (i.e., the area without selecting an application), the standard defines the following files to be (mandatorily or optionally) present:

- *Attributes/Info (ATTR/INFO)*: containing the card capabilities (only mandatory if LDS2 is present).
- *Directory (DIR)*: containing a list of supported applications on the device (only mandatory if LDS2 is present).
- *Card Access (CA)*: containing security infos required for PACE authentication (only mandatory if PACE is implemented).
- *Card Security (CS)*: containing chip and terminal authentication (only mandatory if PACE with chip authentication mapping is implemented).
- *Common (EF.COM)*: containing metadata (version, encoding, etc.) of the application
- *Data Group 1 (EF.DG 1)*: containing the machine readable zone (mandatory).
- *Data Group 2 (EF.DG 2)*: containing the holder's face image (mandatory).
- *Data Group 3 (EF.DG 3)*: containing the holder's fingerprints image (optional).
- *Data Group 4 (EF.DG 4)*: containing the holder's iris image (optional).
- *Data Group 5 (EF.DG 5)*: containing holders displayed portrait(s) (optional).
- *Data Group 6 (EF.DG 6)*: is reserved for future use (optional).
- *Data Group 7 (EF.DG 7)*: containing the holder's displayed signature (optional).
- *Data Group 8 (EF.DG 8)*: containing data features (optional).
- *Data Group 9 (EF.DG 9)*: containing structure features (optional).
- *Data Group 10 (EF.DG10)*: containing substance features (optional).
- *Data Group 11 (EF.DG11)*: containing additional personal details (e.g., localized name, place-of-birth – optional).
- *Data Group 12 (EF.DG12)*: containing additional document details (e.g., issuing authority, date-of-issue – optional).
- *Data Group 13 (EF.DG13)*: containing optional details (optional).
- *Data Group 14 (EF.DG14)*: containing data elements (only mandatory if PACE is implemented).
- *Data Group 15 (EF.DG15)*: containing the public key info for active authentication (only mandatory if active authentication is implemented).
- *Data Group 16 (EF.DG16)*: containing persons to notify (optional).
- *Document Security Object (EF.SOD)*: containing hash values of the data group for integrity checking (mandatory).
- *Country Verifying Certification Authorities (EF.CVCA)*: containing public keys of CVCA for terminal authentication (mandatory).
- Key files for authentication.

The elementary files inside applications need, according to the standard, authentication. The LDS1 authentication needs Basic Access Control (BAC) or the newer Password Authenticated Connection Establishment (PACE), and data groups 3 and 4 additionally needs Terminal Authentication (which is, in contrast to the other methods, based on a public key infrastructure). LDS2 applications (travel records, visa records, additional biometrics) need PACE and Terminal Authentication. All of these methods are defined in the standard. For the lack of a usable implementation of others authentication methods, we are limited to BAC. This method performs cryptographic operations based on a challenge with the passport number, expiration date, and the owner's date of birth as key material. This information is readable on the main page of the passport, but the accessible information is basically just an electronic version of the former (except for DG 3 and 4, which requires additional authentication). The purpose is not to completely shield this information, but to prevent bystanders of a person to obtain its personal information by just reading it out from the passport. In contrast to LDS2, the elementary files in the LDS1 application are defined to be read-only.

Note that, due to many optional elements, the standard is underspecified. This means that more than one implementation is correct, which makes the standard non-deterministic from a modeling perspective (Fig. 2).

3 Learning

We use Learnlib (see Sect. 2.4) to create a setup to learn NFC-based eMRTDs. This section covers the details on the interface, abstraction layer and alphabets. To learn the models we relied on the TTT algorithm and random walks as conformance testing algorithm. We learn the behavior of an eMRTD device with regard to the ICAO Doc 9303 part 9 (file structure and access rules), ISO/IEC 7816-4 (file access and security commands), and ISO/IEC 14443-4 (command and data transmission) standards. The learning setup is based on a previous paper [20], which we extend with the aspect of checking the specification model.

3.1 NFC Interface

To interact with eMRTDs, we created an NFC interface for Learnlib [19]. We connect the developed SUL class via a Socket to an API (based on C++) that operates a Proxmark3 device [7], running a custom firmware enhanced to support automata learning.

3.2 Abstraction

As usual with learning real-world systems, we use an abstraction layer to limit the potentially very large input space. This means that we reduce the input alphabet to sensible commands targeting the data structures from the ICAO standard. Since this includes secure communications, we use the commands (except for authentication-related) in encrypted and unencrypted versions. We also abstract the output to the status code, since it does not contain data and is also always unencrypted. This avoids non-determinism.

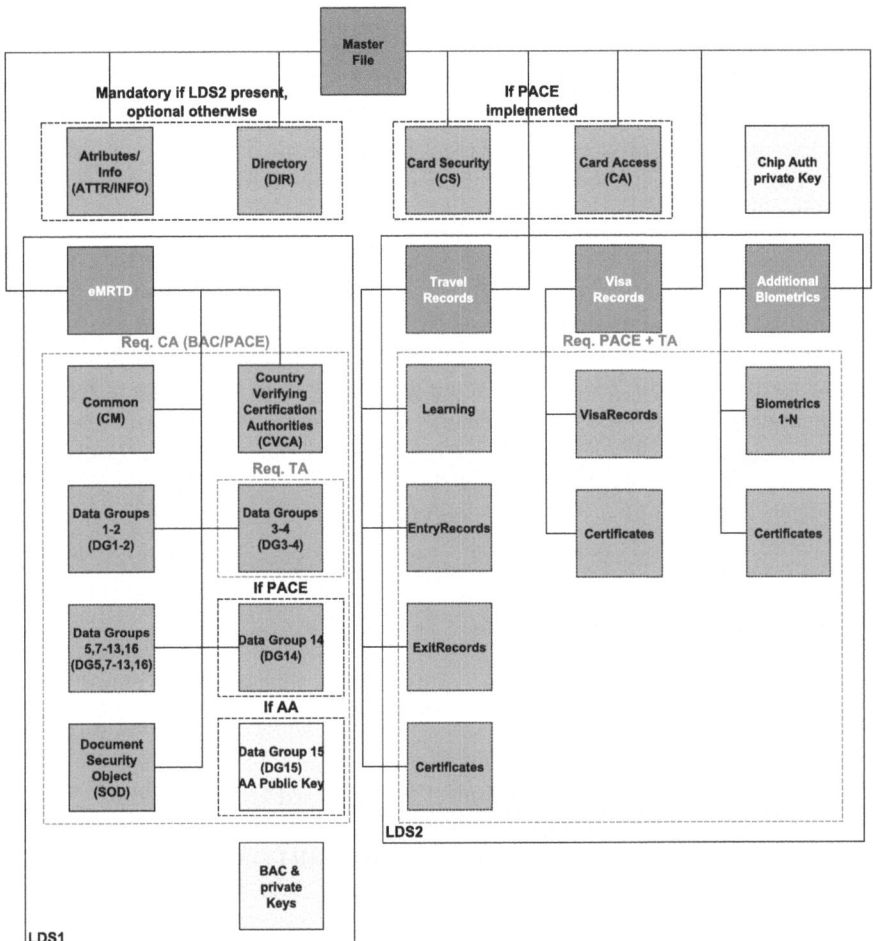

Fig. 2. Logical Data Structure of Machine Readable Travel Documents from [20]. Amber is the master file (MF), Cyan are dedicated files (DF), Blue are Elementary Files (EF), and Green are key files. Solid frames means mandatory files, dashed ones optional files. Solid boxes donate the LDS contexts, dashed black boxes requirements, and dashed red boxes necessary authentication. (Color figure online)

3.3 Input Alphabet

The input alphabet consist of the data structure from ICAO Doc 9303 part 9 accessed with ISO/IEC 7816-4 commands over the ISO/IEC 14443-4 protocol. Concretely, we use the select DF, select EF, GETCHALLENGE, EXTERNAL AUTHENTICATION, READ BINARY, and UPDATE BINARY commands. Limiting to LDS1 (i.e., the eMRTD application), the full alphabet consists of SELECT DF LDS1 (SEL_DF.LDS1) and SELECT EF for the files mentioned (e.g., SEL_EF.CM) in Sect. 2.9, as well as READ BINARY to perform a read operation on selected files. Each of these inputs is used in a plain, unencrypted and a secure, encrypted version (e.g., SSEL_EF.CM for securely accessing the Common file). Additionally, we use a BAC symbol that issues the correct sequence (consisting of a GETCHALLENGE and an EXTERNAL AUTHENTICATION command based on the former) for performing this type of authentication. This also yields a session key that is used for performing the encryption operations in secure commands.

Output Alphabets. The output alphabet does not have to be defined beforehand, but is discovered in-situ by the received answers. However, since we are not interested in the actual data, but rather want to prevent non-determinism (which the learner requires for proper functioning), we abstract the answers by using just the status code as an output. This is enough information to create a model for checking the security properties, mainly to check the proper authentication of data access. This eases also handling the answers of secure commands, as otherwise their data would need to be decrypted first. Using always-unencrypted status codes only, this is not needed.

3.4   Labeling and Simplification

Based on the (by the standard) known status codes, we can issue a simple labeling of the states, that also correspond to atomic propositions if the learned Mealy Machine is seen as an LTS [20]:

- From the initial state, follow the select EF for CardAccess transition
- If output yields 9000, label this state as *EF*
- From the inital state, select the DF for LDS1.eMRTD tansition
- If output yields 9000, label this state as *DF*
- From DF, follow the BAC transition
- If output yields 9000, lable this state as *DF|AUTH*
- From DF|AUTH, follow the encrypted select Data Group 1 transition
- If output yields 9000, label this state as *DF|AUTH|EF*
- From the initial state, select the BAC transition
- If output yields 6985 label the state as *FAILAUTH*
- From FAILAUTH, follow the select LDS1.eMRTD transition
- If output yields 9000 label the state as *FAILAUTH|DF*
- From EF, select the BAC transition
- If output yields 6985 label the state as *FAILAUTH|EF*
- From the DF|AUTH|EF, select the unencrypted READ BINARY transition
- If output yields 6982 label the state as *DEAUTH*

The propositions are: *EF* for a selected elementary file, *DF* for a selected dedicated file (i.e. the LDS1.eMRTD application), AUTH for a successful authentication (i.e., BAC), FAILAUTH for a failed authentication, *DEAUTH* for a revoked authentication.

4   Compliance Evaluation

To determine an implementation's compliance with the standards, we compare a learned implementation model from previous works [20] with a specification model derived from the standards (see Sect. 4.1). As the ICAO standard is under-specified, the results of access operations on (dedicated or elementary) files may have more than one legit result. This means that we cannot model a properly defined Mealy Machine from the standard (since it is non-deterministic), but rather a Mealy-styled LTS (or pseudo-Mealy), with more than one transition target and/or output label for a given input in a given state. However, since we make the comparison operations on LTS with the input/output pair being a combined label, the restriction to a deterministic model does not apply in practice. Due to multiple legit (i.e., standard-compliant) transitions for the same state/input pair, we cannot check for full equivalence. The learned model is a proper (and, thus, deterministic) Mealy Machine (otherwise the learner would crash for failing to handle non-deterministic behavior). Therefore, our learned model can always only cover one (of potentially multiple) state/input transitions. This makes it very likely that the specification displays extra behavior in comparison. For this reason we use preorder instead of simulation for compliance checking – the (learned) implementation model's behavior should stay inside the boundaries of the (modeled and checked) specification behavior.

4.1   Specification Model

We model the eMRTD specification as outlined in Sect. 2.9 in Rebeca by defin-ing two reactive classes: a PCD class that is instantiated with a Rebec called *reader* and a PICC class that is instantiated with a Rebec called *PP* (short for passport). Each of the inputs (e.g., SELECT DF LDS1) is a message server of the PICC, while the respective answers (OK or respective error codes) are message servers of the PCD. Inside the PICC servers, we define the behavior according to the standard given the state variables (e.g., return OK for a secure select of a present file in an authenticated state, while returning an error in an unauthenticated). Listing 1.1 gives an example of the secure SELECT EF CA and CVCA command[2]. It checks (via state variables) if there was a success-ful authentication. If that is the case it sets the EF selected state variable and calls the reader message server for ok (the integer parameter identifies the secure

---

[2] The command is the same for the optional CA file in the common area and the mandatory CVCA file in the LDS1 application area. The difference is just whether the DF LDS1 is selected or not.

SELECT EF CM as originator of the call). Otherwise, it calls the message server for a missing authentication (since the secure command is out-of-context outside of the LDS1 application) or a not found error if the file is not present (which is selected by a non-deterministic assignment). This includes the optionality of files having multiple possible answer paths even if the state (determined by the set state variables) is the same.

Listing 1.1. Exemplary message server for the secure SELECT EF CM command

```
msgsrv SSEL_EF_CA_CVCA (){
    boolean present=?(true,false);
    if(!AUTH) {
        if(present)       reader.FailSec();
        else reader.NoFind();
    }
    else {
        EF=true;
        reader.OK(6001);
    }
}
```

The reader possesses a message server for every (standard-defined) answer code and a reset server that resets intermediately used state variables and is called at the beginning. Except for the message server for an OK message, every answer server and the reset function has local integer variable that is non-deterministically filled with an identifier and an according switch/case statement to determine the function to call next (the default is an error function that should never be reached, which is checked as an assertion by the model checker). This way, all of the possible combinations for inputs are invoked by the model checker. The message server for OK is different, as it sets some intermediate state variables that are used by the model checker to determine whether some specific operations are successfully executed. These intermediate state variables are reset by the reset message server. Listing 1.2 gives an example for the OK and reset servers (note that the list of called functions is arbitrarily truncated for the sake of brevity.

Listing 1.2. Exemplary message server for the OK answer followed by a reset.

```
[...]
msgsrv reset (){
    OK=false;
    rdBinOK=false;
    srdBinOK=false;
    ERROR = false;
    sselEFOK=false;
    int data = ?(1001,2001,2002,2003,3001,4001,6001,6002,6003,7001);
    switch(data){
        case 1001: PP.SEL_DF_LDS1(); break;
        case 2001: PP.SEL_EF_CA_CVCA(); break;
        case 2002: PP.SEL_EF_CM(); break;
```

```
          case 2003: PP.SEL_EF_CS_SOD(); break;
          case 3001: PP.RD_BIN(); break;
          case 4001: PP.BAC(); break;
          case 6001: PP.SSEL_EF_CA_CVCA(); break;
          case 6002: PP.SSEL_EF_CM(); break;
          case 6003: PP.SSEL_EF_CS_SOD(); break;
          case 7001: PP.SRD_BIN(); break;
          default: self.ERR();
      }
}


msgsrv OK(int data){
  switch(data){
          case 1001: break;
          case 2001: break;
          case 2002: break;
          case 2003: break;
          case 3001: rdBinOK=true; break;
          case 4001: break;
          case 6001: sselEFOK=true; break;
          case 6002: sselEFOK=true; break;
          case 6003: sselEFOK=true; break;
          case 7001: srdBinOK=true; break;
          default: self.ERR();
      }
  OK=true;
  reset();
}
[...]
```

Figure 3 shows a simplified state model of a small part of the specified standard, including just selecting the CM elementary file, the LDS1 application and an authentication. The full standard contains far too many states (134) to display here.

4.2 Model Checking

Before using the specification model for compliance checking, we assure its correctness with regard to some basic security properties, as stated below, using model checking. For checking the model, we defined six different rules in LTS that assure the correctness of the security properties of the modeled specification. In particular these rules are:

NoXStates: $\Box(\neg (\neg DF \wedge AUTH))$;
PlainRead: $\Box(\neg (READOK \wedge (\neg EF \vee DF)))$;
ReadFollowsSelect: $(\neg READOK \ \mathcal{U} \ EF) \vee \Box(\neg READOK)$;
SecureRead: $\Box(\neg (SREADOK \wedge \neg(DF \wedge AUTH \wedge EF)))$;
SecureSelect: $\Box(\neg (SSELEFOK \wedge \neg(DF \wedge AUTH)))$;
SecureReadFollowsSecureSelect: $(\neg SREADOK \ \ \mathcal{U} \ \ SSELEFOK) \vee \Box(\neg SREADOK)$; Apart from obvious atomic propsitions like EF, AUTH, and

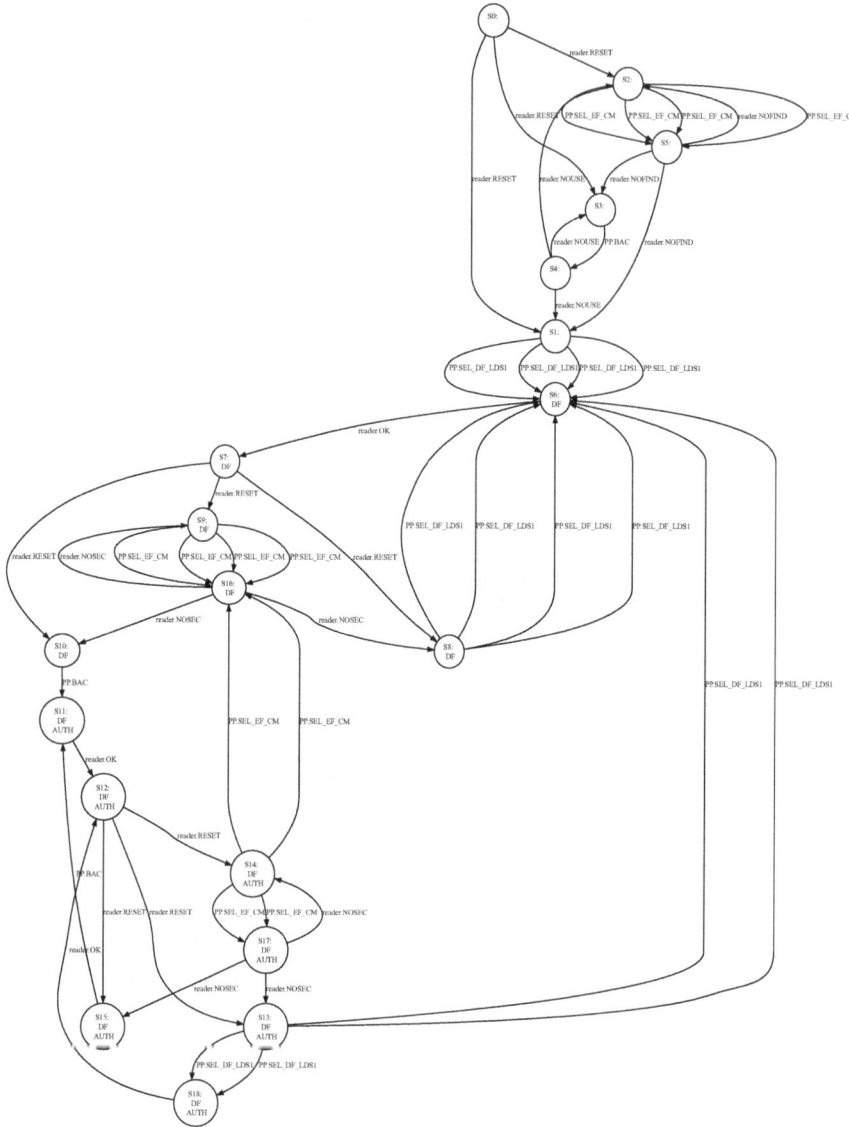

Fig. 3. Example of a simple Rebeca model. It only covers selecting one EF (CM), one DF (LDS1) and a BAC authentication command.

DF, we use READOK, SREADOK, and SSELEFOK, which stand for successful operations and are only set for one state before being unset in the reset message server. NoXStates contains a check for illegal states where authentication is true without an LDS selected (which should not happen because of lacking context for authentication). Plainread says that a (plain EF) READ should not be successful without selected EF or with selected DF (in the latter case, only secure READs should be successful), ReadFollowsSelect sayst that a READ should only be successful when a file is selected or not successful at all. SecureRead says that a secure READ should only successful in an authenticated, DF and EF selected state, SecureSelect says that a successful secure SELECT should only occur in an authenticated and DF-selected state, while SecureReadFollowsSecureSelect says that a secure READ can only occur after a secure SELECT (implying authentication).

4.3 Converting the Specification Model

A full state space export (see Sect. 4.2) comes in an XML format, that can be converted into the Graphviz (DOT) format. However, displaying two communicating reactive systems (see Sect. 3), the format is not compatible with the learned implementation automata, which are Mealy Machines. The Mealy Machines combine the two systems into a single combined state, where the two communication directions are visible in the input/output dualism of the transitions.

We therefore wrote an automated conversion tool that removes the states and transitions concerning the reset function and the respective states for unsetting the successful operation propositions (READOK, SREADOK, and SSELEFOK), as those are just used for checking the model (if certain operations succeed only if certain conditions are met) and should not show up in the specification automaton. Then, it determines the mergable states by first building equivalence classes based on the states' propositions and remove redundant ones. In our case, it is possible to form equivalence classes for merging states this way, because the Rebeca model sets the states' propositions according to system properties relevant for the comparison with a learner, reducing the possible set of remaining ones to the relevant ones, i.e., the set of possible equivalence classes is predefined by the possible combinations of propositions in the model. This was also the motivation of writing a dedicated converter instead of relying on established toolsets. Lastly, for each equivalence class, it replaces reader/PP state pairs with single states and take the transitions from reader to PP as *input* part and from PP to reader as *output* part of the resulting combined transition label. This eventually creates a Mealy-styled LTS with the transitions labeled with input and output. The difference to an actual Mealy Machine is, again, that the we can have more than one transition for the same input in the same state (making the LTS effectively a non-deterministic pseudo-Mealy Machine). This is, however, not a concern for the compliance checking procedure, as we treat the learned implementation (a Mealy Machine) and the specification automaton (a pseudo-Mealy Machine) as LTS with the input/output pairs as labels. This makes the automata comparable by diverse kinds of equivalence relations using standard methods.

Figure 4 shows a comparison of the specification pseudo-Mealy Machine with the learned passport model. For readability, just to demonstrate the concept, we shrinked the showed model the operations SELECT EF CM, SELECT DF LDS1 and BAC. The evaluation, however, covers the full standard specification (see Sect. 5).

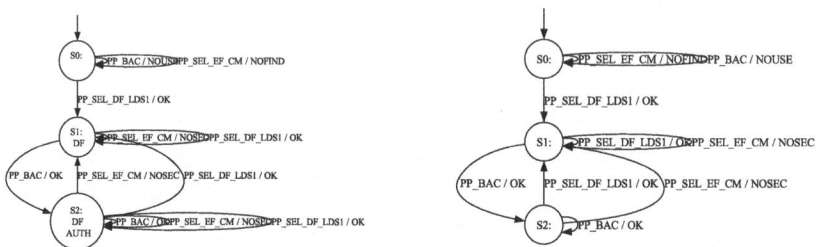

Fig. 4. Simplified example of a Rebeca model converted in a non-deterministic Mealy-style LTS compared to a learned MRTD Mealy model. Note that the difference lies in additional transitions in the Rebeca version, modeling optional behavior. The Rebeca model shows the same behavior as the one in Fig. 3.

5   Evaluation

In this section we briefly outline the achieved results with the described methods. We used the described model-checked ICAO standard's specification model and used trace and simulation preorder to check a learned model of an Austrian passport for its compliance with the specification model. We obtained the learned model in Graphviz format from our Learnlib-based NFC learner (see a labeled, simplified version in Fig. 5), created the specification model using Rebeca in the Afra IDE and verified it with the Modere model checker. We then converted the verified model into a pseudo-Mealy Machine in Graphviz format (see Fig. 6 for a simplified, consolidated version). The full pseudo-Mealy has 6 states and 662 transitions, whereas the original state model from Rebeca has 134 states and over 5300 transitions. This shows the significant decrease of complexity through the Rebeca state model's conversation into a Mealy-styled LTS. The learned model has 6 states and 342 transitions. We converted both Graphviz models into the Aldebaran format and used it as an input for mCRL2's [4] ltsccompare tool, with which we performed simulation and trace preorder checking. The result showed a positive check, i.e. it showed that a simulation preorder relation between the learned model and the specification exists. Hence, the learned model behavior is included in the behavior of the specification. We were therefore able

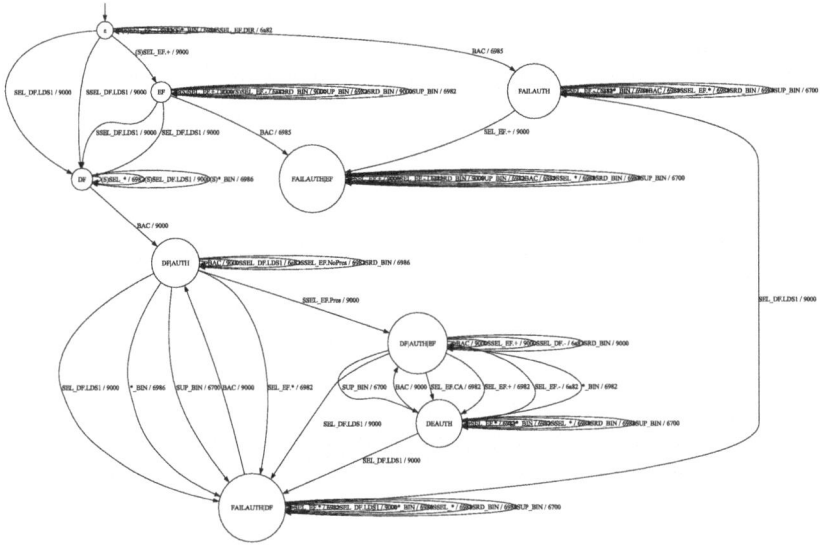

Fig. 5. Labeled model of an Austrian passport learned with TTT from [20].

to demonstrate the passport's compliance with the ICAO standard and, through the model checking, we were able to demonstrate the security of the standard specification (in terms of the data being securely stored on the eMRTD device).

6   Related Work

There are approaches for combining automata learning and bisimulation algorithms [6,9]. However, to the best of our knowledge, there are no approaches for combining model checking, learning and preorder checking as ours. We funded this approach on our method on partly specifying the ICAO eMRTD specification [20] and used the learned model from that work. However, in the former approach we manually modeled the specification pseudo-Mealy Machine using pure graphical notation (i.e., we hand-modeled it in the graphviz format) and did not use a modeling language nor model checking. Using Rebeca and Modere in the present work, we expanded the approach by formally verifying the specification model and, through the automatic conversion to the specification LTS, eliminated sources of error in the specification modeling. We also used the approach of using equivalence checking (bisimulation and trace equivalence) with NFC before, particularly for an automatic compliance checker for the ISO/IEC 14443-3 (the NFC handshake) protocol [19]).

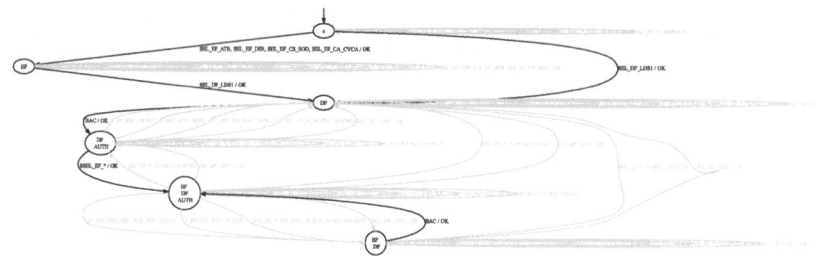

Fig. 6. Example of the modeled ICAO specification. Please note that we simplified the transitions because of the complexity. Solid lines are transitions towards more elevated access rights, light lines are transitions leading towards the same or lower access privileges.

7   Conclusion

In this paper, we demonstrated an approach and a tool chain of automata learning to infer models of systems under test and evaluate their compliance with a specification model in Rebeca, that is formally checked for security properties. We used this approach in practice to automatically mine a Mealy model of an eMTRD device (an Austrian passport). We further created a Rebeca model of the ICAO Doc 9303 part 9 standard and verfied it for security properties (particularly, proper authentication for access to restricted files). We then used the mCRL2 toolset to check the compliance of the mined model with the specification model using simulation and trace preorder, for which we converted the specification model into a Mealy-styled LTS. This way we could show the compliance of the SUT with the verfied standard.

7.1   Discussion

We have limited the current approach LDS1 application of eMRTDs. Furthermore, we were unable to learn another passport (particularly a newer German one), because it uses the more recent PACE authentication for which we do not have a working implementation. Nevertheless, the approach is scalable and can be expanded to cover these areas. Furthermore, the process is transferrable to other systems, mainly depending on the availibility of a learner.

7.2   Outlook

To generalize the approach, we plan to use the vice-versa method, namely converting learned Mealy machines into Rebeca code. This way we can mine models of arbitrary systems automatically, which is very tedious to do manually. Once having these models in Rebeca, we can use Modere for checking them for security and other correctness properties.

References

1. Angluin, D.: Learning regular sets from queries and counterexamples. Inf. Comput. **75**(2), 87–106 (1987). https://doi.org/10.1016/0890-5401(87)90052-6
2. Baier, C., Katoen, J.P.: Principles of Model Checking. MIT Press, Cambridge (2008)
3. Bollig, B., Katoen, J.-P., Kern, C., Leucker, M., Neider, D., Piegdon, D.R.: Libalf: the automata learning framework. In: Touili, T., Cook, B., Jackson, P. (eds.) CAV 2010. LNCS, vol. 6174, pp. 360–364. Springer, Heidelberg (2010). https://doi.org/10.1007/978-3-642-14295-6_32
4. Bunte, O., et al.: The mCRL2 toolset for analysing concurrent systems. In: Vojnar, T., Zhang, L. (eds.) TACAS 2019. LNCS, vol. 11428, pp. 21–39. Springer, Cham (2019). https://doi.org/10.1007/978-3-030-17465-1_2
5. Champarnaud, J.M., Coulon, F.: NFA reduction algorithms by means of regular inequalities. Theor. Comput. Sci. **327**(3), 241–253 (2004). https://doi.org/10.1016/j.tcs.2004.02.048
6. Chen, Y.F., Hong, C.D., Lin, A.W., Rümmer, P.: Learning to prove safety over parameterised concurrent systems. In: 2017 Formal Methods in Computer Aided Design (FMCAD), pp. 76–83 (2017). https://doi.org/10.23919/FMCAD.2017.8102244
7. Garcia, F.D., de Koning Gans, G., Verdult, R.: Tutorial: Proxmark, the swiss army knife for rfid security research: Tutorial at 8th workshop on rfid security and privacy (rfidsec 2012). Technical report. Radboud University Nijmegen, ICIS, Nijmegen (2012)
8. Groote, J.F., Vaandrager, F.: Structured operational semantics and bisimulation as a congruence. Inf. Comput. **100**(2), 202–260 (1992). https://doi.org/10.1016/0890-5401(92)90013-6
9. Hong, C.-D., Lin, A.W., Majumdar, R., Rümmer, P.: Probabilistic bisimulation for parameterized systems. In: Dillig, I., Tasiran, S. (eds.) CAV 2019. LNCS, vol. 11561, pp. 455–474. Springer, Cham (2019). https://doi.org/10.1007/978-3-030-25540-4_27
10. International Organization for Standardization: Cards and security devices for personal identification – Contactless proximity objects – Part 4: Transmission protocol. ISO/IEC Standard "14443-4", International Organization for Standardization (2018)
11. International Organization for Standardization: Identification cards – Integrated circuit cards – Part 4: Organization, security and commands for interchange (2020)
12. Isberner, M., Howar, F., Steffen, B.: The TTT algorithm: a redundancy-free approach to active automata learning. In: Bonakdarpour, B., Smolka, S.A. (eds.) RV 2014. LNCS, vol. 8734, pp. 307–322. Springer, Cham (2014). https://doi.org/10.1007/978-3-319-11164-3_26
13. Isberner, M., Howar, F., Steffen, B.: The open-source LearnLib. In: Kroening, D., Păsăreanu, C.S. (eds.) CAV 2015. LNCS, vol. 9206, pp. 487–495. Springer, Cham (2015). https://doi.org/10.1007/978-3-319-21690-4_32
14. Jaghoori, M.M., Movaghar, A., Sirjani, M.: Modere: The model-checking engine of Rebeca. In: Proceedings of the 2006 ACM Symposium on Applied Computing,

SAC 2006, pp. 1810–1815. Association for Computing Machinery, New York (2006). https://doi.org/10.1145/1141277.1141704

15. Kearns, M.J., Vazirani, U.: An Introduction to Computational Learning Theory. MIT Press, Cambridge (1994)

16. Khamespanah, E., Sirjani, M., Khosravi, R.: Afra: an eclipse-based tool with extensible architecture for modeling and model checking of rebeca family models. In: Hojjat, H., Ábrahám, E. (eds.) Fundamentals of Software Engineering, pp. 72–87. Springer, Cham (2023). https://doi.org/10.1007/978-3-031-42441-0_6

17. Kruger, L., Junges, S., Rot, J.: State matching and multiple references in adaptive active automata learning. In: Platzer, A., Rozier, K.Y., Pradella, M., Rossi, M. (eds.) Formal Methods, pp. 267–284. Springer, Cham (2025). https://doi.org/10.1007/978-3-031-71162-6_14

18. Lee, D., Sabnani, K., Kristol, D., Paul, S.: Conformance testing of protocols specified as communicating finite state machines-a guided random walk based approach. IEEE Trans. Commun. **44**(5), 631–640 (1996). https://doi.org/10.1109/26.494307

19. Marksteiner, S., Sirjani, M., Sjödin, M.: Using automata learning for compliance evaluation of communication protocols on an NFC handshake example. In: Kofroň, J., Margaria, T., Seceleanu, C. (eds.) Engineering of Computer-Based Systems. Lecture Notes in Computer Science, vol. 14390, pp. 170–190. Springer, Cham (2023). https://doi.org/10.1007/978-3-031-49252-5_13

20. Marksteiner, S., Sirjani, M., Sjödin, M.: Automated passport control: mining and checking models of machine readable travel documents. In: Proceedings of the 19th International Conference on Availability, Reliability and Security, ARES 2024, pp. 1–8. Association for Computing Machinery, New York (2024). https://doi.org/10.1145/3664476.3670454

21. Mealy, G.H.: A method for synthesizing sequential circuits. Bell Syst. Tech. J. **34**(5), 1045–1079 (1955). https://doi.org/10.1002/j.1538-7305.1955.tb03788.x

22. Merten, M., Howar, F., Steffen, B., Margaria, T.: Automata learning with on-the-fly direct hypothesis construction. In: Hähnle, R., Knoop, J., Margaria, T., Schreiner, D., Steffen, B. (eds.) ISoLA 2011. CCIS, pp. 248–260. Springer, Heidelberg (2012). https://doi.org/10.1007/978-3-642-34781-8_19

23. Moore, E.F.: Gedanken-experiments on sequential machines. In: Automata Studies, AM-34, vol. 34, pp. 129–154. Princeton University Press (1956). https://doi.org/10.1515/9781400882618-006

24. Muškardin, E., Aichernig, B.K., Pill, I., Pferscher, A., Tappler, M.: AALpy: an active automata learning library. Innov. Syst. Softw. Eng., 1–10 (2022). https://doi.org/10.1007/s11334-022-00449-3

25. Organization, I.C.A.: Machine Readable Travel Documents – Part 9: Deployment of Biometric Identification and Electronic Storage of Data in MRTDs (Eigth Edition) (2021)

26. Rivest, R.L., Schapire, R.E.: Inference of finite automata using homing sequences. In: Proceedings of the Twenty-First Annual ACM Symposium on Theory of Computing, STOC 1989, pp. 411–420. Association for Computing Machinery, New York (1989). https://doi.org/10.1145/73007.73047

27. Russell, B.: Mathematical logic as based on the theory of types. Am. J. Math. **30**(3), 222–262 (1908). https://doi.org/10.2307/2369948

28. Sirjani, M.: Rebeca: theory, applications, and tools. In: de Boer, F.S., Bonsangue, M.M., Graf, S., de Roever, W.-P. (eds.) FMCO 2006. LNCS, vol. 4709, pp. 102–126. Springer, Heidelberg (2007). https://doi.org/10.1007/978-3-540-74792-5_5

29. Tappler, M., Aichernig, B.K., Bloem, R.: Model-based testing IoT communication via active automata learning. In: 2017 IEEE International Conference on Software Testing, Verification and Validation (ICST), pp. 276–287 (2017). https://doi.org/10.1109/ICST.2017.32
30. Vaandrager, F., Garhewal, B., Rot, J., Wißmann, T.: A new approach for active automata learning based on apartness. In: TACAS 2022. LNCS, vol. 13243, pp. 223–243. Springer, Cham (2022). https://doi.org/10.1007/978-3-030-99524-9_12

From LTL to Scenarios: Automatic Test Case Generation for Axini Modeling Language

Maarten Schröder[1], Machiel van der Bijl[2], and Wan Fokkink[3](✉)⬤

[1] Centric, Amsterdam, The Netherlands
[2] Axini, Amsterdam, The Netherlands
[3] Vrije Universiteit Amsterdam, Amsterdam, The Netherlands
w.j.fokkink@vu.nl

Abstract. Axini offers a commercial platform to perform model-based software testing, using models written in Axini's Modeling Language. To verify properties of a system, they use scenario constructs that describe these properties, which are matched against automatically generated test cases. These scenarios are used as alternatives to properties written in Linear Temporal Logic. We provide a translation from a fragment of this logic to scenarios. Moreover, we present a method, using scenarios, to automatically generate test cases, based on the requirements of the system. Experiments show the effectiveness of the method.

1 Introduction

Axini offers a platform where companies can perform model-based testing of their software systems, on what is called the Axini Modeling Platform. Models are built in the Axini Modeling Language (AML). Tests are generated automatically for these models, to verify high-level properties of the system being modeled, as formulated by the system developers. A test consists of one or more test cases, in which inputs are given to both the model and the system, while outputs are received from the system. Meanwhile, the model emulates the system, taking inputs and returning outputs the system is expected to return. Such a model is based on a Symbolic Transition System, which is a state machine that incorporates a defined data control flow.

To check whether all desired properties of a system have been tested by means of the generated tests, Axini has developed a type of function known as a scenario within AML. It entails a particular test trace, consisting of a series of possible test steps, intended to describe a property, which can be matched against the generated test cases. If the test trace described by a scenario can be found within a test case, then that case has verified that scenario. The types of properties depicted in scenarios are those describing how certain inputs can be given to the system and how certain outputs can be sent back.

A scenario is based on a property expressed in Linear Temporal Logic (LTL). However, LTL tends to be too complex to use for a customer trying to express the properties of an AML model of their software system. Therefore Axini wants to use a more intuitive scenario language to describe properties. The scenario language is not fully worked out yet, as it has only recently been developed. Axini wants to know how the scenario language can be expanded to include more of the expressiveness of LTL. The first goal of this paper is to investigate how scenarios can be refined to better express properties for a model in AML, and how scenarios be written based on properties expressed in LTL.

Another important issue is that even if a scenario can be held against test cases, running the generated tests does not guarantee that the corresponding property will actually be checked. Because their test cases do not aim to traverse the model in a way that will verify the property. The second goal of this paper is to investigate how test cases can be automatically generated for AML models so that they cover all properties expressed in scenarios. Scenarios can be used to generate test cases. The same scenarios can then be used to check afterwards whether the properties have been verified.

The paper is structured as follows. Section 2 explains the basics of LTL, AML, and automatic test case generation. In Sect. 3, scenarios are related to LTL formulas. Section 4 discusses automatic test case generation and two case studies. Section 5 mentions some limitations we encountered, and Sect. 6 some alternative approaches to make temporal logics easier to understand. The paper is concluded in Sect. 7.

We are happy to dedicate this paper to Marjan Sirjani, on the occasion of her 60th birthday. Her prolific research at the intersection of software engineering and formal methods covers for instance actor-based languages, model-based systems engineering, and testing. She, moreover, is an active organiser, a social spider in the web of her research community, and a wonderful colleague.

2 Background

2.1 Linear Temporal Logic

Properties of states in a system can be expressed in Linear Temporal Logic (LTL), a modal temporal logic [2]. LTL is built upon propositional logic:

- Each propositional variable is an LTL formula.
- If ψ and ϕ are LTL formulas, then so are $\neg\psi$, $\psi \vee \phi$, $\psi \wedge \phi$, and $\psi \rightarrow \phi$.

LTL contains the following additional temporal operators:

- $\mathbf{X}\psi$: In the next state, ψ will hold.
- $\mathbf{F}\psi$: Eventually in a future state, ψ must hold.
- $\mathbf{G}\psi$: In every state from now on, ψ must hold.
- $\psi\mathbf{U}\phi$: Starting from the current state, ψ will hold at least until ϕ becomes true, which must happen eventually.
- $\psi\mathbf{W}\phi$: Starting from the current state, ψ will hold at least until ϕ becomes true. If ϕ never becomes true, then ψ remains true forever.

– $\psi\mathbf{R}\phi$: Starting from the current state, ψ will hold up until and including where ϕ becomes true. If ϕ never becomes true, then ψ remains true forever.

The verification of LTL formulas has a time complexity linear to the number of states in the model and exponential to the size of the LTL formula [4].

2.2   AML

For their models, Axini has developed a domain-specific language called Axini Modeling Language (AML). It is implemented in Ruby, an interpreted, high-level programming language. AML is designed for writing Symbolic Transition Systems [6]. An AML model is supposed to represent how the system under test (SUT) should work. A user interacts with the SUT by giving it input messages. This user is represented by the program that generates the test cases. When the SUT receives a message, it could give a response back. This response should match the response that would be given if the same input were given to the model.

The language of AML builds a model consisting of states with transitions between those states. A single model is defined by one or more process constructs. Such a process contains AML code. A transition here is a send or receive statement, which involves sending or receiving a message. We explain how the send/receive messages represent the user and the SUT interacting with each other, with the receive messages being the input from the user to the SUT and the send messages being output from the SUT. A send or receive message has a label, and can have additional constraints or updates to variables that have been declared beforehand in the AML code. A constraint mentions what ranges of values certain variables need to have before the message can be sent or received, while an update changes variables after a message is transmitted. The labels that are used in messages are defined in a channel construct. In a channel, stimuli are labels for receive messages, while responses are labels for send messages. A stimulus or response can have additional parameters attached to it that are transmitted with a message, which can be mentioned in the constraint or update part. For a receive message, the parameters are required to be given values in the constraint. Moreover, a response message needs to be sent within a certain timespan from the latest stimulus to the SUT, which is known as a timeout in AML. If the SUT does not respond within this time span, it is considered to have timed out. It is also possible to define a configuration of constants outside of the processes, which can then be referenced within those processes.

There is a distinction between observable and unobservable transitions. Observable transitions have labels that are declared in a channel and can be seen in the test cases. Unobservable transitions are not visible in the test cases and are used for steps within the model that occur internally in the SUT. They are not always defined explicitly in the AML code. There is also a distinction between external and internal transitions. The former is defined in an external channel, which is a channel that can be defined outside of the processes and can be inserted into and then used by every process. This is meant for the user to communicate with the SUT. An internal channel is a channel that is defined only within processes and exists to allow communication between processes. An internal transition is a type of unobservable transition. In one process, its internal channel will have certain stimuli and responses, while in another process it will have stimuli and responses that complement those of the former. For example, if one process has an internal send label a, then another process could have a as an internal receive label.

Figure 1 shows AML code for two processes. A circle depicts a state, which carry a unique numver preceded by an underscore. Processes have an external channel, defining the labels for communication between user and the SUT. They also have an internal channel for communication between the processes. In this example, process name1 can receive input a from the user with a parameter that should be 0. Then it sends a response _i to process name2, which can receive it, since it has a corresponding label _i for input and a proper receive statement. This process will then send output b to the user.

From a single state, it is possible to have multiple outgoing transitions that a tester can choose between. For this purpose, a choice or repeat construct can be used in AML. Within a choice construct, one or more options are defined. Each option can contain a block of AML code, generally consisting of a transition or a series of them. The different options are reflected in a model as different transitions from the state before the choice. The options from choice, while containing their own intermediate states and transitions, by default will end with transitioning to one state that is at the end of the choice. It is however possible for the user to have a transition from an option lead to a different state, so that multiple transitions from one state can ultimately still lead to different states. As for the repeat construct, it works the same as choice, except at the end of an option it will move back to the state from before the repeat, and choose an option again. It will keep doing this until the testing ends or an option is chosen that transitions out of the repeat construct.

In Fig. 2, AML code and corresponding visualisations can be seen depicting a choice and a repeat construct. In the upper part, from the state at the beginning of the choice _0, there are three options containing their own transitions and states. At the end of the options, they come back to one state at the end of the choice by default. In the lower part, from the state _0 at the beginning of the repeat, there are three options containing their own transitions and states. At the end of the options, two of the three come back to the state at the start of the repeat by default. One of them has a stop_repetition command at the end, which causes that option to transition out of the repeat loop.

A behaviour construct is similar to a function. It contains a block of AML code, and can be called via a behave_as command. Once called, the model will behave according to the code inside the behaviour. A behaviour can be terminating, meaning that after it finishes executing it redirects back to where it was originally called, or non-terminating, which means that the code inside will keep being executed until it reaches a transition that goes out of the behaviour.

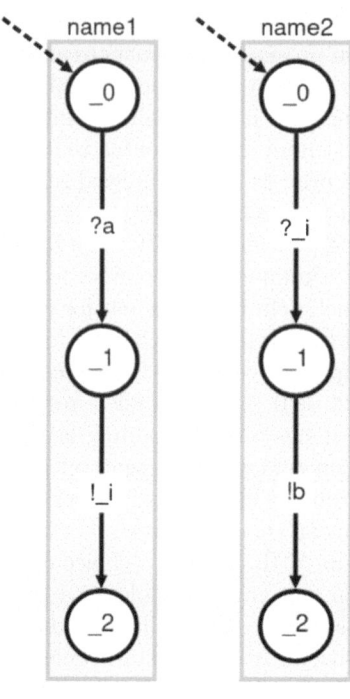

```
timeout 1.0

external 'channel'

internal 'chan'

process('name1') {
  channel('channel') {
    stimulus 'a',
      {'param' => :integer}
    response 'b'
  }
  channel('chan') {
    response '_i'
  }

  receive 'a',
    constraint: 'param == 0'
  send '_i'
}

process('name2') {
  channel('channel') {
    stimulus 'a',
      {'param' => :integer}
    response 'b'
  }
  channel('chan') {
    stimulus '_i'
  }

  receive '_i'
  send 'b'
}
```

Fig. 1. Example AML with two processes

It is also possible to define functions in AML that can be called from within the AML code. These functions are declared and defined outside of the processes and are based on the Ruby language.

Figure 3 depicts a process that starts by moving to a state _1 from where the behaviour behav is called. Within this behaviour, the function func is repeatedly called. In the graphic on the right, the dotted transitions are unobservable transitions. A squared stated is a special state to signal the sequential transition to a subprocess. Since a subprocess is entirely encapsulated again, the state numbering can start with _0 again.

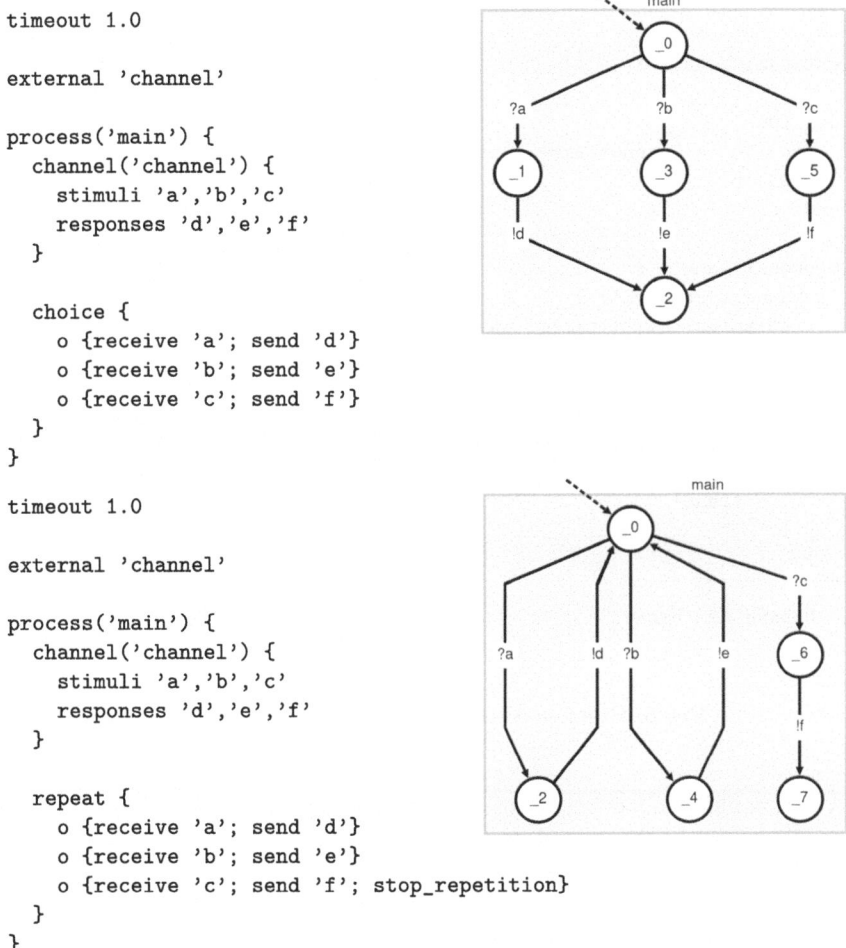

```
timeout 1.0

external 'channel'

process('main') {
  channel('channel') {
    stimuli 'a','b','c'
    responses 'd','e','f'
  }

  choice {
    o {receive 'a'; send 'd'}
    o {receive 'b'; send 'e'}
    o {receive 'c'; send 'f'}
  }
}
```

```
timeout 1.0

external 'channel'

process('main') {
  channel('channel') {
    stimuli 'a','b','c'
    responses 'd','e','f'
  }

  repeat {
    o {receive 'a'; send 'd'}
    o {receive 'b'; send 'e'}
    o {receive 'c'; send 'f'; stop_repetition}
  }
}
```

Fig. 2. Examples AML choice and repeat

2.3 Test Case Generation

AML models are tested via an automatic test case generation program [6]. This program consists of a simulator that starts at the beginning of the model. At each state in the model, it chooses the next transition, or user input. Axini has different programs describing algorithms that determine which transitions are chosen, called strategies. A strategy is set by the person testing before the tests are generated. An example of such a strategy is Local Transition, where a transition is prioritised if it has not been covered before, with the strategy choosing randomly if all the available transitions at a state have been covered. The goal of this strategy is to cover as many transitions in the model as possible. Axini also employs strategies to e.g. cover as many states as possible.

```
timeout 1.0

external 'channel'

def func
  receive 'a', constraint: "param == 0"
  send 'b'
end

process('name') {
  channel('channel') {
    stimulus 'a', {'param' => :integer}
    response 'b'
  }

  behavior('behav', :non_terminating) {
    repeat {
      o {func}
    }
  }

  behave_as 'behav'
}
```

Fig. 3. Example AML with behaviour and function

After a transition has been chosen, the simulator advances on this transition. This will bring it to the next state in the model. This transition is also received by the SUT, which could result in the SUT sending a response back. These send/receive transitions form the test steps. Although unobservable and internal transitions of the model are handled as well, they do not show up in the test cases, as they are not meant to be seen by the user since they cannot be detected within the SUT. Once a number of test steps have completed, the current test case finishes and possibly a new test case is started.

Figure 4 depicts an example test case generation, with two possible test cases. The testing starts at start state _0. In the first test case example, the strategy begins with choosing the input with label a. This leads to state _2, after which the SUT sends the response with label d, leading back to the start state. Suppose the strategy prioritises transitions that have not yet been covered. Since a has been covered, it chooses input b instead. This leads to state _4, where input c can be chosen, which leads to state _6. In this state the SUT sends output e. In the second test case example, the strategy instead begins with choosing the input with label b. As before, this leads to state _4, where input c can be chosen, which leads to state _6. In this state the SUT sends output e. A final state has been reached, so state _2 is not reached in this test case.

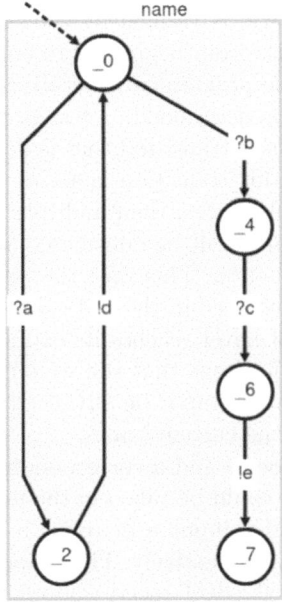

Test Case

step	label
1	?a
2	!d
3	?b
4	?c
5	!e

step	label
1	?b
2	?c
3	!e

Fig. 4. Example test case generation

2.4   Scenarios

To reiterate, tests step through the model, creating a series of test steps, or a test case. A scenario is a construct, designed by hand, that describes a possible test case in AML. Specifically, it describes one or more possible series of send/receive statements. A scenario can then be held against the generated test cases, to see if any test cases follow the behaviour described within said scenario. The idea behind this is to describe a property for a SUT in a scenario as one or more possible series of send/receive statements. If a test case matches a scenario, then that test case has verified the property. The type of properties generally described in scenarios are those stating how a SUT should respond under certain inputs and when it does or does not allow certain inputs. The limited size of test cases does however mean that sometimes a test trace described in a scenario could be encountered in a generated test case, but did not happen in the currently generated ones.

A scenario can be set to be either accepting or rejecting. By default a scenario is set to accepting. This means that the scenario passes when a match is found with a test case. Therefore, a scenario describing a liveness property, which says that something should be able to happen, can be designed using this setting. If a scenario is set to rejecting, this means that it will not pass if a series of test steps is found that matches the described scenario. Such a method can be used for safety properties, where the goal is to check that a certain situation never occurs.

When it is checked whether a scenario is verified by a test case, there is a program that steps through the test case from beginning to end. At the beginning, the scenario is in a start state. The program will iteratively try to see if it can advance a scenario for each transition described in a test step. If the scenario in its current state can follow through on a transition that is described in a test step, then the state that follows after this transition is set as the new current state. If a transition can lead to multiple states, then multiple states are set as the current state and each of these states will be considered when checking if a scenario can follow through on a transition. This way, the program is able to spot different ways for a scenario to be covered in the test case. If a scenario can no longer be advanced at some point, or never reaches its end state, then it has not been covered by the test case. If it happens that the scenarios current state has multiple states and one of these states cannot be advanced, then that state will no longer be considered as part of the current state.

Figure 5 depicts an example of a process and a corresponding scenario. The scenario describes a potential path that could be taken in the process. First, the process on the left allows the user to give input a or input b, after which the SUT should return output f or output g respectively. The property described in the scenario on the right says that after the SUT receives input a, it should send output f. Furthermore, the process allows the user to choose between inputs c,

```
process('name') {                      scenario('scen') {
  channel('chan') {                      channel('chan') {
    stimuli 'a','b'                        stimuli 'a','b'
    stimuli 'c','d','e'                    stimuli 'c','d','e'
    responses 'f','g'                      responses 'f','g'
  }                                      }

  choice {                               receive 'a'
    o {                                  send 'f'
      receive 'a'
      send 'f'                           choice {
    }                                      o {receive 'c'}
    o {                                    o {receive 'd'}
      receive 'b'                        }
      send 'g'                         }
    }
  }

  choice {
    o {receive 'c'}
    o {receive 'd'}
    o {receive 'e'}
  }
}
```

Fig. 5. Example scenario

d, and e afterwards. The property described in the scenario says that after the SUT receives a and sends f, it should be possible for the user to give input c or input d.

3 Relating Scenarios to LTL

The first goal of this study is to investigate how Axini can optimally use scenarios for the representation and verification of properties. In order to optimize the usage of scenarios when writing properties, it is necessary to know how scenarios can be formed based on properties written in LTL.

3.1 Specifying Scenarios in LTL

Scenarios can only be expressed by a fragment of LTL. We explain how scenarios can be expressed properly by means of LTL formulas.

The propositional variables in LTL can be used to represent send/receive statements, including the constraints on those statements. Since a step in a test trace can only handle one send/receive at a time, not more than one variable representing send/receive can be true at any given point. Therefore, the LTL operator **R** should generally not be used when writing properties as LTL formulas, as its two arguments must at some point both be true. Conjunctions should not be used in LTL formulas for the same reason, with the following two exceptions. The first is when the conjunction occurs at depth 0, so that the LTL formula can be split into two formulas, one for each argument of the conjunction. The second is when the conjunction concerns two different transitions that carry the same label, or is between two disjunctions of transitions that have an overlap, so that their conjunction still allows behaviour.

Scenarios can express in a positive way which transitions are possible, but not readily which transitions are impossible. For this reason, the negation operator should be avoided in (or eliminated from) LTL formulas. In particular, with safety properties the goal is often to guarantee that a certain undesirable situation never occurs. These types of properties would be expressed with a negation in LTL formulas. Negation can be implemented indirectly in scenarios, by adding a choice/repeat with all other possible options, i.e., all transitions that are not the transitions under the negation. As mentioned before, a channel defines the labels used in transitions. This means that the total available number of labels is finite and that the total number of possible transitions forms something like a transition space. Therefore, if a property says "not a transition with label a", then this refers to the transitions from the transition space that do not have label a. Thus using negation in a scenario can become unpractical with more complex models, where the transition space could be very large.

Scenarios work by going over the generated test traces. Some aspects of the SUT that are mentioned in properties do not appear in those test cases, such as variables declared in processes. Therefore, it may not be possible for some properties that are partially based around such variables to be tested.

However, it is possible to set a configuration of constants in an AML file, which can be accessed by the scenarios, although these remain constant and are not varied throughout a trace. One way to include variables in scenarios is to add additional statements to the property in LTL where the variables can be used in the constraint of a receive label as parameters. This way, the property in LTL addresses what the values of a variable should be, which can then be incorporated into the scenario.

3.2   Mapping LTL to Scenarios

In order to optimally use scenarios, it is necessary to understand how a property written in LTL can be transcribed to a scenario for an AML model. In this section, it will be shown what a property in LTL looks like as a scenario construct. There are levels of depth to (the parse tree of) an LTL formula. For example, a $\rightarrow$ $\mathbf{X}$(b $\vee$ c) has an $\rightarrow$ operator at depth 0 and a $\vee$ operator at depth 1. Scenarios at depth 0 have a basic scenario construct, which looks as follows:

```
scenario('name') {
    include 'labels.aml'
    *AML*
}
```

Here `labels.aml` is a separate AML file that contains an external channel construct with the labels that can occur in the processes. It is referenced via an include statement, so that the AML code can use the predefined labels in send/receive statements, without having to type out the same channel for each scenario. A model is likely to have multiple scenarios, since the corresponding SUT likely has multiple properties. In this example, *AML* is to be replaced with AML code describing the property starting from depth 0.

Now, for each LTL operator, it will be shown what it looks like as a scenario at depth 0 in further examples. In the following examples, variables a, b, etc. express blocks of AML code. The AML code that describes the LTL formula will be marked red, except if the AML surrounding it deviates from the standard, then it will be marked purple, with the surroundings red. For an LTL formula with depth > 0, the variables a, b, etc. from the AML code describing it can be replaced with AML code describing the LTL formulas from the next depth level in the LTL formula currently being described.

A property is often required to happen at any point within the test cases. For example, a property may describe what a SUT should do for a certain input, where this input could happen anywhere in the test case. Therefore, at the beginning and end of the AML code describing such a property in a scenario, AML code is added that repeatedly sends or receives any message. Adding this code is simplified through a function called **anywhere**, which is called from the scenario and moves through the test case until the property is encountered. The function works like this:

Anywhere

```
def anywhere do
    match_all
    property
    match_all
end


def match_all do
    repeat {
        o {send_or_receive :any}
        o {stop_repetition}
    }
end


scenario('name') {
    include 'labels.aml'
    anywhere {
        *AML*
    }
}
```

As shown in the code example above, the AML code AML* describing the property is passed to anywhere, which calls the match_all function before and after. In match_all there is a repeat construct that either sends or receives any message, or stops repeating. This first match_all allows to step through the test case until a state is reached that contains the first transition related to property, which is replaced by *AML*. If the property is detected, the second match_all allows the test case to complete.

The scenario below describes a situation where under certain circumstance a, which could represent one or more statements, the SUT waits for b, which eventually should happen.

Finally: a → Fb

```
scenario('a-to-Fb') {
    include 'labels.aml'
    anywhere {
        a
        match_all
        b
    }
}
```

A common type of property for AML models is: if a happens in the current state, then in the next state b should happen, written as a $\rightarrow$ **X**b in LTL. In the example below, the scenario at the left describes the property as a liveness property, and the one at the right describes it as a safety property. This means that at the left it is a verification that a $\rightarrow$ **X**b occurs in the test trace, meaning that b occurs after a. At the right it is a verification that a $\rightarrow$ **X**b always holds, meaning that there are no occurrences in the test case of a not being followed by b. Here *not b* is the AML representation of LTL formula ¬b. In AML this represents all transitions that are not b, meaning there is a choice structure with the options containing all those transitions.

Next: a $\rightarrow$ Xb

```
scenario('a-to-b') {                scenario('a-to-b-BAD',:rejecting) {
    include 'labels.aml'                include 'labels.aml'
    anywhere {                          anywhere {
        a                                   a
        b                                   *not b*
    }                                   }
}                                   }
```

A safety property usually expresses something that should not happen. As explained before, to model a negation such as ¬a, a choice construct should be used with the options containing all possible transitions that are not a. Note that if a is a receive, then *not a* only needs to mention receive transitions, and likewise if a is a send. This way of capturing negation only really works if a is a transition or disjunction of transitions and not a larger block of AML code. Therefore, a more complex LTL formula ¬a would have to be rewritten so that the negation is only called on variables that represent a single transition or a disjunction of transitions. In Sect. 3.3, more will be explained on what is allowed and how to rewrite negations.

Negation: ¬a

a is a (disjunction of) transition(s)

```
scenario('not-a') {
    include 'labels.aml'
    anywhere {
        choice {
            *insert as options all sends/receives that are not a*
        }
    }
}
```

In case the negation is over a transition with a constraint, it suffices to change the constraint into its complement. For example, if the constraint of a transition a is foo == 2 && bar > 10, then *not a* is still a but with the constraint foo != 2 || bar < 11.

a is a transition with a constraint

```
scenario('not-a') {
    include 'labels.aml'
    anywhere {
        *a with complement of constraint*
    }
}
```

In case the property is an LTL formula of the form ¬a (i.e., the negation occurs at depth 0), instead of not being used deeper within the formula, it is then allowed to build a scenario modeling a and set it to rejecting.

¬a at depth 0

```
scenario('not-a', :rejecting) {
    include 'labels.aml'
    anywhere {
        a
    }
}
```

A property allowing for multiple possible options for the SUT to enact is generally represented as a disjunction in LTL. In AML disjunction is represented as a choice structure, with the options containing AML code representing the LTL formulas from the disjunction.

Or: $\bigvee_{i=0}^{i=n} a_i$

```
scenario('or') {
    include 'labels.aml'
    anywhere {
        choice {
            o {a_0}
            ...
            o {a_n}
        }
    }
}
```

As explained before, there cannot be two different transitions at the exact same time in an AML model. Therefore, a conjunction of transitions cannot be modeled within a scenario. If a property has a conjuction at depth 0 however, then the property can be split into separate properties where each of those properties is given its own scenario. Another possibility is a conjunction of two disjunctions of transitions that have overlapping transitions. Then a conjunction of the two yields a disjunction consisting of the overlapping transitions.

And: $\bigwedge_{i=0}^{i=n} a_i$ (only at depth 0)

```
scenario('a_0') {                          scenario('a_n') {
    include 'labels.aml'                        include 'labels.aml'
    anywhere {              ...                  anywhere {
        a_0                                          a_n
    }                                           }
}                                          }
```

To reiterate, a weak until operator a**W**b means that a has to be true at least until b becomes true, and if b never becomes true, then a remains true forever. So two different things are allowed to occur within a test trace, the first one being that it keeps getting transition a until b happens, which is modeled trough the first repeat loop in the code below. Otherwise at some point in the test trace, it will keep doing transition a without ending, as seen in the second repeat loop. Since the scenario keeps doing a without ending, it would never trigger the rest of the **anywhere** function if the code were encapsulated in this function. Therefore, the **anywhere** function is left out to avoid errors that would arise from unreachable code.

At the right is the safety property version, which verifies that the weak until always happens correctly. The idea is that a stops being true before b has become true. The conjunction a && *not b* entails that in a given state, the possible transitions contains the overlap between the possible transitions of a and *not b* in said state. Here, *not b* represents all possible transitions that are not b. The overlap a && *not b* basically means that it should contain all transitions or series of transitions that conform to a but not to b. Similarly, *not a* && *not b* consists of a disjunction of all transitions that are neither a nor b. Since it is possible for a or b to consist of multiple transitions in series, a && *not b* and *not a* && *not b* may not produce any overlaps. In that case, it suffices to put a for the former and *not b* for the latter.

Weak Until: aWb

```
scenario('a-W-b') {                    scenario('a-W-b-BAD', :rejecting) {
  include 'labels.aml'                   include 'labels.aml'
  match_all                              anywhere {
  choice {                                 repeat {
    o {                                      o {a && *not b*}
      repeat {                               o {*not a* && *not b*
        o {a}                                  stop_repetition}
        o {b; stop_repetition}             }
      }                                    }
      match_all                          }
    }
    o {
      repeat {
        o {a}
      }
    }
  }
}
```

To reiterate, an until **aUb** operator means that **a** has to be true at least until **b** becomes true and **b** must eventually become true. So just like with weak until there are two repeat loops, one where **b** becomes true and one where it does not, except the one where it does not is put under a rejecting scenario, which is to verify that this situation does not occur. The **a && *not b*** and ***not a* && *not b*** parts mean the same as they do with weak until described previously.

Until: aUb

```
scenario('a-U-b') {                    scenario('a-U-b-BAD', :rejecting) {
  include 'labels.aml'                   include 'labels.aml'
  anywhere {                             anywhere {
    repeat {                               repeat {
      o {a}                                  o {a && *not b*}
      o {b; stop_repetition}                 o {*not a* && *not b*
    }                                          stop_repetition}
  }                                        }
}                                        }
                                       }
```

3.3   Special Cases for LTL and Scenarios

The way that LTL formulas can be expressed into scenario constructs is somewhat limited, and requires the LTL formulas to be written in a specific form. On top of that, since AML code representing an LTL formula can be put inside another AML code block representing another LTL formula, the resulting AML code can become rather unrefined. That is why this section explains some ways that scenarios can be (re)written.

Adding a Safety Scenario. If a scenario models a liveness property, it is often only supposed to occur in this particular way. Then a safety scenario should be added that checks if no deviations occur.

Choice and Repeat. Some of the mappings previously shown have choice structures in their AML content. In some cases, these choice constructs can be replaced by repeat constructs. For example, if one of the options of a repeat construct ends up containing only a choice construct, then the options of the choice construct can be added as options to the repeat construct, instead of adding the whole choice construct. If some AML code came before or after the choice construct, that could be added at the beginning or end of the options.

Weak Until. As can be seen in the example from the previous section, the scenario construct for the weak until is different from others because the contents are not placed within an **anywhere** function. If weak until were to be used in an LTL formula at a depth > 0, then the corresponding AML code would be encompassed by the **anywhere** function of the AML code block containing it. Therefore, the weak until code needs to be rewritten somewhat. To illustrate this, consider an LTL formula c that includes a weak until, say a**W**b. The resulting scenario contains AML code c1 that takes place before the weak until, and c2 that takes place after. The scenario will consist of the choice construct containing the two options representing the two possible outcomes of weak until, but the options now represent the two outcomes of LTL formula c as a result of it containing a weak until.

```
scenario('c') {
    include 'labels.aml'
    match_all
    *AML code representing c1*
    choice {
        o {
            repeat {
                o {a}
                o {b; stop_repetition}
            }
            *AML code representing c2*
            match_all
        }
        o {
            repeat {
                o {a}
            }
        }
    }
}
```

Negation over Finally. It was mentioned before that the negation operator should only be taken over transitions, conjunctions of transitions or $\rightarrow$ operators, and that LTL formulas should be rewritten to accommodate for this. However, with a formula $\neg \mathbf{F}$a this is not going to be so simple. This formula stands for finally a, meaning that in one of the next states, a must eventually hold. The negated form of this would be that in none of the next states, a will ever hold. This results in the following AML code:

```
scenario('name') {
    include 'labels.aml'
    match_all
    repeat {
        o {
            *AML code for not(a)*
        }
    }
}
```

Similar to the second option of the weak until construct, the `anywhere` function has been replaced by a `match_all` function at the start. This will need to be done for any scenario modeling an LTL formula with a negation over finally. Meanwhile, $\neg$a can be rewritten further so that it can be properly mapped to AML code.

3.4   A Mapping Example

We describe an example where the following LTL formula is mapped to scenarios.

$$(a \vee b) \rightarrow (\mathbf{X}(\neg(c \rightarrow \mathbf{F}d)) \wedge \mathbf{X}((e \vee f)\mathbf{W}g))$$

Variables a–g represent send/receive statements. Assume that these are all the labels defined for the channels, from a file `labels.aml`. Before the scenarios can be constructed, the formula needs to be rewritten. Since the conjunction operator is at a depth > 0, we first change the formula to:

$$((a \vee b) \rightarrow \mathbf{X}(\neg(c \rightarrow \mathbf{F}d))) \wedge ((a \vee b) \rightarrow \mathbf{X}((e \vee f)\mathbf{W}g))$$

The formula can now be broken into two parts:

$$h = (a \vee b) \rightarrow \mathbf{X}(\neg(c \rightarrow \mathbf{F}d)) \qquad i = (a \vee b) \rightarrow \mathbf{X}((e \vee f)\mathbf{W}g)$$

This gives rise to the following scenario constructs:

```
scenario('name1') {              scenario('name2') {
    include 'labels.aml'             include 'labels.aml'
    anywhere {                       anywhere {
        h                                i
    }                               }
}                                }
```

Now the formulas of h and i can be broken into:

$$j = a \lor b \quad k = \neg(c \to \mathbf{F}d) \quad l = (e \lor f)\mathbf{W}g$$

Which gives rise to the following scenarios:

```
scenario('name1') {                scenario('name2') {
    include 'labels.aml'               include 'labels.aml'
    anywhere {                         anywhere {
        j                                  j
        k                                  l
    }                                  }
}                                  }
```

Now $j = a \lor b$ can be turned into a choice construct:

```
scenario('name1') {                scenario('name2') {
    include 'labels.aml'               include 'labels.aml'
    anywhere {                         anywhere {
        choice {                           choice {
            o {a}                              o {a}
            o {b}                              o {b}
        }                                  }
        k                                  l
    }                                  }
}                                  }
```

Since k contains a negation over an implication, it is turned into $k = c \to \neg\mathbf{F}d$. Meanwhile, l contains a weak until operator. After simplification this yields the following scenarios:

```
scenario('name1') {                scenario('name2') {
    include 'labels.aml'               include 'labels.aml'
    match_all                          match_all
    choice {                           choice {
        o {a}                              o {a}
        o {b}                              o {b}
    }                                  }
    c                                  choice {
    repeat {                               o {
        o {a}                                  repeat [
        ...                                        o {e}
        o {c}                                      o {f}
        o {e}                                      o {g; stop_repetition}
        ...                                    }
        o {g}                                  match_all
    }                                      }
}                                      o {
                                           repeat {
                                               o {e}
                                               o {f}
                                           }
                                       }
                                   }
               }
```

3.5   :not Label

Allowing the use of the negation operator in scenarios is particularly convenient for specifying safety properties that express something bad will never happen. We therefore extended Axini's code to implement a feature like this. It is now possible to use the label **:not** after a send/receive command. In the options for this statement, one or more possible labels can be added to a novel `notlabels` option. This means that this send/receive statement will match any labels that are not in the `notlabels` part.

For example, if there is a stimulus `Request` and a response `Response`, with property `receive 'Request'` → **X** `send 'Response'`, then a safety scenario would be as follows:

```
scenario('Response', :rejecting) {
    include 'labels.aml'

    anywhere {
        receive 'Request'
        send :not, notlabels: 'Response'
    }
}
```

In this scenario, the `send :not, notlabels: 'Response'` statement will match any send statement that does not send the `Response` message.

Since there may be multiple possible options that need to be checked for in a liveness scenario via choice/repeat, this needs to be reflected as well. If there are two options a and b each containing a not statement, then that would be ¬a ∨ ¬b in LTL, which is not the same as ¬(a ∨ b). In order for the latter to work, a single **:not** statement can contain multiple labels separated by blank spaces as follows:

```
scenario('Response', :rejecting) {
    include 'labels.aml'

    anywhere {
        receive 'Request'
        send :not, notlabels: 'Response1 Response2'
    }
}
```

In this scenario, `send :not, notlabels: 'Response1 Response2'` will match any send statement that sends neither `Response1` nor `Response2`. With this new operator, the scenario construct for a negation operation in LTL, as defined in Sect. 3.2, can be replaced:

```
scenario('not-a') {                scenario('not-a') {
  include 'labels.aml'               include 'labels.aml'
  anywhere {                         anywhere {
    choice {                           send/receive :not,
      *insert as options  ⟹             notlabels: *label(s) from a*
      all sends/receives             }
      that are not a*               }
    }
  }
}
```

4   Automatic Test Case Generation

In this section we study how test cases can be automatically generated such that they cover system properties as expressed in scenarios. Axini currently has several methods to automatically generate tests for the Symbolic Transition System generated from AML code, as briefly explained in Sect. 2.3. We add an additional method, using the existing foundation for Axini's automatic test generation. The novel method consists of a strategy to generate test steps that try to check for properties.

4.1   Generation Strategy

The test case generation strategy that we focus on in the current paper works around the following points:

- At a state in the model, the program selects the transitions from that state that are covered in one or more scenarios.
- The program prioritizes transitions from scenarios that have not been covered yet.
- If the program follows a transition, advance all scenarios on that transition where possible.
- The program always prioritizes an uncovered transition when choosing from the available transitions. If all are covered, it chooses randomly.

A test case consists of multiple steps. Each step stands for a transition in the model being followed. This way, the test moves through the model from state to state. The test cases that are generated can cover a section of the SUT. How much the test cases cover is known as the coverage. The environment in which Axini runs the tests tracks both the transition coverage and the state coverage per process. There are multiple ways test cases can be generated that can lead to a certain coverage. Each method has its own coverage code file and an annotations code file. The coverage file determines which steps should be taken during testing. The annotations file keeps track of which transitions have already been covered in a test case.

In order to generate test cases based on the scenarios, we created a Scenario Coverage file and a Scenario Annotations file. At the start of the testing, the latter file gathers all available scenarios, and builds a simulator for each of them. Such a simulator can move through the transitions described in the scenario. A simulator contains a current state, which consists of all possible states that the scenario could be in. Each scenario starts with a start state, consisting of the initial possible states. Each of these states can have transitions that lead to other states. If a simulator advances on a transition, it sets the potential resulting states as the scenario's current state. A state that could not be advanced on a transition, is removed from the current state.

The model of the SUT consists of states and transitions that are separate from the ones in the scenario simulators. At a state in the model, the coverage file selects the available transitions that match transitions from the current states of the scenarios. Out of these transitions, the strategy picks a transition that has not been covered yet, or a random transition if all available are covered. Note that this is only for receive transitions, as these are the types of transitions that the user can input to a SUT. The SUT could at some point respond to the user via send transitions.

The testing follows through on the chosen receive transition, or the send transition given by the SUT. In the annotations file, this transition is set as covered. All scenarios are advanced on this transition. As a result, a scenario changes its current state, with different transitions available from that state. These transitions can be found by the coverage file for the next step. If one of the potential states from the current state is the scenario's last state, then the scenario is set as covered in the annotations file. When all scenarios have been covered, the current test case generation is stopped and the testing program can start a new test case. At the start of a new test case, the simulators for the scenarios are automatically reset.

When the strategy matches transitions from the model against those from the scenarios, it will only look at scenarios that have not been covered yet. However, there are two problems with this. Firstly, a scenario can have different paths that can be covered and thus it may be good for a scenario to be covered more than once. Secondly, it may be possible that some scenarios cannot get covered, either because they are set to rejecting, or because of a problem with the SUT. As a result the strategy could keep trying to cover a rejecting scenario, which can leave the program unable to cover the rest of the model. The strategy should not be refused to cover rejecting scenarios either, since it would need to be known when it actually is possible to find them. In order to combat this problem, after a set amount of scenario coverage (90%) has been reached, the strategy will start looking at all scenarios. This is admittedly an arbitrary percentage, based on practical experiences. In general, in large models with many scenarios, the coverage percentage can be high (99%), while in small models with few scenarios (like the ones we worked with), the coverage percentage should be lower (90%).

When determining the scenario coverage percentage, the rejecting scenarios are considered covered when they have not been set as covered, since they are not supposed to be. When they do get covered, they are considered not covered when determining the scenario coverage percentage. Thus, if all accepting scenarios are covered and none of the rejecting, the total scenario coverage is 100%.

The solution based on coverage is not entirely foolproof. It may be possible for the strategy to get stuck on scenarios before 90% coverage. That is why there is an extra solution added in. If a chosen transition has already been covered a certain number of times (ten times), then a new transition will be chosen out of all possible transitions at the current state of the model. On the topic of transitions, there is an adjustment in the strategy for encountering a so-called any transition. An any transition is a transition that accepts all labels. When the strategy checks if a transition appears in scenarios, it will not look at transitions that match only if the scenario state contains an any transition. This is so that only interesting transitions will get selected, which refers to transitions that are more likely to advance the scenarios in ways that cover more properties. For example, if there is a scenario that prefers a specific transition and a scenario that is willing to take any transition, then choosing the specific transition will advance both, with the former getting closer to being covered. Also, when advancing scenarios, unobservable and internal transitions are ignored, since they are not included in scenarios.

The example below shows the process and corresponding scenario from Sect. 2.2. Coloured, numbered markers are used to show how the testing strategy tries to choose transitions in the process based on the scenario. First, when the testing arrives at the state before the first choice in the process, it can choose to follow through on either giving input a or input b. Let us say the scenario is at the state at marker 1. Then the testing strategy sees that it should choose the transition with label a. Afterwards, the process says the SUT should send f as an output. The scenario says this should happen as well. If the SUT responds with f, then both the process and the scenario are able to advance to their next states. Now the testing strategy has arrived at the state in the process where it can choose between giving inputs c, d and e. The scenario is at the state where it says the SUT should be able to take inputs c and d. Thus the testing strategy will try to choose between transitioning on giving input c and transitioning on giving input d.

Example Scenario Coverage

```
process('name') {                    scenario('scen') {
  channel('chan') {                    channel('chan') {
    stimuli 'a','b'                      stimuli 'a','b'
    stimuli 'c','d','e'                  stimuli 'c','d','e'
    responses 'f','g'                    responses 'f','g'
  }                                    }

  choice {                       1- receive 'a'
   o {                              send 'f'
   1- receive 'a'
     send 'f'                    2- choice {
   }                                 o {receive 'c'}
   o {                               o {receive 'd'}
     receive 'b'                   }
     send 'g'                    }
   }
  }

  choice {
 2- o {receive 'c'}
 2- o {receive 'd'}
   o {receive 'e'}
  }
}
```

4.2   Evaluation

Experiment. In order to evaluate the code and findings, they were tested in the Axini Modeling Platform (AMP) environment, using two AML demos, based on demos from a training to familiarise trainees with the Axini Modeling Platform and AML. They represent the following simple systems: smartdoor and newsfeed. These are based on systems Axini has seen while working with clients. For each of the models, scenarios were added based on properties written in LTL, which were transcribed using the mapping methods as described earlier. These properties lead to both accepting and rejecting scenarios. For each demo, tests were run consisting of three test cases, with 100 steps per test case. Note that ? and ! in the LTL properties stand for a receive and send message respectively.

Smartdoor: This involves a door that can be automatically controlled by a program that can send open, close, lock and unlock messages to it. The door can then respond by opening, closing, locking, or unlocking itself. It can only do these things under the right conditions (so it cannot open when it is locked for example). For locking and unlocking, a valid passcode is required.

Newsfeed: A news service where an user can enter via a protocol, after which they can request one or more subscriptions. When subscribing, the user can select topics, after which they can receive news messages about these topics.

Results. Figures 6 and 8 show the transitions coverage over the test steps for the smartdoor and newsfeed models, as generated in the AMP environment based on the tests run. Below the graphs the three test cases are listed. The check of whether the properties as defined in scenarios were met is shown in Figs. 7 and 9. These figures show a section of the AMP environment where scenarios can be matched against test cases in order to verify the scenarios. If a scenario is greenlit, then it means that a scenario matched if it is accepting and no match was found if it is rejecting. Otherwise, it would be coloured red. Next to the accepting scenarios, the figure shows where the content of a scenario matches traces of test steps. It does not show this after rejecting scenarios if they passed, because then no test traces match those. If a rejecting scenario fails, it will show where this scenario matches a test trace.

Figure 6 shows the transitions coverage over the test steps for the smartdoor model with a blue line. At the last step, the coverage is 100%. All three test cases completed successfully, with no errors found.

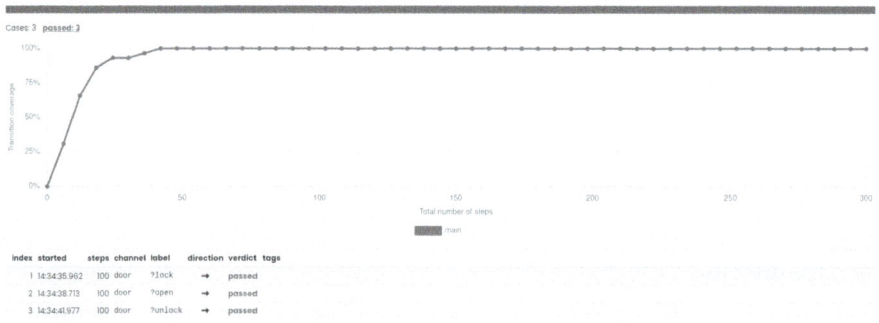

Fig. 6. The transition coverage for the smartdoor model. (Color figure online)

The check whether the properties as defined in scenarios were met is shown in Fig. 7. Green implies for an accepting scenario that it passed and for a rejecting scenario that it did not. All the scenarios are marked green. Next to the scenario name, the places where the scenario matches test steps are shown.

Scenarios

name	kind	verdict	
OPEN-01	accepting	✓	Test case 1: (2 3) (20 21) (86 87) Test case 2: (2 3) (52 53) (86 87) (96 97) Test case 3: (4 5) (18 19) (50 51) (88 89) (60 81)
OPEN-02	accepting	✓	Test case 1: (13 14 15 16 17 18 19 20 21) (85 86 87) Test case 2: (51 52 53) (83 84 85 86 87) (89 90 91 92 93 94 95 96 97) Test case 3: (15 16 17 18 19) (45 46 47 48 49 50 51) (67 68 99) (77 78 79 80 81)
OPEN-03	accepting	✓	Test case 1: (3 4 5) (9 10 11) (77 78 79) Test case 3: (5 6 7) (69 70 71) (69 70 71 72 73) (81 82 83) (81 82 83 84 85 86 87)
CLOSE-01	accepting	✓	Test case 1: (6 7) (32 33) (98 99) Test case 2: (20 21) (66 69) (88 89) (98 99) Test case 3: (14 15) (32 33) (52 53) (76 77)
CLOSE-02	accepting	✓	Test case 1: (3 4 5 6 7) Test case 2: (87 88 89) (97 98 99) Test case 3: (51 52 53)
CLOSE-03	accepting	✓	Test case 1: (13 14 15 16 17) (35 36 37) (49 50 51 52 53) (57 58 59) Test case 2: (21 22 23) (25 26 27) (37 38 39) (73 74 75) (73 74 75 76 77 78 79) (83 84 85) (89 90 91 92 93) (89 90 91 92 93 94 95) Test case 3: (15 16 17) (33 34 35 36 37 38 39) (41 42 43) (53 54 55) (53 54 55 56 57) (53 54 55 56 57 58 59 60 61) (77 78 79)
LOCK-01	accepting	✓	Test case 1: (8 9) (34 35) (56 57) (76 77) Test case 2: (24 25) (36 37) (70 71) (80 81) Test case 3: (40 41) (62 63)
LOCK-02	accepting	✓	Test case 1: (7 8 9) (33 34 35) (49 50 51 52 53 54 55 56 57) (75 76 77) Test case 2: (21 22 23 24 25) (36 38 37) (69 70 71) (73 74 75 76 77 78 79 80 81) Test case 3: (33 34 35 36 37 38 39 40 41) (53 54 55 56 57 58 59 60 61 62 63)
LOCK-03	accepting	✓	Test case 1: (21 22 23) (77 78 79 80 81) (77 78 79 80 81 82 83) Test case 2: (3 4 5) (53 54 55) Test case 3: (5 6 7 8 9) (63 64 65) (69 70 71 72 73 74 75) (81 82 83 84 85)
UNLOCK-01	accepting	✓	Test case 1: (12 13) (48 49) (74 75) (84 85) Test case 2: (34 35) (50 51) (72 73) (82 83) Test case 3: (44 45) (66 67)
UNLOCK-02	accepting	✓	Test case 2: (71 72 73) (81 82 83) Test case 3: (63 64 65 66 67)
UNLOCK-03	accepting	✓	Test case 1: (13 14 15) (13 14 15 16 17 18 19) (49 50 51) (49 50 51 52 53 54 55) (87 88 89) (87 88 89 90 91 92 93) (87 88 89 90 91 92 93 94 95) Test case 2: (73 74 75 76 77) (89 90 91) Test case 3: (19 20 21) (19 20 21 22 23) (33 34 35) (33 34 35 36 37) (45 46 47) (45 46 47 48 49) (53 54 55 56 57 58 59)
BLOCK-OPEN-01	rejecting	✓	
BLOCK-OPEN-02	rejecting	✓	
BLOCK-CLOSE-01	rejecting	✓	
BLOCK-CLOSE-02	rejecting	✓	
BLOCK-LOCK-01	rejecting	✓	
BLOCK-LOCK-02	rejecting	✓	
BLOCK-UNLOCK-01	rejecting	✓	
BLOCK-UNLOCK-02	rejecting	✓	
LOCK-WRONG-PASSCODE	rejecting	✓	
UNLOCK-WRONG-PASSCODE	rejecting	✓	

Fig. 7. The scenarios that were run over the test cases for smartdoor. (Color figure online)

Figure 8 shows the transition coverage for the newsfeed model, using a blue line for the session process and purple for the subscription process. At the last

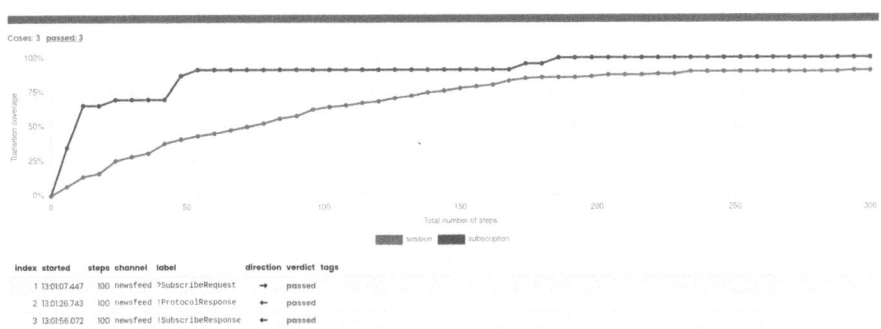

index	started	steps	channel	label	direction	verdict	tags
1	13:01:07.447	100	newsfeed	?SubscribeRequest	→	passed	
2	13:01:26.743	100	newsfeed	!ProtocolResponse	←	passed	
3	13:01:56.072	100	newsfeed	!SubscribeResponse	←	passed	

Fig. 8. The transition coverage for the newsfeed model. (Color figure online)

step, the coverage is 100% for the subscription process and 90.42% for the session process. All three test cases completed successfully, with no errors found.

The check of whether the properties as defined in scenarios were met is shown in Fig. 9. All scenarios are greenlit, meaning that all the accepting scenarios passed and all rejecting scenarios did not.

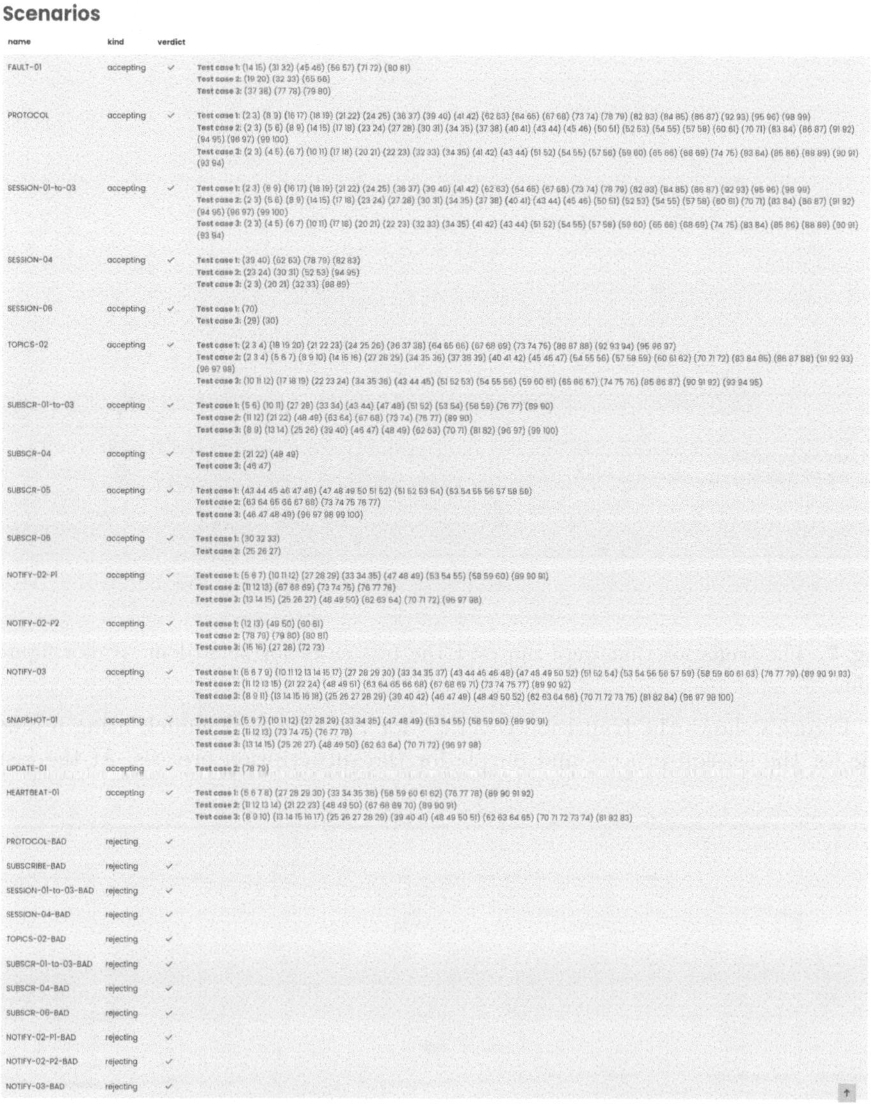

Scenarios

name	kind	verdict	
FAULT-01	accepting	✓	**Test case 1:** (14 15) (31 32) (45 46) (56 57) (71 72) (80 81) **Test case 2:** (19 20) (32 33) (65 66) **Test case 3:** (37 38) (77 78) (79 80)
PROTOCOL	accepting	✓	**Test case 1:** (2 3) (8 9) (16 17) (18 19) (21 22) (24 25) (36 37) (39 40) (41 42) (62 63) (64 65) (67 68) (73 74) (78 79) (82 83) (84 85) (86 87) (92 93) (95 96) (98 99) **Test case 2:** (2 3) (5 6) (8 9) (14 15) (17 18) (23 24) (27 28) (30 31) (34 35) (37 38) (40 41) (43 44) (45 46) (50 51) (52 53) (54 55) (57 58) (60 61) (70 71) (83 84) (86 87) (91 92) (94 95) (96 97) (99 100) **Test case 3:** (2 3) (4 5) (6 7) (10 11) (17 18) (20 21) (22 23) (32 33) (34 35) (41 42) (43 44) (51 52) (54 55) (57 58) (59 60) (65 66) (68 69) (74 75) (83 84) (85 86) (88 89) (90 91) (93 94)
SESSION-01-to-03	accepting	✓	**Test case 1:** (2 3) (8 9) (16 17) (18 19) (21 22) (24 25) (36 37) (39 40) (41 42) (62 63) (64 65) (67 68) (73 74) (78 79) (82 83) (84 85) (86 87) (92 93) (95 96) (98 99) **Test case 2:** (2 3) (5 6) (8 9) (14 15) (17 18) (23 24) (27 28) (30 31) (34 35) (37 38) (40 41) (43 44) (45 46) (50 51) (52 53) (54 55) (57 58) (60 61) (70 71) (83 84) (86 87) (91 92) (94 95) (96 97) (99 100) **Test case 3:** (2 3) (4 5) (6 7) (10 11) (17 18) (20 21) (22 23) (32 33) (34 35) (41 42) (43 44) (51 52) (54 55) (57 58) (59 60) (65 66) (68 69) (74 75) (83 84) (85 86) (88 89) (90 91) (93 94)
SESSION-04	accepting	✓	**Test case 1:** (39 40) (62 63) (78 79) (82 83) **Test case 2:** (23 24) (30 31) (52 53) (94 95) **Test case 3:** (2 3) (20 21) (32 33) (88 89)
SESSION-06	accepting	✓	**Test case 1:** (70) **Test case 3:** (29) (30)
TOPICS-02	accepting	✓	**Test case 1:** (2 3 4) (18 19 20) (21 22 23) (24 25 26) (36 37 38) (64 65 66) (67 68 69) (73 74 75) (86 87 88) (92 93 94) (95 96 97) **Test case 2:** (2 3 4) (5 6 7) (8 9 10) (14 15 16) (27 28 29) (34 35 36) (37 38 39) (40 41 42) (45 46 47) (54 55 56) (57 58 59) (60 61 62) (70 71 72) (83 84 85) (86 87 88) (91 92 93) (96 97 98) **Test case 3:** (10 11 12) (17 18 19) (22 23 24) (34 35 36) (43 44 45) (51 52 53) (54 55 56) (59 60 61) (65 66 67) (74 75 76) (85 86 87) (90 91 92) (93 94 95)
SUBSCR-01-to-03	accepting	✓	**Test case 1:** (5 6) (10 11) (27 28) (33 34) (43 44) (47 48) (51 52) (53 54) (58 59) (76 77) (89 90) **Test case 2:** (11 12) (21 22) (48 49) (63 64) (67 68) (73 74) (76 77) (89 90) **Test case 3:** (8 9) (13 14) (25 26) (39 40) (46 47) (48 49) (62 63) (70 71) (81 82) (96 97) (99 100)
SUBSCR-04	accepting	✓	**Test case 2:** (21 22) (48 49) **Test case 3:** (46 47)
SUBSCR-05	accepting	✓	**Test case 1:** (43 44 45 46 47 48) (47 48 49 50 51 52) (51 52 53 54) (53 54 55 56 57 58 59) **Test case 2:** (63 64 65 66 67 68) (73 74 75 76 77) **Test case 3:** (46 47 48 49) (96 97 98 99 100)
SUBSCR-06	accepting	✓	**Test case 1:** (30 32 33) **Test case 2:** (25 26 27)
NOTIFY-02-P1	accepting	✓	**Test case 1:** (5 6 7) (10 11 12) (27 28 29) (33 34 35) (47 48 49) (53 54 55) (58 59 60) (89 90 91) **Test case 2:** (11 12 13) (67 68 69) (73 74 75) (76 77 78) **Test case 3:** (13 14 15) (25 26 27) (48 49 50) (62 63 64) (70 71 72) (96 97 98)
NOTIFY-02-P2	accepting	✓	**Test case 1:** (12 13) (49 50) (60 61) **Test case 2:** (78 79) (79 80) (80 81) **Test case 3:** (15 16) (27 28) (72 73)
NOTIFY-03	accepting	✓	**Test case 1:** (5 6 7 9) (10 11 12 13 14 15 17) (27 28 29 30) (33 34 35 37) (43 44 45 46 48) (47 48 49 50 52) (51 52 54) (53 54 56 56 57 59) (58 59 60 61 63) (76 77 79) (89 90 91 93) **Test case 2:** (11 12 13 15) (21 22 24) (48 49 51) (63 64 65 66 68) (67 68 69 71) (73 74 75 77) (89 90 92) **Test case 3:** (8 9 11) (13 14 15 16 18) (25 26 27 28 29) (39 40 42) (46 47 49) (48 49 50 52) (62 63 64 66) (70 71 72 73 75) (81 82 84) (96 97 98 100)
SNAPSHOT-01	accepting	✓	**Test case 1:** (5 6 7) (10 11 12) (27 28 29) (33 34 35) (47 48 49) (53 54 55) (58 59 60) (89 90 91) **Test case 2:** (11 12 13) (73 74 75) (76 77 78) **Test case 3:** (13 14 15) (25 26 27) (48 49 50) (62 63 64) (70 71 72) (96 97 98)
UPDATE-01	accepting	✓	**Test case 2:** (78 79)
HEARTBEAT-01	accepting	✓	**Test case 1:** (5 6 7 8) (27 28 29 30) (33 34 35 36) (58 59 60 61 62) (76 77 78) (89 90 91 92) **Test case 2:** (11 12 13 14) (21 22 23) (48 49 50) (67 68 69 70) (89 90 91) **Test case 3:** (8 9 10) (13 14 15 16 17) (25 26 27 28 29) (39 40 41) (48 49 50 51) (62 63 64 65) (70 71 72 73 74) (81 82 83)
PROTOCOL-BAD	rejecting	✓	
SUBSCRIBE-BAD	rejecting	✓	
SESSION-01-to-03-BAD	rejecting	✓	
SESSION-04-BAD	rejecting	✓	
TOPICS-02-BAD	rejecting	✓	
SUBSCR-01-to-03-BAD	rejecting	✓	
SUBSCR-04-BAD	rejecting	✓	
SUBSCR-06-BAD	rejecting	✓	
NOTIFY-02-P1-BAD	rejecting	✓	
NOTIFY-02-P2-BAD	rejecting	✓	
NOTIFY-03-BAD	rejecting	✓	

Fig. 9. The scenarios that were run over the test cases for newsfeed

Qualitative Review. It is worth mentioning that Axini has also conducted a qualitative review among some of its customers. Not surprisingly, temporal logics such a LTL and CTL are generally considered too complex by engineers. That the scenarios of AML use the same language as the models is very much appreciated, as this representation that can be easily visualized makes life of an engineer easier. Experienced users like very much that there are several patterns to use in writing scenarios, which correspond to LTL/CTL operators. The current scenario approach is considered easy to use especially for reachability properties.

5   Limitations

Even if a property can be written in LTL, that does not always mean it can be rewritten into a scenario. The reason is that scenarios can only reference external transitions, given that those are the only ones mentioned in the test cases. If a property relies on a transition that is made internal, then a scenario cannot be written for it. For example, in the newsfeed demo there are two processes with an internal channel meant to model the SUT starting or stopping the sending of notification messages. Any properties based around this aspect cannot be turned into scenarios. The ability of such properties to be turned into scenarios is something that could potentially be improved upon in the future.

Another issue with test cases is that they are of limited size. One can therefore never be completely certain that a rejecting scenario will never occur. Furthermore, it makes weak until and until somewhat interchangeable. Since until relies on something becoming true eventually, it may be that something was about to become true, but the testing ended before it happened. There is also the fact that it may not be interesting to model a property where something does not have to become true. It may therefore sometimes be better to model weak until as until, in order to see if there is even a possible situation where the last part of the weak until becomes true.

When the strategy chooses a transition that could advance a scenario, it can only choose stimuli, because those are input into the SUT by the user. It has little control over any messages the SUT sends and the resulting transitions. Therefore, a scenario that overly relies on responses may not be as likely to get covered. It could be more likely for a scenario to get covered if it starts with a stimulus that may trigger the sought-after responses. On the topic of coverage, the design of a model can influence which transitions are likely to get chosen. If at most points in a model, most stimuli transitions are of label a, but with different constraints, then the strategy will choose from a pool of transitions that mostly have label a if there are scenarios that rely on it. If there are also a few transitions with label b at those points, then scenarios relying on those are less likely to get covered if there are much fewer b than a transitions. The model design is likely the reason why newsfeed did not reach full transition coverage on the session process, since at the starting point there are multiple possible transitions with the same label, but different constraints. At the next state, there are only a few out of many possible paths that can redirect back to this previous state, the StopSession label and an improper protocol request. Thus it is not likely that all transitions at that state will be covered.

6   Making Temporal Logic Easier to Understand

A central motivation for the current work is that Axini wants to make the use of LTL manageable for their customers. There is ample work on increasing the understandability of temporal logic languages. To the best of our knowledge, our approach is unique in its automata-based representation of temporal logic formulas.

Several languages have been proposed with this aim. One such language is FTL [1], which was proposed as a logic for ForSpec, a formal specification language from Intel. It is based on LTL, with the goal of being more expressive, without becoming too complex to understand. It includes constructs to refer to past and future values of Boolean expressions, as well as temporal connectives over time windows. Linear-time was chosen because according to the authors, branching-time logics are too unintuitive. Another is MCL [7], a replacement for the branching-time logic called modal μ-calculus, with the goal of being more concise and readable. Its main ingredients are parameterized fixed points, action patterns extracting data values from transition labels, modalities on transition sequences described using regular expressions and programming language constructs, and an infinite looping operator specifying fairness. In this context, it is also fitting to mention the actor-based formal verification framework Rebeca [9], developed by Mirjan Sirjani and her co-workers, as it targets "modeling issues like the level of abstraction, modularity and usability for practitioners."

Czepa et al. [3] claim that understandability is increased when temporal logic languages abstract away language elements (which is in a sense also the intention of AML's scenarios). In particular it is found that Property Specification Patterns [5], which abstracts away such concepts, is more understandable than LTL. These findings are confirmed by Paulweber et al. [8], who study the effect that certain language constructs have on a language's understandability, specifically languages for an Abstract State Machine. They identify three language constructs: interfaces, mixins, and traits. Interfaces define the protocol or what a language should look like, mixins define state and behaviour information, and traits define stateless behaviour. An experiment was done where the understanding of 105 participants was tested regarding these constructs. Interfaces and traits both have good understandability in roughly equal measure, while understandability of mixins is relatively poor. The authors argue that this is because separation of behavourial and structural elements is more understandable than a mixed representation of the two.

7   Conclusion

In this paper, a method has been described to transcribe properties expressed in LTL to scenario constructs. Moreover, an automatic test generation strategy was developed that generates test steps based on scenarios. This strategy was evaluated using two demo models from Axini. The results from the evaluation show that the strategy is able to generate test cases that verify the scenarios given, while also covering most of the transitions.

It was mentioned in Sect. 5 that properties relying on internal transitions cannot be properly expressed in scenarios. This is because internal transitions do not appear in test cases. As future work, it would be interesting to work on making it possible for this type of properties to be turned into scenarios as well.

Acknowledgments. Jouke Stoel is thanked for his support.

References

1. Armoni, R., et al.: The ForSpec temporal logic: a new temporal property-specification language. In: Katoen, J.-P., Stevens, P. (eds.) TACAS 2002. LNCS, vol. 2280, pp. 296–311. Springer, Heidelberg (2002). https://doi.org/10.1007/3-540-46002-0_21
2. Baier, C., Katoen, J.P.: Principles of Model Checking. MIT Press, Cambridge (2008)
3. Czepa, C., Amiri, A., Ntentos, E., Zdun, U.: Modeling compliance specifications in linear temporal logic, event processing language and property specification patterns: a controlled experiment on understandability. Softw. Syst. Model. **18**(6), 3331–3371 (2019). https://doi.org/10.1007/s10270-019-00721-4
4. De Wulf, M., Doyen, L., Maquet, N., Raskin, J.-F.: Antichains: alternative algorithms for LTL satisfiability and model-checking. In: Ramakrishnan, C.R., Rehof, J. (eds.) TACAS 2008. LNCS, vol. 4963, pp. 63–77. Springer, Heidelberg (2008). https://doi.org/10.1007/978-3-540-78800-3_6
5. Dwyer, M.B., Avrunin, G.S., Corbett, J.C.: Patterns in property specifications for finite-state verification. In: 21st Conference on Software Engineering (ICSE 1999), pp. 411–420. ACM (1999). https://doi.org/10.1145/302405.302672
6. Frantzen, L., Tretmans, J., Willemse, T.A.C.: Test generation based on symbolic specifications. In: Grabowski, J., Nielsen, B. (eds.) FATES 2004. LNCS, vol. 3395, pp. 1–15. Springer, Heidelberg (2005). https://doi.org/10.1007/978-3-540-31848-4_1
7. Mateescu, R., Thivolle, D.: A model checking language for concurrent value-passing systems. In: Cuellar, J., Maibaum, T., Sere, K. (eds.) FM 2008. LNCS, vol. 5014, pp. 148–164. Springer, Heidelberg (2008). https://doi.org/10.1007/978-3-540-68237-0_12
8. Paulweber, P., Simhandl, G., Zdun, U.: On the understandability of language constructs to structure the state and behavior in abstract state machine specifications: a controlled experiment. J. Syst. Softw. **178**, 110987 (2021). https://doi.org/10.1016/j.jss.2021.110987
9. Sirjani, M., Movaghar, A., Shali, A., de Boer, F.S.: Modeling and verification of reactive systems using Rebeca. Fund. Informaticae **63**(4), 385–410 (2004). http://content.iospress.com/articles/fundamenta-informaticae/fi63-4-05

Concurrent Rules Machines

Farhad Arbab[1,2] and Carolyn Talcott[3(✉)]

[1] Centrum Wiskunde and Informatica, Science Park 123, 1098 XG Amsterdam,
The Netherlands
farhad@cwi.nl
[2] Leiden University, Leiden, The Netherlands
[3] SRI, Menlo Park, USA
carolyn.talcott@gmail.com

Abstract. Cyber-Physical systems interact with their environment in complex ways. In addition to exchanging information with other systems, they affect and are affected by their physical/natural environment. Their components run concurrently and may be physically distributed, participating in both synchronous and asynchronous interactions. Existing formal models typically model closed systems, or limited interactions among system components. In this paper we introduce the Concurrent Rules Machine (CRM), a formal model of system behavior that makes explicit interaction with the environment. We define an algebra of operations for CRM composition and decomposition along with equational properties. We illustrate our ideas with a simple cyber-physical system example.

1 Introduction

Cyber-Physical Systems (CPSs) are increasingly ubiquitous. They come in many sizes ranging from autonomous vehicles to tiny medical devices. They may be low risk, or highly safety critical. CPSs interact with, affect, and are affected by their environment, which is often unpredictable. The components of a CPS are inherently open; they execute concurrently, interact both synchronously and asynchronously, and they may be geographically distributed.

A foundational formal framework for developing CPS models should support representation and reasoning about:

- open systems, including interaction with unknown/unpredictable environments
- discrete and continuous change (cyber and physical)
- diverse interactions among components including synchronous and asynchronous discrete interactions, as well as continuous interactions such as flow of a physical quantity among components (e.g., force, energy, liquid, etc.)
- composition operations that model these different interactions
- concurrent and distributed execution
- methods to support scaling in time and space such as symbolic reasoning and abstraction; and compositional design and reasoning

---

Dedication. This paper is dedicated to Marjan Sirjani in celebration of her technical and leadership contributions to advancing computer science.

E. A. Lee et al. (Eds.): Marjan Sirjani Festschrift, LNCS 15560, pp. 266–294, 2025.
https://doi.org/10.1007/978-3-031-85134-6_12

Existing models cover different features. Hybrid system models [7,13,29,30,33] address the combination of discrete and continuous behavior elements (control and plant). Their focus, however, is generally on closed systems. Automata and process algebra models support concurrent or distributed execution and composition with a mix of synchronous and asynchronous interaction, typically as action labels on transitions. [1,3–6,10,15,16,24,34] The usual composition results in a blowup of model size. The environment, if considered explicitly, is viewed as *other components*, a deficient model of the physical world.

Rewriting logic (RWL) is an expressive formalism for specifying concurrent and distributed systems [12,25]. There is a rich algebra of modules (theories), that can be lifted to composition of specific models (terms). Basic rewriting operates on closed systems. Extensions to symbolic rewriting provide an important step towards specifying and reasoning about open system [31]. RWL has no notion of initial state or specific system of interest. We can think of a ground term tm as representing some entity with a (possibly trivial) behavior, given by the rewrite rules. The rewriting process generates one possible behavior (or multiple possible behaviors if the strategy is not deterministic). Unconstrained search generates all possible behaviors. Since there is no pre-determined notion of system or component, RWL has no explicit mechanism for system/component composition beyond basic term formation using constructors. By localness of rule application, term formation induces a corresponding composition of behaviors of subterms and may add behavior due to rules for the top level constructor.

In this paper, we introduce *Concurrent Rules Machines* (CRMs) as a formal model primarily intended for specification and analysis of open, distributed, cyber-physical systems. A CRM is an abstract machine with distributed state and concurrent rule-based transitions that makes the interaction between a system and its environment explicit. The concurrent semantics of CRMs makes them practically compositional, avoiding exponential explosion of their representation under composition. Intuitively, the basic product of two CRMs produces a resulting CRM whose behavior consists of all permissible interleavings and parallel behaviors of the two CRMs.

Contributions. The main contributions of this paper are the following:

- We introduce the Concurrent Rules Machine (CRM) model of computation, defining the structure of a CRM and its operational semantics. A more abstract observational semantics is derived from the operational semantics.
- In the CRM model, interaction with the environment is explicit. This enables reasoning about open systems and supports multiple notions of composition reflecting different forms of component interaction.
- Multiple models of time can be represented in CRMs as well as behaviors in which time is implicit.
- An algebra of CRM components is defined, including several composition operations, and a division relation for reasoning about decomposition. Structural properties of these operations are also presented.
- Importantly, composition scales in the sense that the size of a composed CRM is roughly the sum of the sizes of its component CRMs.
- A simple cyberphysical system is used to illustrate CRM concepts and several algebraic operations.

1.1 Running Example

To motivate and illustrate key elements of CRMs we borrow and adapt the water system example of [22,23]. There are two kinds of component, (i) a water tank with water entering at an inflow port, fin, and draining via an outflow port, fout; and (ii) control components that adjust flow rates: inflow or outflow, or both. We start by considering an inflow controller and assume that the outflow is either fixed at a constant rate, or controlled by some unknown environment entity.

The water tank interface has 2 imports (fin, fout) and one export (wl). Variables fin, fout are rates of water flowing in/out of the tank. Variable wl is the water level. In order to compute the water level at a given step the water tank uses the flows assigned in the previous step. Variables fin, fout are constrained to values in the real interval [0,1] and wl ranges from WLmin to WLmax. WLmin is the lowest level reachable by draining, could be 0 or positive. WLmax is the overflow point. For simplicity we assume units chosen so that $wl' = fin - fout$, where $wl' = dwl/dt$. Thus if fin and fout are constant over the interval [t0,t] then:

$$wl(tx) = wl(t0) + (fin - fout) \times (tx - t0) \text{ for tx in } [t0,t].$$

The inflow controller imports a water level reading, wl, and exports the inflow rate, fin. We assume the controller reads wl at time t and sets fin, which will determine the change in water level until time t1 > t when it repeats this action. Note that the inflow controller does not have access to the outflow rate beyond what it might infer from the inflow and change in wl over time. As a concrete example, assume the inflow controller has two parameters WLminSafe and WLmaxSafe with $0 \leq WLmin \leq WLminSafe$ and WLminSafe < WLmaxSafe $\leq$ WLmax. When wl $\geq$ WLmaxSafe it sets fin to 0; and when wl $\leq$ WLminSafe it sets fin to 1; otherwise it leaves fin unchanged.

Intuitively the water tank component models a physical component while the controller models a cyber component. They interact by the controller reading sensor informant produced by the water tank and the water tank behavior being dependent on flow rates set by a controller.

Plan. The remainder of the paper is organized as follows. In Sect. 2 we introduce notation and concepts used. Sections 3, 4, and 5 introduce key elements of a CRM: Guards, Actions, and Rules. The CRM structure is defined in Sect. 6 and its semantics is given in Sect. 7. Section 8 presents the operations of an algebra of CRMs and Sect. 9 discusses the representation of time. Related work is discussed in Sect. 10. We conclude with a summary and discussion of future work in Sect. 11.

2 Basic Concepts

2.1 Notation

We use $\mathbb{B}$ to denote the set of Boolean values $\{\bot, \top\}$, $\mathbb{N}_0$ to denote the set of natural numbers including zero, $\mathbb{R}_0^+$ the set of real numbers greater than or equal to zero, and

$\mathbf{D} \supseteq \mathbb{B} \cup \mathbb{N}_0 \cup \mathbb{R}_0^+$ to denote a data domain. By **Name** we denote the set of all variable names.[1] We use $new(\mathbf{Name})$ to obtain a fresh new variable name in **Name**.

For a set X, we use $\mathcal{P}(X)$ to denote the set of all finite subsets of X, and X^k, X^*, and X^ω to denote, respectively, the set of all sequences of length $k \in \mathbb{N}_0$, all finite-length sequences, and all infinite-length sequences of elements of X. We use angular brackets to denote concrete sequences, with $\langle\rangle$ denoting the null sequence. We also treat a sequence σ of length $0 \leq k \leq \infty$ over X as a (partial) function $\sigma \in \mathbb{N}_0 \to X$, in order to refer to its $i + 1^{st}$ element as $\sigma(i)$.

We use $f : D \rightsquigarrow R$ to denote f as a *pseudo function* that maps every element of the (domain) set D into a nondeterministically selected element of the (range) set R, where for a $d \in D$, two evaluations of $f(d)$ may or may not map into the same $r \in R$.

We use $Dom(f)$ and $Range(f)$ to refer to the domain and the range of a (pseudo) function f, respectively, and use $\overrightarrow{\emptyset}$ to denote the special function whose domain and range are both empty, i.e., $\overrightarrow{\emptyset} : \emptyset \to \emptyset$.

We do not specify a syntax for defining functions that appear in a CRM, we allow any well-defined mathematical notation that is convenient.

2.2 Utility Functions

A *valuation function* $v : N \mapsto \mathbf{D}$ maps a subset $N \in \mathcal{P}(\mathbf{Name})$ of variable names to values $d \in \mathbf{D}$.[2] We use $\mathbf{V}$ to denote the set of all valuation functions.

The function $revise : \mathbf{V} \times \mathbf{V} \times \mathcal{P}(\mathbf{Name}) \to \mathbf{V}$, below, updates an old valuation function v_1 with a new one, v_2, excluding the latter's value bindings for the names in $N \in \mathcal{P}(\mathbf{Name})$, such that:

$$revise(v_1, v_2, N)(x) = \begin{cases} v_2(x) \text{ if } x \in Dom(v_2) \setminus N \\ v_1(x) \text{ otherwise} \end{cases} \tag{1}$$

Observe that *revise* has the property of idempotency:

$$revise(revise(v_1, v_2, N), v_2, N) = revise(v_1, v_2, \text{ N})$$

Given sets X and Y, we use the pseudo function $fold : (X \times Y \to X) \times X \times \mathcal{P}(Y) \rightsquigarrow X$ to accumulate the images of the elements of a set $S \in \mathcal{P}(Y)$ under an accumulator function $f : X \times Y \to X$ with an initial accumulator value $x \in X$.

$$fold(f, x, S) = \begin{cases} x & \text{if } S = \emptyset \\ fold(f, f(x, s), S') \text{ otherwise, where } s \in S \text{ and } S' = S \setminus \{s\} \end{cases} \tag{2}$$

Intuitively, $fold(f, x, S)$ takes an accumulator function, f, an initial accumulator value, x, and a set, S, and accumulates all elements of S through f to return an element of the

---

[1] We allow $\mathbf{D} \supset \mathbf{Name}$, to support *indirection* (i.e., the value of a variable may be the name of another variable) and *dereferencing*.

[2] We assume the existence of a type system that associates a data type with each variable name in **Name** and ensures that the $\mathbf{D}$ value image of every $n \in \mathbf{Name}$ under every $v \in \mathbf{V}$ is compatible with the data type of n.

same type as x. The accumulator function f itself takes two parameters (the first of the same type as that of x, and the second of the same type as that of the elements of S), and maps them to an image of the same type as x.

Observe that the choice of $s \in S$ to split $S = \{s\} \cup S'$ in each round of recursion of *fold* is nondeterministic. Therefore, every recursive path that $fold(f, x, S)$ takes to exhaustively visit all elements of S reflects a nondeterministic choice out of the $n!$ possible paths, $n = |S|$, in the set of all permutations of the elements of S, mapping each permutation, $s_1, s_2, ..., s_n$ to its image $f(...(f(f(x, s_1), s_2), ...), s_n)$. We call the images of these permutations *alleles*. Thus, generally, $fold(f, x, S)$ is a pseudo function that maps its arguments to one nondeterministically selected allele in its set of all possible image alleles of S under f. However, in the special case where $f(x, s)$ is associative and commutative within the domain of its second argument (or at least over S), the set of image alleles of $fold(f, x, S)$ becomes a singleton and we can treat *fold* as a function: regardless of the nondeterministic splittings of S, the image of $fold(f, x, S)$ is the same unique $y \in X$.

We use the function $foldalleles : (X \times Y \to X) \times X \times \mathcal{P}(Y) \to \mathcal{P}(X)$ to denote the set of all alleles of the pseudo function $fold : (X \times Y \to X) \times X \times \mathcal{P}(Y) \leadsto X$:

$$foldalleles(f, x, S) = \begin{cases} \{x\} & \text{if } S = \emptyset \\ \bigcup_{s \in S} foldalleles(f, f(x, s), S \setminus \{s\}) & \text{otherwise} \end{cases} \quad (3)$$

Observe that by definition, *foldalleles* has the following properties:

1. $|foldalleles(f, x, S)| \geq 1$
2. $|foldalleles(corevise(v), v, A')| \leq |foldalleles(corevise(v), v, A)|$ for action sets $A' \subseteq A$ and valuation functions v.

Intuitively, $fold(f, x, S)$ merely picks a nondeterministically chosen element out of the set $foldalleles(f, x, S)$. We formalize this relationship in Lemma 1.

Lemma 1. $fold(f, x, S) \in foldalleles(f, x, S)$; and $\forall x \in foldalleles(f, x, S)$, x is an image allele of $fold(f, x, S)$.

Proof. We outline a proof. Let $S^!$ be the set of all permutations of all elements in S, with $n = |S|$. Denote ordered sequences in $S^!$ as $S^k = [s_1^k, s_2^k, ..., s_n^k]$, $1 \leq k \leq n!$. Structurally, $fold(f, x, S)$ recursively traverses one permutation $S^k \in S^!$ for a nondeterministic value of $1 \leq k \leq n!$ and returns $f(...f(f(x, s_1^k), s_2^k)..., s_n^k)$. On the other hand, $foldalleles(f, x, S)$ traverses all $S^k \in S^!$, $1 \leq k \leq n!$ and returns $\bigcup_{1 \leq k \leq n!} \{f(...f(f(x, s_1^k), s_2^k)..., s_n^k)\}$.

The significance of Lemma 1 is that in the special case where $foldalleles(f, x, S)$ is a singleton, then the image of $fold(f, x, S)$ is the same unique element in this singleton, regardless of the sequence of nondeterministic choices that $fold(f, x, S)$ makes.

3   Guards

A *guard* $g = p(n_1, n_2, ..., n_k)$ is a function of $k \in \mathbb{N}_0$ arguments that given a valuation function $v \in \mathbf{V}$, maps a sequence of values $d_i = v(n_i), 0 \leq i \leq k$ to a Boolean. We denote the set of all guards as **G**. For $g = p(n_1, n_2, ..., n_k)$, we use g^N to denote the arguments (read variables) of p. For example, let $g_1 = p(\text{wl}) = \text{wl} \leq WLmin$, where $\text{wl} \in$ **Name** and $WLmin \in$ **D** represents some (symbolic) value. Then $g_1(v) = \{\text{wl}\}$.

We use $v \models g$ to denote the evaluation of a guard g in the context of a valuation function v, which produces a Boolean value. For example, if $v(pvwl) = 20$ and the constant $WLmin$ is instantiated to 35 then $v \models g_1$ is true.

4 Actions

An *action* $a \in$ **Name**$^k \times (\mathbf{D}^k \to \mathbf{V})$ is a pair of a finite sequence $\langle n_1, n_2, ..., n_k \rangle$ of $k \geq 0$ argument variable names $n_i \in$ **Name**, $1 \leq i \leq k$, and an *update function* $\lambda(p_1, p_2, ..., p_k)lambexp$. We denote the set of all actions as **A**.

For $a = (\langle n_1, n_2, ..., n_k \rangle, u)$ and $v \in \mathbf{V}$, we use $a^R(v)$ to denote the set $\{m_1, m_2, ..., m_k\}$ of its *arguments* or *read* variables $m_i \in$ **Name**, $\forall 1 \leq i \leq k$ of a in the context of v; $a^U(v)$ to denote the instance of u, the update function of a, in the context of v; and $a^W(v)$ to denote the set of *write variables* of a in the context of v, defined as $Dom(a^U(v)(v(n_1), v(n_2), ..., v(n_k)))$.

We refer to $a^N(v) = a^R(v) \cup a^W(v)$ as the set of *variables* of a in the context of v. Also, we extend our $a^U(v), a^N(v), a^R(v), a^W(v), a^N, a^R$, and a^W notation from individual actions to sets of actions in the obvious way, e.g., the write variables of a set of actions $A \subseteq \mathbf{A}$ is $A^W(v) = \bigcup_{a \in A} a^W(v)$, etc.

Example 1. Consider action $a_1 = (\langle \rangle, \lambda()(\text{fin} := 1))$ where $\text{fin} \in$ **Name**. Then for all $v \in \mathbf{V}$ we have $a_1^R = \emptyset$ and $a_1^W = \{\text{fin}\}$.

Example 2. Consider action $a_2 = (\langle \text{wl}, \text{fin0}, \text{fout0}, \text{wl0}, \text{t0}, \text{t} \rangle, \lambda(wl, fin_0, fout_0, wl_0, t_0, t)(wl := wl_0 + (fin_0 - fout_0) \times (t - t_0)))$ where $\text{fin0}, \text{fout0}, \text{wl0}, \text{t0}, \text{t} \in$ **Name**. Then for all $v \in \mathbf{V}$ we have $a_2^R = \{\text{fin0}, \text{fout0}, \text{wl0}, \text{t0}, \text{t}\}$ and $a_2^W = \{\text{wl}\}$.

Performing an action $a = (\langle n_1, n_2, ..., n_k \rangle, u) \in \mathbf{A}$ in the context of a valuation function $v \in \mathbf{V}$ such that $a^N(v) \subseteq Dom(v)$, applies the update function u on n_i's to yield a new valuation function, v', where generally $Dom(v') \neq Dom(v)$ and the intersection $Dom(v') \cap Dom(v)$ may or may not be empty. We use the function *perform* : $\mathbf{V} \times \mathbf{A} \to \mathbf{V}$ to obtain v' by performing an action $(\langle n_1, n_2, ..., n_k \rangle, u) \in \mathbf{A}$ in the context of $v \in \mathbf{V}$:

$$v' = perform(v, (\langle n_1, n_2, ..., n_k \rangle, u)) \equiv u(v(n_1), v(n_2), ..., v(n_k))) \tag{4}$$

For convenience, we gloss over formal details of lambda expressions and use the typical syntax of imperative programming languages for assignment statements and expressions, if-then-else and loop constructs, and sequential composition to represent actions.

Observe that v', the image of *perform*(), represents merely the "change" that results from performing the action $(\langle n_1, n_2, ..., n_k \rangle, u)$ in the context of v. Intuitively, v' is *not* an "updated version" of v, but rather the "change delta" to v. We use the function *revise*() (Eq. 1) to incorporate the image of a *perform*() into another valuation function. See the CRM semantics defined in Table 1 in Sect. 7.

Example 3. Consider action $a = (\langle c, d, b \rangle, u)$ where $u = \lambda(x, y, z)(x := y * z)$, with $v(b) = 6$, and $v(d) = 3$. Since $(\langle c, d, b \rangle, \lambda(x, y, z)(x := y * z))^W = \{c\}$, we have:

$$\begin{aligned}
v' &= perform(v, (\langle c, d, b \rangle, u)) \equiv \\
&\lambda(x, y, z)(x := y * z)(c, v(d), v(b)) = \\
&\lambda(x, y, z)(x := y * z)(c, 3, 6) = \\
&(c := 3 * 6) = [c \mapsto 18]
\end{aligned}$$

Definition 1 (Equivalent actions). *Two actions $a_1, a_2 \in \mathbf{A}$ are equivalent, denoted as $a_1 \equiv a_2$, if and only if for all valuation functions $v \in \mathbf{V}$ we have $perform(v, a_1) = perform(v, a_2)$.*

4.1 Non-conflicting Actions

Consider two actions $a_1, a_2 \in \mathbf{A}$ and the execution of their sequential composition $a_1; a_2$ in the context of a pre valuation function $v \in \mathcal{V}$. In this case, first a_1 executes in the context of v and its execution produces an "update" valuation function $u_1 = perform(v, a_1)$. Next, a_2 executes in the context of the valuation function $u' = revise(v, u_1, \emptyset)$ and produces the "update" valuation function $u_2 = perform(u', a_2)$. Finally, revising u' using u_2 yields the post valuation function $u'' = revise(u', u_2, \emptyset)$.

Conceptually, in contrast, concurrent execution of a_1 and a_2 in the context of v starts at exactly the same time when both actions "observe" the exact same pre valuation function v. Once both executions complete, they yield two "update" valuation functions $v_i = perform(v, a_i), i \in \{1, 2\}$. Now depending on the order in which we apply v_1 and v_2 to cumulatively revise v, we obtain one of the two post valuation functions $v'_i = revise(revise(v, v_i, \emptyset), v_{3-i}, \emptyset)$, where $v'_1 = v'_2$ may or may not hold. We say actions a_1 and a_2 conflict in the context of a valuation function v if $v'_1 \neq v'_2$, and say they are non-conflicting in the context of v, otherwise.

The significance of non-conflicting actions is that not only they can be executed concurrently, regardless of the order in which their respective resulting "update" valuation functions are used to revise their common pre valuation function, we obtain the same unique post valuation function. We use *nonconflicting* : $\mathbf{A} \times \mathbf{A} \times \mathbf{V} \to \mathbb{B}$ to denote whether or not two actions conflict in the context of a specific valuation function, where:

$$\begin{aligned}
nonconflicting(a_1, a_2, v) &\Longleftrightarrow \\
revise(revise(v, v_1, \emptyset), v_2, \emptyset) &= revise(revise(v, v_2, \emptyset), v_1, \emptyset) \quad (5) \\
\text{where: } v_i &= perform(v, a_i), i \in \{1, 2\}
\end{aligned}$$

We use *neverconflicting* : $\mathbf{A} \times \mathbf{A} \to \mathbb{B}$ to denote whether or not two actions have absolutely no conflict in the context of any valuation function.

$$neverconflicting(a_1, a_2) \Longleftrightarrow (v \in \mathbf{V} \Longrightarrow nonconflicting(a_1, a_2, v)) \quad (6)$$

4.2   Concurrent Actions

To define the valuation function that results from performing a set of actions $A \subseteq \mathbf{A}$ concurrently in the context of a valuation function v, we first define an auxiliary function. The auxiliary function $corevise : \mathbf{V} \to (\mathbf{V} \times \mathbf{A} \to \mathbf{V})$ maps a valuation function $z \in \mathbf{V}$ to another function $corevise(z) \in \mathbf{V} \times \mathbf{A} \to \mathbf{V}$ where:

$$(corevise(z))(v, a) = revise(v, perform(z, a), \emptyset) \tag{7}$$

See Eq. 1 for *revise*.

We use *nonconflicting*(A, v) to extend the notion of non-conflicting pairs of actions in Eq. 5 to sets of actions $A \in \mathcal{P}(\mathbf{A})$: intuitively, a set of actions $A \in \mathcal{P}(\mathbf{A})$ is non-conflicting in the context of a valuation function $v \in \mathbf{V}$ if starting with the pre valuation function v, applying the "update" valuation functions that result from performing all actions in A to cumulatively revise v in any sequential order yields the same post valuation function.

Formally, the set of actions in A are non-conflicting in the context of a valuation function $v \in \mathbf{V}$ if we have:

$$nonconflicting(A, v) \iff |foldalleles(corevise(v), v, A)| = 1 \tag{8}$$

Analogously, we define *conflicting*(A, v) to denote:

$$conflicting(A, v) \iff |foldalleles(corevise(v), v, A)| > 1 \tag{9}$$

We use *neverconflicting* $: \mathcal{P}(\mathbf{A}) \to \mathbb{B}$ to denote whether or not a set of actions have absolutely no conflict with each other in the context of any valuation function.

$$neverconflicting(A) \iff (v \in \mathcal{V} \implies nonconflicting(A, v)) \tag{10}$$

Lemma 2. *For $v \in \mathcal{V}$ and $B \subseteq A \subseteq \mathbf{A}$, nonconflicting$(A, v) \implies$ nonconflicting(B, v).*

Proof. From property 2 of *foldalleles* in Eq. 3 we have

$$B \subseteq A \implies |foldalleles(corevise(v), v, B)| \le |foldalleles(corevise(v), v, A)|$$

By Eq. 8 we have $|foldalleles(corevise(v), v, A)| = 1$. Thus, $|foldalleles(corevise(v), v, B)| \le 1$. From property 1 of *foldalleles* in Eq. 3 we have $|foldalleles(corevise(v), v, B)| \ge 1$. Therefore $|foldalleles(corevise(v), v, B)| = 1$.

Using *corevise*, we now extend the definition of *perform* from performing an action $a \in \mathbf{A}$ (Eq. 4) to performing a set of actions $A \subseteq \mathbf{A}$, concurrently in the context of a valuation function v as follows:

$$perform(v, A) = fold(corevise(v), v, A) \tag{11}$$

Strictly speaking, the image of *perform*(v, A) in Eq. 11 is one nondeterministically selected alternative out of a set of the image alleles of the pseudo function *fold* (Eq. 2).

However, in the special case where $nonconflicting(A, v)$ holds, by Lemma 1 and Eq. 8 $perform(v, A)$ maps to a unique image, which justifies treating the pseudo function $perform(v, A)$ as if it were a true function analogous to $perform(v, a)$.[3]

Lemma 3. *For $z, v \in \mathbf{V}$, and $a, a_1, a_2, a_3 \in A \subseteq \mathbf{A}$ we have:*

1. idempotency:

$$(corevise(z))((corevise(z))(v, a), a) = (corevise(z))(v, a) = v$$

and moreover, if $nonconflicting(A, v)$, then:

2. associativity:

$$(corevise(v))((corevise(v))((corevise(v))(v, a_1), a_2), a_3) =$$
$$(corevise(v))((corevise(v))((corevise(v))(v, a_2), a_3), a_1)$$

3. commutativity:

$$(corevise(v))((corevise(v))(v, a_1), a_2) = (corevise(v))((corevise(v))(v, a_2), a_1)$$

Proof. We sketch a proof as follows.

1. idempotency: Follows from Eq. 7 and the idempotency property of *revise* in Eq. 1.
2. associativity: Let $v_l = (corevise(v))((corevise(v))((corevise(v))(v, a_1), a_2), a_3)$ and $v_r = (corevise(v))((corevise(v))((corevise(v))(v, a_2), a_3), a_1)$. Observe that $\{v_l, v_r\} \subseteq foldalleles(corevise(v), v, B)$ (see Eq. 3). We have $B = \{a_1, a_2, a_3\} \subseteq A$ and $nonconflicting(A, v)$. By Lemma 2, then, we have $nonconflicting(B, v)$, which by Eq. 8 means $|foldalleles(corevise(v), v, B)| = 1$. Therefore $v_l = v_r$.
3. commutativity: Similar to the argument for the case of associativity, above.

Recall that generally $perform(v, a)$ is neither associative nor commutative nor idempotent over a set of actions A (see Eq. 4). By its definition (Eq. 7), then, $(corevise(z))(v, A)$ is also neither associative nor commutative over A. Lemma 3, however, establishes that $(corevise(z))(v, A)$ is idempotent; and if $nonconflicting(A, v)$ holds then it is also associative and commutative.

---

[3] Observe that whereas $v' = perform(v, a)$ for action $a \in \mathbf{A}$ evaluates to an "update change" to v, the evaluation of $v'' = perform(v, A)$ for $A \subseteq \mathbf{A}$ yields a "replacement" for v. Conceptually, an update change to v differs from a replacement for v in that on the one hand, generally, the relation $Dom(v) \subseteq Dom(v')$ may (or may not) hold. On the other hand, $Dom(v) \subseteq Dom(v'')$ always holds because *revise* is monotonic, i.e., for $u' = revise(u, z, N)$ we have $u' \supseteq u$. Thus, a replacement can also harmlessly be considered an update change, i.e., just as for $w = revise(v, v', \emptyset)$ we have $w = revise(v, w, \emptyset)$, we also have $v'' = revise(v, v'', \emptyset)$. Therefore, we ignore their subtle distinction and treat both $perform(v, a)$ and $perform(v, A)$ as expressions that evaluate to an update change for v.

4.3 Sequential Composition of Concurrent Actions

We have assumed that the syntax of actions supports sequential composition of actions $a_1, a_2 \in \mathbf{A}$, which we denote here as $a_1; a_2$ (see the text that follows Eq. 4). We now extend the sequential composition of actions to sequential composition of sets of actions $A_1, A_2 \in \mathcal{P}(\mathbf{A})$, which we denote as $A_1; A_2$. Intuitively, $A_1; A_2$ is a single (composite) action that first performs all actions $a \in A_1$ in some arbitrary order, and then performs all actions $a \in A_2$ in some arbitrary order.

In Sect. 4.1 we showed the valuation function that results from performing the composite action $a_1; a_2$ in the context of a valuation function $v \in \mathcal{V}$. We now use Eq. 11 to define the valuation function that results from performing the action $A_1; A_2$ in the context of a valuation function v as:

$$perform(v, A_1; A_2) = perform(perform(v, A_1), A_2) \tag{12}$$

Observe that whereas the image of $perform(v, a_1)$ is an "update" valuation function for revising v, the image of $perform(v, A_1)$ is a "replacement" valuation function for v, and therefore $revise(v, perform(v, A_1)) = perform(v, A_1)$. See Footnote 3.

For convenience, we also define $perform(v, A; a) = perform(perform(v, A), \{a\})$ and $perform(v, a; A) = perform(perform(v, \{a\}), A)$, where $a \in \mathbf{A}$ and $A \in \mathcal{P}(\mathbf{A})$.

5 Rules

A *rule* $r \in \mathbf{G} \times \mathcal{P}(\mathbf{A})$ is a pair of a guard and a set of concurrent actions. We denote the set of all rules as $\mathbf{R}$.

For $r = (g, A) \in \mathbf{R}$, we use r^G and r^A to denote the guard and the set of actions of r. For $v \in \mathbf{V}$, we call $r^N(v) = (r^A)^N(v)$, $r^R = (r^A)^R$, and $r^W(v) = (r^A)^W(v)$ the *variables*, the *read-only variables*, and the *write variables* of r, respectively. We call $r^S(v) = r^N(v) \cup r^W(v) \cup (r^G)^N$ the *scope* of a rule r, and $r^S = \bigcup_{v \in \mathbf{V}} r^S(v)$, the *superset of the scope* of r. Moreover, we extend our $r^G, r^A, r^N(v), r^R, r^W(v), r^S(v)$ notation to sets of rules in the obvious way, e.g., the scope and the superset of the scope of a set of rules $R \subseteq \mathbf{R}$ are $R^S(v) = \bigcup_{r \in R} r^S(v)$ and $R^S = \bigcup_{r \in R} r^S$, respectively.

A rule $r \in \mathbf{R}$ is *enabled* in the context of a valuation function $v \in \mathbf{V}$ only if $v \models r^G$ and $nonconflicting(r^A, v)$.

Example 4. An inflow controller rule for the case of low water level has a guard that checks that the level is below the safe minimun. When the guard is true, the rule is enabled and fin is set to 1.

```
((<'wl>,\ lambda wl. wl <= WLminSafe), {(< >,\lambda (). 'fin := 1)}))
```

Definition 2 (Equivalent rules). *Two rules* $r_i = (g_i, A_i), i \in \{1, 2\}$ *are equivalent, denoted as* $r_1 \equiv r_2$, *if and only if* $g_1 \iff g_2 \wedge A_1 \equiv A_2$.

We also extend the notion of equivalence from individual rules to sets of rules. We say two sets of rules $R_i, i \in \{1, 2\}$ are equivalent, denoted as $R_1 \equiv R_2$, if and only if $r_i \in R_i \implies \exists r_{3-i} \in R_{3-i}$ such that $r_1 \equiv r_2$.

6   Concurrent Rules Machines

A Concurrent Rules Machine (CRM) is a concurrent transition system that interacts with its environment. A CRM consists of an interface, a set of initialization actions, a set of rules, and a set of termination actions.

Definition 3 (Concurrent Rules Machine). *A Concurrent Rules Machine (CRM) consists of a tuple* $(I, A_0, R, T) \in (\mathcal{P}(\mathbf{Name}) \times \mathcal{P}(\mathbf{Name}) \times \mathcal{P}(\mathbf{Name})) \times \mathcal{P}(\mathbf{A}) \times \mathcal{P}(\mathbf{R}) \times \mathcal{P}(\mathbf{A})$ *where:*

- $I = (Exp, Imp, Sh) \in \mathcal{P}(\mathbf{Name}) \times \mathcal{P}(\mathbf{Name}) \times \mathcal{P}(\mathbf{Name})$ *is its interface where:*
  - *Exp, Imp, and Sh are mutually disjoint,*
  - $\{envstep\} \subseteq Sh$,
- $A_0 \subseteq \mathbf{A}$ *is the finite set of its initialization actions such that neverconflicting*(A_0).
- $R \subseteq \mathbf{R}$ *is its finite set of rules,*
- $T \subseteq \mathbf{A}$ *is a finite set of termination actions such that neverconflicting*(T).

The sets of variable names Exp, Imp, and Sh in the interface I constitute the sets of exported, imported, and shared variable names of the CRM, respectively.

The distinguished shared Boolean variable *envstep* $\in Sh$ coordinates the interaction between a CRM and its environment; see Sect. 7.

We denote the set of all concurrent rules machines by **CRM** and use $\emptyset_{\mathbf{CRM}}$ to denote the empty concurrent rules machine $((\emptyset, \emptyset, \emptyset), \emptyset, \emptyset, \emptyset)$. We use C^I, C^{A_0}, C^R, and C^T to refer to the interface, the set of initialization actions, the set of rules, and the set of termination actions of a CRM $C \in \mathbf{CRM}$, respectively. We use C^{Exp}, C^{Imp}, and C^{Sh} to refer to their respective elements in C^I. We call $C^{W_0} = (A_0)^W$ the *initialized variables*, $C^S = (C^R)^S \cup (A_0)^R \cup C^{W_0} \cup T^W \cup C^{Imp} \cup C^{Sh}$ the *scope* of C, $C^{Rd} = (C^R)^R \cup (A_0)^R \cup C^{Imp} \cup C^{Sh}$ the *read* variables of C, $C^W = C^{W_0} \cup (C^R)^W \cup T^W$ the *write* variables of C, and $C^{Priv} = C^S \setminus (C^{Exp} \cup C^{Imp} \cup C^{Sh})$ the *private* or local variables of C. We use C^{Ro} to denote the set of *read-only* variables of C, defined as $C^{Ro} = C^S \setminus C^W$.

Intuitively, the exported variables in C^{Exp} are the interface variables that C *offers as read-only* variables to its environment: C, another CRM, or the environment can read the values of the variables in C^{Exp}, but only C has the right to change the values of variables in C^{Exp}. The imported variables in C^{Imp} are the interface variables that C *uses as read-only* variables: another CRM or the environment has the right to read or change the values of variables in C^{Imp}, but C may use them only as read-only variables. The shared variables in C^{Sh} are the interface variables that C *shares with* its environment for both read and write: C, another CRM, or the environment may atomically read and/or change the values of variables in C^{Sh}.

Definition 3 restricts the scope of the rules in C^R to the set of interface variables in C^I and the (local) variables initialized by the initialization actions in C^{A_0}. The initialization actions in C^{A_0} must be never-conflicting and they must initialize the exported interface variables in C^{Exp}. Neither initialization actions in C^{A_0} nor rules in C^R may modify the values of the read-only interface variables in C^{Imp}.

Example 5 (Water tank CRM). The water tank component of our running example (Sect. 1.1) can be modeled as a CRM, WL (water level), in the pseudo-code below. In this (and other pieces of) pseudo code, we use the convention that unquoted names (such as t, fin0 or WL.R), represent (global or local) *mathematical variables*, whereas quoted names (such as 'fin, 'time, or'wl), represent *CRM program variables (variable names)* which will be replaced by their respective values that the CRM semantics (see Sect. 7) finds through look-up in its valuation function at run time.

To be concrete, we fix the global parameters as follows: WLmin = 1, WLminSafe = 2, WLmaxSafe = 3, and WLmax = 4. We assume that initially the water level is at WLminSafe. The water level CRM computes the level at the current time (the value of 'time), given the water level at the previous time, t0, and the control settings at t0.[4] When the water level rule executes, the environment has already overwritten 'time, and the control variables. Thus at each step these values need to be cached for the next step. To do so, we introduce private variables 't0 (to store the previous time), to know how much time has passed, and 'fin0 and 'fout0 (to store the values of 'fin and 'fout at the previous time). These variables are set by termination actions. Note that there is no need to cache the value of 'wl as it will have the value at the previous time when the water level rule executes.

```
WL = (WL.I, WL.A0, WL.R, WL.T)
where
  WL.I = ({'fin, 'fout, 'time}, {'wl},{})
  --- the interface with imports ('fin 'fout 'time), exports ('wl)
      and no shared variables ({}).
  WL.A0 = {(< >, \lambda (). 'wl := WCminSafe)}
      --- the initialization action
  WL.R = { (true, {a.wl})}
      --- the rule updating the water level
  WL.T = {(< 'time, 'fin, 'fout >,
          \lambda (t, fin, fout).
              {'t0 := t,'fin0 := fin, 'fout0 := fout} )}
          --- the termination action that caches the
              values of 'fin 'fout and 'time
and
  a.wl = (< 'fin0,'fout0,'t0,'time , 'wl >,
          \lambda (fin0, fout0, t0, t, wl0).
              'wl := wl0 + (fin0 - fout0) * (t - t0) )
```

7   CRM Semantics

Informally, a CRM C iterates indefinitely, performing the actions of some of its rules, in mutual interaction with the environment. In each round, it interacts with the environment to obtain new observation values for its imported and shared interface variables, then nondeterministically picks a subset of its enabled rules whose action sets

---

[4] In cyber physical models, we assume the environment provides a notion of time (see *time* in Sect. 9). The imported variable 'time in our pseudo-code represents *time* in Sect. 9.

are non-conflicting, and atomically performs those actions to revise its current valuation function for its next round. Meanwhile, the environment independently, perhaps continuously, changes the values of some of the interface variables of C. We use the distinguished Boolean variable *envstep* to coordinate the interaction between a CRM and its environment (see multi-steps, below)[5].

Table 1. Semantics of a CRM $C = (I, A_0, R, T)$

Pick $\mathcal{V}^{-1} \in \mathbf{V}$ such that *RequiredVars* $\subseteq Dom(\mathcal{V}^{-1})$; see Equation 13 for *RequiredVars*.

$$\mathcal{V}^i = perform(\mathcal{E}^i, S^i; T)$$

$$\mathcal{E}^i = \begin{cases} revise(\mathcal{V}^{-1}, [envstep \to \top], \emptyset) & \text{if } i = 0 \\ interact(\mathcal{V}^{i-1}, C^{Exp} \cup C^{Priv} \cup \{envstep\}) & \text{otherwise} \end{cases}$$

$$interact(V, P) = \begin{cases} revise(V, xchange(V), P) & \text{if } V(envstep) \\ V & \text{otherwise} \end{cases}$$

$$S^i = pickedacts(E_R^i, \emptyset, \mathcal{E}^i, i > 0)$$

$$pickedacts(F, S, V, I) = \begin{cases} S & \text{if } F = \emptyset \vee (I \wedge Toss()) \\ annex(A, F \setminus \{A\}, S, V) & \text{otherwise, where } A \in F \end{cases}$$

$$annex(A, F, S, V) = \begin{cases} pickedacts(F, S \cup A, V, \top) & \text{if } nonconflicting(S \cup A, V) \\ pickedacts(F, S, V, \top) & \text{otherwise} \end{cases}$$

$$E_R^i = \begin{cases} \{A_0\} & \text{if } i = 0 \\ \{A \mid (g, A) \in R, \mathcal{E}^i \models g \wedge nonconflicting(A, \mathcal{E}^i)\} & \text{otherwise} \end{cases}$$

7.1   CRM Operational Semantics

Formally, we define the dynamic behavior of $C = (I, A_0, R, T) \in \mathbf{CRM}$ as an iterative revision of its valuation function, $\mathcal{V}$, where for $i \in \mathbb{N}_0$, its revised version, $\mathcal{V}^i$, for the ith iteration is derived from its $i - 1^{st}$ iteration version, $\mathcal{V}^{i-1}$, as defined in Table 1. The iteration starts by the environment providing a valuation function $\mathcal{V}^{-1} \in \mathbf{V}$ to initialize those interface variables of C that are not initialized by its initialization actions A_0, i.e., by picking a $\mathcal{V}^{-1}$ such that $Dom(\mathcal{V}^{-1}) \subseteq RequiredVars$ where:

$$RequiredVars = C^{Imp} \cup C^{Sh} \setminus (A_0^W \cup T^W) \tag{13}$$

---

[5] Observe that by Definition 3, *envstep* $\in C^{Sh}$ for every CRM C.

Conceptually, in every round the equations in Table 1 specify two sequential steps through which first the environment of C and then C take turns to change the values of the variables in C^I, the interface of C.[6] For $i \in \mathbb{N}_0$, $\mathcal{E}^i$ represents the valuation function that reflects the incremental modifications that the environment makes to the values of the variables in C^I as round i begins (i.e., before C acts).

The pseudo function $Toss : \emptyset \rightsquigarrow \mathbb{B}$ in the definition of *pickedacts* nondeterministically maps to $\top$ or $\bot$.

Example 6 (Sample WL execution). The listing below gives the sequence of valuation maps of a possible execution of WL when the environment provides time in unit increments (and values of 'fin, 'fout). First the environment writes initial values for time $(= 0)$, 'fin $= 1$, and 'fout $= 0$. The the initialization actions WL.A0 of WL are executed ('wl $= 2.0$) followed by the termination actions WL.T that cache the values of 'time, 'fin, 'fout as 't0 'fin, 'fout. This is followed by alternations between the environment action and execution of the rule WL.R.

time	fin	fout	wl	t0	fin0	fout0	
0	1	.5					Env initiates
			2.0	0	1	.5	WL A0;T
1	0	1					Env writes
			2.5	1	0	1	WL,R ; WL.T
2	1	0					Env writes
			1.5	2	1	0	WL,R ; WL.T
3	1	0					Env writes
			2.5	3	1	0	WL,R ; WL.T
. . . . .							

We can also execute symbolically. Suppose at time 0 the water level is wl_0 and we fix fout to be 0.75. Let fin_j be the value of 'fin at time j. Then wl_j, the water level at time j is given by

$$wl_1 = wl_0 + (fin_0 - 0.75)$$

$$wl_2 = wl_1 + (fin_1 - 0.75) = wl_0 + fin_0 + fin_1 - 1.5$$

. . .

$$wl_{j+1} = wl_0 + \Sigma_{i\in[0,j]}fin_i + (j + 1) \times 0.75$$

Initialization. Initially as round 0 begins, the environment of C must pick an arbitrary valuation function $\mathcal{V}^{-1}$ to give values to at least the set of variables in *RequiredVars* defined in Eq. 13.

---

[6] Of course, in every turn, C may change its own private variables, as well. However, these changes are not directly visible outside of C; the environment will indirectly observe the impact of changes to local variables of C as/if they alter the values of the export and shared interface variables of C.

For $i = 0$ we get $\mathcal{E}^0 = revise(\mathcal{V}^{-1}, [envstep \rightarrow \top], \emptyset)$, where $[envstep \rightarrow \top] \in \mathbf{V}$ is a function that maps the distinguished variable $envstep$ to $\top^7$ (see Eq. 1) Thus we have $\mathcal{E}^0(envstep) = \top$ and for all $x \in Dom(v) \setminus \{envstep\}$ we have $\mathcal{E}^0(x) = \mathcal{V}^{-1}(x)$. Then through $perform(\mathcal{E}^i, S^i; T)$ in $\mathcal{V}^i = perform(\mathcal{E}^i, S^i; T)$, C performs for $i = 0$ the set $S^0 = E_R^0 = A_0$ of its initialization actions, sequentially followed by the set of termination actions T, within the context of the valuation function $\mathcal{E}^0$ to yield the valuation function for the next round (see Eq. 12). This ends round $i = 0$.

Observe that for $i > 0$, depending on the nondeterministic evaluation of $Toss()$, the function $pickedacts(E_R^i, \emptyset, \mathcal{E}^i, i > 0)$ may evaluate to $\emptyset$ regardless of whether or not $E_R^i = \emptyset$. This observation means that a CRM can always refrain from performing the actions of any of its enabled rules in a round $i > 0$. However, the evaluation of $S^0 = pickedacts(E_R^0, \emptyset, \mathcal{E}^0, 0 > 0)$ shows that $S^0 = \emptyset$ only if $E_R^0 = A_0 = \emptyset$. In other words, a CRM cannot "skip" performing its initialization actions in round $i = 0$.

Multi-Steps. In Table 1, the initial valuation function $\mathcal{E}^0$ sets the value of the distinguished private variable $envstep$ to $\top$. Therefore, unless an action in A_0 changes the value of $envstep$, we have $\mathcal{V}^0(envstep) = \mathcal{E}^0(envstep) = \top$.

For $i > 0$, the valuation function $\mathcal{E}^i$ is obtained through (possible) interaction with the environment, formalized as function $interact : \mathbf{V} \times \mathcal{P}(\mathbf{Name}) \rightarrow \mathbf{V}$ in Table 1. The value of $\mathcal{V}^{i-1}(envstep)$ determines whether (1) $interact$ yields $\mathcal{V}^{i-1}$ (if $\mathcal{V}^{i-1}(envstep) = \bot$), in which case C takes another turn without interference by the environment, in the context of the valuation function $\mathcal{E}^i = \mathcal{V}^{i-1}$, or (2) the environment takes a turn (if $\mathcal{V}^{i-1}(envstep) = \top$). Thus, by setting the value of the distinguished private variable $envstep$, C can decide to take one or more steps between every two successive steps by the environment.

Interaction with the Environment. If $\mathcal{V}^{i-1}(envstep) = \top$ for some $i > 0$, the environment takes its turn to incrementally modify the values of some of the interface variables in C^I, an activity that we represent by the pseudo function $xchange : \mathbf{V} \rightsquigarrow \mathbf{V}$.[8] We use the function $revise$ (see Eq. 1) to incorporate these incremental modifications by the environment into $\mathcal{V}^{i-1}$ to produce $\mathcal{E}^i$, the valuation function in the context of which C must determine and perform its set of enabled actions S^i in its next iteration for i.

Generally, nothing prevents the environment from changing the values of the export variables of C (which C offers as read-only to the environment) or the local private variables of C (which only C must be able to modify). To account for this undesirable

---

[7] The default value of $\top$ for $envstep$ in $\mathcal{V}^0$ means that by default, Table 1 ensures that successive steps of the behavior of C are interleaved with updates of its interface variables to reflect the changes in the environment. Of course, C can change this default by changing the value of $envstep$ in its initialization actions or by the actions in its rules.

[8] Observe that having $xchange$ as a pseudo function imposes no restriction on how the environment may behave; the behavior of the environment may neither be computable, nor expressible as a function. Regardless of how/why nature/physics changes certain properties of the environment, intuitively, $xchange$ serves as a *sensor reading function* that modifies the values of some of the interface variables of a CRM, based on its snapshot of, e.g., the energy level of a battery, the velocity of a moving object, the water-level in a tank, ambient humidity, temperature, etc.

fact, we allow the valuation function that is the image of $xchange(\mathcal{V}^{i-1})$ to possibly map some of the variable names in $C^{Exp} \cup C^{Priv}$ to new values. In order to preserve the integrity of the *protected* variables in $C^{Exp} \cup C^{Priv}$, however, the definition of $\mathcal{E}^i$ in Table 1 excludes their modification through the second argument of *interact* (which serves as the third argument of *revise* in the definition of *interact*). This exclusion guarantees that for all $i > 0$ and $x \in C^{Exp} \cup C^{Priv}$ we have $\mathcal{E}^i(x) = \mathcal{V}^{i-1}(x)$.

Enabled Actions. For $i \in \mathbb{N}_0$, the set S^i contains the enabled actions that C decides to perform in its ith round of recursion. The set S^i is recursively constructed by mutual recursion of functions *pickedacts* and *annex*, which together pick a nondeterministic subset of E_R^i. The set E_R^i contains the sets of actions of the enabled rules in round i.

For $i = 0$, E_R^0 contains the set of initialization actions of the CRM C, i.e., $E_R^0 = \{A_0\}$, and we have $S^0 = pickedacts(\{A_0\}, \emptyset, \mathcal{E}^0, \perp)$. Since the condition $\{A_0\} = \emptyset \lor \perp \land Toss()$ in the definition of *pickedacts* evaluates to $\perp$ and $A \in \{A_0\} \implies A = A_0$, we have $pickedacts(\{A_0\}, \emptyset, \mathcal{E}^0, \perp) = annex(A_0, \{A_0\} \setminus \{A_0\}, \emptyset, \mathcal{E}^0)$. By definition, $neverconflicting(A_0) = \top$. Thus $annex(A_0, \{A_0\} \setminus \{A_0\}, \emptyset, \mathcal{E}^0) = pickedacts(\emptyset, A_0, E_R^0, \top)$. Consequently, the condition $\emptyset = \emptyset \lor (\top \land Toss())$ in the definition of *pickedacts* evaluates to $\top$ and we have $pickedacts(\emptyset, A_0, E_R^0, \top) = A_0$. Therefore, $S^0 = A_0$.

For $i = 0$, as we saw above, what $Toss()$ evaluates to is irrelevant. For $i > 0$, the non-deterministic image of $Toss()$ together with the nondeterminism inherent in the choice of $A \in F$ steer the mutual recursion of *pickedacts* and *annex* to nondeterministically pick a "flattened" subset of the action sets in E_R^i that are non-conflicting in the context of the valuation function $\mathcal{E}^i$, as the set S^i of the enabled actions to be performed in round i. Note that the actions in S^i may belong to different rules whose guards evaluate to true. In other words, C does *not* select one enabled rule to perform its actions; it selects a subset of its enabled rules and performs the actions in their action sets. Thus, depending on whether or not C selects one of its enabled rules r, C performs either all or none of the actions in the actions set of r. Note also that C may "idle" in a round if for some $i > 0$, we have $E_R^i = \emptyset$ or if evaluating $pickedacts(E_R^i, \emptyset, \mathcal{E}^i, i > 0)$, $Toss()$ nondeterministically evaluates to $\top$.

Observe that in Table 1 if $\mathcal{V}^{i-1}(envstep) = \top$ for $i > 0$, then we have $\mathcal{E}^i = revise(\mathcal{V}^{i-1}, xchange(\mathcal{V}^{i-1}), C^{Exp} \cup C^{Priv})$. This means that even if $S^i = \emptyset$, through $xchange(\mathcal{V}^{i-1})$, the environment may change the name-value bindings in $\mathcal{V}^{i-1}$, from which we obtain $\mathcal{V}^i$. In other words, interaction with the environment may allow C to progress in round i regardless of whether or not C idles in round $i - 1$.

7.2   CRM Behavior

Observables. Initially, the environment may set the values of all variables in $C^{Imp} \cup C^{Sh}$. The recursive definitions in Table 1 state that in round $i > 0$ the environment can change the values of the variables in the domain of the valuation function that is the image of $xchange(\mathcal{V}^{i-1})$. These changes affect the behavior of C only if they involve the interface variables in $C^{Imp} \cup C^{Sh}$. So, the set of relevant variables whose values the environment changes in rounds $i > 0$ is $(C^{Imp} \cup C^{Sh}) \cap Dom(xchange(\mathcal{V}^{i-1}))$. Combining the two cases, we conclude that the set of C variables whose values the environment changes in the ith round is:

$$M_E^i = (C^{Imp} \cup C^{Sh}) \cap (i = 0 \text{ ? } \textbf{Name} : Dom(xchange(\mathcal{V}^{i-1}))), i \in \mathbb{N}_0$$

From Table 1 we derive the set of variables whose values C may change in the ith round as the write-variables of the set of actions that C performs in round i:

$$M_C^i = T^W \cup \bigcup_{A \in S^i} A^W(v), i \in \mathbb{N}_0 \tag{14}$$

Therefore, the set of all C variables whose values may change (are written) between the ends of rounds $i - 1$ and i is $M^i = M_E^i \cup M_C^i$ or:

$$M^i = ((C^{Imp} \cup C^{Sh}) \cap (i = 0 \text{ ? } \textbf{Name} : Dom(xchange(\mathcal{V}^{i-1})))) \cup M_C^i, i \in \mathbb{N}_0 \tag{15}$$

Binding values to the variables in M^i constitute the difference between the mappings of $\mathcal{V}^{i-1}$ and $\mathcal{V}^i$. Observe that M^i can be partitioned into four disjoint sets of variables: $C^{Exp}, C^{Imp}, C^{Sh} \setminus M_C^i$, and $M_C^i \setminus (C^{Exp} \cup C^{Sh})$. Only C can change the values of its internal variables in $M_C^i \setminus (C^{Exp} \cup C^{Sh})$ and those in C^{Exp}, and only the environment can change the values of the variables in C^{Imp} and $C^{Sh} \setminus M_C^i$. But both C and the environment may change the values of the variables in $M_C^i \cap C^{Sh}$ in the ith round.

Nevertheless, there is no race condition between C and the environment over their shared variables in $M_C^i \cap C^{Sh}$. Table 1 states that C performs its actions that make changes to the values of the variables in M_C^i (through $fold(corevise(\mathcal{E}^i), \mathcal{E}^i, S^i)$) only *after* the environment has made its possible changes to the values of the variables in C^{Sh} to produce $\mathcal{E}^i$. Therefore in the ith round, (1) the values that C reads for the shared variables in $M_C^i \cap C^{Sh}$ are what the environment has set for them in $\mathcal{E}^i$, and (2) in $\mathcal{V}^i$, any change that C makes to the values of the shared variables in $M_C^i \cap C^{Sh}$ overrides the values that the environment may have bound to these variables. Moreover, by Eq. 8, regardless of the nondeterministic choices made by *fold* (see Eqs. 11 and 12), the image of $perform(\mathcal{E}^i, S^i; T)$ is the same unique $\mathcal{V}^i$.

We use O^i to denote the *observable* of the ith round, which we define as the set of name-value pairs $(n, v) \in \textbf{Name} \times \textbf{D}$ for every variable in M^i that acquires a new value through actions of either the environment or C in round i:

$$O^i = \bigcup_{n \in M^i} \{(n, \mathcal{V}^i(n))\}, i \in \mathbb{N}_0 \tag{16}$$

Behavior. We identify a *run* of a CRM C as an infinite sequence $\langle O^0, O^1, O^2, ... \rangle \in (\mathcal{P}(\textbf{Name} \times \textbf{D}))^\omega$ of observables O^i. The *CRM behavior* of C, denoted as $\mathcal{B}(C)$, consists of the set of all of its runs.

Lemma 4. *For* $C^i = ((E^i, I^i, S^i), A_0^i, R^i, T^i) \in \textbf{CRM}, i \in \{1, 2\}$:

$$\begin{pmatrix} E^1 = E^2 \wedge I^1 = I^2 \wedge S^1 = S^2 \\ \wedge \\ A_0^1 \equiv A_0^2 \wedge R^1 \equiv R^2 \wedge T^1 \equiv T^2 \end{pmatrix} \implies \mathcal{B}(C^1) = \mathcal{B}(C^2)$$

8   An Algebra of CRMs

8.1   CRM Containment, Union, and Intersection

For $C_1, C_2 \in \mathbf{CRM}$, we write $C_1 \subseteq C_2$ if and only if C_2 component-wise contains C_1, that is, if and only if $(C_1^{Exp} \subseteq C_2^{Exp}) \wedge (C_1^{Imp} \subseteq C_2^{Imp}) \wedge (C_1^{Sh} \subseteq C_2^{Sh}) \wedge (C_1^{A_0} \subseteq C_2^{A_0}) \wedge (C_1^R \subseteq C_2^R) \wedge (C_1^T \subseteq C_2^T)$.

Analogously, we define $C_1 \cup C_2$ and $C_1 \cap C_2$ for the structures that result from, respectively, the union and the intersection of the corresponding structural components of the tuples that form C_1 and C_2.

Properties of containment, union, and intersection.

– For all $C_1, C_2 \in \mathbf{CRM}$, their intersection $C = C_1 \cap C_2 \in \mathbf{CRM}$.
– For all $C_1, C_2 \in \mathbf{CRM}$, their union $C = C_1 \cup C_2 \in \mathbf{CRM}$ if and only if:
  • The three sets $C_1^{Exp} \cup C_2^{Exp}, C_1^{Imp} \cup C_2^{Imp}$, and $C_1^{Sh} \cup C_2^{Sh}$ are mutually disjoint;
  • $(C_1^{A_0} \cup C_2^{A_0})^W \cap (C_1^{Imp} \cup C_2^{Imp}) = \emptyset$;
  • *neverconflicting*$(C_1^{A_0} \cup C_2^{A_0})$; and
  • *neverconflicting*$(C_1^T \cup C_2^T)$.
– CRM intersection is associative, commutative, and idempotent.
– CRM union is associative, commutative, and idempotent.
– For $C \in \mathbf{CRM}$:
  • $C \cup \emptyset_{\mathbf{CRM}} = C$
  • $C \cap \emptyset_{\mathbf{CRM}} = \emptyset_{\mathbf{CRM}}$

8.2   CRM Product

Informally, the product of two CRMs is a CRM whose behavior is the same as the behavior of the concurrent execution of the two CRMs. As such, the product of two CRMs is very much like their union, except that the union of two CRMs is not always a CRM (see Paragraph 8.1), whereas the product of every two CRMs is always a CRM (see properties of product, below).

Definition 4 (CRM product). *Let $C_1, C_2 \in \mathbf{CRM}$ such that their initialization and termination actions do not conflict, and they share no private variables:*

– *neverconflicting*$(C_1^{A_0} \cup C_2^{A_0})$.
– *neverconflicting*$(C_1^T \cup C_2^T)$.
– $C_1^{Priv} \cap C_2^{Priv} = \emptyset$.

The product of C_1 and C_2, denoted as $C_1 \times C_2$ is $C = (C^I, C_1^{A_0} \cup C_2^{A_0}, C_1^R \cup C_2^R, C_1^T \cup C_2^T)$ where:

$$C^I = (C^{Exp}, C^{Imp}, C^{Sh})$$
$$C^{Exp} = C_1^{Exp} \cup C_2^{Exp}$$
$$C^{Imp} = (C_1^{Imp} \cup C_2^{Imp}) \setminus (C^{Exp} \cup C^{Sh}))$$
$$C^{Sh} = (C_1^{Sh} \cup C_2^{Sh}) \setminus C^{Exp}$$

Intuitively, the product of two CRMs $C_i \in \mathbf{CRM}, i \in \{1, 2\}$, consists of their union after their conflicting elements are symmetrically removed. Conflicts of interface variables are resolved following the policy that export takes precedence over shared which in turn takes precedence over import. Specifically, any $x \in C_i^{Exp}$ that C_i exports remains an export interface variable in $C_1 \times C_2$. If C_i exports a variable $x \in C_i^{Exp} \cap (C_{3-i}^{Imp} \cup C_{3-i}^{Sh})$ that C_{3-i} either imports or shares in its interface, then x remains an export interface variable in the product CRM. If C_i shares a variable $x \in C_i^{Sh} \cap C_{3-i}^{Imp}$ that C_{3-i} imports in its interface, then x remains a shared interface variable in the product CRM.

Properties of product.

- For all $C_1, C_2 \in \mathbf{CRM}$ their product $C = C_1 \times C_2 \in \mathbf{CRM}$.
- CRM product is associative, commutative, and idempotent.
- For all $C \in \mathbf{CRM}$ we have $C \times \emptyset_{\mathbf{CRM}} = C$.
- For all $C_1, C_2 \in \mathbf{CRM}$ if $C_1 \cup C_2 \in \mathbf{CRM}$ then their product and union have:
  - the same behavior: $\mathcal{B}(C_1 \times C_2) = \mathcal{B}(C_1 \cup C_2)$
  - the same interface: $(C_1 \times C_2)^I = (C_1 \cup C_2)^I$

8.3   Hiding

Hiding is an operation that removes an interface variable of a CRM. An interface variable x of a CRM $C \in \mathbf{CRM}$ can be hidden only if x is among the variables that C initializes, i.e., only if $x \in C^{A_0^W}$. Thus, because $C^{Imp} \cap C^{A_0^W} = \emptyset$, a variable x of C can be hidden only if $x \in C^{Exp}$ or $x \in C^{Sh} \cap C^{A_0^W}$.

Definition 5 (Hiding). *By* $\exists[x]C$ *we denote hiding a variable* $x \in (C^{Exp} \cup C^{Sh}) \cap C^{A_0^W}$ *of a* $C \in \mathbf{CRM}$, *where* $\exists[x]C = (I, C^{A_0}, C^R, C^T)$ *and* $I = (C^{Exp} \setminus \{x\}, C^{Imp}, C^{Sh} \setminus \{x\})$.

Removing x from the interface of C makes x a private variable of C, but does not affect any of its rules or actions.

Observe that for $x, y, z \in (C^{Exp} \cup C^{Sh}) \cap C^{A_0^W}$, hiding is associative, commutative, and idempotent. Therefore, we extend our notation for hiding from a single variable to a set of variables, i.e., for a set $S = \{x_1, x_2, ..., x_n\}$ of $0 < i \leq n$ variables $x_i \in (C^{Exp} \cup C^{Sh}) \cap C^{A_0^W}$, we define $\exists[S]C = \exists[x_1, x_2, ..., x_n]C = \exists[x_1]\exists[x_2]...\exists[x_n]C$, where the order is irrelevant.

8.4   Sequential Composition of CRMs

In this section we introduce two CRM sequential composition operators: the cyclic (;) and the sum (+) composition. Each of these compositions combines two CRMs into a composite CRM whose behavior consists of sequences of *macro-steps*, in each of which the first and the second component CRM takes its turn to perform one round of its rule-execution as a *micro-step*. The component CRMs no longer interact with the environment at the end of their turns (i.e., the end of each of its micro-steps); instead, the composite CRM interacts with the environment only at upon the completion of each macro-step.

Definition 6 (CRM cyclic composition). *Let* $C_1, C_2 \in$ **CRM** *such that they share no private variables (i.e., $C_1^{Priv} \cap C_2^{Priv} = \emptyset$). The cyclic composition of C_1 and C_2, denoted as $C_1; C_2$ is $C = (C^I, A_0, R, T)$ where:*

$$C^I = (C^{Exp}, C^{Imp}, C^{Sh})$$
$$C^{Exp} = C_1^{Exp} \cup C_2^{Exp}$$
$$C^{Imp} = (C_1^{Imp} \cup C_2^{Imp}) \setminus (C^{Exp} \cup C^{Sh}))$$
$$C^{Sh} = (C_1^{Sh} \cup C_2^{Sh}) \setminus C^{Exp}$$

$$A^0 = \{\text{turn} := 0, envstep := \bot; C_1^{A^0}; C_1^T; envstep := \bot; C_2^{A^0}; C_2^T; envstep := \bot\}$$

$$R = \{(\text{turn} = 1 \wedge g, a) \mid (g, a) \in C_1^R\} \cup \{(\text{turn} = 2 \wedge g, a) \mid (g, a) \in C_2^R\}$$

$$T = \{(\{\textit{if}(\text{turn} = 1) \textit{ then } a \textit{ fi} \mid a \in C_1^T\} \cup \{\textit{if}(\text{turn} = 2) \textit{ then } a \textit{ fi} \mid a \in C_2^T\});$$
$$\textit{if }((\text{turn} \bmod 2) = 0) \textit{ then } envstep := \top \textit{ else } envstep := \bot \textit{ fi};$$
$$\text{turn} := (\text{turn} \bmod 2) + 1\}$$

where turn $\in$ **Name** *represents a unique fresh new name obtained through new(**Name**) (see Sect. 2.1 for new(**Name**)).*

Intuitively, $C = C_1; C_2$ is a CRM that lets C_1 take a turn to perform C's first micro-step wherein C_1 performs its own choice of its enabled rules once, then lets C_2 perform its respective micro-step to complete a macro-step of C, at the end of which the environment gets to interact with C. The interface of $C_1; C_2$ is the same as the interface of $C_1 \times C_2$.

The initialization actions of C consist of a sequential composition of the initialization and termination actions of its component CRMs (see Eq. 12), and initializing the fresh unique new variable turn $= 0$. Because A^0 sets *envstep* to $\bot$ before every $C_i^{A^0}$, the initialization actions of each component CRM (in $C_i^{A^0}$) can detect whether their respective CRM runs interacting directly with the environment (*envstep* $= \top$), or as a micro-step in some sequential composition (*envstep* $= \bot$), and initialize their respective CRMs accordingly (see initialization of *envstep* in Table 1).

The combination of the initialization action turn $:= 0$ and the termination action turn $:= (\text{turn} \bmod 2) + 1$ yield the following sequence of values for turn: $0, 1, 2, 1, 2, 1, 2, \ldots$. The conjunctions turn $= i \wedge g$ for $i \in \{1, 2\}$ with the guards g of rules $(g, a) \in C_i^R$ restrict C to run only the selected actions of the enabled rules of its component CRM C_i.

The termination action if $((\text{turn} \bmod 2) = 0)$ then *envstep* $:= \top$ else *envstep* $:= \bot$ fi permits C to interact with the environment only after its (micro-step) rounds where turn has the value of either 0 or 2, i.e., only upon completion of every macro-step.

Observe that the initialization actions in $C_1^{A^0}$ and $C_2^{A^0}$, and the termination actions in C_1^T and C_2^T, run concurrently in $C_1 \times C_2$ as in $C_1^{A^0} \cup C_2^{A^0}$ and $C_1^T \cup C_2^T$, respectively. As such, *neverconflicting*$(C_1^{A^0} \cup C_2^{A^0})$ and *neverconflicting*$(C_1^T \cup C_2^T)$ are prerequisites in Definition 4 for $C_1 \times C_2$ to be well-defined. In contrast, in cyclic composition (Definition 6) and sum composition (Definition 7), the initialization actions in $C_1^{A^0}$ run before those in $C_2^{A^0}$, and the termination actions in C_1^T run before those in C_2^T. As such, *neverconflicting*$(C_1^{A_0} \cup C_2^{A_0})$ and *neverconflicting*$(C_1^T \cup C_2^T)$ are not required for cyclic and sum compositions to be well-defined.

The cyclic and sum compositions differ only in when they perform the termination actions of their component CRMs. In cyclic composition (Definition 6), the composite CRM performs the termination actions of its component CRMs at the end of each of their respective micro-steps (including their micro-initialization-steps). In sum composition (Definition 7) the termination actions of component CRMs are performed not at the end of their respective micro-steps, but only collectively at the end of each macro-step.

Definition 7 (CRM sum composition). *Let* $C_1, C_2 \in$ **CRM** *such that they share no private variables (i.e.,* $C_1^{Priv} \cap C_2^{Priv} = \emptyset$*). The sum composition of* C_1 *and* C_2*, denoted as* $C_1 + C_2$ *is* $C = (C^I, A_0, R, T)$ *where:*

$$C^I = (C^{Exp}, C^{Imp}, C^{Sh})$$
$$C^{Exp} = C_1^{Exp} \cup C_2^{Exp}$$
$$C^{Imp} = (C_1^{Imp} \cup C_2^{Imp}) \setminus (C^{Exp} \cup C^{Sh}))$$
$$C^{Sh} = (C_1^{Sh} \cup C_2^{Sh}) \setminus C^{Exp}$$

$$A^0 = \{\mathbf{turn} := 0, envstep := \bot; C_1^{A^0}; envstep := \bot; C_2^{A^0}; envstep := \bot\}$$

$$R = \{(\mathbf{turn} = 1 \wedge g, a) \mid (g, a) \in C_1^R\} \cup \{(\mathbf{turn} = 2 \wedge g, a) \mid (g, a) \in C_2^R\} \cup$$
$$\{((\mathbf{turn} \bmod 3) = 0, \{C_1^T; C_2^T\})\}$$

$$T = \{if ((\mathbf{turn} \bmod 3) = 0) \text{ then } envstep := \top \text{ else } envstep := \bot \text{ fi};$$
$$\mathbf{turn} := (\mathbf{turn} \bmod 3) + 1\}$$

and **turn** $\in$ **Name** *represents a fresh new name obtained from new(***Name***).*

The combination of the initialization action **turn** := 0 and the termination action **turn** := (**turn** mod 3) + 1 yield the following sequence of values for **turn**: $0, 1, 2, 3, 1, 2, 3, 1, 2, 3, \ldots$. The conjunctions **turn** = $i \wedge g$ for $i \in \{1, 2\}$ with the guards g of rules $(g, a) \in C_i^R$ restrict C to run only the selected actions of the enabled rules of its component CRM C_i. The tailor-made rule $((\mathbf{turn} \bmod 3) = 0, \{C_1^T; C_2^T\})$ then performs the composite action C_1^T, C_2^T as an extra micro-step to end each macro-step.

The termination action if $((\mathbf{turn} \bmod 3) = 0)$ then *envstep* := $\top$ else *envstep* := $\bot$ fi permits C to interact with the environment only after its (micro-step) rounds where **turn** has the value of either 0 or 3, i.e., only at the end of every macro-step (including initialization).

Example 7 (Interactive composition of WL and WC). The controller CRM, WC, formalizes the input controller described in Sect. 1.1.

```
WC = (WC.I, WC.A0, WC.R, WC.T)
where
  WC.I = ({'wl 'time}, {'fin}, {})
  WC.A0 = {(< >,\lambda ().'fin := WLminSafe0)}
  WC.R = {wc.r1, wc.r2}
  WC.T = {}
```

where `wc.r1` is the rule described in Example 4 and `wc.r2` is the analogous rule for the case when the value of `'wl` is greater or equal to `WLmaxSafe`.

In composition WL and WC interact: the controller reads the water level written by the water tank and the water level of the water tank is determined by the inflow set by the controller and the outflow set by the environment in the previous step. Thus the water tank rules should fire before the controller rules. To preserve the assumption by termination actions that all (original) imports have been written before the termination actions are executed, the termination actions need to be executed after all components have executed. We choose to expose `'wl` as an export, but to make `'fin` private. These requirements are satisfied by the sum form of sequential composition operation (Sect. 8.4) and the hiding operation (Sect. 8.3). Thus we define:

```
WLWC = Exists['fin](WL + WC)
```

Using the definitions of sum and hiding we obtain

```
WLWC     = [WLWC.I, WLWC.AO, WLWC.R, WLWC.T]
where
  WLWC.I = ['fout 't, 'wl, {}]
  WLWC.AO = { {turn := 0} ; WL.AO ; WC.AO2 ;
              {envstep := false} }
  WLWC.R = {(turn = 1) a.wl)
            (turn = 2, a.wc)
            (turn = 3, WL.T + WC.T)}
  WLWC.T = {if (turn=3) then envstep := true
                        else envstep := false fi;
            turn := (turn mod 3) + 1 }
```

Note that WL and WC satisfy the conditions for sum to be a CRM: combined initialization/termination actions of WL and WC read and write different variables, thus they are conflict free; and WL and WC have disjoint private variables (WC has none).

We illustrate runs with micro steps, with a sample WLWC execution.

Example 8 (Sample run of WLWC). Fix `fout` = .5. Recall `WLmin` = 1, `WLminSafe` = 2, `WLmaxSafe` = 3, `WLmax` = 4, and initially `wl` = 2.00, `fin` = 0. Below, we show the valuation maps `Vij` at each micro step j of step i. To avoid clutter, we show values only where variables are assigned.

	time	fout	wl	fin	t0	fin0	turn	envstep
V0	0	.5	2.00	0	0	0	1	false
v11			2.00				2	
v12				1			3	
v13					0	1	1	true
v21	1		2.50				2	false
v22				1			3	
v23					1	1	1	true
v31	2		3.00				2	false
v32				0			3	
v33					2	0	1	true
....								

8.5   CRM Division

Just as product is an essential operation for composition of simpler CRMs into more complex models, its inverse operation, division, is also useful for decomposition of CRMs into simpler modules, e.g., for analysis, modular replacement, or (dynamic) reconfiguration. Definition 8 establishes which CRMs can be divided by other CRMs.

Definition 8 (CRM divisibility). *Let $C_1, C_2 \in \mathbf{CRM}$. We say C_1 is divisible by C_2 if:*

1. C_1^I *subsumes* C_2^I, *i.e.:*
    (a) $C_2^{Exp} \subseteq C_1^{Exp}$
    (b) $(C_1^{Imp} \cap C_2^{Sh} = \emptyset) \wedge (C_2^{Imp} \subseteq C_1^{Imp} \cup C_1^{Exp} \cup C_1^{Sh})$
    (c) $C_2^{Sh} \subseteq C_1^{Exp} \cup C_1^{Sh}$
2. $C_2^{A_0} \subseteq C_1^{A_0}$
3. C_2^R *subsumes* C_2^R, *i.e.,* $r_2 \in C_2^R \implies \exists r_1 \in C_1^R \wedge r_1 \equiv r_2$
4. $C_2^T \subseteq C_1^T$

Lemma 5. *For all $C_1, C_2 \in \mathbf{CRM}$, $C_1 \times C_2$ is divisible by C_2.*

If C_1 is divisible by C_2, then there exists a C such that $C_1 = C_2 \times C$. Generally, however, C is not unique: there may be more than one unique C whose product composition with C_2 yields C_1. Therefore, Definition 9 defines the result of a division as *a set of quotients*, instead of a unique CRM.

Definition 9 (CRM division). *Let $C_1, C_2 \in \mathbf{CRM}$. The division of C_1 by C_2, denoted as C_1/C_2, is the set of quotients:*

$$C_1/C_2 = \begin{cases} Q & \text{if } C_1 \text{ is divisible by } C_2 \\ \{\emptyset_{\mathbf{CRM}}\} & \text{otherwise} \end{cases}$$

where the set of quotients, Q, is:

$$Q = \left\{ ((E, I, S), A_0, R, T) \,\middle|\, \begin{array}{l} E = (C_1^{Exp} \setminus C_2^{Exp}) \cup E^{xs} \\ I = (C_1^{Imp} \setminus C_2^{Imp}) \cup I^{xs} \\ S = (C_1^{Sh} \setminus C_2^{Sh}) \cup S^{xs} \\ A_0 = (C_1^{A_0} \setminus C_2^{A_0}) \cup A_0^{xs} \\ R = (C_1^R \setminus R_{equiv}) \cup R^{xs} \\ T = (C_1^T \setminus C_2^T) \cup T^{xs} \end{array} \right\}$$

and:

- $(R^S \cup A_0^N \cup T^N) \cap (E \cup I \cup S) = (R^S \cup A_0^N \cup T^N) \cap (C_1^{Exp} \cup C_1^{Imp} \cup C_1^{Sh})$
- $E^{xs} \subseteq C_1^{Exp} \cap C_2^{Exp}$
- $I^{xs} \subseteq C_1^{Imp} \cap (C_2^{Exp} \cup C_2^{Imp} \cup C_2^{Sh})$
- $S^{xs} \subseteq C_1^{Sh} \cap (C_2^{Exp} \cup C_2^{Sh})$
- $A_0^{xs} \subseteq C_1^{A_0}$
- $R_{equiv} = \{r_1 \mid r_1 \in C_1^R, r_2 \in C_2^R, r_1 \equiv r_2\}$
- $R^{xs} \subseteq R_{equiv}$
- $T^{xs} \subseteq C_2^T$

Intuitively, C_1/C_2 produces a set of quotient CRMs the product of each of which with C_2 is behaviorally equivalent to C_1.

Basic Properties of Division

- For all $C_1, C_2 \in$ **CRM**, every quotient $C \in C_1/C_2$ is a CRM.
- Every $C \in$ **CRM** is divisible by $\emptyset_{\text{CRM}}$ and $C/\emptyset_{\text{CRM}} = \{C\}$.
- For all $C_1, C_2 \in$ **CRM**:
  1. if C_1 is divisible by C_2 then $C_1 \in C_1/C_2$.
  2. $C \in C_1/C_2 \implies C \subseteq C_1$.
- For all $C_1, C_2 \in$ **CRM**, $C_1 \in (C_1 \times C_2)/C_2$.
- For all $C_1, C_2 \in$ **CRM**, $C_1 \cap C_2 = \emptyset_{\text{CRM}} \implies (C_1 \times C_2)/C_2 = \{C_1\}$.
- For all $C_1, C_2 \in$ **CRM**, $C \in C_1/C_2 \implies \mathcal{B}(C \times C_2) = \mathcal{B}(C_1)$.

Example 9 (Water system CRM division). To illustrate the utility of division, we start with an in/out controller CRM, WCIO. It has two rule sets: rules in RI read the water level and set `fin` (see Example 7); RO reads the water level and sets `fout`.

```
WCIO= (WCIO.I, WCIO.AO, WCIO.R, WCIO.T)
where
  WCIO.I = ({'wl},{'fin, 'fout}, {}) --- imports, exports, shared
  WCIO.AO = {(< >,\lambda (). 'fin := 0; 'fout := .5)}
  WCIO.R =
    { RI: {wc.r1, wc.r2}
      RO: { (true, {a.wo}) }
    }
  WCIO.T = {}
```

Recall that rules `wc.r1`, `wc.r2` are defined in Example 7. We also define a controller, WCO, for `fout`.

```
WCO = (WCO.I, WCO.AO, WCO.R, WCO.T)
where
  WCO.I = ({'wl}, {'fout}, {}) -- imports,exports,shared
  WCO.AO = {(< >,\ lambda (). 'fout := .5)}
  WCO.R = { RO: (true,{a.wo}) }
  WCO.T = {}
```

Then we have the following: WCO divides WCIO and WC is in WCIO/WCO.

9   Time in CRM

Since the concept of time is inherent in physics, representation of time is essential in formal models of cyber-physical systems. We base our model of time on the concept of *dense time*, and for simplicity represent time values as non-negative real numbers.

We call a stream of real numbers $\delta \in \mathbb{N}_0 \to \mathbb{R}_0^+$ *non-Zeno progressive* if:

1. for every $i \in \mathbb{N}_0, \delta(i) < \delta(i + 1)$, and
2. for every $n \in \mathbb{N}_0$, there exists an $i \in \mathbb{N}_0$ such that $\delta(i) > n$.

We stipulate that:

1. there exists a distinguished variable, ***time*** $\in$ **Name**, whose value ranges over $\mathbb{R}_0^+$ to represent the continuous passage of time.

2. *time* is available as a read-only variable for CRMs to import; and
3. change of *time* is always reported, i.e., $v \in \mathbf{V} \implies time \in Dom(xchange(v))$.

Note that by stipulation 1, above, the values of *time* represent the continuous passage of time. Therefore, the successive values of *time* form a non-Zeno progressive infinite sequence of real numbers in $\mathbb{R}_0^+$.

The availability of *time* provided by the environment does not mean that a CRM is required to import it, neither does it preclude the possibility of a $C \in \mathbf{CRM}$ having its own internal clock manifested as a local, shared, or exported variable *time*. Because time progresses continuously, the value of *time* changes at least as quickly as either C or the environment performs its actions.

We say that a $C \in \mathbf{CRM}$ shows an explicit sense of time in its run σ if *time* $\in C^{Rd}$. In this case, for $i \in \mathbb{N}_0$, by Eq. 15 *time* $\in M^i$ and by Eq. 16 a name-value pair $(time, t)$ exists in every observable O^i in σ. Moreover, by stipulation 1, above, the t values of the $(time, t)$ pairs in successive observables $O^i, i \in \mathbb{N}_0$ form a non-Zeno progressive sequence of real numbers in $\mathbb{R}_0^+$.

10   Related Work

We discuss related work in three areas: rewriting logic, labeled transition systems, and composable semantic models.

Rewriting Logic. Rewriting Logic (RWL) [25,26] is a logic for specifying and reasoning about concurrent and distributed systems. A system is specified by a rewrite theory (Σ, E, R) where Σ is a signature, E is a set of equations used to define functions and relations, and R is a set of rules. RWL and CRM share the feature that in both formalisms behavior is specified by rewrite rules that can be applied concurrently subject to non-conflict constraints. In RWL system states are represented by terms allowed by the signature, while CRM states are maps from variable names to values. RWL provides a means to formally specify the actions of rules, while CRM actions are mathematical functions. In both CRM and RWL the semantics of a system is based on the one step rewrite relation. In RWL this relation is determined by the rules. In CRM the relation accounts for interaction with the environment; CRM rules control only the exported and shared variables.

CRM and RWL both support expressive composition mechanisms. RWL supports a rich algebra of theories. This combined with the use of equationally defined functions to compose system states provides the ability to define many forms of interaction within a composition.

The rewrite relation has been generalized for large classes of rewrite theories to symbolic rewriting either as rewriting modulo SMT [32] or symbolic reachability (using unification rather than matching for rule application) [14,27]. Symbolic rewriting supports representation and reasoning about open systems and system interaction with the environment by rewriting terms with variables. Using symbolic reachability analysis one can often reduce an infinite state space to a finite set of state patterns.

An important aspect of modeling CPS is representing change over time. Timed rewrite theories are a special class of rewrite theories where some rules have duration [28]. This can be used to represent many forms of interactions and change over time.

Labeled Transition Systems. A number of existing formalisms have been used for modeling a system's interaction with its environment by labeling transitions, including finite automata models and process calculi The environment of a component is usually considered to be other components rather than including a physical, possibly non-computable, environment.

Automata may be non-deterministic, but they do not really address concurrency. They are composed by a product operation (that suffers blowup). The processes of process algebra are naturally concurrent and are composed using a parallel construction. In either case the mechanism of interaction is synchronizing of labels representing actions. Neither automata nor processes have explicit interfaces. The networks of communicating automata model [10] supports modeling concurrent executions. Again interactions are by synchronization of actions (also called messages).

Interface Automata [1], abstract from details of how the behavior of a component is generated to focus on observable behavior. The interface automata formalism specifies the temporal order of input and output actions of a component as well as its local events. Interface automata accept only some behaviors generated by the environment and specify a component's behavior only under these inputs. The composition of two interfaces is achieved by synchronizing their shared output and input actions. Two components are said to be composable if they satisfy some conditions on action names, and there is an environment in which the product has non-empty behavior. A notion of adapter for interface automata is proposed in [11] Adapters provide a mechanism to express simple interactions beyond basic synchronization. In contrast, a CRM specifies behavior under arbitrary environment conditions.

IO automata [24] model asynchronous concurrent systems. In contrast to interface automata, an IO automata is required to accept input actions at any time. The semantics includes only fair executions. Two or more IO automata component models can be composed under certain conditions. In the composite automata, actions with the same label must happen together. Component automata may operate at arbitrary relative speeds.

Proposed in 1997 as a formal model for synchronous groupware, Team Automata [15, 34] extend IO automata by removing some of the restrictions on how actions compose. Formally, a team automaton consists of a synchronous product of an underlying set of its component automata. These component automata act as a conceptually identifiable team with some shared context and goals. Acting together, the component automata in a team automaton collaborate and cooperate through joint actions. A team automaton is a synchronous model wherein every one of its automata either participates in one instantaneous action, or it remains idle. The precise manner in which component actions synchronize in team automata to form a joint action is determined by a *synchronization type* assigned to each action, which specifies the range of the number of participating actions.

Constraint Automata (CA) [9] were introduced as an operational semantics for the coordination language Reo. Reo [3–6] is an exogenous coordination language in which interaction protocols are built compositionally out of a set of (user defined) primitive protocols. CA were primarily intended to express the semantics of Reo composite protocols (called circuits) for the purpose of formal verification through model checking [8, 18]. Composition of constraint automata allows both synchronous and asynchronous composition of actions. It uses a strict notion of synchronization that while simpler than synchronization in team automata (by eliminating the need for synchronization types), supports the same expressive power through additional asynchronous components. Moreover, in contrast to team automata (as well as many other automata models), constraint automata support consideration and manipulation of data in specification of the behavior of a system.

Various automata models have been extended to represent time. The monograph *The Theory of Timed I/O Automata* [17] describes the extension of I/O automata to model timed executions. This model allows components to operate on different time scales. Timed constraint automata were introduced for verification of timed interaction protocols specified as timed Reo connector circuits [2, 19].

Labeled transition systems are abstract models with limited means to express the structure of state. Formal verification of a component is done by fixing its environment, which often means other components. CRM models are designed to be executed either concretely or symbolically. A concrete execution represents a behavior of a CRM running in a specific environment. A symbolic execution represents a behavior of a CRM running in any environment whose variables satisfy a set of constraints, that may also involve CRM component parameters.

Time is an essential part of hybrid systems models as physical components model change over time for given input parameters. Formalisms based on hybrid systems such as Differential Logic and hybrid programs model physical behavior of components and the interaction with controllers. [29] A composition algebra for hybrid programs is presented in [22, 23]. Here interaction between components is based on shared variables and analysis is done by fixing a specific environment.

Composable Semantics. The CRM interaction model is inspired by the work on composable semantics for Cyber-Physical System components [20, 21], where component behaviors are expressed as traces consisting of sequences of observations, hiding internal details of cyber and physical processes. A composition operation parameterized by interaction relations is defined. Using interaction relations, diverse interaction mechanisms including forms of synchronization and mutual exclusion can be expressed. Conditions for algebraic properties of composition such as associativity and commutativity are identified. CRM semantics can be mapped to this semantic model and many important interaction relations can be realized by CRM coordination components.

11   Conclusions and Future Work

In this paper we presented the Concurrent Rules Machine (CRM), a model of concurrent (and distributed) computation with explicit representation of interaction of a system with its environment. We defined CRM structure and execution semantics. An algebra of operations on CRMs is defined including different notions of composition (product), hiding, and *division* and key properties of these operations are given. As one intended application of CRMs is modular specification of cyber-physical systems, representation of time is also discussed. The concepts and operations are illustrated by a water tank system example with components representing the water level sensor and the control of input and output flows.

This first step provides the mathematical foundation. Future work includes implementation of a class of CRMs in the Maude rewriting logic system. This will allow modeling and reasoning about complex systems in the context of different environment constraints. The algebra of CRMs can be implemented using Maude's module algebra and reflection. In addition we plan to develop a language for specifying interactive composition in terms of component interfaces. This will simplify developing complete systems and support compositional reasoning. Of course of great interest is developing real world case studies.

References

1. Alfaro, L., Henzinger, T.A.: Interface automata, pp. 109–120 (2001)
2. Arbab, F., Baier, C., Boer, F.C., Rutten, J.J.M.M.: Models and temporal logics for timed component connectors. In: Proceedings of the International Conference on Software Engineering and Formal Methods (SEFM'04), pp. 198–207. IEEE Society Press (2004)
3. Arbab, F.: Reo: a channel-based coordination model for component composition. Math. Struct. Comput. Sci. **14**(3), 329–366 (2004)
4. Arbab, F.: Puff, the magic protocol. In: Agha, G., Danvy, O., Meseguer, J. (eds.) Formal Modeling: Actors, Open Systems, Biological Systems. LNCS, vol. 7000, pp. 169–206. Springer, Heidelberg (2011). https://doi.org/10.1007/978-3-642-24933-4_9
5. Arbab, F.: Proper Protocol, pp. 65–87. Springer, Cham (2016)
6. Arbab, F., Mavaddat, F.: Coordination through channel composition. In: Arbab, F., Talcott, C. (eds.) COORDINATION 2002. LNCS, vol. 2315, pp. 22–39. Springer, Heidelberg (2002). https://doi.org/10.1007/3-540-46000-4_6
7. Babin, G., Ameur, Y.A., Singh, N.K., Pantel, M.: A system substitution mechanism for hybrid systems in Event-B, pp. 106–121 (2016)
8. Baier, C., Blechmann, T., Klein, J., Klüppelholz, S., Leister, W.: Design and verification of systems with exogenous coordination using vereofy. In: Margaria, T., Steffen, B. (eds.) ISoLA 2010. LNCS, vol. 6416, pp. 97–111. Springer, Heidelberg (2010). https://doi.org/10.1007/978-3-642-16561-0_15
9. Baier, C., Sirjani, M., Arbab, F., Rutten, J.: Modeling component connectors in Reo by constraint automata. Sci. Comput. Program. **61**(2), 75–113 (2006)
10. Bowman, H., Gomez, R.: Concurrency Theory: Calculi and Automata for Modelling Untimed and Timed Concurrent Systems. Springer-Verlag, London (2006)
11. Chouali, S., Mouelhi, S., Mountassir, H.: Adapting component behaviours using interface automata. In: 36th Euromicro Conference on Software Engineering and Advanced Applications (2010)
12. Clavel, M., et al.: All About Maude - A High-Performance Logical Framework. LNCS, vol. 4350. Springer, Heidelberg (2007). https://doi.org/10.1007/978-3-540-71999-1
13. Dupont, G., Ameur, Y.A., Singh, N.K., Pantel, M.: Event-B hybridation: a proof and refinement-based framework for modelling hybrid systems. ACM Trans. Embed. Comput. Syst. **20**(4), 35:1–35:37 (2021)
14. Durán, F., et al.: Equational unification and matching, and symbolic reachability analysis in maude 3.2 (system description). In: Blanchette, J., Kovács, L., Pattinson, D. (eds.) Automated Reasoning - 11th International Joint Conference, IJCAR 2022, Haifa, Israel, 8–10 August 2022, Proceedings, vol. 13385 of Lecture Notes in Computer Science, pp. 529–540. Springer, Heidleberg (2022)

15. Ellis, C.A.: Team automata for groupware systems. In: Proceedings of GROUP'97, International Conference on Supporting Group Work: The Integration Challenge, Embassy Suites Hotel, Phoenix, Arizona, USA, 16–19 November 1997, pp. 415–424. ACM (1997)

16. Hopcroft, J.E., Ullman, J.D.: Introduction to Automata Theory, Languages, and Computation. Addison-Wesley Publishing Company, Noston (1979)

17. Kaynar, D.K., Lynch, N., Segala, R., Vaandrager, F.: The Theory of Timed I/O Automata. Synthesis Lectures on Distributed Computing, 2 edn. Springer, Heidelberg (2011)

18. Klüppelholz, S., Baier, C.: Symbolic model checking for channel-based component connectors. Sci. Comput. Program. **74**(9), 688–701 (2009)

19. Kokash, N., Jaghoori, M.M., Arbab, F.: From timed Reo networks to networks of timed automata. Electron. Notes Theor. Comput. Sci. **295**, 11–29 (2013)

20. Lion, B., Arbab, F., Talcott, C.: A semantic model for interacting cyber-physical systems. In: Workshop on Interaction and Concurrency Experience, EPTCS (2021)

21. Lion, B., Arbab, F., Talcott, C.L.: A semantic model for interacting cyber-physical systems. CoRR arxiv:2106.15661 (2021)

22. Lunel, S., Boyer, B., Talpin, J.P.: Compositional proofs in differential dynamic logic dl. In: 2017 17th International Conference on Application of Concurrency to System Design (ACSD), pp. 19–28 (2017)

23. Lunel, S., Mitsch, S., Boyer, B., Talpin, J.-P.: Parallel composition and modular verification of computer controlled systems in differential dynamic logic. In: ter Beek, M.H., McIver, A., Oliveira, J.N. (eds.) FM 2019. LNCS, vol. 11800, pp. 354–370. Springer, Cham (2019). https://doi.org/10.1007/978-3-030-30942-8_22

24. Lynch, N.A., Tuttle, M.R.: An introduction to input/output automata. In: CWI-Quarterly, pp. 219–246 (1989)

25. Meseguer, J.: Conditional Rewriting Logic as a unified model of concurrency. Theor. Comput. Sci. **96**(1), 73–155 (1992)

26. Meseguer, J.: Twenty years of rewriting logic. J. Log. Algebraic Methods Program. **81**(7–8), 721–781 (2012)

27. Meseguer, J.: Generalized rewrite theories, coherence completion, and symbolic methods. J. Log. Algebraic Methods Program. **110** (2020)

28. Ölveczky, P.C., Meseguer, J.: Semantics and pragmatics of Real-Time Maude. Higher-Order Symb. Comput. **20**(1–2), 161–196 (2007)

29. Platzer, A.: Differential dynamic logic for hybrid systems. J. Autom. Reason., 143–189 (2008)

30. Quesel, J.-D., Mitsch, S., Loos, S., Aréchiga, N., Platzer, A.: How to model and prove hybrid systems with KeYmaera: a tutorial on safety. Int. J. Softw. Tools Technol. Transfer **18**, 67–91 (2016)

31. Rocha, C., Meseguer, J., Muñoz, C.: Rewriting modulo SMT and open system analysis. In: Escobar, S. (ed.) WRLA 2014. LNCS, vol. 8663, pp. 247–262. Springer, Cham (2014). https://doi.org/10.1007/978-3-319-12904-4_14

32. Rocha, C., Meseguer, J., Muñoz, C.A.: Rewriting modulo SMT and open system analysis. J. Log. Algebraic Methods Program. **86**(1), 269–297 (2017)

33. The KeYmaera X team. KeYmaera X: An aXiomatic tactical theorem prover for hybrid systems (2022). Accessed 22 Sept 2022

34. ter Beek, M.H., Hennicker, R., Proença, J.: Team automata: overview and roadmap. In: Castellani, I., Tiezzi, F. (eds.) Coordination Models and Languages, pp. 161–198. Springer, Cham (2024)

Verifying ROS-Based Applications Using Timed and Stochastic Timed Automata

Peter Backeman[✉] and Cristina Seceleanu

Mälardalen University, Västerås, Sweden
{peter.backeman,cristina.seceleanu}@mdu.se

Abstract. Robotic systems often operate under real-time constraints, requiring timely responses to sensor inputs. Early consideration of such requirements during design is advantageous. The Robot Operating System (ROS) provides a mature framework for system setup and communication, with ROS 2 offering real-time capabilities. However, determining the maximum reaction time within a ROS-based application is intricate due to complex variable processing and scheduling, especially with periodic and event-triggered tasks. In this paper, we propose a model of ROS-based designs with timed automata semantics, facilitating exhaustive real-time model checking of system behavior. We extend this model to stochastic timed automata, thus incorporating non-deterministic execution time and probabilistic loads, employing statistical model checking for scalability and accuracy. We compare against previous work to confirm the validity of our approach, and show its applicability on a real-world robotic system example.

1 Introduction

This paper is dedicated to Professor Marjan Sirjani, to honor her impactful contributions to the field of formal methods, which have advanced the reliability and correctness of complex systems profoundly, including robotic systems. Marjan's work embodies a vision where robotic systems not only meet functional requirements, but also achieve high standards of dependability, addressing the nuanced interplay of concurrency, real-time constraints, and emergent behaviors [19].

According to this vision, we also consider robotic systems to be subject to real-time constraints that should be obeyed, for example, a system might be required to react to a certain sensor input within a time bound (e.g., door opening when the light sensor is activated). Ensuring such requirements already at early design stages is beneficial and can be done through formal methods. Model checking is an approach that can help establish both liveness and safety properties subject to timing constraints, by employing timed automata as the modeling formalism [4]. When designing a robotic system there are many aspects to take into consideration, e.g., computation and communication issues must be decided upon and addressed. To address this, one can use a pre-existing solution that already solves many challenges; the Robot Operating System (ROS) provides such a framework for setting up nodes and their communication. However,

E. A. Lee et al. (Eds.): Marjan Sirjani Festschrift, LNCS 15560, pp. 295–325, 2025.
https://doi.org/10.1007/978-3-031-85134-6_13

establishing properties of a ROS-based application, e.g., finding an upper bound for the maximum reaction time, is complex as it is affected by the run-time of the involved tasks, respectively, and how the latter are scheduled.

Previous work has helped to establish bounds on reaction times in ROS, through simulation [18]. However, such an approach is hard to extend with non-deterministic behavior, as it is based on simulating one scenario at a time. For example, while task run-time is usually limited by a worst-case execution time (WCET), in practice a task can finish early (and tasks finishing earlier than their WCET can counter-intuitively result in a longer reaction time). Using a model-checking approach, it is possible to investigate multiple traces simultaneously (i.e., corresponding to different task execution times), thus enabling efficient checking of properties in non-deterministic systems. With this in mind, we address the following research question: *How can model checking help analyze end-to-end reaction times in ROS-based applications with non-deterministic properties?*

In this paper, we present a model of ROS-based designs and assign semantics to allow model checking with respect to real-time behavior to help establish such properties, in particular on end-to-end reaction time bounds. We assign semantics in the form of *timed automata* (TA) [2] templates, yielding a precise definition of the underlying behavior of ROS scheduling. We begin with basic semantics and validate it against previous work [18], after which we extend the semantics with non-deterministic execution times and probabilistic loads. For scalability and richness of modeling purposes, we employ the *statistical model checking* (SMC) [13] technique, where properties are guaranteed to a specific degree of confidence. We model and check systems in this paper via the UPPAAL SMC [12] tool. In sum, we present the following contributions:

- Introduction of a pattern-based TA semantics of ROS designs, covering both deterministic and probabilistic running times and loads.
- Validation of our base semantics against previous simulation-based work that uses analytic real-time scheduling theory.
- Application of UPPAAL/UPPAAL SMC to find maximum reaction times in an industrial example, demonstrating the approach.[1]

The paper is structured as follows: after the preliminaries in Sect. 2, we present our formalization of ROS-based application behavior in Sect. 3, followed by our TA semantics in Sect. 4 and its validation in Sect. 5. Afterwards, we extend the semantics in several directions in Sect. 6, and demonstrate with an industrial example in Sect. 7. Finally, related work and comparison to our approach are presented in Sect. 8, and our conclusions in Sect. 9.

2   Preliminaries

In this section, we briefly present scheduling of, and communication between, tasks in the robot operating system and summarize timed automata and UPPAAL as used in this work.

---

[1] Source code is available at: https://github.com/ptrbman/ros2-modeling/.

2.1   Robot Operating System

The Robot Operating System (ROS) is intended to provide developers with a set of open-source software frameworks, libraries, and tools to create applications for robots. The platform offers services for a heterogeneous computer cluster, such as hardware abstraction, device control, implementation of functionalities, message-passing between processes, and package management [16]. The operating system's version ROS 1 underwent a major revision and became ROS 2 [15], bringing many improvements, most notably the Data Distribution Service (DDS) support. DDS acts as middleware for inter-node communication, using the quality-of-service profile to provide real-time communication, scalability, performance enhancement, and security benefits not found native in ROS 1.

The ROS 2 platform has already been used in designing the communication architecture of collaborative and intelligent automation systems [10], or of self-driving cars that require safe and reliable real-time behavior [17]. Most such robotic systems are subject to real-time constraints that, if not met, might result in issues of various severity degrees, from the application failing to perform correctly to a lowered performance of the overall system. Verifying if such undesired issues occur in a ROS-based robotic system, already at a design level, is very desirable. To achieve this, the basic, high-level communication and computation paradigms of ROS need to be given formal semantics, to be amenable to analysis, e.g., via model checking. In this paper, we consider a ROS architecture to consist of *nodes* and *topics*. Communication is done through two paradigms, publish/subscribe and local variables. Whenever a node wishes to communicate data, it can *publish* it onto a topic, or *write* it to a local variable. A node can read data either through *receiving* it from a *subscribed* topic, or *reading* it from a local variable.

Scheduling. A node is a component that has one or more *tasks* (i.e., callbacks) that can be scheduled for execution. When a task is scheduled, a *job* is instantiated and added to the scheduling queue. When a job has finished, it can *publish* its value to a topic, or store it locally on the node. The ROS scheduling works as follows: at each *polling point*, i.e., beginning of a *processing window*, it picks one job from each task (which has queued job) and schedules them according to priority (with timers always having higher priority than subscribers). Next, each of the tasks are executed in order, and afterwards a new polling point is reached. If at any polling point, there are no jobs queued, then the scheduler idles until a task becomes scheduled. The process is illustrated in Fig. 1. In this paper we consider a ROS system with only one host, that is, all nodes are processed on the same CPU.

Reaction Time. In this paper, we are interested in the reaction time of a ROS application. By this, we mean the time that passes between a job (e.g., corresponding to a sensor read) being released (i.e., when the job is instantiated) and the reaction of the system's actuator (i.e., when the actuator job is executed).

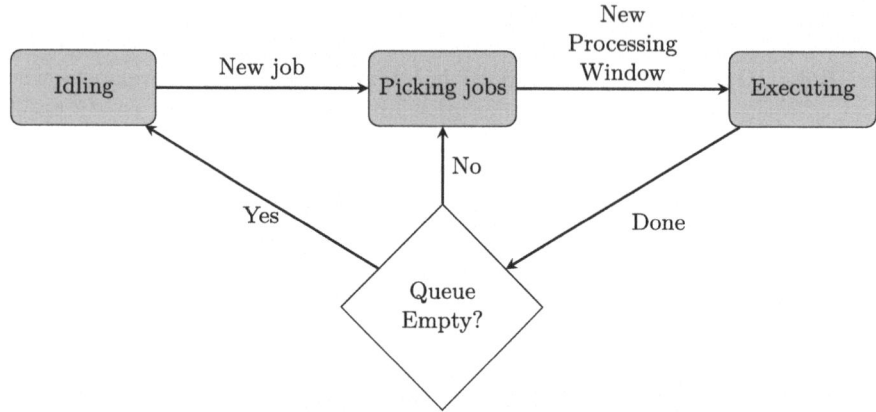

Fig. 1. Scheduler in ROS.

We wish to establish an upper bound, that is, to find the maximum reaction time from a particular sensor being able to observe some data, until the actuator finishes executing, according to the scheduling policy described above.

2.2 Timed Automata and UPPAAL

Formal Syntax. A Timed Automaton (TA), as used in the model-checker UPPAAL [12], is defined as a tuple, $\langle L, l_0, C, A, V, E, I \rangle$, where L is the set of finite locations, l_0 is the initial location, V is the set of data variables, C is the set of *clocks*, $A = \Sigma \cup \tau$ is the set of *actions*, where Σ is the finite set of *synchronizing actions* ($c!$ denotes the send action, and $c?$ the receiving action) partitioned into inputs and outputs, $\Sigma = \Sigma_i \cup \Sigma_o$, and $\tau \notin \Sigma$ denotes internal or empty actions without synchronization, $E \subseteq L \times B(C, V) \times A \times 2^C \times L$ is the set of *edges*, where $B(C, V)$ is the set of *guards* over C and V, that is, conjunctive formulas of clock constraints $(B(C))$, of the form $x \bowtie n$ or $x - y \bowtie n$, where $x, y \in C$, $n \in \mathbb{N}$, $\bowtie \in \{<, \leq, =, \geq, >\}$, and non-clock constraints over V $(B(V))$, and $I : L \longrightarrow B_{dc}(C)$ is a function that assigns *invariants* to locations, where $B_{dc}(C) \subseteq B(C)$ is the set of downward-closed clock constraints with $\bowtie \in \{<, \leq, =\}$.

Invariants bound the time that can be spent in locations, ensuring the progress of TA's execution. An edge from location l to location l' is denoted by $l \xrightarrow{a,g,r,u} l'$, where a is an action, g is the guard of the edge, r is the clock reset set, that is, the clocks that are set to 0 over the edge, and u is a data variable update action. Initially, all clocks are set to 0, and the update action assigns 0 to one or more variables. A location can be marked as *urgent* or *committed*, indicating that time cannot progress in such locations. The latter is more restrictive, indicating that the next edge to be traversed needs to start from a *committed* location.

Example. For illustration purposes, in Fig. 2, we show a simple TA model of a lamp 2(a), and its user 2(b). The lamp has three locations: off, low, and bright. If the user presses a button, modeled by the synchronization variable press!, then the lamp is turned on, that is, the lamp TA synchronizes with the user TA via press?, and changes location from off to low. If the user presses the button again, the lamp is turned off, and the lamp TA moves back to location off. However, if the user is fast and presses the button twice, rapidly, the lamp is turned on and becomes bright, modeled by the lamp TA moving to location bright. The user can press the button arbitrarily at any time or not press the button at all. The clock y of the lamp is used to detect if the user is fast, via the guard $(y < 5)$ over the edge between locations low and bright, or slow, via the guard $(y >= 5)$ over the edge between locations low and off.

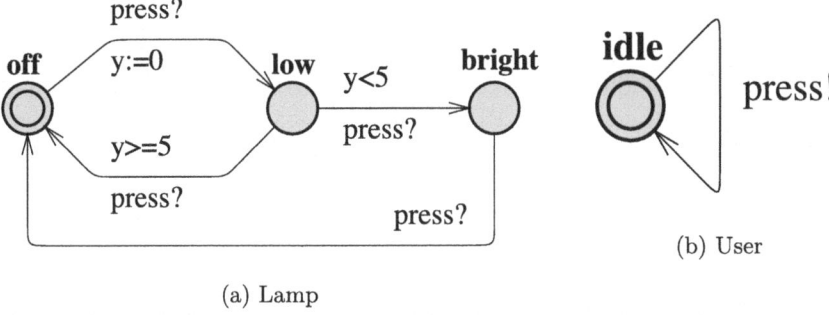

(a) Lamp

(b) User

Fig. 2. A Simple TA model of a lamp and its user

Operational Semantics. The semantics of TA [5] is defined as a *labeled transition system*. The states of the labeled transition system are pairs (l, u), where $l \in L$ is the current location, and u is the clock valuation in location l. The initial state is denoted by (l_0, u_0), where all clocks are initialized to 0: $\forall x \in C, u_0(x) = 0$. Let $u \vDash g$ denote the clock value u that satisfies guard g. We use $u + d$ to denote the time elapse where all the clock values have increased by d, for $d \in \mathbb{R}_{\geq 0}$. There are two kinds of transitions:

(i) *Delay transitions:* $< l, u > \xrightarrow{d} < l, u + d >$ if $u \vDash I(l)$ and $(u + d') \vDash I(l)$, for $0 \leq d' \leq d$, and

(ii) *Action transitions:* $< l, u > \xrightarrow{a} < l', u' >$ if $l \xrightarrow{g,a,r} l', a \in \Sigma, u \vDash g$, clock valuation u' in the target state (l', u') is derived from u by resetting all clocks in the reset set r of the edge, such that $u' \vDash I(l')$.

A real-time system can be modeled as a *network of TA* (NTA) composed via the parallel composition operator ("||"), which allows an individual automaton to carry out internal actions, while pairs of automata can perform handshake synchronization. The locations of all automata, together with the clock valuations, define the state of an NTA. The requirements (queries in UPPAAL) to be verified by model checking on the resulting NTA are specified in a decidable subset of (Timed) Computation Tree Logic ((T)CTL), and checked by the UPPAAL model checker. In this paper, we verify (T)CTL queries of the following kinds (p is a state property):

- **Reachability:** $E \lozenge p$ - The requirement evaluates to true if there exists a path where p eventually holds.
- **Invariance:** $A \square p$ - The requirement evaluates to true if (and only if) every reachable state satisfies p, in other words, for all paths p always holds.

UPPAAL is also capable of handling *statistical model checking* (SMC) [13], where simulations are used to extract information of the system. In UPPAAL SMC, automata have a stochastic interpretation based on: (i) the probabilistic choices between multiple enabled transitions (uniform distribution by default, marked with weighted probabilities otherwise[2]), and (ii) the non-deterministic time delays that can be refined based on probability distributions, either uniform distributions for time-bounded delays, or user-defined exponential distributions for unbounded delays. SMC has the downside of not providing full guarantees of results, but allows handling models of much larger sizes, as well as including probabilistic aspects of the system. UPPAAL SMC uses a probabilistic extension of *weighted metric temporal logic* (WMTL) [6] to provide qualitative analysis, that is, *hypothesis testing*, and *probability comparison*, as well as quantitative analysis, by *probability evaluation*: calculate the probability $Pr[<= bound](\star_{x \leq C} \phi)$ to reach a state ϕ within time cost $x \leq C$ for some network of stochastic timed automata, where $\star$ stands for either *future* ($\lozenge$) or *globally* ($\square$) temporal operator, and $[<= bound]$ denotes the time bound of the executions. In this paper, we focus on probability evaluation only.

3   Formalization of ROS-Based Systems

In this section, we provide a formalization of constrained ROS-based systems. In this work, we model communication via publish/subscribe for inter-node communication and read/write for intra/node communication and the scheduling of tasks on nodes. We assume that each node can be *subscribed* to zero or more nodes, *read* from zero or one variable, *publish* to zero or one topic, and *write* to zero or one variable. We define three kinds of nodes: timer nodes, subscription nodes and data-generator nodes. A *timer node* is triggered at periodic intervals and then schedules a task to publish or write its result. A *subscription node* has a special *triggering subscription*, and schedules a task to publish or write its result whenever data is published onto the triggering topic. Finally, a *data-generator* node is a timer node that has no subscriptions or reads from any variable. For simplicity, we assume that there is only one publishing node per topic.

---

[2] We annotate edge guards with ?*prob* to denote that the edge weight is *prob*.

3.1   Nodes

We define a set of nodes $\mathcal{N}$, a set of topics $\mathcal{T}$ and a set of global variables $\mathcal{V}$. The set of global variables includes a special variable, pd, which is the most recently published data. We define each kind of node separately, as follows.

Definition 1. *A* timer node *is defined as: $tn = TMR(p, d, wcet, S, St, t, rv, wv)$, where:*

- $p \in \mathbb{N}^+$ *is the period,*
- $d \in \mathbb{N}$ *is the delay,*
- $wcet \in \mathbb{N}$ *is the WCET of the main task,*
- $S = \{s_1, \ldots, s_n\}, s_i \in \mathcal{T}$, *are the non-triggering subscribed topics,*
- $St = \{st_1, \ldots, st_n\}, st_i \in \mathbb{N}$, *are the WCET of subscription tasks,*
- $t \in \mathcal{T}$ *is the result-topic,*
- $rv \in \mathcal{V}$, *is the read-variable,*
- $wv \in \mathcal{V}$ *is the write-variable.*

Intuitively, a timer node is activated each p period, with the first activation after a delay of d, (i.e., the second activation is at $p + d$, third at $2p + d$, etc.), creating a job of the main task. The node subscribes to the topics S and uses the data from the variable rv. Whenever a message is received on topic s_i, a job is created to process the retrieved value, with WCET st_i, writing its result to variable $\mathcal{V}(tn^i)$.

Definition 2. *A* subscriber node *is defined as: $sn = SUB(s, wcet, S, St, t, rv, wv)$, where:*

- $s \in \mathcal{T}, s \notin S$, *is the triggering topic,*
- $wcet \in \mathbb{N}$ *is the WCET of the main task,*
- $S = \{s_1, \ldots, s_n\}, s_i \in \mathcal{T}$, *are the non-triggering subscribed topics,*
- $St = \{st_1, \ldots, st_n\}, st_i \in \mathbb{N}$, *are the WCET of subscriptions tasks,*
- $t \in \mathcal{T}$ *is the result-topic,*
- $rv \in \mathcal{V}$, *is the read-variable,*
- $wv \in \mathcal{V}$ *is the write-variable.*

A subscriber node works like a timer node, except that it is triggered whenever a message is published on the triggering topic s, instead.

Definition 3. *A* data-generator node *is defined as: $dn = DGEN(p, d, wcet, t, wv)$, where:*

- $p \in \mathbb{N}$, *is the period,*
- $d \in \mathbb{N}$ *is the delay,*
- $wcet \in \mathbb{N}$ *is the WCET of the main task,*
- $t \in \mathcal{T}$ *is the result-topic,*
- $wv \in \mathcal{V}$ *is the write-variable.*

A data-generator works as a timer except that it has no subscriptions or read-variable.

Example 1. Consider the small system in Fig. 3 with four nodes. One sensor node publishes data to a filter node, which in turn publishes data to the actuator node. There is also an additional sensor node that publishes directly to the actuator. We are interested in measuring the reaction time from the second sensor node to the actuator, that is, to monitor data published by the second sensor and measure the time until it is processed by the actuator. Each component can be formalized (for particular values of WCET, etc.) as:

- first sensor, a data-generator node:
  $s_1 = DGEN(200, 0, 50, \mathcal{T}(s_1), \mathcal{V}(s_1))$,
- second sensor, a data-generator node:
  $s_2 = DGEN(200, 50, 30, \mathcal{T}(s_2), \mathcal{V}(s_2))$,
- filter, a subscriber node:
  $f = SUB(\mathcal{T}(s_1), 30, \emptyset, \emptyset, \mathcal{T}(f), pd, \mathcal{V}(f))$,
- actuator, a subscriber node:
  $a = SUB(\mathcal{T}(f), 10, \{\mathcal{T}(s_2)\}, \{10\}, \mathcal{T}(a), \mathcal{V}(a^1), \mathcal{V}(a))$.

Note that the read-variable for the actuator is $\mathcal{V}(a^1)$, indicating that the value to be used in published data is equal to the value retrieved from the subscription to the second sensor.

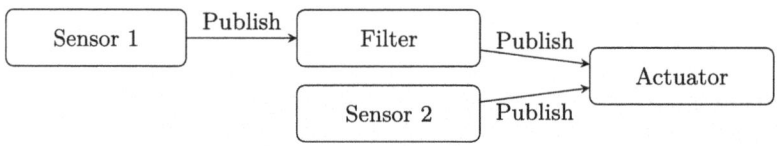

Fig. 3. Small ROS network

3.2   Tasks

Each node contains one or more tasks. All nodes have a *main task* that is responsible for combining all data, compute and publish/write the output. Additionally, every node has for each non-triggering subscription a task responsible for retrieving the published data, process it, and store it in a local variable. All tasks have an assigned WCET. Let τ_n denote the main task of node n and τ_n^i to refer to the subscription task for subscribed topic s_i of node n. For convenience, we introduce a unique topic and variable for each task τ denoted by $\mathcal{T}(\tau)$ and $\mathcal{V}(\tau)$, respectively.

Example 2. The system presented in the previous example contains four nodes. The sensors and filter nodes contain only one main task each: τ_{s_1}, τ_{s_2} triggered by timers and τ_f triggered by a subscription. The actuator node has one main task τ_a triggered by the filter node, and one subscription task τ_a^1 triggered by the second sensor node.

3.3 Job Chains

To define the notion of reaction time precisely, we first present the notion of task chain, and (forward) job chains, respectively.

Definition 4. *A task chain* $\mathfrak{T} = \{\tau_1, \ldots, \tau_n\}$ *is a sequence of tasks such that:*

- *the task τ_1 is the main task of a data-generator, and*
- $\forall \tau_i \in [\tau_1, \ldots, \tau_{n-1}]$ *either:*
  - τ_i *stores its result in* $\mathcal{V}(\tau_i)$ *and* τ_{i+1} *reads from* $\mathcal{V}(\tau_i)$*, or*
  - τ_i *publishes its result to* $\mathcal{T}(\tau_i)$ *and* τ_{i+1} *subscribes to* $\mathcal{T}(\tau_i)$*.*

Definition 5. *A (forward) job chain* $J = \{j_1, \ldots j_n\}$ *is a sequence of jobs such that for a task chain* $\mathfrak{T}$*:*

- $\forall j_i \in J, j_i$ *is an instance of* τ_i*.*
- $\forall i \in [j_1, \ldots, j_{n-1}]$ *either:*
  - j_{i+1} *is the unique earliest job of* τ_{i+1} *that reads the result from* j_i*, or*
  - j_{i+1} *is the unique earliest job of* τ_{i+1} *that receives the result from* j_i *(through subscription).*

Let $release(\tau)$ and $end(\tau)$ represent the release-time and end-time of the task τ, respectively, where $release(\tau), end(\tau) \in \mathbb{N}$.

Definition 6. *For a job chain* $J = \{j_1, \ldots, j_n\}$*, the* reaction time $rt(J) = end(j_n) - release(j_1)$*.*

Example 3. Consider again the small example network in Fig. 3, now executed (according to semantics in next section) with scheduling as presented in Sect. 2.1. The resulting trace is shown in Fig. 4. The job chain $J = \{\tau_{s_2}, \tau_a^1,, \tau_a\}$ has a reaction time of 80.

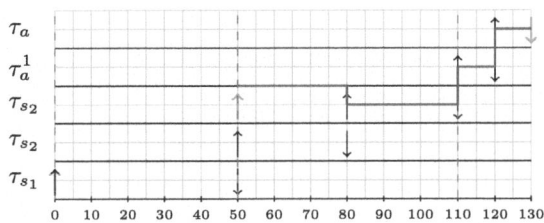

Fig. 4. Schedule for small ROS network example. Processing windows are separated by red dashed lines. An orange upwards arrow indicates the release of a job, a black upwards arrow the start of a job, and downwards indicates the end of a job. The blue line traces the reaction time. (Color figure online)

In this paper, we focus on the case where there is only one host (i.e., executor), on which all functions are executed, and we further assume that there are no cycles in the dependencies between nodes. Then we can define the maximum reaction time for a given ROS system:

Definition 7. *We define the* maximum reaction time *for a task-chain* $\mathfrak{T}$ *as* $max_{j \in J}(rt(j))$, *where* J *is the set of all job-chain instances of* $\mathfrak{T}$.

We acknowledge that for an over-utilized system, no finite maximum reaction time may exist, but for a non-over-utilized system, the maximum reaction time will be finite.

4 TA Semantics for ROS

In this section, we present a formalization of ROS semantics in UPPAAL timed automata. As we focus on analyzing the *end-to-end maximum reaction time*, we do not model how data is processed, but rather the age of data. In particular, we instantiate with a particular task chain $\mathfrak{T}$ in mind, such that the resulting system considers the reaction time of $\mathfrak{T}$. We introduce TA templates that are instantiated depending on the nodes of the ROS application, and the task chain that should be monitored. We begin by introducing the global variables and functions used, followed by each TA template. Finally, we describe how a particular system is instantiated. For simplicity, we assume that each task always publishes to its dedicated topic, and writes to its dedicated variable.

4.1 Constants, Variables, Functions and Channels

Table 1 shows a set of constants, variables, functions and channels. Some constants are used for easier reading, while some have a semantic impact. In particular, BUF_SIZE and MONITORS must be set sufficiently large. In the remainder of this paper we assume that this is the case. Note that PRIO[C], WCET[C] must also be initialized with proper values.

4.2 TA Templates

The semantics are given as template-based instantiation, i.e.,. for each node in the ROS system, we introduce an UPPAAL TA, based on the templates given in this section. Furthermore, each TA is given a unique ID. Since we are interested only in the reaction time of data processed in the task chain $\mathfrak{T}$ under analysis, we can ignore all other data values (however me must remember to trigger subscription tasks). Thus, every task only needs to consider the received or read values from the previous task of the task chain.

Subscriber. A subscriber, $sn = SUB(s, wcet, S, St, t, rv, wv)$, is represented by an instantiated Subscriber TA template using three parameters: *task_id*, *s* and *data_source*. A suitable *task_id* is chosen, and while the triggering subscription *s* is initialized to the counter-part in *sn*, the *data_source* is set to *rv*. The subscriber waits for a message to be published to *s* and then queues a job to publish the result, based on data from *data_source*, to the *task_id* topic (as we assume each task publishes to its own topic). The template is shown in Fig. 5.

Table 1. Constants, variables, functions and channels of the model

Constant	Description
EMPTY	Value for representing empty data
MONITORS	Number of parallel monitors
FIRST_PAYLOAD	Represents the value of the first monitored package
MIN_PAYLOAD	Minimum value of payloads (to reduce state space)
MONITOR_FREE/MONITOR_SENT	Status value of a free/busy monitor
BUF_SIZE	Buffer size of queues
PRIO[C]	Priority of each task
WCET[C]	WCET of each task
deterministic_host	If true, jobs always takes *wcet* to execute

Variables	Description
PAYLOAD	value of next payload value to be sent
LAST_PAYLOAD	value of last sent payload
next_monitor (*nm*)	Index of next free monitor
last_monitor (*lm*)	Index of oldest busy monitor
published_data (*pd*)	Value of last published data
monitor_status[MONITORS]	Status of monitors
monitor_payload[MONITORS]	Payload monitored
QUEUES[C][BUF_SIZE]	Job queues (one for each task)
QUEUES_COUNT[C]	Number of jobs in each queue
JOBS[C][2]	ID and data of scheduled jobs
JOBS_COUNT	Number of scheduled jobs
DATA[C]	Unique variable for each task

Function	Description
waiting_jobs	Returns the number of jobs waiting for the host
queue_job	Add a job to the host queue
dequeue	Dequeue the first job from the host queue
schedule	Sort all jobs in the host waiting list by priority
take_jobs	Take (up to) one job of each task
next_job_idx	Get the index (i.e., task id) of next job
get_data	Get data for a specific task
relevant_payload	True if just published data is monitored
assign_monitor	Assign next free monitor to current package
free_monitor	Free all finished monitors

Channel	Description
new_job	Announce the (possible) scheduling of new job
start_monitor	Signal to start monitoring next data
publish[C]	Unique topic for each task

$$L = \{l\}, \quad \ell_0 = l, \quad C = \emptyset, A = \{s^?\}, V = \{v_{published\_data}\}, I = \emptyset,$$

$$E = \{l \xrightarrow{s^?, \emptyset, \emptyset, queue\_job(id, v_{data\_source})} l\}$$

Fig. 5. Template of a Subscriber

Moreover, for each subscribed topic $s_i \in S$, the Subscriber TA template is additionally instantiated using a suitable $task\_id$, $s = s_i$, and $data\_source$ equal to pd.

Timer. A timer node $tn = TMR(p, d, wcet, S, St, t, rv, wv)$ is represented by an instantiated Timer TA template using four parameters: $task\_id$, p, d, and $data\_source$. A suitable $task\_id$ is chosen, and while the period p and delay d are initialized to the counter-part in tn, $data\_source$ is set to rv. The clock is initialized as $x = p - d$, to ensure that the first activation happens after d. The timer is activated each *period* p. If two or more timers are activated at the same time instant, one of them will use the active synchronization $new\_job^!$ and all others will follow using $new\_job^?$, ensuring that all jobs are added at the same time point. The template is shown in Fig. 6.

In the same vein as for the subscriber node, for each subscribed topic an additional Subscriber TA template is instantiated.

$$L = \{l\}, \quad \ell_0 = l, \quad C = \{x\}, A = \{new\_job^!, new\_job^?\},$$
$$V = \emptyset, I = \{l \mapsto x \leq p\},$$

$$E = \{l_{wait} \xrightarrow{new\_job^!, x=p, x, queue\_job(id, data\_source)} l_{wait},$$

$$l_{wait} \xrightarrow{new\_job^?, x=p, x, queue\_job(id, data\_source)} l_{wait}\}$$

Fig. 6. Template of a Timer

Data-Generator. The template for a data-generator, $dn = DGEN$ $(p, d, wcet, t, wv)$, is represented by an instantiation of the Data-Generator TA template using three parameters: $task\_id$, p, and d. A suitable $task\_id$ is chosen, and the period p and delay d are initialized to their counter-part in tn. The clock is initialized as $x = p - d$, to ensure that the first activation occurs after d. The data-generator is responsible for generating a value each *period* p, then queuing a job of type τ_{dn}. The template is shown in Fig. 7. In addition, location l_{fire} is marked committed.

Monitored Data-Generator: A monitored data-generator is identical to a data-generator with the difference that the edge from l_{fire} to l_{wait} is replaced by:

$$l_{fire} \xrightarrow{start\_monitor^!, \emptyset, x, queue\_job(id, PAYLOAD)} l_{wait}$$

$$L = \{l_{wait}, l_{fire}\}, \quad \ell_0 = l_{wait}, \quad C = \{x\}, A = \{new\_job^!, new\_job^?\},$$
$$V = \emptyset, \quad I = \{l_{wait} \mapsto x \leq p\},$$
$$E = \{l_{wait} \xrightarrow{new\_job^!, x=p, \emptyset, \emptyset} l_{fire},$$
$$l_{wait} \xrightarrow{new\_job^?, x=p, \emptyset, \emptyset} l_{fire},$$
$$l_{fire} \xrightarrow{\tau, \emptyset, x, queue\_job(id, EMPTY)} l_{wait}\}$$

Fig. 7. Template of a Data-Generator

Intuitively, this means that when a monitored data-generator publishes data, a monitor is requested to be started and a payload value is queued. The first task of the task chain $\mathfrak{T}$ should be instantiated as this.

Host. A host is the most complicated template, but has no parameters. The host awaits waiting jobs, and when the latter are present, it picks (up to) one of each task, and schedules them according to their respective priority (through the *schedule* function, called by the *take$_j$obs* function). It then simulates the execution of each job with reading, storing and publishing data accordingly. The host sends a message on the corresponding node-specific topic when it finishes executing a job with the resulting data written to the associated variable. The template is shown in Fig. 8. In addition, locations l_{check}, l_{next} and l_{done} are marked urgent, and l_{loop} is marked committed.

$$L = \{l_{idle}, l_{check}, l_{next}, l_{exec}, l_{done}, l_{loop}\}, \ell_0 = l_{idle}, C = \{x\},$$
$$A = \{new\_job^!, new\_job^?\} \cup \{\mathcal{T}(n)^! \, \forall n \in \mathcal{N})\}\}, V = \{idx, job, data\},$$
$$I = \{l_{exec} \mapsto x \leq WCET[job]\},$$
$$E = \{l_{idle} \xrightarrow{new\_job^?, \emptyset, \emptyset, \emptyset} l_{check}, l_{check} \xrightarrow{\tau, \neg waiting\_jobs(), \emptyset, \emptyset} l_{idle},$$
$$l_{check} \xrightarrow{\tau, waiting\_jobs(), \emptyset, take\_jobs()} l_{next},$$
$$l_{next} \xrightarrow{\tau, \emptyset, x, idx:=next\_job\_idx(), job:=JOBS[idx][0], data:=get\_data(JOBS[idx][1])} l_{exec},$$
$$l_{exec} \xrightarrow{\tau, deterministic\_host \wedge x=WCET[job], \emptyset, DATA[job]=data; pd=data} l_{done},$$
$$l_{exec} \xrightarrow{\tau, \neg deterministic\_host \wedge \frac{WCET[job]}{2} \leq x \leq WCET[job], \emptyset, DATA[job]=data; pd=data} l_{done},$$
$$l_{done} \xrightarrow{publish[job]^!, \emptyset, \emptyset, \emptyset} l_{loop}, l_{loop} \xrightarrow{\tau, JOBS\_COUNT>0, \emptyset, \emptyset} l_{next},$$
$$l_{loop} \xrightarrow{new\_job^!, JOBS\_COUNT=0, \emptyset, \emptyset} l_{check}\}$$

Fig. 8. Template of a Host

Monitor. A monitor is instantiated with two parameters: *actuator*, the last task of the task chain, and the period p of the first task if the chain. The monitor waits for a data-generator to start monitoring and assigns a free monitor (setting the clock to p to allow for worst-case analysis). The location $l_{measure}$ is reached whenever the monitored actuator publishes data, so queries can be over this location to check worst-case reaction times. For compatibility with the validation case, we allow for a second parameter p, which can be set to the period of the data-generator of the first task in the chain. This allows the measured reaction-time to include the worst-case delay from an external event occurring (instead of its measuring). The template is shown in Fig. 9. In this model, location $l_{measure}$ is marked committed.

$$L = \{l_i, l_{measure}\}, \ell_0 = l_i, C = \{x_1, \ldots, x_{MONITORS}\},$$
$$A = \{start\_monitor^? \, \mathcal{T}(actuator)^?, V = \emptyset, I = \emptyset,$$
$$E = \{l_i \xrightarrow{start\_monitor^?, \emptyset, \emptyset, x_{nm}=p; assign\_monitor()} l_i,$$
$$l_i \xrightarrow{\mathcal{T}(actuator)^?, relevant\_payload(), \emptyset, \emptyset} l_{measure}, l_{measure} \xrightarrow{\tau, \emptyset, \emptyset, free\_monitors()} l_i\}$$

Fig. 9. Template of a Monitor

4.3 Instantiation

For a given ROS-based design, each component is instantiated with the corresponding template using suitable values for the parameters. In addition, each component is also given a global integer id (from zero and up), and the global constants PRIO and WCET are set accordingly. The first data-generator node of the task chain $\mathfrak{T}$ is instantiated as a monitored data-generator, while remaining data-generator nodes are instantiated as regular data-generators. The resulting TA network will be deterministic in the sense that the clock values in the monitor automaton will always be the same whenever they are measured at the *measure* location.

Example 4. We instantiate the ROS-based application of Ex. 3 according to the above formula, and obtain five TA: a Data-Generator for Sensor 1 ($task\_id = 0, p = 150, d = 0$), a Subscriber for Filter ($task\_id = 1, s = \mathcal{T}(0), data\_source = pd$), a Monitored Data-Generator for Sensor 2 ($task\_id = 2, p = 150, d = 50$), two Subscribers for the Actuator (($task\_id = 2, s = \mathcal{T}(1), data\_source = pd$) and ($task\_id = 3, s = \mathcal{T}(1), data\_source = pd$)), a Monitor ($actuator = 0, p = 0$), and a Host.

4.4 Queries

Given an instantiated ROS-based application, we can establish an upper bound on the maximum reaction time for $\mathfrak{T}$, using the following TCTL query:

$$A \square \, monitor.measure \rightarrow monitor.x[last\_monitor] \leq t$$

Intuitively, this query checks that reaction times are lesser than t, i.e., that t is an upper bound. This bound is not guaranteed to be tight. We can find a tight bound by using the following query to check if reaction time can exceed t:

$$E \diamond monitor.measure \;\wedge\; monitor.x[last\_monitor] \geq t$$

In order to find an upper bound, the above query is used with $t = 0$. When UPPAAL finds a greater bound t', the query is checked once again with the new bound t'. This process is repeated until UPPAAL states that no greater value exists, establishing the final value of t to be the upper bound. Furthermore, UPPAAL allows the extraction of a trace for a given bound.

Example 5. If we use UPPAAL to query for an upper bound for Example 1, we can the extract trace in Fig. 4. This shows that the figure indeed demonstrates (an instance of) the worst case.

5   Validation

To validate our semantics, we have implemented the case-study ROS system from literature [18], where Teper et al. provide a simulation-based measurement of the maximum end-to-end reaction time. It is a system that consists of: (i) sensors with filters, representing processing of data, (ii) a fusion node, which merges data, and (iii) an actuator at the end of the processing chain. The network is depicted in Fig. 10. The case-study varies the type of the fusion node and the actuator node. Both nodes can either be subscription-based or timer-based, resulting in four combinations, respectively.

For a specific case (Fusion subscription/Actuator timer), each node is formalized as shown in Table 2 (we do not show the other three cases). Note that in our formalization, we must pick a specific task-chain to observe, in this case from Sensor 1 to the Actuator (it can be changed by changing the read-variable of the Fusion node).

In Table 3 the computed maximum reaction times are shown for both the simulation-based measurement of Teper et al. and the model checking-based computation from UPPAAL. Note that we only consider the under-utilized case presented in related work [18]. For the over-utilized system we have different results, as the solution from Teper et al. throws away messages when buffers are overflown. The results show that our semantics seems to agree with the one presented by Teper et al. (at least on the four cases tested).

6   Modeling Non-determinism

In this section, we extend our semantics to capture non-determinism: we allow tasks to execute in less than their worst-case execution time, respectively, and data-generators to generate data with a certain probability only.

Table 2. Formalized validation case

Component	Formal object
Sensor 1	$s_1 = DGEN(420, 0, 10, \mathcal{T}(s_1), \mathcal{V}(s_1)$
Sensor 2	$s_2 = DGEN(420, 0, 20, \mathcal{T}(s_2), \mathcal{V}(s_2)$
Filter 1	$f_1 = SUB(\mathcal{T}(s_1), 10, \emptyset, \emptyset, \mathcal{T}(f_1), pd, \mathcal{V}(f_1)$
Filter 2	$f_2 = SUB(\mathcal{T}(s_2), 20, \emptyset, \emptyset, \mathcal{T}(f_2), pd, \mathcal{V}(f_2))$
Fusion	$fs = SUB(\mathcal{T}(f_1), 30, \{\mathcal{T}(\{\epsilon)\}, \{30\}, \mathcal{T}(fs), pd, \mathcal{V}(fs)$
Filter 3	$f_3 = SUB(\mathcal{T}(fs), 30, \emptyset, \emptyset, \mathcal{T}(f_3), pd, \mathcal{V}(f_3)$
Actuator	$a = TMR(840, 0, 30, \{\mathcal{T}(f_3)\}, \{30\}, \mathcal{T}(a), \mathcal{V}(a^1), \mathcal{V}(a))$

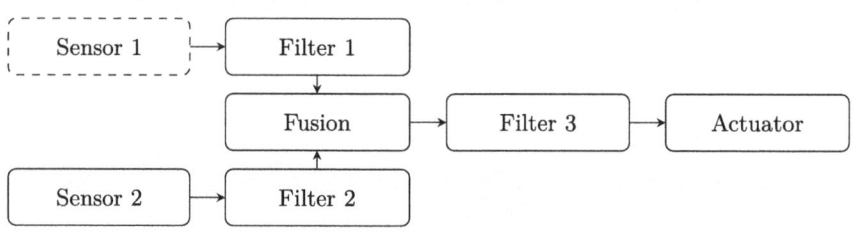

Component	Parameter	Value	Component	Parameter	Value
Sensor 1	*WCET*	10	Sensor 1	*period*	420
Sensor 2	*WCET*	20	Sensor 2	*period*	420
Filter 1	*WCET*	10	Filter 2	*WCET*	20
Fusion Sub1	*WCET*	30	Fusion Sub2	*WCET*	30
Filter 3	*WCET*	30			
Actuator	*WCET*	30	Actuator	*period*	840
Actuator Sub1	*WCET*	30			

Fig. 10. Case-study system and parameter values for subscriber/timer-scenario from literature [18]. Fusion Sub1 is the triggering subscription task of the fusion node, whereas Fusion Sub2 is the first non-triggering subscription task of the Fusion node.

Table 3. Comparison of the simulation approach [18] and (our) model-checking approach. Results indicate the computed maximum end-to-end reaction time in milliseconds.

Case	Fusion	Actuator	Simulation (ms)	Model-Checking (ms)
1	Subscriber	Subscriber	540	540
2	Subscriber	Timer	1320	1320
3	Timer	Subscriber	1470	1470
4	Timer	Timer	2490	2490

6.1 Non-deterministic Execution Time

In the base semantics, the host would always execute jobs for the duration of their respective WCET. However, in general, a job's execution time t is constrained by $BCET \leq t \leq WCET$, where BCET is the best-case execution time. In this extended semantics, we modify the host accordingly, by changing the guard as follows: $x = WCET[job]$ is replaced by $BCET[job] \leq x \wedge x \leq WCET[job]$. Note that this requires the introduction of a BCET-constant for each task.[3]

Example 6. We revisit the small system introduced in Example 1. If we allow for non-deterministic running times (that is, a job's running time is in the interval $[\frac{wcet}{2}, wcet]$), the maximum reaction time is actually increased, demonstrated by the trace in Fig. 11. The reaction time depicted in the graph is $280 - 50 = 230$, greater than 80, the original bound when only worst-case execution times are considered. The reason for the increase in reaction time is due to the filter task being triggered before the second sensor is scheduled (which cannot happen if the first sensor task executes according to its WCET).

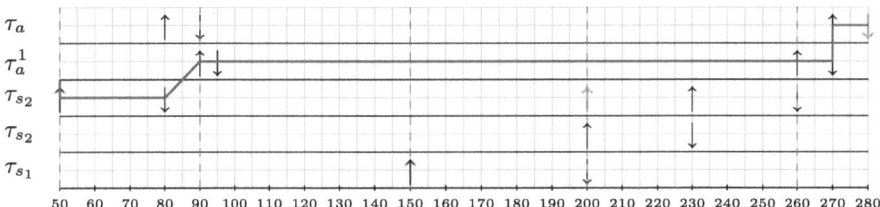

Fig. 11. Schedule for small ROS-based system example with non-deterministic reaction times. Processing windows are separated by red dashed lines. An orange upward arrow indicates the release of a job, a black upward arrow the start of a job, and a black downward one indicates the end of a job. The blue line traces the reaction time. (Color figure online)

6.2 Probabilistic Data-Generator

The sensor, as presented in Sect. 4, would always read a new value each *period*. However, we now introduce a *probabilistic data-generator* which only generates a value each *period* with a probability p. In other words, for each period p, there is a *prob* chance that a new value is generated and thus a job scheduled, in the other cases nothing happens. If $prob = 100$, the behavior is identical to a regular data-generator. The probabilistic data-generator is shown in Fig. 12. Also, location l_{choose} and l_{fire} are marked committed.

---

[3] We assume for convenience that in this paper $BCET[job] = WCET[job]/2$.

Monitored Probabilistic Data-generator is identical to the probabilistic data-generator with the difference that the edge from l_{fire} to l_{wait} is replaced by:

$$l_{fire} \xrightarrow{start\_monitor^!,\emptyset,\emptyset,queue\_job(id,PAYLOAD)} l_{wait}$$

$$
\boxed{
\begin{aligned}
&L = \{l_{wait}, l_{choose}, l_{fire}\}, \quad \ell_0 = l_{wait}, \quad C = \{x\}, A = \{new\_job^!, new\_job^?\}, \\
&V = \{\emptyset\}, I = \{l_{wait} \mapsto x \leq p\}, \\
&E = \{l_{wait} \xrightarrow{new\_job^!,x=p,x,\emptyset} l_{choose}, l_{wait} \xrightarrow{new\_job^?,x=p,x,\emptyset} l_{choose}, \\
&\quad l_{choose} \xrightarrow{\tau,?prob,x,\emptyset} l_{fire}, l_{choose} \xrightarrow{\tau,?100-prob,x,\emptyset} l_{wait}, \\
&\quad l_{fire} \xrightarrow{\tau,\emptyset,\emptyset,queue\_job(id,EMPTY)} l_{wait}\}
\end{aligned}
}
$$

Fig. 12. Template of a Probabilistic Data-Generator

6.3   Statistical Model Checking

When a probabilistic model is chosen, it might no longer be interesting to establish maximum upper bounds, as in many cases these will be the same as for the non-probabilistic case (i.e., the worst case with maximum load). However, the worst case could be very rare, and thus acceptable. Using statistical model checking (SMC) it is possible to find an upper bound which is only violated with a certain (low) chance. For example, the following UPPAAL SMC query yields the probability that the reaction time is observed to be more than t within u time-steps:

$$\Pr[\leq u]\ (\diamond((monitor.measure \wedge monitor.x[last\_monitor] \geq t)))$$

The answer to such a query can be $p \leq 0.05$ with 95 % CI. This means that the probability that the bound of t is violated within u is less than 5 %, and that if we would redo the test, the probability that we would yield the same answer is 95 %. Depending on the application these probabilities could be sufficiently tight to be acceptable.

7   Industrial Example: Camera-Guided Robots

In this section, we present an example inspired from an industrial use case. To assist in production, a factory uses autonomous transport robots to transfer tools and parts as necessary. The robots are guided by a central control system that observes the environment through cameras. The cameras are equipped with a local processor that ensures that pictures are only sent if they changed since last time, that is, if the image is static no data is sent. During production humans can walk around in the same areas as the autonomous robots, and it is important that a collision is avoided by stopping the robot if someone would walk in front of it. Hence, it is crucial to ensure a low maximum reaction time from observing an obstacle through a camera, to sending a stop signal to the robot.

We model each camera as a separate data-generator, each being forwarded to a separate object detection, modeled as a subscriber. All object detection is fused in the fusion timer node. Finally, the managing and actuation is a subscriber node. The resulting ROS design is shown in Fig. 13.

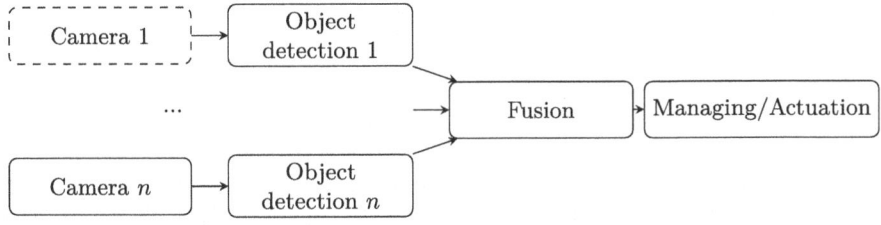

Fig. 13. Industrial example modeled as a ROS Design

We consider configurations with a various amount of cameras and instantiate the suitable templates in accordance with Sect. 4 with parameters and constant values shown in Table 4. Since cameras might not have new information to send, we model them using probabilistic data-generators. For simplicity, we let all cameras have the same probability of being activated at each instant, and we consider different combinations of number of cameras and the probability that a camera will be activated (load). All experiments are run on a 11th Gen i5 @ 2.40 GHz with 16.0 GB of RAM. Run-times are presented for each query and can be seen to mostly be around one second or less.

Table 4. Parameter values for the case-study system

Component	Parameter	Value	Component	Parameter	Value
Camera	$WCET$	20	Camera	$period$	1000
Object Detection	$WCET$	50	Fusion sub	$WCET$	10
Fusion Timer	$WCET$	90	Fusion Timer	$period$	500
Managing/Actuation	$WCET$	50			

We use the queries from Sect. 6.3, to establish if within 10,000 time steps there is less than a five percent chance of the reaction time exceeding 850 with a 95 % confidence interval. The results for the different scenarios are shown in Table 5. From the table, we can see that having more than five cameras already risks overloading the system in such a way as to violate a deadline of 850 time units. Note that since we do not distinguish the cameras from each other, the probabilities that we estimate are for the deadline violation of one camera. Since in most cases, for more than six cameras the deadline requirement is violated, in the following, we only consider cases from one to six cameras. The results in Table 5 are from the perspective on the data from the first camera, and when monitoring other cameras the results remain the same.

Table 5. Results from industrial example. A Yes in column ≤ 850 means that there is less than 5 % chance that the system violates the deadline (within the first 10000 time steps) under that configuration.

#Cams	Load	≤ 850	Time	#Cams	Load	≤ 850	Time	#Cams	Load	≤ 850	Time
1	25%	Yes	0.18	2	25%	Yes	0.19	3	25%	Yes	0.20
1	50%	Yes	0.16	2	50%	Yes	0.19	3	50%	Yes	0.21
1	75%	Yes	0.18	2	75%	Yes	0.20	3	75%	Yes	0.23
1	100%	Yes	0.17	2	100%	Yes	0.23	3	100%	Yes	0.25
4	25%	Yes	0.22	5	25%	Yes	0.22	6	25%	Yes	0.23
4	50%	Yes	0.23	5	50%	Yes	0.24	6	50%	No	0.18
4	75%	Yes	0.23	5	75%	Yes	0.27	6	75%	No	0.13
4	100%	Yes	0.29	5	100%	Yes	0.31	6	100%	No	0.13
#Cams	Load	≤ 850	Time	#Cams	Load	≤ 850	Time	#Cams	Load	≤ 850	Time
7	25%	Yes	0.29	8	25%	Yes	0.34	9	25%	No	0.30
7	50%	No	0.14	8	50%	No	0.13	9	50%	No	0.14
7	75%	No	0.12	8	75%	No	0.14	9	75%	No	0.12
7	100%	No	0.13	8	100%	No	0.12	9	100%	No	0.14
10	25%	No	0.22	11	25%	No	0.19	12	25%	No	0.15
10	50%	No	0.13	11	50%	No	0.14	12	50%	No	0.13
10	75%	No	0.14	11	75%	No	0.14	12	75%	No	0.14
10	100%	No	0.12	11	100%	No	0.13	12	100%	No	0.14

Next, we consider what happens if we extend the time period tenfold. Thus we consider a period of 100,000 time steps and with same reaction time (850), chance (5%) and confidence interval (95%). The results can be seen in Table 6. As expected, the acceptable loads are reduced, since running the system longer increases the chances of bad scenarios to occur: now only two cameras are safe under a 75 % load, and three for a 50 % load. Moreover, the fact that the analysis time is roughly five times longer is also noteworthy.

We can also use modeling to explore alternatives. As an example, we change the fusion node from a timer-based node to a subscription-based one, triggering whenever the first camera produces data (remember, a subscription node is triggered by only one topic), with a WCET of 90. Now there is a substantial difference between the end-to-end reaction times from different cameras. Since the first camera triggers the fusion, its reaction time will be very short. However, if we look at camera three, the performance is very poor, as shown in Table 7, indicating that not even a scenario with two cameras is safe. If the load is 100 %,

Table 6. Use case monitoring 1, with timer-based fusion (period of 500) analyzing 100000 time steps.

#Cams	Load	≤ 850	Time	#Cams	Load	≤ 850	Time	#Cams	Load	≤ 850	Time
1	25%	Yes	0.68	2	25%	Yes	0.82	3	25%	Yes	0.93
1	50%	Yes	0.77	2	50%	Yes	0.95	3	50%	Yes	1.15
1	75%	Yes	0.81	2	75%	Yes	1.09	3	75%	No	1.38
1	100%	Yes	0.91	2	100%	No	1.20	3	100%	No	1.55
4	25%	Yes	1.05	5	25%	No	1.22	6	25%	No	3.04
4	50%	No	1.31	5	50%	No	1.58	6	50%	No	0.19
4	75%	No	1.59	5	75%	No	1.85	6	75%	No	0.14
4	100%	No	1.83	5	100%	No	2.19	6	100%	No	0.13

the scenario *is* safe, since that boils down to a timer-based fusion with a period equal to the period of the first camera.

Table 7. Use case monitoring 2, with subscription-based fusion analyzing 10000 time steps.

#Cams	Load	≤ 850	Time	#Cams	Load	≤ 850	Time	#Cams	Load	≤ 850	Time
1	25%	n/a	0.00	2	25%	No	0.11	3	25%	No	0.13
1	50%	n/a	0.00	2	50%	No	0.12	3	50%	No	0.11
1	75%	n/a	0.00	2	75%	No	0.11	3	75%	No	0.11
1	100%	n/a	0.00	2	100%	Yes	0.18	3	100%	Yes	0.21
4	25%	No	0.11	5	25%	No	0.11	6	25%	No	0.12
4	50%	No	0.12	5	50%	No	0.13	6	50%	No	0.12
4	75%	No	0.14	5	75%	No	0.14	6	75%	No	0.12
4	100%	Yes	0.23	5	100%	Yes	0.28	6	100%	Yes	0.30

Another point that can be investigated regards answering the question: Can increasing/decreasing the period of the fusion node improve the performance of the system? In Table 8, we observe the results (when monitoring the first camera) with fusion periods 250 and 750. It can be seen that both alternatives, in comparison to a fusion time of 500, are performing worse, with only four and cameras being safe for the shorter period and none for the longer period.

Further investigations can be made by additional queries with different confidence intervals, limits on guarantees, etc., to help in gathering insights of the system model, and allow for experimentation with different parameters, aiming to help eliminate poor design choices.

8 Related Work

The closest to our work is the TA-based approach, proposed by Halder et al. [11], which models and verifies safety and liveness properties of ROS applications,

Table 8. Use case monitoring 1, with timer-based fusion period of 250 (above) and 750 (below) analysing 10000 time steps.

#Cams	Load	≤ 850	Time	#Cams	Load	≤ 850	Time	#Cams	Load	≤ 850	Time
1	25%	Yes	0.22	2	25%	Yes	0.24	3	25%	Yes	0.33
1	50%	Yes	0.22	2	50%	Yes	0.25	3	50%	Yes	0.29
1	75%	Yes	0.26	2	75%	Yes	0.28	3	75%	Yes	0.31
1	100%	Yes	0.30	2	100%	Yes	0.28	3	100%	Yes	0.32
4	25%	Yes	0.26	5	25%	Yes	0.32	6	25%	No	1.32
4	50%	Yes	0.29	5	50%	No	0.16	6	50%	No	0.12
4	75%	Yes	0.32	5	75%	No	0.13	6	75%	No	0.11
4	100%	Yes	0.35	5	100%	No	0.11	6	100%	No	0.12
#Cams	Load	≤ 850	Time	#Cams	Load	≤ 850	Time	#Cams	Load	≤ 850	Time
1	25%	No	0.11	2	25%	No	0.12	3	25%	No	0.12
1	50%	No	0.12	2	50%	No	0.11	3	50%	No	0.12
1	75%	No	0.10	2	75%	No	0.11	3	75%	No	0.11
1	100%	No	0.10	2	100%	No	0.11	3	100%	No	0.12
4	25%	No	0.11	5	25%	No	0.12	6	25%	No	0.12
4	50%	No	0.11	5	50%	No	0.11	6	50%	No	0.13
4	75%	No	0.11	5	75%	No	0.12	6	75%	No	0.10
4	100%	No	0.11	5	100%	No	0.11	6	100%	No	0.12

focusing on the communication between nodes, and considering queue sizes and internal timeouts. While the work is carried out at a lower level of abstraction than ours, the authors consider only a publish-subscribe scenario and do not propose methods to enable both end-to-end reaction time verification in deterministic settings, as well as stochastic analysis of reaction time under probabilistic loads. Dust et al. [9] propose a pattern-based modeling and UPPAAL-based verification of latencies and buffer overflow in distributed robotic systems, including all versions of the single-threaded executor in ROS 2, yet the authors do not consider processing chains in their verification, focusing on the node behavior only. Lin et al. [14] propose formal models for the real time publish subscribe protocol using UPPAAL and analyze the protocol's behavior by simulation in Simulink/Stateflow, however the authors do not validate the formal models against the simulation results, as we show in this paper.

Carvalho et al. [7] introduce a model-checking technique for verifying system-wide safety properties in message-passing systems, employing an Alloy extension called Electrum, and its Analyzer. Their approach emphasizes high-level architectural verification of message passing, while our work focuses on timing properties verification. Webster et al. [20] propose a formal verification method for industrial robotic programs using the SPIN model checker, with an emphasis on behavioral refinement and the verification of selected robot requirements.

The Coq-based verification of ROS implementations has been the focus of several works, out of which that of Cowley and Taylor verifies robotic behaviour using linear logic embedding in Coq [8], and that of Anand and Knepper proposes ROSCoq, a framework for developing certified Coq programs for robots, where subsystems communicate using messages [3]. Neither of these works focuses on verifying end-to-end reaction time of job chains, the authors analyzing implementation levels instead.

The work of Hong et al. [19] can be seen as complementary to our work, as it bridges the Timed Rebeca [1] model of a realistic multiple autonomous mobile robots system and its generated ROS 2 demo code, showing the match between the model and the program. Our work does not focus on ROS 2 code generation, hence on such semantic bridge, but on modeling and analyzing formally the main communication concepts of ROS 2, both in a deterministic and a probabilistic context.

9 Conclusions and Future Work

In this paper, we have presented a formalization of ROS semantics in UPPAAL timed automata. To establish its validity, we ensure equal behavior with previous work available in the literature, with respect to the application's timeliness. Afterwards, we have extended it with non-determinism, by allowing variable runtime of tasks, as well as probabilistic data generation, by employing stochastic timed automata. To demonstrate the usability of the approach, we demonstrate how the UPPAAL tool can be used with regular and statistical model checking, respectively, to establish upper bounds of end-to-end timing properties of ROS 2 applications.

Acknowledgments. We acknowledge the support of the Swedish Knowledge Foundation via the synergy ACICS - Assured Cloud Platforms for Industrial Cyber-Physical Systems, grant nr. 20190038, and via the profile DPAC - Dependable Platform for Autonomous Systems and Control, grant nr. 20150022.

A UPPAAL Functions

```
1  bool  waiting_jobs () {
2      int  i;
3      for (i=0; i<C; i++) {
4          if (QUEUES_COUNT[i] > 0) return true;
5      }
6      return false;
7  }
8
9  void  queue_job (int task, int data) {
10     QUEUES[task][QUEUES_COUNT[task]] = data;
11     QUEUES_COUNT[task] += 1;
12 }
13
14
```

```
15 // Right−most job first , i.e., greatest priority first
16 void schedule () {
17     int i, j, tmp_id, tmp_data;
18
19     // Sort first by id
20     for (i=0; i<JOBS_COUNT; i++) {
21         for (j=0; j<JOBS_COUNT−1; j++) {
22             if (PRIO[JOBS[j][0]] > PRIO[JOBS[j+1][0]]) {
23                 tmp_id = JOBS[j][0];
24                 tmp_data = JOBS[j][1];
25                 JOBS[j][0] = JOBS[j+1][0];
26                 JOBS[j][1] = JOBS[j+1][1];
27                 JOBS[j+1][0] = tmp_id;
28                 JOBS[j+1][1] = tmp_data;
29             }
30         }
31     }
32 }
33
34 int dequeue(int task) {
35     int i, tmp;
36     assert(QUEUES_COUNT[task] > 0);
37     tmp = QUEUES[task][0];
38     for (i=0; i<BUF_SIZE−1; i++)
39         QUEUES[task][i] = QUEUES[task][i+1];
40     QUEUES[task][BUF_SIZE−1] = 0;
41     QUEUES_COUNT[task] −= 1;
42     return tmp;
43 }
44
45 void take_jobs () {
46     int i, j;
47
48     assert(JOBS_COUNT == 0);    // Host jobs should be zero
            here
49     for (i=0; i<C; i++) {
50         if (QUEUES_COUNT[i] > 0) {
51             j = dequeue(i);
52             JOBS[JOBS_COUNT][0] = i;
53             JOBS[JOBS_COUNT][1] = j;
54             JOBS_COUNT += 1;
55         }
56     }
57     schedule ();
58 }
59
60 int next_job_idx () {
61     JOBS_COUNT−−;
62     return JOBS_COUNT;
63 }
```

```
64
65 // If value is negative, we don't pick from queue, but from
       node
66 int get_data(int value) {
67     if (value < 0) {
68         return value;
69     } else {
70         return DATA[value]; // Do we need to remove read
               values?
71     }
72 }
73
74 void assign_monitor() {
75     if (lm == -1) {
76         lm = nm;
77     }
78     monitor_status[nm] = MONITOR_SENT;
79     monitor_payload[nm] = PAYLOAD;
80     PAYLOAD = PAYLOAD - 1;
81     if (PAYLOAD < MIN_PAYLOAD) {
82         PAYLOAD = FIRST_PAYLOAD;
83     }
84     nm = (nm + 1) % MONITORS;
85 }
86
87
88 // True if payload is monitored (i.e., not empty or already
       seen)
89 bool relevant_payload(int payload) {
90     int i = 0;
91     if (payload == EMPTY)
92         return false;
93     for (i = 0; i < MONITORS; i++) {
94         if (monitor_payload[i] == payload)
95             return true;
96     }
97
98     return false;
99 }
100
101
102
103
104 // When freeing up, we free up all monitors incl. those
       whose data got thrown away.
105 void free_monitors() {
106     int i;
107     // We could get an old value, in that case it is not in
           the monitored payloads
108     bool old_value = true;
```

```
109    for (i = 0; i < MONITORS; i++) {
110        if (monitor_payload[i] == pd)
111            old_value = false;
112    }
113
114    // If it is an old value, we can just ignore it as it
          has already been seen once
115    if (old_value)
116        return;
117
118    // Free previously used monitors
119    while (monitor_payload[lm] != pd) {
120        monitor_status[lm] = MONITOR_FREE;
121        monitor_payload[lm] = EMPTY;
122        lm = (lm + 1) % MONITORS;
123    }
124
125    // Also free the one just handled.
126    monitor_status[lm] = MONITOR_FREE;
127    LAST_PAYLOAD = monitor_payload[lm];
128    monitor_payload[lm] = EMPTY;
129    lm = (lm + 1) % MONITORS;
130 }
```

B   Graphical Representation of UPPAAL TA

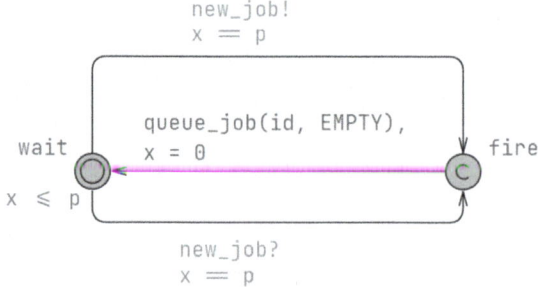

Fig. 14. UPPAAL figure of data-generator.

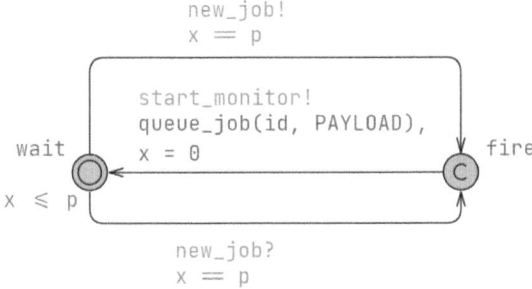

Fig. 15. UPPAAL figure of monitored data-generator.

Fig. 16. UPPAAL graphical representation of subscriber.

Fig. 17. UPPAAL graphical representation of Monitor.

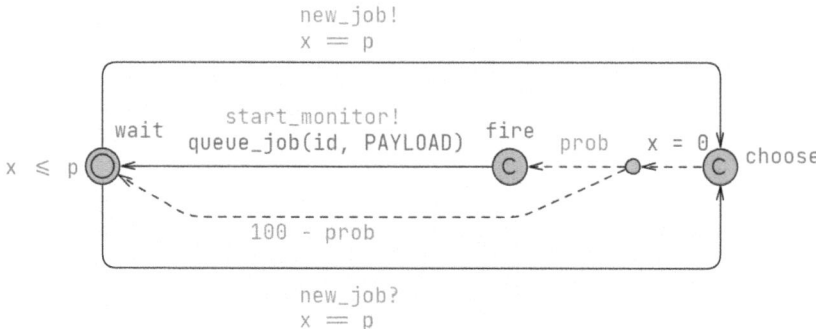

Fig. 18. Template for monitored probabilistic data-generator.

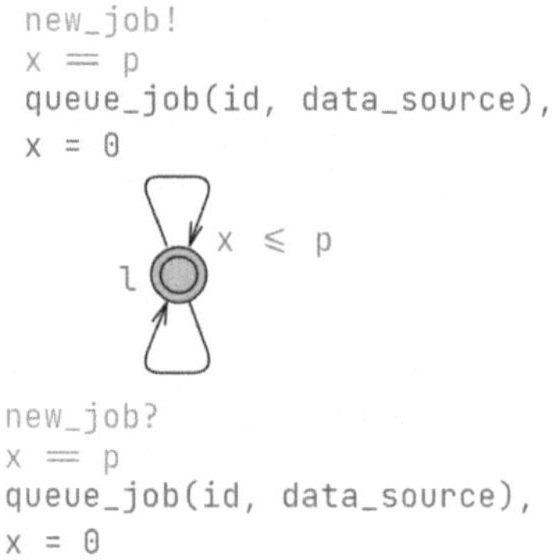

```
new_job!
x = p
queue_job(id, data_source),
x = 0
```

        x ≤ p

```
new_job?
x = p
queue_job(id, data_source),
x = 0
```

Fig. 19. Template for timer.

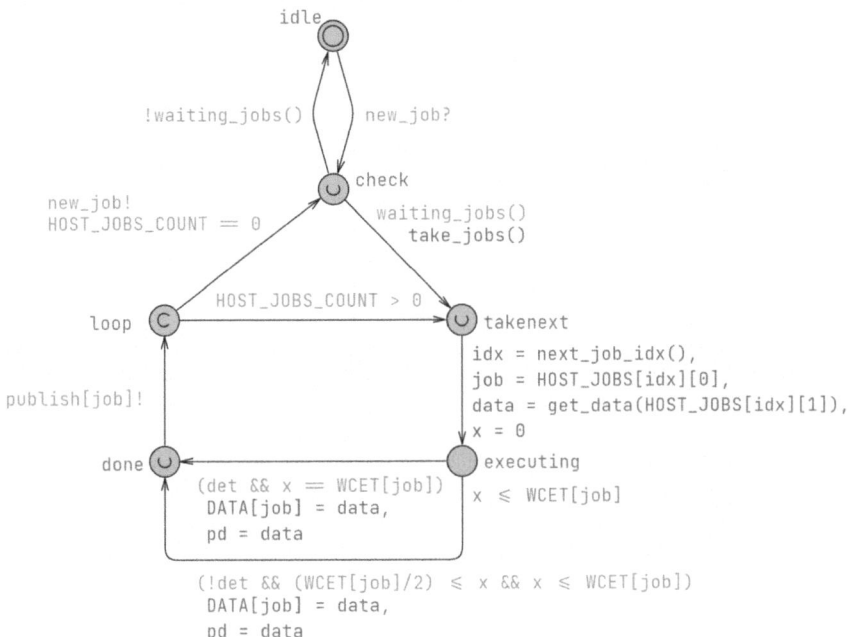

Fig. 20. Template for host.

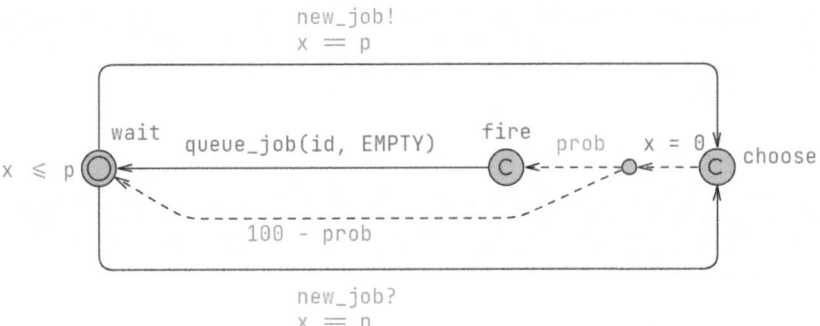

Fig. 21. Template for probabilistic data-generator.

References

1. Aceto, L., et al.: Modelling and simulation of asynchronous real-time systems using timed rebeca. In: Proceedings 10th International Workshop on the Foundations of Coordination Languages and Software Architectures, FOCLASA 2011, vol. 58 of EPTCS, pp. 1–19 (2011)
2. Alur, R.: Timed automata. In: Halbwachs, N., Peled, D. (eds.) CAV 1999. LNCS, vol. 1633, pp. 8–22. Springer, Heidelberg (1999). https://doi.org/10.1007/3-540-48683-6_3
3. Anand, A., Knepper, R.: ROSCoq: robots powered by constructive reals. In: Urban, C., Zhang, X. (eds.) ITP 2015. LNCS, vol. 9236, pp. 34–50. Springer, Cham (2015). https://doi.org/10.1007/978-3-319-22102-1_3
4. Baier, C., Katoen, J.-P.: Principles of Model Checking (Representation and Mind Series). The MIT Press, Cambridge (2008)
5. Bengtsson, J., Yi, W.: Timed automata: semantics, algorithms and tools. In: Desel, J., Reisig, W., Rozenberg, G. (eds.) ACPN 2003. LNCS, vol. 3098, pp. 87–124. Springer, Heidelberg (2004). https://doi.org/10.1007/978-3-540-27755-2_3
6. Bulychev, P., David, A., Larsen, K.G., Legay, A., Li, G., Poulsen, D.B.: Rewrite-based statistical model checking of WMTL. In: Qadeer, S., Tasiran, S. (eds.) RV 2012. LNCS, vol. 7687, pp. 260–275. Springer, Heidelberg (2013). https://doi.org/10.1007/978-3-642-35632-2_25
7. Carvalho, R., Cunha, A., Macedo, N., Santos, A.: Verification of system-wide safety properties of ros applications. In: 2020 IEEE/RSJ International Conference on Intelligent Robots and Systems (IROS) (2020)
8. Cowley, A., Taylor, C.J.: Towards language-based verification of robot behaviors. In: 2011 IEEE/RSJ International Conference on Intelligent Robots and Systems, pp. 4776–4782 (2011)
9. Dust, L., Gu, R., Seceleanu, C., Ekström, M., Mubeen, S.: Pattern-based verification of ROS 2 nodes using uppaal. In: Formal Methods for Industrial Critical Systems (FMICS), pp. 57–75. Springer, Cham (2023)
10. Erős, E., Dahl, M., Bengtsson, K., Hanna, A., Falkman, P.: A ROS2 based communication architecture for control in collaborative and intelligent automation systems. Procedia Manuf. **38**, 349–357 (2019)
11. Halder, R., Proença, J., Macedo, N., Santos, A.: Formal verification of ROS-based robotic applications using timed-automata. In: 2017 IEEE/ACM 5th International FME Workshop on Formal Methods in Software Engineering (FormaliSE), pp 44–50 (2017)
12. Larsen, K.G., Pettersson, P., Yi, W.: UPPAAL in a nutshell. Int. J. Softw. Tools Technol. Transf. **1**(1–2), 134–152 (1997)
13. Legay, A., Lukina, A., Traonouez, L.M., Yang, J., Smolka, S.A., Grosu, R.: Statistical model checking. In: Steffen, B., Woeginger, G. (eds.) Computing and Software Science. LNCS, vol. 10000, pp. 478–504. Springer, Cham (2019). https://doi.org/10.1007/978-3-319-91908-9_23
14. Lin, Q.-Q., Wang, S.-L., Zhan, B.-H., Bin, G.: Modelling and verification of real-time publish and subscribe protocol using uppaal and simulink/stateflow. J. Comput. Sci. Technol. **35**, 1324–1342 (2020)
15. Macenski, S., Foote, T., Gerkey, B., Lalancette, C., Woodall, W.: Robot operating system 2: Design, architecture, and uses in the wild. Sci. Rob. **7**(66), eabm6074 (2022)

16. Quigley, M., et al.: ROS: an open-source robot operating system. In: ICRA Workshop on Open Source Software, Kobe, Japan, vol. 3, p. 5 (2009)
17. Reke, M., et al.: A self-driving car architecture in ROS2. In: 2020 Int. SAUPEC/RobMech/PRASA Conference, pp. 1–6 (2020)
18. Teper, H., Günzel, M., Ueter, N., von der Brüggen, G., Chen, J.J.: End-To-End timing analysis in ROS2. In: 2022 IEEE Real-Time Systems Symposium (RTSS), pp. 53–65 (2022)
19. Trinh, H.H., Sirjani, M., Moradi, F., Cicchetti, A., Ciccozzi, F.: Combining model-based development and formal verification of a complex ROS2 multi-robots system using Timed Rebeca. In: International Workshop on Reliability Engineering Methods for Autonomous Robots - REMARO 2024 (2024)
20. Webster, M., et al.: Toward reliable autonomous robotic assistants through formal verification: a case study. IEEE Trans. Human-Mach. Syst. **46**(2), 186–196 (2016)

An LAGC Semantics for Timed Rebeca

Reiner Hähnle[1]([✉]) [iD], Einar Broch Johnsen[2] [iD], and S. Lizeth Tapia Tarifa[2] [iD]

[1] Technical University Darmstadt, Darmstadt, Germany
reiner.haehnle@tu-darmstadt.de
[2] University of Oslo, Oslo, Norway
{einarj,sltarifa}@ifi.uio.no

Abstract. Timed Rebeca is an actor-based language for modeling and analyzing timed reactive systems. Timed Rebeca has a formal SOS-style semantics, as well as one in terms of rewrite rules. While the latter is suitable for model exploration and bounded model checking, it is less so for the purpose of deductive verification. Since we believe there is great potential in deductive verification of Timed Rebeca programs, as a preparatory step, in the present paper we provide a locally abstract, globally concrete (LAGC) semantics. This is a new approach to the semantic foundation of programming languages. An LAGC semantics is a highly modular, incremental trace semantics, particularly suited to ensure soundness of global program analyses such as deductive verification. We provide the first LAGC-style semantics for Timed Rebeca and discuss possible future applications.

1 Introduction

With her work on Rebeca [20,21], Marjan Sirjani has been a driver for the usage of formal methods in a broad range of applications, based on the modeling and analysis of actor systems [1]. Rebeca has been used to analyze a broad range of systems, clearly demonstrating the usefulness of formal methods for real-world problems, and in particular of the actor perspective in modeling and analyzing real-world systems. In this line of work, Sirjani and her colleagues developed and adapted a range of analysis techniques to actor systems, such as simulation [18], model checking [12,15,23], statistical model checking [11], partial order reduction [2], and rewriting logic [19], in particular for timed systems with *Timed Rebeca* [18].

The development of formal analyses techniques for a modeling language relies on the semantics of the language. For timed actor languages, timing constraints introduce particular challenges related to the synchronization of parallel behavior in the distributed actors [3] and the allocation of time-sensitive resources [14]. For Timed Rebeca, significant effort has gone into formalizing its semantics to match different analysis techniques. At present, Timed Rebeca has an SOS-like semantics [18], as well as a formalization in the rewriting language Maude [19]. The latter is well-suited for bounded model checking and model exploration, however, less so for deductive verification and the analysis of global properties such as fairness.

© The Author(s), under exclusive license to Springer Nature Switzerland AG 2025
E. A. Lee et al. (Eds.): *Rebeca for Actor Analysis in Action*, LNCS 15560, pp. 326–348, 2025.
https://doi.org/10.1007/978-3-031-85134-6_14

$$M \in Model ::= \overline{CD}\ msc$$
$$CD \in ClassDecl ::= \textbf{reactiveclass}\ C\ \{\ KR\ SV\ Ctr\ \overline{MS}\ \}$$
$$KR \in KnownRebecs ::= \textbf{knownrebecs}\{\ d\ \}$$
$$SV \in stateVars ::= \textbf{statevars}\{\ d\ \}$$
$$Ctr \in constructor ::= C(\ d\ )\{\ sc\ \}$$
$$MS \in MsgSrv ::= \textbf{msgsrv}\ m(\ d\ )\ \{\ sc\ \}$$
$$sc \in Scope ::= d\ s$$
$$d \in VarDecl ::= \varepsilon \mid T\ x;\ d$$
$$s \in Stmt ::= for\text{-}stm \mid new\text{-}stm \mid call\text{-}stm \mid \textbf{delay}(e) \mid s;\ s \mid$$
$$\textbf{skip} \mid x = e \mid x =?(\overline{e}) \mid \textbf{if}\ e\ \{\ s\ \}$$
$$for\text{-}stm \in For ::= \textbf{for}\ (s; e; s)\ \{\ s\ \}$$
$$new\text{-}stm \in New ::= x = \textbf{new}\ C\ (\overline{e}) : (\overline{e})$$
$$call\text{-}stm \in Call ::= e.m(\overline{e})\ [\textbf{after}(e)]\ [\textbf{deadline}(e)]$$
$$msc \in mainScope ::= \textbf{main}\ \{\ \overline{InDcl}\ \}$$
$$InDcl \in InstanceDcl ::= C\ x(\overline{e}) : (\overline{e})$$

Fig. 1. Syntax of Timed Rebeca. Overlined identifiers, such as $\overline{e}$, indicate lists or sets and square brackets [ ] indicate optional elements.

Recently, the authors were involved in the design of a denotational semantics, suitable for parallel and distributed systems, named *locally abstract, globally concrete* (LAGC) semantics [7]. In contrast to operational semantics such as SOS [17], which are well-suited to define execution aspects of a model needed for, e.g., simulation or model checking, denotational aspects shift the focus from *how* a model executes to *what* the resulting semantic object will be. LAGC-style semantics was developed to match with calculi for deductive verification [5,7] and can also be used to analyze fairness in asynchronous languages [8]. In this paper, we provide an LAGC semantics for the asynchronous modeling language Timed Rebeca [18].

Paper Overview. Section 2 gives a brief introduction to Timed Rebeca and Sect. 3 explains the basics of LAGC semantics to make the paper self-contained. Section 4 then presents our LAGC semantics for Timed Rebeca and Sect. 5 briefly reflects on our effort in developing this semantics, before Sect. 6 concludes the paper and suggests some lines of future work.

2   Timed Rebeca

Rebeca [21] models the behavior of a system as a set of active objects with encapsulated states, where communication happens via asynchronous message passing. Rebeca is an active object language [4] in the sense that it combines object-oriented features with actors, specifically actors are instances of classes that define how these instances react to messages, and messages are structured like method calls (using dot notation for sending messages). *Timed Rebeca* extends Rebeca with timed constructs.

Various versions of the syntax and semantics of Timed Rebeca [18, 19, 22] have been studied, for example, with timed semantics based on a global clock [19, 22] versus distributed local clocks [18]. In this paper, we consider the syntax and semantics as given in [19].[1] We first explain informally the syntax constructs of Timed Rebeca, then illustrate it with an example of a small model.

2.1   Syntax of Timed Rebeca

Figure 1 shows the syntax of Timed Rebeca as given in [19]. A model M consists of a number of *reactive class* declarations, specifying the behavior of the classes of the actors in the model, as well as a *main block* that statically defines the initial instances of the actor classes. An instance of a reactive class *InDcl* is an actor x of type C in the system model, also called a *rebec*. The meta notation e is for expressions of the appropriate type.

Class Declarations. The declaration of a reactive class *CD* starts with the keyword **reactiveclass**, followed by the reactive class name C. A reactive class declares known rebecs *KR* and state variables *SV*. The former are the statically known rebecs, declared with the keyword **knownrebecs** and may be the empty set. The keyword **statevars** declares state variables of a rebec with a basic (non-class) type. These are initialized to a default value and correspond to object fields. They are fully encapsulated and can only be read and set by sending messages to their owner. Each reactive class has one constructor *Ctr*, used to initialize instances of the class by initializing (some) state variables and possibly sending messages to other rebecs or to itself. The keyword **self** is reserved in the context of the body of a message to refer to the rebec currently executing this message.

Message Servers. A rebec responds to an incoming message by executing the corresponding message server, each reactive class declares message signatures $\overline{MS}$, handled using message servers. Their declaration starts with the keyword **msgsrv**, followed by a name m, the formal parameters, and a message body. The body of a message server *sc* contains local variable declarations and a sequence of statements with standard control structures, including a **skip** statement, sequential composition,[2] variable assignment, random variable assignment of the form $x =?(\overline{e})$, where x is randomly assigned to one of the expressions in $\overline{e}$, an **if** statement, and a **for** loop of the form **for** $(s_1; e; s_2) \{ s_3 \}$, where counters are initialized in s_1, the loop guard is in e, the increment of the counters is according to s_2, and the body of the loop is declared in s_3.

---

[1] The language constructs also differ slightly between these papers: [18] does not consider dynamic actor creation and the **for** loop, whereas a **now**-statement is featured in [22].

[2] The Timed Rebeca grammar [19] has no explicit constructors for empty and concatenated statements. Instead, it admits possibly empty sequences of statements s^*. Since our local rules evaluate one statement at a time, it is more natural to base the grammar on an explicit empty statement **skip** and concatenation $s; s'$. Obviously, both grammars result in an equivalent language.

Actor Configurations. Rebecs may be created statically in the main block, or dynamically using the **new** statement of the form $x = $ **new** C $(\overline{e_1}) : (\overline{e_2})$, which dynamically creates an instance of class C, where the set of known rebecs is initialized according to $\overline{e_1}$, and the constructor of C is immediately executed with the arguments in $\overline{e_2}$. A constructor *Ctr* is very similar to a message server, with the exception that its name is identical to the name of the class.

Communication Structure. Each rebec has a separate FIFO message queue containing its pending received messages. The effect of sending a message is appending the message to the FIFO message queue of the receiving rebec. In Rebeca, the execution of a message server is non-preemptive: The executing rebec does not take the next message from its queue before the running message server is finished. The general behavior of each rebec is a loop which first takes a message from the queue and then executes it in the corresponding message server. The actor is idle when there is no enabled message in the FIFO queue. The order of execution of enabled concurrent rebecs in Timed Rebeca is arbitrary.

Time and Timed Message Passing. The **delay** statement models computation time. Timed Rebeca assumes that all statements other than delays are executed instantaneously, and non-zero computation time must be specified via the delay statement of the form **delay**(t), which indicates the current rebec will be blocked (i.e., it is unable to perform any action) within the next t units of time. Rebecs communicate with each other by sending messages of the form $o.m(\overline{e})$, where o specifies the recipient of the message. The execution of the message is non-blocking, meaning that the corresponding message m along with its arguments $\overline{e}$ is put in the receiver's message queue and the sender continues executing the subsequent statements in the message server. Timed Rebeca's call-statement may include *timing constraints*:

- The **after**(t) tag may be attached to a message and defines the earliest time that the message can be served as t time units after the time when the message was sent. This means that the receiver can take the message from its queue only after t units of time elapsed.
- The **deadline**(t) tag may be attached to a message and defines the expiration time of the message, the last time the message can be served, as t time units after the time when the message was sent.
  This means that the message remains at most t units of time in the receiver's queue, and is ignored[3] later if its processing has not already started.

A deadline parameter can have the special value **Inf**, representing a deadline that never expires. These **after** and **deadline** tags need to be considered for the enabledness of rebecs. In Timed Rebeca, a rebec is enabled if it is not busy handling a message and its message queue has a message with **after**(t) such that t is less than the time in an **after** tag of any messages of any other actor. Such a message is also called an enabled message. This corresponds to an *implicit* model of global time which will later be made *explicit* in our semantics.

---

[3] An implementation may or may not garbage collect expired messages.

2.2   Example: A Thermostat and a Heater in Timed Rebeca

```
1    reactiveclass Thermostat {
2      knownrebecs { Heater heater; }
3      statevars { int period; int temp; }
4      Thermostat(int p, int t) {
5        self.period = p;
6        self.temp = t;
7        self.checkTemp();
8      }
9      msgsrv checkTemp() {
10       if (self.temp >= 30) self.heater.off() deadline(20);
11       if (self.temp <= 25) self.heater.on() deadline(20);
12       self.checkTemp() after(self.period);
13     }
14     msgsrv changeTemp(int delta) { self.temp = self.temp + delta; }
15   }
16   reactiveclass Heater {
17     knownrebecs { Thermostat thermostat; }
18     statevars { boolean on; int delta; }
19     Heater() {
20       self.on = false;
21       self.run();
22     }
23     msgsrv on() { delay(2); self.on = true; }
24     msgsrv off() { delay(2); self.on = false; }
25     msgsrv run() {
26       self.delta = ?(1,2,3);
27       if (self.on == false) self.delta = -1 * self.delta;
28       self.thermostat.changeTemp(self.delta);
29       self.run() after(10);
30     }
31   }
32   main { Thermostat t(h):(5, 25); Heater h(t):(); }
```

Fig. 2. A model of a thermostat and a heating system in Timed Rebeca.

We use a simple example, originally presented in [19], that models a thermo-stat and a heater. The goal of the system is to keep the temperature between 25 and 30°. The system consists of two objects or *rebecs*, a thermostat and a heater. The thermostat checks the temperature periodically. If the temperature is out-side the desired range, the thermostat sends to the heater the appropriate "on" or "off" message. It takes two time units for the heater to turn on or off. The temperature is non-deterministically changed every 10 time units, depending on whether the heater is on or off.

The Timed Rebeca model, shown in Fig. 2, consist of two classes Thermostat (lines 1–15) and Heater (lines 16–31). The main block (line 32) instantiates one rebec for each reactive class. The main block starts the system with an initial temperature of 25 and specifies that the period of checking the temperature by the thermostat is 5.

A Thermostat rebec knows a rebec of type Heater, and has two integer state variables period and temp. The latter models the temperature sensor. Hence, the temperature can be changed simply by setting the temp variable. The Thermostat constructor initializes the two state variables from the values received as arguments, and sends to itself a checkTemp message to initiate its periodic behavior: When temp >= 30 it sends a message to heater to turn it off, when temp <= 25 it sends a message to heater to turn it on, both messages have **deadline**(20). It finally calls itself again, so the periodic behavior restarts after at least period time units, using the tag **after**. Observe that the fields of a rebec (i.e., the state variables and known rebecs) are accessed via a preceding the keyword **self**.

A Heater rebec knows a rebec of type Thermostat, and has two state variables on and delta. The constructor initializes the variable on = false, assigns the default value 0 to delta, and calls itself to run its periodic behavior: it randomly selects a value for delta, then sends a message to the Thermostat with the effect to decrease (increase) the temperature in case the heater is off (on) by delta. It finally calls itself again, so the periodic behavior starts again after 10 time units, using the tag **after**. A Heater receives messages to turn itself on or off which takes two time units, using the **delay** statement.

3 Basics of LAGC Semantics

We briefly introduce the ideas underlying LAGC semantics. For space reasons, we do not give full technical definitions of LAGC, but introduce essential notions in a compact manner (for a fully precise account, see [7]). Remark that this section may be skipped on first reading and consulted if clarifications are needed; it is included to make the paper more self-contained (furthermore, the text contains some excerpts from [8]).

The main principle of LAGC semantics [7] is to strictly separate two phases: The first evaluates statements to sets of parameterized, *symbolic* local traces. The second instantiates the parameters and composes local traces. Composed traces must respect a well-formedness predicate derived from the semantics of the underlying programming language, without referring to program syntax or intermediate structures. Together, well-formed traces over states and events avoid complex data structures in configurations of reduction rules as it is the case in SOS rules [17]. LAGC configurations contain not only the current state, but the whole trace leading to it, including any events that occurred. This richer structure makes it easy to extract information. The modular separation of progress and composition is also crucial for our presentation. It permits an incremental presentation of LAGC for Timed Rebeca.

3.1   States

To permit *symbolic* expressions (i.e., containing variables) occurring as *values* in program states, we use the star expression $*$ to represent an unknown value that cannot be further evaluated. The $*$ symbol does not occur in programs, only in the semantics. We adopt the notational convention of using capital letters for symbolic variables; but symbolic and non-symbolic variables belong to the same syntactic category and some operations transform a symbolic variable into a non-symbolic one. We keep the syntax and semantics of expressions abstract (as does [19]). In the examples we use standard arithmetic and boolean expressions with their canonical semantics informally.

Definition 1 (Symbolic State, State Update). *A symbolic state σ is a partial mapping $\sigma : Var \rightharpoonup Sexp$ from variables to* symbolic expressions $Sexp = Exp \cup \{*\}$. *A symbolic variable is a variable X bound to an unknown value $\sigma(X) = *$. Sexp are expressions that contain symbolic variables. The notation $\sigma[x \mapsto se]$ expresses the* update *of state σ at x with symbolic expression se.*

In a symbolic state σ, its symbolic variables $\mathrm{symb}(\sigma)$ act as parameters, relative to which a local computation is evaluated. They are used to represent, for example, call parameters that cannot be known locally. We assume there are no dangling references.[4] States without symbolic variables are called *concrete*. We denote by $\sigma \subseteq \sigma'$ that state σ' extends (as a mapping) state σ.

Example 1. $\sigma = [x \mapsto Y + 42, Y \mapsto *]$ is a symbolic state with $\mathrm{symb}(\sigma) = \{Y\}$.

Timed Rebeca requires a notion of time that extends the languages that were given an LAGC semantics in [7]. For the semantics, this means that evaluation must track the (global) time when time evolves. In the sequel, the parameter N over non-negative integers serves this purpose.

Timed Rebeca classes are instantiated into rebecs o. These are represented by the domain *RId*. In Timed Rebeca, each rebec is an actor with its own processor; therefore, it is necessary to keep track of the object where semantic evaluation takes place. We use the parameter O for this purpose.

We assume an evaluation function $\mathrm{val}_\sigma^{O,N} : Sexp \rightarrow Sexp$ for symbolic expressions se in the context of a state σ, an object O and execution time N, defined as usual for concrete expressions, and defined as $\mathrm{val}_\sigma^{O,N}(X) = X$ for symbolic variables $X \in \mathrm{symb}(\sigma)$. The evaluation of most expressions simply ignores the parameters O, N, with the exception of the **self** reference, where $\mathrm{val}_\sigma^{O,N}(\textbf{self}) = O$, and fields **self.**v, where $\mathrm{val}_\sigma^{O,N}(\textbf{self.}v) = \sigma(O.v)$.

It is always possible to evaluate expressions without symbolic variables to values and one could define a set of simplification rules on symbolic expressions, but they are not needed in the context of this article. The evaluation function is trivially extended to sets of expressions.

---

[4] A dangling reference is a reference to a variable that is not in the symbolic store.

3.2   Traces and Events

Traces are sequences over states and structured events. For example, the presence of synchronization events makes it possible to express restrictions on call sequences via well-formedness conditions. Symbolic states imply symbolic traces, which motivates to constrain traces by path conditions:

Definition 2 (Path Condition). *A path condition pc is a finite set of Boolean expressions. A fully evaluated concrete pc is exactly one of $\emptyset$, $\{\mathrm{ff}\}$, $\{\mathrm{tt}\}$, $\{\mathrm{ff}, \mathrm{tt}\}$. It is consistent when it does not contain ff. For any concrete state σ, path condition $\mathrm{val}_\sigma^{O,N}(pc)$ is fully evaluated.*

Definition 3 (Event Marker, Conditioned Symbolic Trace). *An event marker over expressions $\overline{e}$ is a term of the form $ev(\overline{e})$. A symbolic trace τ is defined inductively by the following rules (ε denotes the empty trace):*

$$\tau ::= \varepsilon \mid \tau \curvearrowright \nu \qquad\qquad \nu ::= \sigma \mid ev(\overline{e}) \ .$$

A *conditioned symbolic trace has the form $pc \triangleright \tau$, where pc is a path condition and τ is a symbolic trace. If pc is consistent, we simply write τ for $pc \triangleright \tau$.*

Traces can be finite or infinite. Let $\langle \sigma \rangle$ denote the *singleton trace* $\varepsilon \curvearrowright \sigma$. *Concatenation* of two traces τ_1, τ_2 is written as $\tau_1 \cdot \tau_2$ and defined when τ_1 is finite. The final state of a non-empty, finite trace τ is selected with $\mathrm{last}(\tau)$, the first state with $\mathrm{first}(\tau)$, respectively.

Example 2. A conditioned symbolic trace is $\tau = \{Y > 0\} \triangleright \langle \sigma \rangle \curvearrowright \sigma[w \mapsto 17]$, where σ is as in Example 1.

Traces semantically model sequential composition of program statements. Assume τ_r, τ_s are traces of statements r, s, respectively. To obtain the trace corresponding to sequential composition $r; s$, traces τ_r and τ_s must be concatenated, but the first state of the second trace should be identical to (or more precisely an extension of) the final state of the first trace. The chop operator gets rid of the redundant intermediate state.

Definition 4 (Chop on Traces [10,16,25]). *Let pc_1, pc_2 be path conditions and τ_1, τ_2 be symbolic traces, and assume that τ_1 is a non-empty, finite trace. The semantic chop $(pc_1 \triangleright \tau_1) ** (pc_2 \triangleright \tau_2)$ is defined as follows:*

$$(pc_1 \triangleright \tau_1) ** (pc_2 \triangleright \tau_2) = (pc_1 \cup pc_2) \triangleright \tau \cdot \tau_2 \text{ where } \tau_1 = \tau \curvearrowright \sigma, \ \tau_2 = \langle \sigma' \rangle \cdot \tau' \text{ if } \sigma \subseteq \sigma' \ .$$

Chop is well-defined when the first argument is a finite non-empty trace, we only use it this way.

Events are uniquely associated with that state in a trace, where they occur. Events do not update a state, but may extend it with new symbolic variables. To do so, an event $ev(\overline{e})$ is inserted into a trace after a state σ, which can be extended by fresh symbolic variables $\overline{V}$, using an *event trace* $ev_\sigma^{\overline{V}}(\overline{e})$ of length three:

$$ev_\sigma^{\overline{V}}(\overline{e}) = \langle\sigma\rangle \curvearrowright ev(\overline{e}) \curvearrowright \sigma', \text{ where } \sigma' = \sigma[\overline{V} \mapsto *].$$

Given a trace of the form $\tau_1 \curvearrowright \sigma$ and event $ev(\overline{e})$ with fresh symbolic variables $\overline{V}$, appending the event is achieved by the trace $\tau_1 \cdot ev_\sigma^{\overline{V}}(\overline{e})$. Def. 4 ensures that events in traces are joinable: $\tau ** ev_\sigma^{\overline{V}}(e)$ is well-defined whenever $\text{last}(\tau) = \sigma$. If $\overline{V}$ is empty then the state is unchanged, in this case we omit the set of symbolic variables: $ev_\sigma(\overline{e}) = ev_\sigma^{\emptyset}(\overline{e})$.

Example 3. To insert event $ev(Z)$, introducing symbolic variable Z, into trace τ from Example 2 at σ we use the event trace $ev_\sigma^{\{Z\}}(Z) = \langle\sigma\rangle \curvearrowright ev(Z) \curvearrowright \sigma[Z \mapsto *]$. The result is: $\{Y > 0\} \triangleright \langle\sigma\rangle \curvearrowright ev(Z) \curvearrowright \sigma[Z \mapsto *] \curvearrowright \sigma[Z \mapsto *, w \mapsto 17]$.

Traces are assumed to be well-formed, for example the domains of their states match, variables in events are defined, events $ev_\sigma(\overline{e})$ in traces must be aligned with the states before and after, and so on [7].

To enable tracking of the actor where a statement is evaluated, we will tag traces with objects.

Definition 5 (Tagged Trace). *Let $ev(\overline{e})$ be an event, τ a trace, and $o \in RId$ an object. A tagged trace τ^o is defined inductively as follows:*

$$(ev(\overline{e}))^o = ev^o(\overline{e})$$
$$\sigma^o = \sigma$$
$$(\tau \curvearrowright \nu)^o = \tau^o \curvearrowright \nu^o$$

3.3 Making Traces Concrete

Traces with symbolic variables model program executions relative to an unknown context. The symbolic variables in such traces become instantiated when the execution they represent is scheduled in a concrete context. At this point a symbolic trace is *concretized* by instantiating all of its symbolic variables. This results in a concrete trace with a path condition that is either consistent or not. Technically, we use the notion of a *concretization mapping*. A concretization mapping is defined relative to a state. It associates a concrete value to each symbolic variable of the state.

Definition 6 (State Concretization Mapping). *A mapping $\rho : Var \to Val$ is a concretization mapping for a state σ if $\text{dom}(\rho) \cap \text{dom}(\sigma) = \text{symb}(\sigma)$.*

A concretization mapping ρ may also define the value of variables not in the domain of σ. Concretization mappings are canonically extended to events and conditioned traces [7].

Example 4. Consider σ of Example 1 with $\text{symb}(\sigma) = \{Y\}$. We define a concretization mapping $\rho = [Y \mapsto 3]$ for σ with $\rho(\sigma) = [x \mapsto 45, Y \mapsto 3]$. Applying ρ to the trace in Example 2, we obtain $\rho(\tau) = \{3 > 0\} \triangleright \langle\rho(\sigma)\rangle \curvearrowright \rho(\sigma)[w \mapsto 17]$. We adopt the convention to strip away consistent path conditions such as here.

3.4   Continuations

The LAGC semantics evaluates one single statement "locally". Obviously, it is not possible to fully evaluate composite statements in this manner. Therefore, local LAGC rules perform one evaluation step at a time and defer evaluation of the remaining statements, which are put into a *timed continuation*, to be subjected to subsequent rule applications at a later time. Timed continuations extend the continuations of the original LAGC paper [7] to accommodate timed semantics. Syntactically, timed continuations are simply statements s wrapped in the symbol K and tagged by the time when they can be executed: $\mathrm{K}^t(s)$. To achieve uniform definitions we allow the case that no further evaluation is required (i.e., the evaluation has been completed) and use the "empty bottle" symbol ($\mathbb{0}$) for this purpose.

Definition 7 (Timed Continuation Marker). *Let s be a program statement or the symbol $\mathbb{0}$, and let t_0 be a non-negative integer. Then a timed continuation marker has the form $\mathrm{K}^{t_0+N}(s)$, where N is the time parameter.*

4   LAGC Semantics for Timed Rebeca

Local evaluation defines sets of parameterized, symbolic traces that can later be composed into global executions. Local evaluation is defined such that for each statement s and state σ, the result of $\mathrm{val}_\sigma^{O,N}(s)$ is a set of tagged, conditioned, symbolic traces, so-called *continuation traces*, of the form

$$pc \triangleright \tau \cdot \mathrm{K}^t(s') \in \mathbf{CTr} \ ,$$

where τ is a *finite* symbolic trace and s' the remaining statements to be evaluated. Let Θ be the set of traces of s' and ρ any concretization mapping; then the expression $pc \triangleright \tau \cdot \mathrm{K}^t(s')$ is used to describe the set of traces: $\{\rho(\tau) ** \tau' \mid \rho(pc) \text{ consistent}, \tau' \in \Theta\}$. In other words, the traces in this set can be consistently instantiated from τ, and extended by executing s' at time t.

4.1   LAGC Semantics of For

We now define the LAGC semantics of For, the imperative fragment of Timed Rebeca.

The rule for **skip** generates an empty path condition, returns the state σ it was called in, and produces the empty continuation, resulting in a single trace:

$$\mathrm{val}_\sigma^{O,N}(\mathbf{skip}) = \{\emptyset \triangleright \langle \sigma \rangle \cdot \mathrm{K}^N(\mathbb{0})\} \ .$$

The assignment rules generate an empty path condition and traces from the current state σ to a state updating σ at x, and produce the empty continuation.

$$\mathrm{val}_\sigma^{O,N}(x = e) = \{\emptyset \triangleright \langle \sigma \rangle \curvearrowright \sigma[x \mapsto \mathrm{val}_\sigma^{O,N}(e)] \cdot \mathrm{K}^N(\mathbb{0})\} \ .$$

$$\mathrm{val}_\sigma^{O,N}(x =?(e_1,\ldots,e_m)) = \bigcup_{1\leq j\leq m} \mathrm{val}_\sigma^{O,N}(x = e_j) \ .$$

The conditional statement is a complex statement and cannot be evaluated locally in one step, so we expect it to produce a non-empty continuation. The rule branches on the value of the condition, resulting in two traces with complementary path conditions. The first trace is obtained from the current state and the continuation corresponding to the **if**-branch, and the second trace corresponds to an empty else-branch:

$$\mathrm{val}_\sigma^{O,N}(\mathbf{if}\ (e)\ \{\ s\ \}) = \{\{\,\mathrm{val}_\sigma^{O,N}(e)\} \triangleright \langle\sigma\rangle \cdot \mathrm{K}^N(s),\quad \{\mathrm{val}_\sigma^{O,N}(!e)\} \triangleright \langle\sigma\rangle \cdot \mathrm{K}^N(\emptyset)\,\}$$

Timed Rebeca's conditional has an optional **else** branch which we do not model here. It is obvious and not needed in the examples.

The rule for sequential composition $r; s$ is obtained by first evaluating r to traces of the form $pc \triangleright \tau \cdot \mathrm{K}^N(r')$ with continuation r', and then adding s to r':

$$\mathrm{val}_\sigma^{O,N}(r; s) = \{pc \triangleright \tau \cdot \mathrm{K}^t(r'; s) \mid pc \triangleright \tau \cdot \mathrm{K}^t(r') \in \mathrm{val}_\sigma^{O,N}(r)\} \ .$$

If r' is the empty continuation $\emptyset$, it must be ignored. To achieve this the rewrite rule "$\emptyset; s \rightsquigarrow s$" is exhaustively applied to statements inside continuations.

Example 5. We start evaluation of the statement $s_{seq} = (x := 1;\ y := x + 1)$ in an arbitrary symbolic state σ. The rule for sequential composition yields $\mathrm{val}_\sigma^{O,N}(s_{seq}) = \{\emptyset \triangleright \langle\sigma\rangle \curvearrowright \sigma[x \mapsto 1] \cdot \mathrm{K}^N(y := x + 1)\}$. It uses the result of evaluating the first assignment in the context of σ: $\mathrm{val}_\sigma^{O,N}(x := 1) = \{\emptyset \triangleright \langle\sigma\rangle \curvearrowright \sigma[x \mapsto 1] \cdot \mathrm{K}^N(\emptyset)\}$.

We use the semantics of **for** to illustrate that the semantics of a statement can be expressed in terms of the semantics of other statements (here **if** and sequence), without having to expose intermediate states:

$$\begin{aligned}\mathrm{val}_\sigma^{O,N}&(\mathbf{for}\ (s_1;\ e;\ s_2)\ \{\ s_3\ \}) \\ &= \mathrm{val}_\sigma^{O,N}(s_1;\ \mathbf{if}\ (e)\ \{s_3;\ s_2;\ \mathbf{for}\ (\mathbf{skip};\ e;\ s_2)\ \{\ s_3\ \}\}) \ .\end{aligned}$$

Note that this definition is not circular because the evaluation of **if** puts the **for** statement inside a continuation. In practice, loops are rarely used in actor languages such as Timed Rebeca.

4.2   Event Structure

Events in LAGC traces record behavioral aspects that cannot be recovered from a sequence of states alone. In Timed Rebeca, this concerns the creation of rebecs (actors), the invocation and scheduling of messages, and the evolution of time.

Definition 8. *The following events are used in the LAGC semantics for actor and timed constructs. All events but the last are tagged by the object o on which the event is observed.*

- *$newEv^o(\text{createdRebec}, \text{knownRebecs}, \text{constrParams})$ observes the creation of a new rebec createdRebec with known rebecs knownRebecs and constructor parameters constrParams.*
- *$invEv^o(\text{callParams}, \text{callee}, \text{msgName}, \text{callId}, \text{after}, \text{deadline})$ observes the invocation of a message msgName from caller o to callee with call identifier callId and arguments callParams. The message cannot be called before time after is reached and it expires after time deadline. The call identifier is chosen in a way such that it uniquely identifies a message call.*
- *$invREv^o(\text{callParams}, \text{msgName}, \text{callId})$ observes that a called message can be scheduled for execution and stands for "invocation reaction event" [6]. The parameters are a subset of those for invocation events.*
- *$delayEv^o(\text{time})$ observes that the currently executed message on rebec o takes non-zero time to execute and it can continue at the earliest at time.*
- *$timeEv(\text{time})$ observes an advance of the global system clock to time. Since the clock does not belong to any specific actor, it is not tagged.*

Since a call identifier uniquely determines a message call, one can ask why the message name and call arguments are needed as parameters of invocation reaction events. This allows the evaluation of all statements the LAGC semantics to be completely *local*. Rule (1) below needs not only to guess the call identifier, but also the matching call (i.e., the message name and arguments).

To enhance readability, event parameters in the previous definition have mnemonic names. To save space in the semantic rules we use o, o',... for rebecs, e, e', $\overline{e}$,... for (sequences of) expressions, , v, v', $\overline{v}$,... for (sequences of) concrete semantic values, m for message names, i for call identifiers, and t, t',... for time points.

4.3 LAGC Semantics of Dynamic Object Creation

The local evaluation rule for dynamic object creation emits a *new* event and extends the given state σ with the variables declared in the object's class C.

$$\text{val}_\sigma^{O,N}(x = \textbf{new } C\,(\overline{e_1}) : (\overline{e_2})) =$$
$$\{\emptyset \triangleright newEv_\sigma^{\{X\}}(X, \overline{v_1}, \overline{v_2}) \curvearrowright \sigma[x \mapsto X, X \mapsto *, \overline{X.kr \mapsto v_1}] \cdot K^N(X.C(\overline{v_2})) \mid$$
$$X \in RId,\ \text{class}(X) = C,\ kr \in \text{knownRebecs}(C),\ X \notin \text{dom}(\sigma),$$
$$\overline{v_1} = \text{val}_\sigma^{O,N}(\overline{e_1}),\ \overline{v_2} = \text{val}_\sigma^{O,N}(\overline{e_2})\}\ .$$

The rule creates a fresh symbolic variable X to represent the unknown object identity that is returned. The name of the new object is simply guessed; the well-formedness predicate in the composition rules will later check that the name is indeed fresh (see Sect. 4.7). A *new actor* creation event is issued that records the new object, its known rebec parameters, and its initial value parameters. Next, the current state σ is extended with the as yet unknown object X as well as with the known rebec arguments. The continuation of this rule is a call to the constructor function of class C with the values of parameters $\overline{e_2}$. The path condition is empty.

In the creation of new actors, care must be taken to avoid name clashes between the fields of different actors. Concretely, this problem can be solved by systematically prefixing fields by the symbolic identifier X of the new actor, to be concretized later. Here, the names of the known rebec declarations are prefixed by the symbolic actor identifier and mapped to the actual parameter values $\overline{e_1}$. We assume that fields are similarly prefixed by the object identifier when evaluating the constructor function and that field accesses are always prefixed by **self** (for example, **self**.v).

4.4   LAGC Semantics for the Timed Constructs

We now define evaluation rules for the timed constructs of Timed Rebeca. The rule for delay extends the trace with a *delay* event that has as parameter a time $t = N + \mathrm{val}_\sigma^{O,N}(e)$, the absolute time relative to the current global time N, at which the currently executing message can continue. The continuation is empty.

$$\mathrm{val}_\sigma^{O,N}(\mathbf{delay}(e)) = \{\emptyset \triangleright delayEv_\sigma(t) \cdot \mathrm{K}^t(\emptyset) \mid t = N + \mathrm{val}_\sigma^{O,N}(e)\} \ .$$

The rule for asynchronous message passing of m to a receiver e_1 with arguments $\overline{e}$, as well as time constraints **after**(e_2) and **deadline**(e_3), extends the trace with an *invocation* event $invEv(\mathrm{val}_\sigma^{O,N}(\overline{e}), \mathrm{val}_\sigma^{O,N}(e_1), m, i, t_1, t_2)$, then ends with the empty continuation. It has an empty path condition. This corresponds to a *non-blocking* semantics of message calls: The code following the message call can continue executing. Observe that the event includes absolute time point t_1 relative to the current global time N when the message that is appended to the recipient $\mathrm{val}_\sigma^{O,N}(e_1)$ can be earliest scheduled, as well as the absolute expiration time t_2 after which the message cannot longer be scheduled. Messages have a unique identifier i which is guessed during trace composition. The well-formedness rules will ensure that i is unique.

$$\begin{aligned}
\mathrm{val}_\sigma^{O,N}&(e_1.m(\overline{e}) \ \mathbf{after}(e_2) \ \mathbf{deadline}(e_3)) \\
&= \{\emptyset \triangleright invEv_\sigma(\mathrm{val}_\sigma^{O,N}(\overline{e}), \mathrm{val}_\sigma^{O,N}(e_1), m, i, t_1, t_2) \cdot \mathrm{K}^N(\emptyset) \\
&\quad \mid t_1 = N + \mathrm{val}_\sigma^{O,N}(e_2), t_2 = N + \mathrm{val}_\sigma^{O,N}(e_3), i \in MId\} \ .
\end{aligned}$$

The time constraints **after** and **deadline** are optional. When they are not present, they are implicitly added as follows:

$$\mathrm{val}_\sigma^{O,N}(e.m(\overline{e})) = \mathrm{val}_\sigma^{O,N}(e.m(\overline{e}) \ \mathbf{after}(0) \ \mathbf{deadline}(\mathbf{Inf}))$$
$$\mathrm{val}_\sigma^{O,N}(e_1.m(\overline{e}) \ \mathbf{after}(e_2)) = \mathrm{val}_\sigma^{O,N}(e_1.m(\overline{e}) \ \mathbf{after}(e_2) \ \mathbf{deadline}(\mathbf{Inf}))$$
$$\mathrm{val}_\sigma^{O,N}(e_1.m(\overline{e}) \ \mathbf{deadline}(e_2)) = \mathrm{val}_\sigma^{O,N}(e_1.m(\overline{e}) \ \mathbf{after}(0) \ \mathbf{deadline}(e_2))$$

The time model of Timed Rebeca assumes a global clock which has always a positive integer value starting at 0. Observe that when calculating the **after** value t_1 of an invocation event as $N + 0$, this means that the message can potentially be scheduled immediately in the receiver's (FIFO) queue. Similarly, when calculating the **deadline** value t_2 of an invocation event as $N + $ **Inf**, it will evaluate to **Inf** which is greater than any value of N. This means that a message with **deadline**(**Inf**) never expires.

4.5 Message Servers and Classes

The semantics of a message server is a trace that starts with an invocation reaction event corresponding to a previous invocation event. The values of the formal parameters cannot be known locally, so we introduce symbolic variables for them. These are instantiated during trace composition such that the invocation reaction event matches a previous invocation event. At this time also the correct call identifier is guessed.

$$
\begin{aligned}
\mathrm{val}_\sigma^{O,N}(\textbf{msgsrv}\ m(\overline{T\ x})\ \{sc\}) = \\
\{\emptyset \triangleright invREv_\sigma^{\overline{Z}}(\overline{Z}, m, i) \curvearrowright \sigma[\overline{z} \mapsto \overline{Z}, \overline{Z} \mapsto *, \overline{z}' \mapsto d_{\overline{x}'}] \cdot \mathrm{K}^N(sc[\overline{x}, \overline{x}' \leftarrow \overline{z}, \overline{z}']) \quad (1) \\
\mid \overline{z}, \overline{Z} \notin \mathrm{dom}(\sigma),\ i \in MId\ \}\ .
\end{aligned}
$$

There is a subtlety in Timed Rebeca concerning the formal parameters of messages: Not all state variables need to occur among them, some may be initialized with default values. Let $\overline{x}'$ be the state variables in m's class that do not occur in $\overline{x}$. To avoid name clashes in formal parameters $\overline{x}, \overline{x}'$ of different message executions, these are renamed to fresh names $\overline{z}, \overline{z}'$, where the $\overline{z}$ are given symbolic values $\overline{Z}$ and the $\overline{z}'$ default values in the new state $\sigma[\overline{z} \mapsto \overline{Z}, \overline{Z} \mapsto *, \overline{z}' \mapsto d_{\overline{x}'}]$. We repeat the renaming trick for local variables in the following rule:

$$
\mathrm{val}_\sigma^{O,N}(T\ x; d\ s) = \{\emptyset \triangleright \langle\sigma\rangle \curvearrowright \sigma[x' \mapsto 0] \cdot \mathrm{K}^N(\{\ d\ s[x \leftarrow x']\ \})\mid x' \notin \mathrm{dom}(\sigma)\}\ .
$$

Although we elide the exact expression syntax and its semantics, it may be useful to remind the reader of how to evaluate the self reference **self**:

$$
\mathrm{val}_\sigma^{O,N}(\textbf{self}) = O\ .
$$

4.6 The Trace Composition Rules

We observed that local evaluation returns an empty continuation $\emptyset$ when the execution is complete. Therefore, in the composition rules below, the empty continuation may occur as an input and needs to be locally evaluated. The evaluation of the empty continuation yields the empty set of traces:

$$
\mathrm{val}_\sigma^{O,N}(\emptyset) = \{\}\ .
$$

Local traces are instantiated and composed into concrete global ones. Since the code in the body of a message server is non-blocking, sequential and deterministic, there is exactly one trace, provided that the execution starts in a concrete state that assigns values to all the variables of a program [7]. Consequently, no scheduler needs to be defined for the execution of a message, only for *when* messages are executed. However, in general different actors process messages simultaneously at any given time. This is reflected in the semantic configurations.

Definition 9 (Configuration). *An LAGC configuration for semantic evaluation is a pair sh, Σ, where sh is a concrete, tagged trace and Σ is a partial mapping from rebec identifiers in RId to timed continuations of the form $K^N(s)$.*

The task of the composition rule for message servers is to evaluate statements in a concrete state until the next continuation, then stitch the resulting concrete traces together. Given a configuration with *concrete* trace sh having final state σ and a continuation $\Sigma(o) = K^N(s)$, we can evaluate s starting in σ. The auxiliary function now(sh) returns the current global time at the end of trace sh, which we need to schedule and evaluate the continuation $K^N(s)$. The result is a set of conditioned traces from which one trace with a consistent path condition and a trailing continuation $K^N(s')$ is chosen for the execution on o (via tagging the resulting concrete trace $\rho(\tau)$).

Rule (2) models *progress* in the execution of an activated message. A subtle point is that the rule is not applicable when $s = 0$, because then, by definition, the evaluated trace set is empty.

$$\frac{\Sigma(o) = K^n(s) \quad \sigma = \mathrm{last}(sh) \quad n = \mathrm{now}(sh) \quad pc \rhd \tau \cdot K^T(s') \in \mathrm{val}_\sigma^{o,n}(s)}{s \neq 0 \quad \rho \text{ concretizes } \tau, T \quad \rho(pc) \text{ consistent} \quad \mathrm{wf}(sh ** \rho(\tau)^o)} \quad (2)$$
$$sh, \Sigma \to sh ** \rho(\tau)^o, \Sigma[o \mapsto K^{\rho(T)}(s')]$$

Rule (3) models the *activation* of a new message on o. This is only possible, when these conditions are fulfilled: (i) the actor o is idle, i.e. $\Sigma(o) = K^t(0)$ (or it has not yet executed anything); (ii) since the semantics is denotational, there is an invocation event corresponding to the activation in sh; and (iii) the time constraints given at invocation time must be satisfied. The rule "guesses" values for an invocation reaction event fulfilling these conditions and the well-formedness of global traces (Sect. 4.7) will ensure that they hold. In this semantic model, actors are only created once they start processing the first message.

$$\frac{n = \mathrm{now}(sh) \quad (\Sigma(o) = K^t(0) \text{ or } o \notin \mathrm{dom}(\Sigma)) \quad \sigma = \mathrm{last}(sh)}{\mathrm{lookup}(m, \mathcal{G}) = m(\overline{x}) \, sc \quad pc \rhd \tau \cdot K^n(s) \in \mathrm{val}_\sigma^{o,n}(m(\overline{x}) \, sc)} \quad (3)$$
$$\frac{\rho \text{ concretizes } \tau \quad \rho(pc) \text{ consistent} \quad \mathrm{wf}(sh ** \rho(\tau)^o)}{sh, \Sigma \to sh ** \rho(\tau)^o, \Sigma[o \mapsto K^n(s)]}$$

Rule (4) models *time advance*. In this rule, pending(sh, o) is an auxiliary function over traces sh (defined in Sect. 4.7) that expresses that there is a pending message ready to be executed on rebec o. Thus, the premises of the rule express two constraints: (i) there is no non-empty enabled continuation for o at the current time n, and (ii) there is no executable message at current time n for any

o. Rule (4) can then be expressed as follows:

$$\frac{n = \mathrm{now}(sh) \qquad \sigma = \mathrm{last}(sh) \qquad \forall o.\,|\mathrm{pending}(sh,o)| = 0}{sh, \Sigma \to sh ** timeEv_\sigma(n+1), \Sigma} \tag{4}$$

with premise $\forall o.\,\big(\Sigma(o) = \mathrm{K}^t(s) \wedge s \neq \emptyset \implies n < t\big)$

4.7   Well-Formedness

We use the well-formedness predicate $\mathrm{wf}(sh)$ on concrete, tagged traces to ensure that only traces conforming to the Timed Rebeca semantics can be produced by the trace composition rules (2)–(4). The relevant information is contained in the various events emitted during local evaluation, therefore, we define well-formedness inductively over the final event in a trace. The correct evolution of states and delay events is ensured by local evaluation, so no restriction is necessary here. The correctness of time events is guaranteed by a separate condition in the premise of rule (4), so we have four trivial cases:

$$\mathrm{wf}(\epsilon) = true$$
$$\mathrm{wf}(sh \curvearrowright \sigma) = \mathrm{wf}(sh)$$
$$\mathrm{wf}(sh \curvearrowright delayEv(t)) = \mathrm{wf}(sh)$$
$$\mathrm{wf}(sh \curvearrowright timeEv(t)) = \mathrm{wf}(sh)$$

When creating a new rebec on actor o, two conditions must be ensured. First, there cannot be another rebec associated with the name o; second, the known rebecs passed to the new rebec must be known to the caller o'.

$$\mathrm{wf}(sh \curvearrowright newEv^{o'}(o, \overline{o}, \overline{v})) =$$
$$\mathrm{wf}(sh) \wedge \ \nexists o'', \overline{o'}, \overline{v'}.\, newEv^{o''}(o, \overline{o'}, \overline{v'}) \in sh \wedge \overline{o} \subseteq \mathrm{knows}(sh, o') \ .$$

Known rebecs are tracked in the function knows, It extracts from the "new" events in a tagged concrete trace the rebecs known by o: Whenever o is created, by definition it knows the known rebecs $\overline{o}$ passed as the second argument of the event (first equation). Whenever o creates a new rebec o' this is added to its known rebecs (second equation). The third equation deals with initialization and is explained in the subsequent section.

$$\mathrm{knows}(sh \curvearrowright newEv^{o'}(o, \overline{o}, \overline{v}), o) = \overline{o}$$
$$\mathrm{knows}(sh \curvearrowright newEv^o(o', \overline{o}, \overline{v}), o) = \{o'\} \cup \mathrm{knows}(sh, o)$$
$$\mathrm{knows}(sh_{init}, main) = O_R$$
$$\mathrm{knows}(sh \curvearrowright \nu, o) = \mathrm{knows}(sh, o) \ \text{otherwise}$$

Interestingly, the tracking of known rebecs is not modeled in the existing Timed Rebeca semantics [18,19]. It is a clear advantage of the compositional design of the LAGC semantics that this can be added simply by extending well-formedness by one more predicate.

Turning to message calls, the central property that invocation events need to ensure is that each call identifier is unique in a given trace. In addition, the rebec o on which the message is invoked must exist and be known to the caller o':

$$\mathrm{wf}(sh \curvearrowright invEv^{o'}(\overline{v}, o, m, i, t_1, t_2)) =$$
$$\mathrm{wf}(sh) \wedge o \in \mathrm{knows}(sh, o') \wedge \exists o'', \overline{o}, \overline{v}'.newEv^{o''}(o, \overline{o}, \overline{v}') \in sh$$
$$\wedge\, \nexists o'', \overline{v}', o''', m', t_1', t_2'.\, invEv^{o''}(\overline{v}', o''', m', i, t_1', t_2') \in sh \ .$$

The most complex definition is that for invocation reaction events, because two properties must be ensured: The call with identifier i to be executed has not already been selected earlier (second conjunct) and the message can actually be scheduled at the current time. The formula in the third conjunct first retrieves an invocation event with matching callee, identifier, message name, and call arguments, then makes sure that the current time is within the specified bounds. Observe that $\mathrm{now}(sh) \leq \mathtt{Inf}$ is always true.

$$\mathrm{wf}(sh \curvearrowright invREv^{o}(\overline{v}, m, i)) = \mathrm{wf}(sh) \wedge \nexists o', \overline{v}', m'.\, invREv^{o'}(\overline{v}', m', i) \in sh$$
$$\wedge\, \left(\exists o', t_1, t_2.invEv^{o'}(\overline{v}, o, m, i, t_1, t_2) \in sh \wedge t_1 \leq \mathrm{now}(sh) \leq t_2\right) \ . \ (5)$$

Remark 1. By inspection of the well-formedness equations, one can see that delay events are not required in the LAGC semantics. However, they are often useful to reconstruct the full timed behavior from a given trace.

To find the current clock time in a given trace, we simply look for the most recent time event and take its argument:

$$\mathrm{now}(sh \curvearrowright timeEv(n)) = n$$
$$\mathrm{now}(sh \curvearrowright \nu) \qquad = \mathrm{now}(sh) \text{ otherwise}$$

It remains to define the pending function used in rule (4). Let us first make precise what we mean by pending:

Definition 10 (Pending Invocation Event). *A tagged concrete trace sh contains a pending invocation event if:*

1. *sh contains an invocation event for message m, arguments $\overline{v}$, call identifier i, and time constraints t_1, t_2;*
2. *sh contains no subsequent invocation reaction event with call identifier i;*
3. *such an invocation reaction event could be scheduled now.*

The first and third condition correspond to the third conjunct of Eq. (5), the second condition to its second conjunct. This means we can define the pending function with the help of well-formedness as follows:

$$\mathrm{pending}(sh, o) = \{i \mid \exists m, \overline{v}.\mathrm{wf}(sh \curvearrowright invREv^{o}(\overline{v}, m, i))\} \ . \qquad (6)$$

This definition implies that the sh argument is well-formed itself, but since well-formedness of sh is an invariant guaranteed by the trace composition rules, this is no restriction.

Timed Rebeca imposes FIFO order on messages sent to the same actor. As shown in [7, Section 6.2], it is possible to add such constraints to the well-formedness predicate in a compositional manner. With the help of the pending function, the definition becomes succinct. Let the notation $i \prec_{sh} i'$ express that call identifier i appears the first time syntactically before i' in a trace sh. Then we can express FIFO simply by adding to well-formedness of invocation reaction events the constraint that the scheduled event must be the syntactically first event that can be scheduled:

$$\mathrm{wf}_{\mathrm{fifo}}(sh \curvearrowright invREv^o(\overline{v}, m, i)) =$$
$$\mathrm{wf}(sh \curvearrowright invREv^o(\overline{v}, m, i)) \land (i = \min_{\prec_{sh}} \mathrm{pending}(sh, o)) \ .$$

Remark 2. This definition of FIFO embodies a subtle semantic choice: Assume $\mathrm{now}(sh) = 1$ and $invEv^{o'}(\overline{v}, o, m, i, 2, 3) \in sh$, $invEv^{o''}(\overline{v'}, o, m, i', 1, 2) \in sh$ such that $i \prec_{sh} i'$. Then the call with identifier i' is scheduled, because the call with identifier i is not yet pending. But the call with identifier i' might cause a delay beyond time 3, in which case call i is never scheduled, even though $i \prec_{sh} i'$. We implemented *first in first **schedulable** out*, i.e., time constraints take precedence over FIFO constraints. Other semantics, where a queue is blocked until the first pending call is available, can be obtained by adjusting the definition of pending.

4.8 Initialization

For a given Timed Rebeca program, let us denote the rebecs declared in the main block by R. We assign a fixed, unique object o_r to each $r \in R$ and define the set of all initial objects to be $O_R = \{o_r \mid r \in R\}$.

The semantic evaluation of a Timed Rebeca program initially sets the global time to 0 and assigns the object o_r to each $r \in R$:

$$sh_{init} := timeEv_{\sigma_\epsilon}(0) \curvearrowright \langle \sigma_\epsilon^{main}[\overline{r \mapsto o_r}] \rangle$$

The third clause of the definition of the *knows* predicate in Sect. 4.7 ensures that at this point the *main* object knows about all initial rebecs. The semantic evaluation starts in the initial concrete trace $sh_{init} \curvearrowright newEv_\sigma^{main}(main, O_R, \epsilon)$. Observe that this trace is well-formed.

To define the initial configuration, we transform each instance declaration in the main block of the form $\mathsf{C}\ r(\overline{r}){:}(\overline{e});$ into a regular object declaration of the form $r = \mathbf{new}\ \mathsf{C}(\overline{r}){:}(\overline{e});$. This saves us from defining different mechanisms for static and dynamic object creation. Let s_{main} be the sequence of instance declarations in the main block transformed in this way. Now we start semantic evaluation with the configuration

$$sh_{init} \curvearrowright newEv^{main}(main, O_R, \epsilon), [main \mapsto \mathrm{K}^0(s_{main})] \ .$$

For each $r =$ **new** $\mathsf{C}(\overline{r}){:}(\overline{e});$, according to the semantics of **new**, a new object is created with a fresh abstract identifier X_r which must be concretized and assigned to r. The concretization must match the initial state where r has value o_r. Hence X_r, and therefore r, will be bound correctly to o_r. The semantic rule for **new** also adds $o_r \mapsto \mathrm{K}^0(r.C(\overline{e}))$ to the tasks in the configuration, i.e., a call to the constructor C of r's class which initiates program execution.

Let $sh, \Sigma \xrightarrow{*} sh', \Sigma'$ denote the transitive closure of applying rules (2)–(4), expressing that sh', Σ' can be reached from sh, Σ in zero or more steps. We can now formally define the trace set of a Rebeca model as follows:

Definition 11 (Trace semantics of Rebeca models). *Given a Rebeca model* $M = \overline{CD}$ **main** $\{ \overline{InDcl} \}$ *with initially known rebecs* R; *the traces of* M, *denoted* $\mathbf{Tr}(M)$ *is the set of reachable traces from the initial trace of* M:

$$\mathbf{Tr}(M) = \{sh \,|\, sh_{init} \curvearrowright newEv^{main}(main, O_R, \epsilon), [main \mapsto \mathrm{K}^0(s_{main})] \xrightarrow{*} sh, \Sigma\} \ .$$

Observe that the trace set given in Definition 11 is prefix closed. On the other hand, executions in our semantics are infinite; in particular, rule (4) can be applied indefinitely when no further tasks (either progress or messages) can be processed.

Even finite computations end in an unbounded sequence of time advance events. Hence, it might be useful to define *final* configurations:

Definition 12 (Final Configuration). *A configuration* sh, Σ *is* final *when*

(i) $\not\exists o. (\Sigma(o) = \mathrm{K}^t(s) \wedge s \neq \emptyset \wedge \mathrm{now}(sh) < t)$ *and*
(ii) $\not\exists o, t. (\mathrm{now}(sh) < t \wedge |\mathrm{pending}(sh \curvearrowright timeEv(t), o)| > 0)$

Whether a given configuration is final can be effectively computed, because it suffices to consider t until the maximal **after** constraint in sh. Now we can adapt the trace semantics of Rebeca in Definition 11 to finitely terminating traces by choosing traces in $\mathbf{Tr}(M)$ that reach final configurations.

5   Discussion

This paper has proposed an LAGC style [7] semantics for Timed Rebeca [19]. We here analyze our effort. Typically for LAGC semantics, there is exactly one local evaluation rule for each kind of statement, which characterizes its behavior in a succinct manner, independent of context. Rules without events are completely *modular*; i.e., they can be freely modified or added without affecting the remaining definitions. For example, all rules of the For language in Sect. 4.1 are either identical to or minor modifications of existing rules [7, Section 3.1]. Events are used in LAGC semantics to characterize non-local behavior. Of the five event types introduced in Sect. 4.2, three are variations of events in [7, Section 7.2] and one is not strictly required. Also two of the three trace composition rules are variations: the rules for progress (2) and for scheduling message calls (3).

Likewise, traces tagged with a parameter O for the caller object as well as the object-to-task mapping Σ are taken from [7].

The novel aspects in the LAGC semantics of Timed Rebeca concern (i) the handling of time, (ii) initialization including the main block, and (iii) keeping track of known rebecs. Of these, the most interesting is the first. The central concepts we needed are *timed local evaluation* and *timed continuation*s. We believe it is natural that evaluation and continuations not only express *what* to execute, but also *when*. Timed continuations for an LAGC-style semantics were first introduced by Tapia Tarifa [24] to capture time and time-sensitive resources in Real-Time ABS [3,14]. Real-Time ABS is a real-time extension of ABS [13], an active object language that extends Timed Rebeca with non-preemptive suspension points via *await* statements and futures, but has an unordered message queue. Timed Rebeca differs from Real-Time ABS by combining message delay and expiry with a FIFO message queue. This combination requires additional care in capturing the enabledness of pending messages, and its interaction with time advance. In this paper, we have considered a discrete time domain for Timed Rebeca; however, a dense time domain can be realized in a straightforward manner, by forcing the time advance rule (4) to a advance to maximum elapsed time (see [24]). We expect that timed continuations will also be useful in other language settings with timed semantics.

With timed continuations and delay events, the semantic rule for the **delay** statement becomes obvious. The global clock is modeled by time events that are inserted into the current trace by the trace composition rule (4), whenever a program is in a *quiescent* state; thus we opted for a maximal progress semantics, where all pending message calls have been processed before time can advance. Using time events, it is easy to extend invocation (reaction) events to handle delayed message calls, but the advance-time-when-quiescent approach makes executions infinite. For this purpose, we suggest a notion of final configuration (Definition 12) to stop the semantic evaluation.

Handling main blocks uniformly requires the dedicated setup described in Sect. 4.8, because the Timed Rebeca designers chose to have both static (in the main block) and dynamic (with **new**) rebec creation. This issue was not addressed formally in previous semantics for Timed Rebeca (e.g., [18,19]).

To define the "knows" function and use it to check correct usage of known rebecs is a straightforward addition to the well-formedness rules in our setting. As far as we know, this is the first formal semantics which incorporates the **knownrebecs** mechanism in the language semantics.

To summarize, we needed five event types of which two are new (one of them essential), eleven local rules (one for each kind of statement) of which one is new, three trace composition rules of which one is new, and six well-formedness rules of which one is new and one (FIFO) is formulated differently than in [7]. We stress that all additions are *conservative extensions* of the LAGC framework: None of the fundamental definitions needed to be changed, the well-formedness rules merely add conjuncts for the checks of time and known rebecs.

6   Conclusion and Future Work

This paper contributes a LAGC semantics for Timed Rebeca, which is a highly modular, trace-based denotational semantics. We believe this is the first denotational, trace-based semantics for Timed Rebeca. Additionally, the semantics in this paper addresses certain corner-cases of Timed Rebeca that were left open in previous work [19]: the main block and the semantic representation of **knownrebecs**. The latter is particularly tricky for variations of Timed Rebeca that include dynamic creation of rebecs, which allows dynamic topologies, and deserves a semantic treatment.

In general, denotational semantics are challenging to achieve for concurrent languages because scheduling between different parallel activities goes against compositionality. The framework of LAGC semantics addresses this challenge by means of a locally symbolic, denotational semantics that include events, combined with global composition rules to address synchronization between these events. Timed languages add an additional level of complexity to this synchronization; in this paper we have in particular addressed the issue of how constraints on message passing (i.e., delay and deadline) combine with FIFO message ordering and time advance within the LAGC semantic framework. This paper shows how the LAGC semantic framework naturally extends to timed actors in Timed Rebeca.

We believe that the modular nature and succinct formulation of the LAGC semantics for Timed Rebeca makes it easy to understand it and to extend it when further language features are added in the future. The semantics presented in this paper enables the design a calculus for deductive verification [9] for Timed Rebeca programs, following [5,7], and prove its soundness for the LAGC semantics. Furthermore, the non-deterministic scheduling rule (3) of the proposed semantics could be refined into a set of deterministic rules and show some variation of *weak fairness* for it, following [8]. This requires to define a suitable *timed* version of weak fairness, because messages with a **deadline** do not stay enabled.

References

1. Agha, G.A.: ACTORS - a model of concurrent computation in distributed systems. In: MIT Press Series in Artificial Intelligence. MIT Press (1990)
2. Bagheri, M., Sirjani, M., Khamespanah, E., Hojjat, H., Movaghar, A.: Partial order reduction for timed actors. In: Bloem, R., Dimitrova, R., Fan, C., Sharygina, N. (eds.) Proc. 13th International Conference on Software Verification (VSTTE 2021). LNCS, vol. 13124, pp. 43–60. Springer, Heidelberg (2021). https://doi.org/10.1007/978-3-030-95561-8_4
3. Bjørk, J., de Boer, F.S., Johnsen, E.B., Schlatte, R., Tapia Tarifa, S.L.: User-defined schedulers for real-time concurrent objects. Innov. Syst. Softw. Eng. **9**(1), 29–43 (2013). https://doi.org/10.1007/s11334-012-0184-5
4. de Boer, F., et al.: A survey of active object languages. ACM Comput. Surv. **50**(5), 76:1–76:39 (2017). https://doi.org/10.1145/3122848

5. Bubel, R., Gurov, D., Hähnle, R., Scaletta, M.: Trace-based deductive verification. In: Proceedings of 24th International Conference on Logic for Programming, Artificial Intelligence and Reasoning. EPiC Series in Computing, vol. 94, pp. 73–95 (2023). https://doi.org/10.29007/vdfd

6. Din, C.C., Dovland, J., Johnsen, E.B., Owe, O.: Observable behavior of distributed systems: component reasoning for concurrent objects. J. Log. Algebraic Methods Program. **81**(3), 227–256 (2012). https://doi.org/10.1016/j.jlap.2012.01.003

7. Din, C.C., Hähnle, R., Henrio, L., Johnsen, E.B., Pun, V.K.I., Tapia Tarifa, S.L.: Locally abstract, globally concrete semantics of concurrent programming languages. Trans. Program. Lang. Syst. **46**(1) (2024). https://doi.org/10.1145/3648439

8. Hähnle, R., Henrio, L.: Provably fair cooperative scheduling. Art Sci. Eng. Program. **8**(2) (2024). https://doi.org/10.22152/programming-journal.org/2024/8/6

9. Hähnle, R., Huisman, M.: Deductive software verification: from pen-and-paper proofs to industrial tools. In: Steffen, B., Woeginger, G. (eds.) Computing and Software Science. LNCS, vol. 10000, pp. 345–373. Springer, Cham (2019). https://doi.org/10.1007/978-3-319-91908-9_18

10. Halpern, J.Y., Manna, Z., Moszkowski, B.C.: A hardware semantics based on temporal intervals. In: Díaz, J. (ed.) Automata, Languages and Programming, 10th Colloquium, Barcelona, Spain. LNCS, vol. 154, pp. 278–291. Springer, Heidelberg (1983). https://doi.org/10.1007/BFb0036915

11. Jafari, A., Khamespanah, E., Kristinsson, H., Sirjani, M., Magnusson, B.: Statistical model checking of timed rebeca models. Comput. Lang. Syst. Struct. **45**, 53–79 (2016). https://doi.org/10.1016/j.cl.2016.01.004

12. Jaghoori, M.M., Movaghar, A., Sirjani, M.: Modere: the model-checking engine of Rebeca. In: Haddad, H. (ed.) Proceedings of Symposium on Applied Computing (SAC 2006), pp. 1810–1815. ACM (2006). https://doi.org/10.1145/1141277.1141704

13. Johnsen, E.B., Hähnle, R., Schäfer, J., Schlatte, R., Steffen, M.: ABS: a core language for abstract behavioral specification. In: Aichernig, B.K., de Boer, F., Bonsangue, M.M. (eds.) Proceedings of 9th International Symposium on Formal Methods for Components and Objects (FMCO 2010). LNCS, vol. 6957, pp. 142–164. Springer, Heidelberg (2011). https://doi.org/10.1007/978-3-642-25271-6_8

14. Johnsen, E.B., Schlatte, R., Tapia Tarifa, S.L.: Integrating deployment architectures and resource consumption in timed object-oriented models. J. Log. Algebraic Methods Program. **84**(1), 67–91 (2015). https://doi.org/10.1016/j.jlamp.2014.07.001

15. Khamespanah, E., Mechitov, K., Sirjani, M., Agha, G.A.: Schedulability analysis of distributed real-time sensor network applications using actor-based model checking. In: Bosnacki, D., Wijs, A. (eds.) Proc. 23rd International Symposium on Model Checking Software (SPIN 2016). LNCS, vol. 9641, pp. 165–181. Springer, Heidelberg (2016). https://doi.org/10.1007/978-3-319-32582-8_11

16. Nakata, K., Uustalu, T.: A Hoare logic for the coinductive trace-based big-step semantics of While. Logic Methods Comput. Sci. **11**(1) (2015). https://doi.org/10.2168/LMCS-11(1:1)2015

17. Plotkin, G.D.: A structural approach to operational semantics. J. Log. Algebr. Program. **60–61**, 17–139 (2004)

18. Reynisson, A.H., et al.: Modelling and simulation of asynchronous real-time systems using Timed Rebeca. Sci. Computer Program. **89**, 41–68 (2014). https://doi.org/10.1016/J.SCICO.2014.01.008

19. Sabahi-Kaviani, Z., Khosravi, R., Ölveczky, P.C., Khamespanah, E., Sirjani, M.: Formal semantics and efficient analysis of Timed Rebeca in Real-Time Maude. Sci. Comput. Program. **113**, 85–118 (2015). https://doi.org/10.1016/J.SCICO.2015.07.003

20. Sirjani, M.: Rebeca: theory, applications, and tools. In: de Boer, F.S., Bonsangue, M.M., Graf, S., de Roever, W.P. (eds.) Proc. 5th International Symposium on Formal Methods for Components and Objects (FMCO 2006). LNCS, vol. 4709, pp. 102–126. Springer, Heidelberg (2006). https://doi.org/10.1007/978-3-540-74792-5_5

21. Sirjani, M., Jaghoori, M.M.: Ten years of analyzing actors: Rebeca experience. In: Agha, G., Danvy, O., Meseguer, J. (eds.) Formal Modeling: Actors, Open Systems, Biological Systems - Essays Dedicated to Carolyn Talcott on the Occasion of Her 70th Birthday. LNCS, vol. 7000, pp. 20–56. Springer, Heidelberg (2011). https://doi.org/10.1007/978-3-642-24933-4_3

22. Sirjani, M., Khamespanah, E.: On time actors. In: Ábrahám, E., Bonsangue, M.M., Johnsen, E.B. (eds.) Theory and Practice of Formal Methods - Essays Dedicated to Frank de Boer on the Occasion of His 60th Birthday. LNCS, vol. 9660, pp. 373–392. Springer, Heidelberg (2016). https://doi.org/10.1007/978-3-319-30734-3_25

23. Sirjani, M., Movaghar, A., Shali, A., de Boer, F.S.: Modeling and verification of reactive systems using Rebeca. Fundam. Informaticae **63**(4), 385–410 (2004). http://content.iospress.com/articles/fundamenta-informaticae/fi63-4-05

24. Tapia Tarifa, S.L.: Locally abstract globally concrete semantics of time and resource aware active objects. In: Ahrendt, W., Beckert, B., Bubel, R., Johnsen, E.B. (eds.) The Logic of Software. A Tasting Menu of Formal Methods. LNCS, vol. 13360, pp. 481–499. Springer, Heidelberg (2022). https://doi.org/10.1007/978-3-031-08166-8_23

25. Venema, Y.: A modal logic for chopping intervals. J. Logic Comput. **1**(4), 453–476 (1991). https://doi.org/10.1093/LOGCOM/1.4.453

Inside Every Multithreaded Program There Are Active Objects Struggling To Get Out

Frank de Boer[1], Einar Broch Johnsen[2(✉)], Rudolf Schlatte[2], and Silvia Lizeth Tapia Tarifa[2]

[1] CWI, Amsterdam, The Netherlands
F.S.de.Boer@cwi.nl
[2] Department of Informatics, University of Oslo, Oslo, Norway
{einarj,rudi,sltarifa}@ifi.uio.no

Abstract. Multithreading and actors offer different models of concurrency to the programmer. With multithreading, the programmer needs to deal with shared-state and data races, which make programs complex to understand, error-prone and challenging to verify, but potentially very efficient if these issues are mastered to perfection. On the other hand, actors—and their object-oriented incarnation as active objects,—which are inherently concurrent and protect their internal state against races, seem easy to understand and intuitive, but programs may be exposed to deadlocks due to callbacks. Is it possible to simply transition programs from the one concurrency model to the other at will, and thereby get the best of both worlds? We believe such a seamless transition between these concurrency models opens an interesting direction of research that remains to be investigated. As a step in this direction, this paper provides a high-level, informal outline of the translations between multithreading and active object concurrency, highlighting how intuitive or non-intuitive it is to move from one concurrency model to the other.

Keywords: Active objects · Actors · Multithreading · Asynchronous programming · Object-oriented programming

1 Introduction

The title of this paper is inspired by a quote, attributed to Tony Hoare [44]:

"Inside every large program, there is a small program trying to get out."

Reflecting on this quote in the context of concurrency, Marjan Sirjani's work has often championed the simple program trying to get out: the abstract actor-based model that is amenable to automated verification. In particular, her persistent efforts in actor-based modeling and verification in Rebeca [40–42] explores a number of analysis techniques based on formal semantics [35,36], including

E. A. Lee et al. (Eds.): Marjan Sirjani Festschrift, LNCS 15560, pp. 349–363, 2025.
https://doi.org/10.1007/978-3-031-85134-6_15

simulation [35], model checking [27,32,43], statistical model checking [26], partial order reduction [8], and rewriting logic [36]. At the root of this effort lies (we believe) an intuition that actor-based programs [4] are in fact simpler and more intuitive than the competition, namely multithreaded programs (e.g., [7]). In particular, active objects [12], which combine actor-based concurrency with object-based structuring mechanisms seem particularly attractive. In this paper, we expand on this intuition by studying the relation between these two concurrency paradigms. We scope our study to multithreaded programs in Java [33] and active objects in ABS [28]; the further translation of active objects into actors can be achieved via an encoding.

Our study shows that a multithreaded program can be transformed into active objects without affecting the main class structure. This transformation basically consists of a change of the global perspective of the multithreaded flow of control to the local perspective of active objects. That is, instead of the parallel execution of the different threads of method calls (implemented by stacks) the focus is on the parallel execution of the called methods within an object. This paradigm shift is enabled by the basic synchronization mechanisms of the cooperative scheduling of the method execution within active objects, as featured in ABS.

Conversely, modeling a program based on active objects by a multithreaded program requires an invasive and disruptive transformation which involves the introduction of complex synchronization mechanisms, notably mechanisms for suspending and resuming threads which are notoriously complex and error-prone in a multithreaded setting.

Outline. In the following section, we introduce the main programming concepts underlying multithreaded programs (MT, for short) and active objects (AO, for short), respectively. In Sects. 3 and 4 we discuss the relation between the two paradigms.

We abstract from the technical details and provide a high-level, informal outline of the translations between the two concurrency models. This allows us to focus on the main, basic ideas which otherwise would be obscured by the many technical details of the formal syntax and semantics. However, we think this high-level outline provides a clear guideline for a further formalization.

2   Preliminaries

Object-oriented programming abstractions were first introduced in Simula [17,18]. The basic idea is that of an object as an instance of an *abstract data type* which is represented by a *class*. A class specifies the data structures (referenced by 'fields') and the *methods* which describe the data operations. Objects are dynamically created instances of classes. Abstracting from the method implementations, calling a method of an object thus forms the basic operation of an object-oriented program.

One can distinguish two different ways of calling a method of an object. The first one follows the *rendez-vous* pattern of procedure calls in languages like

PASCAL (e.g., [46]). This gives rise to *synchronous* method calls: the caller *suspends* when the method is executed and *resumes* its execution after the method has returned (a value). A sequence of such method calls is called a *thread* (and is usually implemented by a *stack* [19]). This naturally gives rise to *sequential* execution. On the other hand, a method can be called *asynchronously*; that is, the caller continues its execution after the call, without waiting for the callee to respond. This naturally gives rise to the *parallel* execution of the caller and the execution of the called method by the callee, which in turn gives rise to a *co-routine* (used for simulation of parallelism in Simula [17]), a mode of execution of the methods of an object by means of explicit local suspend/resume operations. In the AO language ABS, asynchronous method calls further involve the dynamic creation of *futures* [9]; In ABS, futures are first-class values that act as references to the return value uniquely associated with each method call [13].

In this paper, we consider the AO model of ABS[1] because of its high-level programming abstractions of cooperative scheduling and futures. However, it is worthwhile to mention that these abstractions themselves can be translated into the pure asynchronous AO model of the Rebeca language [43], where methods are executed in a *run-to-completion* mode. A translation of Boolean await statements in ABS [28], for example, can be given by introducing for each occurrence of such a statement a new method. The body of this method consists of a conditional statement statement such that the *syntactic* continuation of the await statement (as given by the method containing this await statement) is executed if the condition of the await statement holds, otherwise a self-call to this new method is executed. Subsequently, all occurrences of await statements (including those appearing in the new methods) are translated into a self-call of the associated method, followed by the return statement (so that the method containing the await statement immediately returns after this self-call). Futures can be modeled by a special class and passing as an additional parameter of an asynchronous method call a newly created instance of this class.

In contrast, in the setting of synchronous method calls, parallel execution of code is achieved by creating *threads*, e.g., via the C function pthread_create or by calling the method start on a Java Thread object. The new thread is started with a programmer-specified "run method", e.g., in C by passing in a function pointer and in Java by either subclassing the Thread class or passing in an object instance of type Runnable. The calling thread continues its execution (run methods do not return a value). Execution of a run method thus spawns a new thread of (synchronous) method calls. In Java, threads further synchronize on so-called *synchronized* methods or blocks, which guarantee *mutual exclusion*, that is, such wrapped code cannot be executed in parallel on a single object.

2.1   Executing Multithreaded Programs

A characteristic feature of multithreaded programs in an object-oriented setting is the presence of one or more threads of execution that *keep their identity* as they

---

[1] ABS webpage: https://abs-models.org/.

```
class C { private int x = 0; private int y = 0; private int z = 0;
    public void m₁(){this.x = this.x+this.z; this.y = this.y+this.z; };
    public void m₂(){this.z = 5; };
}
final C c = new C();
new Thread ( () -> { c.m₁(); } ).start();
new Thread ( () -> { c.m₂(); } ).start();
```

Fig. 1. Example of a Java MT system accessing shared state

```
class C { /*private fields declaration*/
    public void m₁(/*parameter declaration*/){ s₁ₘ₁; s₂ₘ₁; ⋯; sₙ₁ₘ₁;}
    public void m₂(/*parameter declaration*/){ s₁ₘ₂; s₂ₘ₂; ⋯; sₙ₂ₘ₂;}
    ...
}
final C c = new C();
new Thread ( () -> {c.m₁(/*parameter instantiation*/);} ).start();
new Thread ( () -> {c.m₂(/*parameter instantiation*/);} ).start();
...
```

Fig. 2. Pattern of a Java MT system accessing shared state

execute in the context of different objects. Observe that this thread identifier is different from the self-reference **this** typically used by the programmer. When executing a method call in a thread in Java, the self-reference **this** evaluates to the callee object in which the thread executes the method.

In multithreaded programs, it is possible for **this** to evaluate to the same object *at the same time* in multiple threads. If multiple threads change "their" object's state at the same time, data races occur. To illustrate this issue, Fig. 1 shows an example of a Java MT system where both methods m_1 and m_2 start execution concurrently in an interleaved manner via lambda expressions, and as a result, it is unclear if the final state of the fields will be {x=0,y=0,z=5}, {x=0,y=5,z=5}, or {x=5,y=5,z=5}. Such a pattern of interleaved execution is depicted in Fig. 2.

To avoid data races in this setting, all threads have to cooperate and employ locks to define critical sections. Some syntactic sugar can be used to ease this process; for example, Java's **synchronized** methods and blocks guarantee that only one thread executing synchronized code can execute at a time, thus protecting the shared state from races from other synchronized threads. For the example in Fig. 1, by synchronizing the execution of the method bodies, we restrict the final state to be either {x=0,y=0,z=5} or {x=5,y=5,z=5}. Such a pattern of atomic execution with synchronized (atomic) blocks is depicted in Fig. 3, where a method can contain multiple atomic blocks. Note that multiple threads can still execute "on" such an object if they execute code outside the protected code parts. It is worth noting that Java supports *reentrance* [1]: a thread that holds a lock by executing a synchronized method may take the lock again, thus Java supports recursion for synchronized methods. Also note that a thread may acquire locks to multiple objects by nested synchronized method calls, which may lead to deadlocks if, e.g., threads try to acquire locks in different order.

```
class C { /*private fields declaration*/
    public void m₁(/*parameters' declaration*/){ synchronized(this){s₁ₘ₁; s₂ₘ₁; ···; sₙ₁ₘ₁;}}
    public void m₂(/*parameters' declaration*/){ synchronized(this){s₁ₘ₂; s₂ₘ₂; ···; sₙ₂ₘ₂;}}
    ...
}
final C c = new C();
new Thread ( () -> {c.m₁(/*parameters' instantiation*/);} ).start();
new Thread ( () -> {c.m₂(/*parameters' instantiation*/);} ).start();
...
```

Fig. 3. Pattern of a Java MT system accessing shared state with methods that are executed atomically via *synchronized* methods.

```
interface I { Unit method(Int i); }

class C(I o) {
    Int x = 0;
    Unit run() {
        println("Before Boolean await");
        await x > 0;
        println("After Boolean await");
        Fut<Unit> f = o!m(x);
        println("Before future await");
        await f?;
        println("After future await");
    }

    Unit incX() { x = x + 1; }
}
```

Fig. 4. Example of await statements with Boolean and future conditions

Multithreaded program execution can be seen as if, after each atomic statement, execution switches to another thread. This makes correctness proofs for multithreaded code very challenging.

2.2 Executing Active Objects

A characteristic feature of active object programs is that communication and synchronization are decoupled [29]: there is no transfer of control associated with method calls. Each object "owns" its threads. Calling a method creates a fresh thread on the callee object. The caller receives a *future* that represents the fresh thread and can be used to obtain the result of the method call.

Since the object owns its threads, it is not possible for multiple threads to execute at the same time on the same object. This means that all code is implicitly protected as if surrounded by *synchronous* blocks, and that the execution inside an active object is race free by design. Instead, with *cooperative concurrency* [28,29,37], explicit **await**-statements allow the object to switch from executing one thread to executing another thread, leaving the first thread suspended. These **await**-statements can carry a condition that expresses when the current thread becomes eligible to run again. In the simplest case, the condition can be simply *true*. Other conditions include waiting for a future to obtain the result of the method call associated with that future, and waiting for a

Boolean condition over the object state to hold (e.g., a thread can wait until a counter reaches zero). Figure 4 shows a code example with these different **await**-statements. ABS finally supports unconditional cooperative scheduling with the statement **suspend**, which always releases control when executing and is always schedulable when suspended. A formal account of cooperative scheduling in ABS have been given in terms of an operational semantics [28] as well as a recent denotational semantics [21].

From the perspective of verification, since **await**-statements in ABS models are explicit in the code, it becomes feasible to prove object invariants and other correctness conditions of active object code. Thus, active objects can be seen as the maintainers of local invariants [13,20,22]. Another interesting aspect of the active object concurrency model is that a transition system can be translated to active objects with cooperative concurrency in a way that *preserves global properties* [10,15]; this translation enables the use of a transition system model with very expressive synchronization to inductively establish global properties, then obtaining a decentralized active object program with the same global properties.

Of further note is that ABS has a notion of *blocking*: a thread can wait for the result of a future without relinquishing control by having a **get**-statement to a future right after an asynchronous call associated with such future; the **get**-statement will block the active object until the result of the associated method call is available in that future. This behavior can be used to express synchronization similar to synchronous method calls in Java, but does not directly support reentrance. The drawback of this synchronization is that the object cannot switch to another thread, including the one created from the process the original thread is waiting for, in the case of recursion. Such callbacks lead to deadlock; we will explore this area further in the sequel.

3   From Multithreading to Active Objects

A faithful translation of code from the multithreaded (MT) programs to the active object (AO) programs should preserve the interleaving structure of code segments of the multithreaded execution model. The basic idea underlying the translation of a multithreaded (MT) program is to model a synchronous method call directly by an asynchronous method call followed by a so-called **await**-statement which suspends the calling method instance until the called method returns. This suspension allows for the execution of other methods by the object, while the calling thread must wait for the return of the call. We can further model that the entire calling object is blocked for execution during the call by waiting on a **get**-statement instead of the **await**-statement; this models a synchronous call from a synchronized method [29]. However, this approach does not directly support recursive calls; in fact, the semantics of Creol [29] (that was inherited in ABS [28]), treated this case separately—but the proposed solution did not address the general case of reentrance (as we would encounter with mutual recursion between synchronized methods in different objects).

```
interface C {Unit m₁(); Unit m₂();};
class C() implements C {Int x = 0; Int y = 0; Int z = 0;
    Unit m₁(){x = x+z; suspend; y = y+z; }
    Unit m₂(){z = 5; } }
{ C c = new C(); c!m₁(); c!m₂();}
```

Fig. 5. The AO version of the example in Fig. 1.

```
interface C {Unit m₁(/*parameters' declaration*/); Unit m₂(/*parameters' declaration*/); ...};
class C() implements C {/*private fields declaration*/
    Unit m₁(/*parameters' declaration*/){s₁ₘ₁; suspend; s₂ₘ₁; suspend; ⋯; suspend; sₙ₁ₘ₁;}
    Unit m₂(/*parameters' declaration*/){s₁ₘ₂; suspend; s₂ₘ₂; suspend; ⋯; suspend; sₙ₂ₘ₂;}
    }...
{ C c = new C(); c!m₁(/*parameters' instantiation*/); c!m₂(/*parameters' instantiation*/); ...}
```

Fig. 6. The AO version of the pattern in Fig. 2

To model the mechanism of *reentrance* for synchronized method calls from the multithreaded setting in the active object setting, we introduce for each object a *lock* which specifies the thread id and the number of times that this id has acquired the lock. The thread id corresponds to the unique reference to the initial instance of the corresponding thread class. To allow each method invocation of a thread to access its thread id, the thread id is simply passed on as an additional parameter to synchronous method calls. A method instance holds a lock of an object if the lock stores its thread id in the lock with a non-zero counter. A lock is free if its counter is zero. We then extend every method (body) with an initial **await**-statement which checks whether the method instance holds the lock or whether the lock is free. In both cases the counter of the lock is incremented (by one). In case the lock is free the stored thread id is updated, that is, set to the thread id of the executing method instance. Upon return of a method, the lock is simply decremented.

In ABS, the granularity of the interleaving of the execution of different method instances by an object, is controlled by explicit suspend/resume statements (similar to **await**-statements without condition guards). To allow for the arbitrary interleaving needed to model the behavior of multithreaded execution, we need to inject interleaving points in code that would otherwise be "too synchronized" when executing in the active object. In ABS, one simply adds to the different control points a **suspend**-statement which unconditionally releases and resumes control. Figure 5 shows the AO version of the example in Fig. 1, where to capture the interleaved execution inside implicit atomic execution of threads in an AO setting, we introduce a **suspend**-statement after each statement, giving the possibility to another suspended thread to become active and start execution. The AO pattern version of the MT pattern in Fig. 2 is depicted in Fig. 6. Furthermore, synchronized MT methods or blocks are similar to the implicit atomic execution of threads in an AO setting, as can be seen in the depicted AO pattern version in Fig. 7 of the MT pattern in Fig. 3, where capturing various atomic blocks inside one method can be done by adding a **suspend**-statement between the blocks.

The code of an arbitrary Java class may mix synchronized and unsynchronized blocks of execution in different methods. This effect can be translated into ABS by combining the two concerns we have discussed, namely the counting lock for synchronized code over explicit thread identifiers that are passed in synchronous calls, and the injected suspension points to allow arbitrary interleaving on unsynchronized code. Observe that in a *pure actor* setting, these effects need to be modeled by decoupling the translated code into smaller blocks corresponding to atomic statements in Java, that are successively triggered by separate messages, and by renaming the actor to force synchronization for call-backs by providing unique return-addresses to calls that need to be synchronized. This line of encoding was studied in early work by Agha *et al.* (e.g., [2]). This kind of encoding breaks the class method structure of the Java program that we are able to preserve in ABS because of the supported cooperative scheduling and futures.

```
interface C {Unit m₁(/*parameters' declaration*/); Unit m₂(/*parameters' declaration*/); ...};
class C() implements C {/*private variable declaration*/
    Unit m₁(/*parameters' declaration*/){ s₁ₘ₁; s₂ₘ₁; ···; sₙ₁ₘ₁; }
    Unit m₂(/*parameters' declaration*/){ s₁ₘ₂; s₂ₘ₂; ···; sₙ₂ₘ₂;} }
    ...
{ C c = new C(); c!m₁(/*parameters' instantiation*/); c!m₂(/*parameters' instantiation*/); ...}
```

Fig. 7. The AO version of the pattern with *synchronized* methods in Fig. 3.

4   From Active Objects to Multithreading

A faithful translation of code from the active object model (AO) to the multithreaded model (MT) preserves the following properties:

- Only one process at a time executes on an object.
- When a method is called, the calling process continues execution.
- Processes on an object can interleave execution via suspension points.
- Processes can obtain method call results via future variables.

Note that the first two properties are enough to implement pure actor behavior, the remaining points are necessary to realize the active object semantics. We consider two approaches to this encoding problem, by means of thread suspension (Sect. 4.1) and by means of continuations (Sect. 4.2). Both approaches, as presented, create potentially large numbers of threads, so they are most suited to languages like Erlang or Java ≥ 21 (which adds so-called virtual threads) that do not place restrictions on thread count. If thread creation is an expensive operation in the chosen language, for example because each language thread is implemented as an operating-system thread, the approaches in this chapter can be adapted to use thread pools and/or task queues.

```
import java.util.concurrent.*;

interface I { void method(int i); }

class C {
  I o;
  int x = 0;
  public C(I o) { this.o = o; }

  void run() {
    final Future f;
    synchronized(this) {
      System.out.println("Before Boolean await");
      while (!(x > 0)) {
        this.notifyAll();
        this.wait(); // Releases lock
      }
      System.out.println("After Boolean await");

      ExecutorService executor = Executors.newSingleThreadExecutor();
      f = executor.submit(() -> o.method(x));
      System.out.println("Before future await");
      this.notifyAll();
    }
    f.get(); // other methods can run in the meantime
    synchronized(this) {
      System.out.println("After future await");
      this.notifyAll();
    }
  }

  synchronized void incX() { x = x + 1; this.notifyAll(); }
}
```

Fig. 8. A Java translation of cooperative scheduling in ABS, using thread suspension (exception handling elided for brevity)

4.1 From AO to MT with Thread Suspension

AO classes can be directly translated into MT classes, with no special provisions except for synchronization points; this section presents a simplified version of the JCoBox model [37], which was used in the original Java interpreter for ABS. AO method calls, which are asynchronous, are naturally modeled in the MT model by executing each call on a separate thread, but care must be taken to preserve the AO properties. In Java and similar languages, this can be done by wrapping each method call together with its argument values either in a closure (a lambda expression) or in an object implementing the Runnable interface, that is then executed on a MT thread. Figure 8 shows a worked example using the ExecutorService library class that also produces a Java Future object that the caller can use to obtain the method's return value.

AO suspension points are points in code where the MT translation must give up its lock on the object to let other threads execute. Figure 8 shows the encoding of **await** statements both for futures and for Boolean conditions. A future is monotonic in the sense that, once completed, it will always remain available. Boolean conditions, on the other hand, can change between every suspension point, and must be always re-checked before continuing execution.

```
import java.util.concurrent.*;
interface I { void method(int i); }

class C {
  I o;
  int x = 0;
  public C(I o) { this.o = o; }

  synchronized void run() {
    System.out.println("Before Boolean await");
    new Thread(() -> this.run2()).start();
    this.notifyAll();
  }
  synchronized void run2() {
    while (!(x > 0)) { this.notifyAll(); this.wait(); }
    System.out.println("After Boolean await");
    ExecutorService executor = Executors.newSingleThreadExecutor();
    final Future f = executor.submit(() -> o.method(x));
    new Thread(() -> this.run3(f)).start();
    System.out.println("Before future await");
    this.notifyAll();
  }
  void run3(Future f) {
    while (!f.isDone()) { f.get(); }
    synchronized(this) {
      System.out.println("After future await");
      this.notifyAll();
    }
  }
}

  synchronized void incX() { x = x + 1; this.notifyAll(); }
}
```

Fig. 9. Java translation of cooperative scheduling in ABS, using continuations (exception handling elided for brevity)

Note that the transformation also inserts a call to **this**.**notifyAll**() before each suspension point. This is necessary so that threads waiting on a Boolean await can check the await condition. Since in ABS all members are private and can only be changed via method calls, these calls are also sufficient.

4.2 From AO to MT with Continuations

An alternative translation of AO code into the MT model introduces a new method for each suspension point, following the pattern of the translation of ABS **await**-statements into Rebeca discussed in Sect. 2. This section presents a simplified version of this approach, studied by Serbanescu [39]. Figure 9 shows the example of Fig. 4 translated in this style. This translation method introduces one synchronized "continuation method" for each occurrence of an **await**-statement in the AO method such that each such occurrence is modeled by the creation of a fresh thread continuing after the suspension point, passing along local variables in scope at the point of the await. Then, the original thread ends and releases the object lock, letting other methods execute on the object. The continuation of the method can start executing when the await condition is fulfilled.

The body of the continuation of the run method itself starts with a prelude consisting of a transformation of the **await**-statement and its *syntactic* continuation into a *waiting loop* which checks the condition of the **await**-statement. If this condition holds, the loop is exited and the method executes the rest of the AO method. Note that differently from the translation of **await**-statements in the Rebeca language, it is not necessary to spawn a new process each time the condition of the **await**-statement does not hold; instead, the thread checks its await condition multiple times and starts running when the condition holds. As with the other translation, any threads waiting on the object lock are notified before exiting a synchronized method, so they can check their await condition.

5   Conclusion

This paper has discussed differences between MT and AO, and in particular the nature of their basic underlying communication mechanisms. In AO, methods are called asynchronously and as such the generated method invocations are executed in parallel. In other words, the paradigm of AO programming is *intrinsically parallel*. In MT, methods are called synchronously, which imposes a last-in-first-out (LIFO) ordering of the execution of the method invocations, and as such gives rise to an *intrinsically sequential* thread-based execution. Parallel execution of threads in MT is obtained by calling asynchronously the run method (or start method) of an instance of a predefined class Thread.

We have shown that it is straightforward to model a synchronous method call in AO, using the **await**-statement of ABS to suspend the caller. To model the arbitrary interleaving of threads in AO simply requires the introduction of **await**-statements at the interleaving points. This is cumbersome, but only syntactically: It does not complicate the object structures. Thread synchronization is modeled in a straightforward manner by a basic semaphore. This requires the introduction of an additional parameter for a (synchronized) method which denotes the executing thread (i.e., the initial object executing the run method). It should be observed that our outlined encoding from MT to AO relies heavily on the synchronization features of ABS, with asynchronous method calls and cooperative scheduling. The further translation into a pure actor language would require carefully encoding synchronization and call-backs that are naturally supported in ABS through asynchronous message passing and through control restrictions on th e message-interface(e.g., by means of the become-statement in pure actors). On the other hand, modeling arbitrary asynchronous method calls in MT requires quite complex explicit handling of concurrency mechanisms, which gives rise to complicated object structures to handle synchronization points in the AO programs (e.g., wrapping each method call into a proxy of the called object).

We believe a more formal study of these encodings and how they preserve the semantics of the two concurrency paradigms would be an interesting line of research. Research on the relationship between MT on the one side and AO and actors on the other side, is surprisingly scarce. Among interesting work pointing in this general direction, Agha and Palmskog [3] studied how to learn actor structure from the execution traces of MT programs, and de Boer and Hiep [14] the synthesis of actor programs from traces. Haller and Odersky [24] studied how MT execution can be unified with event-based communication. Several papers compare different mechanisms for asynchronous communication with futures (e.g., [23]). Other papers study the extension of AO models in ABS with resource-sensitive behavior [6,11,31,38], these resources act as global synchronizers that affect the intrinsic compositionality of the underlying actor model (for example to model virtualized systems [5,30]). Varela and Agha [45] discuss drawbacks of MT and argue for actors, and Lee [34] highlight challenges with MT and discuss different alternatives, including actors, suggesting that a solution might lie in more abstract coordination languages. Brandauer *et al.* [16] and Henrio and Rochas [25] discuss different ways to overcome the intra-actor sequentialization in the AO model.

References

1. Ábrahám-Mumm, E., de Boer, F.S., de Roever, W.-P., Steffen, M.: Verification for java's reentrant multithreading concept. In: Nielsen, M., Engberg, U. (eds.) FoSSaCS 2002. LNCS, vol. 2303, pp. 5–20. Springer, Heidelberg (2002). https://doi.org/10.1007/3-540-45931-6_2

2. Agha, G.: Concurrent object-oriented programming. Commun. ACM **33**(9), 125–141 (1990). https://doi.org/10.1145/83880.84528

3. Agha, G., Palmskog, K.: Transforming threads into actors: learning concurrency structure from execution traces. In: Lohstroh, M., Derler, P., Sirjani, M. (eds.) Principles of Modeling. LNCS, vol. 10760, pp. 16–37. Springer, Cham (2018). https://doi.org/10.1007/978-3-319-95246-8_2

4. Agha, G.A.: ACTORS - a model of concurrent computation in distributed systems. In: MIT Press Series in Artificial Intelligence. MIT Press (1990)

5. Albert, E., et al.: Formal modeling and analysis of resource management for cloud architectures: an industrial case study using real-time ABS. Serv. Oriented Comput. Appl. **8**(4), 323–339 (2014). https://doi.org/10.1007/S11761-013-0148-0

6. Albert, E., Genaim, S., Gómez-Zamalloa, M., Johnsen, E.B., Schlatte, R., Tapia Tarifa, S.L.: Simulating concurrent behaviors with worst-case cost bounds. In: Butler, M., Schulte, W. (eds.) FM 2011. LNCS, vol. 6664, pp. 353–368. Springer, Heidelberg (2011). https://doi.org/10.1007/978-3-642-21437-0_27

7. Andrews, G.R.: Concurrent programming - principles and practice. Benjamin/Cummings (1991)

8. Bagheri, M., Sirjani, M., Khamespanah, E., Hojjat, H., Movaghar, A.: Partial order reduction for timed actors. In: Bloem, R., Dimitrova, R., Fan, C., Sharygina, N. (eds.) Proc. 13th International Conference on Software Verification (VSTTE 2021). Lecture Notes in Computer Science, vol. 13124, pp. 43–60. Springer, Heidelberg (2021). https://doi.org/10.1007/978-3-030-95561-8_4

9. Baker, H.G., Hewitt, C.: The incremental garbage collection of processes. In: Low, J. (ed.) Proceedings of the 1977 Symposium on Artificial Intelligence and Programming Languages, pp. 55–59. ACM (1977), https://doi.org/10.1145/800228.806932

10. Bezirgiannis, N., de Boer, F., Johnsen, E.B., Pun, V.K.I., Tapia Tarifa, S.L.: Implementing SOS with active objects: a case study of a multicore memory system. In: Hähnle, R., van der Aalst, W. (eds.) FASE 2019. LNCS, vol. 11424, pp. 332–350. Springer, Cham (2019). https://doi.org/10.1007/978-3-030-16722-6_20

11. Bjørk, J., de Boer, F.S., Johnsen, E.B., Schlatte, R., Tapia Tarifa, S.L.: User-defined schedulers for real-time concurrent objects. Innov. Syst. Softw. Eng. 9(1), 29–43 (2013). https://doi.org/10.1007/s11334-012-0184-5

12. de Boer, F., et al.: A survey of active object languages. ACM Comput. Surv. 50(5), 76:1–76:39 (2017). https://doi.org/10.1145/3122848

13. de Boer, F.S., Clarke, D., Johnsen, E.B.: A complete guide to the future. In: Nicola, R.D. (ed.) Proc. 16th European Symposium on Programming (ESOP 2007). Lecture Notes in Computer Science, vol. 4421, pp. 316–330. Springer, Heidelberg (2007). https://doi.org/10.1007/978-3-540-71316-6_22

14. de Boer, F.S., Hiep, H.-D.A.: Axiomatic characterization of trace reachability for concurrent objects. In: Ahrendt, W., Tapia Tarifa, S.L. (eds.) IFM 2019. LNCS, vol. 11918, pp. 157–174. Springer, Cham (2019). https://doi.org/10.1007/978-3-030-34968-4_9

15. de Boer, F.S., Johnsen, E.B., Pun, V.K.I., Tapia Tarifa, S.L.: Proving correctness of parallel implementations of transition system models. ACM Trans. Program. Lang. Syst. 46(3) (2024). https://doi.org/10.1145/3660630

16. Brandauer, S., et al.: Parallel objects for multicores: a glimpse at the parallel language ENCORE. In: Bernardo, M., Johnsen, E.B. (eds.) SFM 2015. LNCS, vol. 9104, pp. 1–56. Springer, Cham (2015). https://doi.org/10.1007/978-3-319-18941-3_1

17. Dahl, O.J., Myhrhaug, B., Nygaard, K.: SIMULA 67 common base language. Technical Report S-2, Norwegian Computing Center (1968)

18. Dahl, O.J., Nygaard, K.: SIMULA - an ALGOL-based simulation language. Commun. ACM 9(9), 671–678 (1966). https://doi.org/10.1145/365813.365819

19. Dijkstra, E.W.: A Discipline of Programming. Prentice-Hall (1976). https://www.worldcat.org/oclc/01958445

20. Din, C.C., Bubel, R., Hähnle, R.: KeY-ABS: a deductive verification tool for the concurrent modelling language ABS. In: Felty, A.P., Middeldorp, A. (eds.) CADE 2015. LNCS (LNAI), vol. 9195, pp. 517–526. Springer, Cham (2015). https://doi.org/10.1007/978-3-319-21401-6_35

21. Din, C.C., Hähnle, R., Henrio, L., Johnsen, E.B., Pun, V.K.I., Tapia Tarifa, S.L.: Locally abstract, globally concrete semantics of concurrent programming languages. ACM Trans. Program. Lang. Syst. 46(1), 3:1–3:58 (2024). https://doi.org/10.1145/3648439

22. Din, C.C., Tapia Tarifa, S.L., Hähnle, R., Johnsen, E.B.: History-based specification and verification of scalable concurrent and distributed systems. In: Butler, M., Conchon, S., Zaïdi, F. (eds.) ICFEM 2015. LNCS, vol. 9407, pp. 217–233. Springer, Cham (2015). https://doi.org/10.1007/978-3-319-25423-4_14

23. Fernandez-Reyes, K., Clarke, D., Henrio, L., Johnsen, E.B., Wrigstad, T.: Godot: all the benefits of implicit and explicit futures. In: Donaldson, A.F. (ed.) Proc. 33rd European Conference on Object-Oriented Programming (ECOOP 2019). LIPIcs, vol. 134, pp. 2:1–2:28. Schloss Dagstuhl - Leibniz-Zentrum für Informatik (2019). https://doi.org/10.4230/LIPIcs.ECOOP.2019.2

24. Haller, P., Odersky, M.: Scala actors: Unifying thread-based and event-based programming. Theor. Comput. Sci. 410(2–3), 202–220 (2009). https://doi.org/10.1016/j.tcs.2008.09.019

25. Henrio, L., Rochas, J.: Multiactive objects and their applications. Log. Methods Comput. Sci. **13**(4) (2017). https://doi.org/10.23638/LMCS-13(4:12)2017
26. Jafari, A., Khamespanah, E., Kristinsson, H., Sirjani, M., Magnusson, B.: Statistical model checking of timed rebeca models. Comput. Lang. Syst. Struct. **45**, 53–79 (2016). https://doi.org/10.1016/j.cl.2016.01.004
27. Jaghoori, M.M., Movaghar, A., Sirjani, M.: Modere: the model-checking engine of Rebeca. In: Haddad, H. (ed.) Proceedings of Symposium on Applied Computing (SAC 2006), pp. 1810–1815. ACM (2006). https://doi.org/10.1145/1141277.1141704
28. Johnsen, E.B., Hähnle, R., Schäfer, J., Schlatte, R., Steffen, M.: ABS: a core language for abstract behavioral specification. In: Aichernig, B.K., de Boer, F.S., Bonsangue, M.M. (eds.) FMCO 2010. LNCS, vol. 6957, pp. 142–164. Springer, Heidelberg (2011). https://doi.org/10.1007/978-3-642-25271-6_8
29. Johnsen, E.B., Owe, O.: An asynchronous communication model for distributed concurrent objects. Softw. Syst. Model. **6**(1), 39–58 (2007). https://doi.org/10.1007/s10270-006-0011-2
30. Johnsen, E.B., Owe, O., Schlatte, R., Tapia Tarifa, S.L.: Dynamic resource reallocation between deployment components. In: Dong, J.S., Zhu, H. (eds.) ICFEM 2010. LNCS, vol. 6447, pp. 646–661. Springer, Heidelberg (2010). https://doi.org/10.1007/978-3-642-16901-4_42
31. Johnsen, E.B., Schlatte, R., Tapia Tarifa, S.L.: Integrating deployment architectures and resource consumption in timed object-oriented models. J. Log. Algebraic Methods Program. **84**(1), 67–91 (2015). https://doi.org/10.1016/j.jlamp.2014.07.001
32. Khamespanah, E., Mechitov, K., Sirjani, M., Agha, G.: Schedulability analysis of distributed real-time sensor network applications using actor-based model checking. In: Bošnački, D., Wijs, A. (eds.) SPIN 2016. LNCS, vol. 9641, pp. 165–181. Springer, Cham (2016). https://doi.org/10.1007/978-3-319-32582-8_11
33. Lea, D.: Concurrent Programming in Java. Addison Wesley (1996)
34. Lee, E.A.: The problem with threads. Computer **39**(5), 33–42 (2006). https://doi.org/10.1109/MC.2006.180
35. Reynisson, A.H., et al.: Modelling and simulation of asynchronous real-time systems using Timed Rebeca. Sci. Comput. Program. **89**, 41–68 (2014). https://doi.org/10.1016/J.SCICO.2014.01.008
36. Sabahi-Kaviani, Z., Khosravi, R., Ölveczky, P.C., Khamespanah, E., Sirjani, M.: Formal semantics and efficient analysis of Timed Rebeca in Real-Time Maude. Sci. Comput. Program. **113**, 85–118 (2015). https://doi.org/10.1016/J.SCICO.2015.07.003
37. Schäfer, J., Poetzsch-Heffter, A.: JCoBox: generalizing active objects to concurrent components. In: D'Hondt, T. (ed.) ECOOP 2010. LNCS, vol. 6183, pp. 275–299. Springer, Heidelberg (2010). https://doi.org/10.1007/978-3-642-14107-2_13
38. Schlatte, R., Johnsen, E.B., Mauro, J., Tapia Tarifa, S.L., Yu, I.C.: Release the beasts: when formal methods meet real world data. In: de Boer, F., Bonsangue, M., Rutten, J. (eds.) It's All About Coordination. LNCS, vol. 10865, pp. 107–121. Springer, Cham (2018). https://doi.org/10.1007/978-3-319-90089-6_8
39. Serbanescu, V., Boer, F., Jaghoori, M.M.: Actors with coroutine support in java. In: Bae, K., Ölveczky, P.C. (eds.) FACS 2018. LNCS, vol. 11222, pp. 237–255. Springer, Cham (2018). https://doi.org/10.1007/978-3-030-02146-7_12
40. Sirjani, M.: Rebeca: theory, applications, and tools. In: de Boer, F.S., Bonsangue, M.M., Graf, S., de Roever, W.-P. (eds.) FMCO 2006. LNCS, vol. 4709, pp. 102–126. Springer, Heidelberg (2007). https://doi.org/10.1007/978-3-540-74792-5_5

41. Sirjani, M., Jaghoori, M.M.: Ten years of analyzing actors: rebeca experience. In: Agha, G., Danvy, O., Meseguer, J. (eds.) Formal Modeling: Actors, Open Systems, Biological Systems. LNCS, vol. 7000, pp. 20–56. Springer, Heidelberg (2011). https://doi.org/10.1007/978-3-642-24933-4_3

42. Sirjani, M., Khamespanah, E.: On time actors. In: Ábrahám, E., Bonsangue, M., Johnsen, E.B. (eds.) Theory and Practice of Formal Methods. LNCS, vol. 9660, pp. 373–392. Springer, Cham (2016). https://doi.org/10.1007/978-3-319-30734-3_25

43. Sirjani, M., Movaghar, A., Shali, A., de Boer, F.S.: Modeling and verification of reactive systems using Rebeca. Fundam. Informaticae **63**(4), 385–410 (2004). http://content.iospress.com/articles/fundamenta-informaticae/fi63-4-05

44. Turski, W. (ed.): Efficient Production of Large Programs. Computation Centre of the Polish Aacdemy of Science (1970). https://www.cs.ox.ac.uk/publications/publication8100-abstract.html

45. Varela, C.A., Agha, G.: What after Java? From objects to actors. Comput. Netw. **30**(1–7), 573–577 (1998). https://doi.org/10.1016/S0169-7552(98)00079-8

46. Wirth, N.: The programming language Pascal. Acta Informatica **1**, 35–63 (1971). https://doi.org/10.1007/BF00264291

A Debugging System
for Language-Parameterized Proofs

Charlesowityear Ly, Eswarasanthosh Kumar Mamillapalli,
and Matteo Cimini[(✉)] [iD]

University of Massachusetts Lowell, Lowell, MA 01854, USA
{charlesowityear_ly,eswarasanthoshkumar_mamillapalli}@student.uml.edu,
matteo_cimini@uml.edu

Abstract. Language-parameterized proofs can express proofs of language properties in a way that does not apply just to one language but, rather, to a class of languages. LANG-N-PROVE is a tool that takes a language-parameterized proof and a language definition as input and produces proofs for the Abella proof assistant.

When a language-parameterized proof is incorrect, the tool blames a proof instruction in the Abella code, but that is not helpful for the user.

In this paper, we develop a debugging system that not only indicates the proof instruction that failed in the original language-parameterized proof, but also strives to describe the context in which such proof instruction has failed.

We have implemented our debugger within the LANG-N-PROVE tool, and we illustrate its application to several examples of debugging scenarios. Ultimately, our debugging system offers informative error messages.

Keywords: Language verification · Mechanized proofs · Debugging

1 Introduction

When we develop new programming languages, it is desirable to determine whether they afford the properties that were intended at the time of design. Over the past years, some attention has been devoted to the development of techniques and tools for *automating* the verification of languages. Results in this area vary greatly in their scope and methods. Rule formats target bisimilarity properties in process algebras [3,26], intrinsic typing of evaluators establishes the type soundness of the language [11], automated theorem proving has been used to determine type soundness [18,27], as well as other noteworthy approaches.

Language-parameterized proofs [13] have been proposed as an approach to language verification that is based on the fact that proofs for languages often follow a schema that does not apply to one language but, rather, to many languages. Language-parameterized proofs then allow us to write proofs in a way that refers to a language definition given as input without knowing the particular

---

C. Ly and E. K. Mamillapalli—These authors contributed equally to this work.

© The Author(s), under exclusive license to Springer Nature Switzerland AG 2025
E. A. Lee et al. (Eds.): Marjan Sirjani Festschrift, LNCS 15560, pp. 364–389, 2025.
https://doi.org/10.1007/978-3-031-85134-6_16

operators, values, and so on, that the language has. To make an example, a part of the progress theorem for the case of **head** *e* calls the canonical form lemma for the list type and then proves the "progress" of **head** *e* by appealing to the existence of two reduction rules (one that handles the empty list and one that handles **cons**). But the progress theorem for the case of **fst** *e* is similar and calls the canonical form lemma for the product type and appeals to the existence of one reduction rule (as pairs are the only canonical form for the product type). Language-parameterized proofs allow language designers to express statements such as "if the operation is an elimination form of the type constructor *c*, apply the canonical form for type *c*" and "for all value forms of type *c*, appeal to the existence of a reduction rule."

LANG-N-PROVE [13] is a tool for expressing language-parameterized proofs. The tool takes a language definition and a language-parameterized proof as input and generates the proof code of the Abella proof assistant [8]. Prior work [13,17] has applied LANG-N-PROVE to express the language-parameterized proofs of the "syntactic approach" to type soundness of Wright and Felleisen [32] (canonical form lemmas, and progress and preservation theorems) for a class of functional languages without subtyping [13] and when subtyping is present [17]. [13] and [17] report applying the proofs to a plethora of language definitions and generating type soundness proofs that machine check in Abella (though some small parts must be manually provided. We refer readers to [13,17] to learn more about it.)

Excerpt of LANG-N-PROVE proof	Generated Abella proof
12 ... 13 for each **e** in **Expression**: 14 **search** 15 ...	26 ... 27 **search.** 28 **search.** 29 **search.** 30 **search.** ✗ 31 **search.** 32 **search.** 33 ...

Fig. 1. Intuition for the debugging problem in LANG-N-PROVE

Problem in Debugging Language-Parameterized Proofs. LANG-N-PROVE generates proofs for the Abella proof assistant. When the language-parameterized proof input is incorrect, Abella may fail. The error message that Abella reports refers to the line number of the generated Abella proof. However, this error message is not helpful because language designers work at the level of the language-parameterized proof. To give an intuition of the problem, let us suppose that we are writing a proof and that after a case analysis on the structure of expressions we wrongly think that each case of expression forms can be simply proved with the proof instruction search. (This instruction is similar to Coq's auto and simply tells Abella to try to derive the goal with the current knowledge.) One of the features of LANG-N-PROVE is that it generates proof instructions by iterating over some grammar of the language given as input. We therefore can write the for-loop in Fig. 1 on the left (within a larger proof). Given a language as input, LANG-N-PROVE generates the series of search instructions in Fig. 1 on the right (within an even larger proof).

Suppose that, contrary to what we expected, search at Line 30 fails in proving the case for an expression form. Through no fault of its own, Abella correctly tells the user that Line 30 of its proof code has failed, but the language designer can hardly understand what the problem is because they work at the level of the language-parameterized proof, to begin with, and also because Line 30 is just one search among many. Each search has no apparent connection to the for-loop that generated them.

It would be desirable to integrate a debugging system into LANG-N-PROVE that can provide more helpful error messages.

Contributions. In this paper, we develop a debugging system for LANG-N-PROVE. One of the main components of our debugger aims at "contextualizing" Abella instructions. We have instrumented LANG-N-PROVE so that when it generates Abella instructions it also attaches the context of the LANG-N-PROVE proof that generated them. For instance, suppose that the search that failed in the for-loop above was for the expression form (*app e e*). Our debugger provides an error message that says that such search was generated by Line 15 of the LANG-N-PROVE proof, that such instruction was in the context of a for-loop, and that it was generated for the iteration element (*app e e*).

Another component of our debugger aims at analyzing the proof instructions specifically produced by for-loops. We consider it an error when the for-loop generates an instruction for, say, iteration element (*app e e*), but Abella uses it in the context of the case for, say, (*if e e e*). This may happen, for example, when the for-loop generated too few instructions for (*if e e e*). That case was then not completed when Abella executes the proof, and so Abella starts grabbing the following instructions, which now are those generated by the for-loop for the next iteration element. (We will see concrete examples of this debugging scenario in Sect. 3 and 4.)

Our debugger includes other components, and Sect. 3 motivates and describes them. This paper makes the following contributions:

– We have developed a debugging system for language-parameterized proofs.
– We have implemented our debugger into LANG-N-PROVE tool.
– We demonstrate our debugger through a series of examples.

Overall, we believe that our debugger provides useful error messages. Our debugger is publicly available [20] and documents all our tests.

Mamillapalli's master's thesis in Computer Science at University of Massachusetts Lowell [21], successfully defended in Fall 2024, is based on the submission for review to Marjan Sirjani's Festschrift (prior to this final version). This present paper differs from Mamillapalli's master's thesis in some ways: The entire Sect. 4 (with its examples) is new in this paper and does not appear in the thesis, the thesis contains an entire chapter with additional examples that are not in this paper, this paper discusses some limitations in Sect. 5 that are not discussed in the thesis, this paper discusses ideas for future work that are not discussed in the thesis, as well as other ways in which this paper differs from the above mentioned thesis.

Structure of the Paper. This paper is organized as follows. Section 2 provides a background overview of LANG-N-PROVE. Section 3 describes our debugging system through a series of motivating examples. Section 4 illustrates our debugger at work with a handful of examples. Section 5 discusses the limitations of our debugger. Section 6 discusses related work, and Sect. 7 concludes the paper.

Dedication. To Marjan on her 60th birthday.

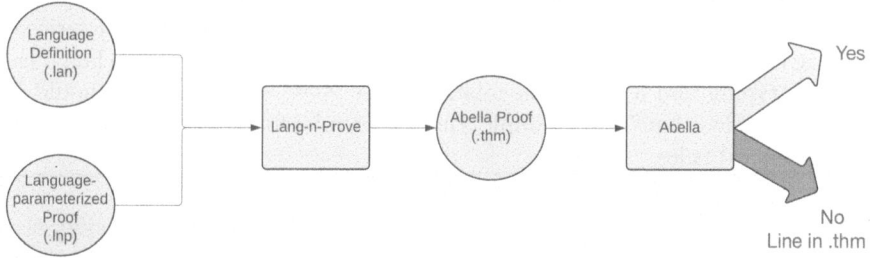

Fig. 2. Pipeline of LANG-N-PROVE

2   Overview of LANG-N-PROVE (Background)

Figure 2 shows the pipeline of the LANG-N-PROVE tool. LANG-N-PROVE takes a language definition and a language-parameterized proof as input and generates an Abella proof, which Abella proof checks. We describe these elements below.

Language Definitions. Language definitions are text files with extension .lan, and they contain a textual representation of operational semantics. For example, the following is the language definition for the λ-calculus with booleans.

We call this file stlc_iff.lan. (By convention, variables R are a shorthand for bindings such as (x)E.)

```
Expression E ::= (tt) | (ff) | (if E E E)
                 | x | (abs T (x)E) | (app E E).
Type T ::= (bool) | (arrow T T).
Value V ::= (tt) | (ff) | (abs T R).
Context C ::= [] | (app C E) | (app V C) | (if C E E).

Gamma |- (tt) : (bool).
Gamma |- (ff) : (bool).

Gamma |- (if E1 E2 E3) : T <== Gamma |- E1 : (bool)
                              /\ Gamma |- E2 : T /\ Gamma |- E3 : T.

Gamma |- (app E1 E2) : T2 <== Gamma |- E1 : (arrow T1 T2)
                             /\ Gamma |- E2 : T1.

Gamma |- (abs T1 R) : (arrow T1 T2) <== Gamma, x : T1 |- R : T2.

(app (abs T E) V) --> E[V/x] <== value V.
(if (tt) E1 E2) --> E1.
(if (ff) E1 E2) --> E2.
```

(This type of textual language definitions is inspired by the Ott tool [30].)

To review operational semantics, languages have a grammar and a series of inference rules. The latter define the relations that are of interest of the language, such as a typing and a reduction relation. The "<==" symbol above should be read as "provided that." For example, the typing rules for if and app correspond to the standard rules

$$\frac{\Gamma \vdash e_1 : \mathsf{Bool} \quad \Gamma \vdash e_2 : T \quad \Gamma \vdash e_3 : T}{\Gamma \vdash \mathsf{if}\ e_1\ \mathsf{then}\ e_2\ \mathsf{else}\ e_3 : T} \qquad \frac{\Gamma \vdash e_1 : T_1 \rightarrow T_2 \quad \Gamma \vdash e_2 : T_1}{\Gamma \vdash (e_1\ e_2) : T_2}$$

The language above makes use of evaluation contexts, which declare which arguments of an expression constructor can be evaluated.

Abella Proofs. It would be natural to describe the second input element (language-parameterized proofs) at this point. However, we prefer to describe the output first, Abella proofs. The reason is that the language for language-parameterized proofs is derived from that of Abella. Abella proofs are in .thm files. (Abella requires other files but we are not concerned with them here.) Below is the syntax of the part of Abella that is relevant to this paper. We refer our reader to [8] for Abella's syntax.

Proof	$th ::=$	**Theorem** $name : f.$ **Proof** $p.$
Proof instr.	$p ::=$	**intros** $\overline{name}$ | **search** | $name :$ **case** $name$
		| $name :$ **induction on** k
		| $name :$ **apply** $name$ **to** $\overline{name}$
		| **backchain** $name$ | $p.p$

where *name* is the name of a theorem or hypothesis, k is a number, and where formulae f specify the statement of theorems. As we are concerned with proofs only in this paper, not formulae, we omit describing the grammar of formulae. Intuitively, they include the standard logical connectives and quantifications.

intros $name_1 \cdots name_m$ applies to a goal of the form $\forall X_1, X_2, \ldots X_n. f_1 \Rightarrow f_2 \ldots \Rightarrow f_m \Rightarrow f$, introduces the variables X_1, X_2, ..., and X_n, and adds, as hypotheses of the current proof, f_1 with name $name_1$, f_2 with name $name_2$, ..., and f_m with name $name_m$. (There may not be one name for each of them but we are not concerned about these details here.) Then, f becomes the new goal. search tries to prove the current goal using the knowledge available to the proof. The proof fails when search cannot prove the goal. $name_1$: case $name_2$ performs a case analysis on the hypothesis $name_2$ while $name_1$: induction on k performs an induction on the k-th formula in the series of implications of the goal. These instructions may open a series of proof subcases to be proven. Also, they may introduce newly derived hypotheses, whose given name is based on $name_1$. induction loads the inductive hypothesis with name $IH0$, if available, IH_k otherwise, for the first available name IH_k. The apply tactic applies a theorem or hypothesis. backchain $name$ is applied for a theorem $name$ of form $\forall X_1, X_2, \ldots X_n. f_1 \Rightarrow f_2 \ldots \Rightarrow f_m \Rightarrow f$. If f unifies with the goal of the current proof and f_1, f_2, ..., and f_m can be derived, then it concludes the proof case. We use backchain $name$ when the theorem $name$ applies to conclude the proof. Proofs can also be sequentially composed ($p.p$).

LNP Proof	$\hat{th}$	::=	for each Z in $\hat{t}$, Theorem $na\hat{m}e : \hat{f}$. Proof $\hat{p}$.
LNP Name	$na\hat{m}e$	::=	$name \mid name\_(\hat{t})$
LNP Formula	$\hat{f}$	::=	$(na\hat{m}e : pname\ \hat{t}_1 \ldots \hat{t}_n) \mid \ldots$ *several other formulae* $\ldots$
LNP Term	$\hat{t}$	::=	$X \mid (opname\ \hat{t}_1 \cdots \hat{t}_n) \mid (X)\hat{t} \mid \hat{t}[\hat{t}/X]$
			$\mid Z \mid n \mid cname \mid \hat{t} =_t \hat{t} \mid \hat{t}$ is $cname \mid \hat{t}$ in $\hat{t}$
			$\mid$ isVar$(\hat{t}) \mid$ ofType$(\hat{t})$
			$\mid$ isEliminationForm$(\hat{t}) \mid$ isErrorHandler$(\hat{t})$
			$\ldots$ *several other operations* $\ldots$
LNP Proof instr.	$\hat{p}$	::=	intros $\mid$ search $\mid na\hat{m}e :$ case $na\hat{m}e$
			$\mid na\hat{m}e :$ induction on $na\hat{m}e$
			$\mid na\hat{m}e :$ apply $na\hat{m}e$ to $na\hat{m}e_1 \cdots na\hat{m}e_n$
			$\mid$ backchain $na\hat{m}e \mid p.p \mid$ noOp
			$\mid$ for each Z in $\hat{t} : \hat{p} \mid$ if $\hat{t}$ then $\hat{p}$ else $\hat{p}$

Fig. 3. LANG-N-PROVE proof language

Lang-n-Prove Proofs. LANG-N-PROVE provides a domain-specific language for expressing language-parameterized proofs. This proof language contains linguistics that are specific to interrogating operational semantics.

Part of the syntax of LANG-N-PROVE from [13] is in Fig. 3. LNP proofs can generate a series of theorems and their proofs with for-loops. (We can generate one single theorem by iterating over a list of one element. The formalism has only one form to keep the syntax tidy.) LANG-N-PROVE makes use of LNP names rather than names. The difference is that while names are essentially strings, LNP names can have a term as a suffix. (We will describe terms shortly.) For example, for each Z in *Type*, Theorem *canonical-form-_(Z)* : ... creates a series of theorems *canonical-form-int*, *canonical-form-bool*, *canonical-form-arrow*, etc., and their proofs, depending on the grammar of types of the language given as input. As before, we are not concerned with formulae, and therefore we omit describing LNP formulae $\hat{f}$ in full. The relevant LNP formula for us is the base case (*name* : *pname* $\hat{t}_1 \ldots \hat{t}_n$). Here, a formula has been given a name and it is in abstract syntax style (top-level predicate name *pname* applied to arguments). The proof language of LANG-N-PROVE is derived from that of Abella. However, it includes a for-loop and an if-statement. Also, intros does not specify names because theorems use formulae with names already, and those names are then given to those formulae. Also, induction specifies the name of a hypothesis rather than a number. noOp is a no-operation and has no effect. noOp will not compile to any Abella proof code. Terms can be metavariables X, LNP variables Z (those bound by for-loops), numbers, category names *cname*, and they can be formed in abstract syntax style, that is, a top-level constructor name applied to a list of arguments. Furthermore, LANG-N-PROVE contains LNP terms that are specific to operational semantics. As LNP terms are numerous in [13], Fig. 3 contains only a few of them so that we can give an idea. $\hat{t}$ is *cname* holds if, after $\hat{t}$ is evaluated, $\hat{t}$ can be derived by the grammar of *cname*. $\hat{t}_1$ in $\hat{t}_2$ holds whenever, after $\hat{t}_1$ and $\hat{t}_2$ are evaluated, $\hat{t}_1$ is an element of the list $\hat{t}_2$. isVar($\hat{t}$) holds whenever, after $\hat{t}$ is evaluated, $\hat{t}$ is a metavariable, ofType($\hat{t}$) evaluates $\hat{t}$, computes the top-level constructor name of $\hat{t}$ and returns the type that its typing rule assigns to it. For example, ofType(tt) = *bool*. isEliminationForm($\hat{t}$) and isErrorHandler($\hat{t}$) hold whenever, after $\hat{t}$ is evaluated, $\hat{t}$ is an elimination form or an error handler, respectively. LANG-N-PROVE determines this and the operations above by inspecting the language given as input, see [13].

3   A Debugging System for LANG-N-PROVE

3.1   Overview of the Debugging System

Figure 4 shows the pipeline of LANG-N-PROVE with our debugging system. (Our additions in red.) Fig. 4 divides the pipeline into two parts. The top shows the first part of the pipeline, which builds the input for Abella. The bottom shows the rest of the pipeline, which analyzes the output of Abella and the .thm file. Essentially, the part of the pipeline at the bottom continues from where the part at the top ends. This section gives a brief overview of our debugging system. Section 3.2, 3.3, 3.4, and 3.5 describe our debugging system in details with motivating examples.

First part of the pipeline:

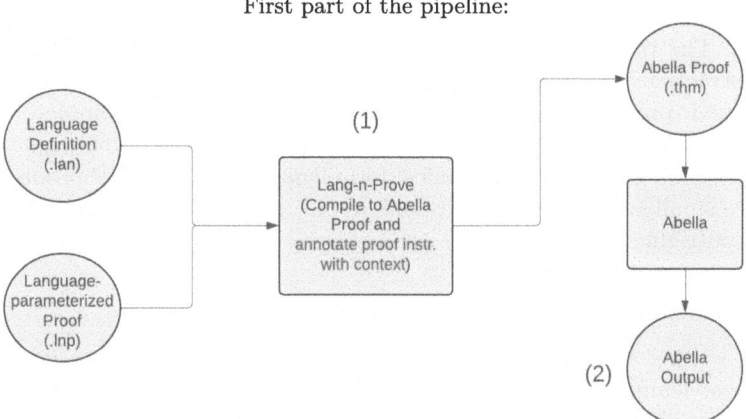

Continuation of the pipeline:

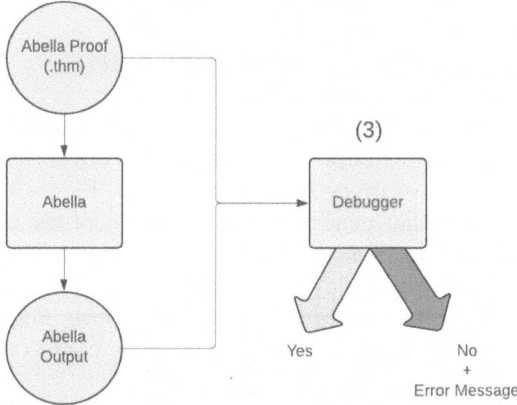

Fig. 4. Pipeline of LANG-N-PROVE with our debugging system. (Color figure online)

(1) We have instrumented the function of LANG-N-PROVE that compiles LNP proofs to Abella proofs so that every Abella proof instruction generated also carries the context it had in the .lnp.

(2) We launch Abella in "annotated mode" on the generated proof and we save the Abella output in order to analyze it after the execution of Abella has terminated. The "annotated mode" provides useful information about the Abella step-by-step execution of the proof given in input.

(3) We have implemented a debugger that takes two elements as input: The Abella .thm proof (where instructions now also inform of their .lnp context) and the Abella output. The debugger analyzes the two inputs and produces an informative error message when it detects an error.

Our debugger has four components. The first component aims at "contextualizing" errors (described in Sect. 3.2). The second component aims at determining whether Abella proofs align with the for-loops in LNP proofs (described in Sect. 3.3). The third component determines whether LNP proofs generate too many instructions for a theorem (described in Sect. 3.4). The fourth determines whether LNP proofs generate too few instructions that do not complete a proof (described in Sect. 3.5). In the remainder, we describe these components by progressively refining a proof for canonical form lemmas. All the LNP proofs in this paper are small variations of the proofs in [13] and [17], or they are from [13] and [17] outright when indicated so.

3.2   Contextual Error Messages

We start writing a language-parameterized proof for canonical form lemmas. To recall, these lemmas establish the value forms for each type constructor. Below are two examples of this lemma for booleans and the function type:

Theorem *Canonical-form-bool* : $\forall e, T,$

Main : $\emptyset \vdash e :$ Bool $\Rightarrow$ *ValHyp* : $(e$ *is value*$) \Rightarrow e =$ tt $\lor e =$ ff

Theorem *Canonical-form-arrow* : $\forall e, T_1, T_2,$

Main : $\emptyset \vdash e : (T_1 \rightarrow T_2) \Rightarrow$ *ValHyp* : $(e$ *is value*$) \Rightarrow \exists T, e', e = \lambda x : T.e'$

The proof is by case analysis on the typeability of e, that is, by case analysis on *Main*. For the sake of example, we first try an obviously incorrect proof that simply strives to prove every case with search. Figure 5 shows our LNP proof. The LNP formula that generates the statement of the theorem is rather complicated because it retrieves the values of the type of e. It is lengthy to describe, and since it does not play a role for us, we omit it. Nonetheless, this statement defines the premises *Main* and *ValHyp* above, and we will refer to these premises throughout our paper. We call this file canonical1.lnp.

```
1  for each ty in Type, Theorem Canonical-form-_(ty):
2    ... language-parameterized statement ... (contains Main and ValHyp)
3  Proof.
4  intros.
5  _ : case Main. # with _ we do not give a name to derived hypotheses
6  for each e in Expression:
7    search
```

Fig. 5. canonical1.lnp

When we run LANG-N-PROVE with the following language with only booleans: (We call this file iff.lan. We show the relevant parts only.)

```
Expression E ::= (tt) | (ff) | (if E E E).
Type T ::= (bool).
Value V ::= (tt) | (ff).
Gamma |- (tt) : (bool).
Gamma |- (ff) : (bool).
```

The generated Abella proof contains a series of **search** similar to those in the introduction section. This Abella proof succeeds the cases for **tt** and **ff**, but fails that for **if** and blames its **search** at Line 10 of the .thm file. As we pointed our earlier, this is not an informative error message. Our solution: We have instrumented LANG-N-PROVE so that every instruction that will appear in Abella proofs also carries their line number (and character number) in the LNP proof. Then we have instrumented the function of LANG-N-PROVE that compiles LNP proofs to Abella proofs so that every time we traverse a **for**-loop or an **if**-statement we record it as a contextual information. (We will be specific on the information we store shortly.) Abella instructions are then generated with a comment that contains the context in which they have been generated. For example, the failing **search** at Line 10 of the .thm file is

$$10 \quad \text{search.} \quad \#7,4\text{-for:}6,0:::(if\ E_1\ E_2\ E_3)$$

The compiler to Abella proofs evaluates **Expression** at Line 6 into its list of grammar items according to the language given as input. Then, it expands the **for**-loop into sequences of instructions. Therefore, the compilation knows the iteration element for which a proof instruction is generated. The comment is structured as follows. It begins with the line and character number of the instruction in the .lnp file. This is position 7,4 in **canonical1.lnp**. After that information, there is a sequence of *entries* separated by the character "-". In this case, there is only one entry. Information within the entry is separated by a colon ":". The first two items **for:6,0** tell us that the instruction was inside the body of the **for**-loop at line number 6 and character number 0. After that, the entry contains two items, both of which are empty strings in this case (that is : : : after **for:6,0**). We will discuss those items in the next section. The last item tells us that the instruction was generated during the loop iteration for the element $(if\ E_1\ E_2\ E_3)$. Our debugger saves contextual information upon traversing **if**-statements, as well. We will show an example in Sect. 4.

Before we speak about the debugging component that we have developed, we shall discuss the structure of the output of Abella (in "annotated mode"). The last lines of the Abella output for our example are the following

```
<a name="10"></a>
<pre>
Subgoal 3:

Variables: E3 E2 E1
Main : {typeOf empty (if E1 E2 E3) bool}
ValHyp : {value (if E1 E2 E3)}
H1 : {typeOf empty E1 bool}
H2 : {typeOf empty E2 bool}
H3 : {typeOf empty E3 bool}
============================
  if E1 E2 E3 = tt \/ if E1 E2 E3 = ff
```

```
Canonical-form-bool < <b>search.</b>
```

We call this a *block*. (To clarify, the term *block* is a name that we have chosen in this paper and we are not aware that it is terminology of Abella.) A block starts with an `<a>` marker followed by a `<pre>` marker.

The `<a>` marker provides the line number in the `.thm` file of the instruction being executed. (Not in general: Technically speaking, this number, say k, is of the k-th instruction read from the `.thm` and processed by Abella. However, LANG-N-PROVE generates the Abella `.thm` with one instruction per line, and therefore that number is exactly the line number in the `.thm` in our case.)

The `<pre>` marker contains the proof state, including the hypotheses, the goal, and the instruction being read, for example. Notice that this marker should end with `</pre>` but, due to the error, the output prematurely ended.

The Abella output contains several blocks. They appear one after another in the Abella output, and each refers to an instruction read from the `.thm` file. (As expected, instructions are read sequentially from the `.thm` file.) The block that we have shown above is the last block in our example.

We have then developed a component that parses the Abella output, stores all the blocks in a list, and can retrieve information from blocks. This component retrieves from the last block the line of the last instruction executed by Abella. In our example, that is Line 10 of the `.thm` file. Then it retrieves the comment of this line and produces an error-friendly message from it. In our example, Line 10 is the one above and our debugger produces the message

"Line 7, character 4 of the .lnp failed. The instruction is in the for-loop at line 6, character 0, and the element of the iteraton is (if E_1 E_2 E_3)."

3.3   Detecting `for`-loops That Are Not in Synch with Abella

This information is useful. We quickly discovered the instruction in the LNP proof that failed, and that it does not work for the case of `if`. We can debug our LNP proof: Since `if` is not a value, its proof case can be proved by contradiction on *ValHyp*. Figure 6 contains our new LNP proof. We call this `canonical2.lnp`.

```
3   Proof.
4   intros.
5   _ : case Main.
6   for each e in Expression iterating Main at 2 :
7       if e is Value
8       then search
9       else _ : case ValHyp
```

Fig. 6. <code>canonical2.lnp</code>

Let us ignore for the moment the directive highlighted in gray. This LNP proof now works for `iff.lan`. However, it fails for `stlc_iff.lan` (functions and booleans). The last block of the output of Abella is

```
<a name="11"></a>
<pre>
Subgoal 4:

Variables: T1 E2 E1
Main: {typeOf empty (app E1 E2) bool}
ValHyp : {value (app E1 E2)}
H1 : {typeOf empty E1 (arrow T1 bool)}
H2 : {typeOf empty E2 T1}
==============================
 app E1 E2 = tt \/ app E1 E2 = ff

Canonical-form-bool < <b>search.</b>
```

This tells us that **search** has failed. However, the case analysis at that point is analyzing $(app\ E1\ E2)$, and we know that our LNP proof does not generate **search** for the non-value $(app\ E1\ E2)$. Something subtle is occurring.

The problem is that the **for**-loop iterates over *all* expressions, but abstraction $\lambda x : T.e$ is not typed as a boolean. Our LNP proof considers such case and generates **search** for it because it is a value. The Abella case analysis (on $\emptyset \vdash e : \text{Bool}$), however, does not offer the case of $\lambda x : T.e$ at all. The mismatch is that the LNP proof thinks that **search** is for $\lambda x : T.e$ while, in actuality, Abella executes it for $(app\ E1\ E2)$. When this occurs, we say that the **for**-loop at Line 6 is *not in synch with Abella*.

We have developed a component that detects **for**-loops that are not in synch. To do so, we have augmented the syntax of LANG-N-PROVE with the optional directive that is highlighted above: **iterating Main at 2**. This directive informs that the loop is connected with the exploration of the case analysis of *Main* and that the element being iterated by Abella will be the second argument of the formula stored as hypothesis *Main* during the execution of the proof.

Then, our instrumentation of LANG-N-PROVE also includes this information as contextual information. (These are the fields that were empty with : : : in the previous section.) LANG-N-PROVE then generates the following line in the .thm

search. #8,9-**for**:6,0:*Main*:2:(*abs T* (*x*)*E*)

Next, we have developed a component of the debugger that retrieves from this line the hypothesis name (*Main* in this case) and the position of the argument (2 in this case), and retrieves from the output of Abella above the term that Abella is analysing during the proof (($app\ E1\ E2$) in this case). With that in hand, we compare it to the last field of the contextual information (($abs\ T\ (x)E$) in this case). This is the term that the LNP proof believes it has generated the instruction for. As the two do not match, our debugger provides an error message that says that the **for**-loop is not in synch with Abella:

"The for*-loop at Line 6, character number 0 is not in synch with Abella. The case analysis was* Main: typeOf empty (app E1 E2) bool *but the element of the iteration was* (abs T (x)E)."

When users do not use the iterating directive in for-loops, the fields above are empty as we have seen before (with : : :), and those loops are not analyzed to see if they are in synch. Our debugger points out the first occurrence in the Abella output for which a loop is not in synch. Also, when there are nested loops, we point out the outermost for-loop that is not in synch.

3.4   Detecting Too Many Proof Instructions for Theorems

Before refining canonical2.lnp, we discuss another problem that might occur with it. We consider a version of stlc_iff.lan where function application appears before abstraction in the grammar: (We call this stlc_iff_inverted.lan)

```
Expression E ::= (tt) | (ff) | (if E E E)
                 | x | (app E E) | (abs T (x)E).
```

And the rest of stlc_iff_inverted.lan is the same of stlc_iff.lan. The proof generated by LANG-N-PROVE for canonical2.lnp when this language is given as input prompts Abella to throw an error for the canonical form lemma of booleans. The for-loop in the LNP proof generates code for 5 cases: tt, ff, if, app, and abs in this order because that is how they appear in the grammar. (We recall that the case analysis on *Main* does not give the case of variables x to prove because the type environment must be empty. We also recall from [13] that for does not iterate over variables x by default.) However, when Abella performs the case analysis on *Main*, it provides only 4 cases: tt, ff, if, and app. As we discussed in the previous section, the case of abs is not given because abs is not typed as a boolean. The proof code for these 4 cases is correct and does prove them. This means that Abella finds itself with a completed proof of the lemma, whereas the LNP proof has generated an extra search instruction for abs. The Abella tool throws an error at the encounter of a proof instruction that does not belong to any theorem. The last block of the output of Abella for this error is

```
<a name="11"></a>
...
Canonical-form-bool < <b>case Mapp : ValHyp (keep).</b>
Proof completed.
</pre>
<a name="12"></a>
<pre class="code">
Abella <
```

The last block (block 12) prematurely ends without `</pre>`, while the second last block (block 11) announces that a proof has been completed. We have developed a component of our debugger to handle this. As Abella has failed, we already know that the last block is about an error. Our debugger checks whether the second last block announces a proof completed. If that is the case, we also retrieve the name of the completed theorem from the second last block. Our debugger provides the error message:

"*The proof of theorem* `Canonical-form-bool` *is completed but the .lnp has generated too many instructions for it.* "

After this message, our debugger also displays the contextual error message of the extra instruction. This message is helpful and says that the extra instruction is the `search` at Line 8 of the LNP proof, and that it was generated by a `for`-loop for the iteration element (*abs T* (*x*)*E*).

3.5 Detecting Too Few Proof Instructions for Theorems

When we have encountered the problem of Sect. 3.3 or that of Sect. 3.4, we learned that our `for`-loop should skip some expression forms. Indeed, the case analysis on *Main* gives cases to prove only for expressions that are typed at the type that is the subject of the canonical form lemma or expressions that can be typed at any type such as function application and `if`.

Figure 7 refines our LNP proof. We call this file `canonical3.lnp`. We now describe how this LNP proof refines that of `canonical2.lnp`.

```
1    for each ty in Type, Theorem Canonical-form-_(ty):
2        ... language-parameterized statement ...
3    Proof.
4    intros.
5    _ : case Main.
6    for each e in Expression:
7        if (ty = ofType(e)) or isVar(ofType(e))
8            then if e is Value
9                    then search
10                   else _ : case ValHyp
11           else noOp
```

Fig. 7. `canonical3.lnp`

The subject of each canonical form lemma is `ty`, which comes from the grammar of types. Line 7 checks that the expression form selected by the iteration has the type `ty` according to its typing rule or that its typing rule assigns a variable to it (as in function application and `if`). If this check is successful then we continue with the treatment that we have seen. Otherwise, we perform `noOp`, that is a no-operation and does not generate any proof instruction. Indeed, the case analysis of *Main* will not consider those cases.

The proofs generated by LANG-N-PROVE with `canonical3.lnp` for both `stlc_iff.thm` and `stlc_iff_inverted.thm` are successful. However, a problem now arises if we add subtyping to, say, `stlc_iff.thm`. LANG-N-PROVE can add declarative subtyping to `stlc_iff.thm` by declaring a specific grammar rule as follows. We call this file `stlc_iff_sub.thm`.

```
Subtyping S ::= (bool) | (arrow Contra Cov).
```

and the rest of `stlc_iff.thm` remains the same in `stlc_iff_sub.thm`. This grammar rule specifies that the first argument of the function type is contravariant (`Contra`) and its second argument is covariant (`Cov`). Based on this grammar rule, LANG-N-PROVE generates the various subtyping rules (see [17] for the details of this). Most importantly for our example, LANG-N-PROVE generates the subsumption rule as the last typing rule of the language

$$\frac{\Gamma \vdash e : T_1 \quad T_1 <: T_2}{\Gamma \vdash e : T_2}$$

Case analysis on *Main* then gives an extra case to prove, that for the subsumption rule. The Abella proof generated with `canonical3.lnp` when the language in input is `stlc_iff_sub.thm` covers for all cases but this last one. The proof ends while the theorem has not been completed.

The last block of the output of Abella for this error is

```
<a name="12"></a>
<pre>
Subgoal 5:

Variables: e S
Main : {typeOf empty e bool}
ValHyp : {value e}
H1 : {typeOf empty e S}
H2 : {subtype S bool}
==============================
 e = tt \/ e = ff

Canonical-form-bool <
```

The last block prematurely ends without `</pre>`. As the LNP proof believes that the proof has been completed, it generated code to start a new theorem at Line 12. (Here, we refer to Line 12 of the `.thm` file and not of the output above.) This new theorem is `Canonical-form-arrow` in our example. However, the command `Theorem` that starts a new theorem cannot be used in the context of an ongoing proof, which expects proof instructions instead, hence the syntax error. If the incomplete proof were to be the last proof and no next theorems to prove followed, then Line 12 simply would not exist in the `.thm` file, i.e., the

11-th line would be the last line of the file. (Here, we refer to Line 11 of the `.thm` file and not of the output above.)

Based on these considerations, we have developed a component for checking whether an LNP proof does not generate enough proof instructions to complete a proof. We check that either the line indicated by the last block (Line 12 in this case) does not exist in the `.thm` file or that this line contains a command that is not a proof instruction. In these cases, we can retrieve the name of theorem that was not completed from the last block. Our debugger provides the following error message:

"*The .lnp proof did not generate the proof instructions for completing the proof of theorem* `Canonical-form-bool`."

To fix `canonical3.lnp`, we need to add the proof code that handles the subsumption rule. This code calls inversion subtyping lemmas, which also must be generated. [17] covers this in details.

4   Additional Examples

This section provides a handful of examples that show our debugger at work.

Another Incorrect Treatment of Operators in Canonical Form Lemmas. This is an example of contextual error message. We modify `canonical3.lnp` to wrongly perform `search` on non-values. We call this file `canonical4.lnp`, shown in Fig. 8. (The modification is highlighted.)

```
1   for each ty in Type, Theorem Canonical-form-_(ty):
2   ... language-parameterized statement ...
3   Proof.
4   intros.
5   _ : case Main.
6   for each e in Expression iterating Main at 2:
7       if (ty = ofType(e)) or isVar(ofType(e))
8           then if e is Value
9                   then search
10                  else search
11          else noOp
12  endfor
```

Fig. 8. canonical4.lnp

The Abella proof generated when the input is `iff.lan` fails. Differently from the example in Sect. 3.3, where the problem was that the `for`-loop ended up not being in synch with Abella, here the `for`-loop is in synch but the instruction is simply incorrect for that case. Our debugger is such that it also saves contextual information when traversing an `if`-statement. The line in the `.thm` file where Abella fails has the following comment:

```
search. #10,19
```
-for:6,0:*Main*:2:(*if E*1 *E*2 *E*3)

-if:7,4: : : (*bool*) = ofType((*if E*1 *E*2 *E*3)) or IsVar(ofType((*if E*1 *E*2 *E*3))

-if:8,14: : : not((*if E*1 *E*2 *E*3) is Value).

We have split entries of this comment in multiple lines for readability (whereas they are all in the same line in the .thm file). The entry for an if-statement stores the line and character number that the if has in the .lnp file. It also stores the condition check of the if and whether it succeeded or not (marked with not). As it is more informative for the user, the condition has variables already instantiated, that is, $e = (if\ E1\ E2\ E3)$ and $ty = (bool)$ above.

From such comment, our debugger produces the message:

"Line 10, character 19 of the .lnp failed.
The instruction is in the for-loop at line 6, character 0, and the element of the iteration is (*if* E_1 E_2 E_3).
The instruction is in the if-statement at line 7, character 4, and the condition was ofType((*if E*1 *E*2 *E*3)) or IsVar(ofType((*if E*1 *E*2 *E*3))
The instruction is in the if-statement at line 8, character 12, and the condition was not((*if E*1 *E*2 *E*3) is Value)."

The information that the instruction that failed was inside the if of not((*if E*1 *E*2 *E*3) is Value) is crucial information for debugging canonical4.lnp.

Canonical Form Lemmas, Still Wrong. This is an example of a for-loop that is not in synch. We add pairs to our language with functions and booleans (stlc_iff.lan). This new language definition contains the following. (Only the parts that are relevant to us. We call this file stlc_iff_pairs.lan).

```
Expression E ::= (tt) | (ff) | (if E E E)
               | x | (app E E) | (abs T (x)E)
               | (pair E E) | (fst E) | (snd E).
Value V ::= (tt) | (ff) | (abs T R) | (pair V1 V2).

Gamma |- (pair E1 E2) : (times T1 T2) <== Gamma |- E1 : T1
                                        /\ Gamma |- E2 : T2.
```

The Abella proof generated with canonical3.lnp when the language in input is stlc_iff_pairs.thm fails. Our debugger displays the message:

"The for-*loop at Line 6, character number 0 is not in synch with Abella.*
The case analysis was Main : typeOf empty (pair E1 E2) (times T1 T2)
but the element of the iteration was (app E1 E2)."

This reveals that the proof code generated for (*pair E*1 *E*2) did not prove the case. Therefore, the instructions generated in the next iteration of the loop, which are for (*app E*1 *E*2), are used by Abella while still trying to prove the case for (*pair E*1 *E*2). This provides useful information. Of course, after reading a message such as that, we still have to look closely because the problem is then specific to the proof we are making. Here, we have generated _ : case ValHyp for (*pair E*1 *E*2) because it is not a value and the condition e is Value fails. (*pair E*1 *E*2) is not a value because we first need to know that *E*1 and *E*2 are values, too (see the grammar of values above). The correct proof does perform _ : case ValHyp because *ValHyp* says that (*pair E*1 *E*2) *is* a value and therefore we do discover that *E*1 and *E*2 are values thanks to that case analysis. (This is because the grammar of values says that (*pair E*1 *E*2) is a value only when *E*1 and *E*2 are values.) That case instruction was accidentally performed because it was borrowed from the else-branch that is meant for operations such as function applications and *if*, where _ : case ValHyp is invoking a contradiction. However, after that case, the proof requires search to close the case.

We can fix the LNP proof by taking into account that some expression forms may not immediately values, such as (*pair E*1 *E*2). That brings us to the LNP proof for canonical form lemmas that has been proposed in [13].

Incorrect Treatment of Elimination Forms in Progress. This is an example of contextual error message. The progress property ensures that a well-typed expression is a value, an error, or takes a reduction step. The proof of the progress theorem sometimes makes use of a predicate *progresses e* that says as much about the expression *e*. The theorem is also sometimes divided into two types of theorems. The first is a series of operator-specific progress theorems that formulate the progress property for each individual expression form. The second is a main progress theorem that invokes such operator-specific progress theorems. Some examples of operator-specific progress theorems are the following:

$progress\text{-}app$: $\forall T, e_1, e_2,$

$\emptyset \vdash (e_1\, e_2) : T \Rightarrow e_1\ progresses \Rightarrow e_2\ progresses \Rightarrow (e_1\, e_2)\ progresses$

$progress\text{-}head$: $\forall T, e,$

$\emptyset \vdash (\text{head } e) : T \Rightarrow e\ progresses \Rightarrow (\text{head } e)\ progresses.$

When an operator-specific progress theorem is about an elimination form, its proof calls a canonical form lemma and appeals to the existence of a reduction rule for each value to handle. [13] presents an LNP proof for generating operator-specific progress theorems. Figure 9 shows a modification of such a proof where we wrongly call search for elimination forms as if their case could be simply proved immediately. The original proof in [13] is rather involved, therefore we do not describe it and we also show the relevant part only in the LNP proof of Fig. 9. We call this file progress-op1.lnp.

The proof generated with progress-op1.lnp for stlc_iff.thm fails because search does not conclude the proof. Our debugger produces the message:

"*Line 6, character 6 of the .lnp failed.*
The instruction is in the if-statement at line 5, character 0, and the condition was isEliminationForm(($if E$1 E2 E3))."

An Incomplete Proof for Progress When Subtyping Is Present. Fig. 10 shows the LNP proof for the progress theorem of [13] (without its statement). This file is called progress.lnp.

The proof is by induction on *Main*. For each well-typed expression form, the inductive hypothesis derive that its arguments progress (as in the *progresses*

```
1  for each e in Expression, Theorem Progress-_(e) :
2    ... language-parameterized statement ...
3  Proof.
4    ...
5  if isEliminationForm(e)
6    then search
7  #  the original Line 6 calls the canonical form lemma.
8  #  see [13].
```

Fig. 9. progress-op1.lnp

predicate), and so we can apply the operator-specific progress theorem. We apply it with `backchain`, which concludes the proof case.

When we apply `progress.lnp` to our language `stlc_iff_sub.thm` with declarative subtyping, the Abella proof fails for the same problem that we have encountered in Sect. 3.5: the case analysis on *Main* now analyzes one more case for the subsumption rule. The LNP proof above, however, covers all cases but that. Our debugger produces the following message:

"*The .lnp proof did not generate the proof instructions for completing the proof of theorem* `Progress-thm`."

```
1  Theorem Progress-thm :
2    ... language-parameterized statement ...
3  Proof.
4  Typing_(0): induction on Main.
5  for each e in Expression:
6    for each i in contextualArgs(e): _ : apply IH0 to Typing_(i)
        endfor.
7    backchain on Progress-_(e)
```

Fig. 10. progress.lnp of [13] (without its statement)

Incorrect Loop for the Main Progress Theorem. This is an example of a `for`-loop that is not in synch. As we have pointed out, for some languages, introduction forms are also values. Their progress case can be proved with `search`. This is the case for `stlc_iff.thm` with values `tt`, `ff`, and abstraction. (Introduction forms such as (`pair` e_1 e_2) need more proof code that explores the progress of e_1 and e_2, instead). If those languages are the intended target of our LNP proofs, we may be tempted to modify `progress.thm` and prove the induction on *Main* with two `for`-loops. The first loop handles the values and the second loop handles the rest of the expressions that are not values. Figure 11 shows the LNP proof of this incorrect attempt. We call this file `progress1.lnp`. (The loop over the rest of expressions that are not values is the iteration at Line 8 over the list difference (`Expression − Value`)).

When we apply `progress1.lnp` to our language `stlc_iff.thm`, the Abella proof fails because the induction on *Main* still includes cases for non-values of `stlc_iff.thm`, such as the function application and `if`. Our debugger detects that the Abella cases do not align with the loop and produces the message:

"*The* `for`-*loop at Line 5, character number 0 is not in synch with Abella. The case analysis was* `Main : typeOf empty (if E1 E2 E3) typ` *but the element of the iteration was* `(abs T R)`."

Our debugger does not prevent from proving a case analysis with two `for`-loops, in general. However, our debugger informs the user if the Abella proof gives to the first loop some cases that are meant for the second loop. This is the scenario above, indeed.

```
1   Theorem Progress-thm :
2     ... language-parameterized statement ...
3   Proof.
4   Typing_(0): induction on Main.
5     for each v in Value iterating Main at 2:
6       search
7   endfor.
8   for each e in Expression - Value iterating Main at 2:
9       for each i in contextualArgs(e): _ : apply IH0 to Typing_(i)
              endfor.
10      backchain on Progress-_(e)
```

Fig. 11. `progress1.lnp`

Correct Abella Proof, Incorrect LNP Proof. This is an example of a `for`-loop that is not in synch. Consider the language `unit.lan` with only the unit type.

```
Expression E ::= (unit).
Type T ::= (unitType).
Value V ::= (unit).

Gamma |- (unit) : (unitType).
```

Suppose that we wanted to develop an LNP proof of the progress theorem that works on languages that contain introduction forms only. Not only so, but also where introduction forms are also values. We have discussed this type of languages in our previous examples. (Perhaps we wanted to focus on this particular class of languages first in order to progressively develop a full LNP proof.) Their characteristic is that one simple `search` proves their progress case. Consider the LNP proof in Fig. 12 for the progress theorem. We call this file `progress2.lnp`.

Our intention is to iterate over expression forms, but we have mistaken the loop at Line 5 and we iterate over types. Since `unit.lan` has only one type and

```
1   Theorem Progress-thm :
2     ... language-parameterized statement ...
3   Proof.
4   _ : induction on Main.
5    for each ty in Type iterating Main at 2:
6      search
```

Fig. 12. progress2.lnp

one value, it so happens that LANG-N-PROVE generates one search that is used for the progress case of the unit value. That is, LANG-N-PROVE generates an Abella proof that succeeds without any problem. Our debugger, however, points out the mismatch between the loop and Abella, and produces the message:

"*This generated* .thm *is valid, all proofs are completed.*
The for-*loop at Line 5, character number 0 is not in synch with Abella. The case analysis was* Main : typeOf empty unit unitType *but the element of the iteration was* (unitType)."

The user can certainly keep and use the generated Abella proof if that particular mechanization was what they sought. However, if the user cared about providing a proof that worked over the intended class of languages, then this error message indicates that the for-loop is not in synch with Abella.

Too Many Instructions When Subtyping is not Present. Fig. 13 summarizes the LNP proof presented in [17] for the progress theorem. This LNP proof is tailored for a certain class of functional languages with subtyping and handles the extra case of the subsumption rule. This file is called progress_sub.lnp.

In particular, the last case is for the typing rule for subsumption and can be proved by applying the inductive hypothesis. (We use backchain to close the case at once.) When we apply progress_sub.lnp to a language that does not have subtyping, say, stlc_iff.thm, then the for-loop in progress.lnp completes the proof. Yet, progress_sub.lnp generates the extra instruction backchain on IH0. Our debugger produces the following message:

"*The proof of theorem* Progress-thm *is completed but the .lnp has generated too many instructions for it.*"

```
Theorem Progress-thm :
  ... language-parameterized statement ...
  ... same exact code of progress.lnp ...
  followed by the following last line
backchain on IH0
```

Fig. 13. This figure summarizes progress_sub.lnp of [17].

5   Limitations

Our debugging system presents some limitations, which we would like to discuss.

The directive `iterating Main at 2` is limited to point to an argument of a formula, that is arg_2 in a formula ($predname\ arg_1\ arg_2\ \ldots\ arg_n$) that is stored with hypothesis name `Main`. However, arg_2 itself may be a constructed term of the form ($op\ arg'_1\ \ldots\ arg'_m$) and the case analysis at play may actually be exploring some arg'_k by cases. Our debugger does not have the capability to specify a subterm.

To detect that `for`-loops are not in synch, we need to fetch the last field of a `for` entry of the comment of an instruction, $\cdots$: ($if\ E1\ E2\ E3$) for example, and compare it with an argument of a hypothesis, for example, the second argument of `Main : typeOf empty (if E1 E2 E3) typ`. This equality check is tricky because Abella may choose different names for variables in some proofs. This equality check is related to α-equivalence, but something more subtle happens because there may be unexplored hypotheses of the proof state that restrict the shape that variables can take. (Unexplored in the sense that if we were to do a case analysis, they would provide the actual shape of that variable.) As further investigation of this subtle problem is needed, we currently approximate this equality check, and there are `for`-loops that we do not catch as not in synch. (The inability to detect all bugs is rather common with static analyses.)

LANG-N-PROVE does not only generate the proof of theorems but also provides various operations for generating the statements of such theorems. Language designers may mistake the LANG-N-PROVE code for generating such theorem statements. However, our debugger does not address them and only strives to debug proofs.

A LANG-N-PROVE proof may fail because the language definition in input is incorrect while the proof itself is correct. In these cases, our debugger blames some point in the proof. It would be interesting to explore ways to understand whether the language definition is at fault and point out an error therein.

Our debugger analyzes the output after the execution of Abella terminates. However, a proof may complete successfully and yet have an instruction of a `for`-loop that is not in synch. This instruction may be very early in the proof code. It would be interesting to adopt more efficient solutions that stem from the research area of *online monitoring* (see [10] for an excellent survey on the topic) where we would monitor Abella in its step-by-step execution of proof instructions and discover the not-in-synch problem immediately when it occurs (rather than letting the proof continue and analyzing the output at the end.)

6   Related Work

Great work has been done to make proof assistants more accessible and user-friendly. It is important, however, to clarify what *is not* an alternative system to ours. The error message systems that proof assistants such as Coq, Isabelle, Agda, and so on, adopt in order to pinpoint errors within one proof, are not an alternative system to ours, as those error messages are related to the broad problem of debugging a mechanized proof. Our work, on the other hand, is about *debugging the algorithms* that traverse and interrogate language definitions and that build proofs by means of that. As far as we know, the ability to express language-parameterized proofs is currently seen in LANG-N-PROVE only. The closest related works to this in the realm of proof assistants are automated proof scripts. Proof assistants such as Coq, Isabelle, and others, can automate the generation of proof instructions with specific scripts. Although they do not traverse and interrogate language definitions given in input, they perform automatic proof generation. When these scripts fail, the error message that is provided is that of the failing instruction that has been generated. This is akin to the problem of LANG-N-PROVE (without our debugger) that we have described in the introduction section.

There are a number of works in automated language verification. Some works use automated proving by feeding a first-order theorem prover [18], while others by using sophisticated automation in higher-order logic programming [27]. In these works, theorems are automated while LANG-N-PROVE strives to *specify* an algorithm that works for classes of languages.

Some works have used type systems for the analysis of the type soundness of languages, both extrinsically [12,16] and intrinsically [11]. The latter has been especially successful [5–7,9,29,31]. Other works [1,4,14,25] automate rule formats [3,26] in order to establish bisimilarity properties of process algebras. These works do not express algorithms for generating proofs for classes of languages. They check one specific property at a time for a language given in input. The error messages they provide points to an error in the language definition for not affording the property. From this perspective, our debugger can learn much from this impressive body of work. The inability to blame language definitions is indeed one of the limitations that we have discussed in the previous section.

7   Conclusion

In this paper, we have described a debugging system for LANG-N-PROVE. Our debugger detects four types of issues in the debugging of language-parameterized proofs. We have implemented our system into LANG-N-PROVE, and we have illustrated its application to several examples (11 examples in total). Overall, we believe that our debugger provides useful error messages.

In the future, we would like to address the limitations that we have discussed in Sect. 5. Prior work has analyzed the complexity of some language-parameterized proofs [15]. The characteristic of such work is that the complexity relates to operational semantics quantities such as the number of typing rules, reduction rules, expression constructors, and others. In the future, it would be interesting to analyze the complexity of our debugging procedures and to do so as relating to these operational semantics quantities, as well. Prior works explore automatic language transformations [22–24] in which a language definition given as input is automatically transformed into another language definition, for example a version of the language with some programming language features added into it. In the future, it would be interesting to explore connecting the capabilities of LANG-N-PROVE with those of automatic language transformations in order to automatically generate proofs about algorithmically transformed languages. We also would like to conduct a study on documenting the journey towards the development of new language-parameterized proofs through the helpful error messages of our debugger. An idea that can put our debugger to the test could be to target language-parameterized proofs for languages with time and probability, beginning with analyzing the few systems that we have experience with [2, 19, 28] as a starting point.

Our debugger is publicly available at [20].

Acknowledgments. This material is based upon work supported by the National Science Foundation under Grant No. CCF-2317257.

References

1. Aceto, L., Caltais, G., Goriac, E.-I., Ingolfsdottir, A.: PREG axiomatizer – a ground bisimilarity checker for GSOS with predicates. In: Corradini, A., Klin, B., Cîrstea, C. (eds.) CALCO 2011. LNCS, vol. 6859, pp. 378–385. Springer, Heidelberg (2011). https://doi.org/10.1007/978-3-642-22944-2_27
2. Aceto, L., Cimini, M., Ingólfsdóttir, A., Reynisson, A.H., Sigurdarson, S.H., Sirjani, M.: Modelling and simulation of asynchronous real-time systems using timed rebeca. In: Mousavi, M.R., Ravara, A. (eds.) Proceedings 10th International Workshop on the Foundations of Coordination Languages and Software Architectures, FOCLASA 2011, Aachen, Germany, 10th September, 2011. EPTCS, vol. 58, pp. 1–19 (2011). https://doi.org/10.4204/EPTCS.58.1
3. Aceto, L., Fokkink, W., Verhoef, C.: Chapter 3 - structural operational semantics. In: Bergstra, J., Ponse, A., Smolka, S. (eds.) Handbook of Process Algebra, pp. 197–292. Elsevier Science, Amsterdam (2001). https://doi.org/10.1016/B978-044482830-9/50021-7
4. Aceto, L., Goriac, E., Ingólfsdóttir, A.: Meta SOS - A maude based SOS metatheory framework. In: Borgström, J., Luttik, B. (eds.) Proceedings Combined 20th International Workshop on Expressiveness in Concurrency and 10th Workshop on Structural Operational Semantics, EXPRESS/SOS 2013, Buenos Aires, Argentina, 26 August, 2013. EPTCS, vol. 120, pp. 93–107 (2013). https://doi.org/10.4204/EPTCS.120.8
5. Altenkirch, T., Reus, B.: Monadic presentations of lambda terms using generalized inductive types. In: Flum, J., Rodriguez-Artalejo, M. (eds.) CSL 1999. LNCS, vol. 1683, pp. 453–468. Springer, Heidelberg (1999). https://doi.org/10.1007/3-540-48168-0_32
6. Appel, A.W., Leroy, X.: A list-machine benchmark for mechanized metatheory: (extended abstract). Electron. Notes Theor. Comput. Sci. **174**(5), 95–108 (2007). https://doi.org/10.1016/j.entcs.2007.01.020
7. Bach Poulsen, C., Rouvoet, A., Tolmach, A., Krebbers, R., Visser, E.: Intrinsically-typed definitional interpreters for imperative languages. Proc. ACM Program. Lang. (PACMPL) **2**(POPL) (2017). https://doi.org/10.1145/3158104
8. Baelde, D., et al.: Abella: a system for reasoning about relational specifications. J. Formalized Reason. **7**(2), 1–89 (2014). https://doi.org/10.6092/issn.1972-5787/4650

9. Benton, N., Hur, C., Kennedy, A., McBride, C.: Strongly typed term representations in coq. J. Autom. Reason. **49**(2), 141–159 (2012). https://doi.org/10.1007/s10817-011-9219-0

10. Cassar, I., Francalanza, A., Aceto, L., Ingólfsdóttir, A.: A survey of runtime monitoring instrumentation techniques. In: Proceedings Second International Workshop on Pre- and Post-Deployment Verification Techniques, PrePost@iFM 2017, Torino, Italy, 19 September 2017, pp. 15–28 (2017). https://doi.org/10.4204/EPTCS.254.2

11. Church, A.: A formulation of the simple theory of types. J. Symb. Log. **5**, 56–68 (1940). https://doi.org/10.2307/2266170

12. Cimini, M.: Early experience in teaching the basics of functional language design with a language type checker. In: Bowman, W.J., Garcia, R. (eds.) TFP 2019. LNCS, vol. 12053, pp. 21–37. Springer, Cham (2020). https://doi.org/10.1007/978-3-030-47147-7_2

13. Cimini, M.: Lang-n-prove: a dsl for language proofs. In: Proceedings of the 15th ACM SIGPLAN International Conference on Software Language Engineering, SLE 2022, pp. 16–29. Association for Computing Machinery, New York (2022). https://doi.org/10.1145/3567512.3567514

14. Cimini, M.: A declarative validator for GSOS languages. In: Castellani, I., Scalas, A. (eds.) Proceedings 14th Workshop on Programming Language Approaches to Concurrency and Communication-cEntric Software, PLACES@ETAPS 2023, Paris, France, 22 April 2023. EPTCS, vol. 378, pp. 14–25 (2023). https://doi.org/10.4204/EPTCS.378.2

15. Cimini, M.: Towards the complexity analysis of programming language proof methods. In: Ábrahám, E., Dubslaff, C., Tarifa, S.L.T. (eds.) Theoretical Aspects of Computing – ICTAC 2023, pp. 100–118. Springer, Cham (2023). https://doi.org/10.1007/978-3-031-47963-2_8

16. Cimini, M., Miller, D., Siek, J.G.: Extrinsically typed operational semantics for functional languages. In: Lämmel, R., Tratt, L., de Lara, J. (eds.) Proceedings of the 13th ACM SIGPLAN International Conference on Software Language Engineering, SLE 2020, Virtual Event, USA, 16–17 November 2020, pp. 108–125. ACM (2020). https://doi.org/10.1145/3426425.3426936

17. Galasso, S., Cimini, M.: Language-parameterized proofs for functional languages with subtyping. In: Gibbons, J., Miller, D. (eds.) Functional and Logic Programming, pp. 291–310. Springer, Singapore (2024). https://doi.org/10.1007/978-981-97-2300-3_15

18. Growo, S., Erdwcg, S., Wittmann, P., Mczini, M.: Type systems for the masses: deriving soundness proofs and efficient checkers. In: Murphy, G.C., Steele Jr., G.L. (eds.) 2015 ACM International Symposium on New Ideas, New Paradigms, and Reflections on Programming and Software (Onward!), Onward! 2015, pp. 137–150. ACM, New York (2015). https://doi.org/10.1145/2814228.2814239

19. Jafari, A., Khamespanah, E., Sirjani, M., Hermanns, H., Cimini, M.: Ptrebeca: modeling and analysis of distributed and asynchronous systems. Sci. Comput. Program. **128**, 22–50 (2016). https://doi.org/10.1016/j.scico.2016.03.004

20. Ly, C., Mamillapalli, E.K., Cimini, M.: The lang-n-prove tool extended with a debugger (2024). GitHub repo https://github.com/mcimini/lnpDebug

21. Mamillapalli, E.K.: A Debugging System for Language-parameterized Proofs. Master's thesis, Miner School of Computer & Information Sciences, University of Massachusetts Lowell (2024), the thesis has not been yet archived at the moment of submission of the final version of this paper. The thesis will be accessible via the UMass Lowell digital library (2025). https://www.uml.edu/library/

22. Mourad, B., Cimini, M.: A calculus for language transformations. In: Chatzigeorgiou, A., Dondi, R., Herodotou, H., Kapoutsis, C., Manolopoulos, Y., Papadopoulos, G.A., Sikora, F. (eds.) SOFSEM 2020. LNCS, vol. 12011, pp. 547–555. Springer, Cham (2020). https://doi.org/10.1007/978-3-030-38919-2_44

23. Mourad, B., Cimini, M.: A declarative gradualizer with language transformations. In: Chitil, O. (ed.) IFL 2020: 32nd Symposium on Implementation and Application of Functional Languages, Virtual Event/Canterbury, UK, 2–4 September 2020, pp. 44–54. ACM (2020). https://doi.org/10.1145/3462172.3462190

24. Mourad, B., Cimini, M.: System description: lang-n-change - a tool for transforming languages. In: Nakano, K., Sagonas, K. (eds.) FLOPS 2020. LNCS, vol. 12073, pp. 198–214. Springer, Cham (2020). https://doi.org/10.1007/978-3-030-59025-3_12

25. Mousavi, M.R., Reniers, M.A.: Prototyping SOS meta-theory in maude. Electron. Notes Theor. Comput. Sci. **156**(1), 135–150 (2006). https://doi.org/10.1016/j.entcs.2005.09.030

26. Mousavi, M.R., Reniers, M.A., Groote, J.F.: Sos formats and meta-theory: 20 years after. Theor. Comput. Sci. **373**(3), 238–272 (2007). https://doi.org/10.1016/j.tcs.2006.12.019

27. Pfenning, F., Schürmann, C.: System description: twelf — a meta-logical framework for deductive systems. In: CADE 1999. LNCS (LNAI), vol. 1632, pp. 202–206. Springer, Heidelberg (1999). https://doi.org/10.1007/3-540-48660-7_14

28. Reynisson, A.H., et al.: Modelling and simulation of asynchronous real-time systems using timed rebeca. Sci. Comput. Program. **89**, 41–68 (2014). https://doi.org/10.1016/j.scico.2014.01.008

29. Rouvoet, A., Bach Poulsen, C., Krebbers, R., Visser, E.: Intrinsically-typed definitional interpreters for linear, session-typed languages. In: Blanchette, J., Hritcu, C. (eds.) Proceedings of the 9th ACM SIGPLAN International Conference on Certified Programs and Proofs, CPP 2020, New Orleans, LA, USA, 20–21 January 2020, pp. 284–298. ACM (2020). https://doi.org/10.1145/3372885.3373818

30. Sewell, P., et al.: Ott: effective tool support for the working semanticist. J. Funct. Program. **20**(01), 71–122 (2010). https://doi.org/10.1017/S0956796809990293

31. Thiemann, P.: Intrinsically-typed mechanized semantics for session types. In: Komendantskaya, E. (ed.) Proceedings of the 21st International Symposium on Principles and Practice of Declarative Programming, PPDP '19, pp. 19:1–19:15. Association for Computing Machinery, New York (2019). https://doi.org/10.1145/3354166.3354184

32. Wright, A.K., Felleisen, M.: A syntactic approach to type soundness. Inf. Comput. **115**(1), 38–94 (1994). https://doi.org/10.1006/inco.1994.1093

Security Threats and Challenges of Digital Twins-Enabled Self-adaptive Systems

Rahul Sankalana Gunawardhana and Narges Khakpour[✉]

Newcastle University, Newcastle upon Tyne, UK
narges.khakpour@newcastle.ac.uk

Abstract. In this paper, we study the security threats and challenges of self-adaptive systems realized using digital twins. We use the MITRE ATT&CK framework to perform threat analysis and identify unique attack vectors specific to these systems. Our results show that the attack surface is broadened in these systems. We further provide an overview of our research findings for reducing the attack surface and present the open security challenges that are specific to such systems.

1 Introduction

Today's complex systems are designed to evolve at runtime and adapt to changing and uncertain requirements, including security-relevant needs such as the application of security patches [29]. These systems are developed using various design paradigms and techniques. Figure 1 shows a conceptual architecture for designing a self-adaptive system in two layers: a *managing layer*, implemented as a MAPE-K (Monitor, Analyze, Plan, Execute, and Knowledge) loop, which controls and adapts the behavior of the *managed layer*, responsible for implementing the system's functionality.

Despite some recent efforts to enhance the security of self-adaptive systems [33,45,56], the research community has mainly focused on developing advanced techniques for designing and implementing these systems without sufficiently considering their security implications [40]. To design effective methods and mechanisms to ensure and enforce security in self-adaptive systems, we need a thorough understanding of the security threats and the attack surfaces they introduce. In this paper, we conduct a security threat analysis on self-adaptive systems implemented using *digital twins* [16]. Digital twins (DT) is a recent technology used to design complex systems where a digital replica (i.e., data models or process models) of a physical system is created to analyze the physical system and offer various services to it. DTs are an effective paradigm for designing and implementing self-adaptive systems, where the digital layer is used to monitor and control the physical layer, as is done in a self-adaptive system. The managed layer corresponds to the physical layer in a digital twin-enabled self-adaptive system, while the managing layer is associated with the virtual layer in a digital twin architecture (See Fig. 1). We use these terms interchangeably in this paper.

© The Author(s), under exclusive license to Springer Nature Switzerland AG 2025
E. A. Lee et al. (Eds.): Marjan Sirjani Festschrift, LNCS 15560, pp. 390–405, 2025.
https://doi.org/10.1007/978-3-031-85134-6_17

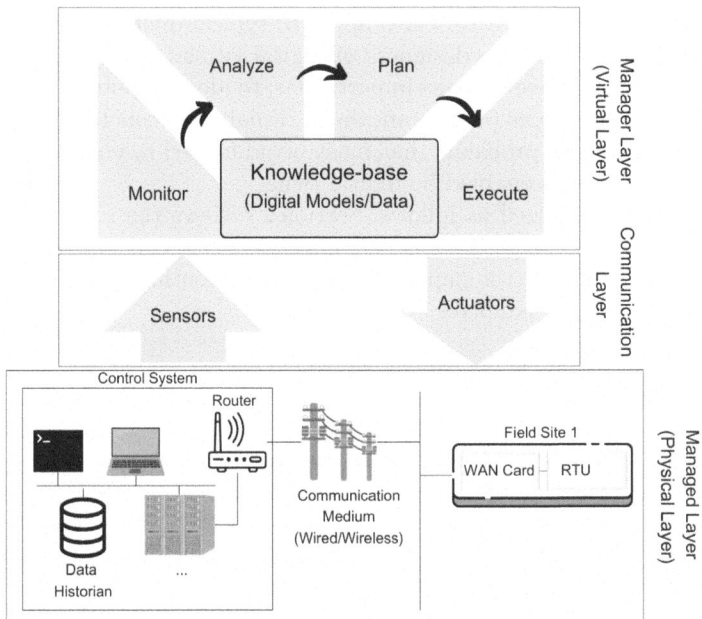

Fig. 1. A self-adaptive ICS architecture enabled with a digital twin (The Digital Twin services are implemented in the MAPE components)

The security of a self-adaptive system relies on both the security of its physical system and its managing layer. While adaptations are crucial for maintaining system functionality and meeting non-functional requirements like performance and reliability, they can also introduce new vulnerabilities and change the attack surface. Thus, it is crucial to understand the impact of adaptation on system security and to control this process in order to enhance overall security. In this paper, we summarize the results of our research within the PROSSES project [5], which focuses on improving the security of self-adaptive systems by making adaptations security-aware. We developed methods to reduce the attack surface of self-adaptive systems by incorporating security considerations into the adaptation process. This approach facilitates self-protection [52] by dynamically minimizing the attack surface through formal threat analysis and integrating security into the decision-making process for selecting adaptations.

The manager layer in a self-adaptive system – corresponding to the virtual layer in a digital twin architecture – broadens the attack surface by introducing new avenues for attacks, some of which are specific to self-adaptive systems. To show this, we map the security threats of existing digital twins-enabled self-adaptive systems to the MITRE ATT&CK framework [4], which is a security knowledge base to categorize adversary tactics and techniques used to compromise systems based on real-world attacks and observations. We identify potential attack vectors and security risks unique to these systems via this analysis. Note that the identified attack vectors also apply to typical digital twins. Therefore, our analysis results can help designers of digital twins in general, and digital-twin-enabled self-adaptive systems in particular, to identify potential attack vectors and develop strategies to mitigate them. Finally, we conclude the paper by discussing several open problems that must be addressed to ensure the security of self-adaptive systems enabled by digital twins.

This paper is organized as follows. Section 2 reviews the related work. Sections 3 and 4 discuss the security of the manager layer and the physical layer, respectively. We conclude the paper in Sect. 5 by presenting the open challenges of digital twins and self-adaptive systems.

2   Related Work

Analysis of Self-adaptive Systems. Formal techniques have been extensively used to model and analyze the safety of self-adaptive systems (see [50] for a survey on formal methods for self-adaptive systems). PobSAM [29] and its extension HPob-SAM [28] are formal models proposed to design self-adaptive systems, where policies are used to control the managed system. These models are formalized using actor-based models [44] and process algebra, and verified using model-checking approaches [30]. However, security verification of self-adaptive systems remains an underexplored area of research. Yuan et al. [53] introduced an architecture-based approach to self-protecting systems and proposed architectural patterns for system protection. In [42], they also analyzed adaptations from an availability perspective to mitigate DoS attacks. Several approaches for the security analysis of dynamic networks have been proposed in the past [7,17,54,55], however, none of these work directly address the security analysis of self-adaptive systems. We will present a summary of our research findings on the security of self-adaptive systems in Sect. 4.

Threat modelling and analysis refers to using models to analyze, evaluate, and describe the threats of a system in order to understand cybersecurity risks, assess them, and analyze their consequences [27,34,39,51]. This process helps in planning more effective countermeasures to mitigate and manage those risks. Several graphical models [34], such as attack graphs and attack trees, as well as formal models, have been used for threat modelling. Further, various knowledge bases have been developed and are employed by designers and practitioners to facilitate threat modelling and analysis, such as MITRE ATT&CK , Common Attack Pattern Enumeration and Classification (CAPEC) [1], Common Weaknesses Enumeration (CWE) [3], and Common Vulnerabilities Enumeration (CVE) etc.

These knowledge bases are often interlinked; for example, an entry in CWE, which represents a class of vulnerabilities, is linked to the related concrete vulnerabilities from CVE. Establishing such links is often done manually based on domain expert knowledge, though there have been attempts to semi-automate this process recently. Izzuddin et al. conducted a threat analysis of smart grid security in [23], where they collected data using a honeypot and manually mapped the data to the MITRE ATT&CK framework. Bhosale et al. [10] present a methodology for manually mapping vulnerabilities identified in Industrial Control Systems (ICSs) to the MITRE ATT&CK framework. They use the Common Vulnerability Scoring System (CVSS) [2] to assess the impact of vulnerabilities but perform the mapping to the MITRE ATT&CK framework manually using expert knowledge. The (semi)–automated approaches include a machine learning-based approach in [35] to map CVEs to MITRE ATT&CK techniques. In this paper, we identify the relevant attacks using the related literature and then map the attacks to the MITRE ATT&CK framework manually based on domain expert knowledge similar to [10,23].

Security of digital twins has been recently studied in several survey papers [6, 25,49]. Alcaraz et al. [6] identify the security requirements of different layers and propose a taxonomy of attacks that can violate these requirements for the various layers of the digital twin. They further discuss the literature and map it to the proposed taxonomy. Wang et al. [49] performed an extensive survey on the Internet of Digital Twins, which has a different focus than our paper. Jeremiah et al. [25] briefly discuss the vulnerabilities of digital twins, but their results are not fully driven by a literature review, and their methodology is not very clear. In contrast to our work that focuses on a specific subclass of digital twins, [6,49] concentrate on a more general class of digital twins, and their literature review is more comprehensive in terms of coverage than ours. However, our method is more systematic, as we use the MITRE ATT&CK framework to perform our analysis.

3 Security Analysis of Managing Layer

In this section, we identify the attack vectors introduced by the managing layer in a digital twine-enabled self-adaptive system using the MITRE ATT&CK tactics that adversaries might use to compromise the managing layer.

3.1 MITRE ATT&CK Framework

The MITRE ATT&CK framework is a knowledge base that comprises various *tactics* representing an adversary's tactical objectives, along with the *techniques* used to achieve those goals at the different stages of an attack, where a technique might consist of a few sub-techniques forming a hierarchy. There are three versions of this framework, tailored for the Enterprise, Mobile, and Industrial Control Systems (ICS) domains. Table 1 presents different tactics that an attacker may use to compromise a system in the ICS domain. The reason that we focus on ICS in this paper is that digital twins are commonly implemented in ICS environments [43], making the ICS matrix particularly relevant for our analysis. Furthermore, designing and ensuring security in ICS environments is often challenging. This is due to the large presence of legacy systems in many industrial settings [37]. They typically have longer lifespans and some of these systems were designed and implemented in an era where cyber security was of no major concern. Further, the integration of these systems with modern network-connected components [24,37] can increase the security risk significantly.

Table 1. MITRE ATT&CK Tactics for the ICS domain [4]

Tactic	Description
Initial Access	Attempting to access the ICS environment
Execution	Executing unauthorized code or manipulating system functions, parameters, and data illegally
Persistence	Maintaining access to the system
Privilege Escalation	Obtaining higher-level permissions
Evasion	Evading security defences
Discovery	Gathering information to identify and assess targets
Lateral Movement	Moving laterally within the ICS environment
Collection	Collecting data and domain knowledge relevant to objectives
Command and Control	Establishing communication with and control over compromised systems, controllers, and platforms
Inhibit Response Function	Disrupting safety, protection, quality assurance, and operator intervention functions to prevent a response to failures or hazards
Impair Process Control	Manipulating, disabling, or damaging physical control processes
Impact	Manipulating, interrupting, or destroying ICS systems, data, and the surrounding environment

3.2 Method

In this paper, we do not consider a specific implementation of digital twin-enabled self-adaptive systems but rather focus on an abstract architecture where a single MAPE-K loop interacts with the physical layer at an abstract level (see Fig. 1). The purpose of our threat analysis is to identify potential attacks, as well as their corresponding MITRE ATT&CK tactics, for each component of a MAPE-K loop. To this end, we identified potential security threats by reviewing the literature on historical attacks, vulnerabilities, and security threats in digital twin systems that support adaptation. We also take into account threats and vulnerabilities that arise in the broader software security domain. This is because the managing layer is essentially a software system, that interacts with a physical layer [11,14]. We limited our search to the references cited in the survey papers [6,25,49] to identify relevant studies which led to the selection of 40 papers for detailed review. We first identified attacks targeting the managing layer using the results of our literature review, and then manually mapped them to the MAPE-K and MITRE ATT&CK frameworks based on domain expert knowledge.

3.3 Literature Analysis Results

By analyzing related attacks on digital twins, we have categorized vulnerabilities into three main groups: attacks arising in the communications layer, those occurring within the virtual layer (managing layer), and attacks that apply to both layers. Attacks related to the physical layer were not considered. The attacks on the communications layer are (i) *physical tampering* [8,22,26,36], which involves deliberately damaging or destroying physical assets to disrupt the virtual layer, and (ii) *sensor spoofing* [22,26], where false input data is provided to sensors to manipulate the perception of the physical layer (data poisoning).

Attacks on the virtual layer fall into three categories: (i) *data manipulation* [19,21,22,26,36], which involves unauthorized modification of stored data or runtime models, (ii) *injection attacks* [15,22,36] where malicious code or data is inserted into the components of the virtual layer, and (iii) *API/software vulnerability exploitation* [8,20–22,26], where API/software vulnerabilities within the virtual layer are exploited.

Furthermore, attacks common to both layers include (i) *supply chain attacks* [8], which target hardware or software components during manufacturing and distribution, (ii) *denial of service* [8,15,19,22,26,36], which interfere with sensors or components to exhaust available resources, (iii) *man-in-the-middle* [8,15,19,22,26,36], which involves intercepting or altering communications between sensors or components, (iv) *unauthorized access* [8,21,22,26], which occurs when illegal access is gained to the virtual or communications layer, (v) *insider attacks* [20,26], which exploit legitimate access privileges to compromise system security from within the organization, and (vi) *side-channel attacks* [8] which extract sensitive information by monitoring physical implementation characteristics such as timing, power consumption, acoustics or electromagnetic emissions.

3.4 Mapping Identified Attacks to MITRE ATT&CK

We followed an approach similar to [10] to map the identified attacks in the literature review phase to the MITRE ATT&CK tactics and the MAPE-K components. Table 2 shows the mapping between the attacks, the MAPE-K components and the MITRE ATT&CK framework. The attacks on the communications layer are mainly applied to the Monitor and Execute components since they directly interface with the sensors and actuators in a MAPE-K-enabled system. Attacks on the virtual layer are associated with the Plan and Analyze components, which function as the virtual layer in a digital twin architecture, facilitating analysis and adaptation. Finally, attacks common to both layers are

Table 2. MITRE ATT&CK Mapping Summary

Attack	Mapped Tactic
Monitor Component	
Sensor Spoofing [22, 26]	Evasion
Physical Tampering [8, 22, 26, 36]	Impact
Man in the middle [8, 15, 19, 22, 26, 36]	Discovery/Collection/Evasion
Denial of Service [8, 15, 19, 22, 26, 36]	Impact/Inhibit Response Function
Supply Chain Attacks [8]	Initial Access
Unauthorized Access [8, 21, 22, 26]	Initial Access/Collection
Insider Attacks [20, 26]	Initial Access/Discovery/Collection/Impact
Side-channel Attacks [8]	Discovery/Collection
Analyze, Plan and Knowledge Components	
API/Software Vulnerability Exploitation [8, 20–22, 26]	Execution
Injection Attacks [15, 22, 36]	Persistence
Data Manipulation [19, 21, 22, 26, 36]	Persistence/Impact
Denial of Service [8, 15, 19, 22, 26, 36]	Impact/Inhibit Response Function
Man in the middle [8, 15, 19, 22, 26, 36]	Discovery/Collection/Evasion
Unauthorized Access [8, 21, 22, 26]	Initial Access/Collection
Supply Chain Attacks [8]	Initial Access
Insider Attacks [20, 26]	Initial Access/Discovery/Collection/Impact
Side-channel Attacks [8]	Discovery/Collection
Execute Component	
Man in the middle [8, 15, 19, 22, 26, 36]	Discovery/Collection/Evasion
Denial of Service [8, 15, 19, 22, 26, 36]	Impact/Inhibit Response Function
Physical Tampering [8, 22, 26, 36]	Impact
Supply Chain Attacks [8]	Initial Access
Unauthorized Access [8, 21, 22, 26]	Initial Access/Collection
Insider Attacks [20, 26]	Initial Access/Discovery/Collection/Impact
Side-channel Attacks [8]	Discovery/Collection

mapped across all MAPE-K components. For each component of the MAPE-K loop, we limit ourselves to provide explanation for a few mappings.

The *Monitor* component in an abstract MAPE-K loop is responsible for receiving input from the sensors in the communications layer. This input contains data about the managed system and its environment. Depending on the domain in which the self-adaptive system is implemented, these sensors may be virtual, or physical components. Therefore, attacks such as sensor spoofing can be utilized to give false information about the managed system in order for an adversary to evade detection. This satisfies the evasion tactic in the MITRE ATT&CK ICS framework. Similarly, attacks such as man in the middle could be utilized by an attacker to discover assets and collect information about the ICS system through data transmitted to the monitoring component and to evade defences by manipulating communications.

The *analyze* component examines the collected data to identify patterns, anomalies, and potential issues. The goal is to determine if any adaptations are necessary based on the current state of the system and its environment. This information is then passed onto the analysis component. Therefore, attacks such as data injections can be utilized to insert malicious goals and adaptations into this component. These malicious goals and adaptations could be utilized by an adversary to maintain access to the ICS environment throughout various system states. Such an attack satisfies the Persistence tactic in the MITRE ATT&CK framework since it would change system configurations which allows an adversary to keep their foothold in the system.

If the analysis component identifies a need for adaptation, the *Plan* component devises a course of action. The planning process considers system goals, constraints, and available resources to create an optimal adaptation plan. Similar to the analyze component, injection attacks could be utilized here to achieve persistence. Moreover, API vulnerabilities could be exploited to run malicious code within the system since the Plan component would have to utilize several system interfaces and resources while carrying out its' operations. Such an attack satisfies the Execution tactic since an adversary would be running malicious code via vulnerable APIs

The *Execute* component implements the chosen adaptation plan, making the necessary changes to the managed system. This may involve adjusting system parameters, reallocating resources, or modifying system behaviour or architecture. Attacks such as denial of service could be utilized by an adversary to stop the execute component from making the planned changes to the system. Such an attack would fall under the Inhibit Response function tactic in the MITRE ATT&CK framework when the denied change is in response to a security concern and it would also fall under the Impact tactic since it would disrupt the overall system operations

The *Knowledge Base* component serves as a central repository of information that supports and works with all other components of the MAPE-K loop. It may contain various information such as system models and architectures, adaptation policies and rules, and historical data among others. This knowledge base is continuously updated and refined based on the system's experiences and adaptations. Similar to other MAPE-K components, the Knowledge Base would be susceptible to attacks such as data manipulation. An adversary could alter or inject malicious data into the Knowledge Base to introduce false information about the system, enabling persistent access or control. The attacker could also manipulate stored data, leading other components such as the Plan and

Analyze to make incorrect adaptation decisions, ultimately degrading system performance or compromising its integrity. The former scenario would fall under the Persistence tactic while the latter would fall under Impact since it disrupts the overall functionality of the system

Limitations and Threats to Validity. We have limited our search to the papers referenced in the survey papers. This means that our literature review is not exhaustive, and there may be relevant studies we have not considered. Furthermore, we restricted our focus to self-adaptive systems implemented using digital twins. Therefore, we did not consider self-adaptive systems that do not explicitly incorporate the MAPE-K loop or do not use digital twin technology, while still offering adaptation services. Therefore, our results may not be comprehensive or complete. Furthermore, the reliance on an abstract model for mapping the identified attacks has a limitation since this mainly utilized conceptual models which may not fully capture the complexities and practical challenges of real-world system deployments. Abstract models, while valuable for theoretical understanding, can potentially oversimplify the intricate interactions and dynamic behaviours inherent in actual self-adaptive systems that should be considered in security analysis.

4   Security of Managed Layer

While the security of the managed layer depends on its design and implementation, due to its separation from the managing layer, the evolution of the system can indirectly influence the security of the managed system by introducing new attack vectors or removing existing ones at the managed layer. This can occur when the managing layer adds a new component that introduces a new vulnerability. These attack vectors are application-specific, as they exist in the components of the managed layer, and do not directly depend on the security of the managing layer. Therefore, the managing layer should make its adaptation decisions to ensure that an evolution does not create security vulnerabilities for the managed layer, and control the attack vector of the managed layer. In the research project PROSSES (Provably Secure Self-protecting Systems) [5], we focused on these types of attack vectors that arise due to an adaptation, and proposed methods to enhance the security of self-adaptive systems by informing the managed layer about security aspects. We pursued two directions of research in this project: (i) threat analysis of self-adaptive component-based systems to offer self-protection by reducing the attack surface of the managed layer, and (ii) designing effective defense mechanisms to protect the managed system against attacks. In this section, we present a summary of our research results from this project.

Security-Aware Adaptations. In today's increasingly complex software systems, many vulnerabilities still remain in the system after being discovered due to factors such as the lack of a patch or knowledge to fix them, cost considerations, or organizational preferences for availability and usability over security [41, 47, 48]. We developed an approach to improve the security of self-adaptive systems containing security vulnerabilities by incorporating security threat analysis into the MAPE-K loop in [32, 33, 45, 56].

We proposed a method for security risk assessment of adaptations in component-based systems [33]. Security risk assessment is usually conducted using measuring some security metrics, which can be either *quantitative* or *qualitative*, depending on the type of measurement. In our approach, we adopt a quantitative method, where security measurements are expressed numerically. The success likelihood of attacks is an example of a security metric. When an adaptation is triggered, there may be multiple *adaptation plans* that can be applied to the system, leading to different final *configurations*. An adaptation plan shows different strategies to adapt the system architecture, and a configuration represents the system architecture in our context, i.e., the list of components and their interactions. Our goal is to make adaptations security-aware by measuring the security level of adaptation plans and considering their security risks when deciding which adaptation to apply. This security analysis aims to minimize the attack surface of the managed system by applying more secure adaptations. When an adaptation is applied, the system transitions through several transient configurations before reaching its final configuration, and we consider the security of the system during the entire transition. We maintain a runtime model of the system architecture, which includes security-relevant information such as detected vulnerabilities. From this model, we generate an attack graph [38] based on the system architecture and its vulnerabilities, which serves as the model for measuring security risks. We then designed several security metrics to assess the security levels of different adaptations, that are used in a utility function by the manager layer to determine the optimal configuration for the system to evolve to in terms of various factors including security risks.

Our approach in [33] lacks formal foundations. To formally reason about attacker behavior and its interaction with system behavior under uncertainty, we extended our approach in [45], where we formalized both attacker and system behavior during adaptation using probabilistic automata and employed UPPAAL [9] for verification. We automatically build probabilistic models from the architectural models maintained at runtime and check the security properties of the attacker or system behavior, specified using PCTL (Probabilistic Computation Tree Logic) [18].

To improve the scalability of formal verification of attacker behavior and make it practical for the analysis of large and complex systems, we proposed an automated approach for scalable security analysis of component-based systems with dynamic architectures in [32]. By leveraging formal abstraction and modular verification, we automatically construct a two-tier probabilistic security model that is maintained and incrementally updated at runtime. Security properties are verified against the top-level abstract model for threat analysis. Our approach has been proven sound, and experimental results demonstrate that it significantly enhances the scalability of security analyses.

Countermeasure Design. Another direction we pursued in PROSSES to reduce the attack surface in the managed layer is designing adaptations that apply effective countermeasures to the system. Designing component-based systems requires evaluating different architectures that integrate system components and countermeasures, i.e., actions aimed at preventing or mitigating attacks. An architecture must adhere to architectural constraints and satisfy both functional and non-functional requirements while selecting the appropriate defense option, considering factors such as security priorities, deployment costs, the overall defense budget, and compatibility with other components. In [46], we utilized model finding and probabilistic verification using a tool-supported framework called HaiQ [12] to design a component-based system that fulfills the required functionalities and also reduces the attack surface. We first identify all architectures that meet the architectural constraints specified in first-order logic and then model-check a set of probability- or reward-based temporal logic properties for each architecture to determine the architecture that offers the most effective defense.

Uncertainty and limited observability of attacker behavior are two key challenges when designing countermeasures for systems. We proposed an approach based on *stochastic games* under *partial observation* in [31] to analyze attack-defense scenarios in systems with vulnerabilities and to automatically synthesize defense strategies. We utilize attack graphs to automatically construct attack scenarios and leverage stochastic modeling and verification using PRISM-games [13] for security analysis and defense/attack strategy synthesis.

5   Discussion

In self-adaptive systems enabled by digital twins, a digital replica of the assets is used at runtime to provide services to the managed system. This enables the creation of a simulation environment for analyzing security and assessing the impact of attacks and defenses on the digital replica, as such tasks can be infeasible, costly, or complex to conduct on real systems. However, the centralization of control in the managing layer can make it easier for adversaries to compromise the system with less effort and cost via the virtualized environment. Hence, to improve the security of the managing (virtual) layer and address the threats identified in Sect. 3, security should be considered during the design and implementation of a DT-enabled self-adaptive system.

The MITRE ATT&CK framework recommends mitigations to protect against attacks, which can be applied to address the attack vectors identified in Sect. 3. This is particularly important to ensure the consistency and integrity of data so that the system operates based on accurate and trustworthy information. In this section, we focus on specific challenges unique to DT-enabled self-adaptive systems that require different mitigation techniques than the general security strategies provided by the MITRE ATT&CK framework.

Consistent Security Requirements. One promising research direction is the development of formal frameworks and methods to specify, analyze, and enforce the security requirements of digital-twin-enabled self-adaptive systems. Let S_p be the security requirements to be enforced in the physical layer, i.e., they are checked against the real implementation of the physical layer. To enforce S_p, the manager layer should define the security requirements S_v, which are checked against the digital replica and other runtime models described at various levels of abstraction, rather than directly against the physical layer. Therefore, to effectively capture and enforce security requirements, suitable formalisms are needed to describe S_p and S_v and to establish formal relationships $\sim$ between them. This is particularly important because these requirements are described at different levels of abstraction, and as the physical layer changes dynamically, so too do the security requirements. This relationship must be maintained throughout the system's evolution and adaptation to ensure that security requirements at both layers remain consistent, correct, and complete.

Secure Modeling and Abstraction. While the physical layer is often equipped with various security controls to enforce security policies, its virtual replica typically focuses on functionality and ignores these security mechanisms. For instance, it is often assumed that the MAPE components have full access to the entire knowledge base, whereas the physical layer implements access control mechanisms to regulate access and privileges. In other words, while access to a component in the physical layer may be restricted by access control policies, its virtual counterpart may be accessed freely. Thus, a key challenge is developing approaches for creating and processing abstract models in a secure manner to ensure that the security policies of the physical layer are enforced at the abstract digital level.

Reasoning under Uncertainty and Partial Observation. While digital replicas are powerful tools, they are essentially approximations that contain uncertainty and incomplete data arising from various factors, such as limitations in sensor and data collection, model simplifications, incomplete data, and the inherent complexity of the systems being modeled. Furthermore, limitations in modeling techniques contribute to the difficulty of perfectly replicating the real world in a digital model. Therefore, it is important to develop techniques and methods for reasoning about security under partial information and observability to ensure security.

Insider Threats. The comprehensive reach and knowledge that a managing layer provides about the managed system can make it easier for insiders to compromise the system. We require techniques and mechanisms to detect anomalies caused by insider malicious activities in self-adaptive systems. The complex nature of a self-adaptive system can make it more difficult to detect and attribute such an attack due to the fact that they might be mistaken for legitimate actions. The autonomous nature of such systems enables the insider to trigger sequences of actions automatically, which makes it difficult to trace the cause and distinguish it from normal operations of the system.

References

1. Common attack pattern enumeration and classification (capec). https://capec.mitre.org
2. Common vulnerability scoring system (cvss). https://www.first.org/cvss/
3. Common weaknesses enumeration (cwe). https://cwe.mitre.org
4. Mitre att&ck. https://attack.mitre.org
5. Prosses: Provably secure self-protecting systems. https://lnu.se/en/research/research-projects/provably-secure-self-protecting-systems-prosses/
6. Alcaraz, C., Lopez, J.: Digital twin: a comprehensive survey of security threats. IEEE Commun. Surv. Tutor. **24**(3), 1475–1503 (2022)
7. Almohri, H.M., Watson, L.T., Yao, D., Ou, X..: Security optimization of dynamic networks with probabilistic graph modeling and linear programming. In: IEEE Transactions on Dependable and Secure Computing, pp. 474–487 (2016)
8. Atalay, M., Angin, P.: A digital twins approach to smart grid security testing and standardization. In: 2020 IEEE International Workshop on Metrology for Industry 4.0 IoT, pp. 435–440, 2020
9. Bengtsson, J., Larsen, K., Larsson, F., Pettersson, P., Yi, W.: UPPAAL - a tool suite for automatic verification of real-time systems. In: Rajeev, A., Thomas, A.H., Eduardo, D.S. (eds.), Hybrid Systems III: Verification and Control, Proceedings of the DIMACS/SYCON Workshop on Verification and Control of Hybrid Systems, 22–25 October 1995, Ruttgers University, New Brunswick, NJ, USA, volume 1066 of LNCS, pp. 232–243. Springer, 1995
10. Bhosale, P., Kastner, W., Sauter, T.: Mapping ics vulnerabilities: prioritization and risk propagation analysis with MITRE ATT&CK framework and bayesian belief networks. In: 2024 IEEE 29th International Conference on Emerging Technologies and Factory Automation (ETFA), pp. 1–8, 2024
11. Brun, Y., et al.: Engineering Self-Adaptive Systems through Feedback Loops, pp. 48–70. Springer, Berlin, Heidelberg (2009)
12. J Cámara, J.: Haiq: synthesis of software design spaces with structural and probabilistic guarantees. In: Kyungmin, B., Domenico, B., Stefania, G., Nico, P. (eds.), FormaliSE@ICSE 2020: 8th International Conference on Formal Methods in Software Engineering, Seoul, Republic of Korea, 13 July 2020, pp. 22–33. ACM, 2020
13. Chen, T., Forejt, V., Kwiatkowska, M., Parker, D., Simaitis, A.: Prism-games: a model checker for stochastic multi-player games. In: Nir, P., Scott, A.S., (eds.), Tools and Algorithms for the Construction and Analysis of Systems 19th International Conference, TACAS 2013, Held as Part of the European Joint Conferences on Theory and Practice of Software, ETAPS 2013, Rome, Italy, 16–24 March 2013. Proceedings, volume 7795 of LNCS, pp. 185–191. Springer (2013)
14. Barna, C., et al.: Software Engineering for Self-Adaptive Systems: A Research Roadmap, pp. 1–26. Springer, Berlin, Heidelberg (2009)
15. Danilczyk, W., Sun, Y., He, H.: An intelligent digital twin framework for microgrid security. In: 2019 North American Power Symposium (NAPS), pp. 1–6, 2019
16. Fitzgerald, J., Gomes, C., Larsen, P.G.: The engineering of digital twins, 2024
17. Frigault, M., Wang, L., Singhal, A., Jajodia, S.: Measuring network security using dynamic bayesian network. In: Proceedings of the 4th ACM Workshop on Quality of Protection, pp. 23–30, 2008
18. Hansson, H., Jonsson, B.: A logic for reasoning about time and reliability. Form. Aspects Comput. **6**(5), 512–535 (1994)

19. He, C., Luan, T.H., Rongxing, L., Zhou, S., Dong, M.: Security and privacy in vehicular digital twin networks: challenges and solutions. IEEE Wirel. Commun. **30**(4), 154–160 (2023)
20. Hearn, M.: Digital twins, the industrial Internet of Things and cyber security threats in connected industry. Cyber Secur. Peer-Reviewed J. **3**(2), 116–123 (2019)
21. Hearn, M., Rix, S.: Cybersecurity considerations for digital twin implementations. IIC J. Innov. **10**, 107–113 (2019)
22. Homaei, M.H., Lindo, A.C., Dıaz, J.A.: The role of artificial intelligence in digital twin's cybersecurity, November 2022
23. Izzuddin, A.B., Lim, C.: Mapping threats in smart grid system using the mitre att&ck ics framework. In: 2022 IEEE International Conference on Aerospace Electronics and Remote Sensing Technology (ICARES), pp. 1–7, 2022
24. Jarwar, M.A., Watson CBE FREng, J., Ani, U.P.D., Chalmers, S.W.: Industrial internet of things security modelling using ontological methods. In: Proceedings of the 12th International Conference on the Internet of Things, 2022
25. Jeremiah, S.R., El Azzaoui, A., Xiong, N.N., Park, J.H.: A comprehensive survey of digital twins: applications, technologies and security challenges. J. Syst. Archit. **151**, 103120 (2024)
26. Karaarslan, E., Babiker, M.: Digital twin security threats and countermeasures: an introduction. In: 2021 International Conference on Information Security and Cryptology (ISCTURKEY), pp. 7–11, 2021
27. Kaynar, K.: A taxonomy for attack graph generation and usage in network security. J. Inf. Secur. Appl. 27–56 (2016)
28. Khakpour, N., Jalili, S., Sirjani, M., Goltz, U., Abolhasanzadeh, B.: Hpobsam for modeling and analyzing IT ecosystems - through a case study. J. Syst. Softw. **85**(12), 2770–2784 (2012)
29. Khakpour, N., Jalili, S., Talcott, C., Sirjani, M., Mousavi, M.R.: Pobsam: policy-based managing of actors in self-adaptive systems. In: Sun, M., Bernhard, S., (eds.), Proceedings of the 6th International Workshop on Formal Aspects of Component Software, FACS@FMWeek 2009, Eindhoven, The Netherlands, 2–3 November 2009, volume 263 of Electronic Notes in Theoretical Computer Science, pp. 129–143. Elsevier, 2009
30. Khakpour, N., Khosravi, R., Sirjani, M., Jalili, S.: Formal analysis of policy-based self-adaptive systems. In: Sung, Y.S., Sascha, O., Michael, S., Mathew, J.P., Chih-Cheng, H. (eds.), Proceedings of the 2010 ACM Symposium on Applied Computing (SAC), Sierre, Switzerland, 22–26 March 2010, pp. 2536–2543. ACM, 2010
31. Khakpour, N., Parker, D.: Partially-observable security games for automating attack-defense analysis. In: 22nd International Conference on Software Engineering and Formal Methods, November, Aveira, Portugal, 2024 (2024)
32. Khakpour, N., Skandylas, C.: Compositional security analysis of dynamic component-based systems. In: The 39th IEEE/ACM International Conference on Automated Software Engineering (ASE 2024), Sacramento, California, United States, 2024. ACM, 2024
33. Khakpour, N., Skandylas, C., Nariman, G.S., Weyns, D.: Towards secure architecture-based adaptations. In: Marin, L., Siobhán, C., Kenji, T. (eds.), Proceedings of the 14th International Symposium on Software Engineering for Adaptive and Self-Managing Systems, SEAMS@ICSE 2019, Montreal, QC, Canada, 25–31 May 2019, pp. 114–125. ACM, 2019
34. Kordy, B., Piètre-Cambacédès, L., Schweitzer, P.: Dag-based attack and defense modeling: don't miss the forest for the attack trees. Comput. Sci. Rev. 1–38 (2013)

35. Kuppa, A., Aouad, L., Le-Khac, N.-A.: Linking cve's to mitre att&ck techniques. In: Proceedings of the 16th International Conference on Availability, Reliability and Security, ARES '21, New York, NY, USA, 2021. Association for Computing Machinery (2021)
36. Li, G., Lai, C., Rongxing, L., Zheng, D.: Seccdv: a security reference architecture for cybertwin-driven 6g v2x. IEEE Trans. Veh. Technol. **71**(5), 4535–4550 (2022)
37. McLaughlin, S.E., et al.: The cybersecurity landscape in industrial control systems. Proc. IEEE **104**, 1039–1057 (2016)
38. Ou, X., Boyer, W.F., McQueen, M.A.: A scalable approach to attack graph generation. In: Ari, J., Rebecca, N.W., Sabrina De Capitani, D.V. (eds.), Proceedings of the 13th ACM Conference on Computer and Communications Security, CCS 2006, Alexandria, VA, USA, October 30 - November 3, 2006, pp. 336–345. ACM, 2006
39. Ou, X., Govindavajhala, S., Appel, A.W.: Mulval: a logic-based network security analyzer. In: Proceedings of the 14th Conference on USENIX Security Symposium, pp. 1–8, 2005
40. Pekaric, I., et al.: A systematic review on security and safety of self-adaptive systems. J. Syst. Softw. **203**, 111716 (2023)
41. Riegler, M., Sametinger, J., Vierhauser, M., Wimmer, M.: A model-based mode-switching framework based on security vulnerability scores. J. Syst. Softw. **200**, 111633 (2023)
42. Schmerl, B., et al.: Architecture-based self-protection: composing and reasoning about denial-of-service mitigations. In: Proceedings of the 2014 Symposium and Bootcamp on the Science of Security, pp. 1–12, 2014
43. Singh, M., et al.: Applications of digital twin across industries: a review. Appl. Sci. (2022)
44. Sirjani, M., Movaghar, A., Shali, A., de Boer, F.S.: Modeling and verification of reactive systems using rebeca. Fundam. Inform. **63**(4), 385–410 (2004)
45. Skandylas, C., Khakpour, N.: Design and implementation of self-protecting systems: a formal approach. Future Gener. Comput. Syst. **115**, 421–437 (2021)
46. Skandylas, C., Khakpour, N., Camara, J.: Security countermeasure selection for component-based software-intensive systems. In: 22nd IEEE International Conference on Software Quality, Reliability and Security, QRS 2022, Guangzhou, China, 5–9 December 2022, pp. 63–72. IEEE, 2022
47. Veracode. Unveiling the state of software security in the public sector, 2023. https://www.veracode.com/sites/default/files/pdf/resources/reports/veracode-state-of-software-security-2023-public-sector.pdf
48. Wang, B., Li, X., de Aguiar, L.P., Menasche, D.S., Shafiq, Z.: Characterizing and modeling patching practices of industrial control systems. **1**(1) (2017)
49. Wang, Y., Zhou, S., Guo, S., Dai, M., Luan, T.H., Liu, Y.: A survey on digital twins: architecture, enabling technologies, security and privacy, and future prospects. IEEE Internet Things J. **10**(17), 14965–14987 (2023)
50. Weyns, D., Iftikhar, M.U., De La Iglesia, D.G., Ahmad, T.: A survey of formal methods in self-adaptive systems. In: Proceedings of the Fifth International c* Conference on Computer Science and Software Engineering, pp. 67–79, 2012
51. Wideł, W., Audinot, M., Fila, B., Pinchinat, S.: Beyond 2014: formal methods for attack tree–based security modeling. ACM Comput. Surv. 1–36 (2019)
52. Yuan, E., Esfahani, N., Malek, S.: A systematic survey of self-protecting software systems. ACM Trans. Auton. Adapt. Syst. **8**(4), 17:1–17:41 (2014)
53. Yuan, E., Malek, S., Schmerl, B., Garlan, D., Gennari, J.: Architecture-based self-protecting software systems. In: Proceedings of the 9th International ACM Sigsoft Conference on Quality of Software Architectures, pp. 33–42, 2013

54. Yusuf, S.E., Ge, M., Hong, J.B., Alzaid, H., Kim, D.S.: Evaluating the effectiveness of security metrics for dynamic networks. In: 2017 IEEE Trustcom/BigDataSE/ICESS, pp. 277–284 (2017)
55. Yusuf, S.E., Ge, M., Hong, J.B., Kim, H.K., Kim, P., Kim, D.S.: Security modelling and analysis of dynamic enterprise networks. In : 2016 IEEE International Conference on Computer and Information Technology, pp. 249–256 (2016)
56. Zeller, S., Khakpour, N., Weyns, D., Deogun, D.: Self-protection against business logic vulnerabilities. In: Shinichi, H., Elisabetta Di, N., Radu, C. (eds.), SEAMS '20: IEEE/ACM 15th International Symposium on Software Engineering for Adaptive and Self-Managing Systems, Seoul, Republic of Korea, 29 June–3 July, 2020, pp. 174–180. ACM, 2020

Ten Years of Spatial Model Checking

Vincenzo Ciancia[1], Diego Latella[2], and Mieke Massink[1(✉)]

[1] ISTI, Consiglio Nazionale delle Ricerche, Pisa, Italy
{Vincenzo.Ciancia,Mieke.Massink}@cnr.it
[2] Formerly at ISTI, Consiglio Nazionale delle Ricerche, Pisa, Italy
Diego.Latella@actiones.eu

Abstract. Model checking has traditionally focused on the analysis of the *behaviour* of concurrent systems. When addressing more complex systems, such as large-scale collective adaptive systems, it quickly becomes clear that a focus on *spatial* aspects of such systems is as much relevant as the behavioural aspects. We provide a guided tour through the various research directions that this new focus on space has generated and is about to generate in the future.

Keywords: Spatial logics · Spatial model checking · Spatial bisimilarity · Logical equivalence · Polyhedral models · Medical imaging · Model minimisation

1 Introduction

This paper provides a (non-exhaustive) guided tour on the research on spatial model checking that we have been carrying out at CNR-ISTI, Pisa, Italy, in cooperation with our collaborators, and that found its origin in the EU funded research project Quanticol [28]. The focus of that project was on the formal verification of properties of collective adaptive systems (CAS). These are generally large systems composed of many similar, independent, interacting objects that are moving through physical space. The objects can be of a widely varying nature, ranging from chemical substances, interacting in chemical reactions, to animals, such as ants or birds, or humans riding shared bikes. Whatever the nature of the objects, it soon becomes clear that for the analysis of such systems their spatial dimension is as important as their behavioural dimension.

In this paper we illustrate a selection of the main issues and questions raised during our quest for a suitable formal spatial framework that was general enough to cope with various forms of spatial models and, at the same time, practical enough to form a suitable basis for automated, large-scale verification techniques such as spatial model checking.

As we will see, the generality of the approach led us to apply spatial model checking also in previously unexplored domains, such as medical image analysis

---

The authors are listed in alphabetical order, as they equally contributed to the work presented in this paper.

E. A. Lee et al. (Eds.): Marjan Sirjani Festschrift, LNCS 15560, pp. 406–424, 2025.
https://doi.org/10.1007/978-3-031-85134-6_18

and surface and volume meshes. Furthermore, it turned out that very useful theoretical results and techniques that made model checking more efficient in the behavioural setting could be adapted to their use for spatial model checking.

This guided tour starts from our first considerations on spatial and spatio-temporal logic and related model checking inspired by our work on CAS in the Quanticol project (Sect. 2). We then pass on to the application of pure spatial logic and model checking in the domain of medical imaging, based on discrete models of space, namely pixels/voxels (Sect. 3). In Sect. 4, instead, we address model checking representations of *continuous* space, in particular polyhedral models. We also show some applications of polyhedral model checking. We see how such discrete and continuous spatial models can be minimised, exploiting spatial forms of bisimulation (Sect. 5) and, finally, we draw some conclusions and provide an outlook on future work (Sect. 6).

2   A First Source of Inspiration: The Quanticol Project

The Quanticol project ran from 2013 to 2017 and had the ambitious goal to develop a formal verification framework for large-scale systems consisting of heterogeneous components that are spatially distributed and have possibly competing goals. The large-scale systems that were considered in the project were related to smart urban transportation and the smart electricity grid. In particular, we studied a smart bike sharing system composed of a fleet of bikes and stations spread around a city where these bikes could be taken from and parked in at the end of a ride. Typical problems of such systems are to make sure that at any time of the day there are a sufficient number of bikes and free parking places in each of the stations to satisfy the need of users. At the same time, one would want to keep the relocation of bikes by little vans to obtain such an equal distribution to the minimum. It is interesting to study to what extent the latter can be obtained by stimulating users to park their bikes just outside the most crowded areas and walk a little further to reach their destination, whenever possible (Fig. 1).

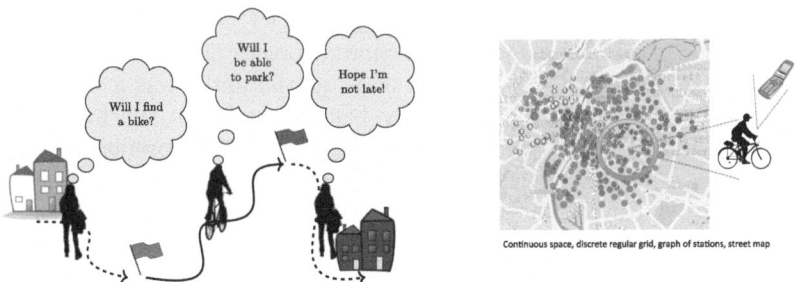

Continuous space, discrete regular grid, graph of stations, street map

Fig. 1. Bike-sharing trips from a user's perspective (left). Various notions of space involved: continuous and discrete (right).

Early 2011 we had started to investigate fundamental aspects of CAS and it was immediately clear that the very nature of such systems, and in particular their relationship with physical space as well as logical spaces (e.g. the Internet and connectivity therein), required formal methods for modelling space(s) and related tools such as model checkers for automatic reasoning about such models. In this context, already for some time we were thinking about the following question: at least in the case of "logical" spaces, that can typically be modelled by general graphs, can we re-interpret *on space* modal operators normally used for expressing temporal properties? For instance, what would be the conceptual spatial meaning of, say, a formula like $\Phi_1 \, \mathsf{U} \, \Phi_2$, where U is the standard temporal logic *until*, if we would interpret it on a graph representing space? Intuitively, such an interpretation of U would convey the idea of characterising an area of points in the space (graph), all satisfying Φ_1, *surrounded* by points satisfying Φ_2.

These intuitions seemed to make sense, although the "mapping" to temporal logics was not at all immediate. For instance, reachability in space is rather different from reachability as interpreted in most of the current approaches to temporal logic. In fact, for branching-time temporal logics[1], the model of time is typically a *tree*, i.e. a partial ordering $(\mathcal{T}, \preceq)$ where every instant $t \in \mathcal{T}$ has a *linearly* ordered set of $\prec$-predecessors in $\mathcal{T}$ as remarked also in the Stanford Encyclopedia of Philosophy:[2]

> "Backward-linearity captures the idea that the past is fixed; forward-branching reflects the openness of the future. At each point in time, there may be more than one path leading towards the future, and each such path represents a future possibility." [31].

When dealing with space, instead, this sort of "backwards determinism", reflected by typical "past-tense" modalities, is no longer acceptable. For instance, we want to be able to express the fact that, from a certain point x in space one can reach (*forward reachability*) a point y which can (or cannot) be reached from (*backward reachability*) a point with certain features. As a concrete example, we can think of a safe exit path from a room bringing to a safe area that cannot be reached by a toxic substance emanating from possibly *yet another* area.

Starting from considerations like the ones above, which we first presented at a Quanticol Project meeting in Edinburgh on Oct. 30, 2013, we initiated a literature study, using the Handbook of Spatial Logics [2] as a main source of inspiration. We found that our intuition of a "spatial until" was a well-founded one, since similar modalities had already been proposed in the literature, in particular by Aiello [1], and the general idea of a spatial interpretation of modal logics dates back to the fourties of the previous century with the seminal work by Tarski and McKinsey on the topological interpretation of **S4**, where the box modality $\square$ is interpreted as topological *interior* (and so $\lozenge$ corresponds

---

[1] Linear-time temporal logics are even more restrictive in this respect.

[2] There are only a few notable exceptions to this interpretation of the past, see for example [34,39], although we are not aware of the existence of any supporting verification tool, such as model-checkers, for the logics presented in these works.

to topological closure) [36]. We also realised two major facts: i) spatial logics were typically interpreted on *topological spaces* and ii) *model checking* was not addressed for them.

We found the restriction to topological spaces too strong a limitation: many interesting "spaces", like general graphs, do not fall in the class of topological spaces. For this reason we focussed on a larger class of spaces, namely Čech *closure spaces* [18], a generalisation of topological spaces that *does* include general graphs. Furthermore, model checking is one of our preferred technologies for formal verification of models based on logics. Thus, our natural move was to study closure spaces, define a logic for them, namely the *Spatial Logic for Closure Spaces* (SLCS), and develop algorithms for model checking finite *closure models*, i.e. closure spaces with valuation functions for atomic propositions [26,27]. The version of SLCS proposed in the above mentioned papers includes a *proximity* unary modality—$\mathcal{N}$—and the binary *surrounded* modality $\mathcal{S}$. A point x satisfies $\mathcal{N}\,\Phi$ if it is in the closure of the set of points satisfying Φ. It satisfies $\Phi_1\,\mathcal{S}\,\Phi_2$ if, for all paths π starting from x, whenever there is an element y on path π that does *not* satisfy Φ_1, there is an element z on path π, occurring somewhere before y, that satisfies Φ_2. In other words, it is not possible to find a path which can "escape" from the area of points satisfying Φ_1, where x lays, without first passing by a point satisfying Φ_2.

As one can see from the above discussion, the *surrounded* operator can be defined using the more primitive notion of *reachability* via paths and, in fact, in [3] SLCS has been (re)defined and the $\mathcal{S}$ modality is replaced by the forward and backward reachability modalities $\overrightarrow{\rho}$ and $\overleftarrow{\rho}$, respectively. A point x satisfies $\overrightarrow{\rho}\,\Phi_1[\Phi_2]$ if a path π exists from x such that there is a point y in π satisfying Φ_1 and all intermediate points in π between x and y satisfy Φ_2. Conversely, x satisfies $\overleftarrow{\rho}\,\Phi_1[\Phi_2]$ if there is a point y satisfying Φ_1 and a path π from y, leading to x and such that all intermediate points in π between x and y satisfy Φ_2. It is easy to see that $\Phi_1\,\mathcal{S}\,\Phi_2$ is equivalent to $\neg(\overrightarrow{\rho}\,\neg(\Phi_1 \vee \Phi_2)[\neg\Phi_2])$. In addition, the above property concerning toxic substances can easily be expressed by the following formula:

$$\overrightarrow{\rho}\,(\texttt{safe} \wedge \neg(\overleftarrow{\rho}\,(\texttt{toxic})[(\texttt{true})))[\texttt{safe}].$$

The theory of closure spaces and the development of topochecker [24], the first spatio-temporal model checker for the logic STLCS, the temporal extension of SLCS, provided a viable way to actually verify spatio-temporal properties of simulation traces of the bike sharing system. The bike sharing system itself was modelled by a stochastic simulator based on Markov Renewal Processes [21, 35]. It simulated a bike sharing system of the size of that of London, with 742 stations randomly distributed in an area of 90 square kilometres, containing 19,000 parking slots, and a fleet of 11,500 bikes making 1,120 trips per hour (see Fig. 2a). The simulator could be used to generate time series of rectangular maps containing the stations and for each station an indication of how full or empty they were. A first question was how well these simulations were in fact corresponding to the data collected on the London bike sharing system itself.

Interestingly enough, assuming that bikes were randomly taken and returned from any station, there was a reasonable correspondence between the curves representing the durations of bikes being hired, as shown by the cyan and violet lines, respectively, in the logarithmic representation of the data in Fig. 2b, but not for what concerns the tail of that distribution. Apparently something was missing, as in reality a part of the bikes were brought back much later than one would expect knowing that the first 30 min rent were for free. What was indeed missing in the simulator was the spatial aspect of taking and returning bikes. Introducing a concept of 'flow', where users do not randomly take and return bikes, but actually change their needs over time, e.g. taking a bike close to their home in the morning and riding to their office in the center, and back in the afternoon, provided a much better match with observational data as shown by the yellow curve in the logarithmic graph in Fig. 2b. In fact, under this assumption there was a much higher likelihood that users find stations full, which required them to spend more time to find a suitable parking place in the neighbourhood, and thus leading to longer than expected hiring times for ca. 7% of the trips, corresponding to the percentage observed in the real system!

But if this was a valid explanation, could we find then such 'clusters' of full stations in the traces produced by the simulator? That was indeed the case, and the STLCS logic was expressive enough to formalise such properties. Figure 2d shows in green the borders of the clusters of stations that eventually become full within the length of the simulation traces that were considered. Clusters of full stations are defined as the *interior* of a set of full stations. The stations coloured in red form the core of such clusters as they are remaining full once they become full during that period and moreover become part of a cluster. These results confirmed that spatial distribution in physical space indeed played a significant role in the analysis of this particular CAS. The analysis was possible by combining several tools: i) the simulator; ii) the spatio-temporal model checker topochecker; iii) the MultiVesta tool to collect the statistical data from the many runs of the simulator and the model checker; iv) the rendering of the model checking result for the initial frame of the trace produced by the simulator (see Fig. 2d). Figure 2c shows a schema of this tool chain.

Besides being applied to the bike sharing system, topochecker has also been used to verify the validity of GPS signals of buses in the public transport system of Edinburgh through the analysis of the street maps on which the GPS signals were projected [24]. That was a first indication of the potential of spatial model checking for the analysis of digital images. The model checker has also been extended to deal with *collective* spatial properties. This extension made it possible to express all properties in terms of the operators defined by the well-known Region Connection Calculus [29].

A signal temporal variant of SLCS has been used to analyse the emergence of Turing patterns as a result of the interactions of chemical substances such as those appearing on the skin of animals [37], as shown in Fig. 3.

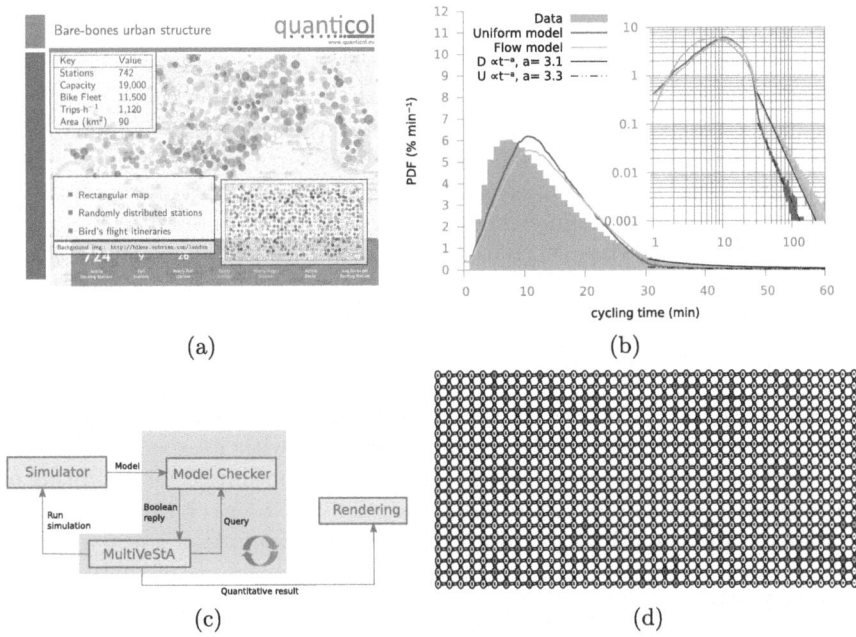

Fig. 2. (a) Configuration of the simulator; (b) Hiring time distribution London; (c) Tool chain; (d) Clusters of full stations found through spatial model checking.

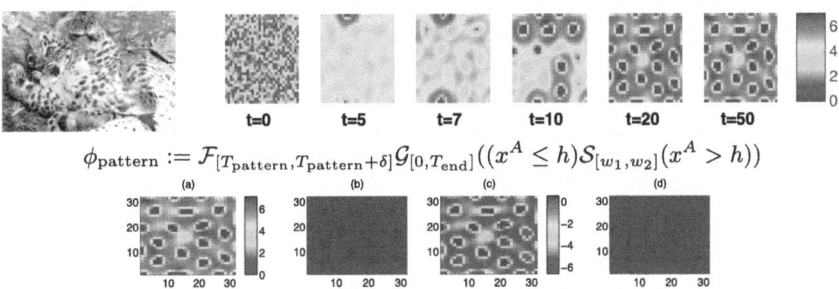

$$\phi_{\text{pattern}} := \mathcal{F}_{[T_{\text{pattern}}, T_{\text{pattern}}+\delta]} \mathcal{G}_{[0, T_{\text{end}}]} ((x^A \leq h) \mathcal{S}_{[w_1, w_2]}(x^A > h))$$

Detecting emergent spots and their persistence in time, including their robustness to small perturbations

Fig. 3. Spatio-temporal analysis of Turing patterns (morphogenesis) in SSTL (Spatial Signal Temporal Logic). The top row shows a time series of the evolution of the spatial concentration of one of the two chemical substances modelled by a reaction-diffusion model starting from a random distribution of the two interacting chemical substances. The bottom row shows model checking results detecting emerging spots (pixels in red in 2nd image), indicating the robustness of the formula results (3rd image) and identifying the core of spots of a certain minimal size (pixels in red in 4th image). (Color figure online)

3   Medical Image Analysis

Digital images can be seen as particular forms of regular graphs, or grids, where each node in the graph represents a pixel or voxel. The latter is a three-dimensional pixel. Pixels or voxels can have particular features (e.g. their luminosity or intensity of their colour). These basic features can be used as atomic propositions in the logical properties. Digital images of particular interest are medical images such as magnetic resonance (MRI) or Computer Tomography (CT) scans. To explore the idea to use spatial model checking on such images we teamed up with domain experts from the radiotherapy and biomedical physics department of the Siena University Hospital in Italy. In a first approach we used topochecker for the segmentation of MRI scans of brain tumours [14], which turned out to give surprisingly accurate results.

Following up on the success of this first result, we decided to develop a dedicated spatial model checker, VoxLogicA[3], together with its specification language ImgQL ("image query language") [5,6] that is optimised for operating on medical images (see [22] for a tutorial). Essentially, VoxLogicA takes as input a digital image and a spatial logic based property (for example, a query involving some aspects of the pixels, such as their intensity, and aspects of those in their direct neighbourhood), and it gives as an output an image where all the pixels of the input image that satisfy the property are shown in a user-specified way, e.g., in a certain colour of choice. This output image can then be shown as a semi-transparent overlay over the original grey-scale MRI image of the brain, as shown in Fig. 4.

In order to assess the general accuracy of our method we applied VoxLogicA to a publicly available set of benchmark MRI images for brain tumour segmentation called BraTS 2017[4] [6]. Figure 4 illustrates some of the intermediate model checking results of our procedure presented in Specification 1. The specification consists of several phases. In the first phase the intensity of the pixels in the image is normalised through the use of percentiles. This allows for the use of fixed thresholds for the dataset to find hyper intense (hl) and very intense (vl) areas in the second phase. These areas are also shown as overlays in the images in the left part of Fig. 4. In the third phase a form of filtering is used to make the hyper and very high intense areas more homogeneous (i.e. small 'specks' of less intense pixels in the same area are added to the hyper and very high intense areas, respectively.). In the fourth phase the gross tumour area is found by checking which very highly intense areas are actually touching the hyper intense areas, leaving out very high intense areas that are disconnected from hyper intense areas. This technique bears similarities with what in the literature is known as 'region growing'. The grow operator has been defined in terms of the basic reachability operator provided by SLCS. Note that the spatial model checker treats the image as a 3D object. The fifth phase uses a form of texture self-similarity function to possibly add small, but not yet captured, areas that

---

[3] VoxLogicA is available at https://github.com/vincenzoml/VoxLogicA.
[4] See https://www.med.upenn.edu/sbia/brats2017/data.html.

are adjacent to the so far found tumour area. Finally, the last phase saves the final tumour segmentation as the gross tumour volume (gtv). This spatial model checking result can then be rendered as an overlay to project onto (slices of) the original brain MRI base image. The gtv, obtained by spatial model checking, and the ground truth, provided by the annotated dataset, are both shown as overlays in the bottom-right image of Fig. 4 where pixels satisfying gtv are shown in pink and pixels that are part of the ground truth (GT) are shown in blue. Both overlays show a very good correspondence for this slice of the example case study.

The images in the benchmark are all manually segmented by experts and it is therefore possible to compare our results with those provided by domain experts. Such comparison is done by calculating a similarity index involving our results and the experts' results that takes false positives and false negatives into account for each image. Similarity indexes, such as Dice-Sorensen, can be directly defined and used in ImgQL; both the resulting layers and the indexes of interest can be saved on the local file system where the user runs the analysis (see e.g. Specification 1 in Fig. 4 lines 16–17).

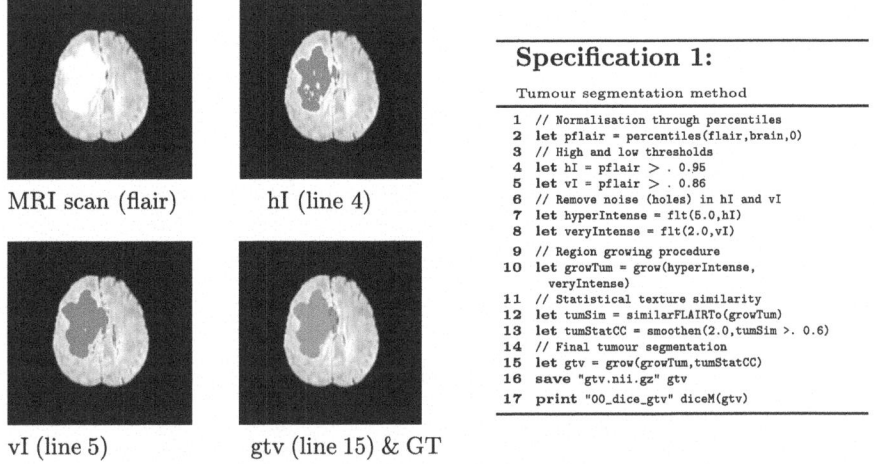

Specification 1:

Tumour segmentation method

```
1   // Normalisation through percentiles
2   let pflair = percentiles(flair,brain,0)
3   // High and low thresholds
4   let hI = pflair > . 0.95
5   let vI = pflair > . 0.86
6   // Remove noise (holes) in hI and vI
7   let hyperIntense = flt(5.0,hI)
8   let veryIntense = flt(2.0,vI)
9   // Region growing procedure
10  let growTum = grow(hyperIntense,
        veryIntense)
11  // Statistical texture similarity
12  let tumSim = similarFLAIRTo(growTum)
13  let tumStatCC = smoothen(2.0,tumSim >. 0.6)
14  // Final tumour segmentation
15  let gtv = grow(growTum,tumStatCC)
16  save "gtv.nii.gz" gtv
17  print "00_dice_gtv" diceM(gtv)
```

MRI scan (flair)   hI (line 4)

vI (line 5)   gtv (line 15) & GT

Fig. 4. ImgQL specification of a tumour segmentation method (right) and resulting example segmentation (left) of a slice of the axial plane of the 3D image Brats17_2013_7_1: Overlays hI (hyper intense voxels), vI (very intense voxels) and gtv (gross tumour volume, in pink) and ground truth (GT) (in blue). (Color figure online)

The results we obtained on the BraTS 2017 dataset turned out to be well in line with the state of the art in segmentation of high-grade brain tumours (glioma). This was both in terms of accuracy of the segmentation and in terms of computational efficiency. We reached on average an 85% coincidence between the manual expert segmentation (ground truth) and the results of the segmentation procedure shown in Fig. 4, for the gross tumour volume (and 91% on average for the clinical tumour volume) [6]. Note that these results have been reached using the same ImgQL specification applied on *all* the relevant cases in the BraTS 2017 dataset (193 cases in total). This was partially made possible due to the simple, but effective, normalisation procedure using percentiles, shown in the first lines of the ImgQL specification.

The segmentation procedure in ImgQL is concise, explainable and user-centric because its high-level steps and derived operators fit the abstraction level at which clinicians are assessing and reasoning about an image. One of the phases in the method is based on the region-growing technique [32]. This is a well-established segmentation technique that is still being further improved and refined (see for instance [33]).

VoxLogicA has also been used for the segmentation of skin lesions in dermoscopic images, such as in nevus segmentation [3], and for the segmentation of tissues in the healthy brain, such as white and grey matter [5].

So far, VoxLogicA has been used via a command line interface. This is sufficient for the technical validation of the tool but hinders usability and a broader uptake by domain experts. Moreover, this requires VoxLogicA users to employ external tools for a set of subtasks: a code editor for the specification, a DICOM viewer to open the base images to be analysed and to inspect the resulting layers, a spreadsheet to analyse the similarity indexes and the file system to handle the dataset of base images and resulting layers. We are actively working on the development of a graphical user interface for VoxLogicA that can be easily adapted to suit the needs of several user classes, such as designers of segmentation procedures, radiologists and clinicians [12].

Fig. 5. A triangular surface mesh of a dolphin [19].

4   Continuous Space: Polyhedra

The spatial model checking techniques we addressed so far target discrete, grid-based structures that can be seen as adjacency spaces, which in turn form a subclass of closure spaces. However, another class of spatial models are polyhedra. These form the mathematical basis for the visualisation of objects in *continuous* space. In the real world we find such structures in domains that exploit mesh-processing such as in computer graphics. Figure 5 shows a simple example of a surface triangular mesh of a dolphin.

Such triangular surface meshes and tetrahedral volume meshes can be very large. Spatial model checking for such structures could be used to highlight or identify interesting aspects of the structures. For example, in the complex medical image in Fig. 6(a) one could be interested in showing a particular organ (Fig. 6(b)) or finding out whether there is a vein that connects to a particular organ (Fig. 6(c)). In a synthetic model of an imaginary building (maze) shown in Fig. 7(a) one could be interested to know whether it is possible to reach a green room from the red room, only passing by white rooms and connecting corridors (Fig. 7(b)). Figure 7(c) shows the use of 3D volume meshes in a brain tumour segmentation case.

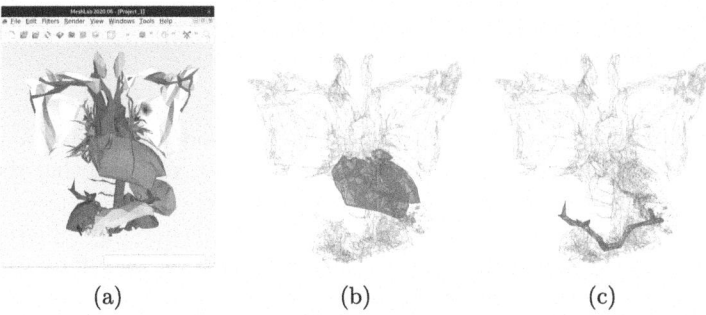

(a)   (b)   (c)

Fig. 6. (a) A 3D medical illustration, courtesy of www.sketchfab.com (copyright: COEUR et vaissaaux by Chair Digital Anatomy - The Unesco Chair of digital anatomy (Paris University) - is licensed under Creative Commons Attribu- tion, see https:// creativecommons.org/licenses/by/4.0/legalcode), visualized using MeshLab [30]; (b) The hearth; (c) Selected vein.

In [8] we addressed model checking for such continuous spaces. More specifically, we considered *polyhedral models* and SLCS_γ, a variant of SLCS for such models. A polyhedral model is composed of a *polyhedron* and a *valuation function*. A polyhedron $|K|$ is the set union of all the components of a simplicial complex K, which, in turn, is a collection of *simplexes* in $\mathbb{R}^n$, for some dimension n, satisfying certain construction constraints. For our purposes, we set n to 3, so that, by definition, the kind of simplexes we are concerned with are just points, segments, triangles and tetrahedra. It is convenient to consider, for each simplex σ, its *relative interior*, or *cell*, $\tilde{\sigma}$. The cell of a point is just the point whereas the cell of any other kind of simplex coincides with the topological interior of the simplex. For instance, the cell of a segment is the segment without its end-points. Note that, given a simplicial complex K, the set $\tilde{K}$ of its cells is a partition of the polyhedron $|K|$. Furthermore, it is easy to see that the cells of a simplicial complex K form a partial order $(W, \preceq)$, where $W = \widetilde{K}$: $\widetilde{\sigma}_1 \preceq \widetilde{\sigma}_2$ if and only if $\widetilde{\sigma}_1$ is included in the topological closure or $\widetilde{\sigma}_2$. Finally, it can be shown that the map $\mathbb{F}$ from $|K|$ to $\widetilde{K}$, mapping each point in the polyhedron to the unique cell containing it, is a continuous function [11, Corollary 3.4].

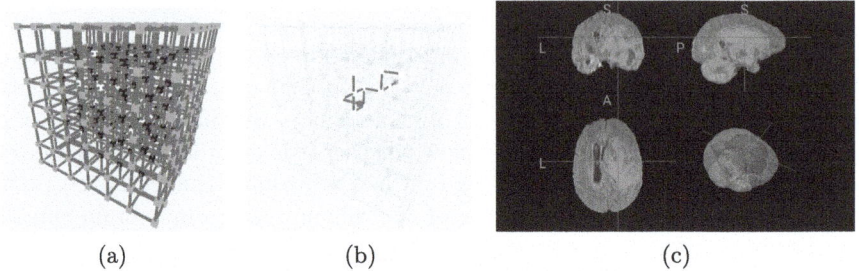

(a)   (b)   (c)

Fig. 7. (a) Maze; (b) Path from red to green room passing only by white rooms; (c) Brain tumour segmentation, axial, sagital and coronal views and 3D volume mesh view of BraTS19_CBICA_AAB_1. (Color figure online)

As usual, the valuation function of a polyhedral model maps atomic propositions to sets of points in the polyhedron. It is, however, required that the image of any atomic proposition be a union of cells. On the basis of the valuation function $\mathcal{V}_\mathcal{P}$ of a polyhedral model $(|K|, \mathcal{V}_\mathcal{P})$, we can define the valuation function $\mathcal{V}_\mathcal{F}$ of its associated poset model[5] $\mathcal{F} = \mathbb{F}(\mathcal{P}) = (W, \preceq, \mathcal{V}_\mathcal{F})$: for each atomic proposition p we have that $\widetilde{\sigma} \in \mathcal{V}_\mathcal{F}(p)$ if and only if $\widetilde{\sigma} \subseteq \mathcal{V}_\mathcal{P}(p)$.

Figure 8 shows a polyhedral model. There are three atomic propositions, **red**, **green**, and **gray**, shown by different colours (8a). The model is "unpacked" into its cells in Fig. 8b. The latter are collected in the cell poset model, whose Hasse diagram is shown in Fig. 8c.

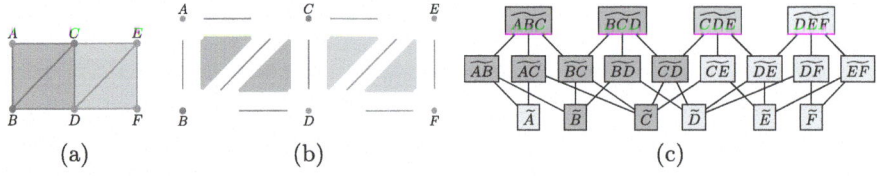

(a)   (b)   (c)

Fig. 8. A polyhedral model $\mathcal{P}$ (8a) with its cells (8b) and the Hasse diagram of the related cell poset (8c).

Besides atomic propositions, negation and conjunction, $\mathtt{SLCS}_\gamma$ provides a reachability operator, γ. Informally, a point x in a polyhedral model satisfies

---

[5] With a little bit of overloading, we let $\mathbb{F}(\mathcal{P})$ denote the poset model associated to polyhedral model $\mathcal{P}$.

the conditional reachability formula $\gamma(\Phi_1, \Phi_2)$ if there is a topological path, i.e. a continuous function from the interval $[0,1]$ to $|K|$, starting from x, ending in a point y that satisfies Φ_2, and such that all the intermediate points of the path between x and y satisfy Φ_1. Note that neither x nor y is required to satisfy Φ_1. Many other interesting properties, such as proximity (in the topological sense, i.e. "being in the topological closure of") or "being surrounded by" can be expressed using reachability (see [8] for details). We have also provided an interpretation of SLCS_γ on poset models using the notion of $\pm$-path as an image on posets of topological paths in polyhedra. An example of the correspondence between a topological path and its $\pm$-path is shown in Fig. 9. We refer the interested reader to the above mentioned work (see [8]) for the relevant formal definitions, here noting only that $\pm$-paths over posets are discrete, finite, and not necessarily directed paths. The interpretation of γ on a poset model $\mathcal{F} = (W, \preccurlyeq, \mathcal{V}_\mathcal{F})$ is the following: $w \in W$ satisfies $\gamma(\Phi_1, \Phi_2)$ if there is a $\pm$-path starting from w, ending in $w' \in W$ that satisfies Φ_2, and such that all the intermediate elements of the path between w and w' satisfy Φ_1. Note that neither w nor w' is required to satisfy Φ_1. It has been shown that, for any polyhedral model $\mathcal{P}$, all SLCS_γ formulas Φ and all points x of $\mathcal{P}$ the following holds: x satisfies Φ in $\mathcal{P}$ if and only if $\mathbb{F}(x)$ satisfies Φ in $\mathbb{F}(\mathcal{P})$ [8]. This result is the theoretical foundation for the model checking algorithm for SLCS_γ on polyhedral models proposed in [8] that actually works on the poset models. The algorithm has been implemented in the tool $\mathtt{PolyLogicA}$.[6]

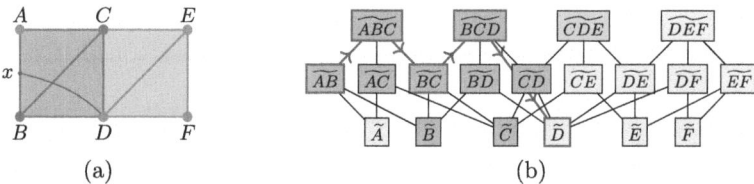

$$\text{(a)} \qquad\qquad\qquad\qquad\qquad \text{(b)}$$

Fig. 9. (9a) A topological path from a point x to vertex D in the polyhedral model $\mathcal{P}$ of Fig. 8a. (9b) The corresponding $\pm$-path (in blue) in the Hasse diagram of the cell poset model $\mathbb{F}(\mathcal{P})$. (Color figure online)

In [10] SLCS_η, another variant of SLCS for polyhedral models, has been introduced by replacing the γ with a weaker modality, namely η. Intuitively, the only difference between γ and η is that a point satisfies $\eta(\Phi_1, \Phi_2)$ if it satisfies $\gamma(\Phi_1, \Phi_2)$ and, *moreover*, it also satisfies Φ_1. Such a relationship between γ and η holds also in the poset model interpretation of the two logics. Clearly η can be expressed using γ, but not the other way around. In other words, letting $\equiv_\gamma^\mathcal{P}$ denote logical equivalence with respect to the interpretation of SLCS_γ on $\mathcal{P}$ and $\equiv_\eta^\mathcal{P}$ denote that of SLCS_η, we have that $\equiv_\gamma^\mathcal{P} \subset \equiv_\eta^\mathcal{P}$. Similarly for the interpretations on poset models: $\equiv_\gamma^\mathcal{F} \subset \equiv_\eta^\mathcal{F}$. In addition, it can be shown that while the

---

[6] $\mathtt{PolyLogicA}$ is available at https://github.com/vincenzoml/VoxLogicA as part of $\mathtt{VoxLogicA}$.

classical ◊ modality can be expressed using γ, this is not the case for η, both in the continuous and the discrete interpretation of the logics [8,10]. On the other hand, being $\equiv_\eta$ a coarser relation, it allows for better model minimisation (see Sect. 5 below), while $SLCS_\eta$ still retains a high expressive power, as will see in the next Section. Also $SLCS_\eta$ is supported by PolyLogicA. Figure 10 shows a 3D maze model and the model checking results of two $SLCS_\eta$ properties using the colours green, white and grey as atomic propositions in the formulas. The cells that satisfy the property are highlighted and shown in their original color, whereas the cells that do not satisfy the property are shown vaguely and in low intensity, just to provide the contours of the original image for visual reference.

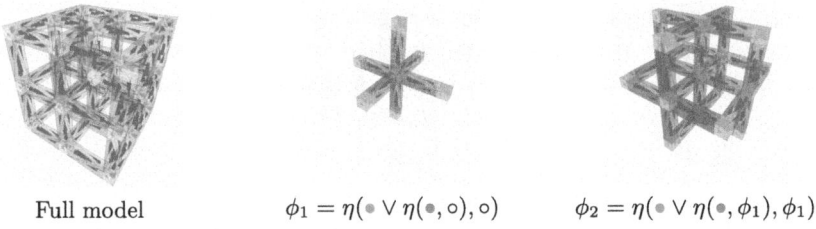

Full model $\phi_1 = \eta(\bullet \vee \eta(\bullet, \circ), \circ)$ $\phi_2 = \eta(\bullet \vee \eta(\bullet, \phi_1), \phi_1)$

Fig. 10. 3D maze model and results of two $SLCS_\eta$ properties.

5   Minimising Spatial Models

Bisimilarity is a fundamental notion both in concurrency theory and in logic. Thus, notions of bisimilarity have also been developed for the models which spatial logics are based on. We refer to some of our earlier work (see [7] and [20]) for an account on notions of bisimilarity for topological spaces and closure spaces respectively, pointing out that in [25] a closure model minimisation procedure has been presented that is based on an encoding of closure models into labelled transition systems as well as a result that links a notion of spatial bisimulation [20] with branching bisimulation on labelled transition systems. The procedure has been implemented in a tool chain that involves, among others, the toolset mCRL2 [13]. Our interest in bisimilarity, apart from its theoretical value, is motivated by the fact that spatial models, and in particular polyhedral ones, are usually very large and therefore model minimisation can be of great importance in order to optimise model checking of such structures. In the sequel we will briefly recall some major results we obtained for bisimilarity with regards to $SLCS_\gamma$ and $SLCS_\eta$.

For *simplicial bisimilarity* [8], written $\sim_\triangle$ and based on topological paths, we have shown that it coincides with logical equivalence with respect to $SLCS_\gamma$ interpreted on polyhedral models. The discrete counterpart of simplicial bisimilarity, namely ±-*bisimilarity*, written $\sim_\pm$ and based on ±-paths, was shown to coincide with logical equivalence of SLCS_γ interpreted on poset models [23]. Thus, in summary, we have:

$$x_1 \sim_\triangle^{\mathcal{P}} x_2 \text{ iff } x_1 \equiv_\gamma^{\mathcal{P}} x_2 \text{ iff } \mathbb{F}(x_1) \equiv_\gamma^{\mathbb{F}(\mathcal{P})} \mathbb{F}(x_2) \text{ iff } \mathbb{F}(x_1) \sim_\pm^{\mathbb{F}(\mathcal{P})} \mathbb{F}(x_2).$$

We obtained similar results for SLCS_η. In particular, in [10] we introduced weaker forms of the bisimilarity relations mentioned above, more precisely: *weak simplicial bisimilarity* ($\approx_\triangle$) on polyhedral models and *weak $\pm$-bisimilarity* ($\approx_\pm$) on poset models. We also proved that they coincide with the appropriate logical equivalence induced by SLCS_η. In summary:

$$x_1 \approx_\triangle^{\mathcal{P}} x_2 \text{ iff } x_1 \equiv_\eta^{\mathcal{P}} x_2 \text{ iff } \mathbb{F}(x_1) \equiv_\eta^{\mathbb{F}(\mathcal{P})} \mathbb{F}(x_2) \text{ iff } \mathbb{F}(x_1) \approx_\pm^{\mathbb{F}(\mathcal{P})} \mathbb{F}(x_2).$$

We presented a procedure that correctly computes the minimal model with respect to weak $\pm$-bisimilarity [9]. Also this procedure works via an encoding into labelled transition systems—different from that presented in [25]—and exploits branching bisimilarity. So, also in this case, the implementation of the procedure can exploit the mCRL2 toolset [13]. Various experiments have been performed showing the effectiveness of the approach. For example, for the model in Fig. 11 consisting of 2,619 cells the structure can be reduced to only 7 cells (in this case due to the symmetry of the mode, see Fig. 12). This reduces the model checking time several orders of magnitude. The less symmetric and much larger model in Fig. 7, consisting of 150K cells reduces to 1225 cells. Further details can be found in [9].

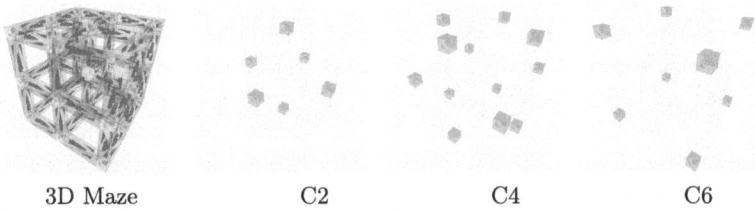

3D Maze   C2   C4   C6

Fig. 11. A 3D maze and some of its equivalence classes.

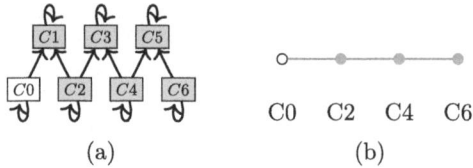

Fig. 12. (a) Minimal poset model; (b) Minimal polyhedral model.

6   Conclusions and Future Developments

The ten years of research on spatial model checking, since its start in the Quanticol project, were characterised by bridging its theoretical foundations, found in the theory of closure spaces, to the development of practical analysis tools such as spatial model checkers and exploring new, possibly impactful domains of application. On the way we met and collaborated with many people who contributed to develop this line of research further or who encouraged us to continue. Marjan was definitely one of them, first when she was a reviewer of the Quanticol project, and later, in a more informal way, when her encouragements were not limited to make us explore new areas of research but also explore other cultures. We are very grateful to her for all those experiences.

Looking forward to future developments, the list of open issues gets longer every week. Here we limit ourselves to just mention a few of them without trying to be exhaustive. First of all, we would like to make our techniques available to domain experts in medical imaging. This would require the development of a suitable graphical user interface that would highly facilitate and support the daily workflows of clinicians and medical physicists. This is ongoing work, and we hope to soon release a first open source version. Furthermore, medical image analysis is also exploring the responsible and explainable use of machine learning that can be shown to adhere to established, rigorous medical guidelines. We are planning to investigate whether, with a hybrid use of logic and machine learning components, one can reach a higher accuracy and reliability than with the individual techniques alone. For example, when considering the brain tumour segmentation example in Sect. 3, instead of just using thresholds to find the hyper intense and very intense areas one could use separate neural networks to learn the concepts of *tumour* and *oedema* tissue separately, roughly corresponding to hyper intense and very intense areas, respectively. The *gross tumour volume* can then be found by using the spatial logic connective touch on the learned tumour and oedema tissue in a similar way as we have seen in Sect. 3. Steps in this direction can be found in [4]. The approach shares some motivations with that of *Intersymbolic Artificial Intelligence* as recently proposed by Platzer [38].

We also plan to further develop the model minimisation approach and to integrate the minimisation techniques in the spatial model checking tools. This step would be very useful for the analysis of large spatial models that are abound in many application domains. Finally, we aim at pursuing the analysis of dynamic spatial models, bringing back time into our spatial logics and exploiting parallel computations made possible by the developments in GPU performance [15,16] and explore the extension of the logic with further operators [17].

Acknowledgement. We would like to thank all the co-authors of the research on spatial model checking and all the people supporting us on this endeavour. Research partially supported by Bilateral project between National Research Council of Italy and Shota Rustaveli National Science Foundation of Georgia "Model Checking for Polyhedral Logic" (#CNR-22-010); European Union - Next GenerationEU - National Recovery and Resilience Plan (NRRP), Investment 1.5 Ecosystems of Innovation, Project "Tuscany Health Ecosystem" (THE), CUP: B83C22003930001; European Union - Next-GenerationEU - National Recovery and Resilience Plan (NRRP) - MISSION 4 COMPONENT 2, INVESTMENT N. 1.1, CALL PRIN 2022 D.D. 104 02-02-2022 - (Stendhal) CUP N. B53D23012850006. MUR project PRIN 2020TL3X8X "T-LADIES"; Shota Rustaveli National Science Foundation of Georgia grant #FR-22-6700.

Disclosure of Interests. The authors have no competing interests to declare that are relevant to the content of this article.

References

1. Aiello, M.: Spatial Reasoning: Theory and Practice. Ph.D. thesis, Institute of Logic, Language and Computation, University of Amsterdam (2002)
2. Aiello, M., Pratt-Hartmann, I., van Benthem, J. (eds.): Handbook of Spatial Logics. Springer (2007)
3. Belmonte, G., Broccia, G., Ciancia, V., Latella, D., Massink, M.: Feasibility of spatial model checking for nevus segmentation. In: Bliudze, S., Gnesi, S., Plat, N., Semini, L. (eds.) 9th IEEE/ACM International Conference on Formal Methods in Software Engineering, FormaliSE@ICSE 2021, Madrid, Spain, 17–21 May 2021, pp. 1–12. IEEE (2021). https://doi.org/10.1109/FormaliSE52586.2021.00007
4. Belmonte, G., Bussi, L., Ciancia, V., Latella, D., Massink, M.: Towards hybrid-AI in imaging using VoxLogicA. In: Margaria, T., Steffen, B. (eds.) Leveraging Applications of Formal Methods, Verification and Validation. Software Engineering Methodologies - 12th International Symposium, ISoLA 2024, Crete, Greece, 27–31 October 2024, Proceedings, Part IV. LNCS, vol. 15222, pp. 205–221. Springer, Cham (2024). https://doi.org/10.1007/978-3-031-75387-9_13
5. Belmonte, G., Ciancia, V., Latella, D., Massink, M.: Innovating medical image analysis via spatial logics. In: ter Beek, M.H., Fantechi, A., Semini, L. (eds.) From Software Engineering to Formal Methods and Tools, and Back - Essays Dedicated to Stefania Gnesi on the Occasion of Her 65th Birthday. LNCS, vol. 11865, pp. 85–109. Springer, Cham (2019). https://doi.org/10.1007/978-3-030-30985-5_7
6. Belmonte, G., Ciancia, V., Latella, D., Massink, M.: VoxLogicA: a spatial model checker for declarative image analysis. In: Vojnar, T., Zhang, L. (eds.) Tools and Algorithms for the Construction and Analysis of Systems - 25th International Conference, TACAS 2019, Held as Part of the European Joint Conferences on Theory and Practice of Software, ETAPS 2019, Prague, Czech Republic, 6–11 April 2019, Proceedings, Part I. LNCS, vol. 11427, pp. 281–298. Springer, Cham (2019). https://doi.org/10.1007/978-3-030-17462-0_16

7. van Benthem, J., Bezhanishvili, G.: Modal logics of space. In: Aiello, M., Pratt-Hartmann, I., Benthem, J.V. (eds.) Handbook of Spatial Logics, pp. 217–298. Springer, Cham (2007). https://doi.org/10.1007/978-1-4020-5587-4_5

8. Bezhanishvili, N., Ciancia, V., Gabelaia, D., Grilletti, G., Latella, D., Massink, M.: Geometric model checking of continuous space. Log. Methods Comput. Sci. **18**(4), 7:1–7:38 (2022). https://lmcs.episciences.org/10348, https://doi.org/10.46298/LMCS-18(4:7)2022. Published on line: Nov 22, 2022. ISSN: 1860-5974

9. Bezhanishvili, N., et al.: Weak simplicial bisimilarity and minimisation for polyhedral model checking. CoRR **abs/2411.11428** (2024). https://doi.org/10.48550/arXiv.2411.11428

10. Bezhanishvili, N., et al.: Weak simplicial bisimilarity for polyhedral models and SLCS$_\eta$. In: Castiglioni, V., Francalanza, A. (eds.) Formal Techniques for Distributed Objects, Components, and Systems - 44th IFIP WG 6.1 International Conference, FORTE 2024, Held as Part of the 19th International Federated Conference on Distributed Computing Techniques, DisCoTec 2024, Groningen, The Netherlands, 17–21 June 2024, Proceedings. LNCS, vol. 14678, pp. 20–38. Springer, Cham (2024). https://doi.org/10.1007/978-3-031-62645-6_2

11. Bezhanishvili, N., Marra, V., McNeill, D., Pedrini, A.: Tarski's theorem on intuitionistic logic, for polyhedra. Ann. Pure Appl. Log. **169**(5), 373–391 (2018). https://doi.org/10.1016/j.apal.2017.12.005, https://www.sciencedirect.com/science/article/pii/S016800721730146X

12. Broccia, G., Ciancia, V., Latella, D., Massink, M.: Towards a GUI for declarative medical image analysis: cognitive and memory load issues. In: Stephanidis, C., Antona, M., Ntoa, S. (eds.) HCI International 2022 Posters - 24th International Conference on Human-Computer Interaction, HCII 2022, Virtual Event, June 26 - July 1, 2022, Proceedings, Part II. CCIS, vol. 1581, pp. 103–111. Springer, Cham (2022). https://doi.org/10.1007/978-3-031-06388-6_14

13. Bunte, O., et al.: The mCRL2 toolset for analysing concurrent systems - improvements in expressivity and usability. In: Vojnar, T., Zhang, L. (eds.) Tools and Algorithms for the Construction and Analysis of Systems - 25th International Conference, TACAS 2019, Held as Part of the European Joint Conferences on Theory and Practice of Software, ETAPS 2019, Prague, Czech Republic, 6–11 April 2019, Proceedings, Part II. LNCS, vol. 11428, pp. 21–39. Springer, Cham (2019). https://doi.org/10.1007/978-3-030-17465-1_2

14. Buonamici, F.B., Belmonte, G., Ciancia, V., Latella, D., Massink, M.: Spatial logics and model checking for medical imaging. Int. J. Softw. Tools Technol. Transf. **22**(2), 195–217 (2020). https://doi.org/10.1007/S10009-019-00511-9

15. Bussi, L., Ciancia, V., Gadducci, F.: A spatial logic with time and quantifiers. In: Gierasimczuk, N., Velázquez-Quesada, F.R. (eds.) Dynamic Logic. New Trends and Applications - 5th International Workshop, DaLí 2023, Tbilisi, Georgia, 15–16 September 2023, Revised Selected Papers. LNCS, vol. 14401, pp. 1–19. Springer, Cham (2023). https://doi.org/10.1007/978-3-031-51777-8_1

16. Bussi, L., Ciancia, V., Gadducci, F., Latella, D., Massink, M.: Towards model checking video streams using VoxLogicA on GPUs. In: Bowles, J., Broccia, G., Pellungrini, R. (eds.) From Data to Models and Back - 10th International Symposium, DataMod 2021, Virtual Event, 6–7 December 2021, Revised Selected Papers. LNCS, vol. 13268, pp. 78–90. Springer, Cham (2021). https://doi.org/10.1007/978-3-031-16011-0_6

17. Bussi, L., Ciancia, V., Gadducci, F., Latella, D., Massink, M.: On binding in the spatial logics for closure spaces. In: Margaria, T., Steffen, B. (eds.) Leveraging

Applications of Formal Methods, Verification and Validation. Verification Principles - 11th International Symposium, ISoLA 2022, Rhodes, Greece, 22–30 October 2022, Proceedings, Part I. LNCS, vol. 13701, pp. 479–497. Springer, Cham (2022). https://doi.org/10.1007/978-3-031-19849-6_27

18. Čech, E.: Topological Spaces. In: Pták, V. (ed.) Topological Spaces, chap. III, pp. 233–394. Publishing House of the Czechoslovak Academy of Sciences/Interscience Publishers, John Wiley & Sons, Prague/London-New York-Sydney (1966), Revised edition by Zdeněk Frolíc and Miroslav Katětov. Scientific editor, Vlastimil Pták. Editor of the English translation, Charles O. Junge. MR0211373

19. Chrschn: A triangle mesh of dolphin (2007). https://en.wikipedia.org/wiki/File: Dolphin_triangle_mesh.png. Accessed 7 Feb 2023

20. Ciancia, V., Latella, D., Massink, M., de Vink, E.P.: Back-and-forth in space: on logics and bisimilarity in closure spaces. In: Jansen, N., Stoelinga, M., , van den Bos, P. (eds.) A Journey From Process Algebra via Timed Automata to Model Learning - A Festschrift Dedicated to Frits Vaandrager on the Occasion of His 60th Birthday. LNCS, vol. 13560, pp. 98–115. Springer (2022)

21. Ciancia, V., Latella, D., Massink, M., Paškauskas, R., Vandin, A.: A tool-chain for statistical spatio-temporal model checking of bike sharing systems. In: Leveraging Applications of Formal Methods, Verification and Validation: Foundational Techniques - 7th International Symposium, ISoLA 2016, Part I. LNCS, vol. 9952, pp. 657–673 (2016). https://doi.org/10.1007/978-3-319-47166-2_46

22. Ciancia, V., Belmonte, G., Latella, D., Massink, M.: A hands-on introduction to spatial model checking using VoxLogicA - - invited contribution. In: Laarman, A., Sokolova, A. (eds.) Model Checking Software - 27th International Symposium, SPIN 2021, Virtual Event, 12 July 2021, Proceedings. LNCS, vol. 12864, pp. 22–41. Springer, Cham (2021). https://doi.org/10.1007/978-3-030-84629-9_2

23. Ciancia, V., Gabelaia, D., Latella, D., Massink, M., de Vink, E.P.: On bisimilarity for polyhedral models and SLCS. In: Huisman, M., Ravara, A. (eds.) Formal Techniques for Distributed Objects, Components, and Systems - 43rd IFIP WG 6.1 International Conference, FORTE 2023, Held as Part of the 18th International Federated Conference on Distributed Computing Techniques, DisCoTec 2023, Lisbon, Portugal, 19–23 June 2023, Proceedings. LNCS, vol. 13910, pp. 132–151. Springer, Cham (2023). https://doi.org/10.1007/978-3-031-35355-0_9

24. Ciancia, V., Gilmore, S., Grilletti, G., Latella, D., Loreti, M., Massink, M.: Spatio-temporal model checking of vehicular movement in public transport systems. Int. J. Softw. Tools Technol. Transf. **20**(3), 289–311 (2018). https://doi.org/10.1007/s10009-018-0483-8

25. Ciancia, V., Groote, J., Latella, D., Massink, M., de Vink, E.: Minimisation of spatial models using branching bisimilarity. In: Chechik, M., Katoen, J.P., Leucker, M. (eds.) 25th International Symposium, FM 2023, Lübeck, 6–10 March 2023, Proceedings. LNCS, vol. 14000, pp. 263–281. Springer, Cham (2023). https://doi.org/10.1007/978-3-031-27481-7_16

26. Ciancia, V., Latella, D., Loreti, M., Massink, M.: Specifying and verifying properties of space. In: Díaz, J., Lanese, I., Sangiorgi, D. (eds.) Theoretical Computer Science - 8th IFIP TC 1/WG 2.2 International Conference, TCS 2014, Rome, Italy, 1–3 September 2014. Proceedings. LNCS, vol. 8705, pp. 222–235. Springer, Cham (2014). https://doi.org/10.1007/978-3-662-44602-7_18

27. Ciancia, V., Latella, D., Loreti, M., Massink, M.: Model checking spatial logics for closure spaces. Log. Methods Comput. Sci. **12**(4) (2016). https://doi.org/10.2168/LMCS-12(4:2)2016

28. Ciancia, V., Latella, D., Loreti, M., Mastiek, M.: Spatio-temporal model checking for collective adaptive systems in QUANTICOL. Ada User J. **37**(4), 223–227 (2016). https://iris.cnr.it/retrieve/ca2cd6d3-b39a-4c29-8b72-8146b59dcdfc/prod_365221-doc_120455.pdf
29. Ciancia, V., Latella, D., Massink, M.: Embedding RCC8D in the collective spatial logic CSLCS. In: Boreale, M., Corradini, F., Loreti, M., Pugliese, R. (eds.) Models, Languages, and Tools for Concurrent and Distributed Programming - Essays Dedicated to Rocco De Nicola on the Occasion of His 65th Birthday. LNCS, vol. 11665, pp. 260–277. Springer, Cham (2019). https://doi.org/10.1007/978-3-030-21485-2_15
30. Cignoni, P., Callieri, M., Corsini, M., Dellepiane, M., Ganovelli, F., Ranzuglia, G.: Meshlab: an open-source mesh processing tool. In: Scarano, V., Chiara, R.D., Erra, U. (eds.) Eurographics Italian Chapter Conference 2008, Salerno, Italy, 2008, pp. 129–136. Eurographics (2008). https://doi.org/10.2312/LOCALCHAPTEREVENTS/ITALCHAP/ITALIANCHAPCONF2008/129-136
31. Goranko, V., Rumberg, A.: Temporal Logics. In: Stanford Encyclopedia of Philosophy. The Metaphysics Research Lab, Department of Philosophy, Stanford University (2023). https://plato.stanford.edu/entries/logic-temporal/. Accessed 23 Nov 2023
32. Gordillo, N., Montseny, E., Sobrevilla, P.: State of the art survey on MRI brain tumor segmentation. Magn. Reson. Imaging **31**(8), 1426–1438 (2013)
33. Hrishikesh Jaware, T., Ramesh Patil, V., Nayak, C., Elmasri, A., Ali, N., Mishra, P.: A novel approach for brain tissue segmentation and classification in infants' MRI images based on seeded region growing, foster corner detection theory, and sparse autoencoder. Alex. Eng. J. **76**, 289–305 (2023). https://doi.org/10.1016/j.aej.2023.06.040, https://www.sciencedirect.com/science/article/pii/S1110016823005082
34. Kurtonina, N., de Rijke, M.: Bisimulations for temporal logic. J. Log. Lang. Inf. **6**(4), 403–425 (1997). https://doi.org/10.1023/A:1008223921944
35. Massink, M., Paškauskas, R.: Model-based assessment of aspects of user-satisfaction in bicycle sharing systems. In: IEEE 18th International Conference on Intelligent Transportation Systems, ITSC 2015, Gran Canaria, Spain, 15–18 September 2015, pp. 1363–1370. IEEE (2015). https://doi.org/10.1109/ITSC.2015.224
36. McKinsey, J., Tarski, A.: The algebra of topology. Ann. Math. **45**, 141–191 (1944)
37. Nenzi, L., Bortolussi, L., Ciancia, V., Loreti, M., Massink, M.: Qualitative and quantitative monitoring of spatio-temporal properties with SSTL. Log. Methods Comput. Sci. **14**(4) (2018). https://doi.org/10.23638/LMCS-14(4:2)2018
38. Platzer, A.: Intersymbolic AI - interlinking symbolic AI and subsymbolic AI. In: Margaria, T., Steffen, B. (eds.) Leveraging Applications of Formal Methods, Verification and Validation. Software Engineering Methodologies - 12th International Symposium, ISoLA 2024, Crete, Greece, 27–31 October 2024, Proceedings, Part IV. LNCS, vol. 15222, pp. 162–180. Springer, Cham (2024). https://doi.org/10.1007/978-3-031-75387-9_11
39. Stirling, C.: Modal and temporal logics. In: Abramsky, S., Gabbay, D., Maibaum, T. (eds.) Handbook of Logic in Computer Science, chap. V, pp. 477–563. Oxford University Press (1993)

Proof Techniques for Behavioural Relations Based on Unique-Solutions of Equations and Inequations

Adrien Durier[1], Daniel Hirschkoff[2(✉)], and Davide Sangiorgi[3]

[1] Université Paris-Saclay, Lyon, France
[2] Univ. Lyon, ENS de Lyon, UCBL, CNRS, LIP, Lyon, France
`daniel.hirschkoff@ens-lyon.fr`
[3] INRIA/Università di Bologna, Bologna, Italy

Abstract. We give an overview of recent work aiming at strengthening Milner's technique of unique-solution of equations. This technique, originally introduced for CCS, is used to establish weak bisimilarity of processes.

We review two improvements of the technique. The first one builds on the contraction behavioural preorder. The second one relaxes the conditions under which unique-solution can be applied by focusing on divergence in processes. We present applications of these techniques to reason about higher-order languages. We discuss how the two approaches, involving contractions and divergences, have been adapted and enriched, and compare them to each other.

1 Introduction

Bisimilarity is employed to define behavioural equivalences and reason about them. In this paper, behavioural equivalences, hence also bisimilarity, are meant to be *weak* because they abstract from internal moves of terms, as opposed to the *strong* ones, which make no distinctions between the internal moves and the external ones (i.e., the interactions with the environment). Weak equivalences are, practically, the most relevant ones: e.g., two equal programs may produce the same result with different numbers of evaluation steps.

A prominent proof method for bisimulation, put forward by Robin Milner and widely used in his landmark CCS book [22], is the *unique solution of equations*, whereby two tuples of processes are componentwise bisimilar if they are solutions of the same system of equations. This method is important in verification techniques and tools based on algebraic reasoning [2,10,30,31]. Not all equations have a unique solution: for instance any process trivially satisfies $X = X$. In Milner's theorem [22], uniqueness of solutions is subject to limitations: the equations must be 'strongly guarded and sequential', that is, the variables of the equations may only be used underneath a visible prefix and preceded, in the syntax tree, only by the sum and prefix operators. This limits the expressiveness of the technique (since occurrences of other operators above the variables, such as parallel composition and restriction, in general cannot be removed), and its transport onto other languages (e.g., languages for distributed systems or higher-order languages usually do not include the sum operator, which makes the theorem essentially useless). A comparable technique, involving similar limitations, has been proposed by Hoare in his CSP book [11].

In this paper we summarise some recent works aiming at improving Milner's unique-solution technique. Two main approaches are described. The first consists in replacing equations with special inequations called *contractions* [39]. The second consists in replacing the most severe syntactic constraint in Milner's theorem with a semantic condition that has to do with *divergence* [4,5].

Other motivations for the work on unique solutions are the following. First, the unique-solution techniques convey the flavour of 'bisimilarity up-to context' techniques, as the equations (or contractions) intuitively bring out those contexts that would be erased in an 'up-to context' proof (indeed there are completeness results with respect to certain forms of up-to context, in CCS-like languages [39]). Thus the study of the unique-solution techniques may bring light into the up-to-context techniques. For instance, in higher-order languages, while there are well-developed techniques for proving congruence [26], up-to context is still poorly understood [12,13,15,25,41].

Another possible interest for the unique-solution techniques is that they can be transported onto other equivalences, including contextually-defined equivalences such as barbed congruence, and non-coinductive equivalences such as contextual equivalence (i.e., may testing) and trace equivalence.

We present Milner's classic technique of unique-solution of equations for CCS in Sect. 2. We then introduce the two improvements that have been recently proposed, namely contractions (Sect. 3) and divergences (Sect. 4). In Sect. 5, we discuss extensions and adaptations of these improved techniques. Section 6 presents a formalisation in the HOL4 theorem prover of the work on contractions. We show the expressiveness of the techniques by presenting applications to higher-order languages in Sect. 7, and we finally compare the approaches involving contractions and involving divergences in Sect. 8.

2   Background

2.1   CCS

We assume an infinite set of *names* $a, b, \ldots$ and a set of *constant identifiers* (or simply *constants*) $K, \ldots$ to write recursively defined processes. The special symbol τ does not occur in the names and in the constants. We recall the grammar of CCS:

$$P := P_1|P_2 \quad \Big| \quad \Sigma_{i \in I}\mu_i.P_i \quad \Big| \quad \nu a\, P \quad \Big| \quad K \qquad \mu := a \quad \Big| \quad \bar{a} \quad \Big| \quad \tau$$

where I is a countable indexing set. We write $\mathbf{0}$ when I is empty, and $P + Q$ for binary sums. Each constant K has a definition $K \stackrel{\triangle}{=} P$. We sometimes omit trailing $\mathbf{0}$, e.g., writing $a|b$ for $a.\mathbf{0}|b.\mathbf{0}$. The operational semantics is given by means of an LTS, and is given in Fig. 1 (the symmetric versions of the rules parL and comL have been omitted).

$$\text{sum} \frac{}{\Sigma_{i \in I} \mu_i . P_i \xrightarrow{\mu_i} P_i} \qquad \text{parL} \frac{P \xrightarrow{\mu} P'}{P \mid Q \xrightarrow{\mu} P' \mid Q} \qquad \text{comL} \frac{P \xrightarrow{a} P' \quad Q \xrightarrow{\bar{a}} Q'}{P \mid Q \xrightarrow{\tau} P' \mid Q'}$$

$$\text{res} \frac{P \xrightarrow{\mu} P'}{\nu a \, P \xrightarrow{\mu} \nu a \, P'} \, \mu \neq a, \bar{a} \qquad \text{const} \frac{P \xrightarrow{\mu} P'}{K \xrightarrow{\mu} P'} \text{ if } K \overset{\triangle}{=} P$$

Fig. 1. The LTS for CCS

Some standard notations for transitions: $\implies$ is the reflexive and transitive closure of $\xrightarrow{\tau}$, and $\overset{\mu}{\Rightarrow}$ is $\implies \xrightarrow{\mu} \implies$ (the composition of the three relations). Moreover, $P \overset{\hat{\mu}}{\rightarrow} P'$ holds if $P \xrightarrow{\mu} P'$ or ($\mu = \tau$ and $P = P'$); similarly $P \overset{\hat{\mu}}{\Rightarrow} P'$ holds if $P \overset{\mu}{\Rightarrow} P'$ or ($\mu = \tau$ and $P = P'$). Letters $\mathcal{R}, \mathcal{S}$ range over relations. We use the infix notation for relations, e.g., $P \, \mathcal{R} \, Q$ means that $(P, Q) \in \mathcal{R}$, and denote as $\mathcal{RS}$ the composition of $\mathcal{R}$ and $\mathcal{S}$. We use a tilde to denote a tuple, with countably many elements; thus the tuple may also be infinite. All notations are extended to tuples componentwise; e.g., $\widetilde{P} \, \mathcal{R} \, \widetilde{Q}$ means that $P_i \, \mathcal{R} \, Q_i$, for each component i of the tuples $\widetilde{P}$ and $\widetilde{Q}$. We use $\overset{\text{def}}{=}$ for abbreviations; in contrast, $\overset{\triangle}{=}$ is used for the definition of constants, and $=$ for syntactic equality and for equations. We focus on *weak* behavioural equivalences, which abstract from the number of internal steps performed.

Definition 1 (Bisimilarity). *A relation $\mathcal{R}$ is a* bisimulation *if, whenever $P \, \mathcal{R} \, Q$, we have:*

1. *$P \xrightarrow{\mu} P'$ implies that there is Q' such that $Q \overset{\hat{\mu}}{\Rightarrow} Q'$ and $P' \, \mathcal{R} \, Q'$;*
2. *the converse, on the actions from Q.*

P and Q are bisimilar, *written $P \approx Q$, if $P \, \mathcal{R} \, Q$ for some bisimulation $\mathcal{R}$.*

2.2 Equations and Milner's Theorem

We recall equations and Milner's theorem, in the setting of CCS. Uniqueness of solutions of equations [22] intuitively says that if a context C obeys certain conditions, then all processes P that satisfy the equation $P \approx C[P]$ are bisimilar with each other.

We use capital letters X, Y, Z for variable of equations. The body of an equation is a CCS expression possibly containing variables.

Definition 2. *Given, for each i of a countable indexing set I, variables X_i, and expressions E_i possibly containing such variables, $\{X_i = E_i\}_{i \in I}$ is a* system of equations. *(There is one equation for each variable X_i.)*

We write $E[\widetilde{P}]$ for the expression resulting from E by replacing each variable X_i with the process P_i

Definition 3. *Suppose $\{X_i = E_i\}_{i \in I}$ is a system of equations:*

- *$\widetilde{P}$ is a* solution *of the system of equations for $\approx$ if for each i it holds that $P_i \approx E_i[\widetilde{P}]$.*
- *the system has a* unique solution *for $\approx$ if whenever $\widetilde{P}$ and $\widetilde{Q}$ are both solutions for $\approx$, then $\widetilde{P} \approx \widetilde{Q}$. The latter means that for each i, $P_i \approx Q_i$.*

Definition 4. *A system of equations $\{X_i = E_i\}_{i \in I}$ is*

- guarded *if, in each E_i, each occurrence of an equation variable is underneath a visible prefix (i.e., a prefix that is not τ);*
- sequential *if, in each E_i, each occurrence of an equation variable only appears underneath prefixes and sums.*

In other words, if the system is sequential, then for every expression E_i, any sub-expression of E_i in which X_j appears, apart from X_j itself, is a sum (of prefixed terms). For instance, $X = \tau.X + \mu.\mathbf{0}$ is sequential but not guarded; using ℓ for a visible prefix, $X = \ell.X | P$ is guarded but not sequential, whereas $X = \ell.X + \tau.\nu a\,(a.\overline{b}|a.\mathbf{0})$, as well as $X = \tau.(a.X + \tau.b.X + \tau)$ are both guarded and sequential.

Theorem 1 (unique solution of equations, [22]). *A system of guarded and sequential equations has a unique solution for $\approx$.* □

3 Contractions

A way of weakening the constraints on the unique-solution Theorem 1 is to move from equations to certain inequations called *contractions* [39].

Intuitively, for a behavioural equivalence $\asymp$, its contraction $\succeq_{\asymp}$ is a preorder in which $P \succeq_{\asymp} Q$ holds if $P \asymp Q$ and, in addition, Q has the *possibility* of being at least as efficient as P. That is, if P can do some work (i.e., some interactions with its environment), then Q should be able to do the same work at least as quickly as P (i.e., performing no more τ-steps than those performed by P). Process Q, however, may be nondeterministic, and may have other ways of doing the same work, and these could be slow (i.e., involving more τ-steps than those performed by P). We now apply the idea of contraction to the concrete case of weak bisimilarity.

Definition 5 (bisimulation contraction). *A process relation $\mathcal{R}$ is a bisimulation contraction if, whenever $P\,\mathcal{R}\,Q$,*

1. *$P \xrightarrow{\mu} P'$ implies there is Q' such that $Q \xrightarrow{\hat{\mu}} Q'$ and $P'\,\mathcal{R}\,Q'$;*
2. *$Q \xrightarrow{\mu} Q'$ implies there is P' such that $P \xRightarrow{\hat{\mu}} P'$ and $P' \approx Q'$.*

Bisimilarity contraction, *written* $\succeq_{\mathrm{bis}}$, *is the union of all bisimulation contractions.*

In the first clause Q is required to match P's challenge transition with at most one transition. This makes sure that Q is capable of mimicking P's work at least as efficiently as P. In contrast, the second clause of Definition 5, on the challenges from Q, entirely ignores efficiency: it is the same clause as in weak bisimulation — the final derivatives are even required to be related by $\approx$, rather than by $\mathcal{R}$. (The bisimilarity contraction is similar but coarser than the *expansion relation* [36].)

Theorem 2. $\succeq_{\mathrm{bis}}$ *is a precongruence in CCS.*

A *system of contractions* is defined as a system of equations, except that the contraction symbol $\succeq$ is used in the place of the equality symbol $=$. Thus a system of contractions is a set $\{X_i \succeq E_i\}_{i \in I}$ where I is an indexing set and expressions E_i may contain the contraction variables $\{X_i\}_{i \in I}$.

Definition 6. *Given a behavioural equivalence $\asymp$ and its contraction $\succeq_\asymp$, and a system of contractions $\{X_i \succeq E_i\}_{i \in I}$, we say that:*

- $\widetilde{P}$ *is a* solution for $\succeq_\asymp$ of the system of contractions *if* $\widetilde{P} \succeq_\asymp \widetilde{E}[\widetilde{P}]$;
- *the system has a* unique solution for $\asymp$ *if whenever $\widetilde{P}$ and $\widetilde{Q}$ are both solutions for $\succeq_\asymp$ then $\widetilde{P} \asymp \widetilde{Q}$.*

When we reason about bisimilarity, the contraction symbol $\succeq$ is interpreted as the bisimilarity contraction $\succeq_{\mathrm{bis}}$, and the equivalence $\asymp$ as the bisimilarity $\approx$. Thus $\widetilde{P}$ being a solution for $\succeq_{\mathrm{bis}}$ of the system of contractions $\{X_i \succeq E_i\}_{i \in I}$ means that $\widetilde{P} \succeq_{\mathrm{bis}} \widetilde{E}[\widetilde{P}]$; and the system having a unique solution for $\approx$ means that whenever $\widetilde{P}$ and $\widetilde{Q}$ are both solutions for $\succeq_{\mathrm{bis}}$ then $\widetilde{P} \approx \widetilde{Q}$.

Lemma 1. *If a system of equations $\{X_i = E_i\}_{i \in I}$ has a unique solution for $\approx$, then also the corresponding system of contractions $\{X_i \succeq E_i\}_{i \in I}$ has a unique solution for $\approx$.*

The converse of the lemma, in contrast, is false: systems of contractions more easily have a unique solution. Indeed, for contraction, the following weak-guardedness condition is sufficient to have a unique solution.

Definition 7. *A system of contractions $\{X_i \succeq E_i\}_{i \in I}$ is* weakly guarded *if, in each E_i, each occurrence of a contraction variable is underneath a prefix.*

Theorem 3 (unique solution of contractions for $\approx$). *A system of weakly-guarded contractions has a unique solution for $\approx$.*

Example 1. The following contractions have a unique solution for $\approx$:

1. $X \succeq \tau.X$
2. $X \succeq a.\boldsymbol{\nu} a\,(\overline{a}|X))$

The corresponding equations do not have a unique solution. The solutions of the contraction (1) are all inactive processes, where a process is *inactive* if it cannot perform visible actions (i.e., if P is the process, then there is no P' and visible action ℓ such that $P \Longrightarrow P' \xrightarrow{\ell}$). The contraction has a unique solution because all inactive processes are bisimilar. Example of solutions for (2) are $a.P$ and $\tau.a.P$, where P is inactive. Any solution of (2) is bisimilar to $a.\mathbf{0}$.   □

4   Divergence

In this section we highlight a different approach, whereby one goes back to equations, but adds a condition based in divergence [6].

4.1   Plain Divergences

In its basic form, the method (inspired by results by Roscoe in CSP [29,30]) essentially says that a guarded equation (or system of equations) whose infinite unfolding never produces a divergence has the unique-solution property. We discuss the approach in CCS, as before.

Definition 8 (Divergence). *A process P diverges if it can perform an infinite sequence of internal moves, possibly after some visible ones; i.e., there are processes P_i, $i \geq 0$, and some n, such that $P = P_0 \xrightarrow{\mu_0} P_1 \xrightarrow{\mu_1} P_2 \xrightarrow{\mu_2} \ldots$ and for all $i > n$, $\mu_i = \tau$. We call a divergence of P the sequence of transitions $\left(P_i \xrightarrow{\mu_i} P_{i+1}\right)_i$.*

Example 2. The process $L \stackrel{\triangle}{=} a.\nu a\,(L|\overline{a})$ diverges, since $L \xrightarrow{a} \nu a\,(L|\overline{a})$, and (leaving aside $\mathbf{0}$ and useless restrictions) $\nu a\,(L|\overline{a})$ has a τ transition onto itself.

We need to reason with the unfoldings of the given equation $X = E$: we define the n-th unfolding of E to be E^n; thus E^1 is defined as E, E^2 as $E[E]$, and E^{n+1} as $E^n[E]$. The *infinite* unfolding represents the simplest and most intuitive solution to the equation. In the CCS grammar, such a solution is obtained by turning the equation into a constant definition, namely the constant K_E given by $K_E \stackrel{\triangle}{=} E[K_E]$. We call K_E the *syntactic solution* of the equation.

For a system of equations $\widetilde{X} = \widetilde{E}[\widetilde{X}]$, the unfoldings are defined accordingly (where E_i replaces X_i in the unfolding), and the syntactic solutions are defined to be the set of mutually recursive constants $\{K_{\widetilde{E},i} \stackrel{\triangle}{=} E_i[\widetilde{K}_{\widetilde{E}}]\}_i$.

Theorem 4 (Unique solution). *A guarded system of equations whose syntactic solutions do not diverge has a unique solution for $\approx$.*

We explain the schema of the proof, considering, for simplicity, a single equation $X = E$. We take a solution P of the equation and a transition $P \xrightarrow{\mu} P'$. The goal is to find an n such that $E^n[P]$ can match this transition *without the need of* P. This means that there is E' with $E^n[P] \overset{\hat{\mu}}{\Rightarrow} E'[P]$, and for any process Q also $E^n[Q] \overset{\hat{\mu}}{\Rightarrow} E'[Q]$ holds.

We look for this n incrementally. If the matching transition $E^m[P] \overset{\hat{\mu}}{\Rightarrow} P_m$ (recall that P is a solution), answering the transition $P \overset{\mu}{\rightarrow} P'$, involves some transitions of P, then $E^m[P]$ does not work. We thus consider a matching transition emanating from $E^{m+1}[P]$, which necessarily starts with the transitions in $E^m[P] \overset{\hat{\mu}}{\Rightarrow} P_m$ that do not involve P. We observe that there are are at least m such transitions, because P is underneath at least m prefixes in $E^m[P]$.

This procedure necessarily stops: otherwise, we could build an infinite sequence of transitions involving only the unfoldings of E, and with at most one visible transition: this would yield a divergence in the syntactic solution of E. Details may be found in [6].

4.2 Innocuous Divergences

Theorem 4 can be strengthened by taking into account only certain forms of divergence. To introduce the idea, consider the equation $X = a.X|K$, for $K \overset{\triangle}{=} \tau.K$: the divergences induced by K do not prevent uniqueness of the solution, as any solution P necessarily satisfies $P \approx a.P$. Indeed the variable of the equation is strongly guarded and a visible action has to be produced before accessing the variable. These divergences are not dangerous because they do not percolate through the infinite unfolding of the equation; in other words, a finite unfolding may produce the same divergence, therefore it is not necessary to go to the infinite unfolding to diverge. Such divergences are called *innocuous*. Formally, these divergences are derived by applying only a finite number of times rule const of the LTS (see Fig. 1) to the constant that represents the syntactic solution of the equation.

Definition 9 (Innocuous divergence). *Consider a guarded system of equations* $\widetilde{X} = \widetilde{E}$ *and its syntactic solutions* $\widetilde{K}_{\widetilde{E}}$. *Given some* i, *a divergence of* $K_{\widetilde{E},i}$ *is called* innocuous *if, when summing up all usages of rule* const *involving one of the* $K_{\widetilde{E},j}$*s (including the case* $j = i$*) in all derivation proofs of the transitions belonging to the divergence, we obtain a finite number.*

Theorem 5 (Unique solution with innocuous divergences). *Let* $\widetilde{X} = \widetilde{E}$ *be a system of guarded equations, and* $\widetilde{K}_{\widetilde{E}}$ *be its syntactic solutions. If all divergences of any* $K_{\widetilde{E},i}$ *are innocuous, then* $\widetilde{E}$ *has a unique solution for* $\approx$.

Remark 1. The conditions for unique solution in Theorems 4 and 5 are a mixture of syntactic (guardedness) and semantic (divergence-free) conditions. A purely semantic condition can be used if rule const of Fig. 1 is modified so that the unfolding of a constant yields a τ-transition:

$$\frac{}{K \overset{\tau}{\rightarrow} P} \text{ if } K \overset{\triangle}{=} P$$

Thus in the theorems the condition that the equations are guarded could be dropped. The resulting theorems would actually be more powerful because they would accept equations not all of which are guarded: it is sufficient that each equation has a finite unfolding that is guarded. For instance the system of equations $X = b|Y$, $Y = a.X$ would be accepted, although the first equation is not guarded.

5   Extensions

5.1   Other Behavioural Equivalences

The techniques reviewed in the previous sections can be applied also to other behavioural equivalences, including behavioural equivalences defined on top of inductive observables. As an example, we briefly discuss below the case of *trace equivalence*.

We write $P \stackrel{\mu}{\Rightarrow}_n P'$ if $P \stackrel{\mu}{\Rightarrow} P'$ is derived using n strong transitions (i.e., we have $P(\stackrel{\tau}{\rightarrow})^m \stackrel{\mu}{\rightarrow} (\stackrel{\tau}{\rightarrow})^{m'} P'$ and $n = m + m' + 1$. If $s = \ell_1, \ldots, \ell_n$, we call s a *trace*, and we write $P \stackrel{s}{\Rightarrow}$ if $P \stackrel{\ell_1}{\Rightarrow} P_1 \stackrel{\ell_2}{\Rightarrow} P_2 \ldots P_{n-1} \stackrel{\ell_n}{\Rightarrow} P_n$, for some processes $P_1, \ldots, P_n$. Similarly we write $P \stackrel{s}{\Rightarrow}_m$ if there are $P_1, \ldots, P_n$ with $P \stackrel{\ell_1}{\Rightarrow}_{m_1} P_1 \stackrel{\ell_2}{\Rightarrow}_{m_2} P_2 \ldots P_{n-1} \stackrel{\ell_n}{\Rightarrow}_{m_n} P_n$, and $m = \Sigma_i m_i$.

Definition 10. *Two processes P, Q of $\mathcal{L}$ are* trace equivalent, *written $P \approx_{\mathrm{tr}} Q$, if for each trace s we have $P \stackrel{s}{\Rightarrow}$ iff $Q \stackrel{s}{\Rightarrow}$.*

Two processes P, Q are in the trace equivalence contraction, *written $P \succeq_{\mathrm{tr}} Q$, if, for each trace s:*

1. *if $P \stackrel{s}{\Rightarrow}_n$ then $Q \stackrel{s}{\Rightarrow}_m$ for some $m \leq n$;*
2. *if $Q \stackrel{s}{\Rightarrow}$ then $P \stackrel{s}{\Rightarrow}$.*

□

Theorem 6. *In CCS, a system of weakly-guarded contractions has a unique solution for $\sim_{\mathrm{tr}}$*

□

In a similar manner, Theorems 4 and 5, concerning divergence, are adapted to trace equivalence. In contrast, both kinds of techniques seem to fail for equivalences allowing infinitary forms of observables. An example is *infinitary trace equivalence*, whereby two processes are equated if they have the same traces, including the infinite ones. For contractions, it is even unclear how the contraction itself for infinitary trace equivalence should be defined. Further, consider the processes $P \stackrel{\mathrm{def}}{=} \Sigma_n a^n$ and $Q \stackrel{\mathrm{def}}{=} P + a.K_a.\mathbf{0}$, where K_a is the process that can perform infinitely many a actions (i.e., $K_a \stackrel{\triangle}{=} a.K_a$): they are not infinitary trace equivalent. However, in an 'infinitary trace' semantics they both are solutions to the (guarded and sequential) contraction

$$X \succeq a + a.X$$

The definition of the contraction for infinitary trace equivalence is irrelevant here, because the processes have no τ-transitions. Similarly, we may consider the equation $X = a + a.X$, whose syntactic solution has no divergences. The process P above is a solution, yet it is not trace-equivalent to the syntactic solution of the equation, because the syntactic solution has an infinite trace involving a transitions.

5.2   Other Languages and Results

We refer to [39] and [6] for extensions of the results to languages defined from a generic signature and for conditions based on rule formats for the transition relation of the language. In the same papers, as well as in [8], one may find extensions to calculi with mobility along the lines of the π-calculus. We discuss extensions to higher-order languages in Sect. 7.2 below.

We refer to the same papers [6,8,39] for other results. These include: abstract formulations of the methods; completeness of the methods (the possibility of being able to use the method to prove all process equalities); the extensions of the results about divergence to behavioural *preorders*; results allowing one to transplant uniqueness of solutions from a system of equations to another one (in the former system divergence may be easier to prove).

6   Formalisation

The paper [44] presents a comprehensive formalisation of Milner's Calculus of Communicating Systems (CCS) in the HOL theorem prover (HOL4), with a focus towards the theory of unique solutions of equations and contractions. Many results in Milner's CCS book [22] are covered, since the unique-solution theorems rely on a large number of fundamental results. Indeed the formalisation encompasses all basic properties of strong, weak bisimilarities (e.g. the fixed-point and substitutivity properties), and their algebraic laws. Further extensions include several versions of "bisimulation up to" techniques, and properties of the expansion and contraction preorders.

The formalisation makes some further refinements to the theory of unique solutions of contractions, in particular concerning the substitutivity problems of weak bisimilarity and other behavioural relations with respect to the sum operator. Thus *rooted bisimilarity* and *rooted contraction*, respectively the coarsest (largest) congruence and precongruence contained in weak bisimilarity and in the contraction preorder when the CCS language includes unguarded sums, are considered. Unique-solution theorems for them are then formulated.

A benefit of the formalisation is that one can take advantage of results about different equivalences and preorders that share similar proof structures. In these cases, when moving between proofs there are only a few places in the proof scripts that have to be modified. The successful termination of a proof gives one the guarantee that the proof is correct, eliminating the risks of overlooking or missing details as in paper-and-pencil proofs.

7   Examples of Applications

7.1   Representation of Functions as Processes

We have used the theory of unique-solutions of equation to study the models produced by representations of functions as processes, precisely encodings of λ-terms under various evaluation strategies, into π-calculus or dialects of it.

In his seminal work [23,24], Milner shows how the evaluation strategies of *call-by-name λ-calculus* and *call-by-value λ-calculus* [1,28] can be faithfully mimicked in the π-calculus. More precisely, Milner shows the operational correspondence between reductions in the λ-terms and in the encoding π-terms. He then uses the correspondence to prove that the encodings are *sound*, i.e., if the processes encoding two λ-terms are behaviourally equivalent, then the source λ-terms are also behaviourally equivalent in the λ-calculus. Milner also shows that the converse, *completeness*, fails, intuitively because the encodings allow one to test the λ-terms in all contexts of the π-calculus — more diverse than those of the λ-calculus.

The main problem that Milner's work left open is the characterisation of the equivalence on λ-terms induced by the encoding, whereby two λ-terms are equal if their encodings are behaviourally equivalent π-calculus terms. The question is largely independent of the precise form of behavioural equivalence adopted in the π-calculus because the encodings are deterministic (or at least confluent).

For the call-by-name λ-calculus, the answer was found shortly later [33,35]: the equality induced is the equality of Levy-Longo Trees (LTs) [19], the lazy variant of Böhm Trees (BTs). It is actually also possible to obtain BTs, by modifying the call-by-name encoding so to allow also reductions underneath a λ-abstraction, and by including divergence among the observables [42].

For call-by-value, in contrast, the problem of identifying the equivalence induced by the encoding has remained open for a long time, for two main reasons. First, tree structures in call-by-value are less studied and less established than in call-by-name. Secondly, existing techniques for reasoning about behavioural relations in the π-calculus appeared not be powerful enough. For call-by-name, for instance, a central role is played by *bisimulation up-to contexts*. Such a technique, however, cannot be directly applied to Milner's encoding. In [8] the problem was solved by exploiting the theory of unique solution of equations, notably the theory based on divergences. Thus the equivalence induced on λ-terms by their call-by-value encoding into the π-calculus turns out to be *eager normal-form bisimilarity* [16,17].

In a similar manner, the theory of unique solutions of equations has been used in [32], where the object of study is extensionality in the representation of functions as processes. (In extensional theories two functions are equated if, whenever applied to the same argument, they yield equal results.) Notably, Milner's original encoding of functions as processes is refined into an encoding that is *parametric* on certain abstract components called *wires*. These are, intuitively, processes whose task is to connect two end-point channels. Three main classes of wires are isolated. The first two are dual of each other; the third has a certain parallel behaviour and is the dual of itself. It is shown that the adoption of the parallel wires yields an extensional λ-theory; in fact it yields an equality that coincides with that of BTs with infinite η, shortly $BT_{\eta\infty}$s. Moreover, the λ-theories produced by the other two classes of wires coincide with the equality of BTs and LTs. All these results rely on the technique of unique-solution of equations (again, in the variant that exploits divergence).

Remark 2. The results above bring up a remarkable agreement between the representation of functions as processes and the classical theory of the λ-calculus. Tree structures play a pivotal role in the λ-calculus. For instance, trees allow one to unveil the computational content hidden in a λ-term, with respect to some relevant minimal information. In BTs the informations are the head normal forms, whereas in LTs they are the weak head normal forms. Indeed, BTs and LTs produce the same local structures as well-known models of the λ-calculus, such as Plotkin and Scott's P_ω [27,43], and the *free lazy Plotkin-Scott-Ankle models* [9,18,19]. In BTs and LTs the computational content of a λ-term is unveiled using the β-rule alone. In *extensional* structures the β-rule is coupled with the η-rule ($M = \lambda x.(Mx)$, for x not free in M). A well-known extensional tree-structure are $BT_{\eta\infty}$s. The equality of $BT_{\eta\infty}$s coincides with that of Scott's D_∞ model [43], historically the first model of the untyped λ-calculus. A seminal result by Wadsworth shows that the $BT_{\eta\infty}$s are intimately related to the head normal forms, as the $BT_{\eta\infty}$ equality coincides with contextual equivalence in which the head normal forms are the observables.

7.2 Higher-Order Languages

As mentioned in the previous section, the unique-solution techniques has been applied and extended to calculi for name mobility in the π-calculus family [6,8,39]. More challenging is the transplant of the techniques onto higher-order languages (intuitively, languages where terms of the language are first-order values and may thus instantiate variables), such as the λ-calculi, Higher-order π-calculi, Ambients (e.g., [12–14,21,37]). A major motivation for this application is that unique-solution techniques have the flavour of 'bisimulation up-to context' techniques; that is, techniques in which, during the bisimulation game, the derivatives of two terms can be rewritten so to remove a common context. Up-to context techniques can be particularly effective in higher-order languages. Unfortunately, proving the soundness of the up-to context techniques can be surprisingly hard. Even in pure λ-calculi, and for the most basic form of bisimilarity (e.g., call-by-name or call-by-value λ-calculus and Abramsky's applicative bisimilarity) long-standing open problems remain about soundness. Higher-order process calculi are the class of languages in which up-to context techniques in the literature are most scarce. Recently, techniques of this kind have been derived exploiting fully-abstract translations into first-order calculi (CCS-like or π-calculus-like) [20]. However fully abstract translations are sensitive to the grammar of the language chosen: a modification to the grammar may break or prevent a fully abstract translation to be defined, or, at the very least, will require a careful re-examination of the full abstraction proof. There are however few direct proofs of soundness, that do not rely on translations into first-order languages; e.g., [21,41] for the Ambient calculus and the Higher-Order π-calculus (HOπ). The Ambient calculus represents a rather special case of higher-order calculus, for processes can move but cannot be communicated. Moving a process is quite different from communicating it as in HOπ: in the former case the process will always be run, immediately and exactly once; in the latter case, in contrast, the process may be copied, and it is the recipient of the process that decides when and where to run each copy. Thus the problems of soundness for up-to context only show up in a limited form in Ambients. The up-to context technique considered in [41] is for environmental bisimilarity. This bisimilarity involves universal quantifications on processes supplied by the environment. Up-to context is essential for limiting the burden due to such quantifications. The contexts used have constraints and are disallowed in certain clauses (which is necessary for the soundness of the technique).

In [7], we have adapted the technique of unique solution of equations (the approach using divergence, as in Sect. 4) to HOπ using, as a form of bisimilarity, *normal bisimilarity* [34]. Normal bisimilarity has been chosen for two main reasons. First, it is the most effective in proofs, because its clauses do not make use of additional universal quantifications on terms, as other forms of bisimilarity such as context bisimilarity or environmental bisimilarity. Second, precisely due to such lack of universal quantifications, the 'contextual' properties of normal bisimilarity are quite delicate. Even proving substitutivity with respect to basic operators such as parallel composition is hard (indeed, usually this is proved by relying on mappings onto other forms of bisimilarity or onto first-order calculi). No direct proofs of soundness of forms of up-to contexts exists for normal bisimilarity.

8   Comparison and Future Work

We briefly compare the method based on contractions and the one based on divergence.

In comparison with the method based on contractions, the main drawback for the method based on divergence is the presence of a semantic condition, involving divergence: the unfoldings of the equations should not produce divergences, or only produce innocuous divergences. Various techniques for checking divergence exist in the literature, including type-based techniques [3,38,45]; a syntactic condition is proposed in [4]. However, in general divergence is undecidable, and therefore, the check may sometimes be unfeasible. Nevertheless, the equations that one writes for proofs usually involve forms of 'normalised' processes, and as such they are divergence free (or, at most, contain only innocuous divergences).

On the other hand, to use contractions for proving an equivalence, one needs also the theory of the associated contraction preorder; moreover there may be processes for which the contraction technique is not applicable simply because the contraction preorder is strictly finer than the equivalence, and therefore one of the processes fails to be a solution.

Formally, the technique based on contraction and the one based on divergence are incomparable. The first can in fact be used also in cases in which the unfolding of the equations produce divergences (plain or innocuous divergences) [6]. On the other hand, when using contraction, a solution is evaluated with respect to the contraction preorder, that conveys an idea of efficiency (measured against the number of silent transitions performed). Thus, while two bisimilar processes are solutions of exactly the same set of equations, they need not be solutions of the same contractions. For instance, we can use our techniques to prove that processes $K \stackrel{\triangle}{=} \tau.a.a.K$ and $H \stackrel{\triangle}{=} a.H$ are bisimilar because they are solutions of the equation $X = a.X$; in contrast, only H is a solution of the corresponding contraction.

In practical cases, from what we have seen so far, it seems that the two kinds of technique are equally applicable, and that the amount of work to be carried out is comparable.

More work is needed to properly understand on which behavioural equivalences and which languages the techniques of unique solution of contractions and of equations work. We mentioned that they seem to work if the observables are finitary. More experimentation is needed to formalise appropriate conditions. In particular, we are thinking about higher-order languages, where often up-to-context enhancements of bisimilarity or of other behavioural relations [40] are not directly applicable. Indeed, in these settings often the definition of the behavioural equivalence or preorder makes use of sophisticated forms of labelled transition systems (e.g., environmental bisimilarity [41]).

Acknowledgments. We are delighted to be able to contribute to the Festschrift in honour of Marjan Sirjani, to whom this paper is dedicated. We would like to take this opportunity for heartily thanking her: both for all her many technical contributions, and for her work in favour of the concurrency of formal methods, including the establishment of the Foundations of Software Engineering (FSEN) conference series, among the most enjoyable conferences that we have had the pleasure of attending.

References

1. Abramsky, S.: The lazy lambda calculus. In: Turner, D. (ed.) Research Topics in Functional Programming, pp. 65–116. Addison-Wesley (1989)
2. Baeten, J., Basten, T., Reniers, M.: Process Algebra: Equational Theories of Communicating Processes. Cambridge University Press, Cambridge (2010)
3. Demangeon, R., Hirschkoff, D., Sangiorgi, D.: Termination in impure concurrent languages. In: Gastin, P., Laroussinie, F. (eds.) Proceedings of the 21th Conference on Concurrency Theory. Lecture Notes in Computer Science, vol. 6269, pp. 328–342. Springer (2010)
4. Durier, A., Hirschkoff, D., Sangiorgi, D.: Divergence and unique solution of equations. In: Meyer, R., Nestmann, U. (eds.) 28th International Conference on Concurrency Theory, CONCUR 2017. LIPIcs, vol. 85, pp. 11:1–11:16. Schloss Dagstuhl - Leibniz-Zentrum fuer Informatik (2017)

5. Durier, A., Hirschkoff, D., Sangiorgi, D.: Eager functions as processes. In: 33nd Annual ACM/IEEE Symposium on Logic in Computer Science, LICS 2018. IEEE Computer Society (2018)
6. Durier, A., Hirschkoff, D., Sangiorgi, D.: Divergence and unique solution of equations. Log. Methods Comput. Sci. **15**(3) (2019). https://doi.org/10.23638/LMCS-15(3:12)2019
7. Durier, A., Hirschkoff, D., Sangiorgi, D.: Towards 'up to context' reasoning about higher-order processes. Theor. Comput. Sci. **807**, 154–168 (2020)
8. Durier, A., Hirschkoff, D., Sangiorgi, D.: Eager functions as processes. Theor. Comput. Sci. **913**, 8–42 (2022). https://doi.org/10.1016/j.tcs.2022.01.043
9. Engeler, E.: Algebras and combinators. Algebra Universalis **13**, 389–392 (1981)
10. Groote, J.F., Mousavi, M.R.: Modeling and Analysis of Communicating Systems. MIT Press, Cambridge (2014)
11. Hoare, C.: Communicating Sequential Processes. Prentice Hall, Hoboken (1985)
12. Koutavas, V., Wand, M.: Small bisimulations for reasoning about higher-order imperative programs. In: Proceedings of the 33rd ACM SIGPLAN-SIGACT Symposium on Principles of Programming Languages, pp. 141–152 (2006)
13. Lassen, S.B.: Relational reasoning about contexts. In: Higher-order Operational Techniques in Semantics, pp. 91–135. Cambridge University Press (1998)
14. Lassen, S.B.: Relational Reasoning about Functions and Nondeterminism. Ph.D. thesis, Department of Computer Science, University of Aarhus (1998)
15. Lassen, S.B.: Bisimulation in untyped lambda calculus: Böhm trees and bisimulation up to context. Electr. Notes Theor. Comput. Sci. **20**, 346–374 (1999)
16. Lassen, S.B.: Eager normal form bisimulation. In: 20th IEEE Symposium on Logic in Computer Science (LICS 2005), 26–29 June 2005, Chicago, IL, USA, Proceedings, pp. 345–354 (2005)
17. Lassen, S.B., Levy, P.B.: Typed normal form bisimulation. In: Proceedings of the Computer Science Logic CSL 2007. LNCS, vol. 4646, pp. 283–297. Springer (2007)
18. Lévy, J.: An algebraic interpretation of the $\lambda\beta\kappa$-calculus; and an application of a labelled λ-calculus. Theor. Comput. Sci. **2**(1), 97–114 (1976)
19. Longo, G.: Set theoretical models of lambda calculus: theory, expansions and isomorphisms. Ann. Pure Appl. Log. **24**, 153–188 (1983)
20. Madiot, J., Pous, D., Sangiorgi, D.: Modular coinduction up-to for higher-order languages via first-order transition systems. Log. Methods Comput. Sci. **17**(3) (2021)
21. Merro, M., Zappa Nardelli, F.: Behavioral theory for mobile ambients. J. ACM **52**(6), 961–1023 (2005)
22. Milner, R.: Communication and Concurrency. Prentice Hall, Hoboken (1989)
23. Milner, R.: Functions as processes. Research Report 1154, INRIA, Sophia Antipolis (1990), Final version in Journal of Mathem. Structures in Computer Science 2(2):119–141, 1992
24. Milner, R.: Functions as processes. J. Math. Struct. Comput. Sci. **2**(2), 119–141 (1992)
25. Piérard, A., Sumii, E.: Sound bisimulations for higher-order distributed process calculus. In: Hofmann, M. (ed.) Proceedings of the FOSSACS. LNCS, vol. 6604, pp. 123–137. Springer (2011)
26. Pitts, A.: Howe's method. In: Sangiorgi, D., Rutten, J. (eds.) Advanced Topics in Bisimulation and Coinduction. Cambridge University Press (2012)
27. Plotkin, G.: A set theoretical definition of application. Technical report. MIP-R-95, School of A.I., Univ. of Edinburgh (1972)

28. Plotkin, G.: Call by name, call by value and the λ-calculus. Theor. Comput. Sci. **1**, 125–159 (1975)
29. Roscoe, A.W.: An alternative order for the failures model. J. Log. Comput. **2**(5), 557–577 (1992)
30. Roscoe, A.W.: The Theory and Practice of Concurrency. Prentice Hall, Hoboken (1998). http://www.cs.ox.ac.uk/people/bill.roscoe/publications/68b.pdf
31. Roscoe, A.W.: Understanding Concurrent Systems. Springer (2010)
32. Sakayori, K., Sangiorgi, D.: Extensional and non-extensional functions as processes. In: 38th Annual ACM/IEEE Symposium on Logic in Computer Science, LICS 2023, Boston, MA, USA, 26–29 June 2023, pp. 1–13. IEEE (2023). https://doi.org/10.1109/LICS56636.2023.10175686
33. Sangiorgi, D.: An investigation into functions as processes. In: Proceedings of the Ninth International Conference on the Mathematical Foundations of Programming Semantics (MFPS'93). LNCS, vol. 802, pp. 143–159. Springer Verlag (1993)
34. Sangiorgi, D.: Bisimulation for higher-order process calculi. Inf. Comput. **131**(2), 141–178 (1996)
35. Sangiorgi, D.: Lazy functions and mobile processes. In: Plotkin, G., Stirling, C., Tofte, M. (eds.) Proof, Language and Interaction: Essays in Honour of Robin Milner. MIT Press (2000)
36. Sangiorgi, D., Milner, R.: The problem of "Weak Bisimulation up to". In: Cleveland, W. (ed.) Proceedings of the CONCUR '92. LNCS, vol. 630, pp. 32–46. Springer Verlag (1992)
37. Sangiorgi, D., Walker, D.: The π-Calculus: A Theory of Mobile Processes. Cambridge University Press, Cambridge (2001)
38. Sangiorgi, D.: Termination of processes. Math. Struct. Comput. Sci. **16**(1), 1–39 (2006)
39. Sangiorgi, D.: Equations, contractions, and unique solutions. ACM Trans. Comput. Log. **18**(1), 4:1–4:30 (2017). http://doi.acm.org/10.1145/2971339
40. Sangiorgi, D.: From enhanced coinduction towards enhanced induction. Proc. ACM Program. Lang. **6**(POPL), 1–29 (2022). https://doi.org/10.1145/3498679
41. Sangiorgi, D., Kobayashi, N., Sumii, E.: Environmental bisimulations for higher-order languages. ACM Trans. Program. Lang. Syst. **33**(1), 5 (2011)
42. Sangiorgi, D., Xu, X.: Trees from functions as processes. Log. Methods Comput. Sci. **14**(3) (2018)
43. Scott, D.S.: Data types as lattices. SIAM J. Comput. **5**(3), 522–587 (1976)
44. Tian, C., Sangiorgi, D.: Unique solutions of contractions, ccs, and their HOL formalisation. Inf. Comput. **275**, 104606 (2020). https://doi.org/10.1016/j.ic.2020.104606
45. Yoshida, N., Berger, M., Honda, K.: Strong Normalisation in the Pi-Calculus. Inf. Comput. **191**(2), 145–202 (2004)

Author Index

E. A. Lee et al. (Eds.): Marjan Sirjani Festschrift, LNCS 15560, pp. 441–442, 2025.
https://doi.org/10.1007/978-3-031-85134-6